THE COMMON PEOPLE

1746–1946

The Common People

1746-1946

BY

G. D. H. COLE

AND

RAYMOND POSTGATE

METHUEN & CO LTD
11 NEW FETTER LANE LONDON EC4

First published October 1938
Second edition revised 1942
Third edition 1946
Fourth edition 1949
Reprinted 1956 with minor corrections
Reprinted three times
Reprinted 1966
4·6
S.B.N. 416 31360 4
First published as a University Paperback 1961
Reprinted three times
Reprinted 1968
1·5
S.B.N. 416 67720 7
Printed by lithography in Great Britain
by Cox & Wyman Ltd, Fakenham

Distributed in the U.S.A. by Barnes & Noble Inc.

CONTENTS

Section IV

THE PEACE WITHOUT A PARALLEL

Section V

ENGLAND UNDER THE REFORM ACT

Section VI

THE GREAT VICTORIAN AGE

Section VII

IMPERIALISM AND SOCIALISM

Section VIII

BEFORE THE FIRST WORLD WAR

Section IX

THE FIRST WORLD WAR

Section X

BETWEEN THE WARS

Section XI

BRITAIN IN 1939

Section XII

THE SECOND WORLD WAR

MAPS AND CHARTS

EIGHTEENTH-CENTURY ENGLAND

CHAPTER I

THE OLD ORDER ENDS

EAST of Inverness, in the Highlands of Scotland, the main road from the South runs through Culloden Moor. On both sides, for a long way, the country is desolate and windy. At a distance, across a boggy field, are relics of a civilization so ancient that it has left no written records, the Stones of Clava. But the stones which attract the rare visitors are nearer: they are the grey tombstones which have written upon them that here is the grave of the MacDonalds, here the grave of the Mackintoshes, and so forth. No individual soldier in the Stuart Army of 1746 has a grave. That was not needed: all that was needed was that each one should be placed in his own clan burial-place. It might almost be said that the soldiers had no individuality of their own. Each one was, say, a Mackintosh: above him was his chief, the Mackintosh, and above him the chief of chiefs, Prince Charles Edward.

Here, in these common graves, is clearly shown the last of a form of government which had ruled humanity for as far back as human history can go—indeed, for further yet, for in a crude form it can be seen in the apes. It was a tribal, a racial, society. The rule of the chieftains over the clans implied, as a logical necessity, the rule of the King over the chieftains. The Hanoverian soldiers, easy targets in their scarlet-and-white, were agents of a power which was determined to break this older power down, and to substitute for it a form of society in which each man was an individual. He might be richer, or better-born, than another, and the law would take due note of that. But this law should run unchanged throughout the country, without regard to local jurisdictions or tribal divisions; each poor man should be free, within its limits, to sell his life and labour, if he could, and each rich man should be free to buy it without fear of dictation from a local chief. Prince Charles Edward's soldiers were no more than so many MacDonalds, each (for all he knew) like to the others, and bound by an indissoluble link; Duke William's were privates of the 51st or some other infantry regiment, each separately enrolled, paid, and noted by his name, coming from anywhere and after his service going to anywhere.

The conflict between this very ancient society and the modern society which was challenging it had not been easily settled. Charles Edward—Prince Edward to most of his contemporaries, "Bonnie Prince Charlie" to later sentimentalists—had broken King George's army at Prestonpans soon after his landing, and had marched as far south as Derby. But on his way he found that the new society had rooted itself firmly into the lands which he had hoped to conquer. He was marching, in the language of Marxian economists, with a feudal army into a bourgeois society. His nominal adherents in England had no desire to support him. Manchester greeted him not by supplying fire-arms but by discharging fireworks. The Lowlands of Scotland, immediately his Highlanders had crossed the border, quietly reinstated the authorities he had expelled.

Since his only supporters were the clans, he was forced to abide by the conditions of tribal warfare. War, for a tribal or feudal society, is a matter of plunder. The Highlanders conquered, plundered, and went home: the Prince had to go home with them. As long as he could hold them together in an army he was invincible. He was their supreme chief, and, at that date, in his young manhood, commanded their respect by outdoing them in everything that they admired. He could outdrink any one of them, finishing a bottle and a half of brandy alone. He could march step for step over the moors with the clansmen and was always to be found in the centre of the battle line. If he was over-fond of women, that was a weakness (or a strength) which his followers mostly admired.

Though he knew it, his followers did not know that these were not sufficient qualifications to gain and hold a kingdom.

Life was now ceasing to be a story of wild infantry charges, cutting down of fleeing foes, drunken orgies, ravishings, and contented withdrawals to the hills with plunder from the towns. After he had retreated to Scotland, the Highlanders once again at Falkirk obliged the Prince by shattering another Hanoverian army, but when they had done this, they returned to their homes to enjoy the plunder. The Prince was left nearly as much alone as if he had been defeated.

The slower, less courageous, but more solid forces of the new society closed steadily on him. William, Duke of Cumberland and son of King George, was in command of them and moved his troops with the serious and sluggish efficiency of an eighteenth-century commander. He occupied the territory that he passed through methodically, in accordance with the text-books of the art of war, and never gave battle unless he had concentrated a marked superiority of troops under his hand.

In April 1746 he was pressing the Prince heavily in the region of Inverness. Lord George Murray, the Prince's ablest commander, conceived the idea of disarranging his plans and breaking this iron pressure by a night attack on his encampment at Nairn on the 15th. It was fairly certain that a descent of some thousands of Highlanders on the Hanoverian soldiers in the middle of the night would lead to a panic and a great slaughter, and the Duke would have to recommence his campaign from the beginning.

The attack was put in hand, but the organization was too casual. Detachments lost their way, and daylight had come before the Highlanders were in sight of the Duke's camp. They returned dejectedly to their base, and flung themselves down on the ground in Culloden Park to sleep off their exhaustion.

While their energy had exhausted itself in a characteristically wild gesture, the Duke moved on with an equally characteristic stolidity. He broke camp and marched forward towards the Prince's army, coming into touch with him on the 16th of April, the next day. Long before the battle began the brightly coloured Hanoverian ranks were clearly visible and the Prince and his advisers had plenty of time to debate whether to fight or retreat. There were ample reasons for retreat: the Duke's troops were double theirs in number—twelve thousand to six thousand—and their own men were exhausted. But their gallant and senseless temper paid no attention to such facts; and despite a few warning voices it was decided to give battle and the troops were deployed to receive the foe. Lord George Murray had the right, the MacDonalds the left. Ceremony and precedence are of enormous importance in a tribal society, and by this division a formal slight of the gravest kind had been given to the MacDonalds. They sulked because the place of honour had been given to Murray; when the clash came they delayed to charge—or even, according to some observers, charged half-heartedly.

The Hanoverians' attack began with a steady artillery fire, which would be trivial to a modern army, but was vexatious and demoralizing to the tribesmen. The killed and wounded can only have reached a very few hundreds, though a horse-man was killed by the Prince's side, but the tired clansmen were badly shaken by it. They charged in their old manner, but some of them charged too soon—or perhaps the Mac-Donalds charged too late; there is no means after two centuries of settling this dispute. The first Hanoverian ranks were, as usual, broken: two regiments were turned to flight or put in disorder. But the second rank stood firm, and the Highlanders were driven back. No other battle that ended a civilization was so brief. Within twenty-five minutes the Stuart army was in flight. "The adjacent country was in a manner covered with its ruins," said an observer. Cumberland's regiments advanced methodically and irresistibly, surprising the sleepers in Culloden Park, and cutting their throats, for that was their General's order.

No rallying was possible for the dejected men. "There was no rendezvous ordered," wrote MacDonald of Lochgarry to a friend, "as we expected to beat the enemy as we had always done before." What few troops collected themselves were dispiritedly, but mercifully, told by the Prince to seek their own safety as quickly as they could. He himself went into hiding; and much, indeed far too much, patience has been spent in discovering and recounting his hardships and wander-ings. "Divine Providence," wrote Father Cordara, "has in

His especial keeping the lives of Princes," and in faith in this maxim he and others have followed the Prince's career through its dreary length till he ended as a hanger-on at Continental courts, heavy, red-faced and bloated, a woman-beater and a drunkard, having destroyed Jacobite loyalty as effectively as Cumberland had destroyed the Jacobite armies.

The historical research spent on him might have been better spent upon the fate of his followers. The brutal order of the Duke on the day of battle was paralleled by his actions afterwards. His cruelty worried even his supporters. "The lord president," he wrote to London, "wishes for lenity, if it can be with safety, which he thinks, but I don't." "I find them a more stubborn and villainous set of wretches than I imagined could exist," he added in further excuse a month or so later.

His ferocity made London society ashamed. The Londoners revived his slang name of Nolkejumskoi: what that peculiar word was meant to convey no one knows, but it was not complimentary. They joked about his enormous fat body, which had to edge itself sideways through a door; they even did not repudiate the nickname of Butcher that the Jacobites fastened on him. But in a sense they were ungrateful and unjust; Cumberland was only doing their work for them, and doing it thoroughly.

The laws that were passed in London seconded and made permanent his achievement. He was breaking the resistance of the Highlanders for the moment; the new laws broke it for ever. The feudal rights and organization of the clans were abolished. No exception was made: the Gordons were treated no differently from others, though they had stayed loyal to King George. Even the most harmless symbols of clan loyalty were prohibited; the wearing of the kilt and even the playing of the bagpipes were forbidden, and the ban was not lifted for some thirty years. The avowed intention of the reforms was that "a sheriff's writ should run" in the Highlands as securely and certainly as it ran everywhere else. This intention was achieved: up to the cliffs of Caithness there was no place at all that was not obedient to Whitehall. All the Highlands observed the laws of Parliament, and lived on the same system as did the Lowlands and Britain.

This extinction of the older society completed a process started long before, a process which alone made it possible for Britain in the next hundred years to become the workshop of the world. There were now no feudal lords to be conciliated or cajoled by the rising employing class. Land-owners, bankers and employers, each with their own type of property to support them, made their political bargaining and conducted their trading without any semi-baronial powers, with private jurisdictions and infeodated supporters, camped threateningly in the countryside.

A similar release was secured in France only by an explosion of far greater violence, which left the country exhausted, and in Germany it was not wholly secured at all.

To defeat the great chieftains, and to pass laws declaring their power at an end, was not enough. This, or something like it, had been done before, and the clans had survived. The country itself had to be changed. The reason for the survival of the clans had been that their moors, mountains and mosses were impassable to troops and to trade. Footpaths and pony-tracks carried all the trade the Highlanders needed, and favoured their method of fighting. What made their defeat, this time, irremediable were the roads which were constructed after Culloden.

A beginning had been made by General Wade after the rising of 1715, but too little had been done to make any serious impression. The roads now made were linked together with the others in the popular mind, and indifferently referred to as "General Wade's military roads," although he was by no means responsible for most of them and was indeed dead before they were all completed. The estimates of the ground covered also vary enormously, from 800 miles to 1,500. But the route of the most important roads when completed is not disputed. One rose from the Lowlands at the head of Loch Lomond, in the west, passed the moor of Rannoch on the right, came down to the sea through Glencoe, turned sharp right and ran straight along the Great Glen (Glen More) of Scotland, where the Caledonian Canal now runs, and ended near Inverness, having cut the Highlands into two pieces. Another, leaving this road at Fort Augustus in the Great

Glen, struck southwards again over the wildest and most inaccessible parts of the Grampians, passing through Blair Atholl and descending to lower ground on the eastern side of Scotland near Perth. The great easterly projection of the country was split by a road which left Coupar Angus (not far from Dundee), rose into the Highlands at Braemar, and ended at Fort George by the extreme north end of the Great Glen.

The roads were hasty. They were not well made, nor intelligently laid out. The bridges were too steep and the foundations were often shoddy. The route unnecessarily crossed hills, when a little thought would have enabled a détour to take the road through a valley. But the roads served their purpose: they split the block of Highland clans into fragments. Once it was clear that the old régime was over, and that buying and selling were for them to take the place of ruling over subjects, the clan chiefs, now landlords, realized that their retainers were an unprofitable expense. Then the Highlands were driven with sudden rapidity through a series of changes which had taken hundreds of years in England. The medieval cry, "sheep devour men" was heard again. The landlords slowly disembarrassed themselves of all their followers who could not be used as shepherds or compelled to rent small farms. In most cases personal loyalties prevented extensive clearances while those who fought at Culloden were still alive. But a first big clearance took place on the Drummond estates as early as 1762, and in 1782 the Glengarry estates followed suit, "and here the rent roll rose from £700 to £5,000 in thirty-two years." By the turn of the century these clearances (which were for sheep, not as later, for deer), were to assume an enormous size, and the people evicted were to be estimated at as many as two hundred thousand.

Thus Hanoverian England made an end at once of the Jacobites and of the ancient order in the Scottish Highlands which was the last hope of the Stuarts. But the England which destroyed the clans, though it was modern by contrast with its beaten antagonist, was still greatly unlike the England of to-day. Though English wealth and commercial power were advancing fast, the great change which we call the "Industrial Revolution" was still to come. Most of the country was still mainly agricultural, and agriculture had not yet gone through the convulsions of enclosure and depopulation which reached their climax during and after the Napoleonic Wars. London was still the only really large town. Steam power, soon to revolutionize industry and transport, was used only here and there for pumping water, and had not yet been applied to turning the wheels of factory machines. Industry was on a small scale, and for the most part scattered over the country in villages or little towns that were hardly more than villages —for there was as yet no considerable economy to be achieved by production on a large scale. Industry, indeed, was advancing fast, though it was held back by the extremely primitive condition of transport. There were, of course, no railways— though a few "track-ways" used for horse-drawn traffic, chiefly from mines, were sometimes called "rail-ways" by contemporary writers. There were few good roads, except between the main centres in the South of England, and no canals, though there were "cuts," sometimes called canals, which linked up some of the navigable rivers. These river navigations were indeed of primary importance all over England, and largely dictated the localization of industry and the density of population in different parts of the country. For, as the badness of the roads rendered them for the most part unusable by wheeled traffic carrying heavy goods, and even difficult and dangerous to travellers on horseback during the winter months, industry and commerce depended mainly on water carriage—almost exclusively so where heavy goods were in question. Trade and population had to settle wherever easy access could be got to navigable water—either close to the sea or along the course of some river which was kept open to navigation under the auspices of a municipal corporation or of a special conservancy. Within easy reach of sea or navigable river the industrial workers lived for the most part, like the agriculturalists, in villages or in little towns that would seem no more than villages to the modern visitor. Countrymen and townsmen, except in London, were far less differentiated than they were to become within the next half-century under the influence of the factory system. And perhaps the greatest difference of all between the England of 1746 and the England of to-day was that for the great mass of the people travel or migration over any great distance was practically out of the question, so that most people lived and died in or quite near the villages in which they had been born.

When a man set out to travel about England in the eighteenth century, he rode on horseback; for that was the easiest way. It was indeed possible to travel by wheel with reasonable comfort from London to Bath or to Bristol; for the roads between England's two leading towns and between London and England's principal pleasure resort had been greatly improved in the early decades of the century. But a Londoner who had business in the North, or a Northerner who had business in London, needed a horse; for the roads between North and South were still so bad as to make travel except on horseback intolerably difficult and slow. As for the common people, they did not attempt such journeys, or, if a rare adventurous workman went far afield in pursuance of his craft, he walked.

Goods, especially heavy goods, where they had to be carried over considerable distances, went by water—by river and by coastwise traffic on board ship. England's navigable rivers—such as the Trent and Severn navigations—were of first importance to eighteenth-century commerce; and it was difficult for any considerable manufacture to be carried on far from a seaport or a navigable river. Some of the smaller seaports were indeed already losing their importance owing to the greater tonnage of shipping; and some of them were silting up as the larger vessels deserted them, and the dues from those that were left no longer sufficed for reasonable maintenance. But the little port, on the sea or on a river navigation, was still a vital economic institution of England in the eighteenth century; and the indispensability of transport by water still dictated the economic configuration of the country. Industrially, England was still hollow—a circumference of activity surrounding a central area which lived largely by self-subsistent agriculture. This is an exaggeration, no doubt; for the West Riding of Yorkshire was already an important industrial area, and there were considerable textile areas in the Midlands and a large and growing iron industry in the Severn valley. But much of central England could not be

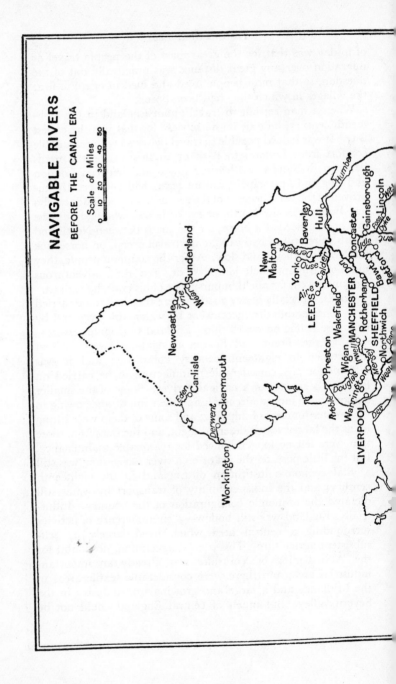

NAVIGABLE RIVERS

BEFORE THE CANAL ERA

Scale of Miles
0 10 20 30 40 50

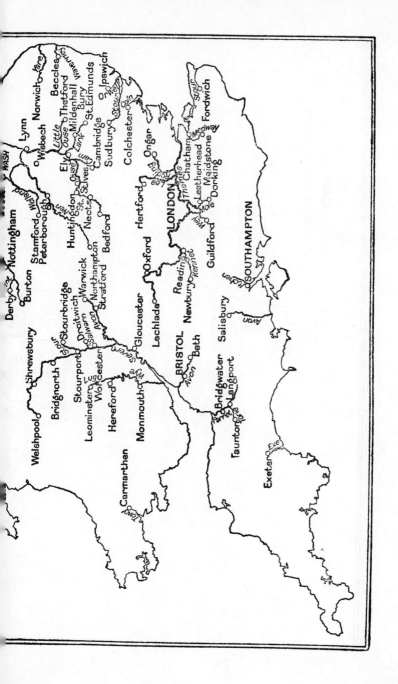

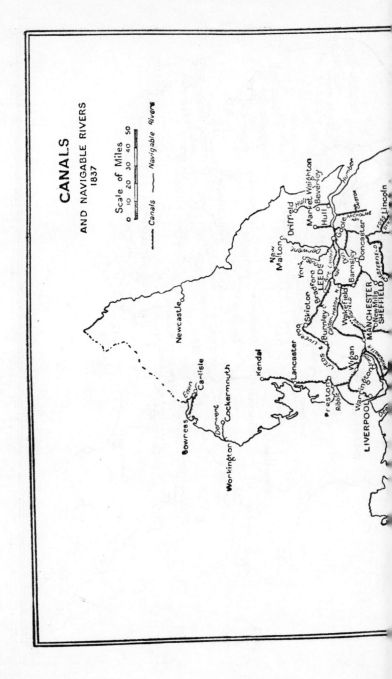

CANALS
AND NAVIGABLE RIVERS
1837

Scale of Miles
0 10 20 30 40 50

——— Canals ——— Navigable Rivers

Bowness
Carlisle
Eden
Workington
Derwent
Cockermouth

Newcastle

Kendal

Lancaster

Preston
Ribble

Warrington
LIVERPOOL

Wigan

Leeds & Liverpool

New Malton
Driffield
Hull
Market Weighton
Beverley
Goole
Humber
Barton

Skipton
York
Derwent
Bradford
LEEDS
Burnley
Calder & Hebble N.
Wakefield
Barnsley
Doncaster
MANCHESTER
New Mills
SHEFFIELD

Trent
Lincoln

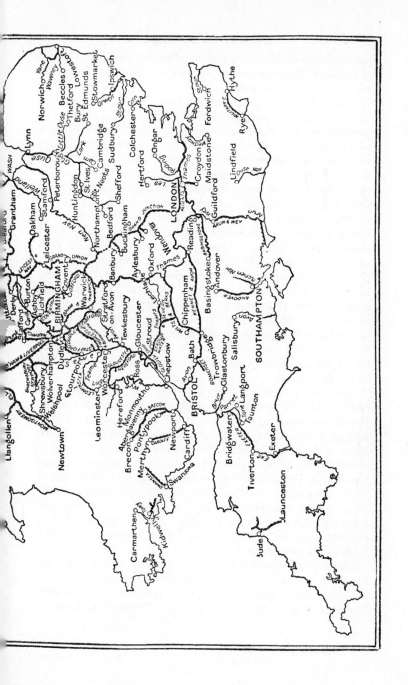

economically developed or industrialized without better means of transport than the contemporaries of Wilkes and Dr. Johnson had at their command.

Where, then, did men live, and how—in this England that was still devoid of the conveniences of modern industry? The uncertainty of population figures in the eighteenth century is well known. It is nevertheless possible to say with fair accuracy which of the counties were more or less populous in relation to their areas. Middlesex, including Greater London north of the Thames, was of course by far the most populous of all; and next to it came Surrey, including Southwark and London's southern suburbs, with a density over the whole county of something over two hundred persons per square mile. Only three other counties—Lancashire, Gloucestershire and Warwickshire—seem to have exceeded one hundred and fifty persons per square mile. Of these the last two had long been among the more thickly populated, whereas Lancashire had risen between 1700 and 1750 from near the bottom almost to the top of the list. The industrial area of the West Riding of Yorkshire was probably still more thickly populated than the comparable part of Lancashire; but even the West Riding contained so much thinly inhabited country as to relegate it to the next group.

Apart from these exceptional areas, England about 1750 can be divided roughly into two areas of varying density. Population exceeded one hundred per square mile in the West Riding, Staffordshire, Derbyshire, Leicestershire, Bedfordshire, Kent, and Durham—which had all been thinly populated at the beginning of the eighteenth century. It also exceeded one hundred in Worcestershire, Somerset, Wiltshire, Oxfordshire, Buckinghamshire, Hertfordshire, Suffolk and Northamptonshire—which had been in 1700 among the more populous counties. To these must be added Devonshire, which had reached a similar density despite the large amount of barren land within its borders.

The rest of England had still a density of less than one hundred persons per square mile. Westmorland alone had less than fifty; but a number of counties—Cumberland, Northumberland, the North Riding of Yorkshire, Lincoln-

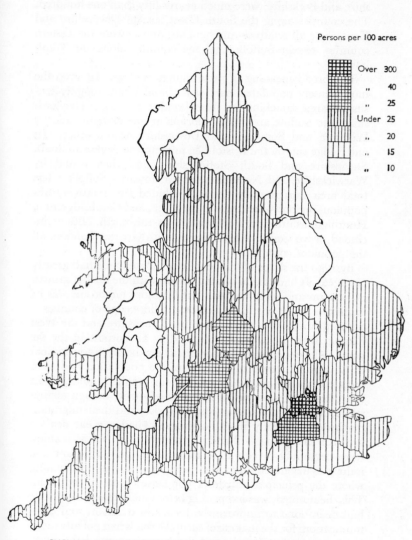

Persons per 100 acres

Over 300
" 40
" 25
Under 25
" 20
" 15
" 10

ENGLAND AND WALES, ESTIMATED DENSITY OF POPULATION IN 1750, BY
COUNTIES

shire and Berkshire, were much nearer fifty than one hundred. The counties along the South Coast, except Devonshire and Kent, were all relatively unpopulous; and so were the eastern counties, except Suffolk, and the counties along the Welsh border.

The broad meaning of these figures is clear. In 1700 the most densely populated part of England was a roughly fan-shaped area stretching out from London by way of Hertford-shire into Suffolk and South Norfolk at one extreme, and by Wiltshire and Somerset into Devonshire at the other. Its outer edge ran by the Bristol Channel up the Severn to South Shropshire and South Staffordshire, and then round by Warwickshire and Northamptonshire towards Suffolk. The total area thus roughly defined included two relatively un-populous regions—Berkshire to the south, and Cambridgeshire, Huntingdonshire and Bedfordshire to the north. But it in-cluded, if we rank northern Surrey with Greater London, all the populous counties.

By 1750 the shape of the densely populated area had greatly changed. It had spread out into Kent, with the further growth of London and its influence. But far more important was its extension to the north, to include a solid wedge of counties— Staffordshire, Derbyshire, Cheshire, Lancashire and the West Riding, with the Durham coalfield as an outpost in the far north, still dependent mainly on its sea-borne trade in coal to London. In 1700 the density of the population had been dictated mainly by the location of the woollen industry. In 1750 this was by no means so exclusively true, though textiles still counted for more than anything else, and their migration northwards, already in rapid progress, had a great deal to do with the change. But coal and iron, as well as textiles, were beginning to count for more, and agriculture and the industries dependent upon it for something less, in determining where the principal centres of population were to be found. This, be it noted, was happening before more than a very little had been done to improve the means of transport and com-munication; for the making of turnpike roads had not advanced far, except in the South, and the improvement of the rivers could not achieve a great deal before the coming of the canals.

CHAPTER II

A JOURNEY THROUGH ENGLAND IN 1746

THERE was a fashion, set early in the eighteenth century by Daniel Defoe's *Tour Through the Whole Island of Great Britain* and John Macky's similar *Journey*, for descriptive guides to the country, embracing not only its antiquities and natural beauties, but some account of its arts and industries and the state of the land and the people. Let us briefly—for our space is scanty—accompany an imaginary traveller on such a journey, round about 1746, over the whole of England. Let us suppose him, in the first place arming himself well against highwaymen, who still infested the major roads, and then leaving Edinburgh behind him, and riding down by way of the flourishing town of Berwick-on-Tweed into Northumberland.

Such a traveller would have found here, till he came quite near to Newcastle-on-Tyne, in the very south of the county, a sparsely populated area, of rough and hilly soil, but an improving agriculture as he went further south. Some way north of Newcastle he would begin to encounter the coal-pits; for the area near the Tyne, in Northumberland and Durham, was by far the most developed of the British coalfields, actively engaged in keeping London supplied with house-fuel.

Newcastle-on-Tyne, in many ways a typical fair-sized eighteenth-century town, had at that time roughly twenty thousand inhabitants, including those who dwelt in Gateshead, outside the city itself, on the south side of the river. These two towns—or rather town and suburb, for the Corporation of Newcastle had leased the control of Gateshead from the Bishop of Durham, who held jurisdiction over it—were joined by a bridge which, like old London Bridge, had houses on it, and was already too narrow and crowded for the volume of traffic which it was called upon to bear. This bridge, after being put in repair in 1770, when its middle arch, previously used as a drawbridge, was replaced in stone, was for the most part swept away in the great floods of 1771 and replaced by a new

PRINCIPAL TOWNS AND PRODUCTS OF ENGLAND, 1746

bridge after a more modern fashion. Newcastle, on the north of the Tyne, had been a walled town, though most of the ancient walls had disappeared and what was left was mainly ruinous, and the houses had spread out far beyond the ancient limits. Outside the old walls, between them and the river banks, was a long line of wharves, reputed the longest in England, except those of Yarmouth. These wharves were used largely for the coal trade, of which Newcastle was the principal centre, though Sunderland had already invaded its monopoly in the supply of the London market. Newcastle, however, had other industries besides coal. Newcastle grindstones were famous all over the world, and the manufacture of hardware was also becoming, in the early eighteenth century, an important local industry.

From the wharves by the river-side the road sloped steeply up towards the walls. Within these, the town had two broad main streets, flanked by good shops and houses and built mostly of stone: for, although the gentry and nobility were by this time beginning to desert Newcastle as a place of winter residence, there were still a good many big stone mansions, as well as public buildings, in the city itself. Apart from the two main streets, and the numerous churches and the ruined castle, the town consisted of a maze of narrow alleys, with buildings constructed largely of timber, though some of the older structures were of stone, and brick was also used to a certain extent. Both Newcastle and Gateshead were built on steep slopes running up from the river; and, the land on the Newcastle side being irregular, the principal buildings were largely perched on high ground, with crowded lesser buildings on the slopes beneath them. Newcastle was notoriously a smoky town, because of the ironworks and its extensive use of coal; and despite its great mansions it was no longer a resort of gaiety or fashion. Perhaps our traveller might have seen its first playhouse being built, in readiness for its opening in 1748; but Newcastle Playhouse was designed for the citizens rather than for the fashionable visitors. Its trading activity, both in foreign commerce and in the sea-borne coal trade with London, gave it a considerable number of wealthy merchants, whose houses were already spreading over the high land round the Town Moor towards Jesmond. The city was proud, too, of its culture; for it was already in possession of a considerable public library, with a librarian salaried at £25 and an endowment of £5 a year for buying books.

Ships of some size could come right up the Tyne as far as Newcastle, though not beyond the bridge. But in fact most of the sea-going vessels came no further than South Shields or Tynemouth. The coals which were brought to Newcastle from the surrounding pits were loaded at the wharves into "keels," or lighters, and thence put on board ship in the roads of Shields. Newcastle Corporation had ancient jurisdiction over the River Tyne right down to its mouth as well as above the city; and this put the control of the coal trade effectively into its hands. The building of both ships and lighters was one of the town's principal industries, carried on not within the city limits but along the river banks between Newcastle bridge and Shields and Tynemouth. At South Shields too were the famous salt-pans, noted for the curing of "Newcastle salmon," which were sent chiefly to London. The Tyne, however, was not a salmon river, the fish being brought mostly on horseback from Berwick-on-Tweed to be cured at Shields.

Apart from its industrial and commercial importance, Newcastle was, even more than Carlisle in the West, England's gateway into Scotland. It was an important "posting-town" —that is, a place where travellers could always get fresh horses from the postmaster and pick up letters that had been left in his care to await their arrival. Commonly, indeed, the traveller going north or south would break his journey at Newcastle for the night. This made it a town of inns and innkeepers, which set itself out for the accommodation of travellers, and prided itself, despite its smoke, on putting a brave face before the world with its public buildings and its fine situation looking across the broad river towards the Durham hills. It was, however, with its crowded alleys, a dark town at night: for street-lighting—with oil-lamps—was not introduced until 1763, and before that there were only such lamps as individual householders chose to keep lighted before their doorways after dark. Even after 1763 the Corporation did not have the lamps lighted when the moon was out.

Like most English towns that had a history behind them, and were not mere villages swollen out by the recent growth of industry, Newcastle possessed its charters from the Crown, and was ruled by a Mayor and Corporation whose jurisdiction extended not only over the city itself, but also, as we have seen, up and down the river, and, by lease from the Bishop of Durham, over the neighbouring suburb of Gateshead. Newcastle's ancient Corporation was of a peculiar type. The franchise rested upon the twenty-four ancient crafts or gilds of the city, and the Common Councillors who chose the Aldermen were themselves chosen one from each of the crafts. This gave the city a relatively wide franchise, including the entire body of merchants and master-craftsmen and a considerable number of journeymen as well. Indeed, in Newcastle the ancient corporations of craftsmen retained much of their activity, though side by side with them there had developed new forms of combination appropriate to the changing times. The Tyne colliery-owners and coal merchants were both closely combined—the Newcastle "Vend" being the most famous of all eighteenth-century capitalist combines, with its elaborate regulations for the control of the output and sale of coal for the London market, including all the devices associated with the working of the most up-to-date cartels of our own day. The "keel-men" again—that is, the lightermen, who plied with their "keels" between Newcastle and the roads of Shields—had recently formed a strong Friendly Society of their own, and there were a good many other Friendly Societies in the town, some of them embryonic forms of Trade Union. Altogether Newcastle in 1746 furnishes an excellent illustration, with its contrasts of medievalism and modernity, of the typical thriving commercial centre of the days before the Industrial Revolution.

For Newcastle stood both in wealth and population high up among the towns of eighteenth-century England. In the whole country there was in the middle of the eighteenth century only one town, apart from London, with a population large enough to give it rank as a considerable place by modern standards. That town was Bristol, with from 80,000 to 100,000 inhabitants, according to the extent of the suburban area included in the count. Norwich came next, with about 50,000 in the city and its suburbs; and Manchester, including Salford and the surrounding villages, had perhaps 45,000. Liverpool had about 35,000 people, and Birmingham nearly 30,000. Thereafter came Hull and Sheffield and Newcastle-on-Tyne, with about 20,000 each, Leeds and Nottingham and Chester with about 15,000, and then towns such as Shrewsbury and Worcester, with not more than 10,000 inhabitants. Over most of the country, towns in the modern sense of the word hardly existed at all—only large villages, or at the most small "market towns" which lived on traffic with the surrounding countryside.

Passing through Newcastle, a traveller in 1746 would have found more coal-pits across the northern part of the county of Durham, mingled with mines of lead and iron, and even some of silver in the western region. As he passed out of the coal region he would have come in South Durham to richer agricultural country, with but few pits and ironworks as yet; for the Tees developed its industries much later than the Tyne or Wear.

Crossing into North Yorkshire he would have found more mines of lead, coal and copper round about Richmond. By way of these and of largely empty moorland country he would have come to York, still reputed the second city in England, though no longer so in population or industrial activity. For York lost its economic importance when the woollen trade deserted it for the neighbourhood of Leeds and Halifax, where the small manufacturers could be free of ancient gild regulations, and could develop their manufactures on lines of individualist enterprise. York, in 1746, had recently made an attempt to introduce the cotton manufacture as a substitute for wool, but without much success. It was of account, not as an industrial centre, but as a cathedral city much in favour as a place of winter residence for the Yorkshire nobles and gentlemen. It was, by contrast with Newcastle, a city of pleasure, with balls and assemblies every night in the season, plays in plenty, and a race-meeting famous all over the North of England. It was reputed to have declined in population with the decay of its woollen manufactures; but it throve well enough as a centre of fashion, rival and complement to Scarborough and Knaresborough, the two chief northern "spas," and as the principal ecclesiastical centre of Northern England, with its magnificent Minster, and its Archbishop, Primate of the Northern Province.

From York a traveller might well have wished to turn away to the west, in order to visit the rapidly developing "clothing district" of the West Riding, which had stolen away the trade of York and scattered the woollen manufacture plentifully over a wealthy and populous countryside. We imagine such a one riding out from York through Tadcaster with its breweries to Leeds and Halifax—the former already the principal mart for the Yorkshire small masters, who wove their own cloth and brought it to market at Leeds Cloth Hall, and Halifax, reputed "the most populous parish in England," at the centre of an area in which almost every farmhouse had a weaving-shed attached to it, and almost every farmer was a manufacturer as well, giving employment to a skilled worker or two in his own house, and, for spinning and preparing the thread, to the wives and children of the cottagers who found employment as craftsmen in his workshop or as labourers on his land.

Large towns in the West Riding the traveller would not have found. Leeds had fewer than fifteen thousand inhabitants in 1746, and Halifax only a few thousands. Bradford was still a village. For the woollen manufacture was scattered in small workshops over the face of the country, and the working craftsman was often still something of a farmer as well as an industrial entrepreneur. Here was a land of independent small masters, often employing as yet little hired labour— embryonic capitalists who were, in the course of the ensuing century, either to turn into fully fledged factory-owners using steam-power, or, if they lost in the race, to become wage-workers under the orders of their more successful rivals.

Let us imagine a traveller passing through this very rapidly developing textile area, which was already undercutting the traditional prices of the western and eastern counties, and then turning back eastwards, to find iron mines increasing in number as he approached Sheffield, with its active trade in many kinds of smith's work, especially knives and cutlery of all sorts. Round Doncaster he would have found an active domestic manufacture of knitted goods; and, if he had a mind, having missed the flourishing "spa" at Scarborough, he could have drunk the waters at Knaresborough instead. When he left Yorkshire, he would have thought of it not only as a great and rapidly advancing centre of the woollen industry, but at least as much as a great place for two things that are often found together—gentlemen and horses. For Yorkshire was a great horse-breeding centre; and no county in England had so many seats of noblemen and gentlemen for the traveller to admire. Yet, except around Halifax, it was not yet a populous county—far less so than most of the counties of the West and East.

Sheffield, already for centuries a home of the edged-tool manufacture, had in 1746 about twelve thousand inhabitants. It was a plainly built town, which was just beginning, by means of the Don Navigation, to develop its trade with distant markets, and to grow into an important industrial centre for plated goods as well as for manufactures of iron and steel. Here was the famous Company of the Cutlers of Hallamshire, incorporated in 1625, which regulated the principal trade of the town. Not far off, at Rotherham and Masborough, were other important centres of the iron trade. It was actually in 1746 that Samuel Walker and his brothers established at Masborough the famous ironworks, soon to rival in importance the Darby works at Coalbrookdale, and to become celebrated for the manufacture of the largest cannon and the finest products of cast iron, as well as for tinplates and steel. These works played a large part in the development of the collieries round Sheffield, especially those belonging to Lord Fitzwilliam and the Earl of Effingham.

From Sheffield the traveller would have passed through Doncaster, then a centre not of coal-mining, but of the manufacture of knit stockings, gloves and waistcoats, to Hull, the principal seaport for Yorkshire and the Midland area served by the Trent and its tributaries. Hull, an ancient town, once the centre of the Greenland fishery, now depended for its prosperity mainly upon the Trent and Ouse Navigations

which were chiefly administered in the town. By means of
these rivers it attracted to itself a large trade in corn, coal,
Yorkshire textiles and Midland knitted goods, gloves and
pottery, beer and malt, and many other products, both for
export, chiefly to Holland and the Baltic, and for the London
market. It was also an important centre for the import of
produce from Europe and of Eastern goods *via* London for
supplying Yorkshire and the Midland Counties. Its chief
industries, which were secondary to its commerce, were shipbuilding and above all sail-making, in which it excelled.

Hull was thus one of England's busiest ports. Its trade to
London was done mainly by whole fleets sailing together, of
as many as fifty or sixty sail, or in wartime, under convoy, a
hundred or more. It had a special Corporation, Trinity
House, for settling disputes between shipowners and seamen,
and numerous endowed charities for seamen, as well as a free
school of good standing. Greenland House, the old centre of
the fishery, had by this time been turned into a corn warehouse
because of the decay of the older trade; but the herring fishery
was still active in nearer waters. The town was close-built
with many narrow alleys; but it had paved streets and was
proud of its buildings, and, in 1746, of a newly installed
"engine for turning salt water into fresh."

Here the traveller would have ended his Yorkshire wander-
ings and crossed over the Humber into Lincolnshire. There
he would have found himself in a pleasant and fertile agricultural country, given over largely to the breeding of fat cattle
and of horses, as well as to sheep-raising. Traversing the
whole length of the county he would have come to Boston,
a flourishing port with a good harbour, by the standards of
the time, much engaged in the trade both with London and
with the Continental ports. Leaving behind him the famous
church-tower known as "Boston Stump"—a noted landmark
for seamen—he would have come by way of King's Lynn,
another and a wealthy merchant town, into the populous
county of Norfolk, then exceeded in population only by
Middlesex, Yorkshire and Devonshire. Here was already an
important corn-growing country, though the great agricultural
improvements of "Turnip" Townshend had hardly begun

to produce their effect, and that other great improver, "Coke of Norfolk," was still to come. Norfolk was still at this stage above all else an active centre of the woollen and worsted manufacture. Norwich was pre-eminently a town of weavers; and there were spinners and stocking knitters scattered over a large part of the agricultural area. Wool, as well as wheat, was a staple product of the county; but the great age of Norfolk wheat-growing was not yet, much of the soil being too light and sandy until it was improved by root-crops, drainage, and agricultural enclosure.

Norwich being one of the principal cities of England, with a population of about thirty-six thousand, excluding the suburbs, we may pause here again to consider what it was like some two centuries ago. Situated ten miles from the sea as the crow flies, and more than twice as far by the windings of the River Yare, it was nevertheless a seaport, the Yare being kept navigable right up to the town. This fact was of importance for its industries, and above all for the worsted manufacture, of which it was the principal centre. Norwich was a city of craftsmen, who carried on their work mainly in long garrets above their houses, and were proud of their craft independence in dealing with the rich merchant clothiers to whom they sold their products. The woolcombers were another important urban craft; and all the villages round the city were largely engaged in spinning and preparing worsted yarn for the use of the Norwich weavers.

Even in 1746, the predominance of the Norwich manufacturers was being threatened not merely by the developing use of cottons, but still more by the rise of the cheaper woollen and worsted manufactures of Yorkshire. For the Yorkshiremen, using new methods and producing what contemporaries denounced as goods of inferior quality, were already undercutting the Norwich craftsmen, and Norwich, unlike other eighteenth-century industrial towns, was hardly increasing its population at all. It remained, in 1746, a busy and flourishing place; but it depended so exclusively on the worsted trade as to be peculiarly vulnerable to the loss of its pre-eminence in that branch of manufacture.

In other respects Norwich was a pleasant town, though not

a place of fashion. On weekdays, there were few people about the streets; for all were busy within doors at their looms or other branches of the worsted trade. But on Sundays and holidays the streets were thronged with people; and Norwich, being built to cover a large area and not crowded together like most of the towns of the time, was then a gay and attractive place, known to eighteenth-century travellers as "the city of gardens and orchards," because many of the houses within, the ancient walls had gardens and fruit-trees. The walls, already in decay, surrounded a larger area then than those of any other town in England. There were five bridges across the river, and the roads were wide. Altogether, Norwich had ground for her citizens to claim her as the principal city of eastern England, rivalled only by London, the metropolis, and by Bristol far away in the West. The traveller, halting there in 1746, would have been unusually prescient if, newly come from Leeds and Halifax, he had predicted how the ancient industry of East Anglia was soon to go down before the competition of the enterprising manufacturers of the upstart West Riding of Yorkshire.

Beyond Norwich the traveller would have come to Yarmouth, the great centre of the herring fishery; and by that route he would have passed into Suffolk, another thriving county, with manufacture of woollen cloth and linen, and an agricultural economy based largely on the production of butter and cheese for the London market. In Suffolk, too, he would have found the seats of noblemen and gentlemen fast increasing in number, and at Bury St. Edmunds a flourishing place of residence and resort for persons of fashion and substantial merchants. Beyond Bury St. Edmunds to the south lay the old "clothing" district of Suffolk and Essex—Lavenham, Long Melford, Sudbury, Stoke-by-Nayland—where the trade for the most part was already in decay. Turning east, however, towards Colchester, he would have again found woollen manufactures in a flourishing condition; for Colchester was as celebrated for its "white bays" as for its oyster-fishing. In Essex he would have found a rich country of mixed tillage and pasture, with many woodlands used for the supply of timber. Hereabouts barley was grown in great plenty, and there were

also hop-gardens. Harwich was a busy little port, much used
for the sea route by passengers to the Continent. All along
the coast were active fisheries and also a great industry of
fowling for the London market; and in the flat moist lands
near the coast and the Thames estuary were great numbers of
cattle, often brought there to be fattened up after journeying
long distances on their four feet in readiness for the Londoners'
consumption.

At this point, instead of journeying to London, let us imagine
the traveller taking boat and crossing by Tilbury and Graves-
end into Kent. Here he would not find so many manufactures,
though Maidstone was active in the thread trade and there
were still in Canterbury weavers of Walloon descent. Chatham
already had its busy dockyard for the Navy; and the Medway
was noted for its salmon-fisheries. But most of the country was
still agricultural, as much of it remains to-day—hops in the
north, sheep and corn in the Isles of Sheppey and Thanet, and
great quantities of fruit, especially apples and cherries, as well
as wheat and cattle. Faversham was noted for its trade in
pigs for London, and forestry products were important,
especially in the centre and south. Many visitors came from
London to drink the waters at Tunbridge Wells, or to seek
a retreat in the many beautiful villages during the summer
months.

As we passed by the Yorkshire "Spas"—Scarborough and
Knaresborough—in silence, we may pause here to get a
glimpse of Tunbridge Wells. First developed in the seventeenth century as an inland "watering-place," Tunbridge
Wells had become, by 1746, the favourite resort of London
citizens in search of a healthful holiday not too far from home.
Charles II and later Queen Anne had advertised the value of
its chalybeate waters; and round the Wells, fitted out by Lord
Abergavenny early in the previous century, had grown up
a regular town of lodging-houses and shops, rooms of assembly,
coffee-houses and the like, well built in a spacious fashion to
attract the gentry and those citizens who were eager to follow
pleasure where the gentry led. Tunbridge Wells was Bath
upon a smaller scale, and with less of wealth and fashion. It
knew well how to cater for the favourite eighteenth-century

habit of drinking the waters, and therewith for dancing, promenading, frequenting assemblies, plays and concerts, matchmaking to the heart's content, and gaming as well, though in 1746 the new laws against public gaming-houses had caused a sharp falling off in this part of its flourishing business of pleasure.

From Kent the traveller would have passed into Sussex, coming at once upon many mines of iron and forges for the iron-casting scattered among the already diminishing woodlands in the eastern part of the county. He would have already found the forges threatened with the exhaustion of their supplies of fuel—for the trees must be preserved for the use of shipbuilders for the Royal Navy as well as for the merchant marine. Great guns—great by eighteenth-century standards, though they would seem mere pop-guns now—were among the most important products of the Sussex iron industry, which was essentially a small-scale manufacture carried on by tiny squads of workers in forest clearings remote from towns. Next to iron, glass-making was the leading Sussex industry. In the rich deep soil of the Weald agriculture flourished. Sheep and cattle were bred, and oats grown over a large area. Malting was also a thriving business—largely for the big capitalist breweries in London. But Sussex was not highly populous, or, as yet, a place of much fashionable resort. Brighthelmstone, or Brighton, was still hardly more than a fishing village.

In Hampshire, which comes next on the road, shipbuilders were active round the coast, especially by the inlets of Southampton Water and Beaulieu River, wherever a convenient "hard" by the mouth of a navigable river made it possible for timber to be brought cheaply from the interior. Southampton was a busy port, and there was great activity round the naval dockyard and arsenal of Portsmouth—an important military as well as naval centre. Inland the country was chiefly agricultural, though there was a not very flourishing woollen manufacture towards the north. The New Forest was still a wild area as some of it is even to-day—for the numerous plans for its settlement had come to nothing. The soil of Hampshire is good; and there was much growing of corn and raising of cattle, and also of bacon for the London market. Honey too was an important product, and the timber industry was still of account, though here too it was decaying with the depletion of the forest area. There was some iron manufacture, but much less than in Sussex. These two counties—Sussex and Hampshire—were much less thickly populated than Kent or Essex, Norfolk or Suffolk—largely because of the absence, save on a quite small scale, of the pervasive woollen manufacture, and because the outward stream of suburbanites from London had not yet flowed significantly over their borders.

A traveller might make hence a brief journey across to the Isle of Wight, where he would find sheep reputed second only to those of the Cotswolds for their wool, together with fine pastures for cattle as well as sheep, fisheries, and an active trapping and shooting of rabbits, hares and wildfowl for the London market.

Thence he could cross back into Dorset, a county rich in corn and cattle and important for its timber. He would find the famous Purbeck quarries, producing freestone and some marble, an industry of clay-getting for tobacco-pipes, and the noted Bridport rope and cable manufacture, based upon local hemp. Here too he would see fishermen and fowlers in great numbers; for Dorset was famous for its wildfowl.

Passing into Devonshire, the traveller would reach in the Western Counties the third great centre of the woollen manufacture—a regional industry far greater at this time in its total extent than that of either Yorkshire or East Anglia. Exeter was famous for its serges, and a town of much resort; and this and other branches of the woollen manufacture spread over a good part of the county in its older-inhabited regions. Agriculture, of course, flourished too—corn and cattle and a great raising of sheep for wool. There had been in the first half of the century much activity in the improvement of hilly and barren lands, by means of manures brought from the seashore. But large areas remained uncultivated, including the great stretch of Dartmoor. In some of this barren country were mines of tin and lead, and some of silver. Dartmouth and Plymouth were already important naval harbours, though not dockyard centres comparable with Portsmouth or

Chatham. Fishing was actively carried on along most of the south coast and to a less extent on the north.

From Plymouth the traveller would cross into Cornwall, a land of ports, fishermen, and mines, with prosperous agriculture in its fertile valleys. Cornwall has many havens, among which Falmouth stood then, as it stands now, pre-eminent; and the fishing industry was of great importance. The mines were of tin and copper, with some silver and gold, and china-clay was mined or quarried around St. Austell. In the tin and copper areas the "free" miners had their ancient institutions still working. The Court of Stannaries settled claims and did something to regulate the trade, which was not yet affected by the coming competition with the large-scale exploitation of the newer copper-mines in Anglesey. Apart from mining there was little industry—unless the making of M.P.s be so regarded; for in that Cornwall, with its many "rotten boroughs", some under Crown influence, was first of all. A traveller would probably have been most struck by the alien character of the people, who thought and to some extent still spoke in a foreign tongue.

In Cornwall we have again passed outside the area dominated by the woollen manufacture. But we come back to it in Somerset, crossing North Devon by way of Exmoor on our route. Somerset in the mid-eighteenth century was probably fifth in populousness among English counties, next after Norfolk, with only Middlesex, Yorkshire and Devonshire well ahead. Somerset the traveller would have found exceptionally rich in agriculture as well as in industry, in corn as well as in cattle reputed among the best in England, and in sheep. Somerset cheeses were well thought of, and Bristol and the rapidly growing resort of health and fashion at Bath provided excellent markets for a wide diversity of agricultural products. Bristol, easily the second-largest city in England, was still the great centre for the export of cloth, as well as for imports from all parts of the American continent. Taunton cloths had a high reputation for quality, and there were spinners scattered throughout the hamlets, and many large villages and small market-towns given over chiefly to weaving. Mining in the Mendips had not quite died out, and there was active quarrying in the county for the famous Bath and Bristol stone, which was in much request for building not only at Bath, but as far afield as London.

Here were two towns which, for widely different reasons, both deserve more than a passing mention. Bath in 1746 was at the height of its glory under the rule of the famous Beau Nash—easily the leading pleasure resort of all England, though one of its attractions had been lost, much to Nash's pecuniary damage, by the Act of 1745 which suppressed public gambling. At the beginning of the century Bath had been a small town, almost confined within its ancient Roman walls, though it had long been noted as a resort for invalids, who went there to bathe in the waters—not to drink them till Bath entered on its second life as a "watering-place" in the latter part of the seventeenth century. Thereafter growth was rapid. The first Pump Room was opened in 1704, followed within four years by a Theatre and an Assembly Room for the fashionable visitors. While Nash looked after the gaieties of the place, Wood, as architect and Pope's friend, Ralph Allen, of Prior Park, set to work building a new and spacious city in place of the narrow and crowded purlieus of the old town. Bath was planned, as no other town in England has been planned since the days of the Romans, with long terraces of stately houses and walks and gardens for the visitors' pleasure. It wears still much of the look which Wood and Allen gave to it two centuries ago—which they were busy giving to it when our imaginary traveller would have come upon it in the course of his pilgrimage.

But Bath, of course, was planned not for the common people, but for the rich—not, indeed, for the nobility and gentry in any exclusive sense; for its citizens had a clear eye for the main chance, and set themselves out to attract the well-to-do merchant or tradesman as well as the upper classes. Matches could be made at Bath for all who had daughters to marry and money to spend; and the serious business of the search for health soon became quite a secondary matter when Nash and his satellites had organized the city as a haunt of fashion and pleasure, and perhaps above all else, of matchmaking as we see it pictured in the stories of Smollett, or, later, Jane Austen.

From Bath to Bristol was but a short journey, even in those days; and Bristol, as we have seen, was the second city in England. Here too were "Hot-Wells," and some coming of visitors to bathe and drink the waters. But Bristol was primarily a commercial city, very busy with import and export trade, especially to and from the West Indies and the American continent. Its merchants were notoriously jealous of their privileges and of their independence of the merchants of London. The populous country behind the city supplied them abundantly with woollen goods for export, and they also did a thriving export trade in bottled beer and cider to the West Indies and the American plantations—so much so that glass-bottle making ranked among Bristol's leading industries. Moreover, the position of the town allowed it, by means of the Severn and Wye navigations and the Bristol Channel ports, to gather to itself most of the trade of Wales and the border counties; and it also did much business with Ireland, though there Liverpool was already becoming a formidable rival.

Architecturally, Bristol was closely built, with many narrow streets and alleys crowded round the quays and wharves upon the River Frome. Ships came right up to these quays, though vessels of the greatest burden were forced to remain lower down the Avon, into which the Frome runs in the heart of the city. Bristol in 1746 was very proud of the new crane installed upon its quay, designed by the ingenious Mr. Padmore of Bath, who had also made much-admired engines and trackways for bringing the stone from the quarries to rebuild his native town. Already the Bristol Corporation was clearing away houses in order to enlarge the space about the quays and improve the convenience of the crowded central part of the city. But Bristol remained a city with little dignity of appearance to match its commercial importance.

Bristol stands on the River Avon, on the frontier between Somerset and Gloucestershire, with a foot in each county. In the area behind it lay, in the eighteenth century, the central grazing ground of the famous Cotswold sheep, and sheep-rearing and the woollen manufacture dominated the economy of both counties. The Stroud valley was noted for the high quality of its woollen goods, and especially for its scarlet dyeing. Tewkesbury woollens were also of high quality and value. But Gloucestershire had other industries as well. It raised corn and timber, and was noted for bacon and cider, and for its salmon-fishing. Round Gloucester and towards the Forest of Dean were iron manufactures, and also steel-making; and Dean Forest produced coal, and had free miners with laws of their own under the Crown, not unlike those of the Cornish Stannaries.

From Gloucestershire, leaving Monmouth to the west—for that belongs rather with Wales—the traveller would have passed into Herefordshire, the county of the "four W's"— wheat, wool, wood, and water—this last because of the high reputation of the salmon-fisheries of the Wye. In Hereford-shire the woollen manufacture was found in certain areas, notably round Kineton; but the county as a whole was noted more for the high quality of its raw wool than for manufac-tures. Here, as in Gloucestershire, the cider-makers were active; for cider was still comparable in importance with beer as a national drink, at any rate in the West, and the full, dark, Herefordshire cider commanded a big export market in Ireland and the West Indies. Perry, too, was extensively made in Herefordshire, both for bottling and for local consumption.

Passing into Shropshire, we leave the country of sheep and woollen manufactures behind, and come into an area of hills and valleys in which wheat and barley were extensively grown and cattle raised. Here again there was plenty of timber, and there were also coal-pits to serve the rapidly advancing iron industry of Coalbrookdale, where the Darbys had already learnt to practise the art of smelting the metal with coal instead of charcoal—though charcoal had still to be used for the finer processes. Coal-pits and ironworks gave Shropshire consider-able industrial importance, though it was still predominantly an agricultural county, known from the number of ¡ortified seats along the Welsh Marches as the "County of Castles." Shrewsbury, on the Severn, was not only the principal market-town for all the country of the Welsh border, but also an important social centre, noted for its good gentlemen's houses and its air of gaiety and solid comfort.

Out of Shropshire the road led into Cheshire, a county

abounding in gentlemen's houses and parks, predominantly given over to pasture and tillage. Here corn and cattle were the basis of the agricultural economy; and the dairying industry yielded a plentiful supply of cheese as well as milk and butter. But there were also some mines of metal and coal, a large manufacture of salt, a button-making industry at Macclesfield, and a glove industry centred upon Congleton. In this county the principal city was, of course, Chester, or West Chester, as it was commonly called in the eighteenth century. At the time of our traveller's visit Chester was fighting almost its last battle to retain its status as a port in face of the growing competition of Liverpool. In the early part of the century, the Dee had been so silted up that sea-going vessels could no longer come up to the city, but were forced to discharge their cargoes six miles or more away. But in 1732 an Act of Parliament was passed—followed by a further Act in 1741—for cutting a new channel right up to Chester; and by the time of which we are writing ships were again loading and discharging at the ancient quays. Chester, however, did not succeed in regaining its old position as a commercial centre: it was important rather as a port for passengers journeying between England and Ireland, and as a market-town and social meeting-place for the farmers and gentlemen of the county.

Its ancient walls were already kept by the Corporation as a pleasure-walk; and the famous "Rows" were alternatively admired for their picturesqueness or censured as dark and dirty, obscuring the shops and houses and violating the Augustan canons of contemporary taste. But, if the "Rows" were a matter of dispute, Chester's planned appearance with its four broad streets forming a cross was generally admired. The city was proud too of possessing, even in 1746, an excellent water supply pumped by engines from the Dee, and of keeping its streets and walks clean and sweet, according to the standards of the time. It had some textile manufactures, largely in the hands of Dutch settlers; but its chief industry was the making of clay tobacco-pipes, and caring for travellers and gentlefolk and farmers in its numerous inns.

Crossing the Mersey by the one available bridge at Warrington—for elsewhere the swift current and the wide mud-flats and marshlands beside the river allowed no passage—the traveller would have advanced into Lancashire. Warrington itself was an important and thriving town, until about this time of more account than its neighbour, Liverpool. Indus-trially, Lancashire was an important centre of the woollen and linen manufactures, in conjunction with which a cotton industry was already beginning to grow up, based as yet largely on mixed tissues of wool and cotton, or of linen and cotton. Manchester was the chief centre of these rapidly developing textile trades; and Manchester was already a very important place. At and around Warrington metal industries flourished, especially in the making of nails and wire and other similar products; and in South Lancashire the small-scale foundations of the engineering industry were already being laid. Coal-pits for the supply of the metal industries and of house-coal for Manchester were already being opened up in considerable numbers. For the rest, Lancashire, save the ancient town of Preston, was still largely agricultural; but, except round Ormskirk, its agriculture was for the most part not advanced in technique. Oats were the principal cereal crop, and there was also flax-growing for the linen industry. The reputation of Lancashire oxen stood high: indeed, the county was more notable for pasture than for tillage. It was already growing very populous in the south; but there was as yet nothing to foreshadow its coming predominance. The West Riding of Yorkshire, and not Lancashire, was still the leading centre of the textile industries of the north.

Here we must pause to say something of the two rapidly growing towns which were soon to become, after London, the greatest cities in England. Throughout the eighteenth century observers marvelled at the extraordinary increase of Liver-pool's trade and prosperity. It was already, by 1746, the equal of Bristol in imports and exports of merchandise; and, unlike Bristol, it had engaged extensively in the highly profitable trade in slaves from Africa to the West Indies and the American plantations. The Goree Piazzas in Liverpool, where the slaves used to be herded together by the quays, still remind the modern visitor of this unsavoury aspect of Liverpool's rise to wealth. The slave trade from Liverpool had begun in 1709, and by 1746 there were already between fifty and sixty vessels regularly engaged in it.

But apart from this revolting commerce, which was suppressed in 1806, Liverpool was prospering chiefly because of the great growth of the trade in goods with the Americas. Its rise had begun in the seventeenth century; but as late as 1700 it had still fewer than six thousand inhabitants. By 1746 it had at least twenty thousand, without its suburbs, and by 1800 nearly eighty thousand. Until the second decade of the eighteenth century it was hampered by the lack of an enclosed harbour, the vessels having to ride in the open roads behind the protecting bar at the mouth of the Mersey. But in 1709 an Act was obtained for building a wet dock—the first in the country outside London—and by 1746 this dock had been enlarged and improved, so that it would hold a hundred vessels. The town, under a Corporation noted for its progressive policy, had not only built and lighted the docks, but had also in 1709 secured a special Act for improving the supply of water, and had promoted several other Acts for developing the river navigations—Mersey, Weaver, and Dove—on which it depended for marketing its goods in the interior of the country, as well as for securing an abundance of commodities for export.

Eighteenth-century observers seldom failed to praise the enlightened policy of the Liverpool Corporation as one of the chief sources of the town's prosperity. This is the more remarkable because it was purely a closed corporation, recruiting itself by co-option without any element of election by the main body even of the wealthier citizens. It excluded Dissenters from membership, and chiefly recruited itself, and obtained its better-paid officers, from a narrow group of governing families. Its competence, nevertheless, must be taken as proved; and by contemporary standards it was remarkably honest as well as competent in the management of the extensive property belonging to the borough. In 1746 it had not yet gone so far as to make public provision for lighting or cleaning the streets—these obligations still resting, as elsewhere, on the individual householders. But in 1748 it secured an Act for this purpose—the first obtained by any town in England out¯side London.

Manchester, in 1746, occupied a very different position from Liverpool, in that it possessed no municipal corporation at all. It was under the rule of a manorial "Court Leet," which appointed a Boroughreeve and two Constables to supervise the "policing" of the town, with the aid of a number of subordinate executive officers. The Court Leet, at which every householder was obliged to attend, levied rates on the inhabitants, and undertook the duties of municipal government over an area much larger than that of the town. For it was not until 1765 that the citizens obtained, under the first of a series of private Acts of Parliament, the power to appoint Commissioners of their own to watch and light the streets, and not until about 1780 that the new Commissioners began seriously to impinge upon the jurisdiction of the manorial court.

Manchester, as a mere manorial village, despite its population, sent no members to Parliament till 1832, and had no municipal corporation till later still. The population, about 1746, could be variously stated at anything between fifteen thousand and thirty thousand, according to the area covered by the survey. For the town itself, fifteen thousand was probably an ample estimate, with another two thousand or so for Salford; but the manor and parish covered much wider areas, and included many populous villages. In 1770 the parish of Manchester, together with Salford, had over forty thousand people.

Though unincorporated as a borough, Manchester was an old town, and had been an important textile centre throughout the seventeenth century, when it was active in the manufacture of linen goods as well as of the so-called "Manchester cottons," which were in fact made of various textile yarns. But it had been growing fast in the first half of the eighteenth century, and had already earned the name of the "first village in England." It was not, however, in 1746, growing so fast as Liverpool, nor was there anything to foreshadow its coming predominance as the metropolis of northern England. In appearance, it was a busy, squat town, with little to attract the traveller except its ancient parish church and a very few other old buildings, including the Grammar School, founded in 1519, and noticed by a reference book of 1751 as having "three masters, with excellent salaries"—with the further comment that "the foundation boys have certain exhibitions for their maintenance at the University." We may here observe that a traveller could have found, in nearly every town through which he passed, some sort of endowed school, either based on an ancient religious foundation, or instituted later by some local benefactor of note. Some of these endowed schools were in decay, and their revenues improperly applied; but many were in a fairly flourishing condition, though they had been largely diverted from their original purpose of providing for "poor scholars" to caring for the children of the better-off citizens. The children of the poor, if they went to school at all, attended dame-schools or similar establishments, often kept by very poorly educated persons, whose remuneration was but a tiny pittance. In the villages, the parson often kept the school, like Parson Adams in Fielding's *Joseph Andrews*. In the towns most of the poor had to pay for such schooling as they got; and for the most part they could afford but little. There had been an active movement for the establishment of Charity Schools in the first third of the eighteenth century; but the interest then displayed was largely transferred to foreign missions after 1750. Not till near the end of the century did Methodism and the Evangelical Movement cause a growing section of the rich to busy themselves anew about the charitable education of the poor; and even then there were many misgivings about the dangers of teaching poor people ideas above their station.

There were other towns in Lancashire besides Liverpool and Manchester and Warrington. Preston and Lancaster, among others, were ancient boroughs; and, in all, six Lancashire towns sent members to Parliament. But these other towns were small; and most of the county population outside Liverpool and Manchester lived in the southern part of the county, in manufacturing villages which were to turn within the next half-century into crowded and hideous, black and insanitary factory towns.

In 1746 few visited the thinly populated and mountainous county of Westmorland. Here agriculture provided

CP · C

for little, except for the subsistence of the local population. There was, however, one town of considerable importance. Kendal and the neighbouring villages were busily occupied with manufactures of wool and cotton, with hat-making and with stocking-knitting; and Kendal ranked as a considerable place—far more so than Appleby, the little county town.

Across the county border the road passes into Cumberland, another area of relatively sparse population. Here were more cattle on the hills, and the valleys also were largely given over to stock-breeding. Fishermen and fowlers were numerous along the coast; and some of them were pearl-fishers. Here too were miners in considerable numbers. There were copper-mines at Keswick and Newland, coal-mines round about Whitehaven, a black-lead-mine—the only one of its kind in England—near Keswick. Especially had the mines been developing round Whitehaven, from which Ireland was largely supplied with coal. A new harbour had been built there for the coal trade under Queen Anne, and further improvements were in progress under an Act of 1740. Cockermouth and Ravenglass were also coastal towns of some trade. Carlisle, despite its navigable river, was not. Its two thousand inhabitants were mainly engaged in the fustian trade, or in the ordinary services of a small market-town. Industrially, Penrith, with its tanneries, was more important than Carlisle.

CHAPTER III

A JOURNEY THROUGH ENGLAND IN 1746 (continued)

THE traveller has now completed his circuit of the maritime and border counties of England, in which the chief wealth of the nation lay; for, as we have seen, under eighteenth-century conditions of transport manufacture except for a local market was nearly impossible, save for very light or easily transported ware, in any neighbourhood not within easy reach of the sea or of a navigable river. At the date of our assumed journey, canal-making had not begun. There were, indeed, certain "cuts," straightening out the bends of rivers or providing an easier outlet to the sea, or joining together two navigable streams so as to provide through connections. But the canal proper, that is, the waterway which alters its level by means of locks, was still to come, with the Duke of Bridgewater's successful measures for getting the coal from his collieries to the Manchester market, and for giving Manchester itself an outlet to the Mersey and the sea.

The inland counties, then, depended for their access to markets on the nearness of navigable rivers; and the dredging and maintenance of these waterways was an activity of the greatest importance to eighteenth-century industry and trade. Nottingham and the East Midlands would have been unable to develop as manufacturing centres without the Trent, by far the most important waterway of eastern England. The country between Wiltshire and London depended on the Thames navigation, and in the West the Severn opened up the iron centres of Shropshire and the textile and other manufactures of the West Midlands. Birmingham suffered greatly from lack of transport facilities till the coming of the canals. That is largely why the Birmingham and Black Country manufacturers had to concentrate on the lighter wares, which could be carried by packhorses to the nearest convenient place whence they could be taken further afield by river and sea.

We may picture the traveller, on this occasion, returning from Carlisle to Manchester, and thence going south-east, and coming soon into Derbyshire, over high country by way of Glossop to the already famous Spa at Buxton. Around him here is the country of the High Peak, with Dovedale stretching away to the south. In this mountainous country were numerous mines and quarries—of stone for millstones and whetstones, and of crystal, marble and alabaster. Coal was also actively mined in the north-east, around Chesterfield, and there were iron mines and antimony mines as well. But the most famous Derbyshire mines were the lead-mines of the Peak—the chief source of England's supply of lead, despite the difficulties of transport. In the south of the county the soil was rich; and here was the usual mixture of corn and cattle. The woodlands also were of economic importance.

Derby, the county town, was a place of perhaps five thousand inhabitants, and, but for one recent development, not of great economic importance. It was a corn market for the surrounding country, and also a market for wool; and it had an active industry in malting and brewing, Derby beer being sent to London in considerable quantities. The making navigable of its river, the Derwent, which runs into the Trent, had recently linked it to the important Trent navigation; but what made it most worth a visit in 1746 was the famous silk-mill of Sir Thomas Lombe, fitted with machinery smuggled out of Italy in 1734—for which service to native industry Lombe had been rewarded by Parliament with a grant of £14,000. Lombe's mill stood on an island in the river facing the town; and its secrets were jealously guarded.

From Derby we may picture the traveller passing, by way of Burton-on-Trent—then more famous for its bridge and its horse-races than for its beer—into Staffordshire, where, for the most part, an economy similar to that of Derbyshire prevailed. Here again were coal-pits, iron-mines, copper-mines, lead-mines and quarries of alabaster. Marl was produced for the pottery industries of the towns around Stoke-on-Trent; but the china and earthenware trades were not of great national importance till Wedgwood and Spode revitalized them later in the century, nor could they expand save to a very limited extent till the Grand Junction and other canals gave them better supplies of raw materials and also outlets for their wares to Manchester and the sea, and southward through Birmingham to the London market. Staffordshire at this date was more important for its metal manufactures than for its potteries; for already in the south of the county was the spreading Black Country, with Wolverhampton as its centre, given over to the making of nails and iron utensils of many sorts and kinds. In agriculture, Staffordshire made no great mark. Its produce was mainly for local consumption, and much of its soil was poor and thinly cultivated.

From South Staffordshire the traveller could have crossed into Worcestershire, a county of rich pasture and tillage, especially in the moist, fertile vale of Evesham. Here was much fruit-growing—of apples, pears and cherries—much making of cider and perry, and also, over the rest of the county, of cheese. There was salt at Droitwich, glass-making and iron-working at and round Stourbridge, on the borders of the Black Country, and a considerable textile industry at both Kidder-minster and Worcester, which was a glove-making centre as well—for Worcestershire was a border county between the textile area of the West and the metal-working area of the West Midlands. Worcester, a city of about ten thousand people, was in those days a considerable place, but noted for low wages and poverty as well as for industrial activity.

Next the traveller would have come into Warwickshire, with Birmingham upon its north-western edge. Corn and sheep were the staple products, with dairying and cheese-making and an active tribe of maltsters. There were forests, especially that of Arden, and coal- and iron-mines in the north of the county. Further south, Coventry was still a textile town, engaged in silk-weaving and ribbon-making. But the rising industrial centre was Birmingham, with its countless light, small manufactures of metal goods, especially of brass and copper and steel. In 1746, Birmingham with its environs had from twenty to twenty-five thousand inhabitants, and had doubled its population within half a century. Like Manchester it was not a borough, but remained under manorial govern-ment; but in fact, after the seventeenth century the Lord of the Manor ceased to exercise any real jurisdiction over it, and it was managed by a manorial Court Leet in which the appoint-ments to office were in the hands of the resident householders. It was thus in fact, though not in theory, much more demo-cratically administered than Manchester, or than most of the incorporated towns. But it had not done much by way of local improvements: its civic development began in 1771, when a new body of Street Commissioners was set up; and thereafter the municipal control passed gradually from the ancient Court Leet to the new Commission.

Birmingham in the mid-eighteenth century was already pre-dominantly a town of many small manufacturers, active in providing novelties and semi-luxuries to meet an expanding demand. It was growing fast, despite difficulties of transport, which were even more serious for its supply of raw materials, such as copper from Anglesey or Cornwall, than for the marketing of its light products, which had for the most part a high value in relation to their bulk and weight.

South of Warwickshire comes Oxfordshire—a county of transition. On one side Oxfordshire bordered upon the Western textile area. Witney's blankets were famous, and yielded high wages; and there were woollen manufactures round Chipping Norton at the edge of the Cotswold Hills. Elsewhere the county was predominantly agricultural. It grew much fruit as well as corn, and had excellent pastures for cattle. Burford was famous for saddlery, Banbury for cheese as well as cakes, and Henley in the south-east for malt. Oxford city produced scholars, but at this time none too efficiently, as Jeremy Bentham and Edward Gibbon among others have austerely explained.

Travelling on towards the South, the wanderer would reach Berkshire, again a mixed agricultural economy. Here were many sheep on the downs, as well as cattle, with corn-growing in the valleys, of which some were very fertile, and plentiful woodlands of oak and beech. Here too had been an active textile trade, though it was now decaying. Reading was famous for canvas for the sails of ships, as well as for malt. Newbury still made broadcloth, as it had done since the Middle Ages. Round Windsor was a country noted for cattle as well as forest timber.

Of counties south of the Thames, Surrey alone is left. Here again we touch London, with Southwark expanding rapidly to the south, and the other villages along the riverside becoming considerable places and joining up to form a continuous line of building from Greenwich to Wandsworth. Gentlemen's and rich merchants' seats were abundant in the country round London. Wimbledon, Richmond and Croydon were flourishing places, and Epsom Spa a pleasant village of popular resort for many amusements besides the racing. Over the county as a whole large estates abounded. Agriculturally, Surrey mingled barren heaths in the centre with rich soils near its borders. Corn and walnuts and vegetables were grown, and sheep and cattle raised. Reigate produced fuller's-earth, and there were a few scattered remnants of a decaying manufacture of textiles round Guildford and Godalming. But mainly the county was agricultural, and dominated by the gentlefolk, except where it had been sucked into London's orbit.

In Buckinghamshire, the traveller would have reached the proverbial county of "bread and beef." Its chief activities were directed towards supplying London with corn and cattle, and with timber from the beech-woods. Wycombe was noted already for manufactures of wood; and round Newport Pagnell the poor got or eked out a meagre income by making bone-lace. But most of the county prospered by its good land and its proximity to the London market.

In Hertfordshire the soil is much less good, but eighteenth-century opinion set much store by the excellence of the air. Wheat, barley and malt were produced; but much of the land was woodland, and there were many fine and highly prized gentlemen's seats. At Barnet, another "Spa," the traveller could have taken the waters, and at Ware he could have observed the works of the New River Company, which, since the seventeenth century, had been the principal supplier of London's water for domestic use.

Middlesex, predominantly the metropolitan county, was in 1746 being encroached upon by London very much more rapidly than Surrey. In outer Middlesex beyond London was a land of highly productive soil, some naturally fertile and some greatly improved by drainage and manure. It produced fruit and vegetables, as well as corn and cattle; and it was, like its neighbour Hertfordshire, a land of country houses and highly esteemed estates.

Once more avoiding London, to which we shall come last of all, the traveller has turned his horse's head northwards. In Bedfordshire again the gentlemen's seats were many; but here the traveller would have found himself back in a country of corn and cattle and not of woodlands. There was much making of butter and cheese, and raising of poultry, chiefly for London. Round Olney the manufacture of bone-lace spread across from the Newport Pagnell area; but of more importance was the active straw-hat manufacture of Dunstable and Luton —another domestic industry in which wages were low, and often a supplement to agricultural earnings, though many families lived altogether by lace-making at a very low standard which often involved the necessity of parish relief.

Huntingdonshire the traveller would have found a fertile county, of moist air, much denuded lately of its woodlands. It had famous markets and fairs at St. Ives and St. Neots, and was noted for its excellent pastures, especially the lovely water-meadows around Huntingdon itself. Cattle and corn predominated; and even here London was not too far away to dominate the economy.

In Cambridgeshire the traveller would reach the Fen Country—a land of many cattle. Here too was excellent arable land for corn-growing, and an active trade in wild-fowl. Royston was famous for malting, and Newmarket for horse-breeding as well as for racing and hunting. Manufactures were not many—paper-making and, in the villages, basket-making being the most important. Cambridge had its ancient University; and hard by Cambridge was held the world-famous Stourbridge Fair, to which resorted merchants and salesmen from all over the country, with goods of all sorts, from textiles to hardware, and from amusement booths to agricultural produce.

Northamptonshire, Cambridgeshire's western neighbour, was a flourishing agricultural county, rich in both pasture and tillage, and containing many noble seats. As a manufacturing centre, it was not yet important, unless saltpetre for gunpowder be classified as a manufacture. It had some patches outlying from the textile industries further north, and some tanning and leather-working; but its importance in the boot industry was yet to come.

Leicestershire, too, except for the stocking trade at Leicester and in the surrounding villages, was almost purely agricultural, and very rich, especially in pasture-land. It bred the largest sheep in England, though not of the finest wool. Its woodlands were of importance; and, in tillage, it specialized in beans and peas and similar crops. It had also a coalfield already developing round what is now Coalville, though this was not of great extent. Next to Leicestershire, little Rutland had a largely similar agricultural economy, but with more corn and cattle and timber, and fewer sheep.

Finally, the traveller would have reached Nottinghamshire, very fertile in the south-east, and thickly wooded, especially about the "Dukeries" in the east and north. Here, among the woodlands of Sherwood Forest, were some of England's greatest estates. Newark, as well as Nottingham, was a thriving centre of trade from its vantage-point on the Trent. Mansfield was the home of an active malting and brewing trade, and Worksop contributed liquorice. The coal trade was beginning to develop on an expanding scale; and for the rest corn and timber, and the framework-knitting trade of Nottingham and the neighbourhood—to be associated later with the name of "King Ludd" and the Luddites—together with the Trent navigation gave the county its industrial importance. It was, however, not yet a populous county; it had fewer people than agricultural Northamptonshire, or than Derbyshire with its more developed mines.

All eighteenth-century observers were agreed that Nottingham—a place of about ten thousand people in 1746—was an exceptionally pleasant town. Perhaps this was partly due to the prodigality with which it refreshed the traveller with its excellent ale—for which, and for its malting industry, it was specially famous. But it was also because the town was remarkably neat and well built, with a great many good houses occupied by resident gentry as well as merchants. The poorer inhabitants, in the town as well as in the surrounding villages, subsisted largely by knitting on the stocking-frame; but there were also glass-houses and a growing manufacture of earthenware, which had recently profited by the increase of tea-drinking. Nottingham was also a market-town, with important horse-fairs and a racecourse which drew visitors from all over the country; and, most important of all, it was the centre of the Trent Navigation, which we have had occasion to mention already in the course of this narrative. Like many other ancient towns, it had considerable borough property, largely assigned under trust to the maintenance of its bridges—the famous Trent Bridge, with its causeway, was nearly a mile long—and of its free school.

Nottingham was chiefly concerned with the navigability of its river—from Nottingham to the sea. But in the first part of the eighteenth century the Corporation of the city had spent much money and energy in resisting proposals to make it navigable as far up as Burton; for the merchants of Nottingham feared the loss of the considerable profits which they drew from their position at the head of the navigable water. Before 1746 this resistance had been defeated, and both Burton and Derby had become inland ports. But the warfare was not over. Barges from Nottingham were refused accommodation at the wharves higher up the river, where local interests laid claim to a monopoly of the carrying trade; and Nottingham retaliated by trying to exclude the up-river barges, or mulcting them by means of special tolls. Over all the areas served by navigable rivers, similar quarrels between local vested interests were going on, each town trying to secure some special monopoly or privilege at the expense of its neighbours. This rivalry, added to the deviousness of the rivers and the shallowness of many of their reaches at certain seasons, made river transport highly inconvenient; but even so it was far easier and cheaper, for heavy goods, than transport by land. England in 1746 was waiting for the canal era; but it had not yet matured the art of making artificial waterways with locks and a supply of water regularly maintained.

Thus, the traveller would have completed his circuit of all the English counties. It is not necessary to take him journeying round Wales or Scotland after the same fashion. Wales was, in 1746, still a country of little industrial importance; for the great growth there of the coal and iron industries was only just beginning, and Glamorgan was thought of rather as a fruitful agricultural county, prosperous by reason of its nearness to the Bristol market, than as an industrial centre. There was, indeed, already an active coal trade from Swansea and Neath—then much more important industrial ports than Cardiff—to Bristol and further afield; and the iron industry was developing both behind Swansea and further east. But it had not reached considerable dimensions; and in North Wales, Wrexham was still regarded much more as the metropolis of the flourishing Welsh flannel manufacture than as the centre of a coalfield.

Scotland, too, was relatively undeveloped in 1746, even in

the areas between the Clyde and the Forth. There had been, indeed, from the time of the Union of the Scottish and English Parliaments, a great increase in trade, of which Glasgow and the Clyde valley, well situated for the rapidly increasing commerce with the West Indies and the American continent, were able to secure the largest share. Glasgow became a great *entrepôt* centre, importing sugar, tobacco and other colonial produce and re-exporting the bulk of its imports, not to England, but by way of Alloa and the Firth of Forth, to which there was only a short land haul of twelve miles, direct to Holland, the Baltic, and other parts of Europe. To a substantial extent Scotland sent to America, in exchange for these products, not Scottish but English goods. But through the first half of the eighteenth century there had been a very rapid growth of the linen industry, most of all in Forfarshire around Dundee, but also, for finer-quality linens, in Lanarkshire and the neighbouring counties. Linen, to be superseded towards the close of the century, except at Dundee, by cotton and wool, was easily Scotland's leading manufacture. The coal and iron fields, except in the neighbourhood of Edinburgh, were still relatively undeveloped as late as 1746; and the woollen manufacture, though widespread, produced chiefly coarse woollens for local consumption.

Scotland was, in fact, in 1746 still not only an agricultural country, but a country practising an exceedingly backward subsistence-agriculture based on open fields, with an elementary rotation of crops and a survival of the ancient practice of opening the arable land to cattle after the harvest. The Act of Union had greatly stimulated the production of cattle, which were sent in rapidly increasing numbers to England. But they were lean cattle, sent to be fattened across the border; and it was but slowly that, first in Midlothian and the border counties and then further north round the Clyde and right up the east coast as far as Aberdeen, methods of cultivation and breeding were improved. In Scotland there were no enclosures in the English sense; for in the Scots law land ownership was unlimited by customary tenant rights, and enclosure could be achieved by *fiat* of the landlord, without the sanction of a special Act of Parliament. Nevertheless, the old methods gave

way but slowly; for the great Highland clearances for sheep-
runs belong to a period after the middle of the eighteenth
century, and did not reach their height till after 1800.

CHAPTER IV

EIGHTEENTH-CENTURY LONDON

IN this description of the economy of Great Britain at
the point at which our narrative begins, there is so far one
district missing; and that is London, the most important of all.
London, in 1746, had at any rate one thing in common with
the London of to-day. It astonished men by its size, by its
capacity for growth, by its propensity for spreading over the
surrounding countryside and swallowing up formerly independent towns and villages. Defoe, who described London in
1725, wrote about its expansion in terms very like those that
might be used by an observer at the present time. London was
already the greatest city in the world, in point of bigness; but
then as now it was a city whose limits it was impossible precisely to define. The distinction between London and Greater
London existed in 1746, as it does to-day; and Greater
London was no easier to define than it is now.

Let us try, first of all, to compare the extent of Defoe's
Greater London and of our own. For although Defoe wrote
two decades before the date which is the starting-point of this
history, the new building that took place between 1725 and
1746 had the effect rather of filling up vacant spaces within the
area marked out by Defoe than of actually extending the
boundaries of the Metropolis. Defoe's Greater London was
not very different save in density of building from the London
of 1746.

In 1938, according to the latest population estimates, much
less than half the population of Greater London lived within the
area administered by the London County Council. This area
was first marked out by the Metropolis Management Act of
1855, which set up the L.C.C.'s predecessor, the Metropolitan

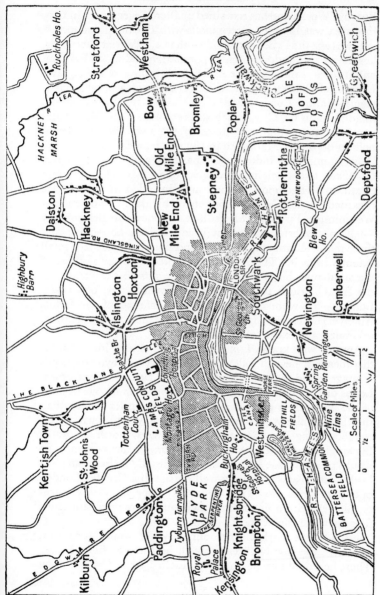

Board of Works, and has remained unaltered ever since. In 1855 this area was broadly coterminous with Greater London.

If we take the L.C.C. area only—that is, a district containing less than half London's present population and much less than half its area—and compare its limits with those of the Greater London of Defoe's day, we shall get some idea of what eighteenth-century London was. The L.C.C. territory includes, in addition to the City, which still retains its Lord Mayor and ancient Corporation, the areas of the twenty-eight Metropolitan Boroughs established in 1899, to replace a considerably larger number of independent parishes and district boards. Of these twenty-eight Boroughs, only two—Holborn and Southwark—had most of their area included in what Defoe regarded as the Greater London of his day. Five others—Westminster, Finsbury, Shoreditch, Stepney and Bermondsey —fell to a substantial extent inside Defoe's boundary; and three more—Lambeth, Deptford and Battersea—fell to a small extent within it. The remaining eighteen—to say nothing of the numerous boroughs and districts outside the control of the L.C.C. which now form unquestionably part of Greater London—fell wholly outside the area marked off by Defoe. And yet Defoe was inclined to exaggerate, rather than to minimize, the extent of London.

Anyone who knows London can get a clearer idea of what this means if he will follow an imaginary surveyor on a pilgrimage round the frontiers of London as Defoe set them down. Let us picture him starting out from a point on the north bank of the Thames, a good deal nearer Westminster Abbey than the Tate Gallery. From this point he would turn north, roughly along Horseferry Road, and keep north as far as Buckingham House—now Buckingham Palace—whence he would pass to Hyde Park Corner. Thus all Chelsea, Knightsbridge, and Kensington lay well outside the Greater London of two centuries ago. They were still independent small towns or villages, with a life of their own, and there were still green fields between them and London.

From Hyde Park Corner our surveyor would turn east, taking in the line of Piccadilly, till he came to Bond Street. There he would turn north, till he reached Oxford Street, along which he would go, only deviating to include one or two projections of houses on the north side. At St. Giles's Circus, where Oxford Street meets Tottenham Court Road, he would turn north for a little way, and then east again past the British Museum—called in those days Montagu House—taking in a fraction of what is now Bloomsbury. At Southampton Row he would go north a little way, and then east by Guilford Street, noting the newly built Foundling Hospital. He would cross right over Grays Inn Road; for King's Cross and Euston were both outside Greater London, though there was an outlying group of buildings at St. Pancras. East of Grays Inn Road the boundary becomes harder to define; for the houses were already reaching out to join Islington past Mount Pleasant, and there was much new building in the neighbourhood of Sadler's Wells. It was already a moot point whether the village of Islington was not best regarded as part of Greater London; but Defoe left it outside. To the east of this projection towards Islington Defoe's boundary followed what is now the line of Old Street, leaving some houses away to the north, but including within his circuit a good deal of yet uncovered ground. For at this point the open spaces occupied by the Artillery Ground and Moorfields stretched down almost into the heart of the City.

Next, proceeding along the line of Old Street, the surveyor would include Shoreditch and would then go to the south-east, round the northern verge of the New Town of Mile End. Bethnal Green and Old Mile End were still well outside the area of continuous building, which ended in this region approximately where, to-day, Whitechapel Road turns into Mile End Road. To the south of this point he would turn sharply to the west, leaving outside his circuit a large open space, then partly occupied by rope-walks, where the Commercial Road area is now. But to the south of this space he would turn east again a little north of the river, so as to include Wapping and Shadwell, and would continue as far as Limehouse. Poplar and Blackwall beyond Limehouse were indeed already almost joined to London; but they could still be regarded as independent places not yet quite swallowed up in the London area.

From this point the surveyor would cross the Isle of Dogs, still largely empty, and pass over the river by boat to the water-gate at Deptford, already stretching out towards Greenwich, which was not yet quite joined to London. From Deptford in the east Defoe's London extended to Lambeth in the west, at a point roughly opposite the point north of the river from which we set out. But on the south side our surveyor would have found, for most of the way, only a thin strip of built-up land along the riverside, with only one considerable stretch of building away to the south, in the area of Southwark to the south of London Bridge. For London Bridge remained, until the opening of old Westminster Bridge in 1750, the only dry way across the river. Elsewhere the Londoner whose business took him across the Thames had to go by ferry or wherry: and this fact mainly dictated the geography of South London up to 1750. Southwark itself, served by the bridge, spread away already a good distance to the south. Apart from this projection the line of buildings was thickest at Rother-hithe, or Redriff, and Bermondsey, which were already considerable places, whereas, west of the Borough, the districts of Newington and Lambeth were still thinly peopled. London was experiencing its first "ribbon-development" along the Kent and Croydon Roads past St. George's Church in Southwark.

Such was the London of 1746; and in some directions there were serious obstacles to its further growth. The land left open to the east was largely low-lying marsh, then regarded as undrainable and uninhabitable, though much of it is now filled up with the habitations of the poor. In other directions the natural obstacles to growth were much less formidable; and outside Defoe's London a good deal of the hilly country in Middlesex and Surrey was already being dotted with the country villas of prosperous London traders. It is a broadly accurate generalization that, as London has grown, the richer people have moved out first, occupying the higher ground, whereas the low-lying lands have been filled up later by the smaller houses and cottages of the less prosperous folk. Round London, at any rate, the rich live high, and the poor low; and this was beginning to be true a good deal earlier than two centuries ago.

So much for London's limits: now for what it was like. Our account of it had best begin with the river; for important as London was, and is, in the field of manufacture, it is of still more significance as a port. ".The whole river from London Bridge to Blackwall," wrote Defoe's editor in 1747, "is one great arsenal: nothing in the world can be like it." Here, in the Pool of London and below the Pool between Limehouse and Deptford, lay the shipping which was the foundation of the City's commercial greatness. But in this crowded area there were great difficulties over the loading and unloading of vessels. There were as yet no docks in the modern sense— these were to come only at the beginning of the nineteenth century. Ships had to lie in the river, and to discharge and take on board their cargoes chiefly by means of lighters from the wharves and quays which lined both banks.

Over these wharves there were constant troubles. In 1558 there had been appointed a number of legal quays, at which alone goods liable to duty could be landed; and these quays, long absurdly inadequate, still constituted the only legally recognized accommodation. But the practice had grown up of allowing ships to unload elsewhere, at what were called "sufferance wharves," five on the north and eighteen on the south bank of the river. Even so the facilities were inadequate; and there were many complaints of combination among the owners of the wharves to raise prices at the expense of the merchants. During the eighteenth century there were numerous projects for providing further accommodation. But these all broke down, and the situation remained practically unaltered till the Napoleonic Wars.

Nevertheless, the Port of London did manage to handle a quantity and variety of goods that was prodigious by contemporary estimation. London was the centre of the great East India trade, which brought back from the East a vast variety of goods which were largely re-exported all over Europe. The trade with France, Spain, Portugal and the Mediterranean was mainly carried on from London; and the London merchants traded to the West Indies and the American continent as well as to the East. To London colliers from Tyne and Tees brought the major part of the coal mined in Durham

and Northumberland; and from Hull came the merchandise
which reached the sea from Yorkshire and the Midland
Counties by way of the Ouse and Trent Navigations. London
was, in addition, an important centre for shipbuilding and
repairs. It had, according to Defoe's editor of 1747: "3 Wet
Docks for lying up, 22 Dry Docks for repairing, and 33 Yards
for building Merchant Vessels, including the building of
lighters and hoys, but excluding all boat-builders, wherry-
builders, and, above-bridge, barge-builders."

The commerce of London thus centred round the Pool and
the reaches immediately below it, and here and in the City
itself was London's most congested area. But Londoners
manufactured goods, as well as carried them about; and the
London craftsmen, of whom something will be said later, were
as noted for their skill as the London "mob" was for its
drunkenness, brawling, and lack of manners, especially
towards strangers. Gin-drinking was in its heyday in 1746;
and, whereas beer-houses needed licences from the Justices,
the sale of spirits was wholly unrestricted, so that in 1725 there
were reckoned to be in London over six thousand places at
which gin was openly sold. "Gin," wrote Henry Fielding in
1751, "is the principal sustenance of more than an hundred
thousand people in this Metropolis." Dram-drinking had
probably a good deal of the responsibility for making London
so turbulent a place, and the reaction from it was largely the
making of the Methodist movement.

Of London's industries and workpeople we shall speak later.
Here we must turn to the question of its organization and
government. Then, as now, no single authority had any sort
of jurisdiction over the whole London area. The twenty-six
wards represented on the Common Council of the City of
London, including the "liberties" outside the walls as well
as the ancient city, covered only a fraction of the entire
London area. Westminster was an independent city by itself,
and the rest of the area was split up among a number of
parishes and other authorities. For certain purposes the City
jurisdiction extended over a wide area—for the regulation of
markets, for example, and for matters connected with the
business of the port. But there was no authority capable of

taking care of London's growth, or of planning its development in a comprehensive way.

The City Corporation, under its Lord Mayor, consisted of 26 Aldermen, one for each ward, the 2 Sheriffs, who were also Sheriffs for Middlesex, and 236 Common Councillors, in addition to a number of other officers. Throughout the eighteenth century the City was jealous of its privileges and its independence of the Crown and the King's Government, and solidly Whig, and even at times Radical, in a political sense. Side by side with this municipal organization there existed the 91 City Companies, still keeping a real connection with the trades over which they held jurisdiction, and differing greatly among themselves in wealth and social composition. Certain companies, notably those of the Porters and Watermen, were strongholds of Radical sentiment, dominated by their rank and file membership of working craftsmen, and jealous of their privileges and monopolies, but also ready to demonstrate noisily and often turbulently in support of any radical agitation. The wealthier City Companies, on the other hand, were closely controlled by the leading merchants, and were already even more concerned with their elaborate social festivities than with the business of regulating the London trades, save for the purpose of excluding unlicensed competitors, or keeping the poorer masters and working journeymen safely in their place. The Halls of the leading companies were among the most imposing of London's public buildings, ranking with Wren's churches, the public offices, and such establishments as East India House and the Bank of England. The Mansion House had not yet been built as the Lord Mayor's official residence; and the Bank, originally conducted at the Grocers' Hall, had only opened its own premises in 1734.

London's streets in the middle of the eighteenth century were still, despite the rebuilding after the Great Fire, in many cases little more than narrow alleys, noted for dirt and darkness. But there were some broad and well-built thoroughfares, even in the City, along which the coaches rumbled over the cobbles. There was still no public provision for paving the streets, though many abortive attempts had been made to get

Paving Acts through Parliament. Westminster ultimately got its Act in 1762, and the City followed in 1776. Till then the householders were individually responsible to the magistrates for keeping the streets in decent repair.

London's maze of narrow alleys, opening off the main streets, remained a notable feature of the City long after 1746 —indeed, well into the nineteenth century. Narrowness, darkness, and noise were accentuated by the creaking shop-signs still hung out on hinges before the shops and offices. The City still had its bars and gates to obstruct traffic, until their removal in the 1760's. In 1746 travellers might have seen the heads of the executed Jacobites exposed on Temple Bar; but they were the last heads hung there, though later the corpses of pirates continued to swing from the gallows by the river's edge at Wapping.

The Fleet Ditch had been arched over, and Fleet Market opened on the cleared ground, by 1737; and that had done something to mitigate the nuisance of London's stench. But rubbish still littered the streets, and open drains ran along many of them, half-choked with refuse. Noise was as much a nuisance as smell. Hawkers, the messengers of the penny post, and many other vendors went about ringing bells. Street-singers abounded; and wheeled traffic made a terrible din in the narrow streets.

The shops, however, with their glass fronts and their fine show of wares, were already much admired, and admitted to be superior in display and luxury to those of any other city in the world. For the gentry and the men of letters, as well as for citizens and men of business, coffee-houses abounded, and were commonly used as clubs are now—for reading the papers, meeting friends, and furnishing the needy scribbler with a respectable address. Many coffee-houses became resorts for men of a particular business, or party, or occupation—Lloyd's for insurers, Almack's for Whigs, the Bedford for playwrights and actors, and so on.

The greater inns, both in the City and in the Borough south of the river, were already important as travel and transport centres, for carriers, stage-wagons for the poorer travellers, and stage-coaches for those who could afford better accommodation, as well as for post-chaises hired by travellers on official business, or by wealthy men for their private journeys. But till about 1750 the coaches lacked springs, and jolted horribly along the cobbled streets as well as on the ill-made roads.

Westminster Bridge was actually a-building in 1746, and was not opened till 1750. London Bridge, still the only dry crossing, had houses on it, and was far too narrow for the traffic till the City Corporation widened it and removed the houses, in 1757.

Such was the city; but already the West End had a different aspect. In the country north and south of the Tyburn Road— now Oxford Street—new squares and houses were being built fast for the rich, on spacious lines and with some attempt at town-planning on the great estates which were being broken up. Cavendish and Hanover Squares had been built nearly thirty years, and new streets and squares were being made around them. Mayfair was still unbuilt, the scene of an annual fair in May, from which it derives its name. Piccadilly was full of builders' yards and storehouses interspersed with houses; but at Hyde Park Corner a great mansion, formerly Lanesborough House, had already become St. George's Hospital in 1734. The road to Knightsbridge and Kensington was already an important thoroughfare. But Tothill Fields, between Westminster and Chelsea, remained open marshy ground. Hyde Park itself was a rural tract, and not a made park like Kensington Gardens. Hyde Park, and still more St. James's Park, were favourite popular resorts; but Kensington Gardens, open to the gentry, were kept firmly closed against all who were "meanly dressed."

Round London, from Vauxhall and Ranelagh to Marylebone, Islington and Hackney, were countless tea-gardens and pleasure resorts, of every degree of exclusiveness or promiscuity. The Londoners loved to find their way to a bit of country near the town. They liked to go about in crowds, and to amuse themselves with spectacles. The Lord Mayor's Show —still largely a watermen's pageant, held in boats upon the river—was a real popular entertainment even more than the executions at Tyburn (by Marble Arch), which still attracted spectators of all classes.

With crowded buildings, little air, and next to no sanitation, it is not surprising that London was unhealthy. In 1746 the death-rate for the country as a whole was probably about 35 per 1,000. For good country parishes it was under 30: for London about 50 per 1,000. It was said that three-quarters of all the children born in London died before reaching five years of age. This proportion had fallen to about 40 per cent by about 1800. But London grew despite its high death-rates, by reason of constant immigration from the country.

In 1746 there was a movement afoot for the improvement of hospitals and medical charities. Both the London Hospital and St. Bartholomew's were then re-building. But John Howard, when he visited them forty years later, thought ill enough of them for dirt and lack of air and good water. The dispensary movement had not yet begun, the first in London being founded in Red Lion Square in 1769. Even midwifery had made little advance. The Lying-in Charity for poor women, which did something to train midwives, was begun only in 1757.

Smallpox was very prevalent, and inoculation, known from 1720, was not at all widely practised, though the Middlesex Hospital was actually founded in 1746 as a smallpox hospital for the encouragement of inoculation. The prisons, mostly at least as evil and insanitary as John Howard found them a generation later, were great spreaders of infection of all sorts, but especially of the notorious "gaol-fever." At the "Black Sessions" of 1750 at Newgate, four out of six judges on the bench caught the infection and died, and so did forty jurymen and officials of the court. But even this holocaust did not bring reform. Not till 1774 did the Gaol Distemper Act order the justices to keep the prisons clean; and Howard's reports show that little was done in spite of the Act.

These particulars close our account of London on a melancholy note; but they do not mean that, apart from conditions arising out of its bigness, London was worse than other places. It presented, no doubt, more glaring contrasts between luxury and wretchedness, and it was more given to gin in its poorer quarters and to gambling and wine-drinking among the rich. But it had its compensations, especially for the well-to-do and for the better sort of artisans, who could earn much better wages in London than anywhere else, and could afford to keep out of the slum areas, and live under tolerably comfortable conditions. Hogarth's London of "Gin Lane" was a very real part of the London of his day; but it was not by any means the whole.

CHAPTER V

CHANGING INDUSTRIES

WE have seen that the growing industries of eighteenth-century England were not predominantly urban. By far the greatest of English industries before the Industrial Revolution was the making of woollen and worsted stuffs; and that was carried on principally in three areas—the south-western counties from Devonshire to Gloucestershire and Oxfordshire, the eastern counties from Norfolk to northern Essex, and the West Riding of Yorkshire, which was more and more challenging with its cheaper fabrics the predominance of the older centres. Next to the woollen industry, with its close association with the land and the ruling aristocracy based on land, stood the iron industry, barely yet learning to emancipate itself by the use of coal in smelting from the pervasive trouble of shortage of timber. The lack of charcoal had already driven it out of its ancient home in Sussex to the Severn Valley and South Wales and Cumberland in search of further woodlands for demolition. The wars of the eighteenth century were good customers to the iron industry, before the days of Watt's steam engine and the "iron road"; but the iron-masters were in serious difficulties for lack of fuel, until the technique of using coal was gradually perfected in the course of the century. Until that had been achieved, much raw iron had to be brought from abroad to keep the finishing branches of the developing industry adequately supplied.

These two industries, based on wool and iron, far surpassed all others in importance until the Industrial Revolution came to raise up a new industry—that of cotton—to a position of pre-eminence based on the new technique of factory production. Apart from small-scale crafts, carried on mainly by small groups of highly skilled handicraftsmen, cotton was the first really urban industry; and even the cotton industry, in its earlier stages, while it depended on water power, was largely located in villages or small towns outside the great centres of population. But in 1746 the cotton industry was still of quite minor importance, far exceeded by the lead and copper trades, by brewing, by coal-mining, by shipbuilding, and even by such textile trades as linen, hosiery and silk.

Wool was, in 1746, still the main basis of England's prosperity and growing importance in foreign trade. The preponderant position of the woollen and worsted industries largely dictated the character of agricultural production. A large part of the cultivated area was pasture, for feeding flocks of sheep which were valued far more for the wool than for the meat; and this use of the land bound the landed aristocracy close to the merchants who bought the raw wool from the farmers, saw to its conversion into yarn and finished piece-goods, and thereafter exported to all the markets of the world the surplus which was not absorbed by the home consumers. The land-owners and merchants were partners in the exploitation of eighteenth-century England's principal industrial asset—the sheep; and naturally they regarded with a jealous eye any rival manufacture, such as that of cotton goods, which threatened wool's monopoly.

Now, the woollen and worsted industry of the eighteenth century was for the most part what economic historians call a "domestic" industry. This means that it was carried on chiefly, not in factories or even large workshops, but in cottages and small domestic workshops which were the actual homes of the workers. Especially in the older centres of the industry, in the western and eastern counties, the actual producers were individual piece-workers, labouring for the most part in their own homes, as the virtual wage-employees of great capitalist merchant-clothiers, who bought the raw wool from the farmers, handed it out to spinners to be made into yarn, and then again sent the yarn to handloom weavers to be made into cloth, which might then be bleached, dyed and finished either by further sub-contractors or by direct wage-earners employed by the merchant in his own establishment. The need for a supply of water, and for somewhat more capitalistic methods of work in the dyeing and finishing processes made these suitable for some degree of factory concentration even before the advent of mechanical power. But until the coming of power-driven machinery there was no similar motive for concentration of the other processes of production.

There was, however, an important contrast between the two principal occupations of spinning and weaving. The weaving of cloth was a skilled trade, though not esteemed of so high a skill as such urban crafts as bootmaking, tailoring, painting and coach-building, or so highly paid. It was, however, skilled enough to be essentially a full-time occupation and to retain some vestiges of the old system of apprenticeship; and the weaver was seldom anything besides a weaver, though he might lend a hand on the farms at harvest time. The weavers lived for the most part, not scattered among the agricultural labourers throughout the countryside, but in large, predominantly industrial villages, where they formed in effect concentrated communities of industrial wage-earners. They showed this repeatedly throughout the eighteenth century by their efforts to form combinations for the regulation of wages either by collective bargaining, or, more often, by appealing to Parliament or to the County Justices to fix their wages in accordance with the wage-fixing statutes which were then (and remained until 1813) unrepealed.

The spinners, on the other hand, were generally regarded as unskilled workers, and were far more widely scattered over the countryside. It took the labour of several spinners to keep a weaver supplied with yarn, especially after the invention of Kay's flying shuttle in the 1730's; and during the next thirty years the weaver was often held up by the shortage of yarn. But spinning could be readily carried out by the labour of women and children; and on an ever-increasing scale it furnished employment to the wives and families, not only of the weavers themselves, but also of countless agricultural labourers in rural villages in which no weaving for the market was carried on. From the standpoint of family earnings spinning, till it moved into the factories after the inventions made later in the century, was usually a by-employment, eking out the exiguous wages of the agricultural labourer, or the somewhat higher piece-work earnings of the handloom weaver or other village craftsman.

This was the broad structure of the woollen industry in its older centres in the South of England—especially in the south-west. But even in the South there were substantial differences from place to place. The Norwich worsted weaver retained far more independence and a higher craft status than the woollen weavers of the south-western counties; and there was, even in the south-west, an important difference between the weaver who owned his own loom and the weaver who rented one from a merchant or from a professional owner of looms for hire. But there was a far broader difference between the woollen and worsted industry of the South of England and that of its rapidly developing rival, the West Riding of Yorkshire. For the Yorkshire industry was based, not upon the rich merchant-clothier employing piece-working craftsmen who were virtually wage-earners under the domestic system, but upon the small working master with a worskhop of his own, usually attached to a house or farm-house—for he was often a small farmer as well as a master-craftsman. In Yorkshire, as elsewhere, spinning was an unskilled trade, carried out mainly as a by-employment by cottagers, usually the wives and families of the agricultural workers and artisans. But weaving was in the hands of craftsmen who owned not only their own looms, but also the materials on which they worked, and usually took their finished products for sale to the cloth-market in Leeds or Halifax. These small master-craftsmen employed the cottage spinners to make the wool, which they bought or raised themselves, into yarn; and they often employed a journeyman or two to weave it for them at a wage in their workshops. Their places of work were embryo factories, without steam-power; and when power was introduced—sometimes water-power at first, to be superseded later by steam—many of them were able to convert their workshops into fully-fledged factories, and to set up as capitalists employing labour on a larger scale.

In fact, the small master-craftsmen of the West Riding were soon to show their skill in adapting themselves to the new technique of factory production: whereas in the South the merchant-clothier was too much the gentleman, and too inexperienced industrially, to become a factory-entrepreneur, and the "domestic" weavers, without capital or independent access to the market, had no means of applying the new technique for themselves. Consequently, the West Riding beat Norwich and the south-western counties out of the market; and what had been the principal centres of the English woollen industry lost their ability to produce on economic terms—with devastating reactions on the local standard of living, and to the accompaniment of wholesale unemployment. This, we may note, has been largely blamed to the account of the enclosures which were proceeding simultaneously.

In comparison with the woollen industry, the iron industry was already being carried on, in 1746, under a "factory" system. The tiny ironworks of Sussex, each employing only a handful of workers, had been crushed out by shortage of fuel; and the developing ironworks of Coalbrookdale, of South Wales, of Cumberland, and of Yorkshire and the north-east coast were based on relatively large aggregations of capital and on the direct employment of relatively large groups of wage-earners, among whom coal-miners, as well as metal-workers, were often included—for the iron-masters often got the coal they needed by means of labour directly employed. The woollen industry, especially in the south-west, was in 1746 at the stage of merchant-capitalism, dominated by rich merchant-clothiers largely active in the export trade; but it had, save in the finishing processes, no incentive to adopt large-scale production before the advent of power-driven machinery. The iron trades, on the other hand, had to use power earlier—often in the form of water-power till the steam-engine was adapted by Watt for other purposes besides pumping. They were more dependent both on fluctuating government demand for their products, and on the economies of large-scale integrated production, even before power-driven machinery came into use. In this sense, iron was in the eighteenth century a far more "capitalistic" industry than wool or cotton, because it offered far more benefits from production on a relatively large scale.

Macpherson, in his *Annals of Commerce*, made an estimate of the relative importance of the chief British manufacturing industries in 1785; and this, with a few comments to allow for the principal changes, can be taken as indicating roughly their relative importance forty years earlier. In Macpherson's estimate, only three manufactures—those based on wool, iron and leather—had an annual value of more than £10,000,000. The woollen industries were easily first, at nearly £17,000,000: iron and its manufactures came next, at over £12,000,000. Third stood the leather industries—tanning, currying, boot and shoe making, saddlery, and so on—at £10,500,000. The leather trades, unlike the woollen and iron trades, were mainly urban, carried on by skilled craftsmen in the towns. But in boot and shoe making and in saddlery there was already some spread of workshops outside the urban areas, and some approach to large-scale marketing of products made under a domestic system.

After these three great industries there was a very wide gap, the next in importance, the silk trade, being valued at only £3,350,000, and the next after silk, flax, at no more than £1,750,000. Lead came next, at £1,650,000, and then porcelain and tin, each at £1,000,000. The cotton trade was still valued at under £1,000,000 a year, even in 1785, when spinning factories were already being established at a prodigious rate. After cotton came hemp, at under £900,000, paper, at under £800,000, and glass at £630,000. The list does not include coal-mining or brewing, building or shipbuilding, which were not regarded as manufactures; but apart from these it gives a not inadequate picture of the broad character of English industry before the Industrial Revolution. In 1746 cotton, porcelain and glass were certainly of smaller relative importance, and the woollen industry had a still longer lead over all the others; but with these exceptions it is unlikely that the relative magnitudes had greatly changed.

A traveller such as we have described would have noted in his passage that various industries were being carried on before his eyes. But it would be too much to expect that he would investigate precisely how they were carried on; nevertheless, this question is of the first importance for the historian. How were these industries in fact conducted? The large factory, employing a considerable number of workers, already existed; but it was very exceptional. Lombe's silk mills at Derby and such metal-working establishments as the Darby works at Coalbrookdale stand out as the principal instances of large-scale manufacture under factory conditions. It follows that there were very few large industrial employers—certainly not nearly enough to constitute a recognizable social class. The typical capitalist was still the merchant, who employed only a small body of workers under his own roof—clerks and salesmen, buyers and travellers, and perhaps a few skilled workers in some special processes, such as woolcombing, or finishing goods made by domestic workers in their own homes. Beside the capitalist merchants, whose main business was commerce over long distances, and especially with foreign countries, the industrial employers were in most cases men of small substance. The urban master-craftsman, descendant of the medieval gild master, was still no more than a workshop employer, often dealing directly as a retailer with the final consumer, or else selling to a merchant who was in that case apt to reduce him virtually to the status of a sub-contractor. The small country employer was usually even more dependent on the merchant for marketing his wares, though it was in some cases easier for him to expand the scale of his operations, because he was less under the jurisdiction of a bench of magistrates set on enforcing the traditional rules and customs of the trade. But even where expansion was possible there was, until the advent of power-driven machinery, little to be gained economically by gathering large bodies of workers together in factories; and the merchants, who dominated the situation, dealt habitually with a large number of small producers, some of whom were small employers of hired labour, while others worked alone or only with the help of their immediate families.

As for the workers, they can be divided, for our present purpose, very broadly into three main classes: skilled artisans, following a recognized trade after a regular period of apprenticeship, less skilled craftsmen, sometimes apprenticed workers, but regarded as possessing only a lower degree of skill, and labourers—among whom the eighteenth century classified all miners, the majority of metal-workers other than highly skilled mechanics, transport workers, and a host of workers of very varying real skill outside the recognized skilled trades. The lines of demarcation between these three groups were, of course by no means clear; but the broad division roughly represents the class-structure of the time.

The highly skilled artisans belonging to the first group were for the most part urban workers following one or another of the traditional skilled trades—printers, tailors, bootmakers, bakers, coachmakers, craftsmen in the building trades, watchmakers, millwrights and instrument makers, and so on. With them belonged such special grades as the woolcombers, who were to some extent migratory; but the main body of skilled workers in the textile trades was regarded rather as belonging to the second group. In London, for example, the Spitalfields silk weavers were much less highly thought of, and much worse paid, than the artisans in the group of trades mentioned above. These craftsmen of lower status were far less concentrated in the larger corporate towns, and there was among them far greater local diversity of wages. They were rapidly increasing in relative numbers with the expansion of the textile trades under the domestic system. In the newer industries, the line between them and the labourers is by no means easy to draw; for new sorts of skill were constantly emerging with the development of new technical methods of production.

CHAPTER VI

HOW THE PEOPLE LIVED

IT is possible to get some idea of the relative economic position of these broad grades of workers by appealing to such scattered wage-figures as are available for the middle of the eighteenth century. Fortunately there exists, in a book published in 1747, a detailed account of the wages and conditions of most of the trades then carried on in London; and it is easiest to begin with certain observations based directly on this list. London wages were, as we shall see, on the whole a great deal higher than those paid in other parts of the country; and London prices were also notably higher in those days of slow and expensive transport.

In the first place, shopkeeping naturally bulks large among London occupations; and in 1747 it was still very common for the shopman to live in his employer's house as a journeyman after his apprenticeship was over. In the shopkeeping trades, the money-wages paid were often additional to board and lodging; and in some related occupations the employee got his food as well as his money-wage. This, however, did not apply to the main body of journeymen in the producing trades, who were paid either a weekly wage or by piece-work. In most of the skilled trades, including shopkeeping, there was a regular system of apprenticeship; and it was usual for a premium to be charged for taking an apprentice, the charges varying greatly from trade to trade—from say £5 to £10 in the less highly paid manual crafts to £50 or even £100 in the superior branches of shopkeeping. The Elizabethan statutes which forbade unapprenticed workers to follow a recognized craft being still in force, the apprenticed men enjoyed a sort of monopoly, and this helped to keep their wages well above those paid even to relatively skilled workers in trades which lacked a regular system of apprenticeship.

Let us begin with what we should call nowadays the nonmanual workers. A shopman out of his apprenticeship in one of the more prosperous London trades seems to have received, as a general rule, about £20 a year in wages in addition to his board, rising to £30 or even £40 for experienced men in responsible positions. In some cases, however, the rates were a great deal lower, at £10 or £15 a year, the lower pay generally going together with much lower premiums for the original apprenticeship. Experienced clerks in merchants' offices seem to have been paid about £1 a week, or more, or about the same as shopmen when they received their board as well. Ushers, or assistant schoolmasters, are set down as receiving £10 to £20 a year in addition to their board; and the author notes that they could often better their position by becoming clerks to merchants.

THE PYRAMID OF ENGLISH SOCIETY, 1688

Gregory King's Estimate of the Class-Structure of the time of the English Revolution. (All figures represent households, including dependents.)

Royalty and Nobility, 7,000

Baronets and Knights, 20,000

Squires 30,000	Upper Merchants 16,000	Upper Clergy 12,000
Upper Civil Service 40,000		Army and Navy Officers 36,000
Liberal Arts 75,000		Lawyers 70,000

Upper Freeholders 280,000

Lesser Merchants 48,000	Lesser Clergy 40,000	Lesser Civil Servants 30,000

Lesser Freeholders 660,000

Farmers 750,000

Shopkeepers and Innkeepers 225,000

Artisans 240,000

Soldiers, Sailors and Seamen 220,000

Labourers 1,275,000

(including agricultural labourers, miners, and industrial labourers)

Cottagers and Paupers 1,300,000

(including workers in domestic industries)

Vagrants. 300,000

THE PYRAMID OF SOCIETY
IN THE UNITED KINGDOM

ABOUT THE END OF THE
NAPOLEONIC WARS,
based chiefly on Patrick
Colquhoun's estimate.
Figures, *in thousands*, include
dependent members of
family, but not other
members of household.
Total population
about 17 millions.

3

50

20 20

Royalty and Nobility

Baronets, Knights
and Squires.

Upper Clergy, Merchants and Bankers
Upper Civil Servants and Lawyers

Independent
Gentry 150

20

Upper Doctors and other Professionals

Army and Navy
Officers 70

75 Lesser Clergy

300 Upper Freeholders

200 Shipowners and Lesser Merchants,
Shipbuilders, Engineers and Builders

250 Lesser Professionals, Civil Servants,
and Dissenting Ministers

Innkeepers 375

Shopkeepers
and Hawkers 600

Master Craftsmen
and Manufacturers 450

Lesser Freeholders 900

Farmers 1300

Teachers, Actors, Clerks and Shopmen 320

Artisans and other
Skilled Workers

4500

Agricultural Labourers,
Miners, Road and Canal
Workers, and Seamen 3500

Personal and Household
Servants 1300

Soldiers and Sailors 800

Paupers, Vagrants, Prisoners,
and Lunatics 1900

CP : D

Turn next to the skilled craftsmen in the better-paid trades. For most of these the usual wage for a good London journeyman seems to have been about 15s. a week, without board, with an upper limit varying from 18s. to 20s. for craftsmen of special skill or experience. On piece-work higher earnings were possible in some trades, though hardly common, and liable to serious irregularity. Most piece-workers seem to have been able to make about 3s., or sometimes 3s. 6d. a day in the better-paid trades, though in a few—coach-making, fan-making, gilding, goldsmith's work, and so on—it was possible to make up to 4s. or more.

But below these best-reputed skilled trades there were others, also regarded as skilled, in which the earnings were substantially lower. Stay-makers (Tom Paine's original trade), trunk-makers, glaziers, loom-makers, leather-dressers, breeches-makers, cabinet-makers and chair-makers were among the trades in which the ordinary wages were only about 12s. a week, with an upper limit of 15s. Piece-workers in trades of this standard could earn only from 2s. to 2s. 6d. a day in normal cases; and some skilled piece-workers, such as the Spitalfields silk-weavers, often earned as little as 10s. a week, though 12s. was probably nearer the general average, and some exceptional workers earned on occasion at least twice this amount.

Finally, "labourers," by which was meant workers not following a definite trade which had to be entered normally by way of regular apprenticeship, seem to have got 10s. a week, or even less, though exceptionally they might rise to about 12s. Women's rates are not quoted in many cases; but where they are, for definite trades, the figure is usually about 8s. per week, with the possibility of considerably higher piece-work earnings for exceptional skill. Rates as low as 7s. are given for women in certain of the dressmaking trades.

These figures cannot, of course, mean very much absolutely; for there is no real way of comparing the cost of living in eighteenth-century London with that of to-day—so greatly have habits and the necessary expenses of life changed. Accordingly, the figures are of use rather in showing the relative situations of different grades of workers than as telling us a great deal about the actual standards of life.

If these were London wages round about the middle of the eighteenth century, what was the position in the provinces? No figures of the same order of completeness exist for provincial industries: nor is any comparison easily possible for an exact date. But when Arthur Young composed his famous *Tours Through England* in the 1760's and 1770's—that is, about twenty years after the London survey quoted above—he noted down a large mass of data about wages and conditions in every area he visited; and the lapse of twenty years is of little account, for in the eighteenth century, though piece-work earnings varied greatly according to the state of trade, time-rates of wages were altered in most trades only at long intervals, and then not usually to a great extent. Not till the price-upsets which accompanied the Napoleonic Wars did wages cease to be largely customary, and begin to vary much from year to year. It matters a good deal more that Arthur Young's figures, especially those relating to piece-work earnings, were obtained chiefly by means of inquiries from merchants and employers, and may easily tend to overestimate what was actually being earned during an average or normal week.

Nevertheless, Young's figures, while they show relatively high wages here and there, give on the whole an impression of a very low standard of living among the skilled workers under the domestic system. Young himself presents, on the basis of his observations, a summary statement of average earnings, in which he makes some allowance for loss of wages through unemployment, and attempts to compare the level of industrial and agricultural workers' earnings in certain broad divisions of the country. His general conclusion is that in the Western Counties the average for industrial earnings was about 11s. a week, and for agricultural labourers' earnings about 5s. 10d. In the Southern Counties he puts industrial earnings at 9s. 4d., and agricultural earnings at 6s., and in the Eastern Counties industrial earnings at only 6s. 6d., and agricultural—in the neighbourhood of towns only—at 8s. Young thus found a very low level of industrial wages in East Anglia, combined with a higher standard than elsewhere for agricultural workers, at any rate near the towns. In the pastoral West he found the industrial workers, chiefly in the woollen trades, to be much better paid, but agricultural workers worse off than anywhere else. For the three areas taken together, he estimated average industrial earnings at only 8s. 3d. a week, and agricultural earnings at 7s. 9d.

Unfortunately, Young gives no precisely comparable figures for the North of England, which is excluded from the survey just mentioned. He did, however, give in his *Northern Tour* a large number of figures for the industrial workers of Lancashire and Yorkshire. Thus, in the Leeds district he puts the average earnings of men weavers, allowing for unemployment, at only 6s. or 6s. 6d. a week; and at Manchester he found skilled men only getting 5s. or 6s., and some as little as 4s. Women's rates at Manchester he found varying from 2s. 6d. to 7s. a week, the same rates being often paid to men and women where both sexes worked at the same trades. In the iron trades at Rotherham he put foundrymen's earnings at 7s. to 10s. a week, and highly skilled forgemen's at an average of 12s. to 14s., whereas at Crowley's great ironworks at Newcastle-on-Tyne he estimated that wages ranged from 1s. to 2s. 6d. a day. Miners got 10s. to 12s. a week near Rotherham, and about the same at Wakefield, and at Newcastle they ranged, he says, from 1s. to 4s. a day on piece-work, with free coal in addition. In the rapidly developing Potteries he found men getting from 7s. to 12s. a week, and women from 5s. to 8s. In Birmingham men earned from 7s. upwards, and women from 2s. 6d. to 7s. a week. Building craftsmen in Staffordshire got from 1s. 6d. to 1s. 8d. a day, and labourers 1s. 4d., as against £15 a year for agricultural workers. Farm wages over the northern counties as a whole ranged from 5s. 6d. to 9s. 6d. a week, with from 6s. to 7s. as the most usual rates. Woollen weavers at Kendal got from 9s. to 10s. a week, but cotton weavers, who were mainly women, only about 4s. 3d.

It would be possible greatly to lengthen this catalogue; but enough has been cited to illustrate the extreme diversity of the provincial rates, and their general tendency to be a good way below the wages of the skilled London craftsmen. There were indeed some high wages for exceptionally skilled men, such as the Rotherham forgemen. Dyers in Norwich, for example, are given as earning 15*s*. a week; but this must refer to a narrow group of exceptionally well-paid men. Woolcombers are given as getting 13*s*. on the average in the Western Counties, 12*s*. to 14*s*. in Essex, 10*s*. 6*d*. in Kendal, 7*s*. in Norwich, and from 6*s*. to 12*s*. in Leeds. Blanket weavers in Witney earned from 10*s*. to 12*s*. a week, and the more skilled grades of pin-makers in Gloucester from 12*s*. to 15*s*., as against 7*s*. and 9*s*. for the lower grades. Porcelain workers in Worcester earned from 12*s*. upwards.

So far, we have taken our evidence from the London *General Description of Trades* of 1747, and from Arthur Young's *Tours*. It is, however, possible, with the aid of Miss Gilboy's recently published study of *Wages in Eighteenth-Century England*, to supplement these contemporary sources by the results of more recent research, based largely on unpublished documents. Miss Gilboy's figures, which relate mainly to the building trades and to agricultural labour, make it possible to present, for London and the Home Counties and the West of England and, much more tentatively, for the North, a very broad estimate of the movement of builders' and agricultural labourers' wages throughout the country up to the outbreak of the Napoleonic Wars. These estimates can be regarded as only very rough and provisional; but they are based on wider research for certain parts of the country than any previous figures. They are given in the form of broad estimates of daily wages, and therefore do not, like some of Arthur Young's figures, take account either of high piece-work earnings or of wages lost by reason of unemployment or under-employment —which were undoubtedly both very prevalent.

According to Miss Gilboy's figures, and to the summary tables which we have based chiefly upon them, money-wages were in all cases appreciably higher in 1790 than at the beginning of the century. But the extent of the rise, and the periods at which it occurred, differ considerably. Thus, in London, the typical craftsman's wages in the building trades rose from 2*s*. 6*d*. a day to 3*s*. a day between 1700 and 1720; but there was no further general rise till after 1780. In the Home Counties, on the other hand, wages rose between 1770 and 1780, and again after 1790; but there are not sufficient data to show what happened between 1700 and 1770. In the West of England the craftsmen's wages remained generally unchanged between 1700 and 1750, and then started to rise, remaining throughout a long way below the London rates. In the North of England, for which the particulars are even less adequate, wage-rates seem to have remained unaltered from 1700 to 1760, and then to have risen, but to have remained lower than in the West until after 1790.

For labourers in London wages are shown as rising from 1700 to 1710, and then as stationary till after 1730. They rise between 1730 and 1740, and then are given as unchanged, apart from temporary fluctuations, right up to 1790. In the Home Counties, on the other hand, they are shown as unchanged between 1710 and 1750, rising to 1760, and then falling again to 1770, and rising in 1780 above the 1760 level, but remaining unchanged in 1790.

For agricultural labour in the Western Counties the figures, such as they are, show wage-rates unchanged between 1700 and 1740, and then actually lower in 1750 and 1760, rising again in 1770 to the earlier level, and continuing to rise in 1780 and 1790. In the North, on the other hand, agricultural wages show an unchanged level from 1730 to 1760, and a renewed and sharper rise from 1760 to 1790—probably on

DAILY WAGES IN THE EIGHTEENTH CENTURY

	1700 s. d.	1710 s. d.	1720 s. d.	1730 s. d.	1740 s. d.	1750 s. d.	1760 s. d.	1770 s. d.	1780 s. d.	1790 s. d.	1800 s. d.
Craftsmen's wages—chiefly skilled building operatives											
London	2 6	2 8	3 0	3 0	3 0	3 0	3 0	3 0	3 0	3 4	—
Home Counties	—	—	2 0	2 0	2 0	2 0	2 2	2 0	2 6	2 6	3 0
West of England	1 8	1 8	1 8	1 8	1 8	1 8	1 10	2 0	2 0	2 4	—
North of England	1 6	1 6	1 6	1 6	1 6	1 6	1 6	1 8	2 0	2 0	—
Labourers' Wages, chiefly builders in London, chiefly agricultural workers in other areas											
London	1 8	1 10	1 10	1 10	2 0	2 0	2 0	2 0	2 0	2 0	—
Home Counties	—	1 4	1 4	1 4	1 4	1 4	1 6	1 4	1 7	1 7	—
West of England	1 2	1 2	1 2	1 2	1 2	1 0	1 1	1 2	1 3	1 4	—
North of England	9	9½	10	10	1 0	1 0	1 0	1 2	1 6	1 8	—

account of mining and manufacturing growth improving the market for agricultural produce, and compelling the farmers to pay higher wages because of the competition of other employments.

All these figures, which are based on broad deductions from Miss Gilboy's evidence, must be taken as very approximate indeed. But they do very roughly indicate the general movement in building and agriculture. We have set them out in the form of a table, for which we, and not Miss Gilboy, must be held responsible, as it represents ℴot her figures, but our deductions from them. (See page 76.)

In order to get some idea of the meaning of these wage-changes in relation to purchasing power, it is necessary to relate them to the movement of prices. We begin with the price of wheat, in the form of a five-year average based on the average official prices of each year for British wheat.

BRITISH WHEAT PRICES, 1696–1800
Five-year Averages (per Quarter)

	s.	d.			s.	d.			s.	d.
1696–1700	55	7	1731–5	..	31	0	1766–70	..	49	1
1701–5	32	11	1736–40	..	37	2	1771–5	..	51	6
1706–10	46	3	1741–5	..	28	11	1776–80	..	40	2
1711–15	46	7	1746–50	..	33	0	1781–5	..	48	7
1716–20	35	5	1751–5	..	35	5	1786–90	..	47	3
1721–5	35	6	1756–60	..	42	4	1791–5	..	53	8
1726–30	41	4	1761–5	..	38	6	1796–1800		73	0

This sequence of prices shows no continuous upward tendency till the middle 'sixties; but it does show a large enough fluctuation to involve, in face of the very slowly changing wages, a great instability in the standard of living, as far as this depended upon wheaten bread. This comes out even more if account is taken of the yearly movements, which are flattened out by the use of the five-year average. Thus in 1709 and 1710 two bad harvests drove up the price of wheat to from 71*s.* to 72*s.* a quarter. So high a price was not reached again till 1795, when the wartime inflation had begun; but in 1757, a notably bad year, the price rose to 55*s.*, falling as low as 27*s.* 1*d.* by 1761. In 1767 it rose to 59*s.* 1*d.*, and thereafter it was usually over 40*s.*, the lowest recorded price being 34*s.* 10*d.* in 1779. These prices were nothing to those of the famine years during the wars—for in 1800 wheat averaged nearly 114*s*. a quarter—but the fluctuations were big enough to cause very large variations in the standard of living from year to year.

It has, however, to be borne in mind that by no means the whole of the population lived on wheat. It is common among modern investigators, and it was common among many contemporary writers, who were apt to think mainly of conditions in the South of England, to describe eighteenth-century England as pre-eminently a nation of wheat-eaters. But even at the end of the century there was a considerable part of the population that did not eat wheat at all, or ate it at most only on rare occasions and as a peculiar luxury. About 1760 it was estimated, on the basis of figures of the sale of grain all over England, that about 3,750,000 people ate wheat, as against about 860,000 who ate rye, 710,000 who ate barley, and nearly 600,000 who ate mainly oatmeal. The consumption of oatmeal, as the staple article of diet, was confined to the North and the North Midlands; and in these areas taken together the number of oatmeal eaters exceeded the wheat eaters. In the North, wheat, rye and oats were consumed in about equal quantities, but much less barley was used. In Lancashire and the North Midlands oats came first and wheat a good way behind, with barley and rye about equal at one half of the consumption of wheat. Wales ate mainly barley and rye, with a little wheat and practically no oats. Over the rest of the country wheat easily led all the rest. Barley was also consumed to a fair extent in the south Midlands and the south-east, but not in the West. Oatmeal was hardly eaten at all, save as a supplementary article of diet, except in the North.

Everywhere in the countryside, and to a considerable extent in the towns as well, the ordinary labouring population lived mainly on cereals. Over most of the South, the labourer got no meat at all, except an occasional bit of bacon. Even if he fattened a pig himself he usually sold a good part of the meat. In the Home Counties, north of the Thames, and in the South Midlands the labourer got a little more meat than this, but in Norfolk and Suffolk almost none at all. In the North the miners in both Cumberland and Durham ate meat as a staple

article of diet; but the agricultural workers lived chiefly on rye,
barley and oatmeal. In the West, again, there was usually no
meat for the labourer, except a little bacon.

Nevertheless, the writers of the eighteenth century, from
Daniel Defoe near its beginning to Arthur Young near its end,
continually dwelt on the superiority of the British labourer's
standard of living over those of the labourers in Continental
countries. Thus Defoe, in *Giving Alms No Charity*, refers to "the
dearness of wages, which in England outgoes all nations in the
world." Arthur Young, ninety years later, estimated in his
Travels in France that wages were, on the average, 76 per cent
higher in England than in France, and that the English
labourer lived 76 per cent better than the French. This conclusion was based on taking the English labourer's wage at an
average of 8s. 5d. a week, over the country as a whole, not
including harvest money or special allowances or, apparently,
the subsidiary earnings of wives and children; but presumably
such payments were also excluded from the French figures.

In view of these and other contemporary judgments, it is
desirable to get as clear a view as we can of the actual living
standards of labourers in the eighteenth century. For the
poorest sections of the population in both town and country,
we can get some idea of these standards from the numerous
tracts dealing with the poor laws; and we have also a great
deal of information about the standard diets prescribed for the
inmates of various poorhouses, though it is by no means
certain that these diets were in nearly all cases actually supplied. Where they were supplied, there can be no doubt that
the inmates fared a good deal better, in respect of food, than
the general body of independent labourers.

Unfortunately, we are most fully equipped with facts about
the standard of living towards the end of the century, when
rising prices, especially after the outbreak of war in 1793, must
have seriously upset the previous standards. Eden, whose
three volumes on *The State of the Poor*, published in 1797, are
our principal source of information, collected most of his
budgets from all parts of the country between 1794 and 1796.
But it is noticeable that most of Eden's budgets show the poor
as expending a good deal more than they are shown as having

received from all sources of family income; and it seems probable that his statistics show in fact rather what the poor had been able to buy before the rise in prices than what they were actually getting in 1795 or 1796. We can therefore use them as giving a general guide to standards of living in the latter part of the eighteenth century, especially as they are fairly well confirmed by other contemporary evidence from the pre-war period, drawn from Arthur Young, from Davies's *Case of the Labourers in Husbandry*, and from numerous poor law sources.

From Eden's budgets we get a picture of agricultural labourers earning, in different parts of the country, mostly from 7s. 6d. to 10s. a week, though an exceptional man here and there got 11s. or even 12s. These figures exclude harvest money, which might bring in a pound or two more during the year. But family earnings depended greatly on whether the wife also worked for pay, and on the earnings of children. In fact, the majority of wives did supplement the family income, most often by spinning or some similar home occupation, but sometimes by going out to work. Their earnings were put at from less than 6d. to as much as 2s. a week, with 1s. or 1s. 3d. as a fairly common figure. Children's earnings naturally varied much more, according to their ages. A good many households got as much as 2s. or 3s. a week from this source; but some, with large families of young children to feed, got nothing at all. Total family earnings, on an annual basis, varied between £50—a single abnormally high figure—or £40 and under £18, the commonest amounts ranging from £24 to about £35.

On what were these incomes spent? Rent was a primary charge, except for the minority who lived in rent-free "tied" cottages, or had their rent paid for them by the parish on grounds of poverty. Rents varied, according to district, from about £1 10s. to £2 a year in most areas; in a few they were put at less than £1 10s. and in Norfolk the annual rent was given as £3 3s. In Suffolk it was £2 10s. £1 15s. to £2 represents a rough average.

Fuel was another serious expense, though the poor, wherever they could, collected it from the woodlands, and were often heavily punished for stealing it. Eden's estimates of the cost of fuel actually bought—mainly wood, but including coal in some areas—range in most cases from £1 10s. to £2 10s. a year, though there are both much lower and much higher figures. Boots and clothing, which Eden also estimates on an annual basis, show so wide a variation that little can be made of the figures. Clearly the labourers lived in many cases largely on the cast-off clothes they were given by the gentry, or by their relations who were in service with the rich. Including boots, Eden gives figures as low as 10s. 6d. a year for the expenditure of families in Suffolk, with four and five children to clothe, and as high as £12 for an Oxfordshire household earning £50 a year, and £8 13s. for a Yorkshire labourer whose total family income was under £18. Clearly the poor spent on clothes what they could, after meeting the costs they could not avoid. It is plain from Eden's budgets that an increase in total income was at once reflected in a higher expenditure on boots and other clothing.

Food, however, necessarily absorbed most of the ordinary labourer's income. Eden's budgets show weekly expenditure on cereals, including oatmeal and other grains besides wheat, but excluding potatoes, of from 5s. 2d. to 14s. a week, excluding families with fewer than three children. The commonest figures are 8s. to 10s. a week, or well above the man's weekly earnings. In the North expenditure on cereals was a good deal lower—from 4s. 6d. to 6s.—because oatmeal was eaten much more, barley partly replaced wheat, and potatoes were used a great deal more than in the South or West. By Eden's time the labourers in most areas had begun to eat potatoes; and they were to be driven to substitute them more and more for wheat during the period of war prices. But in the North potatoes had long been a regular article of diet, costing the labourer, by Eden's figures, from 1s. to 1s. 6d. a week. Only Somerset, at 1s. 9d. a week, showed a higher expenditure on potatoes than the Northern Counties.

Meat, as we have seen, was usually outside the range of the labourer's purchasing power, beyond a little bacon, or perhaps an occasional stew. Eden's budgets show many households buying no meat at all, and most spending only from 9d. or less to 1s. 6d. a week, though a very few spent as much as 3s. Cheese was eaten instead in some parts of the country, notably East Anglia; but in many areas little or no cheese was consumed. The Northern labourer, who had potatoes, seems to have tasted neither meat nor cheese.

As for milk, the labourer saw little of it, even for young children, except in the North of England, where it was widely used with oatmeal. The remaining expenditure on food was for butter, tea, and sugar; and these Eden's investigators usually lumped together, so that it is impossible to give separate figures. The grouped expenditure upon them varied greatly, from 8d. to 10d.—and even in some cases 6d.—a week among the poorer labourers, to 1s. 6d. or 2s., or in a few cases rather more. Seldom was more than a very few pence put down as spent on beer, though the Suffolk investigator—perhaps either a thirsty soul or a strong Puritan—put down the normal expenditure in that county at 1s. a week. Half the households are returned as buying no beer at all. No doubt, many of them brewed their own; for home-brewing died out only in the early years of the nineteenth century, largely as a consequence of the malt tax. But, even before this impost, malt and hops and the other ingredients were not cheap: so this does not explain the absence of any allowance for them in the returns.

There remained absolutely necessary expenditure for lighting, which was in fact usually by rush-light, for wax candles were a luxury far beyond the means of the poor. Rush-lights —tiny bowls of fat or tallow with a rush for wick—cost as a rule from 4d. to 7d. a week, but are entered at 9½d. for a plutocrat with nearly £1 a week. Then there was soap—usually from 2d. to 6d. a week—and thread for sewing or knitting—usually from 2d. to 3d. or 4d. Finally, the labourer was bound to incur—unless the parish paid—expenses for sickness, for his wife's lying-in, and for other contingencies. Eden's investigators allowed nothing at all in half the cases for these costs of living, and in the other cases put them sometimes as low as 5s. a year and sometimes as high as £3 to £4. Such figures clearly mean but little. But it is interesting to observe that in only one area—Somerset—did the local investigators allow anything at all for the cost of sending the children to school.

With these figures to guide us, let us set down a rough standard budget of expenditure for 1795 for a labourer in the South of England with four or five children at home.

TYPICAL LABOURER'S BUDGET
LATE EIGHTEENTH CENTURY

			per week			per year	
			s.	d.		£	s.
Cereals	..	..	9	0	..	23	8
Potatoes	..	..		9	..	1	19
Cheese	..	..		3	..	0	13
Meat	..	..	1	0	..	2	12
Sugar, Tea and Butter			1	0	..	2	12
Milk	..	..		3	..	0	13
Beer	..	..		3	..	0	13
Thread	..	..		3	..	0	13
Clothes and Boots	..				..	2	0
Fuel	..	..			..	2	0
Rent	..	..			..	1	10
Sickness and contingencies					..	1	0
						41	12

But it is certain that the ordinary labourer in 1795 did not, even when he had children of earning age, get anything like this amount. If he himself got 9*s*. a week, his wages would just pay his bread bill. If his wife earned 2*s*. weekly—a high figure —she could pay for the meat, sugar, butter and tea. If his children earned half a crown between them, they would just cover the last four items on the budget. But with total family earnings, on this basis, of just over £35 a year, there would be left a deficit of £6 10*s*. After the rise of prices in the last decade of the eighteenth century, it is no wonder that the labourers were driven more and more to the parish to eke out their meagre earnings.

It would, of course, have been greatly preferable to present these budgets in terms of quantities consumed, rather than in money. But that cannot be done; for most of Eden's budgets give only figures of expenditure. We can, however, in one or two cases give details of actual consumption. Here, for example, is the budget, from Eden, of a labourer at Streatley, with a wife and four children at home. Two of the children, aged fourteen and twelve, were out working on farms: the other two, aged seven and five, were not working. Three other

children were living away, in service. The man earned 8s. a
week in winter, and as much as 12s. in summer. His wife
earned 1s. 6d. a week. The total family income was £46—the
family being thus a long way above the ordinary level of
labouring households.

This family bought weekly:

8 half-peck loaves	at 1s. 9d. each.
2 lb. of cheese	at 7d. per lb.
2 lb. of butter	at 9d. per lb.
2 lb. of sugar	at 9d. per lb.
2 oz. of tea	at 3s. per lb.
½ lb. of oatmeal	at 3d. per lb.
½ lb. of bacon	at 3d. per lb.
2d. worth of milk.	

Their annual charges were:

	£	s.	d.	
Soap, candles, etc.	2	7	4	
Fuel	1	0	0	(most being gathered free in the
Rent	2	5	0	woods)
Shoes	1	10	0	
Other Clothing	4	12	0	

On this basis, their annual expenses, at 1795 prices, worked
out at nearly £64, or £18 more than the family earnings. Yet
their diet does not err on the side of excess. It was actually
about what the family could have got before the rise in prices.

So far, we have confined ourselves to budgets from the
agricultural areas. Eden and other contemporary authorities,
being mainly interested in the poor law aspect of the question,
give few urban budgets and very few of skilled workers. Eden
does, however, give a few for miners from Cumberland and
Durham, and one or two from other trades. Here is the
budget of a Durham miner in the early 1790's, on an annual
basis:

	s.		s.		s.		s.
Rent ..	30	Barley	150	Meat ..	50	Candles, Soap,	
Fuel ..	32	Wheat		Butter ..	50	etc. ..	30
Boots and		and Rye	50	Milk ..	30	Potatoes ..	28
Clothes ..	100	Oatmeal	104	Tea and Sugar	40		

The total expenditure comes to £34 14s. Earnings are given
as £32. Clearly this man's family did not buy bread, but grain
and oatmeal, from which the cereal diet was prepared at home.

Here, for comparison, is the budget of a Cumberland miner, at about the same time:

	s.		s.		s.		s.
Rent ..	60	Barley	110	Butter ..	60	Candles, Soap,	
Fuel ..	20	Wheat ..	—	Milk ..	36	etc. ..	40
Boots and		Oatmeal	80	Cheese ..	20	Potatoes ..	80
Clothes	104	Meat ..	200	Tea and Sugar	70		

Total expenditure is £44: earnings are given at the same amount. This miner and his family, relatively well off, ate much more meat, and also many more potatoes, but did not eat wheat at all.

Here, again, is the budget of a Durham stonemason:

	s.		s.		s.		s.
Rent	40	Barley ..	130	Butter ..	30	Candles, Soap, etc., in-	
Fuel	40	Wheat ..	—	Milk ..	30	cluded with Clothes.	
Boots and		Oatmeal ..	60	Tea and Sugar	40	Potatoes ..	40
Clothes	80	Meat ..	60				

Again, no wheat is eaten. Total expenditure comes to £27 10s. Earnings are given as £28. None of these budgets allows anything for sickness or contingencies.

By way of contrast, take a Cumberland miner, cited by Eden. He spent 27s. on rent and 34s. 4d. on fuel, and only 9s. on meat, and 26s. on all other items except oatmeal, which cost him 234s. In other words, he practically lived on oatmeal porridge.

It would be satisfactory to be able to set against these figures of wages, expenditure and consumption some general measure of the movement of the cost of living. But the data for such a measure do not exist. The only available index of the cost of living is that compiled a few years ago from contemporary British records by the American statistician, Silberling, and that only begins in 1779 and measures rather urban than rural costs of living. It weights meat nearly as heavily as wheat, and does not include barley at all. It can be regarded at most as applicable only to the very best-paid workers, all the rest being far more dependent on the fluctuating prices of cereals, and far less on meat and other prices.

Silberling's index, for what it is worth for our purpose, shows the cost of living as rising by 22 per cent from 1779 to

1782, falling to only 4 per cent above the 1779 level in 1785, and then rising again by 1790 to the same height as in 1782. In 1800 it was actually 107 per cent above the level of 1779, and 70 per cent above that of 1790.

There is always a danger, in studying the past, of reading back into it the notions and circumstances of our own time. We must not make this mistake in dealing with social classes and working conditions in the eighteenth century. It must not be forgotten that in many trades, though not of course in all, the class division between master and workman was in 1750, or even in 1800, by no means comparable with what it is to-day. In many of the London trades, for example, it was possible in the middle of the eighteenth century for a journeyman to set up for himself with only a very small capital, which he quite often acquired by marriage. In the *General Description of All Trades*, from which the account of London wages has been taken, an estimate is given of the approximate capital needed by a journeyman in each trade in order to be able to start in business for himself. For the manual crafts £100 is a frequent figure; for some as little as £50 is mentioned as enough. In shopkeeping £500 is more often recommended, and in some trades substantially more; and a few are cited as open only to men of fortune. In provincial towns considerably smaller sums than these were adequate; but against this has to be set the fact that in England's two greatest industries, based on wool and iron, the road to independent mastership was by no means easy. The iron and coal trades already needed large capital for their successful exploitation, though in the coal trade it was still possible for a man of little capital to get a contract to work a mine on behalf of a superior proprietor, employing his own hired labour, and paying a rent or royalty, or sometimes both. In the woollen industry it was much easier to become a small master in Yorkshire than in the Western Counties, where the entire trade was dominated by the rich merchant-clothiers and the great majority of the workers, however skilled, were shut out under the domestic system from the hope of ever becoming more than piece-workers virtually in the clothier's employment.

In the urban crafts, on the other hand, the social line

between master and journeyman was by no means sharp.
Friends and near relations were often on opposite sides of this
line, and marriage frequently overstepped it. Moreover, in
certain trades, such as building, a man might employ others
as a master on one contract, and then change places on the
next occasion with someone whom he had employed, and shift
back again later on.

With this fact goes another. Educationally and culturally,
there was a far deeper cleavage between the skilled apprenticed craftsmen and the unapprenticed labourers below them
than between these craftsmen and their employers—except of
course in the few trades which were already being organized
on a basis of large-scale production, such as iron-working and
brewing. The skilled craftsman knew how to read and write.
He was quite commonly, at any rate in many districts, a
Dissenter, attending the same chapel with his employer; and
in quite a substantial number of cases he had actually lived in
his employer's house and fed at his table. These facts made
strongly against any common consciousness of the entire
manual working class in face of their employers. That consciousness could hardly come into being until the employer
had become a capitalist factory-owner, remote from the practice of the work which his capital set in motion, until the old
social relation of apprentice and master had died out, and
until the line of division between skilled craftsmen and
labourers had been blurred, and in some cases wholly obli-
terated, by the advent of power-driven machinery.

SOCIAL MOVEMENTS
IN THE EIGHTEENTH CENTURY

CHAPTER VII

THE UNREFORMED PARLIAMENT

ALL these classes were subordinate to a government that consisted, in theoretically equal parts, of King, Lords and Commons. If an inquirer pursued his questions beyond theory into practice he would learn that already, of the three, the House of Commons was the predominant partner. But if he assumed from this that the Commons were in any way what their name would naturally suggest, he would be ridiculously mistaken.

The composition of the House of Commons in the eighteenth century was of a character so eccentric—to use no more severe a term—that it is surprising that it retained as it did the reputation of being in some degree a representation of the people. The process of corruption had been partly a natural decay due to the shifting of population since medieval days, partly a deliberate development in the interest of the king or a limited number of aristocrats. Large towns like Manchester and Leeds had no representation; for though Cromwell had redistributed seats so as to enfranchise them, Charles II had cancelled his changes. Empty or half-empty towns such as the Cinque Ports—New Romney had eight voters—were represented, generally by two members. Gatton had six houses and one resident elector. Old Sarum, the "accursed hill," near Salisbury, contained nothing but a thornbush.

These boroughs had been denuded by natural decay; others, notably the Cornish boroughs, had been deliberately created to be bought and sold, or to be the property of the Crown or of a rich man. The right to nominate their members was on occasion sold as easily and openly as any other form of property. Thomas Holcroft, the dramatist, attended a sale of the borough of Gatton at which "the celebrated auctioneer scarcely noticed the value of the estate. The rental, the mansions, the views, the woods and waters, were unworthy of regard, compared to what he called *an elegant contingency.*" "No tempestuous passions to allay," said the salesman of his prospective purchaser, "no tormenting claims of insolent electors to evade, no tinkers' wives to kiss, no impossible promises to make, none of the toilsome and not very clean paths of canvassing to drudge through; but, his mind at ease and his conscience clear, with this elegant contingency in his pocket, the honours of the State await his plucking and with its emoluments his purse will overflow."

Even in those boroughs which retained a fair number of electors the tendency was towards increased corruption rather than towards less corruption. A vote in a borough with a narrow electorate was a valuable privilege, the more valuable the smaller the electorate, and the tendency of those possessing it—who were very often also the municipal corporation—was to restrict their own numbers and diminish fresh entries as far as possible. Thus, as the franchise varied from town to town, many boroughs which still had population enough to give them the right to be represented were, nevertheless, as venal as Gatton. Totnes had 78 voters at the end of King George III's reign, Bodmin had 36, Rye had 14, and Winchelsea had 7.

Boroughs which were really representative did still exist. Westminster had a "scot-and-lot" franchise—that is, a franchise based on the payment of certain small municipal taxes —which gave the vote not only to the lower middle class, but to the artisan class. Preston and Coventry were in a similar position; London with four members and a 10,000 odd electorate was only a degree less democratic, though its electoral machinery was based on the medieval organization of the City Companies. Middlesex, on its northern borders, though technically a county, was already becoming partly urbanized and had a fairly wide freeholder franchise; Southwark on the south had democratic elements in its voting body, as also had Liverpool. But these names, with Newcastle

Bristol, Norwich and Nottingham, practically exhaust the list of even partly representative boroughs.

The county representatives, the "knights of the shire," were in general more esteemed and more estimable. Two knights were returned from every English shire, regardless of its size and population, and one each from the shires of Scotland and Wales. After the Union, there were also two members from each Irish county. The freeholder franchise was general, and the electorates were far from insignificant. Generally, it is true, the county representatives were drawn from the families of the largest landlords in the area. But this was by choice of the lesser gentry: they wished to be represented by their wealthiest or most aristocratic colleagues, and these representatives did not wholly neglect their constituents' interests. In 1763, indeed, the representatives of Hereford and other western counties were largely responsible for overturning a Chancellor of the Exchequer because of an excise project which injured the cider trade. About 1780 Sir George Savile and Christopher Wyvill, the Yorkshire reformers, found that it was possible to appeal to the county electors behind their representatives, and for this appeal to have a certain limited effect upon the behaviour of their M.P.s.

Thus, the county representation was largely a direct and genuine representation of the smaller gentry and the large farmers. But even to this statement two qualifications must be made. In the first place, the Scottish counties, which returned one member each, were constituencies as fictitious as any borough. Edinburghshire had 96 electors, Wigtownshire 53, and Inverness-shire 32. All Scottish seats, boroughs as well as counties, were indeed utterly venal. Their introduction into the English Parliament under Anne had merely been an introduction of 45 purchasable seats, of which 39 were steadily in the possession of the Government or the King. For all practical purposes, Scotland had no representation at all.

The second qualification to be made is that only in unusual circumstances could the votes of the county members be effective. There were 122 county members—80 from England, 12 from Wales, and 30 from Scotland. There were 4 university members, from Oxford and Cambridge, who certainly could never be classed as democratic. But there were 429 borough members—12 and 14 from Wales and Scotland respectively, and 403 from English boroughs. Control of Parliament, therefore, lay in the hands of the borough members.

The condition of borough representation has already been described. The distribution of borough seats among the counties made it still more improbable that Parliament could in any way adequately represent the people. Borough seats were allotted to various parts of the country without regard to population. Cornwall, by far the greatest centre of Crown influence, actually returned 42 borough members. Wiltshire, a more populous county because of the clothing trade, came next with 32, followed by Yorkshire and Sussex with 26 apiece. Devonshire and Hampshire had 24 each, Dorset 18, Somerset and Kent 16 each, Suffolk 14, Lancashire, Buckinghamshire and Surrey 12 each, and Norfolk, Lincolnshire and Shropshire 10. On the other hand the following counties had each only two borough members—Bedford, Cambridge, Cheshire, Derby, Durham, Huntingdon, Leicester, Monmouth, and Westmoreland—and there were six or fewer in Cumberland, Hertford, Warwick, Northumberland, Nottingham, Essex, Gloucester, Hereford, and Oxford, though several of these were among the most populous counties.

As a result, a very small number of voters were able to control the decisions of the House of Commons. Wilkes, in introducing his Reform Bill in 1776, analysed recent divisions of the House and showed that, upon the highest recorded figures, the command of 254 seats was sufficient to secure a majority. "This number of 254 is elected by no more than 5,723 persons, generally the inhabitants of Cornish and other very insignificant boroughs, perhaps by not the most respectable part of the community." At that date, he said, the inhabitants of the southern part of the island were estimated to exceed 5,000,000.

The corrupt boroughs were roughly divisible into four classes. Some were controlled by a narrow oligarchical borough council, itself often renewed by co-option. There were no fixed registers and each would-be voter had to make good his claim at each election, a process encouraging the growth of oligarchy. Boroughs, such as these already described, were regularly on the market, and required to be repurchased at each election. Sometimes the burgesses had no functions beyond selling votes. On rarer occasions, when the auction was very open, the House might intervene to rebuke and punish. In one case, but one alone—Grampound, 1821—actual disfranchisement followed, and the two seats left free were transferred to Yorkshire. In a very few other cases the area of the offending borough was enlarged, by throwing into it a part of the surrounding county, and so increasing the number of voters. Generally, however, no interference was made with what was recognized as a common and legitimate traffic. The second class was owned by a single peer or wealthy man: these were no more than a form of property and any attempt to eliminate them without full compensation would have been highly resented. Another consisted of boroughs whose control was shared between two or more proprietors; when the proprietors fell out there would be a conflict, and to the unwary this conflict might appear to be a genuine political disagreement. The fourth class consisted of boroughs owned by the Crown, which were generally put at the disposal of the Government of the day.

As time went on, these various forms of control became stronger rather than weaker. At the end of the reign of George III—according to the *Black Book* of 1820—144 peers nominated 300 M.P.s, and the government and 123 persons together nominated 187 more, thus making an actual majority however high the division figures might be. Nevertheless, the House continued solemnly to pass at the beginning of each session a resolution to the effect that for any peer to concern himself in elections was "a high infringement of the liberties of the Commons." It should be remembered, too, that the knights of the shire, reflecting the opinions of the smaller gentry, were moderate Whigs at best and in many cases Tories; their occasional interest in reform—even in the case of the most enlightened county—Yorkshire—meant no profound democratic feeling, but rather the resentment that a gentleman would feel at the sight of an ill and corruptly administered estate. They would very much have disliked being compared to or classed with the "mob" in Westminster, and were very cautious even in their alliances with the London merchants.

When seats in Parliament were for sale, or were the private property of well-to-do individuals, it was a natural consequence that the allocation of governmental offices which were dependent upon Parliament should be equally corrupt. Perhaps the most startling feature of eighteenth-century government is the enormous number of sinecures and of ill-earned pensions. Such sinecures and pensions were indeed (as Horace Walpole argued) more worthy of respect than incomes derived from landed property, as landed property might well pass to unworthy persons, while pensions and sinecures were at least awarded for some real or imagined service to the government. This statement was unduly optimistic: pensions and sinecures were at least as often awarded because the recipient was connected by blood or marriage with some important politician. Soon after George III made his chief favourite, the Scotsman Lord Bute, into the equivalent of Premier, the pensions list was found to contain sixty-three Macs, twenty-five Campbells, an uncertain number of Hamiltons, and a large number of other Scots names.

The noblemen, or relatives of noblemen, who received these posts were not particular concerning the titles and functions they nominally assumed. They consented to become clerks, tide-waiters, searchers, gaugers, craners, wharfingers and packers. A baroness was "sweeper of the Mall in the Park," and Lord William Bentinck was "clerk of the Pipe," whose duties included that of waiting upon the man who held up the Lord Chancellor's robe on State occasions. If the duties were performed at all, it was by underpaid deputies. In 1782 (to anticipate), it is true that Acts for an "economical reformation" were passed, which restricted such pensions and sinecures to £90,000 a year. But there was no body of persons interested in enforcing such a prohibition: after a momentary restriction, old habits were resumed, and even exaggerated during the French wars, and the description given above remains in general terms true until the year 1832.

Such usurpation of funds existed locally as well as nationally. In nearly every borough there were foundations, or old-established taxes, which had originally been constituted to provide for certain necesary administrative duties or reliefs, and which now only went into the pockets of privileged persons. Bishop Pretyman Tomline, the younger Pitt's tutor, was discovered in such a type of embezzlement, but few thought the worse of him for it. This century also saw the completion of the process by which the educational establishments, set up by medieval charity for the use of the poor, were finally taken over by the wealthy. The colleges of Oxford and Cambridge, famous schools like Eton, were permitted to disregard wholly the provisions of their statutes, and in certain cases Fellows with tender consciences were allowed, when repeating their oath, to omit the clauses conferring the benefits of the schools on " poor scholars."

While public money was taken freely for the performance of non-existent services, it was inevitable that genuine public services should be underpaid and inefficient. Many of the ordinances of eighteenth-century parliaments appear oppressive, but in judging them it must always be remembered that their execution was generally ineffective. All the instruments of coercion that an eighteenth-century Government possessed were more or less ineffective. Peculation and jobbery were universal in the army; and, partly for this reason, the British army's reputation, except in India, stood lower than the victories listed in the school-books current to-day would suggest. Victories on the Continent were discounted as secured with the help of allies and mercenaries; across the ocean British generals lost an empire. The record of the navy on the other hand was one of victory, but peculation and theft were common enough there too, for the post of purser on a ship of the line was regarded as worth £1,000 to its holder.

The police were far from formidable. The City police, it is true, were not inefficient: the streets of London perhaps were not intolerably disorderly. But this was exceptional: immediately outside the city boundaries chaos ruled. No ordinance to which any large body of persons objected could be enforced by the watchmen or the Bow Street Runners. Gaming-houses, apart from clubs, were nominally forbidden, but 43 such houses existed in London outside the City boundaries. Their entrances were "barricadoed" and furnished with "bludgeon men" whose duty it was to knock out any police officer who might be unwise enough to attempt to interfere. Such an event was, indeed, rare: police officers sometimes did raid a gaming-house, but most usually for personal revenge, as a punishment for failure to bribe, or in order to confiscate for themselves the money that was on the tables. By the end of King George III's reign the annual turn-over of the 43 houses mentioned was estimated at slightly over £7,000,000. Spasmodically, energetic justices like Fielding would start and direct "drives" for the suppression of the more ostentatious crimes, but after their energy was exhausted the streets returned to their previous state.

Milk retailers, at the places where they met to take delivery from the farmers, commonly had in the yard a pump, which they facetiously named the Black Cow, and with which they openly diluted the milk in view of the police and without interference. The poorer population of London and any large town every Sunday, and many weekdays, would pour out into the country with bags in their hands and strip the lands of unwary farmers of fruit, vegetables, and any other consumable or saleable products. For protection, a farmer had to rely on the strong arms of himself and his sons: there were no police in the country and the town police were unconcerned. In consequence, the fields immediately adjoining built-up land, which should have been the most valuable as market-gardens, did not fetch so high a price as fields rather further out.

The chief police station was in Bow Street, whose "Runners," with their bright scarlet waistcoats, performed as far as it was performed at all the duty of a detective force. The watchmen, frequently aged men, performed or failed to perform the duties of a constable on his beat. Both branches of the force were paid little by way of salaries, but made their incomes from perquisites and fees, as did the magistrates' clerks and other officers.

It is not to be imagined that such a system of aristocratic corruption and inefficiency passed unattacked. It was already fashionable to criticize the privileges of birth and title. The elder Pitt owed a great deal of his popularity to his being known as the Great Commoner. When his wife destroyed that distinction for him by taking the title of Chatham, the Londoners showed their disappointment by calling her Lady Cheat'em. "I am in such a passion I cannot tell you what I am angry about—why, about Virtue and Mr. Pitt, two arrant cheats!" wrote Horace Walpole of the same event. But the populace of London forgot its annoyance in twelve months, and the Walpole who wrote this denunciation was the admiring son of the most corrupt premier England had ever known. When the agitation of Wilkes made democratic principles into serious politics, he at once abandoned his ideals in alarm and wrote with complete naïveté: "I wish we do not soon see quarrels of a graver complexion than squabbles for places and profit."

Such opposition was rootless and almost factitious; it was the "parlour Bolshevism" of a later age. Any historian of the middle of the eighteenth century is forced to catalogue a series of convincing reasons for discontent, and then to record contentment. Almost without exception all classes of society were indifferent to the vast collection of abuses listed above. For this, the main reason was without question that they were prosperous, except in the recurring "bad years," which were often marked by bread riots in the towns. The first half of the eighteenth century showed a steady, if slow, increase in real comforts and in civilization for all classes in England. No one who benefited by this was inclined to oppose seriously the system which might be supposed to have produced this advance. All he required was that some sufficiently plausible excuse might be produced for him to continue to support it; and this was provided by the theory of "virtual representation."

This theory claimed that by a happy series of accidents the grotesque parliamentary system gave exactly the correct weight to the opinions of those who should properly govern the country—that is to say, to men of rank, assisted by those who had made fortunes in commerce. The trio that nominally governed the country—King, Lords, Commons—would not have done in its crude state. Since James II had been summarily dismissed, the power of the first had been properly diminished. It was assumed that the next occupant of the throne would be as conveniently inert as had been Anne, George I and George II. The Commons were in theory the equals in power of, if not greater than, the Lords. If they had in fact been "commons," it would not have done. The governing class might have been impeded in its task of governing. As it was, the system of pocket boroughs gave this class the tempered authority it required. Even the artisan class, through certain constituencies, had the small and respectful voice to which it was entitled. Reformers—if they had themselves the money or could interest a member of the governing class—could and did purchase boroughs and so call attention to necessary reforms. When the dispute with America flared up it was seriously proposed that the colonists should settle the matter by purchasing a sufficient number of seats to see that their interests were not neglected. The aristocracy was by these means also continuously refreshed by an immigration of successful business men. A "nabob" returning from India, or a merchant who had made his fortune in the West Indian trade, purchased a small strip of land to make himself a freeholder and then bought the most convenient borough that was in the market for himself or for his nominee. Sir Josiah Child, the East India merchant, actually rose so high as to become a peer, Lord Castlemain. The noble owners of boroughs frequently were most broadminded in overlooking plebeian origin in those whom they permitted to sit for them: in 1775 one of them actually nominated and returned an ex-waiter.

A philosoph'al observer, therefore, in the year 1746 could see a Constitution in which the throne was happily inactive, the landed class controlled the government, but was salutarily supported by and admixed with the commercial interest, and the lower orders were not condemned to complete silence. Had he conjectured what elements were in the future likely to be eliminated, he would probably have pointed to the democratic elements. It is a natural error to read into the eighteenth-century mind our own knowledge of the future. Before the American and French Revolutions it was more natural to assume that parliamentary government was moving towards extinction. The Russian, Spanish and German empires had either never had effective parliaments or had long dispensed with them; the remains of parliamentary government were in the next few years quietly disposed of in Sweden and France, and the largest other State of importance which retained a parliament was Poland, whose approaching destruction for that very reason was easily predictable.

In such circumstances it is not surprising that the first entry into politics of what were called the lower orders was not of a grave or determined character, but rather sporting and even frivolous. They joined in the uproar created by John Wilkes mostly because they were in the mood for a certain turbulence: that the conflict was prolonged and general principles raised was due largely to the courage and wit of the peculiar champion whom they had adopted.

CHAPTER VIII

WILKES AND LIBERTY

THE case of John Wilkes, which was to stir the "lower orders" from a century-long slumber, and to start a political agitation which is still not completed, began in the year 1763, and at its commencement the London populace took no more active part than that of an applauding audience. Wilkes was M.P. for Aylesbury, a seat for which he had been cheated into paying £7,000, and a follower of the rich and important aristocrat, Lord Temple, brother-in-law of the elder Pitt. His personal character was scandalous; he was a prominent member of the recently dissolved Monks of Medmenham—the so-called Hell Fire Club, a society whose improprieties shocked even the eighteenth century; he was senselessly extravagant with money; and though he was witty, his wit was invariably cynical and indecent. It was only later shown that he was personally honest, very daring, and a political campaigner of genius. At this moment, he was directing in the interests of his patron Temple a periodical called the *North Briton*, which had

had a success and circulation uncommon among political journals. It had intervened powerfully in a struggle which seemed of profound importance to the Whig oligarchy of the day, but which had not as yet roused any wide interest outside. The new King, George III, had determined to recover for himself the power which was nominally his, but which his predecessors had abandoned. The control of Parliament being a marketable thing, haggled over by well-to-do aristocrats, he had seen that it was perfectly possible for himself, an individual richer and more highly placed than any Duke, to enter into the competition and by the use of the same methods as the Whig dignitaries to outbid them and control Parliament for himself. The process was long and tortuous. His first instrument for this purpose, a Scotsman named Lord Bute, had carried it a certain way, but had been forced to retire after he had secured the removal of both Pitt and Temple from office. His successor was Temple's brother, George Grenville, and when it was discovered that he proposed to follow the same policy as Bute, Temple in his annoyance permitted his follower Wilkes to publish a violent attack.

The attack was printed on 23 April, 1763, in Number 45 of the *North Briton*, a number which for a short while became nationally famous. It was far from immoderate in phrasing, but its essential crime was that it attacked the King's Speech, and George III, really or for show, chose to consider this a grave insult. He, or his advisers, decided to make this publication an excuse for a direct blow in the face of the oligarchs who were resisting his influence. A "general warrant" was issued for the apprehension of the printer and author of "Number 45." Forty-eight persons were arrested and questioned on this warrant before Wilkes was detained; when he was seized he declined to answer questions on the pretext of his privilege as an M.P. The case was brought before Chief Justice Pratt, a judge of high probity, who ruled in two successive judgments that Wilkes's privilege should have protected him from arrest, and that general warrants were illegal. The first direct blow of the royal fist, therefore, had completely missed its mark. The populace of London was vociferously amused, and the printers, proof-readers and booksellers who had been dragged from their beds to prison under the general warrant, immediately commenced actions against the Government, and had the experience, rare to the common people, of being awarded appreciable sums of money as compensation.

Such a check could, however, be only temporary. The Government prepared a second attack more carefully. A suit was brought against Wilkes for "Number 45" in the ordinary way, and before a sympathetic judge, Lord Mansfield, in the Court of King's Bench. A loyal M.P., Samuel Martin, after careful revolver practice, challenged Wilkes to a duel and wounded him severely. The House of Commons was induced to pass a resolution condemning "Number 45." In the House of Lords, a fellow-member of the Hell Fire Club, Lord Sandwich, produced and read part of an obscene poem called "The Essay on Woman," of which Wilkes had at one time begun to print a dozen copies at his private press: this was also formally condemned. Wounded and not improbably intimidated, Wilkes retired to Paris for a rest. In his absence he was first expelled by the House of Commons, and then, for not standing his trial, declared an outlaw by the Courts. The sympathy of the town remained with him, but few disputed the verdict of the *Annual Register* that "the ruin of that unfortunate gentleman" was "completed."

That this verdict was upset was due to the courage of the unfortunate gentleman. Five years after, in 1768, the advance of the single Royal corrupter at the expense of the divided ducal purchasers of seats had not only put the power of the Crown high enough for Wilkes to despair of a rehabilitation, but had also compromised or disunited most of those whom he regarded as his natural protectors. He decided that he must rely upon himself and his humbler supporters alone, and defying his outlawry returned to London for the election that year. So slow were eighteenth-century police methods that he was able at his ease to present himself as a candidate first for London, where he failed, and then for Middlesex, where he received 1,292 votes against his rivals' 827 and 807. The people of London, whose appreciation of his courage had now been intensified by a fear of the King's growing ambition, received him with such tumultuous fervour that he was able to play with the authorities. He spent a week's ostentatious holiday at Bath, before he surrendered to justice. Even then, Lord Mansfield declined to try him on the ground that the sheriffs had not produced him on a writ of *capias utlagatum* and he was therefore not perceptible to the court. He spent yet another week amusing himself in the West End before he sent his own footman to ask the sheriff to be kind enough to arrest him, and his lawyer to tell the Attorney-General that the matter had been seen to. While he was in prison awaiting trial, the people demonstrated in St. George's Fields outside the walls, and the Scotch regiment in charge cleared the fields with a volley which left six dead and many more wounded. Three of the military pursued a demonstrator, turned a corner, and thinking they had found him, killed an innocent farmer work-.ing in an outhouse nearby.

This "Massacre of St. George's Fields" changed the temper of the Wilkites, especially when the Government congratulated the regiment responsible. An insurrection, or at least very severe rioting, began to be not impossible, and Lord Mansfield, the judge before whom Wilkes was to appear, decided to apply lenitives. He declared Wilkes's outlawry (on a worthless excuse) to be bad in law, cancelled it, and proceeded to sentence him for "Number 45" and the "Essay on Woman" to the relatively light penalties of £1,000 fine and twenty-two months' imprisonment.

In prison, Wilkes was no more than confined. He had his own food, his friends and visitors, and could lead as riotous a life as he chose. For once in his life, however, his energies were really directed to politics, and seconded by friends of considerable activity. Among these were Serjeant Glynn, a distinguished lawyer, John Horne (afterwards Horne Tooke), a clergyman whose habits and wit were similar to his own, and several of the more influential City merchants. The first victory of the camarilla that met in prison was to secure the return of Glynn for the second Middlesex seat at a by-election, the second to elect Wilkes an alderman of the City. But on 2 February, 1769, the House of Commons, impelled by the Government, which was impelled by the King, counter-attacked by expelling Wilkes from the House for publishing an inflammatory account of the Massacre of St. George's Fields.

A writ for a new election in Middlesex was issued.

The election was held on the 16th of the month, and Wilkes was returned unopposed. There was some curiosity as to what the Government could do now.

By resolution of the House of Commons it expelled Wilkes again, and ordered a third election, for March 16. An opponent for Wilkes, Mr. Charles Dingley of Golders Green, was found, but he did not even find a voter to nominate him, and Wilkes was returned a third time. The House expelled him again.

By this time the capital was in an uproar. The contest had now become far more than a sporting entertainment. Not only had lives been lost, but a House of Commons which had been bought by the King had raised a grave question of principle by overriding the choice of a democratic constituency on purely political grounds. Well-to-do persons who might have hesitated in other circumstances to support Wilkes against the King came to his aid with considerable sums of money subscribed through a Society of Supporters of the Bill of Rights; but his chief champions were from the long-silent class of workers and small employers, who burst into the arena with unexpected noise and violence. Mingling their trade demands with their sympathy for "Wilkes and Liberty," the weavers, hatters, hat-dyers, Southwark joiners, watermen, tailors and glass-grinders at one time or another came out on strike. The merchant sailors for a short while actually tied up the Port of London, and the coal-heavers marched on the Houses of Parliament and were only induced to quit Palace Yard by the eloquence of Sir John Fielding, the blind magistrate and half-brother of the famous novelist. "It has been said," observed a Wilkite pamphlet, "that in the neighbourhood of St. James's Mr. Wilkes's enemies are forty-five to fifteen; in the City his advocates are forty-five to fifteen; and in Wapping his staunch friends are forty-five to none at all."

This remained a true description of the Wilkite movement as long as it existed. But it was not one that was best fitted for success at an eighteenth-century polling-booth. When, for the fourth election, the Court at last secured a serious candidate, named Luttrell, the predominating influence of property showed that a slight, very slight, weakening had occurred in the Wilkite ranks. The figures were:

J. Wilkes	..	1,143
H. L. Luttrell	..	296
W. Whitaker	..	5
D. Roche ..	..	0

The next day the House of Commons, losing all restraint, not merely declared Wilkes expelled, but declared that Luttrell "ought to have been returned," and, to the astonishment of all London, formally seated him as member for Middlesex.

It was about the time of this violently provocative action that Franklin made his famous judgment that if Wilkes had had a good character and George III a bad, the King would have been turned off the throne. The opinion was based almost wholly upon the state of London: he had noticed that "not a door or window shutter" was unmarked with the figures 45 for fifteen miles out of town, "and this continued here and there quite to Winchester, which is 64 miles." But a journey even to Winchester does not carry one deeply into England, and the rage and excitement of London was not yet extended to the rest of the country. The Wilkites could, it is most probable, have occupied the City and defied the armed forces which the Crown had immediately to hand. But such an action by London would not (as a similar action in Paris did in 1789) have led to a successful rebellion. The provinces of England were not filled with the bitter, stormy hatred of the provinces of France. Wilkes and his admirers, to gain their support, had to start a campaign. To do this they had to improvise not merely organization but principles, and in both cases their cynical and frivolous chief provided instruments which are still being used.

Their main weapon was the introduction, or at least revival, of *public meetings* as a method of expressing opinion and influencing the Government. These meetings were called for the purpose, generally, of drafting and signing a petition to the King or the Commons; they were addressed by itinerant Wilkite speakers, who covered a regular "planned tour" as if they had been modern organizers. Occasional meetings of

county freeholders were not unknown, though they were
unusual except at elections; apart from them, this most essential and apparently natural expression of democracy had
largely disappeared. Their second weapon was inducing
electors to issue instructions to their representatives, usually to
protest against the Middlesex election decisions. This provoked far bitterer resentment than the other: Whigs who
had been willing enough to vote for Wilkes against the King
were enormously angered at being offered orders, which
they held to be "derogatory of the dignity of senators," and
continued to resist until the whole Wilkite agitation had
disappeared.

From such records as have survived, the Wilkites' movement
seems to have stirred deeply the Home Counties, the South-
west, most of East Anglia and most of the Midlands, Yorkshire
and Durham and Northumberland. Scotland, Wales, the
counties west of the Pennines, and Ireland, were little affected:
the American colonies were indeed excited, but the results of
that lie outside the scope of this book. The number of electors'
signatures secured in the petitions reached the quite surprising
total of 60,000.

To the plain demand for a reversal of the Middlesex decision
there was by degrees added a complete radical programme, of
which the programme of the Wilkite candidate (Frederick
Bull) for the London by-election of 1773 gives the best summary. It was for shorter parliaments, exclusion from the
Commons of all pensioners and placemen, "to establish a fair
and equal representation of the people in Parliament," and to
redress various separate grievances. Moreover, while it was
not possible to force the Commons to bend to the public will,
at least the organization of the City was still amenable. When
Wilkes was released in 1770, he commenced a campaign which
rapidly extirpated any traces of royal influence in the capital.
His nominees became Lord Mayors, he himself a sheriff. He
stopped the press-gang operating in London, and when the
Commons attempted to arrest printers for printing reports of
their debates, arrested their messenger for assaulting a freeman—an action which ultimately resulted in a further highly
valuable extension of the freedom of the Press, after the House

had again humiliated itself by sending two London M.P.s to the Tower in a vain attempt to prevent any further reporting. He introduced greater humanity in the treatment of prisoners, and even of the oxen at Smithfield. As Lord Mayor in 1774 he raised the "assize" of bread (i.e., increased the size of the penny loaf), and steadily enforced the jurisdiction of the livery-men of the City gilds against interloping merchants, in those trades where workers and working-masters still controlled the companies and applied to him for enforcement.

It was at the end of this year that Wilkes's movement reached its highest peak of success and at the same moment began to disintegrate. Its chief was Lord Mayor, and was re-elected to Parliament (this time taking his seat) with twelve followers whom he called The Apostles. But this little knot was unable to effect anything against the King, who now had Parliament completely in his hand, and Wilkes's Reform Bill when it was introduced was treated with jocularity. The City's opposition had to remain merely vocal, and the leaders of the movement began to dispute among themselves. The arrogance and frivolity of Wilkes turned against him Horne Tooke and some of the richest of the City merchants—John Sawbridge, James Townsend, Frederick Bull and Richard Oliver. On top of this came the American War in 1775: Wilkes's cause was in most minds identified with the Colonies and their early defeats depressed the popular enthusiasm. Initially, the outbreak of the war had done Wilkes's cause good: commercial centres well beyond his previous influence resented it as unnecessary and a dislocation of trade: the list of cities which now for the first time petitioned against the Government includes Norwich, Liverpool, Manchester, Birmingham, Wolverhampton, Dudley and even Glasgow. But the war proved eventually a fillip to trade, in effect merely transferring profits from West India and other merchants to the providers of war materials, pro-vender and ships. The enthusiasm of the newly won towns quickly disappeared; the county gentlemen who had grumbled remembered that in wartime loyalty to their King overrode everything else; even in London and Bristol the influence of the new rich began to eclipse the older-established men who had favoured Wilkes. A society called the White Hart

Association, chiefly of large contractors, was formed in London, which supported the King by the effective method of withholding as far as possible employment from the liverymen who expressed "democratic" views. In 1778 they were able to elect their candidate, Esdaile, a court supporter and contractor, as Lord Mayor.

A counter-raid was made immediately by Wilkes himself; he worked up a fresh mass agitation upon a proposal to raise a London regiment for the American War, and was able to defeat it. Further, authentic news now began to be received of serious British defeats which shook the King's position. Weymouth, Gower, and other prudent aristocrats who had been on his side deserted in good time to the Whig opposition. Early in 1780 the House of Commons actually carried a famous resolution "that the influence of the Crown has increased, is increasing, and ought to be diminished." The end of George III's attempt to restore the power of the throne was clearly in sight. It had, indeed, enormous though it bulks in contemporary opinion, never had a considerable chance of final success. Any real support for a powerful king had been broken at Culloden; George's success depended upon the King invariably being cleverer at the game of parliamentary purchase than his oligarchic rivals.

Within two months—April to June—of this famous resolution, the Wilkite movement was destroyed. It had rested upon a precarious alliance of the City magnates and the working class, only possible because of the continuity of interest, and of possible promotion, which linked the often illiterate and operative freeman of a company with his superiors. Before Wilkes's programme and ingenuity had joined them together, the richer merchants had supported Lord Shelburne, Lord Chatham or some other Whig peer, and the rank and file had been supine. Were Wilkes to disappear the same thing might recur. Now in June 1780 he was removed from the scene by a wholly unexpected explosion whose reasons are to this day partially obscure.

The King, though a bigoted Protestant, had made certain attempts, especially by the "Quebec Act" of 1773, to use Catholics against the Americans. He was suspected of a desire to raise Catholic troops, with Catholic officers, who would not take the customary oath. There remained also, from Puritan days, a general suspicion of the Catholics as servile by nature and the adherents of absolute authority in politics as much as religion. In short, if a suitable instrument could be found, it was not impossible to deflect the anger of Wilkes's followers into an attack on the Catholics, precisely as, before the Revolution, Tsarist agents turned the discontent of Russian workers and peasants into a pogrom against Jews.

The instrument does not, in this case, seem to have been an agent of any person or any group: the explosion was, as near as can be in politics, a spontaneous combustion. Lord George Gordon, the instigator of the riots, had no other advisers but his own feeble mind and a bundle of half-crazed Protestant tracts, the most venomous of which came from a Scottish source, the "heritors of Carluke." He was the youngest son of the Duke of Gordon, and sat for the pocket borough of Ludgershall. The Government, needing the borough for its own purposes, arranged with the Duke to make Lord William Gordon Lord Admiral of Scotland in return for Ludgershall being turned over to them. Here was proof, to Lord George, that the Popish plot was directed against him personally. On Friday, the 2nd of June, 1780, he attended the House of Commons to present a petition against a recent and mild Catholic Relief Act. Large and angry crowds escorted him, decorated with Wilkes's blue cockade despite the disapproval of the originator. They gravely manhandled some of the members, tearing the wigs off two lords and chasing a bishop across the leads of several Westminster houses. When they were persuaded to disperse, they robbed a number of Catholic chapels on their way home.

After a lull on Saturday, the same persons, as far as could be judged, resumed their activity on a larger scale. Moorfields, a Catholic district, was sacked and burned on Sunday. On Monday Smithfield and parts of Wapping were devastated, all Catholic houses being carefully pillaged and then burned. Even sympathizers with religious tolerance found their houses destroyed: so too did judges and lawyers for their presumed desire to support the law. No adequate authority to check the riot existed. Most of Wilkes's poorer followers were in the

front ranks of the rioters; some of his richer ones were charged
with complicity, but most of them had timorously retired
behind their own shutters.

Newgate, the new prison, the Catholic houses round Red
Lion Square, and a number of judges' houses went up in flames
on Tuesday. At this Wilkes himself suddenly moved: he compelled the terrified Lord Mayor to call out the *posse comitatus*
and meanwhile set out himself with a small force of volunteers
to put down the riot. He found the King's Bench prison, the
Fleet, and nearly all other prisons except the Tower in flames;
Langdale's Holborn distillery blazing, and the ardent Protestants trying to drink the flaming whisky as it ran down the
gutters from the stove-in vats; unknown corpses lying in the City
streets, and the parks full of frightened refugees. The sky at
night was red, stated the *Annual Register*, with the fires of thirty-
six separate conflagrations, and unceasingly there continued
"the tremendous roar of the authors of these horrible scenes."

Wilkes with his small body of troops first received outside
the Bank of England the shock of the attack of those who had
been his followers; he fired "six or seven" volleys and killed
several rioters, including their chief, a young man on a white
cart-horse. For a short while he carried on the struggle almost
alone: before long reinforcements arrived, through the King's
peremptory instructions, but peace was not restored till the
14th. Among Wilkes's prisoners was the one-time printer of
the *North Briton*, charged with burning down the house of
Lord Mansfield.

This sudden and short explosion blew the democratic movement into pieces. Wilkes disappeared from active politics. The
operative liverymen and the richer merchants no longer formed
a single block united against the Crown. The short and
simple initial period, in which the democratic movement is
concentrated under one leadership for the convenience of the
historian, comes to an end. Henceforward it is scattered and
various. But it is not for that reason weaker; indeed, the disappearance of the curious character who had for a short time
been its dictator meant that before long the people of England
would find their own leaders and not select them from the
entourage of a peer.

CHAPTER IX

THE RIGHTS OF MAN

THE elimination of Wilkes did not mean that the citizens of London abandoned the principles he had inculcated. He remained himself an amused witness of their fidelity, and when a crowd of adherents of the French Revolution broke his windows, refused to prosecute. "They are only," he said with great truth, "some old pupils of mine, set up in business for themselves." Bull, Sawbridge, and the other City magnates ventured out after the turmoil of the Gordon Riots and resumed their old principles, more chary of "exciting the mob" and less likely to ignore the Whig aristocrats. The London juries continued to return, for sixty years or more, verdicts based upon the principles of individual liberty which Wilkes had taught them—indeed, so indocile were they in general to Government wishes that the phrase "the London disease" was coined to describe their disrespectful state of mind. Horne Tooke, and other less ribald persons, continued a privateering campaign of their own. Many of the aristocracy realized that the Wilkite upheaval meant that it would be wise to anticipate the discontent of the lower orders by a prudent reform of Parliament from above. Both the Duke of Richmond and the younger Pitt (Lord Chatham's second son) presented in the early 'eighties projects for reform which were similar to Wilkes's rejected bill. In 1782 what was at the time regarded as an immense step forward was taken by the passing of the "economical reformation" bills. These quaintly named Acts were the result partly of the agitation of the Yorkshire county members, partly of the eloquence of Edmund Burke; their main effect was to cut down the distributable sinecures and pensions to £90,000 per year, and so to defeat the long-drawn-out campaign of the King to control Parliament. They could not have been passed but for the success of the American rebellion. Their passage did not mean that the King became a mere cipher. He was to be there for years as an obstacle, preventing necessary reforms and opposing toleration, interfering with ministers and insulting individuals; but he was no longer able to control Parliament. His last move was to put the younger Pitt in as Prime Minister: shortly afterwards he discovered he had chosen not a servant but a master. When circumstances changed, he had already become intermittently insane, and unable to assert any coherent or continuous will.

Meanwhile the reform movement had halted at the point of "economical reforms"—reforms which were acceptable to the aristocracy because they checkmated the King without interfering with their own freedom. Neither the Duke of Richmond's bill nor Pitt's was passed, and the contest between the forces of reform and the opposition became more sullen and dangerous. For this there were two reasons, the one economic and the other "ideological." The second was the influence of the American Revolution; the first was the change in economic conditions.

The relatively good temper of the Wilkite agitation, and the placidity which preceded it, were due to the steadily growing comfort of the average Englishman. While this lasted, no serious upheaval was to be feared. Round about 1755 or 1760 it began to come to an end. As we have seen, no trustworthy figures exist for the eighteenth-century cost of living, but wages changed rarely and slowly, and the price of wheat is consequently a fairly reliable index of the cost of living, in the South at least. As has been shown, from about the middle 'sixties the price of wheat climbed fairly steadily, whereas before at the worst it had suffered from occasional violent fluctuations.

With the consequent increasing pressure the theory of "virtual representation" which suggested that the Parliamentary system by a probably divine accident was the wisest conceivable no longer carried conviction, while the progress of the United States seemed to provide a living example to the contrary. It has been the misfortune of the British revolutionary movement to depend too greatly upon foreign object-lessons, American, French or Russian; but the flaws of the new republic at this date were too small to be perceived across the Atlantic. It was for many years highly civilized, in a rather small-town eighteenth-century manner; it spent nothing on lords or kings; its administration was reputed to be cheap and on the whole honest; it meticulously conserved individual liberty and the freedom of the Press. It served for many years as a platform example, and it had further provided in its Declaration of Independence almost a complete theory of popular control.

"We hold these truths to be self-evident," stated that document, "that all men are created equal, that they are endowed by their Creator with certain inalienable Rights, that among these are Life, Liberty and the pursuit of Happiness. That, to secure these rights, Governments are instituted among Men, deriving their just powers from the consent of the governed, that whenever any form of Government becomes destructive of these ends, it is the Right of the People to alter or to abolish it, and to institute new Government."

Practically every clause of this was offensive and seditious and would have served as a text for a sermon against the British administration; and, indeed, in many cases did.

In every town of any size, and even in many rural areas, there were a few who advocated imitating the American example, and some of them rose to prominence enough to be called leaders. Three of these, while certainly not working-class in origin, were equally certainly neither aristocrats nor hangers-on of the aristocracy. Dr. Richard Price, in his day an expert on population, taxation and other economic problems, was a Unitarian, and a leader of large influence among the middle-class Dissenters who met in the Revolution Society to celebrate the "Glorious Revolution" of 1688. In his *Discourse on Civil Liberty* he ardently defended the American Revolution; and his Sermon on *The Love of Our Country*, welcoming the French Revolution, immediately provoked Burke's famous *Reflections on the Revolution in France*. His advocacy of the new principles ended with his death in 1791, but his importance as a philosopher gave his words a weight which it is easy now to overlook. Joseph Priestley (1773–1804), a still more Radical Unitarian, is still honoured in modern text-books as a chemist of genius rather than deep learning—he discovered oxygen and several other gases, all the while adhering to an obsolescent "phlogiston" theory, by which even his own dis-coveries were almost incomprehensible. But his political logic was better than his chemical: he advocated from his study American principles with a vehemence that disquieted Price himself. Major John Cartwright (1740–1824) was above the other two in origin; he might well have had a good career in the Navy but for his refusal to serve under General Howe against the Americans. His pamphlet, *Give us Our Rights!* can be compared to a text-book: other publications were more exciting, but it stated the arguments more completely, dis-passionately and lucidly than they, and men returned to it in their more reflective moments. From 1780 onwards he advocated direct and pure democracy, with a single-minded-ness and simple-mindedness that excited at first ridicule and eventually respect. He continued his agitation for forty-four years, without discretion and without fear, living on a diet chiefly of raisins and weak gin-and-water, and introducing his political principles into every discussion which gave him the smallest opening.

But in 1787 there landed in England a propagandist whose powers and reputation greatly surpassed theirs. Thomas Paine (1737–1809) was English by birth, and had been no notable success as a staymaker or an exciseman, though he had demonstrated where his sympathies lay by a pamphlet upon the excisemen's grievances. He had quitted England for America in despair, but in his new country his pamphlet *Common Sense* and his periodical *The Crisis* had so electrical an effect in rallying and comforting the American rebels that Cobbett later, with his usual picturesque exaggeration, said that "the real cause" of the American Revolution was "some beastly insult offered to Mr. Paine while he was in the Excise in England." Tom Paine later became the equivalent of Foreign Secretary to the American Congress; and even though he had lost this post through impetuousness and indiscretion, he came back to England with the reputation of being the inspirer and one of the organizers of victory.

His principles, as outlined by himself, shortly after his arrival, were broadly as follows. Men are naturally equal, and enjoy equal natural rights, derived from God. No process of history can alter this natural equality: nor can any generation bind its successors. Circumstances change, and each generation has a complete right to judge for itself how it will manage its affairs. The purpose of government is to organize and make effective those natural rights which individuals are unable to secure for themselves acting alone, or in Paine's phrase: "The individual converts from natural into civil rights all those rights in which the power to execute them is defective," such as the right to be judge in his own cause. Every civil right grows out of a natural right, or "in other words, is a natural right exchanged." It follows that the power which exists in civil rights cannot be used to invade men's natural rights, which the individual retains in full when he is living in society. Under a republican government the welfare of the whole nation is the object; under a monarchical, the interests of an individual override those of the nation; under an aristocratic, the interests of one class override them. The "rights of man" means the right of all men to equal representation.

Indeed, equal representation of all men lies at the very foundation of Paine's doctrine. Earlier "democratic" theorists of the eighteenth century had despaired of making democracy effective in large States because they thought of democracy as involving the direct participation of all the citizens in the work of government. Paine, on the other hand, puts unquestioning faith in representation as the means of making democracy real. "By engrafting representation upon democracy, we arrive at a system of government capable of embracing and confederating all the various interests and every extent of territory and population." Government, says Paine, "is nothing more than a natural association" through which the natural equality of men takes a civic form. It follows that all hereditary government and all class privilege are illegitimate. "All delegated power is trust: all assumed power is usurpation." It follows too that no government has any right at all to interfere with the absolute freedom of thought of every individual; for the right to think freely is a natural right, and the power to "execute" this right exists sufficiently in the individual himself. Paine will not accept mere toleration as adequate. "Intolerance is the Pope armed with fire and

faggot, toleration is the Pope selling or granting indulgences."
Natural rights demand equal freedom for all; and Paine held
strongly that the diversity of opinion is good in itself and leads
to human progress.

These principles, and in particular Paine's demand for equal
representation, were shortly taken up by an advocate with
a more tremendous voice. In 1789 the Estates General of
France met; on October 5 of that year Louis XVI under the
clear pressure of force signed the Declaration of the Rights of
Man. It contained seventeen clauses, but no principles not
already enunciated by the Americans: its greater length was
due to its more constructive phraseology and its drawing of
specific deductions, such as the need for freedom of the Press.
For a short while it seemed as though the French Revolution
was about to reproduce on a vaster scale the peaceful success
of the American: not until the September massacres of 1792
did the outside world receive a shock of horror. Till then the
feeling of the British reformers was best expressed in the
address of the Belfast Volunteers (14 July, 1791). "Go on then
—great and gallant people, to practise the sublime philosophy
of your legislation . . . and not by conquest but by the omni-
potence of reason to convert and liberate the world." But
already the aristocratic circles which had been willing enough
before to advocate a granted reform had taken alarm: the
French Revolution was laying hands upon the privileges of
a similar class in France, and an English revolution would
almost certainly do the same.

The most famous and almost the first to appear as a denun-
ciator was the chief opponent of severity against the Americans,
Edmund Burke, who in 1790 published his *Reflections on the
Revolution in France*, a bitter attack which was widely circulated.
Within a few months Paine answered it by his *Rights of Man*,
a pamphlet which had perhaps a greater influence than any
other single work of its kind in the last two hundred years.
Reprinted continually, circulated legally and "bootlegged," it
was for years the inspiration of reformers and the chief object
of the Government's alarm and perquisitions. The first part
was largely a defence of the French against Burke: it set the
sufferings of the common people against Burke's sentimental

picture of the troubles of Marie Antoinette and told him that he "pitied the plumage and forgot the dying bird." The second part, published later, applied what Paine held to be French principles to England. The programme was, in fact, considerably in advance of what most of the Deputies would have supported; its provisions were not to become practical politics again for over a hundred years. It proposed, among other things, to abolish the Poor Law, to establish a graded estate-duty on all estates with over £500 a year, starting at 3*d*., and rising to 20*s*. in the £ for revenues above £22,000 a year, to remove all sinecures (and ultimately the useless expense of the King and Court), and to secure disarmament by arbitration treaties. Estimating the population at 7,000,000, it argued that these economies would quite early permit of the abolition of indirect taxation, and of a grant of £4 per year per head for each child under fourteen, and a £6 per head pension to all over fifty. A maternity benefit of £1 per child could also be instituted, and a large residue would remain for a national system of education and for the provision of work for the unemployed by the State.

These proposals were received enthusiastically in both France and England. In France Paine was elected to the Convention (where he later took his seat and by his ignorance of French was prevented from cutting any considerable figure), and in Britain innumerable societies sprang up, largely to propagate his ideas. Many earnest gentlemen substituted for the National Anthem at public functions a melancholy song beginning, "God Save the Rights of Man," and the legal sales of Paine's book by 1793 amounted to nearly 200,000 copies. A prosecution was commenced in 1792 against its author, who, in the flush of success, declined to consider it seriously, although a special proclamation against seditious publications had just been issued. Indeed, accompanied by Horne Tooke, he appeared at a meeting of Surrey freeholders summoned to hear the proclamation and distributed a hundred copies of his book and a thousand of a smaller pamphlet. Both he and Horne Tooke delivered speeches pointing out that the convener of the meeting, Lord Onslow, held a £1,000 sinecure with a £3,000 pension.

He spoke on September 12 at the meeting of a London society called the Friends of Liberty, and the next night to a group of friends which included William Blake repeated, as far as he could remember it, his enthusiastic oration. When he rose to go, the poet, who had more knowledge of reality than his worldly-wise friend, put his hand on his shoulder and said: "You must not go home, or you are a dead man." He hurried him, half against his will, to Dover by a roundabout route. Twenty minutes after his ship had left the harbour, the order for Paine's arrest reached the town.

THE INDUSTRIAL REVOLUTION AND
THE FRENCH WAR

CHAPTER X

THE AGRARIAN REVOLUTION

SEVENTEEN HUNDRED AND EIGHTY-NINE—the year of the French Revolution and the Fall of the Bastille—is one of the great dates in European history. It is of infinitely greater significance, even for Great Britain, than 1688—the year of that "Glorious Revolution" which brought William III to the throne of England. It means far more, at least for Europe, than 1776, the year of the Declaration of Independence by the North American States. For the French Revolution, however mixed its causes and however uncertain its objectives may have been, marks for Europe the end of an age and the unloosing of new democratic forces and ideas which are still actively working themselves out to-day. It announces too an epoch of war; for within a very few years the new régime in France became the centre of a conflict involving almost all Europe. Great Britain went to war with France in 1793; and thereafter, save for a brief interval of two years in 1801–3 and the false peace of 1814 before the "Hundred Days," the war lasted until 1815. From 1812 to 1815 Great Britain was at war with the United States as well as with France, over the right of British ships to blockade the Continental ports against American vessels. And though the Bourbons were put back after Waterloo, and Napoleon was exiled to St. Helena, no coalition of Great Powers could avail to put back the old Europe. In France the peasants had seized the land, and they kept it; and over half Europe the Revolution and Napoleon between them had made a holocaust of obsolete feudal institutions and ideas, though the completeness of the destruction varied greatly from place to place.

While these great political events were in progress, there was proceeding side by side with them an economic revolution which was to give a profoundly new meaning to political change. The powers of production—men's ways of wresting a living from the gifts of nature—were being fundamentally transformed.

The political events which led to Paine's flight were sufficiently exciting: when, a few months later, there was added to them the declaration of war between France and Great Britain, the tension was too great to escape the notice even of the most indifferent. Yet, great though the political changes were, the economic were at least equally important. It is of the nature of economic change to proceed far less than political change by way of great events—revolutions, wars, conquests and dynastic alterations—to which definite dates can be assigned. Economic changes are, by comparison, gradual and cumulative, though at times they occur with remarkable speed and decisiveness. In economic matters, dates often mislead more than they illuminate; for socially what matters most is not when a discovery is made, but when it is widely taken up. The period of the Napoleonic Wars is remarkable not so much for its great inventions—though these were numerous—as for the momentum and speed of actual economic change, which the war in some directions hastened and in others held back.

Over most of Europe, the long and destructive war was inimical to economic development. It did, indeed, foster certain forms of growth—for example the metal industries of France and later Belgium, on which Napoleon chiefly relied for munitions of war. But on the whole the diversion of manpower to fighting instead of production, especially in France, and the repeated devastation of many of the most important economic areas, necessarily impoverished Europe; while the British command of the seas cut off from extra-European commerce both France and the countries which were from time to time under her control, and thus denied these areas a share in the rapidly expanding profits of colonial, American and Eastern trade.

Great Britain, on the other hand, remained an uninvaded island, with free access to the world's markets, except that part of the European market which was from time to time closed, save to the growing host of smugglers, by the economic exigencies of war. Privateers doubtless added to the uncertainties of British commerce; but on the whole Great Britain kept the command of the seas. Not until the quarrel with the United States ripened into war in 1812 did the British merchants suffer any serious hindrance to their exploitation of markets and sources of supply in all the continents outside Europe.

War conditions were thus of a sort, on the whole, to foster the development of British industry, and certainly to give it a long lead over the industries of the continental countries. But even more profoundly for the moment the wars affected British agriculture. Before 1789 Great Britain was already, on balance, an importer of wheat; for she imported more in bad seasons than she exported when the harvest was abundant. But she was not yet far from self-sufficiency. The war period, however, witnessed a great expansion in the demand for wheat, partly because population was rising fast—why, we shall consider hereafter—and partly because of the abnormal war demand for provisions to feed British, and often Allied, soldiers abroad. Wheat prices rose sharply—to prodigious heights in years when harvests were bad; and high prices put a premium on wheat-growing, and caused immense efforts to be made both to increase the yield and to extend the cultivated area. Meat prices also rose rapidly; and there was a demand for better breeds of cattle and sheep and for more pasture-lands, despite the conversion into arable of much land previously used as pasture.

In the decade 1781–90 wheat averaged 47s. 7d. a quarter. In the following three decades, which include the war period and the years of post-war unrest to 1820, the averages were 63s. 6d., 83s. 11d., and 87s. 6d. By five-year periods the figures are even more startling:

BRITISH WHEAT PRICES, 1786–1825
Five-year Averages

	s.	d.		s.	d.		s.	d.
1786–90	46	3	1801–5	80	0	1816–20	80	10
1790–5	53	8	1806–10	87	11	1821–5	57	3
1796–1800	73	5	1811–15	94	3			

But even these figures do not reveal the height of prices in the famine years. Wheat rose to 113s. 10d. a quarter in 1800, and to 119s. 6d. in 1801, to 106s. 5d. in 1810, and to 126s. 6d. in 1812. These are yearly average prices. At some places and at some times, even higher figures were reached. And wheat was the commodity on which the standard of living of the common people depended most of all.

Naturally, these immensely high prices put vast sums into the pockets of the farmers and also of the landlords, who were able to raise their rents to unexampled heights. Naturally too they stimulated wheat-growing on an unprecedented scale. The war prices, far more than anything else, were responsible for the prodigious advance of the enclosure movement, which reached, during the war years, the full dimensions of an agricultural revolution. There can be no doubt that the open-field system, under which a large part of England was still cultivated up to the end of the eighteenth century, was inefficient and stood formidably in the way of technical progress in agriculture. Under this system, the arable area consisted largely of narrow strips of land which, even if they had ceased to be periodically re-divided, split up each cultivator's holding into a number of often widely separated fragments. The baulks of uncultivated land separating these strips seriously reduced the cultivable area; and the tenants had to pursue a course of cultivation laid down for the village as a whole, and commonly settled in accordance with an ancient customary rotation of crops. Moreover, after harvest much of the arable area was laid open for grazing by the animals belonging to the various tenants and proprietors: this manured the land, but made growing of winter crops impossible.

Even apart from the effects of the war in stimulating agricultural development, the period was one of great and rapid progress in agricultural technique. The great improvement had begun much earlier, with the epoch-making work of Jethro Tull (1674–1741), whose book *Horse-hoeing Husbandry*, published in 1733 and later re-popularized by William Cobbett, taught farmers the virtue of pulverizing the soil and applying capital to extracting its full capacity. Lord Townshend—"Turnip Townshend" (1674–1738)—was establishing the famous Norfolk four-course rotation during the 1730's; and to him succeeded T. W. Coke of Norfolk (1752–1842), a universal improver, who not only discovered the art of growing rich wheat crops on the light lands of the Eastern Counties, but was also a great breeder of cattle and sheep, whose manure fertilized that sandy soil. His senior contemporary, Robert Bakewell, of Dishley in Leicestershire (1725–95) ranks first among those who, during the second half of the eighteenth century, revolutionized the arts of sheep- and cattle-breeding, so that the weight of the beasts offered for sale at Smithfield and other markets increased by staggering amounts, and the supply of meat grew faster than the supply of corn. There were parallel improvements in land drainage, in agricultural implements, and in the arts of timber-growing; and under these combined influences the annual value of well-farmed lands grew rapidly, and skilled farmers as well as improving landlords amassed large fortunes.

With this progress in the arts of agriculture the old conditions of land tenure and rural life became more and more intolerable to progressive farmers. These men wanted opportunity to pursue improvements on their own initiative, without waiting for the agricultural education of the entire village—which, moreover, could hardly be promoted except by example. They wanted to select their own rotation, to grow winter as well as summer crops, to improve their lands by drainage and manuring, and to have them protected from weeds growing on their neighbours' holdings, and from the incursions of wandering beasts. They wanted, themselves, to raise improved breeds of sheep and cattle, which they could not hope to do without winter fodder as well as better cared-for pastures and a breakaway from traditional methods of breeding. They wanted to drain, fence and improve the land, in order to increase its output; and these incentives became immensely greater with the rise in prices and demand during the Napoleonic Wars—for the wars made improved land-utilization a patriotic duty as well as a source of profit. This largely accounts for the rapid increase in the number of Enclosure Acts passed through Parliament, setting up in each case a special Commission to settle the terms of enclosure, the compensation to owners of existing legal or customary rights, and the methods of fencing and draining to be applied to the enclosed lands, which consisted partly of the old open fields, and partly of the common pasture and waste land previously in the possession of the village as a whole.

There was, of course, nothing novel about the process of enclosure in itself. Enclosure of English lands had been going on for centuries, from the days of the great enclosures for sheep-farming against which More and Latimer had protested in the sixteenth, and Laud in the seventeenth century. Enclosures, for both pasture and arable, had been proceeding steadily all through the eighteenth century, at first mainly without legislation, by agreement or by the high-handed action of great landlords, latterly by means of private Acts setting up special Commissions supposed to represent the interested parties. Probably these Commissions acted less arbitrarily than the landlords had done in earlier days; but as the total scale of enclosures increased, and as more and more of the common lands were taken over, the social consequences became much more oppressive to the poorer people, and above all to those who could advance no clear legal title to their land or, even if they could, were unable to afford the expense of hedging and draining the land allotted to them, so as to conform to the Commissioners' requirements. These poorer people were driven wholesale from their tiny holdings, deprived of their rights of common for geese or pigs, driven to become hired labourers or to seek work in the towns or in the coal-mines. Their strict legal claims were generally met, but their equitable claims were almost wholly ignored; and the proposals of Arthur Young and others that every big enclosure scheme should include provision for settling poor households on smallholdings of their own were hardly ever acted on. The war prices put so high a premium on corn-growing by up-to-date methods that, from the 1790's, enclosure went on at an unprecedented rate, and with less care than ever for its effects on the village communities.

Much has been written of the social wrongs and hardships caused by these enclosures to the common people. There is no doubt of the reality of these hardships; but in dwelling upon them it is necessary to bear certain closely related facts in mind. During the Napoleonic Wars the main uses made of enclosure were, first, to extend and improve the use of the arable area, and secondly to secure new lands for pasturage. The arable land encroached on the old pastures, and new pastures were found by calling into use waste lands which had, till then, hardly been put to any economic end. But arable cultivation employs a large amount of labour in comparison with the amount used on pasture land. Accordingly, the effect of enclosures for extending or improving the arable area was on the whole the employment of more agricultural labour and not less. Pasturage needs fewer workers; but the extension of pasturage to waste lands could hardly act as a serious depopulating influence. How then did it come about, as it undoubtedly did, that the enclosure movement was accompanied by a large displacement of rural population?

It should be noted that we are here discussing the English and Lowland enclosures, and not the notorious "Highland clearances," which stand on quite a different footing. The Highland crofters were displaced in their thousands during the latter part of the eighteenth and the early part of the nineteenth century in favour, not of larger arable farms, but of vast sheep-runs, on which very little labour was employed. In that instance, the reasons for depopulation and distress are immediately apparent; but the same is not the case with the enclosure movement further south.

The answer to our question is twofold. In the first place, the most serious rural depopulation in England occurred not before but after 1815; for after the end of the war the premium on corn-growing was in fact greatly reduced, despite the maintenance of a very high duty on imported wheat by the dominant landlord interest, which sought thereby to preserve the increased rents imposed during the war. Secondly—and this is even more important—there was a most powerful force at work, wholly apart from the enclosures, tending to depopulate the rural area. In the eighteenth century, as we have seen, industry, largely carried on under the "domestic system," was tending to spread itself out more and more over the countryside, so that a large proportion of the population outside the towns lived not by agriculture, but wholly or partly by industrial pursuits.

The most widely spread of all these manufacturing occupations of the country people was spinning—chiefly of wool, but also of cotton, linen or flax, and other textile substances. But in the latter part of the eighteenth century, with the advent of new technical inventions for the carding and spinning of cotton—Hargreaves's jenny, Arkwright's water-frame, Crompton's mule, and many others—the preparing and spinning processes began to migrate swiftly from the scattered villages all over the country to the new factory areas. Weaving, which was already more concentrated in large industrial villages, was brought only later under the factory system; but from about 1800 the power loom, invented by Cartwright in 1785, but uneconomic until it was improved by later inventors, began to make rapid progress, and this became faster still about 1815, when falling prices gave a strong incentive to employers to resort to new methods designed to lower the costs of production.

Weaving had always been a skilled trade; but the carding and spinning of wool and other textiles were unskilled processes carried on largely by women and children as a source of auxiliary earnings, in households whose chief breadwinner might be either a weaver or some other sort of craftsman, or an agricultural labourer, or a cottager tilling a tiny patch of land and pasturing a few geese or perhaps a pig or cow on the common waste. With the disappearance of auxiliary earnings from spinning or other industrial by-employments the cottagers and agricultural labourers underwent a severe fall in their standard of life, quite apart from any enclosure of the land; and many of them sank into destitution and were driven to apply to the parish for poor relief. This, up to 1815, was probably a far more potent cause of rural depopulation—or, far more often, of over-population, because the new "redundant" cottagers were usually unable to migrate to other districts—than the enclosure of the land could be as long as its main purpose was the extension of the arable area.

But at the same time sharply rising prices made the customary wages of the labourers employed on the land wholly inadequate to support a tolerable standard of life, not only where these wages had previously been eked out by industrial by-employment of the labourer's family, but even where no such by-employment had been common. Agricultural wages did, indeed, rise during the war period. Our knowledge is very far from complete; but a comparison of the available data for a large number of counties suggests that, on the average, they rose from about 8s. 6d. a week in the period before 1793 to about 14s. round about 1810, falling again to 13s. in 1814–15, and to 12s. in 1816, and thereafter to less than 10s. in the next few years. But this average conceals the truth; for in the southern counties wages rose less than elsewhere during the wars. In Sussex, for example, the rise seems to have been from 9s. in 1790 only to 13s. in 1810, with a subsequent fall to 12s. or less, and in Wiltshire wages seem hardly to have risen at all.

Upon these wages, even when they could be secured, life could not be sustained in the years of very high corn prices; and the labourers were driven wholesale to the parishes for relief. But the surplus rural population was greatest in those areas where the cottager's standard of living had previously depended largely upon industrial earnings. For, now that the households whose members had been deprived of these earnings by the migration of industry and at the same time dispossessed of their meagre agricultural incomes by enclosure were competing for employment as labourers on the enclosed farms, there were very many who could not find regular work at any wage. In bad years the wages of the regular farm labourers had to be supplemented by poor relief; and in good and bad years alike there came to exist a surplus of unemployed country labour which had to be maintained by the parish. These surplus workers were partly set to work at the statute-labour of road-making, of which the obligation still rested on the parishes save where roads had been taken over by the Turnpike Trusts; and partly the labourers were sent the round of the farmers in the district, and these in turn employed the wretched "roundsmen" of whose bare subsistence they had in any event to meet the cost through the poor rate.

This was the notorious Speenhamland system of poor relief —so called from the Berkshire village of Speenhamland, now a part of Newbury, where it was first formally introduced by the county justices of the peace. Under the Speenhamland system, which rapidly spread over most of the South of England, but never extended in the same form to the Northern Counties or to Scotland, the justices directed the poor-law authorities to relieve the unemployed and to supplement the wages of the employed at a rate fluctuating with the price of the gallon loaf and with the number of persons in the household, so as to provide a bare minimum standard of subsistence. Under these conditions the common people of the "over-populated" villages of Southern England lived miserably amid the growing wealth of the farmers and landlords, as long as the war lasted. After the war their lot became yet more wretched; for then the fall in arable cultivation and the further decay of village industries swelled the total of unemployment, while the fall in prices made the farmers more determined to keep down the rates, and caused them constantly to revise, always in a downward direction, their estimates of the income on which a labourer and his family could somehow contrive to exist. Already, during the wars, the labourers were being adjured to imitate the Irish and their own compatriots in the North by substituting potatoes for wheaten bread. But after 1815 the pressure upon them to live more "abstinently" became greater still.

Why, it may be asked, did not these starvelings migrate in search of employment to the growing factory towns? Why did they not follow their lost industrial employments northwards, and secure the factory wages which, low as they were, were at least a good deal higher than the starvation relief accorded under the Speenhamland system? The answer is that for the most part such migration was utterly beyond their power. Before the coming of the railways the distance over which unskilled labour could move was very short. A skilled artisan, with money in his pocket and perhaps a chain of trade clubs with which he could make contact, could move easily enough over a wide area. An unskilled worker without resources who attempted to follow his example was likely, before he had proceeded far, to be arrested as a rogue and a vagabond, and deported from the parish into which he had come back to his parish of origin, for fear he should become a charge upon the local rates. The Settlement Acts, which, even after their modification in 1795, made every "pauper" chargeable upon, and removable to, his parish of "settlement," confronted the unskilled worker who had the will to migrate in search of work with insuperable obstacles to movement over long distances; and the growing factory areas were a terribly long journey away from the "over-populated" rural counties of Southern England. It was far easier for an Irish labourer to cross the seas and find employment in Lancashire or Yorkshire, than for a "redundant" worker from Sussex or Wiltshire or Somerset to make the land journey under the jealous watch of a host of parish authorities who stood in fear of becoming responsible for his maintenance if he established a settlement in their area. For if a worker could succeed in remaining in a parish for a year he lost his original settlement and became chargeable to that parish. Cottages were often pulled down to make it harder for new-comers to effect a settlement.

Thus, it was usually impossible for the "surplus labour" of the South to find employment in the factories of the North. This fact can be verified by reference to the Census returns from the beginning of the nineteenth century; for the Census records the birthplaces as well as the actual residences of the people. From the successive decennial Censuses we find that few of the workers employed in the developing factories of Lancashire, Cheshire and Yorkshire came from the Southern Counties. They came rather, attracted by the higher factory wages, from the adjoining counties—from Derbyshire, Staffordshire, Nottinghamshire and North Wales—and from Ireland—while the Scottish industrial areas were filled up with Irish migrants as well as with dispossessed Highland crofters; for in Scotland there was no State poor law—and no Settlement Act to make land migration as difficult as it was on English soil.

In England the difficulties of migration immensely aggravated the sufferings of the rural population after the decline of the "domestic" industries. Very gradually, migration was achieved, mainly by a series of short-distance movements, but for the most part not until after the period with which this chapter deals. The village labourer, however wretched his lot might be in the Southern counties, was without a way of escape. He was "on the dole"; and the dole of those times

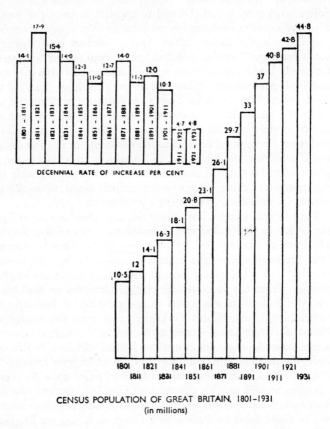

DECENNIAL RATE OF INCREASE PER CENT

CENSUS POPULATION OF GREAT BRITAIN, 1801–1931
(in millions)

was infinitely more wretched than the dole which even the most niggardly authority deems sufficient for the unemployed worker of to-day.

CHAPTER XI

THE REVOLUTION IN INDUSTRY

MEANWHILE, principally in the North, the Industrial Revolution was going on apace, and the factory system was developing fast in the textile areas of Lancashire, Yorkshire and the East Midlands and in certain parts of Scotland. It is customary, for convenience, to date the beginning of the "Industrial Revolution" from about 1760; but this does not mean that there were no considerable industrial establishments in Great Britain before that date—much less that capitalism came into existence about then. There were many large establishments, and many great employers of labour, long before the new factory system began to develop in the Lancashire cotton industry round about 1770, and before England began to be covered with a network of canals constructed by capitalist enterprise. Coal-mining, for example, on the North-east coast, the iron industry in Coalbrookdale and elsewhere, the brewing industry in London, and the silk industry at Derby, all employed in the early eighteenth century large-scale methods of production involving the concentration of considerable bodies of workers about the establishment of a single employer. Moreover, the "domestic" system, under which the main body of workers laboured at home, or in very small workshops under a small master who was often really a sub-contractor for a capitalist merchant, was itself for the most part highly capitalistic. The "domestic" worker was in most cases virtually a piece-working wage-earner, not even always owning his own tools—for the more expensive implements, such as knitting-frames, were often rented from capitalist owners, or supplied by the capitalists who put out the work. Often, the domestic worker did not own the materials on which he worked, but received them from the capitalist merchant and worked them up for a piece-work price; and even where the worker did nominally own the materials, they were often supplied on credit by the merchant, who thereafter

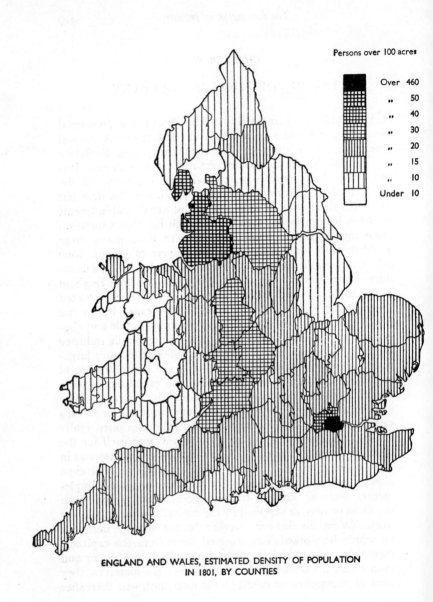

Persons over 100 acres

Over 460
„ 50
„ 40
„ 30
„ 20
„ 15
„ 10
Under 10

ENGLAND AND WALES, ESTIMATED DENSITY OF POPULATION
IN 1801, BY COUNTIES

deducted the price from the sum due to him for the finished goods.

The domestic system, as it existed for example in the woollen industry of the Western Counties and largely elsewhere—Yorkshire, as we have seen, was somewhat different —was a system of capitalist production with the aid of wage-labour. It differed from the factory system in that the workers were not for the most part gathered together into large groups working on the capitalist's premises, and in that the representative capitalist figure was far less the industrial employer than the merchant, who might conduct certain key-processes, such as wool-combing or cloth-finishing, in his own establishment, but left most of the productive operations in the hands of piece-workers, or sometimes small masters, scattered over a large part of the country.

This system was, of course, never possible in certain industries. Coal-mining, as soon as it advanced beyond a quite primitive stage, involved fairly large units of exploitation. So did the iron industry, as soon as it could no longer get its fuel from the untouched forests, and had to resort to coal instead of charcoal as its principal fuel. Moreover, the iron industry had been tending towards large-scale units even before coal had been more than experimentally introduced, as the cost of plant increased and the manufacture left its old centres in Sussex and settled down in new areas under larger capitalists, who purchased forests and riverside sites for its better exploitation.

It is still uncertain when coal was first successfully used for the smelting of iron; for Dud Dudley's claims to have used it in the seventeenth century are disputed. Certainly it was used by the Darbys at Coalbrookdale quite early in the eighteenth century. But even then its use did not spread at all rapidly, because of the difficulty of preventing the carbon in the coal from making the iron brittle. All through the first half of the eighteenth century the British iron-making industry languished for want of fuel, and pig and bar iron had to be brought in more and more from abroad, especially from Sweden and the Baltic. Meanwhile, the demand for iron goods continued to expand fast; and Great Britain's iron manufactures continued to grow on a basis of imported materials.

The problem facing the inventors was in fact twofold. Manufactured iron in the eighteenth century had two alternative forms—cast-iron and wrought-iron. Cast-iron, hard and brittle, was used for making certain types of finished iron goods, such as stoves and grates, rollers and cooking-pots or kettles. Wrought, or malleable, iron was the material of the smith's trade, used in making most kinds of finished goods. The smith used coal for the finishing processes; and accordingly the smithing trades were already centred round the coalfields.

Iron was first made in the blast-furnace, which produced pig-iron, or, alternatively, cast-iron objects made by ladling the molten metal straight into moulds of the required shapes. This was done in foundries, whereas iron destined for smiths' use was allowed to cool in the pig, and then reheated and made into bar-iron, which could then be slit and rolled into smaller rods or bars for the smith to work on. Bar-iron was made in forges, as distinct from foundries, and worked up in slitting and rolling mills.

At the beginning of the eighteenth century both cast-iron and bar-iron needed charcoal. But as early as 1709 the first Abraham Darby was making cast-iron and iron pigs with coke at the Coalbrookdale works. His son, in the 1730's, was still making bar-iron with charcoal out of pigs made with coke. As the century advanced more and more producers learnt to make pig-iron, and cast-iron objects, with coal, and they secured a substantial economy in the use of wood-fuel. But, strong as were the inducements to devise new methods, in order to reduce the dependence of industry on imported bar-iron, satisfactory bar-iron could not be made throughout with coal fuel until in the 1780's Henry Cort of Portsmouth and Peter Onions of Merthyr simultaneously invented the puddling process, and Cort added to it the invention of the rolling mill. Thereafter the iron industry expanded rapidly, in its primary as well as in its finishing sections; and of course the Napoleonic Wars gave it a further stimulus, and enabled the iron-masters to make high profits, which were then applied to the expansion of business on lines of large-scale capitalist production.

In the meantime James Watt, in partnership with Matthew

Boulton, one of the leading capitalists in Birmingham, had perfected his invention of the steam-engine. There had been steam-engines, or rather "fire-engines," as they were commonly called, long before Watt's day; but both Savery's fire-engine of 1698 and Newcomen's improved model of 1705–6 were adapted principally for pumping operations, and had even so an enormously high fuel consumption which made it difficult to use them extensively at any great distance from supplies of coal. Watt's first patent, of 1769, was important chiefly because of the large economy which it achieved in fuel. Much more revolutionary in its effect was Watt's later patent of 1781, which embodied his successful invention of a rotary motion, enabling his engine to be used directly to supply machine-power. Before this steam-engines had been chiefly used for raising the level of water—for example, in pumping out mines or in connection with urban water-supply. They had also come quite widely into use for supplying motive-power to machinery by indirect means: thus water raised by the engine was used to turn waterwheels in connection with a wide variety of operations. But Watt's patent of 1781 enabled steam-power to be applied directly, and was thus truly the beginning of the age of steam. Thereafter steam-power invaded one industry after another, giving an immense impetus to the growth of the factory system, and largely freeing the industrialists from the necessity of placing their factories on rivers capable of yielding abundant water-power. Economy in the use of fuel was Watt's first achievement; and it was not lost when he added to it the application of rotary motion. But the second achievement, though it would have accomplished far less without the first, overshadows it in revolutionary importance.

Before Watt had made his improved steam-engine, the factory system was already spreading fast, especially in the cotton industry, on a basis of water-power. In 1733, John Kay of Bury, then working at Colchester, took out his patent for the "flying-shuttle." This device, for speeding up the work of the handloom-weaver, had directly nothing to do with the factory system; for the weavers who adopted it in increasing numbers through the rest of the century continued to work, without power, under the domestic system. Its effect was, by enabling the weavers to weave more cloth, to expand rapidly the demand for yarn; for in the growing world-market for British cloth more could readily be sold. Thereafter the problem of the merchant-clothiers was to secure sufficient supplies of yarn to keep the weavers employed up to the full capacity of the market; and this set men looking eagerly for some means of speeding up the spinners' output in order to enable them to keep pace.

We have no space to tell here the story of the successive inventions by which this need was met—Lewis Paul's rollers of 1738 and his carding machine of 1748, Arkwright's improved rollers for spinning in 1769, Hargreaves's spinning-jenny patent of 1770, and Arkwright's water-frame as improved in 1775. These were the principal among a large number of inventions—often of disputed authorship—by means of which both the preparing and carding processes and the actual spinning of yarn were greatly speeded up. When, in 1778, Samuel Crompton combined the principles of Hargreaves's jenny and Arkwright's rollers into the spinning-mule, the technical conditions for the transference of spinning from the cottage to the factory were complete; for Arkwright's patent of 1769 had already embodied the idea of using power to move his machine. At first, indeed, Arkwright used the power of horses; but in 1771, at Cromford, he began to use water-power. Steam-power came later, the first successful steam-engine for use in a spinning mill not being erected in Manchester till 1789, though one had been used in Nottinghamshire in 1785. The first large growth of textile factories was based not on steam, but on water. On this basis cotton-spinning rapidly became a factory industry in the years between 1770 and 1790, when water-power was first applied to the spinning-mules at New Lanark, ten years before Robert Owen became its owner. Wool and other textiles followed some way behind cotton; but they too went over to the factory system by slower stages. The spinning-wheel began to disappear from the cottages of the poor all over the country; and the most important source of supplementary earnings for families in the rural areas went with it.

Weaving, meanwhile, remained under the domestic system; and now the boot was on the other leg. The spinning factories could turn out yarn, at any rate in the cotton industry, much cheaper and much faster than it could be made into cloth by the existing body of handloom-weavers. Consequently there came a rush of fresh workers into the trade; but in spite of this the cotton-weavers' wages rose for a time to unexampled heights, thus further encouraging the advent of additional labour. In or about the year 1800 cotton-weavers' wages in Bolton are said to have reached an average of 25s. a week— partly, no doubt, as a result of advancing war-prices, but also because there was an actual shortage of workers in relation to the demand.

The new labour which now flocked into cotton-weaving was attracted from many sources—from the weavers of other textiles, from the ranks of agricultural labour, and, not least, from Ireland, where the decay of the native cotton and linen industries, largely owing to British discrimination against them, added to the dire poverty of the people a further incentive to emigration. Irish weavers flocked into Lancashire and Glasgow, and many Irish who were not weavers followed them and learnt the trade.

But the prosperity of the handloom-weavers was short-lived; for the power-loom was on its way, and weaving too was destined before long to pass under the domination of the factory system. Cartwright had patented his power-loom as early as 1785, and set up a factory to use it at Doncaster in 1787. He used horse-power at first, but introduced a steam-engine in 1789. But his factory failed, possibly through bad management, but more probably because the power-loom was still only in an experimental stage; and his next attempt, in 1791, in partnership with the Grimshaws of Manchester, was wrecked when his factory was deliberately burnt to the ground.

Weaving machinery, in fact, met with an organized resistance from which spinning machinery had been wholly exempt. Under the domestic system, the spinners were a widely scattered body of unskilled workers, mainly women and children, with no organized power of resistance. The weavers, on the other hand, were skilled men, already used to combination and

CP : F

bitterly resentful of the threat which the power-loom presented to their means of living. Undoubtedly their resistance delayed its introduction; for until its economic advantages had been incontestably proved most capitalists were reluctant to incur the odium and the material risk of employing it. Gradually, however, Cartwright's machine, improved with later devices by himself, by Samuel Horrocks and by William Radcliffe, inevitably made its way. Radcliffe himself dates its widespread use in Lancashire from about 1806; and thereafter it extended its sway rapidly—fastest of all in the years of depression and falling prices after 1815.

However, the handloom-weavers' sufferings from the competition of the power-loom came principally after 1815, and belong rather to the next chapter of our story. Their troubles during the years of war were due more largely to the repeated interruptions to trade caused by the war itself, especially after the outbreak of hostilities with the United States in 1812. For, whereas the cotton used in England and Scotland in the eighteenth century had come chiefly from the West Indies and Central America, and also from India, by 1812 the Southern States, with their abundant armies of negro-slaves, had become the principal source of supply, as they have remained ever since. Not till the wars were over, and the immediate post-war crisis had been surmounted, could Lancashire go full steam ahead with its factories for weaving as well as for preparing and spinning cotton.

Meanwhile, over the country as a whole, population was rising fast. In 1801, at the date of the first Census, it was nearly 9,000,000; in 1811 over 10,000,000; and in 1821 12,000,000. Density per square mile probably at least doubled between 1721 and 1821; and there was also an immense change in the distribution of the population over the country. Towns grew fast, especially in the new industrial areas, as factories increased in size and number. The mining areas became populous; and the relative population and importance of Southern England, including the old centres of the woollen industry in East and West as well as the agricultural districts, sharply declined.

There has been much debate concerning the reasons for this

very rapid increase of total population, coming after centuries of very slow growth—for the population was probably about 5,000,000 in 1600, and did not rise by more than three-quarters of a million during the ensuing century. Much stress used to be laid on the effects of the break-up of the old village economy and the movement to the factory towns in swelling the birth-rate. It used to be said that the village worker, when he removed to the town, rose earlier to his maximum earnings, found it easier to set up a household of his own at an early age (for many of the farm-hands lived in), and lost the prudential restrictions everywhere imposed by the conditions of a peasant economy. But, though these contentions have some force, they probably account for only a small part of the change. In communities at a low standard of living, the death-rate is usually far more potent than the birth-rate in determining the natural increase of population; and among death-rates the rate of infant mortality counts for far more than any other.

The new industrial system assuredly did not "strive officiously to keep alive." But neither did it kill, even as fast as the older economic system which it displaced. Vital statistics are notoriously inaccurate for the eighteenth century, and sadly deficient for the early decades of the nineteenth; but there is no denying the weight of evidence that points to a sharply falling death-rate over the period during which the factory system was being actively introduced. A large part of this fall must undoubtedly be attributed to the decrease in infant mortality. According to an estimate for London published in the *Lancet* in 1835, the death-rate for children was halved between 1750 and 1830. In the first half of the eighteenth century, according to the same estimate, nearly three-quarters of all the children born died before reaching five years of age: a century later the proportion dying was under one-third. Figures for the industrial districts are unobtainable on a comparable basis; but it seems clear that, whereas in the eighteenth century the larger towns had, apart from immigration, an excess of deaths over births, after about 1800 most of them had a natural increase. The factory system may have stunted and maimed its victims; but it did not kill them off nearly fast enough to offset the sharp decline in infant and child mortality.

Why did this decline occur? Various answers have been given—the spread of purer water-supply, the advance in medical knowledge and midwifery, the extension of vaccination (but that came too late to serve as an explanation), improved sanitation—even the higher value which the employment of children in the factories caused to be set on child labour. Of these probably purer water and midwifery counted for most. Dr. William Smellie virtually founded scientific midwifery in the mid-eighteenth century; and thereafter the number of lying-in hospitals and charities increased greatly, and the training of midwives rapidly improved. In the British Lying-in Hospital, which opened in 1749, the rate of maternal mortality was reduced by four-fifths between the first ten years' working and 1799–1808, and that of infant mortality by five-sixths. Over the same period many towns provided themselves with an improved supply of water, and there was a considerable advance in drainage. Water-closets, though not yet common, were widely introduced by the better-off households and in institutions; and the cesspools into which the filth was emptied at first, often with highly insanitary results, were gradually replaced by connections with house-drains and public sewers. Bad as the conditions of public health still were when Chadwick and Southwood Smith studied them in the eighteen-forties, there can be no doubt that in 1815 they were a good deal better in the larger towns than they had been during the greater part of the eighteenth century.

Indeed, it is more than possible that after 1815 there was an actual worsening of conditions in the rapidly developing factory towns, where houses were being run up wholesale by contractors intent chiefly on cheapness, and the older residential areas were being rapidly converted into slums as the well-to-do citizens moved further out. The sanitary reformers of the latter years of the eighteenth century, such as Dr. Percival and Dr. Barnes of Manchester, were able to make some headway. Their successors were swept aside by the inrushing sea of immigrants in search of employment, many of them wholly unused to urban life, and not a few bringing with them the habits involved in a desperately low standard of living, such as prevailed in Ireland. The worst housing conditions in the industrial towns belong to the period described by Chadwick and his collaborators, and by Engels in his *Condition of the Working Classes in England in 1844*. Up to 1815 things were, on the whole, probably getting slowly better rather than worse, as far as sanitation and disease were concerned. Certainly mortality was falling; and that was the main cause of rapidly rising population. Immigration counted for relatively little over the country as a whole; and as for the birth-rate, the evidence, though incomplete, points rather to a fall than to an increase.

This, of course, does not affect the fact that population *was* rising at a prodigious rate. This rise, as we have seen, made the country permanently dependent on foreign corn, despite the increase in the arable area. It also provided a rapidly increasing home market for industrial products; for, irregular as employment was, the new-comers had mouths to feed and bodies to clothe as well as hands to labour. There is no means of measuring the increase in total production; but it was undoubtedly very large. The quantity of raw cotton consumed in the United Kingdom rose from 5,000,000 pounds in 1781 to 124,000,000 in 1810 and 164,000,000 in 1818. The quantity of iron produced is estimated to have risen from under 70,000 tons in 1790 to 400,000 in 1820. That of coal raised was trebled between 1800 and 1840. Even of wool the total yarn consumption rose from 58,000,000 lb. in 1780 to 80,000,000 in 1820. As for exports, they were about 30 per cent greater in volume in 1815 and 1816 than at the beginning of the century; but in face of the set-back to trade during the later years of the war and the sharp fall in prices after 1815, the £55,000,000 at which they were valued in 1800 was not reached again until 1844.

In the main, the increasing wealth of the country was either wasted on war or consumed at home. The richer classes doubtless reaped by far the greatest proportionate share by way of the rise in rents and the rapid increase in industrial profits, together with the swollen interest on the National Debt. But factory wages, low as they were, were probably higher, even in relation to the cost of living, than the previous earnings of unskilled workers under the domestic system; and there is no reason for doubting Francis Place's testimony that wages rose sharply among the skilled urban artisans. For these workers, still practically untouched by the advent of machinery, found their labour in growing demand with the rise in total wealth and in the incomes of the richer classes, on whom they chiefly depended for their market. Place's figures relate mainly to London, which benefited in this way more than any other area, and they give too favourable a picture. But what figures there are for other towns bear out his general conclusion.

According to Place's testimony, a typical wage for a skilled artisan in London at the beginning of the war in 1793 was 22*s.* a week. This is somewhat higher than the figures which we gave earlier; for these indicated a rate of about 20*s.* for 1790. Place says that London artisans' wages rose steadily until 1813, when they stood at about 36*s.* a week—a rise of nearly 64 per cent. This was definitely less than the accompanying rise in the cost of living, which, according to the Silberling index, rose by 76 per cent between 1793 and 1813, and by over 92 per cent between 1792 and 1813. Prices, however, were exceptionally high in 1812–13; and if these years are left out, the rise in wages had only lagged a little behind that of retail prices. Place goes on to say that from 1815 to 1834, the level of money-wages for London artisans remained unchanged, whereas the cost of living fell sharply from 1815 onwards. If his figures can be accepted, the skilled London workers lost something in purchasing power during the war; but their standard of living rose sharply during the next decade. If, however, as we are inclined to suggest, Place's figure of 22*s.* in 1793 is 2*s.* too high, whereas his figure of 1813 is roughly correct, then wages rose during the war by 80 per cent— enough to keep pace with the cost of living except in one or two famine years.

Outside London it seems clear that even the skilled workers were a good deal less fortunate. Wages in the shipyards seem indeed on the average to have risen by nearly three-quarters for skilled shipwrights—a highly organized trade—in such ports as Liverpool and Glasgow. Skilled millwrights, and other engineering mechanics, did less well, their money-wages rising by much less than half—probably nearer one-third—between 1793 and 1815. Skilled workers in the woollen trades got about 40 per cent more on the average. Builders seem to have done better, at any rate in the growing factory towns. In Glasgow, for example, carpenters got from 8s. to 12s. a week in 1793, and about 18s. in 1815, and in Edinburgh 9s. 6d. in 1793, and from 15s. to 18s. in 1815. In Macclesfield, however, carpenters' wages rose only from 18s. to 24s. For London one source gives the rise as from 18s. to 30s. (but this may be an average including labourers as well as craftsmen). Another source gives a rise from 20s. to 35s. All these figures are for summer wages: in winter less was earned, owing to lost time and shorter working hours.

Miners' wages in Scotland seem to have risen from 2s. 6d.–3s. a day before the war to nearly 5s. in 1811–12: but thereafter they dropped back sharply to 4s. in 1813, and lower still about 1820. Miners' earnings were, in fact, already very sensitive to changes in prices and industrial activity, and showed much bigger fluctuations than wages in the majority of trades. For cotton factory operatives it is unfortunately impossible to quote any figures before 1806, for lack of data. From that year wage-rates seem to have been rising slowly until about 1810, from an average of perhaps 11s. to perhaps 11s. 6d. a week for workers of all classes. Thereafter the rates seem to have remained stable till 1815; but in the last years of the war earnings fluctuated greatly because trade was much upset by the European blockade and by the American War, which interrupted supplies of new cotton. After 1815 wages fell, but not so much as prices.

On the other hand, the handloom-weavers, after reaching a high wage-level towards the end of the eighteenth century, experienced a sharp decline towards 1805. Between 1805 and 1808 the average wage of a cotton-weaver was estimated to have fallen from 23s. to 13s. over Lancashire as a whole, and in Bolton, for which we have fuller figures than for most towns, from 25s. to 15s. Thereafter there was a recovery to about 18s. (Bolton 24s.) in 1814, followed at once by a catastrophic **drop,** which brought the Lancashire average down by 1818 to no more than 8*s*. (Bolton 9*s*.). By 1815 the handloom-weavers in the cotton industry were already at starvation point; for the introduction of the power-loom had pushed them into a position in which they could get work only by reducing their wage-claims to a desperately low level in order to compete. Nevertheless, for some time after this, fresh labour—chiefly from Ireland or from the agricultural areas—continued to come into the doomed craft, making the situation yet worse.

It remains to consider the position of the agricultural labourers—still by far the largest body of workers. Their situation will be dealt with more fully in a later section, in connection with the Poor Law and the Speenhamland system of poor relief after the war; and we shall deal here only with wage-movements in a narrow sense. Over the country as a whole, agricultural wages seem to have risen from the beginning of the war to about 1806, when the average level was rather more than 50 per cent above that of the early 1790's— from about 9*s*. to nearly 14*s*. a week, according to one estimate, which is perhaps rather high for both dates, and definitely too high for the Southern and Western Counties, and for East Anglia. In Sussex, for example, wages rose only from 9*s*. a week to 13*s*.

Moreover, after 1806, agricultural wages in most counties stopped rising, though the cost of living continued its upward trend. From 1806 to 1812 the rates seem to have been nearly stable; and from 1812 they began to fall, the average descending, for the country as a whole, to 13*s*. in 1814–15, and to 12*s*. by 1816, and continuing its fall to under 10*s*. in the 1820's.

Even apart from the loss of auxiliary industrial earnings and of many perquisites which had been common in the eighteenth century, the wages of the labourer undoubtedly fell in purchasing power over the goods on which he mainly lived— especially cereals. In 1792 wheat had been at 42*s*. a quarter, and in 1793 at 49*s*. 3*d*. It was at 126*s*. 6*d*. in 1812, and 109*s*. 9*d*. in 1813. These were exceptionally bad years; but even after the war wheat cost 96*s*. 11*d*. in 1817 and 86*s*. 3*d*. in 1818. No wonder that, especially in the bad years of scarcity, the labourers and their dependents were driven to rely largely on the parish for the means of life.

CHAPTER XII

PARLIAMENT AND THE CLASS SYSTEM

So much for the economic picture of Great Britain during the critical period of the Napoleonic Wars. It remains to present, very briefly, a companion political picture. Throughout the war period there was no change at all in the basis of political representation in the House of Commons apart from the addition of the Irish members in 1801. The House of Lords, indeed, received a very large number of new recruits. As a result of the Act of Union in 1801, there appeared in the House thirty-two Irish representative peers, including four Irish bishops. But apart from this the reign of George III was throughout its length by far more fertile than any previous reign in the creation of new hereditary titles. George III actually created or called out of abeyance no less than 254 peerages of Great Britain or the United Kingdom, not including 268 Irish peerages. At the death of George II the House of Lords numbered under two hundred: by the time George III died its numbers had doubled. These new peers mostly came from the ranks of the landed aristocracy, including the existing Scottish and Irish peers. Apart from a very few great merchants and bankers, peerages were not yet conferred upon the richer members of the commercial or industrial capitalist classes, until, like the great clothiers of earlier times, they had sanctified themselves by retirement from business and become by inherited landholding a part of the recognized aristocracy.

The House of Commons remained unchanged except for the Irish; but as commercial wealth increased a large number of great financiers bought themselves seats in Parliament as well as landed estates. There were a whole tribe of Barings in both the Unreformed and the Reformed Parliament; and such army contractors as John Maberly, and such City financiers as the Alexanders, and Sir Manasseh Lopez, readily bought seats.

But the class structure of English society was changing much more rapidly than the basis of political representation. During the war, in order to finance the extraordinary expenditure, the Government was compelled to impose an income-tax which, in response to the clamour of the propertied classes, was promptly taken off as soon as the war ended. The assessments under this tax help to give some idea of the main sources of incomes for the wealthier classes at the end of the war period. For the year 1814–15 the total income brought under review was roughly £177,500,000. Of this £39,400,000 arose from the ownership of lands, a further £16,250,000 from the ownership of houses, and £4,500,000 from manorial rights, tithes, and the ownership of mineral rights—making over £60,000,000 from land and house property. A further £38,400,000 was derived from the occupation, as distinct from the ownership, of lands and houses—making in all nearly £100,000,000 attributable to the landed interest and to the more substantial householders in respect of buildings. As against this the interest on the public funds accounted for nearly £29,000,000—to be met, of course, out of the taxes. Incomes from public offices, pensions and sinecures, came to £11,750,000—making nearly £41,000,000 in all payable out of public revenues. Finally, the total recorded income from all trades and professions taken together amounted to £38,300,000.

These figures are doubtless very inaccurate; for it is common knowledge that the income-tax was very widely evaded. But they do broadly indicate the continued preponderance of the landed and agricultural interests among the wealthier sections of the community up to 1815.

Patrick Colquhoun, near the beginning of the century, made in his *Wealth, Power and Resources of the British Empire*, published in 1814, a general estimate of the national income, which he then proceeded to apportion among the principal classes in the community. This estimate bears out the same conclusions. Very broadly summarized, it shows the following results:

	£
Aristocracy (Nobility, Gentry, Royalty and Upper Clergy, not including next group)	60,000,000
State Service and Pensions	8,000,000
Professions (rest of Clergy, Law, Medicine)	17,000,000
Agriculture (landholders apart from aristocracy, including freeholders and farmers, but not including labourers) ..	74,000,000

					£
Trade and Industry (excluding innkeepers and publicans, and also wage-earners)					37,000,000
Innkeepers and Publicans					9,000,000
Working Classes (artisans, labourers, miners, etc., including agricultural labourers)					82,000,000
Paupers, Vagrants and Criminals					10,000,000
Total Income					£297,000,000

According to these figures, the working classes, even including the last group, received less than one-third of the national income. The aristocracy, without its receipts from public offices and pensions, received over 20 per cent. The agricultural interest, excluding both aristocratic landlords and labourers, received nearly 25 per cent, while the entire trading and industrial interest, apart from the working class, got only 15 per cent, of which £9,000,000, or 3 per cent of the total, was estimated by Colquhoun as going to what he called "eminent merchants." It is significant that Colquhoun had no separate category of "eminent" industrial employers. Such as there were he lumped in with the merchants; for the merchants were still considered as the typical capitalist class. But even with this inclusion the "eminent merchants" got only a very little more than the innkeepers and publicans.

It is impossible for this period to attempt any separation between the incomes of the industrial and the agricultural working class. As long as the domestic system lasted, their fortunes were far too closely intertwined, and they represented too largely the same households for separate estimates to be made. The Census of 1811, taken on a basis of families, showed 35 per cent of all the families in Great Britain as occupied in agriculture, as against 44 per cent in trade, manufactures and kindred occupations, and over 20 per cent as unoccupied or unclassified; but in the circumstances of the time no great reliance can be placed upon these figures, as the occupations of individuals, as distinct from households, were not recorded until 1841. Colquhoun's estimate, based on a total population of fourteen millions, assigned roughly nine millions to the working classes, including paupers and vagrants, three millions to the freeholders and farmers, three-quarters of a million to the traders and employers, half a million to public employees and the professional classes together, four hundred and thirty-seven thousand to the class of innkeepers and publicans, and four hundred and twenty-five thousand to the aristocracy—all these groups including families and dependants. But the two final figures especially are overweighted because Colquhoun includes domestic servants among dependants—so that they need to be reduced at least by over half in order to get at the correct proportions.

All these figures are highly unsatisfactory; but no better ones are to be got. They clearly indicate a society still dominated by the landed interests, even though by 1811 the number of households recorded as employed in agriculture was not much more than one-third of the total in Great Britain. Colquhoun's estimates, which include Ireland, are based for this reason on a higher proportion of agricultural households.

But though the landed interest was still predominant in 1815, the manufacturing classes were increasing rapidly. The industrial employers, however—even the new factory owners—had in 1815 still for the most part no pretensions to be regarded as gentlefolk. Nor were most of them yet rich, by the standards of the gentry, or yet employers of large bodies of workers. The typical factory of the early phases of the Industrial Revolution, say of 1815, remained small, even by the standards of ten years later; and the typical employer was still too busy building up his capital in order to enlarge his establishment to launch out into extravagant spending, or to spare much thought for politics, until the troublous years after 1815 set him thinking about his political rights. He was busy accumulating capital; but he had not yet accumulated very much, and what he had he ploughed back promptly into his business, in order to take advantage of the expanding opportunities that came with the installation of power-driven machinery and the employment upon it of a larger body of workers. The employer at this stage was often truly a man of "abstinence"—to use the phrase beloved by the economists who constituted themselves his defenders. He "abstained" from sumptuous living in order to accumulate capital; and it was natural that, making a virtue of abstinence in himself, he should regard it as still more a virtue in his employees. For every penny spent on consumption, and so abstracted from the funds available for capital accumulation, was apt to seem mere waste to men eager to seize the chances offered by the revolution in productive technique. Moreover, this early industrialism was very keenly competitive. Though many rising capitalists made fortunes, many more failed; and hardness was often a quality indispensable for success.

Among the recipients of income there were two categories which are not large enough, perhaps, to rank as classes, but which loomed very huge in contemporary eyes. The expenditure on the royal family, and in particular on the King, was disproportionately heavy. His Majesty's exact income was not disclosed, although in the opinion of reformers "there could be little doubt he was the richest individual in Europe, perhaps in the whole world." In 1817 the extra money voted by Parliament for the use of the King and the Prince Regent, above the customary royal income, was £500,000, of which over £20,000 was spent on snuff-boxes. The family on which this money was expended was unloved and unlovable: the *Black Book* said publicly of the Duke of York that "the character of his royal highness exhibits a strange compound of bigotry, avarice and profligacy," and Wellington said privately that "they are the damnedest millstones about the neck of any Government that can be imagined."

Second to the royal family in unpopularity were the Bank of England and the whole fraternity of stock-jobbers. In face of rising war prices, and subsequently of post-war deflation, anything connected with finance roused the hatred and suspicion of farmers and tradesmen nearly as much as of working men —or sometimes even more. Stock-jobbers equalled sinecurist tax-eaters in public contempt. At the centre of this swarm of financial iniquity was believed to be the Bank. Its profits were indeed large, but hardly large enough to account for the widespread hatred. They had risen (after the payment of dividends and bonuses on a generous scale) from £89,872 in 1792 to £1,066,025 in 1815. But the main grievance did not lie in the Bank's own profits. Then as now, the Bank was controlled by the ring of financial houses which dominated the City of

London. It stood in the public mind as the symbol of the sinister interests which had forced up the rates of interest and made huge underhand profits by buying up Government stock at one price from the State and re-selling it to the public at a higher figure. Every loan issued during the Napoleonic Wars provided large rake-offs for the City—in addition to handsome presents for persons whom the Government wished to bribe or to reward for their "political services." It was a common practice to issue war loan at a reduced price to a selected body of favoured individuals, among whom the City bankers and the leading public contractors were always to be found, in company with lesser fry such as journalists whose opinions found favour with those in authority. The general public, on the other hand, paid full price or more for what it bought; for the insiders were always adepts at rigging the market. The practice was, no doubt, partly analogous to modern underwriting; but the "rakes-off" were usually excessive, and it was extended to form an entirely illegitimate system of bribery and corruption.

Periods of rising prices are, of course, always a godsend to the speculator. But the bankers and stock-jobbers were even more unpopular in the period of financial deflation which followed the return of peace. For, when values are falling, those who are in the know stand much the best chance of passing the losses on to others. Farmers and landowners who, in the collapse of prices after 1815, saw ruin staring them in the face, whereas the stock-jobbers appeared to be richer than ever, were naturally furious: nor were their tempers improved when the financiers promptly bought up the great estates which came into the market during the years of distress.

There was yet another cause for the unpopularity of the Bank of England. In 1797, under stress of war conditions, the Bank was authorized to suspend cash payments; and though banknotes were not made legal tender, people had to take them whether they liked it or not, because there was no better money to be had. Paper money was intensely unpopular, especially with the country people who had always been used to dealing in hard cash. But with prices rising more money was needed, and only paper was available. Therefore banks sprang up all over the country, each with its own issue of notes; and before long the banks were issuing so much paper as to cause prices to rise faster still.

Now, in fact, the Bank of England's paper was a good deal better money than that issued by many of the country banks; for the "Old Lady" had large reserves behind her and was relatively cautious in the manufacture of notes. But farmers and tradesmen who were ruined by bank failures—of which there were very many, especially in market-towns—did not distinguish. They regarded the Bank of England as the central fount from which the stream of intrinsically worthless money flowed; and they blamed the Bank for the unsoundness of the entire system. The Bank, urged on by the Government, was doubtless responsible for some part of the war inflation; but the chief unsoundness really arose from the ease with which anyone equipped with a plausible manner and a small printing press could set up as a country banker and get his notes accepted as long as prices remained high. There were, indeed, many quite sound banks in the larger centres; but during the post-war deflation a great many of the gimcrack country banks collapsed; and the farmers and tradesmen blamed their ruin on the paper-money system and the Bank of England.

Not only were many banks unsound. It was also in those days appallingly easy to forge banknotes. Between 1797 and 1817 there were no less than 309 capital convictions for this crime, and in the majority of cases the forgers were actually executed. In addition, 522 convictions were secured for owning or passing forged Bank of England notes. Committee after committee was set up to inquire into the best method of preventing these forgeries; but it was some time before a satisfactory method of secret signs and watermarks was devised and put into operation. Between 1812 and 1818 over £100,000 of forged notes were actually discovered in circulation.

These facts, taken together, explain the venom of contemporary references to the villainy of bankers and stock-jobbers. From Cobbett downwards, every Radical orator continually denounced them; and no appeal was surer to go straight to the heart of an audience of farmers or small-town tradesmen. Every great depression carries with it a storm of abuse directed against high finance, and a plentiful crop of currency schemes and other projects for amending the monetary system. The years after the Napoleonic Wars were particularly fruitful in such things; and the people of Great Britain had then even more obvious cause than ever after for regarding the financier as the principal villain of the piece.

CHAPTER XIII

ENGLAND AND THE FRENCH REVOLUTION

WE have run far ahead of our narrative in attempting to describe the condition of Britain during the Napoleonic Wars. We broke off our story at the moment when Paine had embarked for France, his mind full of the rosiest dreams, not only of the future of the French Revolution but of the prospects of his own country. But both he and his friends greatly exaggerated to themselves their own popularity in the country. Effigies of Paine had been burnt already by crowds in provincial towns, and in 1791 a more serious warning had been given by a riot in Birmingham. The anniversary of the storming of the Bastille (July 14th) had been celebrated by the local society of "The Friends of Freedom" at a dinner in an hotel. In revenge a mob collected together that night and burnt down dissenting chapels—for the Church was active against the Revolution and the enemies of the Church were presumed to be revolutionaries. The mob then left the centre of Birmingham for Fair Hill, where Priestley had what was possibly the best-equipped laboratory in England. He himself was brought away in time by a friend, and paced the road quietly, listening while the mob methodically destroyed all his records and instruments, ending by breaking his wine bottles, flooding his cellar, and drinking themselves stupid till they lay in heaps in his garden, to which they had retired after setting the house on fire. Priestley himself went shortly afterwards to America, never to return: the mob next day extended its activities to the destruction of the homes of less well-known reformers. The authorities did not interfere with it until its appetite for destruction was satisfied: even the highest circles, while nominally deploring the riot, actually encouraged it. "I am not sorry," wrote the Marquis of Buckingham, and the King told Dundas, "I cannot but feel better pleased that Priestley is the sufferer."

It seemed highly amusing to the "Church and King" party that the defenders of "the people" should be harassed by the people itself. In the next two or three years the clergy and landowners were to make a very considerable use of mobs. These two castes had not previously exercised their full influence: in the Wilkes agitation they had not been so severely frightened, their opponents had been more formidable, and Wilkes himself had made no mistakes. Now, the employers and merchants who had supported Wilkes were sometimes hostile, mostly neutral, and at the best guardedly sympathetic to the Painites; the nobility and clergy were severely scared by the progress of the French Revolution; and their opponents were dependent for their prestige upon politicians across the Channel who neither cared for nor understood their difficulties. Nevertheless, the Church and King mobs which were raised showed very little proof of genuine political enthusiasm: quite a small show of force would have put them down. This was proved the next year (December 1792) when a similar mob attempted to repeat the Birmingham coup in Manchester. They were unfortunate enough to select as an easy victim Thomas Walker, a very bellicose and well-to-do merchant who had been Borough-reeve (the equivalent of Lord Mayor). As soon as he ascertained that the constables were not going to afford him any protection, he and his friends fired over the heads of the mob. The loyalists fled in terror, though no one was hurt, and the riot came to a sudden and complete end.

Such energy, however, was unusual, and in most cases a mob would have its way. The year 1792 saw the two forces, of reform and reaction, balancing. Honest enthusiasm for the French Revolution brought members into the reform societies: prudent fear for their persons or popularity took them out again. The record of many societies has unquestionably perished: it is mere accident, for example, that has preserved the information that as late as March 1793 there were between thirty and forty societies in Norwich alone. Most of these would be smallish bodies meeting at a tavern, often under the chairmanship of a middle-class member. As soon as governmental disapproval became marked, the landlord, fearing for his licence, most frequently withdrew his permission for the meetings, and the chairman resigned his office. This frequently meant the end of the society, and the mortality of such associations was as noticeably high as had been their birth-rate.

The three most important societies in London were the Friends of the People, the Society for Constitutional Information, and the London Corresponding Society. The first named, founded in 1791, was, surprisingly for such a name, a very moderate Whig body, including Charles (afterwards Lord) Grey among its members. It consisted, in fact, of Foxites without Fox: it is doubtful, indeed, whether its members were what would be called democrats to-day at all, though they were certainly in favour of freedom. But while it existed, it counselled moderation and to a certain extent acted as a screen and protection for its more violent or low-born allies. The Society for Constitutional Information had been founded as long ago as 1780, with Sheridan and several earls among its members. It had long been languescent and its revival in 1791 was due to the energy of Horne Tooke; its membership was chiefly middle-class. Among its chief members was Major Cartwright: its influence and propaganda were at one time very considerable. The Friends of the People and the Constitutional Society were both dining clubs, holding their meetings in respectable restaurants over dinner—or rather, when they had dined—and based on annual subscriptions running into guineas. Very different—and much more alarming—was the London Corresponding Society, with its much bigger membership, its weekly subscription of one penny, and its meetings in taverns or coffee houses. Its membership varied sharply from time to time: it was at one time put as high as ten thousand. This was probably an exaggeration, but it is fairly safe to assume that in 1792, '93 and '94 its membership was over three thousand, after the initial few weeks of its existence. (It was constituted on 25 January, 1792.) The subscription was 1*d.* a week and its membership was over-whelmingly working-class—artisan or small tradesman. Weavers, watchmakers, carpenters, shoemakers and cabinet-makers were the trades chiefly represented. It was organized in "sections" of thirty members (though this number was after a while exceeded) which were represented by delegates who were subject to recall. Its chief activities were the printing of pamphlets and the holding of meetings and discussions: there is no valid evidence of any military organization or prepara-tions. Its objects were brief—universal suffrage and annual parliaments. When an opposing organization charged it with demanding "no king, no parliament" it repudiated both pro-positions with equal anger.

Outside London the strongest English reform centres were Norwich, Sheffield and Manchester. The Birmingham reformers had been cowed, and Burke's influence had pre-vented a large spread of the new doctrines in Bristol. Possibly the strongest (for all figures are conjectural) and certainly the most daring reform movement was found in Scotland. Here the struggle between the two factions began earlier and was more bitter than elsewhere. Scottish education was already far superior to English, and the "lower orders" more quickly appreciated the arguments of Paine's *Rights of Man.* Church and King mobs were less easy to collect. On the other hand, Scottish government, whether by the lairds or the kirk, had always been more oppressive and inquisitorial than English: very little care for the rights of the subject was likely to impede the authorities.

The first large success of the reformers, and one which made conflict certain, was the holding of a "Convention" in Edin-burgh in December 1792. The title "Convention" was pleasantly dangerous and exciting, in view of events in France, and the delegates indulged in some harmless imitation of French forms, even taking an oath "to live free or die." But in essence the Convention was no more than what we should call a delegate conference for propaganda purposes. The most active and "left-wing" delegate, Thomas Muir, a young lawyer, said nothing that was not strictly constitutional, and a rather fiery address from the United Irishmen, a more revolutionary and also more formidable society in Ireland, was not accepted. The Convention separated after giving a powerful fillip to reform propaganda all over Scotland, and to the fears of its opponents.

The ensuing months were spent in agitation and counter-agitation. Minor prosecutions were instituted, which mostly ended in the Government's favour, but no wholesale suppression followed. Nevertheless, the outlook for the Scottish as much as the English reformers was darkening. In May 1793 the House of Commons refused by 282 votes to 41 even to consider petitions asking for reform, thus in effect closing to the reformers the constitutional approach. On 1 February, 1793, Britain and France had gone to war, and further association with the French became automatically a crime, besides being abhorrent to the average patriot. But the progress of the French Revolution itself was the greatest inconvenience to the reformers. The French leaders paid no attention to Thomas Muir when he begged them to refrain from cutting off the King's head, or to Tom Paine when he urged the same thing from his place in the Convention. British public opinion, in all classes, had been at best approaching the point where it would demand, in a pacific manner, a reformed Parliament and a strictly constitutional monarchy. The reformers were shortly forced to defend a republic, the execution of a king, and the confiscation of the property of the Church and the nobility. Before long only their hardiest followers stood by them. They did not themselves advocate these things; they merely defended them in another country; but the distinction was too fine for the public to attend to it. Nor was their position made easier by their acknowledged chief and inspirer: when Paine was tried in his absence he annihilated the chances of the defence by sending to court a letter in which he spoke of the complete lack of need for "such a man as Mr. Guelph, or any of his profligate sons."

When Muir returned to Scotland from his fruitless mission to the French, the Scots judiciary believed that their opportunity had come to crush the movement that he represented. "Gentlemen," said the Lord Advocate at the trial in August 1793, "this is the moment which I have long and anxiously

looked for." The charge was treason; the evidence, except the
evidence of opinion, was negligible. But the verdict could not
be in doubt; or if it had been, the presiding judge would have
seen that it did not remain so. He was Robert M'Queen, Lord
Braxfield, the Lord Justice Clerk and one of the most pre-
judiced judges of Scottish history; he afterwards served as a
model for R. L. Stevenson's "Weir of Hermiston." "Come
awa', Maister Horner," he said to a juryman who delayed,
"Come awa' and help us to hang ane o' thae damned scoun-
drels." The evidence showed no arming, no conspiracy, and
no preparations for violence on Muir's part. It was not even
clear that Muir's own society's claim for a "more equal
representation" reached as far as modern democracy. "Two
opinions," it was said, "divided the society; one for confining
the right of voting to landed property, the other for every man
having a vote." But M'Queen was not diverted by such considerations. He told the jury—in words which have been
smoothed out by the reporter, for he spoke broad Scots and the
Edinburgh Gazetteer was once punished for the offence of merely
reproducing his words as he said them—he informed the jury,
then: "Two things must be attended to that require no proof.
First, that the British Constitution is the best that ever was
since the creation of the world and it is not possible to make it
better." He became too confused to say what the second thing
was: "his Lordship" merely says the report, "said he never
liked the French all his days, but now he hated them." But he
was clear enough for the jury of landlords: he received the
verdict he wished and gleefully sentenced Muir to fourteen
years' transportation. A few weeks later Fyshe Palmer, an
energetic reformer who had spoken in more northerly towns,
especially Dundee, received a seven years' transportation
sentence at Perth on similar evidence.

The Scottish reformers replied to these sentences by calling
another Convention, which met in October 1793. It was
similar to the first, but more angry and more "Frenchified."
The Edinburgh authorities were indignant at the impudence,
but uncertain how to act, and the Convention had actually
dispersed unharmed when the secretary, William Skirving,
recalled it to meet some delegates who had arrived from the

London Corresponding Society and other English bodies. The language used at these resumed meetings became more violent: a "secret committee" was appointed, later becoming a Committee of Ways and Means; and it was resolved that the Convention should be re-summoned if Habeas Corpus was suspended, or certain other acts of tyranny took place—though what it should then do was not clear.

At this the authorities acted. Skirving, two London delegates named Joseph Gerrald and Maurice Margarot, and a few others were arrested, and the Convention forcibly dissolved. The first three were brought to their trial early in 1794, before the exultant M'Queen. The question before the jury again was by the evidence confined to whether it was sedition or not to advocate a parliamentary reform, and the result was to declare that in Scotland it was so. Even if the advocates had no seditious intention, it was nevertheless sedition, M'Queen instructed the jury. He was so certain of his verdict that he could afford to jest. When Gerrald said proudly that Christ too had been a reformer, "muckle he made o' that; he was hangit," answered the judge. The defendants were not put down by his sardonic ferocity: Margarot, indeed, stood up to him defiantly and demanded to examine him from the dock. M'Queen, declining to take an oath, nevertheless cautiously asked him what questions he wished to put, and the following strange dialogue ensued:

Q. Did you dine at Mr. Rochead's at Inverleitch in the course of last week?

The Lord Justice Clerk (*M'Queen*). And what have you to do with that, sir?

Q. Did any conversation take place with regard to my trial?

L.J.C. Go on, sir.

Q. Did you use these words: "What should you think of giving him an hundred lashes, together with Botany Bay?" or words to that purpose?

L.J.C. Go on: put your questions, if you have any more.

Q. Did any person, did a lady, say to you that the mob would not allow you to whip him? And, my lord, did you not say that the mob would be the better for a little blood? These are the questions, my lord, that I wish to put to you. . . .

L.J.C. Do you think I should answer questions of that sort, my Lord Henderland?

Lord Henderland. No, my lord. . . .

Lord Esgrove. What may have been said in a private company cannot in any way affect this case. . . .

Lord Swinton. My Lord, not one of them are proper.

Lord Dunsinnon concurred, but in the opinion of many people M'Queen had been discredited, and an uncomfortable debate followed in Parliament. The Lord Justice Clerk became an instrument which could only sparingly be used. But courage did not save Gerrald, Skirving and Margarot: fourteen years' transportation was allotted to each. Their sufferings remained an inspiration to democrats for years, though they are now almost forgotten. Half a century later the Corn Law poet, Ebenezer Elliott, wrote:

> *O could the wise, the brave, the just,*
> *Who suffered—died—to break our chains,*
> *Could Muir, could Palmer from the dust,*
> *Could murdered Gerrald hear our strains!*

Skirving was so ill-treated on the voyage that he died on landing. Gerrald died soon after. Muir was rescued by a United States boat and after wandering half across the world died of exhaustion in France. Palmer died a prisoner in Spain, having been captured on his way home after the expiry of his sentence. Margarot alone survived to return to England.

For transportation was not, as it is easy to suppose, merely an enforced voyage to Australia, dreaded by the eighteenth-century convict only because of his fear of foreign travel. The journey itself occupied many months, round the Cape of Good Hope and through the Indian Ocean. If the convicts were free of chains, it was exclusively by special kindness of the commander—a kindness extended only to favoured criminals. The mere journey would be regarded by a modern sailor as an appalling hardship; in an eighteenth-century sailing-ship—which would seem to him a mere walnut-shell—without ventilation and sanitation, and fed upon the rations which convicts received, it is doubtful if he would survive it. Certainly, a death-rate of 20 per cent among the convicts was nothing out of the ordinary. On their arrival they found a land which was very nearly uninhabited—for transportation to Botany Bay had only been begun in 1787—and they were "farmed out" to settlers as if they were slaves. Their duty was to clear the bush and perform all the hardest and most menial work. For a failure, or imagined failure, they were liable to be flogged, and often were flogged. Sometimes, when they were working in chained gangs, one of them would die in the heat of the sun; the corpse would remain chained to its fellows until nightfall, for an earlier release was impossible. It is not surprising that in the popular imagination a sentence to transportation was only one degree less terrifying than a sentence to death.

But the immediate effect of these sentences was to increase rather than diminish the agitation in Scotland. Pamphlets, including one that gave Margarot's trial in full and is said to have been issued in 100,000 copies, were spread about the country, secret drilling began, and minor conflicts occurred in the streets. Patriotic plays were hooted in the Edinburgh theatres and "God Save the King" was drowned in cries of: "The sow's tail to Geordie!" A further lesson was needed, in official opinion, and it was soon provided. Robert Watt and Samuel Downie, two members of the Ways and Means Committee of the suppressed Convention, were arrested and charged with organizing an insurrection. A special commission, since M'Queen was discredited, tried them, and their trial was a fair one. Perhaps because of that, something went wrong. The case was complete; the chief agent, Watt, confessed and was sentenced to death, his fellow being pardoned later. But it is known that Watt was a police spy, and his confession, which gives the outline of an elaborate organization, bears several evidences of unreality. If it had been the confession of a spy, used to convict others, while its writer went free, the story would be a simple one. But Watt was executed; certain of the more horrible penalties of treason were omitted, but he was drawn to the Tolbooth on a hurdle, hanged, and then beheaded.

Whether a hideous error had been made or not, the effect of the cruel scene was immediate. Momentarily, though it was to revive later, the Scottish reform movement was terrorized. However, the fate of the people, in the current phrase, did not depend upon Scotland, but upon England. Here the reformers had certain advantages which the Scots had not. Their leaders were, perhaps, less inexperienced. Certainly the judiciary was more circumspect, less inhuman, and with a greater respect for informed public opinion. Furthermore, they had the services of an advocate of genius.

Thomas Erskine, afterwards Baron Erskine of Clackmannan, and possibly England's worst Lord Chancellor of modern days, was at this time at the height of his powers as a pleader. Passionately partisan, learned in the law, conceited, eloquent, violent in language and in gesture, he terrified guilty witnesses and often innocent ones as well. His overbearingness, his rages, and his courage were essential to defeat a campaign such as the Government had projected. He bullied officials, he bullied rival counsel, he bullied even the judges; but he flattered the juries and he prepared his cases with care and erudition. Checked, even checked justly on a small point, he knew how to fling himself into a diplomatic fury. "Good God!" he shouted at the judge in the Walker case, on such an occasion, "Where am I? Am I in a British court of justice? How is a man to defend himself? How are my clients to be exculpated?"

He appeared for the defence in one of the earliest important English cases of 1794, when the same Thomas Walker of Manchester who dispersed the Church and King mob in 1792 was charged with treason. Erskine was able to cast considerable doubt upon the evidence of the chief witness, Thomas Dunn, who claimed as a member of Walker's society to have perceived preparations for insurrection. The fact was that Dunn, and another man not produced in court, had been organized and drilled in false evidence by a magistrate, the Rev. Mr. Griffiths. Unable to prove all this, Erskine nevertheless was able to produce witnesses to show that Dunn had called on Walker and apologized for his perjuries. Dunn first denied this, then seemed to admit it; the judge then demanded of him why he said those things to Mr. Walker. "I went there when I was intoxicated, the same as I am now," replied the witness, and brought the trial to an abrupt end. Walker was discharged; Dunn was given two years for perjury; the Rev. Mr. Griffiths was not disturbed.

Manchester, however, despite this victory, was no longer a stronghold of reform. The growing strength of the repression had reduced the popular societies to little more than shadows in all provincial towns, except possibly Sheffield. London was the only centre where the reformers were undismayed, and even here the lesser societies had dissolved or fallen into insignificance: only the London Corresponding Society remained upright. That it did so was largely due to the personality of its secretary, Thomas Hardy, a working shoemaker of high organizing ability. He was marked out from his fellows by his taciturnity; unlike them, whose great fault was loquacity and "mistaking a resolution for a revolution," he never spoke but to the purpose in hand. It was deposed in evidence that at one highly important meeting he said nothing at all but "read without comment," addressed to a fellow committee-man, Richter, a footman, who was improving the resolutions by his own ejaculations. Among his most important assistants were the one-time Wilkite Horne Tooke, Thomas Holcroft, an ex-jockey and now a popular dramatist, and John Thelwall, an orator who ingeniously disguised his propaganda, at need, as commentaries on Roman history.

In the second week of May the Government arrested all these men and half a dozen others, at the same time securing the suspension of Habeas Corpus and announcing the discovery of a huge revolutionary plot. They had determined to put down the revolutionary movement for good, considering that once Hardy and his colleagues were dealt with no resistance to them would remain. They held them in prison for several months— May to October—throughout a very hot summer cross-examining them and going through the Society's papers again and again. Sorrow as well as illness depressed the prisoners; Mrs. Hardy, from shock of an attack on her house by the mob, died in childbirth, leaving an unfinished note to her husband saying: "You are never out of my thoughts, sleeping or waking." Most of them were well aware that the Government would gladly see them transported or executed, and if they failed to realize their danger it was quickly brought home to them. Pitt, the Prime Minister, and Dundas, the Home Secretary, judged the case important enough to take a personal part in preparing it. An experienced gentleman like Horne Tooke they treated with great reserve and exact legality, but the working-men they bullied unscrupulously, telling them that they were compelled by law to answer incriminating questions. Sharp, an engraver, was among those who remained obstinate, and Pitt said in front of him, with a gesture of despair, "Well! We can do without his evidence. Let him be sent to prison and hanged with the rest of them in the Tower." But the Government secured no evidence of an insurrectionary plot— not because of the fortitude of the prisoners, for several of them broke down, but because no evidence was there, and the Government had not yet fallen, except in Scotland, to fabricating evidence as it did twenty years or so later. It was compelled to base its case upon the undeniable fact of the prisoners' democratic opinions, and to endeavour to secure a verdict that it was illegal to propagate such views.

Hardy did not come to trial till October 1794. If he were hanged, wrote Grey to his wife, "I do not know how soon it may come to my turn"; and less aristocratic heads felt the same fear. The Government's leading counsel was John Scott, afterwards famous, or infamous, as Lord Eldon: Hardy's defender was Erskine. The trial was an obstinate and long-drawn-out struggle; it lasted nine days, and the evidence fills four printed volumes. When at last the jury retired, to be absent three hours, there was "an awful silence and suspense." The tension so affected the foreman of the jury, a Mr. Buck of Acton, that on their return he delivered the verdict in a whisper scarcely to be heard in court, and fell down in a faint the moment he had spoken. But stronger voices than his were there to pick up his "Not Guilty" and shout it triumphantly through the court and to the waiting crowd outside. The other trials then followed a less dramatic course: Horne Tooke jeered at the Attorney-General and clowned in the dock, and the Lord Chief Justice slept through the prosecution's speech against Thelwall. The verdicts were foregone conclusions, and the Government abandoned the other prosecutions, Holcroft being removed protesting because he was not allowed to deliver the eloquent and philosophically important speech which he held prepared in his hand.

So resounding a victory might be expected to lead to a revival of the popular cause. It did not; after the rejoicings were over the decline was resumed. Partly, this was due to the greater powers assumed by the Government. In 1795–6 there were passed the "Two Acts," the first of a long series of enactments arming the Government against their fellow-citizens, which made writing and speaking as much treason as overt acts, made inciting to hatred of the Government a "high misdemeanour," made public meetings illegal except when licensed and political lectures and reading-rooms also dependent on licences and subject to control by the magistrates. These enactments hamstrung the Society's propaganda. In addition, the magistrates, stimulated by the Government, made extensive use of their power to close taverns which were regarded as centres of Radical activity, and many innkeepers had to turn some group of Radicals from their doors for fear of losing their livelihood.

But there was a further, more deep-seated reason. The British Reform movement depended almost wholly upon the inspiration of the French Revolution and of Tom Paine's writings. There were other writers, later realized to be of great importance, but they were relatively unheeded. William Godwin, in his *Political Justice*, provided a philosophical basis for the movement, but his book was published at three guineas, Mary Wollstonecraft wrote one of the first answers to Burke, but it was not widely read and her most important work, in defence of the rights of women, had to wait a hundred years for a popular audience. Wordsworth, Coleridge, and Southey were inspired by the French Revolution to some great and some fairly good poetry. But their influence, like Shelley's later, was as small at the moment as it was great in the future, and their most popular member, Southey, though he hated industrialism to the end, became politically a reactionary.

Of all their writings only Godwin's *Political Justice* deserves notice here, for it did exert an indirect influence upon the young intellectuals of the day. Of all Radical writings, it is rationalistic in the most complete and unqualified sense. All government, it states, is illegitimate, because it rests on coercion and not on individual appreciation of the need for rational conduct: even voluntary association is to be kept down to a minimum, because it interferes with the free action of the individual reason. Men are to associate only in small communities, with occasional consultation over wider areas, and with no coercion at all.

Among evil institutions Godwin included, not only government, but above all else inequality. He believed profoundly that men's productive powers were enough to provide a "frugal sufficiency" for all. To those who, like Malthus, answered that, but for the checks on population imposed by vice and misery, the numbers of the people would at once press upon the narrow means of subsistence, Godwin answered, first, with a denial that the shortage need exist under a more rational system, and secondly by asserting that under such a system men could be trusted to act reasonably in keeping the number of mouths well within the means of filling them.

In ultimate ideas, then, Godwin was the extreme revolutionary. But he had no belief at all in revolutionary action. The new society, he thought, must come by persuasion and the spread of enlightenment and not by force. He defended the English "Jacobins" of the Corresponding Societies manfully when the Government attacked them. But he did not agree with their policy. His hatred of coercion extended to hatred of coercing the evil-doer. But it also made him a powerful influence for penal reform. His attack, in his best novel, *Caleb Williams*, on the horrors of the system of transportation was read far more widely than *Political Justice*. But it was from *Political Justice* that Wordsworth and Coleridge received their youthful inspiration; and from the same source Robert Owen derived many of his ideas—above all the idea that character is formed by environment, and that most of the evil in the world is due to bad instutitions and can be removed by rational education under conditions of social justice.

Paine, however, was the immediate leader of popular opinion, and he had failed to prevent the execution of the French King, had lost his influence in the Convention, and after the fall of the Gironde had even been imprisoned. But his misadventures had not inclined him to compromise; rather, they had moved him to more implacable logic. In 1796 and 1797 he published a second great work, *The Age of Reason*, in which, without regard to the dictates of prudence, he submitted the institutions and sacred books of the Christian Church to the same type of logical analysis to which he had already submitted monarchy and aristocracy. The book is an able and elementary exposition of what later became the "Higher Criticism." The claims of Moses to authorship, the pedigree of Christ, the account of the creation, the sanguinary habits of Jehovah and similar problems are dissected, and at the end very little is left of the Bible, or of the institutions of Christianity. The book is not atheist, but Deist; but that was no help to its defenders. Only the broadest-minded Unitarian could tolerate it, and the dissenters, who till then had been consistent if timid recruits to the reform movement, were henceforward as horrified as the bishops themselves.

It was hard enough for the British reformer to be charged with the wish to wreck all Christian establishments, but it was even harder because the mainspring of his own inspiration was failing. While Robespierre was alive, the torrents of blood poured out by the Terror had shocked and sickened many potential supporters. But it was still, up to the very day of the 10th of Thermidor, possible for the more austere revolutionary to draw inspiration from France. The men in charge of the Revolution were at least going forward, at whatever price, towards liberty, equality and fraternity. If they did not spare others, neither did they spare themselves, and compromise and corruption were as unknown to them as were fear and mercy. But with the fall of Robespierre the idealistic period of the Revolution was over. It was not possible for anyone at all to draw inspiration from Barras or the Abbé Sieyès. The British reformers had the task of defending the excesses and the decadence of a revolution in which they themselves had ceased to believe.

Only where national feeling reinforced social discontent was there strong enough enthusiasm to carry such a burden. The London Corresponding Society dwindled to a shadow, and the only active organizations were the United Scotsmen and the United Irishmen. (There may have been an organization of "United Englishmen," but its strength, its exact name, and even its existence are matters for dispute.) The United Scotsmen were powerful in 1797 and 1798: their oath survives and some information about their organization. Pikes were, probably, being manufactured fairly freely, but the United Scotsmen never came into conflict with the authorities, except perhaps at Tranent in August 1797. Here the Cinque Ports cavalry were called out against a population holding seditious opinions, and charged them as if they had been a foreign enemy, killing them in the corn-fields "like partridges." Eleven dead were officially reported; other bodies were found at the reaping of the harvest. Spies disrupted the organization and it seems to have disappeared about 1798.

The history of the United Irishmen, their unsuccessful revolt in 1798 and its aftermath in Emmet's rebellion of 1803, lies outside this narrative. But they intervened, indirectly at least, in England in the year 1797. In April and May of that year the Spithead fleet twice mutinied: these mutinies were not political, but far more in the nature of a strike against intolerable conditions. The pay of the seamen had remained the same as in the days of Charles II—19*s*. a month; it was in arrears, sometimes even for years; the food was even on paper insufficient, but was shorn of one-eighth of its nominal quantity by the universal and almost recognized peculation; port-leave was withheld—a very real grievance; the discipline was brutal and administered without restraint by commanders who were often of a violent temper. Certain admirals, such as Lord Howe, were deservedly loved, but despite romantic historians many more were deservedly hated for the example of cruelty which they set.

> "*Damn and blast old Admiral Jervis*
> *For he was no sailor's friend*"

was the seamen's song about Lord St. Vincent, and their verdict on many others.

During the second Spithead mutiny a delegation arrived at the Nore to organize the small fleet there in support; it came out duly on May 12. The Admiral was sent ashore, together with a selection of minor officers whom the men had decided to dismiss as bullies. Almost immediately they received the news that the Spithead mutineers had returned to work, satisfied by considerable concessions in the matter of food and wages. The expelled Spithead officers were not in fact put back in their command (though this was not formally promised) and written pardons had been granted to the mutineers. The Admiralty announced that the same concessions would be applied to the Nore, and waited for the seamen to resume duty.

They refused to do so. Their demands were confused, ranging from requiring a personal visit from Lords of the Admiralty to Sheerness to demanding a revision of the articles of war. Port-leave and payment of wages in arrears were probably the most serious of these, after the dismissal of brutal officers. "Dam my eyes if I understand your lingo or long proclamations," wrote Henry Long, seaman on the *Champion*, to the Lords of the Admiralty, "but, in short, give us our due at once and no more of it; till we go in search of the rascals the enemys of our country"; and most of his fellows would have echoed him. But others had more advanced views; Parker, their "Admiral," signed and probably wrote a manifesto which menacingly said: "The Age of Reason has at length revolved" (though it added, "we do not wish to adopt the plan of a neighbouring nation, however it may have been suggested"), and the red flag hung from the riggings.

After a few days the Nore mutineers were reinforced by nearly all Admiral Duncan's fleet, which had been bottling up the Dutch in the Texel; encouraged by this, they blockaded London, stopping all trade for several days and making over a hundred captures. There were many Irish among the sailors, and almost certainly many United Irishmen. These latter gained influence as the Admiralty remained obstinate, until at last they carried a resolution to take prizes and hand the fleet over to the French "as the only Government that understands the Rights of Man."

This month (May 12 to June 16) was a period of the acutest danger for the British Government. Even if the Fleet did not desert, only two ships were left with Duncan pretending to blockade the Dutch Fleet. Had the wind been more favourable and the French and their allies more alert, the long-expected invading force could have been landed without interference, and what would have been the consequence it is impossible to predict. King George's ministers were saved by the daring and ingenuity of a captain. With the permission of his superiors he took out a boat's crew one night and sank the buoys and put out the lights marking the shallows and sandbanks of the Thames estuary. The Nore mutineers found themselves trapped: no sailor would face those treacherous waters uncharted and without pilots. The crews began to fight within the vessels, but the decision was not in doubt. One by one the ships pulled down the red flag, and dropped down to Sheerness to surrender. Some of the ringleaders escaped in long-boats: Parker, the "Admiral," was hanged.

Under the influence of the mutiny, a number of repressive Acts were passed in 1797, including one which provided the penalty of transportation for administering unlawful oaths; and in 1798 another Act required the registration of newspapers, and punished the editor, printer, publisher, and even the casual possessor of a copy of an unlicensed sheet.

The mutiny was the last serious effort of the reformers in the British Isles. When, in 1799, further Acts strengthening the Government's powers of repression suppressed by name the London Corresponding Society, the United Irishmen, the United Scotsmen, and the United Englishmen, the last three were already practically extinct and the Corresponding Society expired without a struggle. One last tiny effort, like the final twitch of a dying body, was to occur in 1803, when a gallant army officer of Irish descent, Colonel Despard, with a few very poor and very weak followers, was denounced by a spy for plotting to kill the King and seize the Bank of England. Very little trust can be put in the spy's story, but it is known that Despard had been in touch with the unhappy Robert Emmet, and some ejaculations of his which have been preserved suggest that he believed he was part of an international plot of grave importance. But his following seems to have been microscopic; despite the intervention of Lord Nelson he was hanged and carried whatever secrets he had with him to the grave.

The reformist or revolutionary movement—the two adjectives may be used indifferently, for to advocate reform was in these years a revolutionary act—passed out of existence. It might almost be said that only two propagandists survived as links into the new century, Horne Tooke and Major Cartwright. They were dissimilar in almost every personal characteristic—Cartwright was dull, patient, respectable and tactless, Horne Tooke was witty, unreliable, disreputable and a polished gentleman—but they were alike in their indomitable courage and their possession of a vast erudition which they consistently misapplied, Horne Tooke incorrectly expounding philology and Major Cartwright misdescribing Anglo-Saxon political institutions. But if these two eccentric figures were the only ones which remained in the public eye, the propaganda of Thomas Hardy and Tom Paine was not for that reason forgotten. It was no longer safe to speak publicly about the *Rights of Man*, but the book itself remained hidden in many weavers' cottages and on dissenters' bookshelves: where its physical body was for safety's sake destroyed its arguments were printed indelibly in the readers' minds.

When the pressure of the war should be lifted it was certain that the reformers' principles would be revived and the anger of the people would be the sharper for its long suppression.

CHAPTER XIV

THE COMBINATION ACTS

BUT though political struggle was effectively made impossible, human life went on and some form of struggle was inevitable. Economic, or apparently economic, conflict in part took the place of political; there was no time, even in this most oppressive period of British history, in which the people were wholly quiescent. Yet an endeavour was made by their rulers to make even economic resistance impossible. The act against illegal oaths passed in 1797 against the Nore mutineers was used to break up existing Trade Unions; the Combination Acts of 1799 and 1800 outlawed them altogether.

But before the origin and provisions of these Acts are explained, it is necessary to go back a little in history to explain what were the societies which they suppressed and how they arose.

The history of Trade Unionism in the eighteenth century is one that can never be written; it was partly deliberately concealed, partly naturally so. With a certain amount of diffidence it may however be said that nearly all Trade Unions were a spontaneous coming-together of bodies that were already in existence and conceivably had been in existence for a long time. In most towns—the societies of which we are speaking were almost wholly urban—there would be one or more sociable clubs for each craft. The members of these clubs would be journeymen who had served their apprenticeship: unskilled workers, if they had such societies, have left no traces of them in history. The members sometimes would have been masters in the old days, and not infrequently some called themselves masters still, in such trades as felt-making, for example. In the seventeenth century this class had not infrequently attempted to use the "courts of yeomanry" in the gilds to arrest economic development and secure their own continued status as real masters, but without any success. Dependent now on work given out to them by richer masters, they were almost indistinguishable from the ordinary journeymen who worked in their own homes under the domestic system, and were as interested in maintaining trade customs, wages and piece-rates as the rest of the domestic craftsmen.

None of these trade clubs was a direct descendant of the old gilds, nor is it possible to claim any great antiquity for them. Clubs of journeymen hatters and compositors certainly date back to the seventeenth century, or possibly earlier; but even their claims to a continuous history are shaky and those of others, excepting the woolcombers, not even plausible. But in the eighteenth century journeymen's clubs of all crafts were well established and of great vitality.

Less established—indeed, ephemeral but recurrent—were county-wide or even larger unions of trades such as wool-combing, weaving, and other occupations which were run upon the "domestic system" already described. Intermittent references show that these workers were already in the habit of combining for short periods to achieve certain ends, often effectively. But these combinations, though they sometimes showed great activity for a time in petitioning Parliament to regulate their wages, or even in conducting wage-movements of their own over an entire county, seem to have been of brief continuous life: had any observer considered eighteenth-century working-class organizations worthy of study, it is almost certain he would have taken the urban trade club as their essential and most important unit.

These clubs met sometimes in coffee-houses, but more often in taverns—for there was no other available place of meeting. Sometimes the society would take its name from the public-house which sheltered it, as in the case of the Globe Coach-makers, or the Marquis of Granby Society of Carpenters; sometimes (we may conjecture) the reverse would happen and the house became named, say, the Jolly Painters, or the Bricklayers' Arms. The objects of the club were firstly—and most importantly—to buy beer and have cheerful evenings; secondly, to initiate and accept apprentices into the trade after they had served their legal time, with a solemn and rather ridiculous ceremonial possibly copied from the Freemasons; thirdly, to run sickness and burial funds; fourthly, to provide a "house of call" for the masters where skilled workers could be regularly found—a primitive Labour Exchange; fifthly, to insist on existing trade customs such as the limitation of apprentices being preserved, in which the members would usually have the support of the small working masters, who were for many years often to be found actually in their ranks. These, were, in all probability, all the usual objectives of these societies; not every society had them all, some had only a few, some no doubt stopped at the first. But given these objects, it was only natural that to them should be added, from time to time, that of defending wage-rates when attacked or even increasing them when the cost of living rose. Ostensibly, for reasons of prudence, the society would always remain in appearance only a friendly society.

Such societies were called *trade clubs*; a federation or union of them was a *trade union*. The trade club, later called a "lodge" and much later a branch, remained, however, even after the federation the most vital organ of the Union in the majority of cases. Always it imposed on the larger body its own ceremonial and habits of mind. Festivity was still to be a chief object: the earliest recorded Plumbers' Union actually paid its officers in beer. "Inside" and "Outside Tylers" (doorkeepers) protected the meetings, Presidents, Vice-Presidents and Wardens examined applicants about their fitness for membership, dressed in top-coats, three-cornered hats and false moustaches. Each new member was usually bound to loyalty by an alarming oath, enforced by a property sword at his breast and a painted skeleton before his eyes—no superfluous precautions, for there was no legal remedy for pilfering of funds or treachery of any kind. Continually, the more serious members of the union deprecated the attention spent on drinking and dressing-up, but their words were not to be effective for another fifty years. As late as 1843, the Chartist chief, Feargus O'Connor, was welcomed to Aberdeen by the United Bakers in their full lodge attire, consisting of startling "rich pink muslin suits with splendid turbans."

Such trade clubs, in trades where there was not much displacement of labour or introduction of new machinery, were regarded with almost as much complacency by the masters as by the men. They were unlikely to be disturbed; but when they united together, nationally or over a smaller area, they became much more formidable and more likely to be repressed. It was generally allowed—subject to the uncertainty of eighteenth-century law and the capriciousness of its enforcement—that such unions were of doubtful legality. There were about forty Acts forbidding them in specific trades, and almost any judge would decide that a confederation of workmen to raise wages was illegal. But a combination to secure the regulation of wages by Parliament, or to enforce the wages decreed by justices under a Parliamentary Act, was another matter: Parliament had received without complaint petitions from bodies with such objects and had even consented to meet their prayers. Furthermore, any action to repress them had to be brought before the High Court. Before this procedure could be completed the strike of which the employer complained would be over. Certain working men would indeed be punished, possibly rather viciously, but the complainant would not benefit.

It is not surprising then, that there are clear traces of fairly powerful unions in the eighteenth century. These unions are all of skilled or semi-skilled workers. Incidental references show that the Glasgow Coopers had a strong society in 1752, the London Sailmakers (called a "burial society") in 1740, and the Newcastle Shoemakers as early as 1719. The Woolcombers had a West of England Society by 1741: in 1752 the Norwich woolcombers left the town and camped out for several weeks, imitating the Roman plebs, until their demand for the dismissal of an unapprenticed man was granted. The London Brushmakers were another early union, the London Tailors had in 1720 "7,000 or upwards" of members. The London Goldbeaters were in possession of large union funds by 1777; the Liverpool Shipwrights, by a freak of electoral chance, had votes and played a predominant part in choosing the two M.P.s. The Spitalfields silk-weavers secured a regulatory act in 1773 (which controlled their wages and conditions) partly through their organization and partly by the aid of the Wilkite Lord Mayor. The "Original Society of Painters" dates from 1779: other references show numerous societies of worsted weavers, framework knitters, Sheffield grinders and other trades, and printers. The hatters in 1771 had a national federation.

It was against such a union, "a combination of journeymen millwrights within the Metropolis and twenty-five miles round" that the House of Commons received a petition from a group of master millwrights on 5 April, 1799. The petition was referred to a Committee which reported, as might have been done at any time during the eighteenth century, that such a combination should be repressed, and power be given to the magistrates to fix millwrights' wages. But this procedure, which had been universally accepted in the earlier part of the century, was now being seriously questioned, ever since the repeal of the Woollen Cloth Weavers' Act in 1757. It was doubted whether the power of magistrates to fix wages was salutary, though whether the discouragement of combination was equally unwise was not even considered. Wilberforce, whose zeal for negro liberty was only equalled by his enthusiasm for repressing insubordination in white workers, took the opportunity to demand that the affair of the millwrights be used as an occasion to introduce a general law providing summary remedies against combinations. After a certain amount of parliamentary delay, Wilberforce's proposal was adopted, and the bill was passed with too great speed for any effective opposition to be organized. When it was law, protests began to pour in, and an amending bill was passed the next year, but the changes it made were designed mainly to improve the legal drafting and gave no appreciable relief.

The Acts, as passed, made liable (for the first offence) to three months in gaol, or two months' hard labour, any working man who combined with another to gain an increase in wages or a decrease in hours, or solicited anyone else to leave work, or objected to working with any other workman. The sentence was to be given by two magistrates, who should not belong to the trade involved. Appeal was forbidden unless "two sufficient sureties in the penalty of twenty pounds" were provided. Such sureties were outside the means of most working men, and the sustaining of a defence was made more difficult by a provision that anyone who contributed to the expense of a person convicted under the Act would be fined £10 and the receiver of the subscription another £5. The removal of a conviction by *certiorari* (a process which guards against biased or interested judges) was specifically forbidden, and a further provision which excited great indignation was that defendants were forced to give evidence against one another. Appeals were, however, allowed; and, when the workers could find money to appeal, the convictions granted by the magistrates were very often quashed on the score of irregularities in the procedure. This was partly because the higher courts, in this as in many other fields, objected to the extension of the magistrates' jurisdiction, and were continually on the look-out for technical flaws. In most cases, however, the victims of the magistrates had no money to pay for an appeal.

The Acts also nominally forbade employers' combinations, without the provision about evidence and without a penalty of imprisonment. But this prohibition was never enforced, though employers' combinations were open and frequent in the next quarter of a century. Gravener Henson, a Nottingham bobbin net-maker, and a patient and able adviser and friend of the working men, made the only pertinacious attempt to enforce this portion of the Act. He was met in official circles with such consistent opposition and refusal to act that he abandoned the task in despair.

Attempts have been made to argue that the effect of the Combination Acts was small. The reasons put forward are, in brief, that the Acts did not apply to Scotland, that most recorded cases were, as before, taken to the High Courts under existing laws, and that many unions undoubtedly continued to exist. But these objections do not stand up to serious examination. Influenced by the passing of the Acts, the Scottish judges henceforward re-interpreted the Common Law so as to hold all combinations illegal, and the Scottish workers were soon no better off than the English. That most recorded cases are before the High Court is not surprising. The intention of the Acts was to make combination an offence that could be dealt with summarily in order that strikes might be broken. The proceedings of courts of summary jurisdiction were not recorded: to this day, police-court proceedings are not extensively noticed in the Press and in the eighteenth century they were scarcely printed at all. What the Act did, in addition to providing a summary procedure and thus making punishment (with a comparatively light sentence) speedier and easier, was to make conviction much less uncertain in the case of serious "offenders," who were still prosecuted in the High Court under Common Law. Such leaders could now be accused before a judge of Common Law conspiracy to violate the statute, and proof of the mere fact of combination, without any proof of further action, was enough to secure a conviction. It is certainly true, as will be seen, that unions continued to exist. Some of them did so by resorting to methods of great secrecy and, occasionally, intimidation. Others were shattered and driven out of existence. In fact, their life or death depended on the caprice of the magistracy. In corporate towns, where trade clubs had for long been known and were viewed with indulgence, they were likely to be undisturbed, unless they attracted the hostile attentions of the borough magistrates by their militancy. In the county areas, their existence depended on the lethargy of the county magistracy. This was disturbed fairly frequently by pressing circulars from the Home Office, and their life was short and uncertain. In mining areas, the magistrates were also the coal-lords, and the miners were in consequence fairly continuously repressed. The miners were in any case a class of workers with very few rights: the Scottish miners were indeed only formally released from bondage by an Act of 1755 which had to be amended in 1799 to make it effective.

The previous forty-odd Acts which had prohibited combinations in separate trades had had for theoretical justification the argument that magistrates were empowered to fix wages and that combinations were interfering with the sphere of the law. This excuse no longer remained when the comprehensive Combination Acts were passed. The workers pathetically endeavoured to enforce the existing laws for wage-fixing and the regulation of industry, but as soon as they did so the instrument broke in their hands. The West of England and Yorkshire weavers hired an attorney in 1802 to prosecute employers for failing to observe the Elizabethan Acts prescribing conditions of apprenticeship and methods of wage-fixing. Parliament promptly suspended the Acts dealing with that industry, and annually renewed the suspension. A number of London societies combined in 1810 to try a similar enforcement in London: they received an occasional conviction without costs, while heavy costs were granted against them if any flaw could be detected. Lord Ellenborough ruled on appeal that any trades which were new or had substantially varied since the days of Elizabeth (such as that of engineer) were outside the Acts. The next year, on a plea requiring the Kentish justices to hear a petition for fixing wages, he granted a *mandamus* remarking that though the judges must hear the petition they need not fix a wage. No wage, naturally, was fixed. Apprenticeship provisions, which it was less easy to ignore, were from time to time enforced. The same Lord Ellenborough in 1813, in an action brought by the operative saddlers, sustained the apprenticeship provisions. Great alertness, however, as well as considerable courage, was needed to enforce them. In the building trades, for example, by the end of the war it was alleged by the operative masons that apprenticeship had "wholly disappeared"—a patent exaggeration but one certainly pointing to a great weakening of the custom.

The most cruel, or most laughable (according to the social class of the observer), deception of the working class was that of the Scottish cotton-weavers. In 1812 they appealed to the Quarter Sessions to fix wages. The employers, denying the power of Quarter Sessions, appealed to the Court of Session. The Court declared that the magistrates had the power to fix wages, and the operatives returned to the original Court. Now the employers refused to attend, but the magistrates required the attendance of 130 witnesses from the operatives before they would endorse the rates proposed. Eventually they declared the rates reasonable, but failed to make an order enforcing them. The case had cost the working men £3,000, and the employers almost unanimously refused to accept the result. Immediately a nation-wide strike broke out to enforce the magistrates' rates. The police then arrested the leaders under the Common Law for the crime of combination; they were sentenced to various terms of imprisonment and the strike was broken.

Eventually, the Acts empowering judges to fix rates were repealed in 1813, and the apprenticeship Acts in 1814. By the end of the war there was not even a pretence of protection for the worker.

Long before this the great majority of workers had realized that they must rely on themselves alone. Certain unions which were favourably placed, in trades not much affected by the economic changes, were able to retain and even improve their position by cautious action and apparently individual abstention from working for "black" masters. The cashbook of the Preston Joiners' Society, dating from 1807 and possibly the oldest remaining trade union document, records a placid and discreet existence, in which money is received from initiations and spent on beer, while the officers in consultation with the employers are apparently able to prevent any unfortunate incidents. This uneventful history goes on till 1833. When an occurrence such as inducing a blackleg to cease blacklegging has to be noted it is charitably and prudently entered as "to Poor Brother for Leaving Town . . . 3/6." There were many other societies whose history must have been similar. George White, clerk to the Committee which secured the repeal of the Acts in 1824, even made the statement that "shoemakers, printers, papermakers, shipbuilders, tailors, etc.," had been unaffected by the Acts; this, though an extreme exaggeration for the writer's purposes at the moment, had a kernel of truth. Such societies continued to exist and their relief of "tramps" (travelling members on the road seeking for work) in particular was not interfered with, though it might conceal a discreet form of industrial pressure, in cases where men were "tramping" because of a dispute. Unions which were active or in unprotected trades, however, rarely had so peaceful a history. The Society of Ironfounders, founded in 1810, is traditionally stated to have had to meet at night on the moors in the Midland area, and its books and records were buried in the ground. The London tailors had "all but a military system. Their orders come from the Executive and are always obeyed. There are upwards of twenty regular or *Flint* houses of all in London: each house has a delegate and they elect five other delegates who are technically called the Town." Violence, as was later admitted by the Seamen's Loyal Standard (a union concealed in a friendly society) might be used against blacklegs; even if it was not, the impact of working-class public opinion could express itself in other highly deterrent ways. The Coventry Weavers' Aggregate Committee punished a breach of its rules, by member or non-member, by having the offender tied on to an ass, face to tail, and driven about the town "exposed to the ridicule and violence of the mob."

But, in general, despite these protections, the story of the years from 1800 to 1815 is industrially one of defeat and oppression. The Acts placed the working men at the mercy of two classes, the English gentlemen and the English employers. They depended on the fairness of the first for the application of the law, and on either for the law to be put in motion—for the magistrates, using spies and informers, were often more active than the employers in starting prosecutions. Their fate was what might have been expected. "However heavy the sentence passed" upon men accused of combination, wrote Francis Place, "and however rigorously it was inflicted, not the slightest feeling of compassion was manifested by anybody for the unfortunate sufferers. Justice was entirely out of the question: they could seldom obtain a hearing before a magistrate, never without impatience or insult. . . . Could an accurate account be given of proceedings, of hearings before magistrates, trials at sessions and in the Court of the King's Bench, the gross injustice, the foul invective, and terrible punishments inflicted would not, after a few years have passed away, be credited on any but the best evidence." And again, of a section of workers most in need of protection, he writes, "the sufferings of persons employed in the cotton manufacture were beyond credibility; they were drawn into combinations, betrayed, prosecuted, convicted, sentenced, and monstrously severe punishments inflicted on them; they were reduced to and kept in the most wretched state of existence."

Penalties applied for combination had included, before the repeal of the Acts, public whipping, but for the most part imprisonment and ruin sufficed. For the usual procedure, one instance must suffice, a very notorious one in the centre of the kingdom. The compositors on *The Times* were in 1810 prosecuted for the crime of combination. They were sentenced to terms of imprisonment ranging from nine months to two years. Sir John Sylvester—"Bloody Black Jack"—in sentencing them denounced them for "a most wicked conspiracy" to injure "the very employers who gave you bread." Less typical, but in no way reprobated, were the proceedings against the Durham miners, who, in the winter of 1809, came out on strike against an attempt by the coal-owners to vary the period of their "binding" to the miners' disadvantage. So many "leaders" were arrested that Durham gaol and the House of Correction were overfilled and the surplus were imprisoned in the Bishop's stables. The strike momentarily ended in a truce, negotiated by the Rector of Brauncepeth and the captain of the militia, whom the miners trusted when they would not their employers, but ultimately the use of the law broke the men's resistance.

CHAPTER XV

"KING LUDD"

THE natural recourse of the workers was to rioting and violence. Sometimes, since early nineteenth-century police were inefficient and timorous, this could be quite effective. The cotton-weavers, when Parliament in 1808 refused their appeal for a minimum wage Act, went on to quite extensive rioting, which was for the moment successful in stopping any attempt to degrade their condition. But they too were shortly afterwards defeated by a circumstance that undid many other efforts to keep up the standard of living. This was the sudden fluctuation caused by war demands. Throughout this period, with the brief intermission of the Peace of Amiens, Great Britain was at war with Napoleon. The chief industries, coal, iron and clothing of all kinds, but expecially the last, were subjected to sudden expansions and contractions. Shortly after the 1808 riots the Orders in Council and the Berlin Decrees together heavily damaged the cotton goods market, and the American War in 1812 completed the ruin: the weavers were soon glad enough to take whatever wages the employers offered them. Prosperity had laid the foundations for such disasters: the origin of the collapse lay in the inrush of un-qualified persons into handloom-weaving as a result of the high prices reigning at the beginning of the period and the rapid increase in the supply of factory-spun yarn. The Committee on Handloom Weavers in 1835 worked out an average scale of weekly earnings of weavers in this period. In the period 1797 to 1804 these were 26s. 8d.; from 1804 to 1811, 20s.; from 1811 to 1818, 14s. 7d. With these, the Committee calculated the weaver could purchase (in equal quantities of flour, oatmeal, potatoes and meat) 281 lb. of food in the first period, 238 lb. in the second, and 131 lb. in the third.

Only two ways out remained to the workers. The one was to wreck the establishments of employers who paid unfair rates, or used labour-saving machinery. The other was to agitate for the reform of the State which held them down and prevented them from organizing to relieve their misery. Both were highly dangerous. The first was a counsel of desperation, and was not taken widely till 1811, though as early as 1802 the Somerset shearmen were destroying gig-mills (machines for raising the nap on cloth, instead of hand-teasing); and, finding no evidence, the Lord Lieutenant, seeking to put them down, complained "the working clothiers are unfortunately true to each other." The second was one which the workers themselves were slow to adopt. It required the very bitter experiences of the war to turn them from "Church and King" men to reformers; but by the time of Waterloo it had largely been done By 1812 the woolcombers, who had a powerful national organization, were reputed as generally seditious and Republican. Similarly in 1811, the renewed rejection of an appeal for a minimum wage Act had taught the cotton-weavers the same lesson. "Had you possessed 70,000 votes" reported back their committee to the weavers "for the election of members to sit in that House, would your application have been treated with such indifference, not say inattention? We believe not."

No relaxation whatever of industrial oppression was permitted the sufferers. But some instalment of political liberty was to come. The interlude of the Peace of Amiens (March 1802 to May 1803) was too brief to make a change, and the peace-time Prime Minister, Addington, was little more than a shadow of Pitt, who resumed his office when war began again. But everything which is based on human lives, even political tyranny, must have a term. In the first month of 1806 the chief organizer of the repression was removed. "At last Mr. Pitt died," reports Madden, the historian of the United Irishmen; "it was a joyful day. The prisons were thrown open, where many an honest man had lain for many days." The relief was greatest in Ireland; there was no such general gaol-delivery in England, but the relief here also was genuine, Later, Ministers were to show that they could be more cruel and less scrupulous than Pitt, but none were to excite the same sustained dislike and contempt. Partly, no doubt, this was because sycophants had praised the "heaven-born Minister" to nausea, but far more because he was generally believed to have done evil knowing that it was evil. Sidmouth might, later, be presumed to know no better; but Pitt had been a reformer, just as he had advocated Catholic emancipation, and had sacrificed both causes. At the height of the oppression he had told his friends that "Tom Paine was quite right"; but that private opinion did not affect his public actions. So, not wholly fairly, since he honestly held the war to be of over-riding importance, he was held to have willingly persecuted those on whose side he knew justice to be, and was rewarded with the peculiar hatred reserved for those who are treacherous as well as cruel.

The intermission secured by his death was not long and not in itself important. The story can be told in a very few sentences. A predominantly Whig ministry, called the "Ministry of All the Talents" and including Fox, took office and held it for a little over a year. It passed one Act of great importance and beneficence, but it was an Act which con-ferred no relief upon the English or Scottish people: it was the Act abolishing the slave trade. For the rest it did no more than show that the opposition Whigs would make no essential change in the Government; and, Fox being dead, it fell in 1807 to make way for the first of a series of Governments which differed in few respects from that of Pitt.

But in a very dark room a small light appears brilliant; the small relief of 1806 was a great thing to those who experienced it, the more so that the liberties they had recovered could not be at once withdrawn. It was not made possible, it is true, to advocate the dethronement of the King, the establishment of a Republic, the expropriation of the aristocracy, or the destruc-tion of the Church, still less to organize (as had once been done) bodies to achieve any or all of these things. But it was once more possible to demand, in discreet phraseology, a radical reform of Parliament, and to expose specific acts of oppression or corruption. Moreover, an endeavour was made again to use what channels of constitutional protest existed, though the organization of societies to that end remained throughout the war too dangerous to be widely attempted.

The most notable of these endeavours was the Westminster election of 1807. Westminster was a constituency of over

10,000 electors, but it had not till this year been a sure popular seat—indeed, on occasion it was regarded as a pocket borough in the gift of a couple of dukes. Francis Place, an ex-working man, now a master-tailor in Charing Cross, in this year took (according to his own account, which probably exaggerates his importance) almost single-handed the task of organizing it on behalf of the Radicals, as they were beginning to be called. Their candidate was Sir Francis Burdett—a well-known reformer, who himself gave no assistance, not believing that so large, poverty-stricken and ignorant an electorate could be merely persuaded instead of being bribed into voting. To the general surprise he was elected by a handsome majority, his colleague being another reformer, Lord Cochrane, the famous sailor. Sheridan, the official Whig candidate, polled so badly that Lord Cochrane as a matter of civility withdrew his inspectors so that Sheridan might poll the same voters over and over again until his figure seemed not indecently small.

From the date of this exciting election the reform movement began to revive. The Parliamentary leadership (indeed, one might say membership, for he had few or no consistent followers) devolved on Burdett, who was exceedingly rich from his marriage with Miss Sophia Coutts. Lord Cochrane, Samuel Whitbread, the brewer, M.P. for Bedford, and Matthew Wood, the London M.P. and City alderman, were now, or later, almost as energetic, but there were few others. Three years later Sir Francis staged a conflict with the House which was clearly modelled on Wilkes's example and had nearly as great a success. John Gale Jones, the organizer of a Covent Garden debating society, having been sent to Newgate by the House for holding a discussion on the exclusion of strangers from the House, Burdett delivered a speech demanding his release. He then published the speech; the House of Commons, declaring this a breach of privilege, voted to send him to the Tower. Burdett immediately fortified his house and arranged with the City authorities to have any emissaries who attempted to seize him arrested. This trick had been successfully carried out by Wilkes in 1771 on the occasion of an attempted arrest of printers for publishing an account of parliamentary debates. But Wilkes was more skilled at timing than his imitators; the

City authorities were not on hand when the soldiers came. Burdett had to be satisfied with a melodramatic arrest, being seized while he was instructing his son to construe the text of Magna Carta from the original Latin. But though he was confined in the Tower for a few weeks, his popularity and the cause of reform were considerably benefited, and another Wilkite device was revived in the presentation to the House of Commons of insulting addresses and petitions from Middlesex and Westminster electors.

What Burdett and others began to do with the spoken word, an equally powerful agent was beginning to do with the written. William Cobbett (1763–1835), perhaps the most powerful political pamphleteer in English history, in 1806 considered himself to be an opponent of Parliamentary reform, which he still intermittently denounced. A farmer's boy by origin, then a private soldier, then a teacher of English and highly successful pamphleteer and journalist in America, he had returned from that country with a hatred of democracy and an acrid patriotism. Armed with these and a bitter pen, he had founded the *Political Register* to attack Jacobinical ideas and defend his ideal of England. Gradually he realized that the conditions in England were not in fact what he had imagined them to be, but in 1806 he looked confidently to his friends in the new Government to put an end to the corruption and oppression which he had observed, and to restore the peaceful idyllic England of squire and farmer which he believed he remembered from his youth. When they did nothing he found himself forcibly in alliance with men like Burdett and Cochrane; this was one forward step in his education. Another was made in 1809 when he took a large part in exposing very nearly the highest person in the land—the Duke of York, Commander-in-Chief—for taking part in the corrupt sale of commissions through his mistress. This led to a sharper and decisive lesson: the Government turned on him immediately after for an article denouncing the flogging of British soldiers under guard of German mercenaries, when they had demanded arrears of pay. Cobbett was made personally aware of the danger of defending the poor and defenceless: he was fined £2,000, sent to prison for two years and ordered to find sureties for good behaviour for seven years to follow.

One other propagandist requires mention, though his voice was far feebler than Cobbett's. Thomas Spence (1750–1814) came gradually back into the public eye at this time, having received a little passing notice in the days of the Corresponding Society. "Spence's Plan" was a scheme of land nationalization by which parishes would own the land and rent it out, so providing for all public expenditure. Spence's arguments anticipated much of Henry George's more famous and effective thesis. His personal oddness, bitterness and unsociability, the result of poverty and suffering, kept him lonely. He conducted his propaganda by pushing a large closed barrow from which he sold his Plan, his "IMP'ORTANT TRI'AL OV TOMIS SPENS" (for he was also a spelling reformer) and other papers. His ideas were sounder and more far-reaching than those of many who looked patronizingly on him. His followers were very few, very poor and very simple-hearted; his importance lies not so much in himself as in the organization he left behind, the "Spencean Philanthropists," whose innocence was to enable the Government agents to use them for an exceedingly vile purpose.

The use of spies as provocative agents, the purpose to which we refer, was not a new one. Used once against the Jacobites, it had been practised, for political purposes, under Pitt, especially against the Irish: the earliest known occurrence of an industrial spy seems to be one in 1807. It was not applied on any extensive scale in industry however until after his death, in the years 1811 and 1812, in the first cases of what are known as the Luddite riots.

These riots were the reply to oppression of men who had been deprived of any other means of resistance. They were not a "mass movement" in the modern sense—that is to say, the Luddites did not constitute the bulk of the population in the counties (Nottinghamshire, Yorkshire, Lancashire and Cheshire) where they mainly operated. They were a picked band of daring and desperate men, who received the passive support and countenance of their fellow workers. It is not certain whether they were supported by the existing clubs or unions or not. They claimed to be directed by one Ned Ludd, whose "office" was said to be in Sherwood Forest. If such a person existed at all, it is not known who he was. He was certainly believed in by large numbers of persons, and the Luddites clearly had some organizing brain behind them.

In Nottinghamshire the Luddite campaign began, intermittently, as early as the spring of 1811, but did not get into full swing until November and went on till February of the next year. It was not directed against new machinery in this case (despite the statement of the House of Lords Committee later) but against the abuse of old machinery. The framework knitters (stockingers) of this county had found their livelihood half-ruined by the war, and on top of this their condition was sharply worsened by the selling on a large scale of "cut-ups" made on "wide frames." A stocking frame is narrow, but there were in existence a large number of wide frames for knitting pantaloons and fancy stockings called "twills." Twills had gone out of fashion; pantaloons, whose chief market was the Continent, could not be sold because of the war. Unscrupulous owners had their weavers weave large pieces of cloth on the now idle wide frames and then cut the pieces by scissors into the shape of stockings, gloves, or whatever it might be. These "cut-ups" were then stitched up: having no selvedges like the true stockings they rapidly fell into pieces. But the shoddy was ruining the market. The Luddites appeared in village after village and smashed the wide frames, and any other frames worked by unapprenticed labour. A good many of the masters, though they did not approve of the methods, approved of the results. Certainly, there was no stopping the Luddites. Troops ran up and down helplessly, baffled by the silence and connivance of the workers. Nottingham Town alone was safe: outside, a thousand illegal frames were broken and a large amount of shoddy stuff forcibly destroyed. As a result, the "cut-up" trade was sharply checked and wages temporarily rose as much as two shillings a dozen pieces.

Parliament, frightened and vicious, passed a Bill making frame-breaking (already punishable by fourteen years' transportation) a capital offence. But, unfortunately for the hopes of the Home Office officials, most of the Nottingham Luddites who were ever captured had been caught before the Bill was passed. When the assizes came on in March, therefore, it did not appear possible to hang them, unless the judge, Mr. Justice Bayley, consented to convict for burglary in addition. But this judge was a man of kindly sentiment and a regard for the law: though he sentenced the seven men found guilty to transportation for seven or fourteen years, he saw no reason to bring in the death penalty by a trick, and even wrote privately to the Government suggesting that it should diminish the penalty as the cases deserved lenience. His advice was rejected, and it was made certain that he would not preside at the trial of any more Luddites.

No assistance for any of the Luddites came from the official opposition in Parliament. Grey, Grenville, and the other Whigs saw nothing that called for their intervention. Sir Francis Burdett, Samuel Whitbread and a few others alone protested in the Commons against the Bill for the death penalty: in the Lords, Byron added a more famous but equally ineffective plea in his most memorable speech there. "Suppose it passed," he said of the Bill. "Suppose one of these men, as I have seen them—meagre with famine, sullen with despair, careless of a life which your lordships are perhaps about to value at something less than the price of a stocking-frame—suppose this man (and there are a thousand such from whom you may select your victims) dragged into court to be tried for this new offence by this new law, still there are two things wanting to convict and condemn him; and these are, in my opinion, twelve butchers for a jury and a Jeffreys for a judge."

The judges who dealt with the Lancashire Luddites of 1812, Baron Thompson and Mr. Justice Le Blanc, did not perhaps deserve the name of Jeffreys; but neither they nor their colleagues in Cheshire and Yorkshire were swayed by any untimely sentimentality. The outbreaks which they aided in repressing were more alarming than the Nottingham explosions; or at least were made to appear so. In Lancashire and Cheshire, the chief objects of the machine-breakers were the power-looms. In Yorkshire the shearing-machines, which had thrown the cutters (or "croppers") out of work, were the main enemy. The Luddites broke them down with "Great Enoch," the heavyhammer made by Enoch and James Taylor, who also made the shearing-frames.

> *Great Enoch still shall lead the van,*
> *Stop him who dare! Stop him who can!*

they sang, and for weeks the boast was justified. Mixed up with machine-breaking was what was no more than hunger-rioting. Famine was a general as powerful as Ludd: the magistrates denounced alternately plots to wreck factories and to sell potatoes forcibly at 1*d.* a lb. cheaper. Food riots on a large scale occurred at Oldham and Middleton; they were intimately linked up with an attempt to wreck Burton's power-looms in the latter town. Mr. Burton, defending his looms, killed five Luddites, and for this his house was burned down. The owner of Rawfolds Mill in Yorkshire, in April 1812, similarly drove off the Luddites, who till then had been almost unresisted, and his fire left two men dying. He was reputed to have refused them water or a doctor unless they would name their fellow Luddites. They died silent; but one or perhaps two attempts were made to assassinate him in revenge. An equally ruthless manufacturer, William Horsfall, was actually murdered at the end of the same month.

Such events were enough to put more courageous persons than the northern manufacturers in a panic; but further evidence was provided—almost, provided by themselves—to increase their terrors. "B," a spy whose real name was Bent, worked up to the best of his ability a national plot for an insurrection, based upon an illegal oath which he himself produced. Stones, another spy whose reference letter was "/S/", economically brought his father into the same business, and "/S/" and "Old /S/" continually received their wages from the local magistrates, of whom the most credulous and violent was a Colonel Fletcher of Bolton. Stones's chief objective was to collect enough people to burn down the power-loom factory at West Houghton. Two rallies were called by him vainly, though he told the weavers that "those who did not attend would be in greater danger than those who did attend, and would be torn out of their beds." The second rally ended in a dispirited and unsuccessful attempt to parade on Dean Moor, which turned out to be fatal to those who were afterwards identified by spies. When West Houghton factory was in fact burnt down on 24 April 1812, it seems to have been a spontaneous movement which the Stones family had not controlled at all.

Numbers of the Lancashire employers and magistrates were now convinced that a general rising would occur on May 1. Where they drew this information from, and why this date should so early in history have been a bogy, is unknown; but the insurrection was a phantasm. The day passed without disturbance. Yet this was not the most absurd of their suspicions. One of the most preposterously mendacious of the informers, a man called Lawson, announced that the chief organizer of insurrection went by the name of Lord Lovat. A warrant was duly issued, by the credulous Home Secretary, for the arrest of this peer, though even Sidmouth might have been (one would have thought) suspicious at the citing of a name which was that of the chief supporter of the Young Pretender in 1745.

No Lord Lovat was found, and Lawson was discredited, but the work of the spies as a whole was undemolished. The sentences at the assizes on the unhappy men who were caught reflected the fears of their governors. Fourteen death sentences were pronounced by the Cheshire Commission, and two of these were actually executed. In Yorkshire six men were given seven years' transportation for administering illegal oaths. Seventeen others were hanged, and one transported for life. In Lancashire, the activities of Bent and the Messrs. Stones were largely responsible for the convictions, and the sentences are perhaps worthy of close inspection. Four persons (including a woman of fifty-four) were sentenced to death for forcing dealers to sell bread, butter and cheese at a lower price than they would have done otherwise. An honest (or, in the opinion of the prosecution, an obstinately seditious) juror prevented any convictions for the riot at Burton's Middleton mill. Fifteen men or boys were sentenced to seven years' transportation for accepting or administering Stones's or Bent's oaths. Three men and a boy of sixteen were sentenced to death for the burning of West Houghton mill. The boy, Abraham Charlson, had three soldier brothers, and had acted as a sort of sentinel at the burning, pacing up and down with a scythe. He was young for his age, and when he was brought to the scaffold he "called on his mother for help, thinking she had the power to save him."

Against this black picture one lighter incident may be put. Nadin, the active and unscrupulous Deputy Constable of Manchester, worked up a case against no less than thirty-eight Lancashire reformers with the aid of a spy named Fleming. The counsel for the defence were Scarlett, Brougham and Williams. The evidence of the spy was torn to pieces by the lawyers and the judge directed the jury accordingly. Every man was acquitted.

But a single success like this did not save the Luddites. Their movement collapsed, having met with no successes except in Nottinghamshire. Even here the revival was short-lived. Prudently, the stockingers followed up their temporary success by organizing a national union, with Nottingham as centre and *Taisez-vous* as motto. In 1813 it had 2,390 members and £195 funds. It lasted for little more than a year: in 1814 a committee of the employers broke it into pieces. This committee was in itself a "combination" and illegal under the Combination Acts, but though it used these Acts to stamp out the Union nobody thought of invoking the law against it.

THE PEACE WITHOUT A PARALLEL

CHAPTER XVI

BRITAIN AFTER WATERLOO

PEACE came at last, on Napoleon's final fall in 1815, after the episode of the "Hundred Days." As long as the war lasted the question of Reform, which had seemed urgent after the American War of Independence, could be thrust aside; for there was no will to deal with domestic grievances until the country was at peace.

Great Britain emerged from the war far richer as a country than she had been in 1793; for both agricultural and industrial production had greatly advanced. But if the total wealth was greater, much more had the burden of public debt increased. Before the American War of Independence the total National Debt had been under £150,000,000; and that had seemed a monstrous total to the people of the time. After the American War it stood at nearly £260,000,000; and Adam Smith and his contemporaries regarded such a burden as almost past bearing. But by 1816 the total debt, including unfunded debt, had reached about £860,000,000, or more than one-third of the estimated capital wealth of the nation. On the average, each citizen of the country owed his fellow-citizens nearly £45—or, to put the situation in a truer aspect, the poorer citizens owed the rich the best part of the total, for under the current system of taxation, especially as the income tax was promptly repealed as soon as the war was over, it was clear enough that the poor would be called upon to foot the bill.

It is the way of wars, at their ending, to cause first a furious and short-lived boom, and then a slump, far deeper and more prolonged. For when peace returns there are always both urgent orders that must be placed, almost regardless of cost, and optimistic producers and traders who hope to make a good thing out of the reopened markets. But before long the trouble begins. Some countries, if not all, have been impoverished by warfare; and after their most immediately clamant needs have been met the buying drops away, and the stocks of goods got ready by the optimists begin to pile up unsold.

There are apt, too, to be currency troubles; for in modern times at least no great war has ever been financed without some sort of inflation. In 1814 the British wholesale price-level was roughly twice as high as it had been in 1790. By 1816 it was only about one-third above the pre-war level; and, after a brief rally, in 1818, it resumed its fall, sinking to well below the pre-war level before 1830. Now, falling prices, even when most of the costs of production are falling too, discourage industry; for who that can wait will buy at once when he hopes to buy cheaper by waiting? Falling prices, moreover, raise the real value of all debts fixed in money. In this period they kept raising the real burden of the national debt; and they also discouraged merchants and employers from borrowing capital, which would have to be repaid later at an increased cost in real goods.

Nothing, however—nothing, that is, within the imaginations of contemporary statesmen and financiers, save a few such as the Attwoods, who, though leading bankers, were denounced as cranks—could check the fall in prices. With the cessation of the special war demand and the spread of unemployment, wheat prices, as we have seen, came down from 126s. 6d. a quarter in 1812 to 65s. 7d. in 1815. There was panic among landlords and farmers; and Parliament promptly rushed through an almost prohibitive Corn Law in order to keep up the price. No wheat at all was to be brought into Great Britain from abroad until the price rose above 80s. a quarter. For the time being, wheat, owing to bad harvests as well as to the law, responded. It rose to 78s. 6d. in 1816, and 96s. 11d. in 1817. Then it fell again, to 86s. 3d., 74s. 6d., 67s. 10d., 56s. 1d. and 44s. 7d. in the five following years. Farmers, with high rents still to pay, became active in county movements, and many who had bought their land at war prices with borrowed money were ruined. Then, gradually, rents came down, and prices again rose—to 53s. 4d. in 1823, 63s. 11d. in 1824, and 68s. 6d. in the boom year, 1825. Thereafter, up to 1832, the price varied between 58s. 6d. and 66s. 4d. These were prices too high for the poor; but it became clear that the grossly inflated war prices were gone for ever. Even the Corn Law was modified in 1828, despite the protests of those whom Cobbett called the "agriculturasses," prohibition being abandoned in favour of a sliding scale of duty. When wheat was under 62s. a quarter, imported wheat was dutiable at 25s. 8d. For every rise of 1s. in the price there was a shilling off the duty, up to 73s. When that price was reached, wheat could be brought in at a nominal duty of 1s.—but it never was.

In 1815, during the short-lived boom, British exports were valued at well over £51,000,000—more than £3,000,000 above the previous record of 1810. They fell to under £42,000,000 in each of the two following years, and, after a recovery in 1818, fell again to £35,000,000 in 1819, when quantities as well as prices were sharply reduced. For in that year the export trade to Europe and to the American continent—then of approximately equal importance—both fell off together, that to North America catastrophically, following speculative attempts to expand the West Indian and North American markets at far too rapid a rate. The result at home was widespread unemployment and distress, accompanied by active wage-cutting—first and foremost in the expanding factory trades, but thereafter, as home demand fell off, in nearly every branch of production.

The worst-off of all were, indeed, the handloom-weavers. For as we have seen, the advance of the power-loom in the cotton industry—it did not happen until later in the woollen trades—was already reducing the handloom-weaver to the condition of a "marginal" worker. The progressive employer would seek to instal in his factory enough power-driven machinery to meet the minimum demand for his wares—for he could not afford to leave his valuable machinery unemployed. More and more, the handloom-weavers were getting only the residue of the work, after the factories had taken what they could; and consequently the home-workers bore most of the brunt of depression in the bad years. This explains **why**

"Luddites" in Lancashire and Yorkshire went about wrecking the new machines, and why even Ricardo, greatest among orthodox economists, was impelled to add to the later editions of his *Principles of Political Economy* a chapter in which he expressed his doubts concerning the benefits of machinery to the working classes. Most of the economists were not troubled by such doubts, though they were expressed by Malthus as well as Ricardo. As soon as the worst of the post-war troubles were over, the economists stooped to conquer the poor. They supplemented their manuals for perusal by the educated classes with special manuals for the vulgar, designed to teach them, despite appearances to the contrary, the real benefits of the factory system.

Lord Brougham and Charles Knight and their collaborators sent all over the country, through the Society for the Diffusion of Useful Knowledge (which Thomas Love Peacock called the "Steam Intellect Society") and other publishing and lecturing agencies, a flood of instruction in orthodox principles of economics and finance. *The Results of Machinery*, *The Relations of Capital and Labour Considered*, and countless other manuals were distributed by thousands in the hope of bringing the industrious classes to a better frame of mind.

In these instructive works it was explained to the people that, in spite of appearances, machinery was in process of conferring upon them abundant benefits, and that the interest of capitalists and labourers were, whatever misguided agitators might say, fundamentally the same. It was argued, on principles laid down by the Ricardian school, that the laws of political economy made the sums available for the payment of wages strictly dependent on the accumulation of capital—the famous doctrine of the "Wages Fund"—and that, in view of this fact, the enlargement of wealth by machine-production would automatically increase the size of the wages fund.

Less emphasis was put on another side of the Ricardian doctrine, on which the Socialist economists were prompt to seize. This was that wages tended always to subsistence level, because population always tended to increase up to the point at which it could be barely maintained by the available supply of food. This pessimistic view, associated with the name o

Malthus, appeared to mean that the poor could never improve their position, however greatly the production of wealth might increase. But it was toned down by the Malthusians, who insisted that the subsistence level was not purely physical but conventional, so that it was possible for it to rise or fall, and that it could be raised if the poor, by exercising self-restraint, kept down the number of competitive workers to such a level as to make labour scarce. For the "Wages Fund" would then be shared out among a smaller number of workers; and the "subsistence level" would rise.

The propagandists of the Society for the Diffusion of Useful Knowledge and similar bodies therefore preached to the workers "moral restraint" in getting families, and not Trade Union bargaining, as the only effective way of raising wages; and so influential were the classical economic doctrines that Francis Place held this opinion almost as devoutly as McCulloch or James Mill. Nor had the followers of Malthus and Ricardo any hesitation in proclaiming machinery a blessing to the poor, although Ricardo himself, observing the actual conditions of his time, had, as we have seen, admitted his own doubts upon the matter. Lord Brougham and his friends scouted such hesitations: whatever might be the sufferings of the hand-loom weavers, or of other skilled workers whom the new machines had displaced, they were confident that the enlargement of productive power must in the long run be of material benefit to the workers as well as to the capitalists. Nor were they wrong—in the long run; but they ignored or minimized the immense sufferings which were inflicted upon large sections of the working classes while the transition was in progress.

This propaganda on behalf of the new capitalism did not, indeed, begin on any large scale until the immediate post-war troubles were over; and it came less as a spontaneous movement from the orthodox than as an answer to dangerous doctrines of the opposite sect. No sooner was the war over than "the philanthropic Mr. Owen of New Lanark," model employer and owner of the greatest cotton factory of the day, came south to plead the cause of the poor. He demanded for them the protection of an effective Factory Act—for the elder

Peel's Factory Act of 1802, reputed the first of the Factory Acts, applied, even if it had been observed, only to the special class of "pauper apprentices" in the cotton mills; and that class had been dying out even when the Act became law, as with the expansion of the factory districts the supply of "free" child labour increased. Owen wanted an Act to prohibit all labour under ten years of age, to limit hours of labour to ten and a half, including meal-times, for all workers under eighteen, and to provide paid inspectors to secure enforcement of these reforms. His crusade was not wholly abortive; for largely as a result of it the elder Peel secured his second Act in 1819. But this fell far short of Owen's demands. It applied only to cotton mills; it put the minimum age for employment at nine instead of ten: it limited hours only to twelve, and only up to sixteen years of age; and finally, the vital provision for inspection was dropped. The workers got little enough out of Peel's Act; yet even that little was hard to get in face of the embittered hostility of most of the employers and the apathy of the county justices who were supposed to administer the law.

But Owen came south from New Lanark to advocate far more than a Factory Bill. He had become convinced that the entire basis of the industrial system was wrong—that competition in profit-making necessarily involved misery for the mass of the people, and that the remedy was to substitute for it a system of universal co-operation. Profoundly impressed by the immense enlargement of the productive powers which the Industrial Revolution was bringing about, Owen believed that the problem of poverty was well on the way to solution, and could be solved as soon as men consented to work together at solving it, instead of each scrambling against the others for a larger share. He believed, therewith, that men's moral ideas were also radically wrong, in that they sought by savage punishment to repress wickedness and inculcate virtue, instead of recognizing that men in the mass were what their environment made them, and that the way to virtue and happiness was to provide them with an environment in which their good qualities would have room to grow. This denial of men's responsibility for their conduct was soon to lead Owen into public denunciation of all the orthodox religions; for was not the belief in man's natural wickedness and in his responsibility for it the cardinal tenet of them all? But at the first this aspect of Owen's teaching was not widely known; and for the moment he received a sympathetic hearing even in highly respectable quarters.

Immediately, what Owen had to urge was that, instead of doling out relief to the poor in niggardly fashion through the poor rates or through agencies of private charity, society should set the unemployed to useful work by settling them in "Villages of Co-operation"—called by Cobbett, who disliked the idea, "Mr. Owen's Parallelograms of Paupers"—in which they would be able easily to provide for their own subsistence. "Mr. Owen's Plan" we shall have to consider more fully in a subsequent section. Here it concerns us as the starting point for the movement which, under Owen's leadership, was to sweep over the country in the years immediately after the Reform Act of 1832.

Robert Owen had not only a plan for dealing with unemployment and setting up a new industrial system based upon— and not like Cobbett's and later O'Connor's projects in opposition to—the new forces set in motion by the Industrial Revolution. He had also at least the germ of a new economic theory in sharp contrast to that of the orthodox economists. For in his *Report to the County of Lanark* (1820) upon his scheme, he propounded a new doctrine of value and exchange, and set out to replace money by a new currency based upon the "labour-time"—the "socially necessary" labour-time, as Marx would have called it—spent by the worker in production. This idea, which he was to seek to apply later in his Labour Exchanges, was the germ of the anti-capitalist theories of value which began to gain wide acceptance among the more educated workers during the eighteen-twenties. William Thompson's *Principles of the Distribution of Wealth* (1824), Thomas Hodgskin's *Labour Defended* (1825), and numerous other books and pamphlets followed up the idea, building upon Ricardo's doctrine that the relative values of commodities were chiefly determined by the amounts of human labour directly or indirectly incorporated in them the conclusion that labour, as the sole source of value, was also the only legitimate claimant to the product of industry.

These were the subversive notions which Brougham and the Society for the Diffusion of Useful Knowledge set out to answer. Through the 'twenties and 'thirties there went on, side by side with the material struggle of the workers, an active battle of ideas. These contests came indeed to a head only after the Reform Act had been passed, and had left the workers voteless while it set their employers firmly on the road to political power. But the ideas, as well as the movements, were growing steadily from 1815 onwards; and Robert Owen, far more than any other man, was their original inspirer.

Meanwhile the Industrial Revolution went on. During the years immediately after 1815, despite the prevailing depression, the textile industries, with cotton far in the van, were passing over more and more swiftly to the factory system. The hand-loom-weavers, their numbers swollen during the preceding decades, were left to fight a hopeless battle against the machines. In the coal industry, especially on the North-East Coast, mines were driven deeper, and the number of accidents increased, despite Sir Humphrey Davy's invention of the safety-lamp in 1815. The output of iron grew fast—from about 250,000 tons in 1810 to nearly 700,000 in 1830. Raw cotton consumed in production increased from 94,000,000 lb. in 1815 to over 273,000,000 in 1831. The woollen manufacture expanded much more slowly; but the quantity of yarn used rose from about 80,000,000 lb. in 1820 to 94,000,000 in 1830. The building industry, next to the cotton trade, increased most rapidly of all. The number of houses in Great Britain grew from 2,100,000 in 1811 to 2,850,000 in 1831, the average number of persons per house remaining unchanged at 5·6.

This last activity brought with it a great change in the building industry in the larger towns. The building "contractor," who undertook to erect whole factories and blocks of houses, partly replaced the small masters in the separate crafts, and this caused a rapid growth of Trade Unionism and unrest which prepared the way for the Builders' Union of 1832. At the same time, new skilled crafts, based on the technique of the machine, were being developed in the factory areas. With the advent of Crompton's mule, spinning of cotton became pre-dominantly a men's trade, and the factory spinners soon began to develop into a highly organized skilled craft, till in 1829 a large proportion of them joined up for a time, under Doherty's leadership, into a Grand General Union. Over the same period the steam-engine makers and other new metal-working crafts were growing up and becoming conscious of their common skill and need for unity. The Steam Engine Makers' Society was formed in 1824, and that of the Journeymen Steam Engine Makers in 1826. As machines came to be made all of metal instead of wood, the old craft of millwrights, who had organized powerful societies in the eighteenth century, became far less important; and in addition to the steam-engine makers, other trades, such as the ironfounders, boilermakers and blacksmiths, began to form combinations of their own.

Up to 1824, the Combination Acts, passed in 1799 and 1800, remained in force, though as we have seen Trade Unionism despite them was never at all completely suppressed. From the repeal of the Acts in 1824—even under the less liberal amending Act of 1825—Trade Unions were able to grow openly. They did grow fast, though, apart from their outburst of activity during the great boom and the following crisis of 1825, their activity remained mostly on a small scale till the Reform agitation was over. John Gast, the leader of the ship-wrights in London, and John Doherty in Manchester, had made, as early as 1818, the first attempts to organize a Trade Union movement wide enough to include all trades. But the first practical "General Union" was Doherty's National Association for the Protection of Labour, formed in 1830, the direct precursor of Owen's Grand National Consolidated Trades Union of 1833-4.

Over this period we have been describing, the post-war deflation of the currency had run its course. The gold stan-dard, suspended under the exigencies of war finance in 1797, was restored in 1821 under an Act of 1819. William Cobbett vigorously denounced this policy, not because he loved paper-money—he was indeed one of the stoutest critics of inflation—but because he claimed that deflation was monstrous injustice without an "equitable adjustment" to scale down the interest burden of the National Debt. Cobbett, and many others, including Attwood and the advocates of paper-money (that is, of credit based on production instead of gold) prophesied ruin as a result of the return to the gold standard. But though the real burden of the debt mounted with the fall in prices, the wealth of the country mounted faster still. Moreover, something was done to reduce the money burden. The total debt had fallen to well under £800,000,000 by the time the Whigs came to office in 1830; and revenue remained high despite the abandonment of the income tax. Customs receipts rose from £10,500,000 in 1815–16 to £16,500,000 in 1831–2, although prices had fallen very sharply in the interval. But the growth of indirect taxation, of course, meant that the poor were bearing most of the burden.

With the incomes of the richer classes, at any rate as soon as the immediate post-war crisis was over, rising rapidly in purchasing power, a huge stimulus was given to the investment of capital both at home and abroad. There was now both a far larger investing class than ever before, and a widening field for investment in industry and commerce. While the war lasted, the mounting National Debt had absorbed a large part of the available capital; but, now that the debt was being actually reduced, the upper and middle classes had to look for other outlets for their money. At home, they found these outlets most of all in the rapid development of the canals, which, beginning as far back as 1755, with the planning by Brindley of the Duke of Bridgewater's Worsley Brook Canal, had reached large dimensions before the end of the century, and went on apace until railways began to challenge their supremacy from the opening of the Stockton and Darlington Railway in 1825. The most active period of canal building was over by 1800; but even after that date about 600 miles, out of a total of 2,300, were built, and these included the famous Caledonian Canal, which was begun in 1803.

Side by side with the canals, there grew up further openings for investment in what are now called "public utilities." Gas-lighting began to be introduced at the beginning of the century, and water-companies were promoted for supplying the growing towns.

CP : H

In the meantime manufacture and mining, as distinct from transport and public utilities, continued to be financed by individual capitalists or private partnerships, without the protection of limited liability. In 1725 Parliament had passed an Act prohibiting altogether the formation of joint stock companies; and this prohibition was maintained until 1825. It did not prevent Parliament, whenever it so desired, from granting the privilege of incorporation to a particular company by means of a private Act; and this, on the model set to some extent by the Turnpike Trusts, as well as by the Bank of England and the East India Company, was done freely in the case of canals, and later railways, and of undertakings for the supply of gas or water, or for insurance against fire. No similar privilege, however, was accorded to firms engaged in ordinary manufacture; for there was a widespread opinion, supported by Adam Smith's authority, that joint stock enterprise was inefficient except in the conduct of routine business, and limited liability was widely denounced as an encouragement to the corrupt evasion of the payment of business debts.

In these circumstances, the new factory system had to be financed without the aid of joint stock companies or of limited liability. Many of the new industrial enterprises—witness Robert Owen's Chorlton Twist Co. of 1795, and his New Lanark Co. of 1800—did in fact take the name of companies; but in the eyes of the law they remained merely unincorporated partnerships of individuals whose liability for their debts was unlimited. This led to great practical inconveniences, especially as these "companies" could neither sue nor be sued in their collective names, but only in those of the actual partners. But still more the absence of limited liability made the risk of investing in them much too great for the mere passive investor who did not intend, or had not the knowledge, to keep an active watch over the conduct of the enterprise.

How, then, was the considerable capital needed for the building and running of the new factories actually supplied? No one answer is possible; but, in the first place, a great many of the new factory owners began on quite a small scale, and then gradually enlarged their establishments by putting back the greater part of their profits into the business. The successful factory using the new methods of pioduction was often in a position to make very high profits, and thus to expand its operations rapidly even without calling on outside capitalists to supply it with additional financial resources.

This, however, is only a part of the explanation; for the new employers, in order to make a start at all with factory production, had in most cases to get control of a good deal more capital than they actually possessed, and many of the factory owners expanded their scale of operations much further than they could have done if they had depended entirely on the accumulation of profits. They acquired the additional resources which they needed in any or all of three ways—by borrowing at fixed interest, by forming syndicates of partners in conjunction with moneyed men who were ready to back them, or by obtaining credit from merchants or bankers.

In order to understand how this system worked, it is necessary to go back to the conditions of the domestic system. Under that system, the merchant was the principal financier of industrial operations, sometimes buying the raw material and then handing it out to a succession of craftsmen who worked it up into a finished form at piecework prices—so that the merchant financed the entire "period of production," including the payment of wages as well as the lock-up of working capital in other forms. Alternatively, the merchant often sold the material to the craftsmen, but made the sale on credit, and was recouped out of the price of the finished goods: so that in this case too he financed the "period of production" in a somewhat different way. The merchants were thus fully accustomed, before the advent of the factories, to financing productive operations.

This made it natural, when factories began to replace individual workers or small workshop masters under the domestic system, for the rich merchant houses largely to take over the business of financing factory production. They did this extensively by granting credit to the factory owners for materials supplied. But they also went much further than this, both by granting loans for the purchase of additional machinery and the payment of wages during the period of production, and by becoming actual partners with promising factory employers in order to enable them to expand rapidly their supply of some product for which the merchants felt certain of finding a ready market. The merchant, with a swiftly expanding world-market before him as factory costs of production fell, was eager to secure a larger supply of the new factory products; and he could hope to get them only by being ready to supply a large part of the requisite capital, and often to take an actual share in the risks of capitalist production.

There can be no doubt that in the earlier stages of the Industrial Revolution the bulk of the new capital needed for creating and working the new factories came from the merchants. It must be remembered that at this time, except in London, the business of banking was only being slowly differentiated from that of the merchant. The provincial banks began largely as merchant businesses, dealing in goods. This led them into the financing of industry; and, by way of acting as financiers to the industrial capitalists, some of them were drawn on to drop their merchant businesses, and concentrate wholly on banking. Others turned into industrialists; and yet others finally dropped industrial financing, and reverted to purely merchant activities. But for the time being the merchants, as merchants, supplied the largest part of the capital for new factory enterprise.

Of course, not all the capital came in this way. There were industrialists, such as Matthew Boulton, who were wealthy enough to build up new factories mainly out of their own resources. There were rich men, such as Dr. Roebuck, Watt's first financier, who applied their own wealth to the creation of factories. There were syndicates of a few rich men, not necessarily drawn from the merchant class, who made a regular business of financing promising young factory *entrepreneurs* by entering into a series of partnerships with them, each for a separate factory. Richard Arkwright made himself a partner with a number of people in this way, and became the controlling financial influence in quite a cluster of separate enterprises. Moreover, especially in the case of coal-mining and the other extractive industries, the great landlords, whose wealth had been largely increased by enclosure and the war-time rise in rents as well as by urban development, became the principal financiers, working their mining properties either directly through managers or indirectly through contractors to whom they extended credit, or even lent capital.

Thus, in one way and another, the money was forthcoming to finance the new forms of industrial enterprise; and the methods of advancing it helped to link closely together the interests of the new class of industrial employers and those of the older wealthy classes of landowners and merchants. This helps to explain why, whereas France experienced a Revolution, Great Britain underwent only a Reform of Parliament.

CHAPTER XVII

WAGES AFTER 1815

WHAT was happening, meanwhile, to the workers and to their conditions? According to Silberling's index of retail prices, the cost of living, in terms of commodities, rose by 87 per cent between 1790 and the peak year, 1813. It then fell very sharply, and in 1822 was back at the pre-war level. Thereafter, it rose again, to a peak of 28 per cent above that level, in the boom year, 1825; and then it fell again, to only 6 per cent above 1790 in 1829. In 1832 it was 9 per cent above the level of 1790.

The available statistics are far too inadequate for it to be possible to present any companion picture of the general course of wages. A broad impression can, however, be given. At the time of the outbreak of the war with France in 1793, 9s. a week was a frequent agricultural wage in the Southern Counties, and 8s. in the North. By 1810 about 13s. was being paid in the South and Southern Midlands, where the Speenhamland system was in force, whereas in the North, where the system did not exist, wages had risen as high as 15s., and in some places higher. In the West Riding, for example, 16s. 6d. was being paid in 1813.

Before the end of the war agricultural wages had begun to fall, and by 1822–3 they were down to 8s. or 9s. in the Eastern Counties—the great wheat-growing area. In the South, except in Wiltshire and the West, where they were about 8s. 6d., they seem to have ranged from 10s. to 12s., and in the North to have fallen to 9s. or 10s. Thereafter, they rose again in the North, to 12s. in Yorkshire and even 14s. in Lancashire, but changed little in the South until after 1834. Thus, at the end of the period with which we are dealing, agricultural wages had risen from an average of about 9s. a week in the seventeen-nineties to 11s. or 12s. in 1832, whereas, according to Silberling's index, the cost of living had risen by less than 10 per cent.

There is, however, serious reason to believe that Silberling's index by no means reflects the real movement in the agricultural labourer's cost of living. This index is based mainly on urban living conditions, and assigns an undue weight to commodities which the labourer could not afford to buy. The labourer lived mainly on cereals, even when he was not driven to subsist on potatoes; and accordingly he suffered terribly in the years of high cereal prices. In 1832, indeed, wheat, at 58s. 11d. a quarter, was only 4s. 2d. above the price of 1790; but, as we have seen, it had been at 126s. 6d. in 1812, and, even after the war, at 96s. 11d. in 1817. Since 1820 the price had never exceeded 70s.; but in the ten years ending in 1832 wheat averaged nearly 62s. a quarter, whereas in the decade ending in 1790 it had averaged under 48s. The agricultural labourer's real wage position was at the best no better than it had been before the war; and in the meantime enclosure had robbed him of the means of eking out his income by keeping pigs or geese on the common land, or perhaps tilling a patch of his own, and his family's by-earnings from industry had mainly disappeared with the advent of the factory system. In addition, the conditions of employment had been stiffened up, and a good many valuable perquisites, such as gleaning after harvest and the receipt of food in the farmer's house, had been largely lost. On the whole, there is no doubt that there had been a very great worsening in the position of the main body of agricultural workers.

What then of the workers in industry? For the factory workers it is impossible to get any impression earlier than about 1806. For that year, Mr. G. H. Wood has estimated the average earnings of all classes of factory workers in the

Manchester area at about 11s. a week, rising to about 11s. 6d. in 1810, and thereafter falling by slow stages to little above 10s. in 1832. These figures, however, include women and children, who formed the larger number of factory workers. For cotton-spinning, which became, with the advent of the mule, a skilled man's occupation, Mr. Wood puts the average wage as high as 26s. in 1806, rising to 30s. in 1810, and thereafter falling to as little as 21s. in 1824, and, with many intermediate changes, reaching about 24s. 6d. in 1832. For power-loom weavers, men and women together, no figure can be given before 1816, when weavers in the Hyde area averaged about 14s., falling to about 11s. by 1832.

Of the handloom-weavers there is of course a still more desperate story to tell. Mr. Wood puts their average earnings in the cotton industry at about 19s. in 1800, rising to 23s. in 1805, but falling to 13s. in 1808 and 12s. 6d. in 1811. Then came a brief recovery, to nearly 18s. in 1814, followed by a sharp drop to 8s. by 1818, and as little as 6s. by 1832, by which time handloom weaving in the cotton trade was at the point of death, and the number of unemployed weavers had become very great. G. R. Porter's fuller figures, for the Bolton area, show an even deeper reverse of fortune, from 25s. between 1800 and 1806, down to 15s. in 1808, up to 19s. in 1810, down to 14s. in 1812, up again to 24s. in 1814, and then down to 8s. in the early 'twenties, and 5s. 6d. in 1832.

There remain the miners, and the skilled artisans in the older crafts. For the miners, paucity of data makes any general picture impossible. The only full series of figures relates to Scotland, where the day wage seems to have risen from 2s. 6d. or 3s. in the early 1790's to nearly 5s. in 1811–12, then fallen by stages to about 3s. 6d. in 1821, risen to 5s. 3d. in the boom of 1825, and fallen again to about 4s. by 1832. Such figures as exist for the most important mining area, the North-East Coast, do not conflict with this impression; for there the average day-rate seems to have been about 2s. 9d. in 1795, and about 3s. 9d. in 1832.

For skilled craftsmen in London, Francis Place gives, as we have seen, a far more optimistic estimate. According to Place's figures, the skilled London craftsman got 22s. in 1793, at the outbreak of the war. This rose to 25s. in 1795, 27s. in 1802, 30s. in 1807, 33s. in 1810, and 36s. 6d. in 1813—after which Place says that the common wage remained unchanged right up to 1832, despite the fall in the cost of living. This estimate must, however, relate only to a very limited number of highly skilled workers. London builders certainly earned very much less—about 18s. in 1793, rising by stages to 30s. in 1810, falling to 27s. in 1815, rising again to 30s. in 1824, and, for a moment, to 33s. in the boom of 1825, and then falling again to 30s. in 1827–30, and to 27s. by 1835.

The wages of provincial artisans were a good deal lower than this. In Manchester, bricklayers got 22s. 6d. from 1810 to 1821, and 25s. in 1822, and then, after several fluctuations, fell as low as 17s. in 1832. Manchester carpenters were rather better paid, at 25s. from 1810 to 1821, at 26s. in 1822, and, after a drop to 22s., at 24s. in 1832. In Glasgow carpenters got 18s. in 1810, but only 14s. in 1819, and no more in 1832. Tailors in Manchester got 18s. 6d. in 1810, 21s. 6d. in 1815, 18s. 6d. in 1819, 21s. in 1825, and 18s. in 1832. Manchester shoemakers got 16s. in 1810, 18s. in 1821, and 15s. in 1832. Woolcombers at Leicester fell from 20s. in 1818 to 14s. 3d. in 1832.

London compositors were better paid than any other group whose wages are known. For book-printing, they got 33s. in 1801, rising to 36s. in 1811, and remaining steadily at the same level till 1832. Compositors on morning newspapers got even more—40s. in 1801, 48s. in 1810, and still 48s. in 1832. Compositors on evening papers were about midway between these rates.

In general, the available evidence points to a considerable improvement in the economic position of certain bodies of skilled artisans, especially in London. Nor is this at all difficult to understand. The general increase in the wealth of the country created a larger demand for the products of the skilled trades. But these trades were not, for the most part, much affected at this stage by the competition of machinery or by the factory system. Despite the repeal in 1814 of the Elizabethan statute confining their crafts by law to regularly apprenticed workers, they were able to a great extent to preserve their monopoly of labour and their control over the apprenticeship system; for even while the Combination Acts were in force they maintained their strongly organized local Trade Clubs, and the actual shortage of labour made these too powerful to be lightly challenged by the small masters who were still the typical employers in this type of trade.

Outside London, the skilled artisans were for the most part much less strongly organized, though in a few places, such as Liverpool, their monopolies in certain trades were very strong —the Liverpool shipwrights being cited before the committee which considered the repeal of the Combination Acts in 1824 as an outstanding example of "Trade Union tyranny." Even these favoured workers, however, earned only 27s. a week in 1822 and 30s. in the boom of 1825, after which they fell again to 27s., and remained at that wage till after 1832. Especially, the artisans tended to be much less strongly entrenched in the new towns which had not been important centres of craft industry before the Industrial Revolution. Partly for this reason, but also because London was far more continuously prosperous than any of the Northern industrial centres, the London artisans tended in the years after the war to improve their relative economic position.

On the whole, however, wages in 1832 were exceedingly low; and the principal benefit of the great increase in productivity due to the advent of machinery had clearly gone to the richer classes. The low level of agricultural wages, the extreme poverty in Ireland, and, in Scotland, the depopulation of the Highlands by the great "clearances" which reached their height in the first part of the nineteenth century, caused a steady flow of seekers for work into the developing industrial areas, and helped greatly to keep down wages. In addition, the rapid growth of population, from less than 11,000,000 in 1801 to over 16,500,000 in 1831 (excluding Ireland), assured an abundant supply especially of juvenile labour for the developing factories.

Up to the early years of the nineteenth century, indeed, the factory owners constantly complained of an actual shortage of child labour. This was partly because the early factories employed an even larger proportion of children than the factories of the period after 1815. It was also because there had not yet been time for the industrial towns to grow in response to the demand, and because parents, until they were driven by sheer economic necessity, were often unwilling to send young children to face the hardships of factory labour. Moreover, as we have seen, the period of acute rural depopulation did not really set in until after 1815; nor was it easy, in view of the Settlement Acts, for the surplus agricultural workers of the South to migrate to the Northern factory areas..

To this early period of labour shortage belongs the "parish apprenticeship" system, under which many thousands of children from London and other large towns, having become inmates of pauper institutions, were shipped in droves to the new factory areas, there to be bound apprentices to some cotton lord who undertook to feed and clothe them in a barrack built specially for their occupation, and even to give them a minimum of schooling in his factory school. This system, which, as we have seen, Peel's "first Factory Act" of 1802 was designed to bring under some sort of regulation, died out rapidly as soon as local supplies of child labour became available; for the factory owners soon found that "free" labour, which they could engage and discharge at will, came cheaper than pauper labour which they were bound to maintain throughout the period of apprenticeship, whether trade was good or bad. In bad times, the "free" factory children had to be kept by their parents, or out of the local poor rates, of which the factory owners paid only a relatively small part.

Wages, then, except in a few privileged occupations, remained very low in purchasing power, despite the fall in prices after the war period. But, the lower the wages, the more the price of wheat mattered; for when wages were very low most of the money had to go in buying bread, and there was little left for dearer commodities, even if these had fallen in relative price. This fact, as we shall see later, counted for a great deal in ranging the sentiment of the factory workers behind the demand for the repeal of the Corn Laws, despite the assertions, common among their leaders, that the employers wanted it only in order to reduce wages yet more. If the subsistence theory of wages, then generally preached by the orthodox economists, had been correct in the rigid form in which it was often advanced, the Corn Laws could not have had any lasting effect in lowering the working-class standard of life. But it is certain that the high price of wheat, whether or not it was due to the Corn Laws, did have this effect, and no less certain that the extreme fluctuations of prices, from year to year and even from week to week, caused acute misery in times of shortage. It is also true that, in view of the abundance of the less skilled types of labour, and the difficulties in the way of Trade Unionism outside a few skilled trades, wages were bound in any case to remain very low during this period —certainly the most miserable in working-class history since the beginning of the Industrial Revolution.

CHAPTER XVIII

THE POST-WAR CRISIS—ROBERT OWEN'S "PLAN"

PEACE—the real ending of the war, after the final episode of the "Hundred Days"—meant distress. "On the day on which peace was signed," Robert Owen wrote in his *Autobiography*, "the great customer of the producers died." Unemployment spread everywhere over the country; there was a catastrophic fall in prices, which meant ruin to a host of farmers and small employers and involved for the workers a drastic cutting-down of wages as well as an acute shortage of work. In the metal and mining industries workers were dismissed by thousands; in the textile trades short-time became almost universal for those who were able to keep any work at all. All over the countryside, both wages and poor law allowances were drastically curtailed by farmers and landowners who regarded the existing burdens as intolerable in face of the fall in agricultural prices and demand.

The National Debt, on the other hand, was immensely swollen in real value by the deflation of prices. The State's creditors reaped the advantage; but a clamour went up from the entire possessing classes against the excessive burdens of national and local taxation. The Government was bidden to economize in order to reduce the taxes; the unpopular income tax was swept away by Parliament on the plea that pledges had been given that it should be taken off as soon as the war was at an end. As this tax alone, despite the large extent to which it could then be evaded, did place substantial burdens on the rich, its abolition made the tax system bear still more inequitably upon the poorer classes, who were compelled, as consumers, to pay in indirect taxation the huge sums needed for meeting the swollen interest upon the Debt.

Between 1793 and 1816 the annual interest charge on the National Debt rose from under £9,500,000 to over £31,500,000 out of total post-war expenditure of about £55,000,000. Substantially more than the total sum needed to meet the debt charge was raised by taxes on commodities, one-third from customs and two-thirds from excise duties falling mainly on goods popularly consumed. Tea was taxed nearly 100 per cent *ad valorem*, and yielded between £3,000,000 and £4,000,000 a year. Sugar yielded roughly equal amounts, and tobacco not much less. Beer yielded another £3,000,000, and there were very heavy taxes on such indispensable goods as soap, candles and paper—to say nothing of the duties which were imposed on the raw or half-manufactured materials used in producing the great majority of necessary commodities.

Moreover, under the Corn Law, which was hurried through in 1815 for the protection of the agricultural interest, wheat was altogether excluded from importation until the price rose above 80s. a quarter (or 67s. in the case of wheat from the North American colonies). When the home price reached this level wheat could be brought in duty-free; but the protection given to the home producers was enough to keep the price-level intolerably high. The cost of a four-pound loaf of bread in London averaged over 1s. in the critical years 1816–18, and over the same period wheat averaged more than 87s. a quarter.

In these circumstances, the post-war collapse of industry was bound to lead to terrible distress. Despite drastic scaling-down of the rates of relief, the sums expended for poor relief, which had been under £2,000,000 before the war, and about £5,500,000 in 1815, rose to nearly £7,000,000 in 1816, and nearly £8,000,000 in the following year; and, in addition, considerable sums were expended out of voluntary funds raised for the relief of distress. Despite this expenditure starvation walked through the land, producing the inevitable reaction in hunger-riots, machine-breaking and other spontaneous outbursts of popular misery. At the first, there was some disposition in high quarters to take emergency action for relieving the wretchedness of the poor. But the spread of desperate unrest soon quelled this mood of charity, which was replaced by vindictive repression. Not content with passing savage sentences upon hunger-rioters, machine-breakers and all who were driven by misery to become "disturbers of the peace," the Government turned upon all Radicals and Reformers wherever their proposals and protests could be twisted into threats of sedition or incitements to the poor to rebel. In order to suppress the "agitators" the Habeas Corpus Act was suspended in 1817 and 1818, and Sidmouth passed in 1817 his "Gagging Bills," which were amplified two years later by the even more ferocious severity of the "Six Acts."

Before the war was over, there had been some revival of the movement for political reform. Major John Cartwright had begun to organize his Union and Hampden Clubs, and in every considerable town there was at least an organized nucleus of Radicals demanding a really representative Parliament based on manhood suffrage and a drastic reform of the tax system.

The Radicals, in face of the post-war crisis, redoubled their agitation, and began especially to demand the abolition of pensions and sinecures and what they called an "equitable adjustment" of the National Debt—by which they meant an enforced reduction of interest at least equivalent to the fall in the general level of prices. They argued that it was monstrously inequitable to take off the income tax, which bore chiefly on the rich, while leaving them in possession of an unchanged money income derived from the Debt, and now, in face of the fall in prices and production, representing a greatly increased proportion of the entire national income. Their protests were intensified as soon as it was known that the Government was contemplating an early return to the gold standard; for it was held that this, involving further deflation of incomes and prices, would hand over to the *rentiers* a still greater proportion of the national wealth.

However, most of the Radicals stressed in their propaganda the sheer impossibility of expecting that reforms would ever be granted by an unreformed Parliament representative almost exclusively of the classes which benefited by the prevailing injustice. William Cobbett, "Orator" Henry Hunt, Major Cartwright, William Hone, T. J. Wooler, William Benbow, Richard Carlile and the other Radical leaders of popular opinion used their demands for financial reform chiefly as a means of reinforcing their case for a drastic reform of Parliament, and sought to concentrate the scattered activities and protests of workers, small farmers and other distressed sections of the population upon the major issue. Parliamentary Reform alone, they kept saying, would clear the way for a real change of system. In the years after 1815 the general mass of popular discontent came to be centred, as never before, round this one demand for a Reformed Parliament. Even the sheer hunger-riots of starving labourers, miners and factory workers came to be more and more transmuted into movements for a radical change in the British Constitution.

William Cobbett, greatest of Radical journalists, speedily made himself the outstanding leader of the crusade. In 1816 he began to publish, side by side with his regular *Weekly Political Register*, which was far too expensive to be bought by the workers, a cheap twopenny *Register*, dubbed by his enemies "Twopenny Trash," in which he appealed directly to the workers in town and country to throw their weight behind the Reform movement. Cobbett's *Addresses to the Journeymen and Labourers*, issued first in his cheap *Register* and re-issued as pamphlets, reached a circulation hitherto unexampled. At the end of 1816 his *Register* is said to have been selling 60,000 copies a week—many times the circulation of any contemporary newspaper. Other working-class journals speedily sprang up to meet the growing demand for Radical literature, among them notably Hone's *Reformist's Register*, Wooler's *Black Dwarf* (to which Cartwright was a frequent contributor), Carlile's *Republican* and John Gast's *Gorgon* of 1819 (the first Trade Union newspaper).

As the distress deepened in 1816, the reformers redoubled their agitation. Everywhere in the growing factory districts there was widespread unrest, the outcome of sheer hunger. The employers, faced with falling prices, set to work to cut down the costs of production by every possible means. Wages were sharply reduced; and the great mass of home workers still outside the factory system felt everywhere the intensified competition of the new machines. The depression fell with exceptional severity on the large body of handloom-weavers in the textile areas. Up to 1815, though the handloom-weavers had felt the growing competition of the power-loom, they had been just able to stand up against it, thanks to the high level of prices. But now, as prices fell, more and more employers installed power-looms in order to cut their costs; and the hand-loom-weavers were compelled to accept lower and lower wages determined by the competition of the new machines (except in fancy lines such as pattern weaving, which had not yet been mechanized). Even so, they secured only such work as was left over after the growing number of power-looms had been fully employed. For the employers, having expended capital in installing the new machines, made it their first object to keep these in full employment, and put out to the handloom-weavers only the residue of the trade. Consequently, the handloom-weavers, whose numbers had been greatly swollen during the previous decades by the increased supply of yarn made possible by the mechanization of spinning, found their livelihood rapidly destroyed. They were driven in thousands to the Poor Law for relief; and it is no wonder that in their misery some of them turned to smashing the power-looms which seemed to them to be the source of their distress. "Luddites," they were called, because their attacks upon the factories recalled to men's minds the Luddite troubles of 1811 and 1812. But whereas the earlier Luddites had been for the most part in revolt, not against the factory system, which at that time had hardly invaded their trades, but only against certain special menaces to their standards of living, such as the introduction of "cut-up" hosiery, or gig-mills, these post-war "Luddites" set themselves against the factory system as a whole, because it now threatened the entire body of handloom-weavers with extinction. In many places mills were burnt down and machinery destroyed.

These disturbances were never more than sporadic, and in the years of distress and unrest immediately after 1815 they were relatively few, partly no doubt because of the severity which had been used in suppressing the Luddites only a few years before. In the strikes of 1818, for example, acts of violence were exceptional; and the numerous arrests of strike leaders, such as Ellison and Baggulay, were made on charges of conspiracy or combination, without the added accusations of riot or offences against property. The most extensive machine-breaking did not take place until 1826, when the unfortunate handloom-weavers had already lost all hope of securing a tolerable wage either by striking or by agitating for a legal minimum wage. In that year, after the collapse of the boom of 1825, the drastic reduction of wages was met by a fairly extensive outburst of machine-breaking, directed against the hated power-looms, in Manchester, Burnley, Bury, Blackburn, Haslingden and several other textile towns. The soldiers were called out to suppress the rioting; and in an affray at Chadderton seven workers were killed and a large number wounded. The usual round of arrests followed; and in the subsequent trials ten of the weavers' leaders were sentenced to death—the sentences being commuted to transportation for life—and thirty-three others to varying terms of imprisonment. This was almost the last widespread rebellion of the handloom-weavers, whose cause was in fact already lost. In later movements of unrest the factory workers, and not the handloom-weavers, were to take the lead.

The political reformers for the most part realized, as early as 1816, the hopelessness of this instinctive struggle against the new economic order. Accordingly they sought to persuade the starving workers that their real enemy was not the machine, but the money power which controlled it. Manhood Suffrage and a Reformed Parliament, said the Radicals, would destroy the power of the bankers, the cotton lords, and the mine-owners to exploit the poor. It would sweep away unjust taxes, redistribute incomes, and unloose the pent-up powers of plenty upon a regenerated world. The political reformers saw, indeed, but dimly the new economic order to which democracy would open the door. Many of them still thought far less in terms of a regenerated factory system than of a return to an older order in which there would be no great çapitalists to exploit the poor, and the old relations between small working masters and journeymen would be somehow miraculously restored. They were inclined to attribute all the evils of the time to political corruption and financial oligarchy, and to believe that economic problems would settle themselves if only the political system could be purged by the institution of a democratic franchise. The political reformers, or most of them, never understood the Industrial Revolution. They continued, in a changed economic world, to preach the political gospel of the rights of man, without adapting it to the conditions of a new age.

Robert Owen and his followers fell foul of them precisely upon this ground. Owen, a self-made man, who at the age of twenty was already at the head of one of the most important cotton-mills in Lancashire, had bought in 1800 the great mills at New Lanark originally founded by David Dale in association with Richard Arkwright. There he had proceeded to demonstrate that profits could be made without subjecting the workers to the intolerable exploitation which most employers regarded as belonging to the order of Nature. Owen paid good wages, by the standards of the time; and he paid them regularly, even when, during the war, the New Lanark mills had to be closed for lack of supplies. He reduced the hours of labour and refused to employ any child at less than ten years of age, though six was then quite a common age for starting work in the mills. He provided full-time schooling up to ten years for the children not only of his own employees, but those of other families who chose to send them to his schools. He built improved houses, with better sanitation, laid out roads and places of recreation, and set up stores at which he sold goods of high quality at cost price. Owen was the model employer of his day; and visitors came from all over the world to see the wonderful establishment which he had built up in beautiful surroundings upon the banks of the Clyde.

But Owen, long before 1815, had it in his mind to be much

more than a model capitalist employer. He was firmly convinced that the entire basis on which the social system rested was wrong. Against the principle of "competition" upheld by the orthodox economists he upheld the principle of "co-operation"; and he believed that if men would but co-operate instead of competing in the production of wealth, it would be easy to achieve reasonable abundance for all, to make an end of wars and of national as well as individual rivalries, and to institute a world order of peace and universal well-being.

For men's failure to achieve this Owen blamed above all the false notions which were everywhere preached about human nature and morality. He held that the religions of his day were principally to blame; for the priests taught assiduously that each man's business was to save his own soul. The evils of Society were put down to individual wickedness, whereas they really proceeded from the false notions in which men were brought up, and the demoralizing environment in which they were compelled to live. *Men's character is made for them and not by them*, Owen never wearied of proclaiming; and by "character" he meant, not the individual disposition of each person—for he insisted that each child must be given the fullest possible chance of developing its peculiar bent—but the make-up of social and moral ideas instilled into the community as a whole by education and environment.

Owen believed that, if children were brought up under good living conditions, both moral and material, and taught from infancy the virtue of human co-operation and fellowship instead of personal salvation and personal aggrandizement, society would speedily acquire a different "character," and men would set to work to use in common the means to plenty which lay ready to their hands, instead of each man seeking opportunity to exploit his fellows, and the rich blaming the poor for their wickedness and improvidence. In his own factory Owen, when he had at last secured a group of partners, including Jeremy Bentham, who were prepared to give him a fairly free hand, insisted on paying only a limited dividend on the invested capital, and applying all the surplus profits for the benefit of the workers.

In order to make a model factory amid the wretchedness of

the times, Owen was compelled to create far more than a factory in the modern sense. He had in effect to build up a model community, in which he, as owner and manager, was responsible for the entire conduct of affairs—for houses, roads, shops, schools, places of entertainment and recreation, as well as for the factory itself. In this way there was born in his mind the vision of a world consisting wholly of "Villages of Co-operation" not unlike the great New Lanark establishment, but differing from it in that they would be exchanging their products one with another on fair and equal terms, and that all capitalist exploitation and all predatory government would have disappeared. This vision lay at the back of all his subsequent propaganda of Co-operation and Socialism.

Owen's fundamental ideas about the false basis of existing society had been set forth in his *New View of Society*, published in parts in 1813–14. But in this work two aspects of his doctrine, though implied, were not yet plainly stressed. One was his hostility to all existing religious systems and his advocacy of a "Rational Religion" based solely on the idea of human brotherhood and co-operation. The other was his frontal attack on the entire system of capitalist profit-making. In 1815, when Owen first came forward to champion his ideas on the solution of the post-war miseries of the people, he was still thought of, not as a Radical or revolutionary leader, but as a great employer who was also a great philanthropist and a man of ideas which, though cranky, merited attention because, by the world's standards, he was a success.

Till the war ended, Owen had contented himself with trying out his ideas in his own establishment. But when he saw the desperate confusion of the post-war period—the intense exploitation of those at work by long hours and intolerably low wages, while millions of willing workers could find no work at all, the rapid decline of actual production in face of a rapidly increasing power to produce wealth, the outpouring of money in doles barely sufficient to keep the workless from starvation, whereas the money could have been used in setting them to supply one another's needs—he came forward to advocate his gospel to the wider world. He wanted, first, a Factory Act to keep within bounds the exploitation of those in work, and secondly, a large-scale experiment in settling the workless in Villages of Co-operation, modelled on New Lanark, in which they would be able to provide usefully for their own subsistence and would cease to be a burden upon the public. Owen wanted far more than this—for he looked forward to the spread of his projected Villages of Co-operation over the whole world, and to the entire supersession of the capitalist system. But he wanted the Government to make a modest beginning with a Factory Act and a substitution of his system for that of unproductive poor relief.

At first, some members of the governing classes gave a measure of respectful attention to the "philanthropic Mr. Owen's schemes." Even Sidmouth listened to him; and Ricardo, the economist, as well as the Duke of Kent, Queen Victoria's father, sat on the committee which he formed to further his immediate projects. At this stage, Owen's appeal was to the rich and powerful; for he did not believe that the poor, down-trodden as they were and subjected to an anti-social environment, were yet capable of self-government or of instituting a new order. For that they would need to be educated; and accordingly the governing classes must be converted first. Owen had so great a faith in human reason that he never, to the end of his life, despaired of converting anybody. It always seemed to him that, if the truth were but told often enough, it was bound to be believed.

Soon, however, it became clear that the rich had no intention of acting upon his proposals. His Factory Bill was so mutilated that he gave up advocating it, and left the elder Peel to pilot what remained of it to the Statute Book in 1819. Meanwhile, as he went on urging the rest of his "Plan," the wider implications that lay behind it began to be understood. In one of his public addresses Owen said what he really thought of the religions of his day; and thereafter all the Churches were against him. He made plain, too, his desire to subvert the entire capitalist and competitive system; and that set against him the great body of profit-seekers, large and small. But Owen, so far from moderating his utterances to placate his critics, became more and more Utopian and all-inclusive in the projects which he advanced. In his *Report to the County of*

Lanark (1820), which contains the best account of his developed doctrines, he added to his earlier proposals an attack on the whole monetary system, and a demand for a new standard of value, based on labour instead of gold, as an assurance of fair and equal exchanges between the real producers of wealth.

By this time Owen had lost the ear of the governing classes; and he had not yet found articulate followers among the poor. His insistence that the real revolution must be economic rather than political, and that only education in a changed environment would fit the masses for self-government, antagonized the Radicals, who regarded him as a reactionary opponent of Parliamentary Reform. Already, Owenite Socialism was influencing the minds of a number of the younger workers, such as the printer, George Mudie, who founded in 1821 the first working-class Owenite society. But not till some years later was Owenism to become an important factor in the working-class movement; and in the meantime Owen himself, despairing of the corruption of the Old World, had gone to America, where he attempted, by founding his settlement of New Harmony, to demonstrate the quality of his projects in the purer atmosphere of the still young and uncontaminated United States.

CHAPTER XIX

REVOLT AND REPRESSION—PETERLOO AND THE SIX ACTS

UNEMPLOYMENT reached its worst in 1816, when distress was everywhere. The first serious troubles occurred in London: and the spark that set the general repression alight came from a tiny group of followers of Thomas Spence, the land reformer. Spence himself had died in 1814, but the Society of Spencean Philanthropists, originally formed in 1812, carried on the advocacy of his doctrines under Thomas Evans, Thomas Preston, Arthur Thistlewood and the two Watsons, father and son. The Spencean Society, like most Radical bodies of the time, was afflicted with Government spies, who sent regular reports of its proceedings to the Home Office. Lord Sidmouth, the Home Secretary, either greatly exaggerated the influence which it was able to wield, or decided to use its activities as a convenient excuse for instituting a general repression.

In 1816, at the height of the post-war distress, the Spenceans decided to hold in London a public demonstration in support of Spence's plan of land nationalization and the "single tax." They invited Henry Hunt, the leading orator of the Radicals, to be their speaker; but Hunt, who had no belief in Spence's ideas, would only address a demonstration in favour of the orthodox Radical programme. In the end, two meetings were held on the same day in Spa Fields—the first by the Spenceans, and the second, after they had done, by Hunt and the orthodox Radicals. The London mob, active as ever, used the occasion to march through the streets; and some rioting and a little looting took place in the City.

Upon this, Sidmouth and the Government either felt, or professed, immense alarm, declaring their belief that a general rising was in preparation. Copies of Spence's Plan and reports of the proceedings of the Spenceans, supplied by informers, were adduced in proof of this conspiracy. Both Houses of Parliament appointed "Committees of Secrecy" to examine the evidence of treasonable intentions. On their alarmist reports, the Habeas Corpus Act was suspended, and the Spencean leaders, arrested at an early stage, were put on trial for high treason.

There may have been among Spence's followers a few real revolutionaries, though most of the "Philanthropists" clearly entertained no insurrectionary ideas. At all events the alarm professed by the Government was quite ridiculous if it was based upon the wild talk of the tiny group of extremists in London. The truth must be that the widespread unrest in the industrial areas had made Lord Sidmouth and his colleagues ready to seize on the tiniest fragment of evidence that came their way. In addition to arresting the Spenceans, Sidmouth sent to magistrates throughout the country a series of letters exhorting them to the utmost severity in suppressing all forms of treason and sedition, and his office set to work to draft a series of Bills, imitated from those which had been used in suppressing the Corresponding Societies twenty years before.

Under Sidmouth's Gagging Acts of 1817, all public meetings were forbidden except under licence from the magistrates. All reading-rooms and similar places of meeting were also put under the licensing system, so that public-houses and coffee-houses could be arbitrarily closed if they were suspected of harbouring Radical groups. More drastic penalties were laid down for uttering treasonable or seditious words in speech or writing; the judges and magistrates were given to understand that the Government would be fully behind them if they used their powers to the furthest limit. Nor was this all. The Home Office itself sent spies and provocative agents, headed by the notorious Oliver, out into the country to mix with the local Radicals and, under pretence of being themselves insurrectionaries, to report upon all seditious proceedings; and the magistrates in the industrial areas were further encouraged to employ similar agents of their own.

Meanwhile, the trial of the Spenceans came on. But to a London jury the evidence, resting, as it did, entirely on the word of a Government spy, by name Castles, who had played the vile part of an *agent provocateur*, seemed far too flimsy; and after James Watson had been acquitted, the rest of the prosecutions had to be dropped. The Government, however, intensified its measures against the impending "insurrection"; and at length the "overt act" for which it had been waiting was procured for it by the work of its leading spy. The proceedings in the North of England, culminating in the "Derbyshire Insurrection" of June 1817, assured Sidmouth that he had been right, after all, about the state of the country.

Before this, the tragic history of the year 1817 had opened with the attempted March of the Blanketeers. This was a movement, chiefly among the starving Manchester handloom-weavers, but supported by the spinners as well, for an organized march of the unemployed to London, for the purpose of presenting to the Prince Regent petitions for Reform and the relief of distress. The marchers were to carry blankets and such provisions as they could provide, and were to sleep by the way in churches, enlisting support for their movement in the towns through which they passed. This movement was quite open, and nothing was done to stop it until the actual day on which the marchers were to be given their send-off at a great meeting in St. Peter's Fields, Manchester. Upon this meeting the soldiers descended, dispersing the demonstrators and arresting Baggulay and Drummond, the two leaders of the march. But some contingents had already set off before the soldiers arrived; and these, harried by soldiers and yeomanry, were broken up and their leaders arrested at various points along the route. No organized body of marchers got beyond Derby, though one man, Abel Couldwell, actually reached London and duly presented his petition. The rest either scattered to their homes or were committed to jail as vagrants, or after spending varying periods in prison without trial, were released because the Government did not know what to do with them.

So ended the first "hunger march" of the unemployed. But even while the Blanketeers were arranging to proceed to London to present their grievances, Government informers from Lancashire and Yorkshire were sending in their sensational stories of an impending general insurrection in the North. Everywhere spies and provocative agents were at work. Such men as Oliver, Castles and Edwards were mainly responsible for stirring up the so-called revolutionary conspiracies which they were rewarded for denouncing. While Castles was active in London, Oliver was busy in the North; and the official spies were able to produce enough stories of impending violence to induce the magistrates to make wholesale arrests among the Radical leaders—which could be done the more easily because, after the suspension of Habeas Corpus, there was no necessity to bring the victims to trial.

In March and again in June the magistrates pounced upon meetings of working-class delegates and arrested them all. These men were supposed to be engaged on making plans for a general insurrection; but apart from the evidence supplied by paid spies and informers, there is nothing to show that any such movement existed. Wild talk there doubtless was; but of any organized conspiracy there is no untainted evidence at all. No one can read to-day, without disgust, the facts set forth in Mr. and Mrs. Hammond's *Skilled Labourer*, on the unimpeachable authority of the Home Office official papers, and the evidence furnished by such contemporary writings as Samuel Bamford's *Passages in the Life of a Radical*, written by one who was himself arrested at this time and kept in prison without any offence being proved against him.

Throughout the spring of 1817 the spy, Oliver, was going to and fro in the industrial districts, posing as a delegate from the London "Physical Force Party." Wherever he went he assured the local Radicals that the rest of the country was ready for a general insurrection, and only that particular place was lagging behind. In most areas he had no success in provoking the Radicals to take up arms; but in Derby, where the frame-work knitters were even nearer starvation than the rest of the textile workers, an unemployed knitter named Jeremiah Brandreth believed what Oliver said, and a small band of men from Pentridge and some neighbouring villages set out with such arms as they could gather to march upon Nottingham. They believed that they were but one contingent among many; but in fact they were alone. Only at one other place, Hudders-field, did a few of Oliver's dupes assemble in arms; and they dispersed at once when they found how few and weak they were.

The Derbyshire "rebels" fared worse. They marched through the night, meeting no other contingents, till they came in sight of a small party of soldiers sent from Nottingham to intercept them. They fled at once; but most of them were captured. Thirty-five were tried for high treason; twenty-three were found guilty. Of these eleven were transported for life, and three more for fourteen years. Four, including Brandreth, were hanged. The others had their sentences commuted to various terms of imprisonment. Oliver, who was responsible for the whole wretched affair, had done his work well; but his name was not allowed to be mentioned at the trial. The prisoners, by taking up arms, had convicted themselves. There was no need to mention the spy who had induced them to commit this folly.

There was a further reason for keeping Oliver's name out of the case. The Yorkshire reformers, before the trials came on, had discovered what manner of man he was, and he had been publicly exposed in the *Leeds Mercury*. So great was the feeling that Oliver's Huddersfield victims, who were tried at York before Baron Wood, a fair judge, were acquitted. But the blood of the Derbyshire victims sufficed to demonstrate to the satisfaction of the governing classes the need for Sidmouth's repression.

Meanwhile, under threat of arrest, William Cobbett had fled the country; and from 1817 to 1819 he conducted his *Weekly Register*, with William Benbow as his helper in England, from the United States. Radical journalists and pamphleteers were jailed in dozens, and their publications confiscated, only to appear immediately under new names or in other forms. The Government found itself quite unable to suppress the agitation, especially as it did not venture to deal so summarily with middle-class Radicals, such as Sir Francis Burdett, as with mere working men. In 1817 the Hampden Clubs ventured to hold a national delegate conference in London, and to put forward claims for Radical Reform; and they were not suppressed, though a few of the middle-class leaders were put in prison for short periods.

Then, towards the end of 1817, came a rapid revival of trade, which reached in 1818 the dimensions of a boom. The sheer hunger movement died away for the time, and the year was filled with strikes in which the workers sought to win back at least a part of the wages that had been taken from them during the depression. The storm centre was again in Lancashire, where, despite the Combination Acts, both spinners and weavers succeeded in creating for the time extensive Unions of delegates from the various textile towns. Combinations also existed, often under the guise of friendly societies, in many other trades; and the strike movement actually began with the brickmakers, followed by the carpenters, before it spread to the cotton workers and miners. The brickmakers and carpenters secured wage advances without being molested by the law; and then came the extensive strike movement of the spinners for the restoration of the 20 per cent cut in their wages which had been made since 1815. The weavers, far more scattered and ill-organized, followed the spinners' lead; and numerous other trades joined the movement, which spread from Lancashire into the neighbouring counties and received financial support from trade societies in many parts of the country, including the principal London trades.

At the height of this movement, the first recorded attempt was made to bring all the workers together into a "General Union of Trades," sometimes called by the name of the "Philanthropic Hercules." Delegates were sent to the London trades, which, under the leadership of the shipwright, John Gast, interested themselves in the movement. But the attempt was premature. It was promptly blotted out in the suppression of the great strikes which had inspired it.

For, as soon as the Trade Unions showed their strength, the employers and the magistrates took action. The spinners' and weavers' strikes were both broken, partly because hunger forced the strikers back to work, but also by the arrest and conviction of their leaders, on the charges of combination and conspiracy. The weavers, aided by public sympathy, did secure wage-advances in some mills; but when the strike had been broken elsewhere, most of these were quickly taken away. The more strongly organized spinners secured no concessions at all. They were forced back to work at the old wages, and their Union was broken.

The boom was short-lived. By the middle of 1819 depression was as deep as it had been two or three years before. There was a fresh round of wage reductions; and once more misery led to a revival of the mass-movement for political reform. The severity of government repression had been somewhat relaxed as the troubles died down in 1818, and reformers had been rather more free to speak their minds; but at the signs of renewed agitation the Government was ready to act again. 1819 will go down to history not only as the year when it was decided to restore the gold standard, and thus to make permanent the deflation of the previous period, but also as the year of the Peterloo Massacre and of the Six Acts.

In August 1819, the Manchester Reformers held a great open-air demonstration in St. Peter's Fields, where the hapless Blanketeers had assembled two years before. Their chief speaker was to be Henry Hunt, already "wanted" by the Government for his Radical speeches. Hunt, knowing that the magistrates had in mind to arrest him, offered to give himself up before the meeting; but his offer was ignored. Instead, the authorities waited until the great crowd had assembled, and Hunt was actually addressing it. Then suddenly forces of yeomanry and soldiers rode in upon the crammed demonstrators, striking right and left with the flat of their sabres. For a time the crowd managed to give way, and Hunt was actually arrested before the serious trouble began. Then, who knows why, a stampede started. The yeomanry began to charge in earnest at the helpless crowd, which fled in panic. Eleven persons were killed and many hundreds injured, some by sabre cuts and some by being trampled underfoot by the horses of the yeomanry or by the fleeing crowd. Two women and a child were left among the dead.

Among decent-minded people, this horrible massacre, known in derision as "The Battle of Peterloo," provoked an immediate revulsion of feeling. Lord Fitzwilliam was deprived of the lord-lieutenancy of Yorkshire for organizing a protest, and there were numerous meetings in many parts of the country, Whigs as well as Radicals lending support. But the Government congratulated those who were responsible for the massacre; and under cover of the anger which it had caused, fresh repressive measures were at once hurried through Parliament.

The Six Acts of 1819 far outdid in severity either Sidmouth's Gagging Acts of 1817 or Pitt's measures of the 1790's. The magistrates were given fresh powers for the summary conviction of political offenders without the delays involved in prosecutions at the Assizes. They were authorized to search private houses, as well as places of public resort, to confiscate weapons, to suppress all drilling or training in the use of arms, and to put down any meeting of which they disapproved. In addition the penalties against blasphemous and seditious publications were greatly stiffened up; and the entire Radical Press was threatened with suppression by the extension of the heavy tax on newspapers to periodical publications of every sort, whether or not they contained news. This last measure was directed especially at such publications as Cobbett's cheap *Register*, Carlile's *Republican* and Wooler's *Black Dwarf*, which had hitherto been treated not as newspapers but as periodical pamphlets outside the scope of the tax. The attack on "blasphemous and seditious" publications was aimed not only at these Radical journals, but also at Radical literature generally, and perhaps especially at the reprints of Paine's *Rights of Man* and *Age of Reason*, which had been selling extensively among the workers. Richard Carlile, in 1819, had reprinted Paine's *Theological Works* as well as his political writings; and the charge of atheism (though Paine was in fact a Deist) conveniently reinforced the case against the advocates of political reform.

These drastic measures were not successful. No Radical journals which paid the new tax could hope to secure any working-class circulation; for the tax alone was fourpence a copy. Such papers as Cobbett's larger *Register*, which did pay the impost, were henceforth sold only to well-to-do Reformers or to societies or inns or coffee-houses which risked suppression by buying them for their members or visitors. But Cobbett also continued to publish his cheap *Register* without a stamp; and Carlile and other Radical journalists at once made up their minds to defy the law. From 1819 onwards the "unstamped" Press played an important part in the Radical movement. Its editors, printers and publishers, and hundreds of those who sold it, were sent to prison again and again. But the fight went on, and gradually proceedings came to be taken only occasionally against some paper to which the Government felt especially strong objection. Carlile, for example, after repeated imprisonments, was let out in 1825, and thereafter left alone. But his claim that he had "accomplished the liberty of the Press in England" was premature. When the "great unstamped"—as the Radical journals published in defiance of the newspaper tax were called—again became active and numerous during the closing years of the Reform struggle, prosecutions were renewed, though not with quite the old frequency or severity. Not till 1834 did Henry Hetherington, Carlile's greatest successor in the struggle, win from Lord Lyndhurst the legal judgment that his *Poor Man's Guardian*, which its editor and many others had previously been convicted for selling without a stamp, was after all a perfectly lawful publication, because it was not in fact a "newspaper" but only a "periodical pamphlet." Even after 1834 there were occasional prosecutions. The newspaper tax was reduced to one penny in 1836; but not until 1855 was it finally abolished, after a long agitation in which Richard Cobden, as well as William Lovett, had played a leading part.

CHAPTER XX

THE RISE OF THE TRADE UNIONS

GEORGE III, who had been long insane, died at last in 1820, and the Prince Regent became George IV—the most disreputable and unrespected monarch who has ever sat upon the British throne. His reign opened with a comedy which, of no political importance in itself, had powerful repercussions on the cause of Reform. The King had long been living apart from his consort, Caroline of Brunswick; and as far back as 1806 there had been a parliamentary enquiry into her conduct —known as "the delicate investigation." This had ended in Caroline's exoneration from the graver charges, but she was censured in the report for "levity of conduct." The trouble was renewed in 1813, when as Princess Regent she protested against the restrictions placed on her intercourse with her daughter, the Princess Charlotte. On both these occasions Cobbett and other Radicals had espoused her cause, less for her own sake than because it gave them a stick wherewith to belabour the Government and draw attention to the notorious immorality of the Prince Regent.

In 1820 a far more serious issue arose. George was King; but was Caroline Queen? The King said no, and demanded from his ministers a Bill of Pains and Penalties to deprive her of her claims. Radicals and some Whigs rushed eagerly to her defence. The Government was sorely embarrassed by the scandal; but the King would not allow them to give way. He had been, since 1818, collecting evidence against her with a view to a divorce; the Bill was to dissolve the marriage as well as to deprive Caroline of her right to the title of Queen. The

House of Lords was presented with the evidence collected against her by the "Milan Commission," which had been sent out at George's behest; the sordid details were reported in the newspapers, and made the theme of countless squibs. William Hone and the Cruikshanks devoted their talents as parodists and caricaturists to the story of Caroline's—and of the King's —amours. Monarchy, rather than the Queen, seemed to be on its trial. Never in history had the Republican movement been given so magnificent a chance.

The House of Lords passed the Bill of Pains and Penalties by a bare majority of nine votes; and in face of such a division the Government did not dare to pass the Bill on to the Commons. It had to be withdrawn; but the King would not give way. On the day of the Coronation, with the issue still unsettled, Caroline tried to force her way into Westminster Abbey. She was repulsed; but the scandal remained. And then, to the immense relief of King and Government, the Queen died, and the huge agitation which the Radicals had stirred up in her support abruptly ended.

The Queen Caroline case comes into this history, not for its own sake, but because of the part which it played in organizing the Radical forces, in discrediting the monarchy, and in weakening the Government's repressive power. Never after 1820 was the old ferocity of repression restored. Journalists and working-class agitators continued to be sent to prison in considerable numbers, but the sentences were less savage, and for the most part the advocates of Reform and even of Trade Unionism were henceforth left alone, unless there were exceptional reasons for proceeding against them. The Six Acts were more repressive than previous legislation; but the actual repression became markedly less.

This was doubtless due in part to the continued recovery of trade. After the crisis of 1819 economic conditions began to mend slowly. Trade was still poor in 1820, and only fair in 1821; but 1822, 1823 and 1824 were years of prosperity, leading up to the prodigious speculative boom of 1825. After the Queen's death there spread over the country an atmosphere of remarkable tranquillity. Ireland, indeed, where Daniel O'Connell founded the Catholic Association in 1823, was working up to a new burst of unrest. But in Great Britain better times brought a temporary quiet.

Before this quiet, however, there was an epilogue. Whether or no any section among the Spencean Philanthropists had really contemplated insurrection in 1817, the tiny group that held together during the ensuing years of repression did undoubtedly turn to thoughts of violence. *Agents provocateurs* were still among them; and under this sinister influence Arthur Thistlewood and about a dozen associates, chiefly of the working class, formed the plot known as the "Cato Street Conspiracy" of 1820. Their plan was to surprise and kill the ministers at a Cabinet meeting; a Government agent, Edwards, assisted in, if he did not draw up, the scheme, and a special notice of a fictitious "grand Cabinet dinner" was inserted in one of the newspapers to bring the members to the point of action. When they met on the evening, they were raided in a barn in Cato Street (off Edgware Road), and in the struggle Thistlewood killed one of his attackers. The leaders of this feeble conspiracy were hanged, but the suspicions of the spy's activities and the inquisitiveness of Alderman Wood made it impossible to use the same provocative agent again.

These vermin were very active about the same time in Scotland, spreading reports about an impending general insurrection, and using the same tactics as Oliver had used three years before in Derbyshire. Their efforts met with much the same measure of success. At Bonnymuir, in the spring of 1820, a small body of Scottish colliers and weavers, egged on by spies, took up arms, and were scattered in a skirmish with a body of soldiers. Here again, exemplary executions followed, and among the victims was Andrew Hardie, ancestor of James Keir Hardie, who was to become the first leader of the Labour Party.

The Bonnymuir affair arose out of a widespread strike movement among the Scottish colliers. But from 1820 onwards there were, over most of the country, relatively few strikes, as Great Britain began to settle down to enjoying the full advantage which her long lead over all competitors gave her in exploiting the markets of the world. Between 1819 and 1824 the quantity of British exports rose by nearly 40 per cent, and the increase was much greater in exports to the American continent, both to the United States and to the newly liberated Republics of South and Central America, whose independence Canning recognized in 1824, when he "called in the New World to redress the balance of the Old." The increase was much smaller in exports to Europe, which was still slowly recovering from the devastation wrought by the long war. But Europe's backwardness as a purchaser involved also her backwardness as a competitor; and the British industrialists had the lion's share of the world market to themselves. Working in keen competition one with another, they exploited their opportunities by means of intense price-cutting, as is shown by the fact that the greatly increased volume of goods exported was accompanied by a relatively small rise in their total value—from £35,000,000 to under £38,500,000. In these circumstances there was little or no advance in wages, though of course the workers gained something as a result of the falling level of prices, especially as, thanks to good harvests, the price of bread fell despite the virtual prohibition of imports.

It was in the comparative tranquillity of the years after 1820 that Francis Place began his campaign for the repeal of the Combination Act of 1800 and for the statutory legalization of the workers' movement. He was able to secure the support of a group of Radical M.P.s, headed by Joseph Hume, and of some of the leading economists, including J. R. McCulloch. Place, in his own account of the affair, gives the impression that he managed this agitation almost alone, and that there was no enthusiasm for repeal among the Trade Unionists themselves until he took up their case. The truth appears to be that most of the Trade Unionists, with the experiences of the years 1815 to 1820 in their minds, felt little hope that anything would be done to redress their grievances by an unreformed Parliament. The Trade Unions wanted repeal, but did not expect to get it till they had won Reform. Place was more hopeful, especially as he knew that the fear of revolution had largely subsided, and that the Government, preoccupied with foreign affairs and the amendment of commercial policy, was for the moment looking another way.

The story of Place's and Hume's success in packing the Parliamentary Committee of 1824, presenting it with a carefully marshalled body of evidence from employers as well as workmen hostile to the Combination Laws, and finally rushing a repealing Act through Parliament before the opponents of the measure, or even the Government, were aware of what was happening, is a remarkable example both of Place's mastery of the arts of political wire-pulling and of the casual fashion in which the work of government and administration was carried on before the "new brooms" of 1832 had swept the old system away. The illegality of Trade Unionism rested not only upon the Combination Acts passed in 1799 and 1800, but still more on the interpretation given by the judges to the Common Law. Apart from the Acts of 1799 and 1800, and from the earlier Acts prohibiting combinations in particular trades, the courts had come to regard all working-class combinations as criminal conspiracies in restraint of trade, punishable at Common Law. The only exceptions had been in favour of combinations for the sole purpose of taking action to secure the observance of the Elizabethan and other statutes regulating wages and apprenticeship; and by 1814 this exception had been swept away with the repeal of these statutes. Thenceforth all combinations were liable to be treated as criminal conspiracies, except pure Friendly Societies, which had been given special statutory recognition in the 1790's, on terms designed to secure their good behaviour by requiring their rules to be submitted to the magistrates. Friendly Societies, were, however, usually let alone by the law, even if they did not comply with these conditions. An inquiry of 1815 revealed a membership of nearly a million in societies of which records could be obtained; and there must have been very many more. Trade Unions often disguised themselves as Friendly Societies, or carried on their friendly activities through a separate Society; but such bodies seldom, if ever, applied for recognition under the Act. A new Act in 1819 caused more Societies to enrol; but there is no sign that, even thereafter, legal recognition was effectively opened to Trade Societies, even of a purely "friendly" type.

Francis Place and his friends now set to work to sweep all these restrictions away, and to give Trade Unionism immunity from prosecutions under Common as well as Statute Law. With Joseph Hume's aid, Place succeeded so well in packing the Parliamentary Committee and selecting the witnesses who gave evidence before it that the repealing Act of 1824 included everything that the Trade Unions desired. Neither the more aggressive Trade Unionists, who might have given the show away, nor the genera body of reactionary employers, who would have been strongly against giving Trade Unionism any legal recognition, were allowed a chance of appearing before the Committee. Before most of them had even heard that a Bill was in contemplation, Hume's Committee had reported, and the Bill drafted by it had become law. Place and his Benthamite and economist supporters mostly held the view that the effect of this far-reaching legalization would be not to stimulate, but to discourage, Trade Union action; for as devout believers in the idea that wages were ruled by the inexorable laws of Political Economy, and that Trade Union action was powerless to affect them save within a narrowly restricted field, they held that freedom to combine would soon teach the workers the futility of kicking against the pricks, and induce them rather to collaborate with the employers in increasing the "wages fund"—which depended on the employers' profits— than to wage a useless war against Capitalism. Place did not mean by this that working-class combinations would disappear; for he was a firm believer in the utility of small Trade Clubs of skilled journeymen for regulating the conditions of labour. What he did mean was that the wider Unions of Trades—*Trades* Unions as distinct from mere journeymen's clubs—would be given up, and that the workers would recognize the underlying community of interest between Capital and Labour.

Actually the repealing Act of 1824 was speedily followed by a great outbreak of strikes. The Trade Clubs and Trade Unions, which had hitherto often disguised themselves as Friendly Societies in order to evade the ban of the law, came out into the open, with publicly issued codes of rules and public appeals for members; and almost at once there were strikes, or threats to strike, over a large part of the industrial districts. This was in reality due not so much to the removal of the legal ban as to the economic situation. In 1824 the growth of trade was already reaching the dimensions of a great speculative boom, involving a huge investment of capital both at home and abroad, a rapid inflation of credit, and the making of great fortunes on the Stock Exchange and by industrial speculation.

In these circumstances one body of workers after another came forward with demands for higher wages, especially as the boom was accompanied by a sharp rise in the cost of living. Bread, which had cost on the average roughly 8¼d. for the 4-lb. loaf in London in 1822, rose to nearly 10½d. in 1824, and averaged nearly 11d. in 1825. Wage movements were doubtless more numerous and more open because of Hume's Act; but they would have occurred on a large scale even if there had been no change in the law.

In due course, the speculative boom of 1824–5 ended in a crisis which brought with it many bankruptcies, a great writing-off of capital losses, and a widespread industrial slump. Before the end of 1825, and throughout the following year, trade was deeply depressed. At once employers in one industry after another set to work to claim back the wage concessions which had been made during the boom; and there was a second wave of industrial disputes, in which the Trade Unions, especially among the miners and textile workers, offered resistance to these reductions. Thus, in the years 1824–5, two strike waves, of an opposite character, came in rapid succession; and the blame for all these industrial disturbances was of course laid by the employers and the Government on the mistaken policy of giving legal sanction to the workmen's right to combine.

Nevertheless, the old legal restrictions on combination were not put back. Place's Act of 1824 was indeed much modified by the amending Act of 1825, by which the Government sought to confine the legalization of Trade Unionism within very narrow limits. But the Act of 1825 still left combination lawful, as long as the Trade Unions confined themselves to peaceful bargaining about wages and hours, took care not to lay themselves open to charges of inducing breach of contract, and did not in any way "molest" or "obstruct" either employers or blacklegs. These restrictions meant in effect that it was exceedingly difficult to conduct any strike—at any rate any considerable strike—without serious danger of falling foul of the law; for the courts were apt to place a very wide inter-pretation on the notions of "obstruction" and "molestation," including under them even the attempt peacefully to persuade a workman to abstain from work. But, though many Trade Unionists were convicted of offences under the 1825 Act, even the bare recognition which it gave to the right of combination made a great difference to the status of Trade Unionism. The Trade Unionist was no longer an outlaw, liable to prosecution for mere membership of a trade society. The Unions were not driven again underground. After 1825 they no longer dis-guised themselves as Friendly Societies, but for the most part pursued their activities openly, and were no longer so con-tinually harried by the law.

This Trade Union victory was one sign among many of the changing times. Peel had succeeded Sidmouth as Home Secretary in 1822; Huskisson, at the Board of Trade, was busy reforming the tariff on less illiberal lines, which included a modification of the Corn Laws; Canning at the Foreign Office was giving support to liberal movements abroad. The Ministry was still hostile to parliamentary Reform; but its policy had become definitely less reactionary and oppressive. The British governing classes were preparing themselves for a readjustment to the new social system created by the Industrial Revolution; and the new ministers were not unwilling to do something to meet working-class claims, in the hope of lessen-ing the support of the workers for the Radical cause. More-over, the argument of the Benthamites that freedom to com-bine was really a part of the essential freedom of trade carried some weight, especially when it was accompanied by an assurance that prohibition positively encouraged combina-tion, by causing the workers to attribute their sufferings to legal oppression instead of recognizing in them the working of inexorable economic laws.

The workers, however, undiscouraged by their defeats in 1825 and 1826, persisted in forming combinations; and Trade Unionism continued to grow apace. Trade improved in 1827, and still more in 1828, and after a set-back in 1829, was again reasonably flourishing in 1830. Thereafter a renewed depression set in; and the final struggle over the Reform Bill was fought out in a period of economic adversity. This fact, indeed, helps to explain its course. The workers would have been less ready to riot for Reform in 1831 and 1832 if unemployment had been less acute.

Trade Unionism grew strongly through the years of improving trade after the crisis of 1825. Old Unions, such as the London Shipwrights, came out into the open; in numerous cases local trade clubs of craftsmen began to link up into Unions which aimed at covering the whole country; and many new Unions and local societies were formed. Among the skilled craftsmen, the Steam Engine Makers (1824), the Journeymen Steam Engine Makers (1826) and the Friendly Society of Carpenters and Joiners (1827) were attempts to form open combinations on a national scale. The miners on the North-East Coast re-formed in 1825 the Northumberland and Durham Colliers' Union, which had been broken after the struggles of 1810; and under the leadership of John Doherty the cotton spinners set to work to re-create their central organization, which had fallen to pieces after the struggles of 1818.

John Doherty, who had come to Lancashire from Ulster in 1817, was in this period easily the leading figure in the Trade Union movement in the North. An ardent Owenite, he regarded Trade Unionism not only as a means of protecting working-class conditions, but also as an instrument for changing the basis of the economic order. He aimed not merely at creating a powerful and inclusive society of cotton spinners extending to every area in Great Britain, but also at welding together the entire working class into a closely united body for mutual protection and for the creation of a new social system. Beginning with his own trade, he led the cotton spinners in their resistance to the wage reductions demanded by the employers in face of the trade depression of 1829. The workers were defeated; but the moral which they drew from their failure was that they must build up a Union powerful enough to prevent one district from undercutting and blacklegging on another. In pursuit of this object Doherty, towards the end of

1829, got together in the Isle of Man a conference representing the Scottish and Irish as well as the English spinners, and persuaded it to create the Grand General Union of All the Spinners of the United Kingdom.

This, however, was only the first step. Doherty had already made in 1826 an attempt to create an inclusive Union of all trades; but he had apparently become convinced that this could succeed only if it could be built up round a solid nucleus of trade organization. Having won over the spinners, he next set to work to make their Union the starting-point for a wider combination. In March 1830 he started the *United Trades Co-operative Journal* to advocate his Trade Union and Owenite ideas; and in June he succeded, at a widely representative conference, in launching the National Association for the Protection of Labour, which every trade society in the country was invited to join.

Hardly had this been done when the parent body, the Spinners' Union, became involved in a series of local strikes for wage advances, to which the employers responded with a general lock-out. Trade, which had improved for a time, again grew worse, and the men were starved back to work on the old terms. The Spinners' Union survived; but it was greatly weakened. The Scottish and Irish branches broke away; and it was all Doherty could do to hold the English sections together.

Meanwhile, the National Association for the Protection of Labour, fostered by the growing mass excitement, as the struggle for Reform grew more intense, spread rapidly to new areas. The hosiery, lace, silk and other textile workers of the East Midlands came in with their numerous local societies; and with them came a wide variety of other trades in the Midland Counties. The Potters' Union, organized with Doherty's help in 1830, joined up almost at once, and set to work to organize a Co-operative Pottery, which lasted only a few months. Miners from some areas in Lancashire joined at an early stage; and under their influence a national delegate conference of miners drawn from the Yorkshire, Lancashire, Midland and Welsh coalfields decided to become a section of Doherty's all-embracing body, though it does not appear that most of the groups represented ever contributed to its funds or owed it more than a shadowy allegiance. In Yorkshire, the woollen and worsted workers, instead of joining the National Association, which sent missionaries to organize them, formed a separate body of their own, usually known as the "Leeds Trades Union" or the "Clothiers' Union." This body, faced with implacable opposition from the Yorkshire employers, became a secret society, and waged bitter industrial warfare until it was broken up by a great lock-out, in the course of which the "document" was presented, in 1834. By 1831 the National Association and the bodies loosely associated with it could claim a combined membership of at least 100,000, without counting the Leeds Union; and its published accounts show that, in Lancashire and the Midlands, most of the societies which joined it took their membership seriously enough to pay substantial dues to the centre at Manchester.

Nor were these organizations alone. There was also a widespread Trade Union revival in areas beyond Doherty's sphere of influence. The Northumberland and Durham Colliers' Union had languished after 1825; but in 1830 it revived under the leadership of Thomas Hepburn, and succeeded in winning an extensive strike, despite the generally depressed condition of trade. In London the various trades joined together in a Metropolitan Trades Union, which entered into some sort of loose relationship with the National Association. And, last but not least, the excitement spread from the industrial workers to the downtrodden labourers in the villages, and there occurred that tragic episode in the history of the English countryside which Mr. and Mrs. Hammond have graphically described as "the Last Labourers' Revolt."

The labourers did not, indeed, at this stage form Trade Unions. Their revolt was a matter of instinct rather than of deliberate organization; and from first to last it had no general co-ordination and no national leaders.

In order to understand this movement, it is necessary to go back to what was said earlier about the Speenhamland system of poor relief. As long as the war lasted, the extension of arable cultivation served to keep up the demand for rural labour, despite the progressive decline of village industries. Moreover, the farmers and landlords were reaping high profits, and the burden of poor rates, which were used to supplement wages in face of the rising prices, was not severely felt. But after 1815 the arable area gradually declined, and pasturage, which requires less labour, was extended in its place. At the same time the sharp decline in agricultural values made the farmers far more resentful of rate burdens, especially as the numbers of unemployed who had to be kept entirely out of the rates were being increased both by the fall in rural employment and by the continued migration of industry to the towns.

Accordingly, throughout the period between 1815 and 1834, the justices and the parish authorities were continually revising their ideas of the minimum real income on which the poor could be kept alive. The use of wheaten bread was denounced as wanton extravagance; and the labourers were recommended to take to potatoes and oatmeal instead. Wages were simultaneously beaten down on the ground of the fall in prices and the farmers' diminished capacity to pay. The labourers, employed and unemployed, were living throughout this period under conditions of steadily increasing misery. Anyone who doubts this can study for himself the first-hand account of their situation which Cobbett has given in his *Rural Rides*, written between 1820 and 1830—that fascinating medley of acute observation, impassioned invective, and no less impassioned love of the English country and the English people, that remains as alive and as moving to-day as it was more than a century ago.

Rural misery had been responsible ever since 1815 for sporadic outbreaks in years of exceptional distress. Ricks had been burnt, and there had been hunger-riots again and again in the famished areas where too much food was being produced. There had even appeared village Messiahs, announcing a Second Coming; and the despairing labourers had followed after them as they would have followed anyone who promised them a way out of their troubles. But the agricultural uprisings of 1830 were on a far larger scale than any that had occurred before. They spread from village to village over all the Southern Counties from Kent to Wiltshire and Dorset, and throughout the Eastern Counties and a considerable part of the Midlands. There was behind them no formulated common programme; but almost everywhere the outbreaks followed much the same course. The labourers destroyed the threshing-machines and other new implements which reduced the demand for labour. They burnt the ricks of exceptionally harsh landowners or farmers, while showing no enmity to the farming class as a whole—indeed, not a few of the farmers seem to have sympathized with the movement.· They demanded from the Church and the landlords a remission of tithes and a general lowering of rents, and from the farmers the higher wages which these reforms would make them able to pay. From the Poor Law authorities they claimed living rates of relief, based on a tolerable diet; and almost the only acts of personal violence which marked the revolt were directed against the harsher overseers of the poor, some of whom got a ducking in the village pond.

Throughout the whole affair the labourers neither killed nor wounded one single person. But their moderation did not save them when the Government, with the aid of the soldiers who were sent into the rural districts, got the upper hand. Special Commissions of judges were sent out to try the offenders. Nine men were hanged, 457 transported, and nearly as many more sent to prison for varying terms. Included among the victims were some middle-class people who had too plainly shown their sympathy with the revolt. Henry Cook of Micheldever, a lad of nineteen, who had committed the enormity of knocking off the hat of a member of the Baring family during an altercation, was among those who were hanged. The story persisted long that the snow would never lie upon his grave.

This savagery was suffered by the wretched labourers at the hands not of the old Tory aristocracy which had governed the country for so long, but of the new Whig Government which was even then pressing forward its measure of parliamentary Reform. The Whigs, in fact, were no more prepared than the Tories to tolerate any sign of independence on the part of the village workers. For the Whig leaders too were of the squire-archy, and accustomed to regard the labourer as a serf without rights; and their espousal of the cause of Reform in the interest of the rising middle class made them more determined than ever to demonstrate their hostility to subversive forces. Henry Cook and his fellow-victims were butchered by Lord Melbourne to salve the Whig conscience and assure the Tories that the aristocracy need fear nothing from a Whig Reform.

By 1831 the revolt was over. But the threat from the industrial workers remained. In the case of the miners, the great landowners, who were also the great coalowners of the North, exacted speedy vengeance for the concessions which they had been compelled to make. In 1832 Hepburn's Colliers' Union was broken in pieces after a desperate strugle, and the South Wales miners were also involved in a pitched battle with the colliery owners, in which they too went down to defeat.

By this time, Doherty's National Association for the Protection of Labour was already breaking up, as each section became too preoccupied with its own special conflicts to have energy to spare for building up the wider movement. The National Association virtually ceased to exist; but most of the Unions which Doherty had helped to call into being survived and remained active despite the adverse state of trade and employment. The Spinners' Union, the Potters' Union and the Clothers' Union lived on to play their part in the great Trade Union struggle of the years after the Reform Act; and the Midland and other sections of the National Association also held together in a number of regional Federations which united the workers of different trades over considerable areas. Most of these regional bodies were subsequently merged in Owen's Grand National Consolidated Trades Union.

In face of the depression, however, the Unions in the textile areas, beaten in their wage struggles, were turning more of their attention to the campaign for a new Factory Act, in which they had the support of a considerable number of the more progressive employers. The Ten Hours' movement, which was to achieve its first success in the Factory Act of 1833, and actually to win the Ten Hours' Day fourteen years later, in 1847, was born in the troubled years which followed Doherty's success in welding the cotton spinners into a powerful Union and persuading the woollen and worsted workers and the Midland hosiery workers to build up parallel organizations of their own.

Side by side with the rapid development of Trade Unionism after 1824, there was growing up a second movement, which was destined for a brief period to link its fortunes with those of the Trade Unions, and then in defeat to part company with them and go its own unforeseen but highly successful way. Co-operation was beginning to take root among the workers, in forms mainly based on the Socialist ideas associated with the name of Robert Owen.

Owen, as we have seen, left Great Britain in 1824 in order to try out his gospel in the New World. At that stage, Owenism had not attracted any substantial measure of working-class support. But no sooner did Trade Unionism begin its rapid growth than many working men began to see a close affinity between the Trade Unionist and the Owenite gospels. They, like Owen, were in revolt against the evils of capitalist, competitive society; they, like him were in search of a new social order based on the idea of human brotherhood. They began to re-interpret Owenism in their own terms, turning his proposed "Villages of Co-operation" from gifts to be offered by the governing classes to the poor into self-governing workers' associations to be created by the efforts of the workers themselves. There sprang into existence Owenite societies, such as the London Co-operative Society of 1824, with a mainly working-class membership. James Watson, one of the outstanding leaders of the London working-class Radicals, and William Lovett, later to be a leading figure in the Chartist movement, were at the head of this Society, which began to gather funds for the establishment of a Co-operative Community, and in 1826 set up *The Co-operative Magazine*.

Owen was not the inventor of Co-operative Societies. The earliest known examples date back to the eighteenth century. In the 1760's, rising bread prices induced the dockyard workers of Woolwich and Chatham to start Co-operative Corn Mills; and there were more such mills, at Hull and elsewhere, during the Napoleonic Wars. In Scotland, there were early Co-operative Stores at Fenwick, in Ayrshire, in 1769 and at Govan, near Glasgow, in 1777; and a number more date from the early years of the nineteenth century. Oldham had a Co-operative Supply Company in 1795. But none of the experiments in

Co-operation before Owen seems to have been more than an isolated venture, or to have been animated by any conscious social philosophy. To Owen belongs the credit for starting Co-operation as a social movement, with definite anti-capitalist aims and the hope of instituting a new "Social System."

Soon Owenite Co-operative Societies began to be formed in many other areas, under the leadership sometimes of working men and sometimes of Owenite sympathizers among the middle classes. Some of these Societies were purely propagandist bodies, preaching the Owenite gospel in its new form based on the idea of workers' self-government. But many of them took almost at once to shopkeeping, not so much for its own sake as because they hoped to use it as a means of building up resources which could be applied in due course to the founding of "Villages of Co-operation," or, as a half-way house, to the establishment of self-governing workshops in which the members could find employment free from the miseries of capitalist exploitation. Moreover, some of the Trade Unions, especially when they became involved in strikes, began to set up "Union shops" in which they employed their workless or striking members; and the Co-operative Stores served these Union Shops as agencies for the disposal of their products.

The growth of these movements from about 1827 was extra-ordinarily rapid. In that year Dr. William King founded the Brighton Co-operative Society; and its organ, *The Co-operator*, first issued in 1828, soon became the chief journal of the movement. Doherty, then busy organizing the cotton spinners and preparing his wider Union of all trades, gave the movement his full support. By 1830 there were already over three hundred Co-operative Societies of various kinds in active existence.

CHAPTER XXI

THE STRUGGLE FOR REFORM

WHILE the rapid growth of economic organization was proceeding among the workers, the political Reformers were gathering their forces for the final struggle. After the tumults of the distressful years immediately following the war had died down, it seemed for a time as if the Radical movement had spent its force, and as if the country might settle down again under the old constitution, provided only that the governing classes were prepared to interpret that constitution in a new way. For a few years after 1815 the old governing class had pursued the old methods of repression and had ruled openly in the interests of the landed aristocracy. But this was possible only as long as the immediate threat of revolt, arising out of the misery of the poor, solidified the richer sections of the population behind the Government as the defender of order and property. As soon as trade improved and the hunger of the poor became less insistent, the fear of revolution waned, and differences began to manifest themselves between the old and the new rich. The rising class of merchants and industrial employers in the Midlands and the North began more openly to express resentment at an economic policy designed to suit the interests of the landowners, but calculated to obstruct the growth of industry and commerce. Protests, which had been widespread already during the latter years of the war, were renewed with growing vehemence. The new rich complained that the taxes, which bore heavily upon trade and industry, allowed the landowners to escape almost scot-free, that the numerous imposts on the necessary raw materials of production hampered economic development, and that the prohibitive Corn Law of 1815, by raising the costs of production, had the same effect. The middle classes began to clamour for a change of policy, and to agitate for a reform of Parliament as the only means of securing it. They began to join forces with the Radicals and the workers in the demand for Reform.

In these circumstances, the governing classes had either to face the united hostility of the middle classes and the workers, or to attempt to buy off the less radical sections of the opposition. Through the whole of the period from 1820 to 1832 there was proceeding in Parliament a struggle between the "die-hards" and the moderates, as well as a struggle between the advocates and opponents of Reform. Of genuine Radicals there were in the Unreformed Parliament but a tiny handful; but the Whigs, still in continuous opposition up to 1830, were becoming more and more committed to a reform of the electoral system. In their ranks were many who remained hostile to any far-reaching measures that could be construed as an attack on the rights of property, or even as seriously endangering the aristocratic principle. These "moderates" favoured no more than a modest measure of electoral redistribution, which would abolish the rottenest "pocket boroughs" and transfer the seats to a carefully limited electorate in the more populous counties and the big industrial towns. But there were others who wished to go much further than this, and to establish some sort of uniform franchise over the whole country, wide enough to give votes to the middle but not to the working class. The Whig leaders who inclined to the second group by no means intended to make Great Britain a democracy—even a "middle-class democracy." They meant rather to reinforce the claims of the Whig, instead of the Tory, aristocrats to govern the country by ranging the middle class behind the Whig party. They looked forward to a Reformed Parliament still consisting mainly of aristocrats, but of aristocrats prepared to govern in conformity with the interests of the industrialists and merchants.

The Tories, on the other hand, were against Parliamentary Reform. But they too were divided. One section wanted to go on ruling the country in the old way, ignoring the pretensions of the new rich. But a second group, headed by such men as Canning, Huskisson and the younger Peel, held that the one chance of preventing electoral Reform lay in a voluntary change of attitude on the part of the existing aristocracy. This group wanted the Tories, and not the Whigs, to govern the country; and it hoped that, if the Tories showed themselves more attentive to the needs of industry and commerce, the new rich would give up clamouring for a change in the Constitution.

From 1822 onwards this new Toryism got its chance. Peel set to work to amend the savage criminal law. Huskisson carried through large changes in the tariff, simplying the rates of duty and removing or reducing many excessive taxes on raw materials; and he also gratified his Liverpool constitutents by modifying the Navigation Laws and negotiating Reciprocity Treaties with the United States and numerous other countries. Meanwhile Canning, as Foreign Secretary, set his face against the reactionary Holy Alliance in Europe and opened up new markets for British manufactures by giving diplomatic recognition to the new South American Republics.

These measures, however, in the end strengthened the Reform cause. The middle classes accepted what Canning and Huskisson and Peel gave them, and asked for more. Despite the blandishments of the "liberal Tories" they rallied to the Whig side, and began to push the Whigs towards a more definite attitude on the question of Reform. The middle classes were still for the most part prepared to accept aristocrats as governors; but they insisted on their right to settle which set of aristocrats should govern.

The Reform movement thus gathered force; and the economic crisis of 1825 added greatly to its strength. But the Reformers did not form at all a homogeneous group. On the right of the movement were the Whig aristocrats, desiring no more than the minimum of change that would suffice to allay middle-class discontent and to consolidate their own ascendancy. To their left were the more advanced Whigs, headed by Brougham and Durham, who held that nothing short of a clean sweep of the rotten boroughs and a new electoral system based on the middle classes would meet the needs of the time. To the left of Brougham and his *Edinburgh Reviewers* were the Benthamites, or "Philosophic Radicals," weakly represented in Parliament, where Hume was their principal spokesman, but with a very powerful following among merchants and manufacturers and in the professional classes. The Benthamites, following their master's conversion, were by this time advocates of Manhood Suffrage; but most of them regarded so sweeping a change as practically out of the question, and were prepared to join forces with Brougham and Durham in order to push the Whigs as far as they could be persuaded to go. The Benthamites, mainly of the middle classes, had their working-class supporters, such as Francis Place and his Westminster Radicals; and Place and his friends were to Hume and the parliamentary Radicals what Hume was to Brougham and Brougham in his turn to Lord Grey and Lord John Russell.

To the left of Place, now grown old in the service of the movement and economically a fierce adherent of Benthamite and Ricardian doctrines, stood the main body of the working class, demanding nothing less than full Manhood Suffrage. But the workers too were divided. One group, probably the largest and including a good many farmers as well as industrial workers, looked to Cobbett for leadership. A second, especially strong among the London and West Country artisans, followed Henry Hunt. Sir Francis Burdett, long Member for Westminster and the close political associate of Francis Place, had by this time become much cooler in the cause of Reform, and had largely lost his influence; and Major Cartwright, who continued his indefatigable efforts right up to his death in 1824, never commanded a large independent following. But though Cobbett and Hunt were the outstanding leaders of working-class Radicalism, their ascendancy was by no means unquestioned. To their left stood numerous local societies of working men, often Trade Unionists and Owenites as well as Reformers, who disbelieved in the possibility of Parliament reforming itself, and dreamed of unconstitutional action, or even of armed revolt, as the means of redressing their economic grievances and re-establishing society on a new basis of equality and freedom. From about 1830, the National Union of the Working Classes—at first, not national, but a London body, with its headquarters at the famous Rotunda in the Blackfriars Road—became the rallying-point for this extreme section. It founded branches in a number of provincial towns, and these soon came into conflict with the branches of the National Political Union led by Burdett and Place.

One factor that now counted for a great deal in strengthening the British Reform movement was the growing unrest in Ireland, where Daniel O'Connell's Catholic Association, founded in 1823, was rapidly making a continuance of the British authority in Ireland impossible without large concessions to the Catholic claims. The Government suppressed the Association in 1825; but it revived instantly in a new shape, and by the time of O'Connell's triumphant return at the Clare election of 1828 it had become plain that the choice lay between concession and open war in Ireland. O'Connell, though elected, could not as a Catholic take his seat in Parliament; but his exclusion only made the agitation more intense. In 1829, to the fury of the old Tories, Peel and Wellington gave way. Parliament passed the Catholic Emancipation Act, and the King, who hated it, gave his assent. The Act saved the British rule in Ireland, but it wrecked the Tory Government. In the following year, against the squabbling and divided Tories, the Whigs under Lord Grey came to power; and the country knew that Parliamentary Reform would be pressed forward at last.

The Irish agitation helped the British Reformers in two distinct ways—by forcing Catholic emancipation and thus breaking the Tory party, and by providing an object-lesson in the effectiveness of mass action from below. Moreover, the numerous Irish workers in Great Britain played everywhere an active part on the extreme left of the Radical movement. In the propaganda of the National Union of the Working Classes, "Repeal of the Union"—that is, of Pitt's Act of Union of 1801, which had destroyed the Irish Parliament—ranked almost as equal to the demand for Parliamentary Reform in Great Britain. The Irish both in London and in the factory areas took the lead in stirring up the worst-paid sections of the working class, which when roused were also the most turbulent. Even before the days of Feargus O'Connor's ascendancy, the eloquence of Irish orators helped to spread to Great Britain the revolutionary spirit of the Irish peasants.

In 1830 the spirit of revolt received a fresh impetus from Europe. Revolution broke out in both France and Belgium. The French people dethroned the reactionary, Charles X, and set up the "*bourgeois* monarch," Louis Philippe, in his stead.

The Belgians, united to Holland against their will by the victorious Allies after Napoleon's fall, proclaimed their national independence. There were nationalist and democratic risings in Poland, Saxony, Brunswick and Hanover. A new wave of revolutionary feeling seemed to be sweeping across Europe; and in this international upheaval the forces of Labour and Socialism played for the first time a noticeable, albeit a subordinate, part. The proletariat made its first significant appearance on the streets of European cities.

The European Revolutions, especially those in France and Belgium, had a profound influence on the situation in Great Britain. They undoubtedly affected the results of the General Election which chose the first Parliament of William IV; for the election followed hard upon the "Days of July" in Paris. The new Parliament contained a Whig majority. Lord Grey was in power.

The Reform movement in the country had been rapidly gathering momentum before the revolution in France. At the beginning of 1830 Thomas Attwood, the Birmingham banker and currency reformer, had taken the lead in forming the Birmingham Political Union; and thereafter similar Unions were rapidly formed in most of the leading towns. In the following year, under the leadership of Place and Burdett, these bodies were linked up into a National Political Union, which was thereafter the outstanding representative of the main body of Reform opinion outside Parliament.

The Birmingham Political Union was not formed on a class basis. A large part of its membership consisted of working men, but its leaders were mainly of the middle class. It stood primarily for Radical middle-class opinion, as distinct from Whiggery, and it rallied behind it those sections of the working class which were content to seek Reform through an alliance of middle-class Radicals and workers rather than by means of a proletarian revolution. Over a large part of the country the organization of the Political Unions followed the Birmingham model. They enrolled the workers, or at any rate the better-paid artisans, as members; but they were led by members of the middle classes. But in some districts, especially in the North, the workers themselves assumed the lead, and the

Political Unions were predominantly working-class societies with only a sprinkling of middle-class members. In some towns two societies were founded side by side, one by the workers and one by the middle-class Radicals, and the two bodies then worked together in more or less uneasy alliance.

Until the Whigs had produced their Reform Bill, it was not necessary for the Radical societies precisely to define their attitude. Their leaders, middle-class and working-class alike, all wanted a far more radical reform than they believed the Whig Government capable of proposing; and accordingly their combined efforts were directed to organizing a pressure of public opinion that would push the Whigs as far leftward as possible. At this stage Place was devoting his efforts principally to two things—first, to organizing the existing constituencies in order to mobilize all the more Radical elements among the electorate and to secure for the new election, which he expected confidently before long, the largest possible muster of Radical, as distinct from merely Whig, candidates; and secondly, to obtaining pledges to support, after their election, a Radical measure of reform from as many as possible of the new members. Attwood meanwhile was already urging that all the Reformers should pledge themselves to refuse payment of taxes unless a really Radical Bill were passed; and Place was prepared to give qualified support to a contingent threat of tax-refusal, provided that the pledge was so worded as not to bring those who signed it prematurely into danger with the law.

At length the Whigs produced their Bill; and the Radicals were taken aback at the success which their propaganda had achieved. They had supposed that the Whigs would advance no further than the disfranchisement of a number of rotten boroughs, and the transference of the seats to the more populous counties and the growing towns. But actually the Whigs, under Brougham's and Durham's influence, and in fear of revolution unless they could destroy the unity of the Radical front, had decided to go very much further, and to establish over the whole country a uniform electoral system, with qualifications differing only as between town and county seats, on a basis broad enough to enfranchise the entire urban middle class and the main body of farmers. The workers in the towns and the labourers and small-holders in the counties were to be left voteless. But the middle class was to be offered full partnership with the existing electorate, and there was to be a thorough redistribution of seats to make the new voting rights effective. The ballot, which had been in the forefront of the Radical programme, was refused; but apart from this the Bill went much further than any section of Radical opinion had believed it possible for the Whigs to be impelled.

As soon as the terms of the Bill were known, it became indispensable for the various Radical groups to define their attitude towards it. There appeared at once wide differences among them. A large body of middle-class opinion, even among those who had joined hitherto in the demand for Manhood Suffrage, the Ballot and the rest of the traditional Radical programme, were satisfied with the Bill as it stood, and well content to desert their allies in return for the offer of membership of the governing class. The Benthamites, or Philosophic Radicals, for whom Manhood Suffrage had been an article of faith, did not take up this attitude; but they too were quite content, if they could secure as large an instalment of their full programme as the Bill offered, to postpone the rest to the indefinite future. They were not, however, by any means confident that what the Whigs promised the Whigs would or could perform. They were certain that the Parliament elected in 1830, in which there was no real Reform majority, would never pass the Bill; and they very much doubted whether the Whigs would face the necessities of a struggle which would involve new elections, the coercion of the House of Lords, and in all probability a contest with the Crown before the issue was settled. Accordingly they were determined to maintain the Radical united front of middle classes and workers, and to use it to keep up to the end the struggle for "the Bill, the whole Bill, and nothing but the Bill." Without abandoning their insistence on the Ballot as a necessary condition of free elections, they were prepared to postpone even the Ballot and to concentrate all their forces on securing that the Bill as it stood should become law

The working-class groups which were associated with Place

and the Political Unions shared in the main the attitude of the
Benthamite Radicals, though they were naturally more disposed to keep up a vocal clamour for Manhood Suffrage, and
to point out that the Whig Bill meant the sovereignty of the
employing class. For though they would be left voteless, and
would even lose the influence they already had in the few
"open" constituencies such as Westminster, they were prepared to believe that Radical Reform must come by instal-
ments, and that they would be able to repeat the success just
gained by popular pressure in a renewed agitation for a more
Radical Bill before many years had passed. They were not
content; but they were ready to storm the first lines of the
aristocratic defences before attempting to take the citadel.

The groups of workers who stood to the left of Place were
in a more difficult dilemma. Cobbett and Hunt and countless other leaders up and down the country had been un-
sparing in their denunciations of Whigs and Benthamites
alike, telling the workers that the Whigs and the cotton-lords
would unite to betray them, and that they had nothing to hope
for save from their own efforts. They no more than Place
had believed that the Whig Bill would go nearly as far as it did.
They had expected to find themselves free to denounce a proposed alliance of the aristocracy and the rich capitalists
against the workers and the small middle class. They found
themselves faced with a Bill which offered to take the entire
middle class into the electorate, and accordingly threatened to
leave the workers to fight their battle utterly alone. Moreover,
they knew that, whatever they said, a large section among the
workers would follow Place's lead in agitating for the Bill as
it stood.

In this difficult situation the working-class forces divided.
Cobbett, after an attempt to insist on the inclusion of the
Ballot as a condition of support, rallied his followers behind the
demand for the whole Bill as a first instalment of Reform, without ceasing to adjure the workers to "watch the Philosophical
villains" as well as the Whigs, and to stand ready to act against
a new betrayal. On the other hand the National Union of the
Working Classes and a few of the Northern Reform societies
cried out fiercely against a measure which proposed to hand

the workers over to the mercies of the capitalist class, and sought to rally the working-class forces behind a demand for nothing less than Manhood Suffrage. Henry Hunt, who had been elected as M.P. for Preston in 1829 against the powerful Stanley interest, shared the view of the extreme left; but his Preston constituents were all for the Bill, and he found himself in the House of Commons compelled to vote with the Whigs, though he continued to speak against them. In effect, it had become plain, as soon as the Whig Bill was issued, that the choice for the Radicals lay between working for the Bill and adopting a definitely revolutionary attitude; and, faced with this choice, most of the leaders rallied to the Bill, either because they were against revolution or because they felt it to be hopeless.

The Whig Bill was carried on second reading in the House of Commons by a single vote. That meant that, even apart from the attitude of the House of Lords, there was no chance at all of carrying it through Committee without large modifications, which public opinion would certainly not be prepared to accept. The Whigs had either to give way to the Tories, now reinforced by Whig malcontents who regarded the Bill as a betrayal of the Whig aristocracy, or to face a new election—and the consent of the King was needed for a dissolution. Lord Grey, convinced that nothing less than the Bill would avert the danger of revolution, decided on the second course. With many misgivings—for he disliked the Bill—the King gave way. A second General Election was held in May 1831, and the Whigs came back to Parliament with a greatly increased majority. The Bill passed through the Commons without difficulty or substantial change. It was sent up to the House of Lords in October; and the Lords promptly threw it out.

The peril in which the Bill stood in 1831 solidified the popular forces in its support. Its working-class opponents were left in a small minority, and the main mass of working-class Reformers rallied to the Political Unions in the struggle for the Bill. When the Lords rejected it, a revolution backed by the middle-class as well as the working-class Reformers seemed fully possible. All the Reform bodies clamoured for a creation of peers sufficient to ensure its passage. The Whigs had to go on, or face revolution. But they hesitated to ask the King to swamp the House of Lords by making new peers; for he might well refuse, and then revolution would be unavoidable. Grey introduced his Bill with minor changes, again passed it through the Commons, and sent it back to the Lords who, in April 1832, carried the second reading by a majority of nine votes.

But the House of Lords had not yet done with the Bill. Driven to accept the inevitability of some sort of Reform, the Lords set to work to amend the Whig measure. Grey thereupon resigned. Then followed the political crisis known as the "Days of May." Wellington, who hated all Reform, tried to form a Tory Ministry to carry through a Bill just sufficient to prevent revolution. But Peel and most of the Tories in the House of Commons refused to follow him. Grey came back to office with a pledge from the King to create, if need arose, enough new peers to ensure the passage of the Bill. But the threat was now enough. The House of Lords gave way, and the Reform Bill of 1832 became law.

This, however, is only the parliamentary side of the story. The issue was really decided in the weeks of turmoil which followed the Lords' rejection of the Bill in October 1831. For in those weeks it became manifest not only to the Whigs but to many Tories as well, and to almost the whole class of merchants and financiers, that nothing less than the Bill would now avail to prevent revolution. The Bristol Riots, in the course of which the workers had command of the city for several days, the burning of Nottingham Castle, the sack of Derby jail, and the appearance of angry crowds in the streets of London, where the King's carriage was molested, gave the governing classes warning of the temper of the people. The middle-class Reformers, though they were ready enough to use these demonstrations of force as arguments for the Bill, were in no mind to see their hopes of a *bourgeois* Parliament drowned in a Red Revolution; and they rallied all their forces behind the Whigs to secure the passage of the Bill. The Political Unions were amply supplied with money for propaganda; and they used it in consolidating their hold in opposition to the forces of the extreme left. The National Union of the Working

Classes and the other opponents of the Bill, who had seemed in October about to assume the leadership of the workers, found themselves again isolated. In the final crisis of May 1832, Place and not Hunt was in control of the situation, working in close alliance with the middle-class Reformers. It was he who took up again Attwood's proposal to refuse payment of taxes, and carried his famous slogan: "To stop the Duke, go for gold," proposing to the middle classes a run on the Bank of England's gold reserve as a means of preventing Wellington from forming a government. Never since 1688 had Great Britain been so near actual revolution as in 1831; never in all the troubles of the next two decades was she to come so near to it again.

It is by no means unimportant to bear in mind that the struggle over the Reform Bill was fought out at a time of deep industrial depression. Trade had been very bad in 1829; and then, after a partial recovery in 1830, it slumped again, and remained depressed during the next two years. The crowds that seized Bristol, burnt Nottingham Castle and created disturbances in many parts of the country were impelled by hunger as well as by zeal for Reform. If trade and employment had been good in 1831, it is at any rate arguable that the rejection of the Bill by the Lords would not have been followed by an unescapable demonstration of popular force, and that the Whigs, instead of pressing on with "the whole Bill," would have compromised with the reaction and accepted a much less comprehensive measure. As matters stood, the depression forced their hands; and when the crisis recurred in 1832, with trade still bad and unemployment widespread, Peel and his "moderate" Tories were not prepared to risk the danger of a new outburst of popular wrath.

The Bill therefore became law, and the combatants, now getting ready for a new General Election, were free to count up their gains and losses. Under the new system, the franchise in the boroughs was extended to all "Ten Pound Householders"; and in the counties the "Forty Shilling Freeholders" were reinforced as voters by the tenant farmers who paid £50 or more in rent—a reform which went beyond the original intention of the Bill, having been introduced as an amendment during its passage through the House of Commons. Even after this enlargement the electorate remained small in relation to the whole adult population, five out of every six adult males being still without a vote. The Scottish electorate, moreover, was much smaller in relation to population than the English, and the Irish was smaller still. In the counties there was in England one voter to every 24 inhabitants and in Wales one to every 23, whereas in Scotland there was one to 45, and in Ireland one to 115. In the boroughs the electorate was rather larger in relation to inhabitants—one to 17 in both England and Wales, one to 27 in Scotland, and one to 22 in Ireland. On the average each M.P. in the United Kingdom represented 36,500 inhabitants and 1,235 voters, whereas in England alone the proportions were one to 27,800 and 1,314.

But the magnitude of the change did not lie solely, or even mainly, in the increased number of electors. The redistribution of seats was at least as important. Over 200 seats were removed from the control of the borough-mongers. In England alone 56 boroughs returning 111 members were wholly abolished, 30 other boroughs were reduced from 2 seats to 1, and the combined borough of Weymouth and Melcombe Regis from 4 to 2. Instead, 22 large towns, including the new parliamentary boroughs in London, received 2 members each, and 20 more a single member. The number of English county members rose from 94 to 159, the more populous counties being divided up into smaller constituencies and the disfranchised boroughs thrown into the county areas. Towns such as Manchester, Birmingham, Leeds, Bradford, Sheffield, Merthyr Tydfil and Swansea received representation for the first time; and in London, where the City still returned its 4 members, new constituencies were created for Finsbury, Marylebone, Tower Hamlets and Lambeth, in addition to the old constituencies of Southwark and Westminster.

It remained to elect the new Parliament; and that was done in December 1832. The result was a Whig but not a Radical triumph. About half the members of the first Reformed Parliament were gentlemanly Whigs who could be relied on to regard the Reform Act as final and definitive, and to oppose any projects of further change. About a quarter were Tories,

divided between the two factions of "diehards" and "Peelites"
—for Peel was already setting about his task of reconditioning
the Tory, or Conservative, Party to meet the needs of a new
era of capitalist ascendancy. The remaining quarter consisted
of O'Connell's Irishmen, bent on repeal of the Act of Union,
and a small group of Radicals, ranging from the philosophic
Radical, Joseph Hume, to the ex-ploughboy, William Cobbett,
with Thomas Attwood of the Birmingham Political Union
about midway between. Of the working-class leaders, Cobbett
alone secured election. Hunt was beaten at Preston; and
actual working men were still outside the pale. Cobbett, when
he divided the House on a really Radical motion, could command about a dozen followers among the more extreme
middle-class Radicals, or, if some of the Irish voted with him,
as they sometimes did, perhaps twice as many. Moderate
Whigs, with the frequent support of the Peelites, controlled the
parliamentary situation. If the Tory diehards had been beaten
the working classes had been beaten too. For now that the Act
was law, extra-Parliamentary agitation had lost much of its
force. The workers were speedily to find themselves at grips
with the Reformed Parliament.

The new Parliament was immensely stronger than the old.
For, of the forces hitherto ranged against the Government,
most of the wealthier and more influential elements had now
gone over to the Government side. The middle classes, or
rather the Whig aristocracy governing on their behalf, had
freedom to rule Great Britain in full accordance with the
requirements of advancing Capitalism. There were, indeed,
struggles still to come between the new voters and the old,
between the middle classes and the landed aristocracy which
had admitted them to a share in power. It took fourteen more
years to repeal the Corn Laws, and nearly thirty to complete
the free trade system. But for the moment the tide was with
the middle classes; and they set to work promptly upon the
rest of their immediate programme.

ENGLAND UNDER THE REFORM ACT

CHAPTER XXII

OWEN AND THE TRADE UNIONS

THE 1832 revolution, consequently, had handed political power over to the middle class from the aristocracy. The new rulers indeed contrived for many years to act through members of the upper class. Scarcely a member of the Grey Cabinet was not either a peer or an heir to an old or recent peerage. But these Whigs, and in due course the Tories who succeeded them in office, were directly responsive to middle-class opinion and needs. They were even less than the old Governments responsive to working-class opinion, for they had now no fear of it. The working class had been kept outside, and the exclusion was entirely successful.

But no man, as Juvenal says, ever became utterly abominable all at once; many members of the new Parliament which met after the passing of the Bill had their minds filled, as by the swirl of dust that had not settled, with the diplomatically vague catchwords of liberty which had been shouted during the struggle. Under the influence of what severer critics such as Bright were to condemn as thoughtless good-nature they passed in 1833 the first effective Factory Act, which was even more significant for the promise of future benefits than for its own provisions. Other Factory Acts existed; Peel's 1819 Act had been amended by Acts passed under J. C. Hobhouse's initiative in 1826 and 1830. But these, limited in any case to the cotton industry, had been largely nullified by the absence of machinery to enforce them. The new Act appointed four inspectors for that purpose, thereby ensuring that not only it but all subsequent Acts would be better obeyed. Moreover, the investigations of these inspectors and the facts which they brought out were largely responsible for pushing later Parliaments further along the path of industrial legislation which most of the M.P.s disliked and feared.

The Act itself was not very generous. It dealt only with textiles, specifically excepting silk; it limited the hours of children under thirteen to eight, and under eighteen limited them to twelve. Indirectly it thus stopped some of the worst evils of the employment of children, but it was far from satisfying the promoters of the reform, headed by Lord Ashley, who was later to become famous as Lord Shaftesbury. Their object was a general "ten hours" Act. Such an Act would nominally apply only to women and children, since it was hopeless to offer Parliament a Bill which openly restricted the hours of adult male workers, as this would be denounced as an infringement of liberty. But the Ten Hours' Committees correctly reasoned that it would be unprofitable for millowners to run their machines for longer than they could keep the female workers to their task; and in fact the gains of the female operatives were always shared by the male.

The movement, after Hobhouse had dropped it, had been restarted effectively in 1831 and its parliamentary spokesman had been Michael Sadler, a Tory soon thrown out by the Reform Act. Its most numerous adherents were of course working-class, but some of its most effective supporters were not. Ashley was heir to, and later owner of, an enormous Dorset estate, Fielden was a great millowner in Todmorden, Wood another employer who is said to have spent £40,000 on the cause, and Oastler a bailiff or estate-manager of high Tory views and passionate temper.

For a little while longer, too, the pre-Reform temper lasted in the juries. It died, partly for class reasons, but partly also because the new Governments rarely permitted the persecution and political tyranny that had been the custom of the old régime; the "London disease" was ended by the removal of its causes. Before it disappeared, it gave one of its most remarkable manifestations, and one that demonstrated an important strengthening of the powers of State against revolution and disorder. The new London police, whose organization was due chiefly to Sir Robert Peel and who for that reason retained for years the names "bobby" and "peeler," were an organized, disciplined and minatory force; necessarily they threatened not only the burglars, footpads and cut-throats who were the pest of London, but political malcontents as well. Moreover, Francis Place had given the new inspector, a Mr. Thomas, advice on how to break up London crowds which were now dangerous instead of useful. "I advised Mr. Thomas when he saw a mob prepared to make an attack, to lead his men on and thrash those who composed the mob with their staves as long as any of them remained together, but to take none into custody; and that if this were done once or twice, there would be no more such mobs."

In May 1833, the National Union of the Working Classes held a meeting in an open space off Calthorpe Street, by the Gray's Inn Road. Mr. Thomas's police now applied their new tactics: they set upon the meeting, which does not seem to have been turbulent, closed up the exits, and beat it "for nearly one hour." Lethal weapons were not used by the police, but the scene, by witnesses' accounts, was highly disagreeable. One especially enthusiastic constable, Cully by name, attacked a man who struck back with a knife and killed him. The inquest was held nearly a fortnight later: so great was the resentment at the police that the jury refused to return a verdict of murder. They disputed with the Coroner nearly two hours: in the end, to the satisfaction of the angry crowd outside the court-house, he had to accept a verdict of justifiable homicide.

The first attacks upon the newly enthroned class were not, however, insurrectionary, or indeed political in form at all. They were economic, or rather, they were what a later generation would have called syndicalist. Ever since 1828, after the end of the 1825–6 slump, Trade Unionism had been reviving. Many unions or clubs had been founded, but their progress remained sedate until after 1832. The Trade Union onslaught of 1833 and 1834 can be compared to a thunderstorm with much more exactness than that comparison is generally used. Like a storm, the movement rose unexpectedly and from almost invisible origins. Its chief characteristics were a great noise and the appearance of being about to cause a great deal of destruction (or a great clearance). It provoked great alarm, and it passed almost as suddenly as it had risen, leaving very few permanent changes behind it.

The anger which suddenly inflated the existing Trade Unions to an enormous size had its direct reason in the deception of the Reform Bill. It was illogical, but very natural, that the fraud of that year should have disgusted the thinking workers not merely with the ingenious politicians who had deceived them, but with politics altogether, and that they should have turned to a method which appeared to disregard wholly the dishonesties of Parliament

> '*Tis twelve months past, just yesterday, since earth and sky and sea*
> *And rock and glen and horse and men rang loud the jubilee;*
> *The beacons blazed, the cannons fired, and roared each plain and hill*
> *With the Bill—the glorious Bill and nothing but the Bill!*
>
> *But now each holds his hands up in horror and disgust*
> *At this same document—once termed the people's trust*
> *That at the last was to bring grist to all the nation's mill.*
> *Oh, curse the Bill, ye rogues, the Bill, and nothing but the Bill!*

So wrote a working man in a Glasgow paper; his anger was typical of many others. They felt they knew exactly what class had tricked them and why. The theory of the class struggle now for the first time appeared overtly in British history as a dominant belief. The practice of the class war, for the next fifteen or twenty years, was to fill domestic history to the exclusion of most other things: it was recognized by both those who deplored it and those who fought on one side or the other. The opposition between the middle class (the word "capitalist" was rarely used) and the working class was more universally taken to be the key to current history than it has ever been since or before, except perhaps in twentieth-century Russia.

The most natural instruments of such a conflict were, of course, the Trade Unions, which directly set man against master in satisfying conflict. For the first few months after the passing of the Reform Bill the revival of Trade Unionism was probably confined to the local clubs. But later in the year 1832 John Doherty's Cotton Spinners' Union revived, and that year the Operative Builders' Union was formed at Huddersfield.

This was the only Union which in the whole of British history united all the building crafts in one body. It had seven "governments"—masons, painters, plasterers, plumbers and glaziers, carpenters, bricklayers and slaters: builders' labourers were presumably organized with their proper craftsmen (as masons' labourers, and so forth), for there is no trace of a labourers' "government." Figures of membership are lacking: it appears probable, however, that at one time the members were 60,000 in number or more. It was made up partly of wholly new societies founded by itself, partly of existing trade clubs and trade societies which were swept up by it and greatly increased its membership. During 1832 and 1833 it acted as a signal advertisement for Trade Unionism by conducting a series of local strikes, chiefly in Lancashire, against the practice of "general contracting." The smaller masters agreed with it that customers should contract separately with master-painters, master-carpenters, master-plumbers, etc., instead of with a general contractor who broke trade customs and screwed small masters down to the level of journeymen; they viewed the Union's action with benevolence, and the strikes were everywhere successful. (They did not for long save the little master from his approaching doom at the hands of the big contractors. The massive additions which were being made to the new industrial cities could not be handled by innumerable working masters.)

Other individual unions which rose to strength enough to keep their individuality were the Potters' Union, the Clothiers' Union, and the regional Associations in Northampton, Derby, Leicester and other Midland areas, which were survivals of Doherty's National Association. The Potters' membership in the autumn of 1833 numbered 8,000. The total union membership at that time was estimated at 800,000.

But all this was overshadowed by the enormous Grand National Consolidated Trades Union, founded in October 1833 (not, as has previously been believed, in February 1834). What membership it had is uncertain: the official journal estimated it at "half a million" and contemporary reports suggest that this may not be inaccurate. The actual, registered paying membership of the Union (if we were able to discover it) would probably be only a percentage of its effective membership: trade clubs and trade societies put themselves "in union" with the larger body almost automatically, but that they returned carefully and paid for all their membership, or that the newly-sworn members paid their threepence a month steadily, is as improbable as that the machinery of Grand Lodges and District Lodges written in its constitution was ever in full working order.

Every sort of trade, without distinction of craft or sex, was swept into the new Union. Its branches reached as far as Exeter, Pembroke, Belfast and Aberdeen. The trades it covered included farm-workers, miners, tailors, gas-workers, shearmen, sweeps, bonnet-makers and bakers. The Unions mentioned above (and no doubt some unmentioned others) held apart, but despite them a vast new membership was brought in casually and without order. We hear of "Miscellaneous Lodges," which would presumably be either local Owenite societies enrolled *en bloc*, or workers in trades which had no unions of their own on the spot, and of "miscellaneous females" who would be women workers. But the exact classification of the lodges of "Ancient Virgins" who rioted at Oldham on behalf of an eight-hour day can probably never now be discovered.

The programme of this rather turbulent and excited mass of workers was provided almost entirely by one man, Robert Owen. Owen's previous views and experiments have already been described, and he was justified in claiming that his principles had not changed at all since about 1817. But a variation in method did occur, and this was due to the contacts of his friends and himself with the unionists, but particularly to his experience of the Labour Exchange of 1832. This experiment, though he now referred to it as a "mere pawnshop," had been far more successful for a time than any of his other projects. It was an extablishment in the Gray's Inn Road (with branches or satellite stores in London and the provinces) at which "industrious persons" or societies deposited the products of their industry—clothes, potatoes, doors, metal-work and anything—which were then valued at their cost in labour time (sixpence per hour; skilled labour a higher rate; material

allowed for at market prices) and put on sale after a commission had been added for the use of the Exchange. The
producer received notes for "one hour," "two hours" and so
forth, which were then used to purchase other goods in the
Exchange. The success was enormous: the Exchange was
jammed with goods and with purchasers, and its "labour
notes" were even accepted outside its walls. Private banks
still issued notes, and large firms issued their own tokens, so
public opinion was not unprepared. The management was
largely left by Owen to delegates of working-class co-operative
producers' societies: during the year November 1832 to
November 1833 a clear profit was shown. The decline of the
whole experiment in the ensuing year was unnoticed in the
more exciting events outside. It was due to several causes,
some merely accidental. A dispute with the landlord forced
the Gray's Inn Road Exchange out of its original building, and
it lost much of its clientele and suffered from theft in the
process; Owen's religious views offended the wives of the
workers, who controlled the shopping; the proportion of slow-
selling objects deposited became excessive: before long regulations had to be made requiring equal quantities of cash and
labour notes to be paid for meat and food, so great was the
demand for these; groceries, a little later, were at three-fourths
cash and one-fourth notes. Some time about October 1834
the Exchange was closed; the provincial exchanges soon after
or before.

But for the time it seemed a success, and brought Owen
into contact with the working class in action. Till then he had
unconsciously assumed that the working class was to be helped
and enlightened, that it was a material to be pitied and improved rather than a number of active individuals who might
help themselves. Once he had seen the Exchange at work, his
speeches and letters became full of happy surprise at the intelligence, energy and competence of the lower orders.

He rapidly convinced himself that the Trade Unions would
in a very brief space of time—five years—transform existing
society into a Socialist community by taking over industry and
running it co-operatively, and that within five months they
could secure a large number of immediate benefits. Nor were

the members of the Unions in any way disposed to question his prophecies. "It is my impression," wrote Welsh, an architect who was one of his chief propagandists in the Builders' Union, "that with your assistance and counsel we can plant a giant Tree the top whereof shall reach to Heaven and afford shelter to succeeding generations."

Owen addressed the Builders' Parliament (i.e. that Union's annual meeting) in November 1833, and persuaded it to form itself into a Builders' Guild, for the co-operative erection of buildings, and to concentrate its industrial energy on securing an eight-hour day—the latter a wise and the former an exciting decision. In a public lecture immediately afterwards he announced the form of the future society: "I now give you a short outline," he said, "of the great changes which are in contemplation and which shall come suddenly upon society like a thief in the night." All trades, he explained, would form "parochial lodges," which would contain all members of a craft and control that craft; all these lodges would send delegates to "county lodges," which again would send delegates to ten provincial lodges, which would control the trade of the province. Delegates from these last would meet in London with the delegates of other "companies" of other trades and arrange the economic life of the nation. *The Man*, a sympathetic paper, warned the politicians that "the Trade Unions have dispensed with their services and have refused to let them have a finger in the pie." *The Pioneer*, the Union organ, more excitedly said: "See into what a position this mode of pursuing things resolves itself. Every trade has its internal government in every town; a certain number of towns comprise a district, and delegates from the trades in each town form a quarterly district government; delegates from the district form the Annual Parliament; and the King of England becomes President of the Trade Unions."

There are no sufficient records, but it seems not improbable that up to the time when these wild hopes were officially published—December 1833—the Unions had been, if not generally successful in their struggles, at least not usually defeated. Even as late as March of next year (London Gasworkers' dispute) partial successes were achieved. But they were then exceptional: in the New Year the current changed. The chief reason for this was a deliberate decision of the employers. Owen's followers were not the only people to believe that these vast changes were possible. The middle class was scared and angry. John Fielden, a big employer of Todmorden, founded and with John Doherty's aid largely ran an Owenite "National Regeneration Society" to secure the eight-hour day and other Owenite ends by co-operation of employers and employed. So far as the employers were concerned, he was wasting his breath. Very few stood aside from the new determination to stamp the Unions out of existence. The means which were chosen were known as "the Document," a pledge which all employees were required to sign. It bound them to renounce the Union and to refrain from supporting other members of the Union. At intervals during the years 1833 and 1834 it was presented in various towns and various industries. Wherever it appeared, it meant a strike. Even when the employers did not take the offensive, the men, intoxicated by their new hopes, not infrequently precipitated a conflict. "Do not for a moment," wrote the Manchester masons to their employers, "suppose that *Union* is a bubble so easy to burst or that it is nothing more than sounding brass or a tinkling cymbal. We must tell you that our Laws like those of the Medes and Persians are unalterable." Such men were spoiling for a fight, and when it came they welcomed it without reflection. They did not even calculate that, financially, co-operative production and big strikes could not be afforded at the same time. Despite big conflicts in Lancashire and Birmingham, the Builders' Union began to build its own Guildhall in the latter city. When the employers' attack led to what was practically a general lock-out in Derby (the "Derby turn-out") involving 15,000 workers, the Consolidated equally enthusiastically began to set the victims to co-operative production. But before long the multitude of conflicts threw the finances into disorder. Three consecutive levies discouraged the membership without providing sufficient pay for locked-out men or for those on strike. The Builders' Guildhall stopped still for lack of funds and the "Derby brothers" broke and streamed back to work in April 1834.

But before this the most vicious blow had been struck by the Government. As early as 1830 Peel, the retiring Tory Home Secretary, had pointed out to the incoming Whig, Lord Melbourne, that Trade Unions were a grave danger. In 1832 the Duke of Wellington, as Lord Lieutenant of Hampshire, had complained of those dangerous bodies, saying (quite untruly) that half the labourers in the county were unionists. A closely reasoned report by Nassau Senior, the once famous Whig economist, reinforced the Tory Duke's appeal and urged the total suppression of the Trade Unions. The Government was merely awaiting a convenient time to strike. The judiciary was already acting energetically. Miners were being punished for "illegal conspiracy" on announcing an intention to strike, shoemakers for picketing, tanners under the Master and Servant Laws for "leaving work unfinished," and convictions for "molestation" were common. The Government attack was more unexpected and more shattering than these. Six farm labourers of the village of Tolpuddle in Dorsetshire were arrested for swearing men into a Lodge which was intending to join (it does not seem that it had in fact joined) the Consolidated. They had not commenced, or even threatened a strike. They were tried before an ambitious and newly appointed Welsh judge, John Williams, on 18 March 1834 and sentenced to seven years' transportation, a punishment whose horrible character has already been described.

Great agitation followed this vindictive decision. Owen organized, with the assistance of the Consolidated and the independent Unions mentioned already, many petitions and a monster procession of Trade Unionists in London, which even unfriendly estimates could not put below 27,000. But the protests were wholly unsuccessful, and though they revived the members' enthusiasm for the moment with the temporary inspiration of anger, in a few weeks the agitation died down, and it was impossible for Union organizers or propagandists not to realize the fate that was quite likely to be theirs if they showed any noticeable energy.

To official repression, financial disorder and unsuccessful strikes was shortly added internal dissension. Robert Owen fell out with his two chief assistants, James Morrison, a brick-

layer, editor of *The Pioneer*, the Union journal, and J. E. Smith,
a lecturer and a sort of clergyman, editor of Owen's own
journal *The Crisis*. These two men, far more clear-headed than
those who surrounded them, had for several issues been
preaching what to-day would be called the strategy and tactics
of the class-struggle. They urged reform of the Union structure,
abstention from trivial conflicts, consolidation and conserva-
tion of energy for one well-considered attack—"a long strike,
a strong strike, and a strike all together"—and generally an
informed and directed hostility to the employers. Smith's
economic analyses (signed "Senex") are astonishingly modern
and intelligent: reading them torn from their context, few
critics would believe that they antedated Marx. But though
this advice corresponded to economic reality, it increasingly
vexed Robert Owen. "Both men and masters are producers,"
he believed, and although he had launched against the capitalist class the most formidable attack it had ever yet sustained,
he was wholly unwilling to countenance even verbal warfare
against it. His mind was already, indeed, partially withdrawn
from the outside world. He had begun to live among the
fantasies in which he ended his life. He had, for example,
previously announced that the millennium had commenced on
1 May 1833. What he meant by this, what it meant to him
or to his followers it is impossible to conceive. But it is clear
that it was this apocalyptic manner which endeared him to
them, and indeed secured his victory over Smith and Morrison.
All the objective facts were on their side, but Owen's disapproval was enough to close down *The Crisis*, which Smith
edited, and to expel Morrison's *Pioneer* from its position in
favour of a new official journal of the Consolidated.

   This occurred in the summer of 1834, when the Consolidated
was already shaken, and soon to disappear. In July the
presentation of the "Document" stamped it out in South
Wales. In May the Clothiers' Union had been similarly shattered. In August and September the Builders' Union was
broken by a London dispute. The exact date of the disappearance of the Consolidated is unkown. It is seen for a moment
in October 1834, when its Executive, from some obscure
petulance, is refusing to meet even Owen himself; it is never

heard of again. Morrison, exhausted and disappointed, died in 1835; Smith took to occultism and family journalism, withdrawing from the real world in his own manner. Owen, apparently unaware that he had even received a check, announced that "The British and Foreign Consolidated Association of Industry, Humanity, and Knowledge" would take the place of the Union, and proceeded on his equable way.

Some traces remained. The Potters' Union secured a "green book" of prices in 1835 and survived to 1837. The Scottish builders' and printers' Unions were not immediately suppressed. Elsewhere, the place of the Consolidated Union was taken by bodies with other methods. The extinction of the Union in Wales led to the revival of the "Scotch Cattle," a secret organization which enforced its conditions by murdering those who failed to observe them. Similarly in the Glasgow cotton trade the same system of terrorism was revived. In 1837 a number of Glasgow cotton spinners were arrested and charged: arson and something very little different from murder were more or less proved against them. But so general was the belief that this had been their only refuge, that subscriptions for their defence arrived from trade clubs all over the country, and the sentences were not to death but to transportation. It is also true that clubs which had existed before the Consolidated remained in existence, and often stayed absorbed into national unions.

Nevertheless, the end was almost wholly failure. The reasons for this are worth considering. It is probable, at the least, that the sublime objects of the Consolidated Union could never have been achieved. But a far more powerful and competent Trade Union organization could have survived, if the advice of Smith and Morrison had been followed, instead of that of Owen. The Unions that remained had, in general, the membership that they had had in 1832: the whole period of the Consolidated had passed by without leaving any effects, despite the enormous enthusiasm that it had generated.

This need not have happened, and, objectively, all arguments must have been in favour of the propaganda of Smith and Morrison. Yet the disapproval of Owen was enough to extinguish them. This was, as has already been suggested, directly because of the apocalyptic nature of his speeches. He announced with absolute conviction that the millennium was about to arrive—with a minimum of exertion by his listeners— or even that it had arrived. Because of their economic conditions, which will be described later, the working class of Great Britain was prepared to accept these affirmations. Psychologically, the great majority of the British working class was in those years, and for fifteen more years to come, diseased: as it had indeed always been in a greater or lesser degree since the eighteenth-century equilibrium had been broken up. Unable to find any rational methods of escape, it turned to irrational. It demanded a sure promise of happiness—of food, rest from overwork, clothing and what delights it could imagine—within its own lifetime. It found this in prophetic religions; one of the legitimate ways of regarding Owenism is to class it among the Messianic religions which arose in the early nineteenth century in more luxuriance than at any other proximate time.

The existing churches did not provide the necessary relief. The Church of England, though reform was already menacing it, was still the upper-class preserve of the eighteenth-century Establishment. It adhered to its practice—indulge the rich and keep down the poor, *parcere superbis et debellare subiectos*. This is not, indeed, true of the Evangelicals, who ever since the days of Porteous had a deep interest in social conditions and whose greatest ornament was the famous Lord Shaftesbury. But the remedies that they offered were personal reform and piety. Only later, and reluctantly, did they even advocate legislative reforms for the very worst abuses. These were methods which were slow, and the people demanded a quick relief. The Methodists—Cobbett's "nasty, canting, dirty, lousy Methodists"—and their fellow Nonconformists believed that the meek and righteous would be compensated in an after life and that to attempt to overthrow existing inequalities was "infidel and irreligious." Further, the doctrine of original sin showed that Owen's environment principle ("man's character is formed *for* and not *by* him") was un-Christian.

Such dogmas were unsatisfactory: more enterprising prophets took the vacant places. As late as 1851 the Mormons had 222 churches with 30,000 sittings. George Turner, one of the most successful prophets, not only promised immediate rewards to his followers, but actually announced the date on which the Lord would take over the government of the world and reward the faithful. The date was in 1817, the Cabinet was named, its salaries fixed, and one of the advantages of the new régime was to be that the power of men and women to enjoy each other was to be increased "and that an hundred-fold." The date passed uneventfully, but the new Church was undismayed. John Ward succeeded to Turner, and the Church extended as far as Australia, where its practices became demonstrably pathological. Joanna Southcott, still unforgotten, and perhaps the most important, announced that she was pregnant with Shiloh, the new Messiah. She died of dropsy, but her followers were unaffected by such external facts: they continued numerous and certain of the imminent coming of the Kingdom of Heaven up till 1885, when the last prophet, J. J. Jezreel, died. (Indeed, they may not yet be extinct: in 1928 their pressure induced a bishop to open what was alleged to be "Joanna Southcott's box"; he found in it some tracts, an old novel, and a booby-trap made with a horse-pistol, which had fortunately collapsed through the passage of time.) John Wroe, who added to Joanna's teaching an order that the male faithful must grow their beards, was the instructor and ordainer of J. E. Smith, the theorist of the Consolidated. Lindsay, Thorn and Boon were other religious leaders of the same type, now happily forgotten; Edward Irving, more persistent after death, has left us a "Catholic Apostolic Church" which still exists.

These Churches, and others which there is no room to discuss, depended for their appeal upon the promise of a heaven which could be secured by merely believing the prescribed set of propositions, and which would shortly appear on this earth. Such exactly was the Owenism of the Consolidated. The members had little conception of the means needed to attain to the new state of society. They were content to be informed that the millennium had commenced owing to the decision of "the benevolent Mr. Owen"; or, less, but not much less absurdly, that merely by their will they could achieve a fundamental change in five months.

This essential delusion, almost an insanity, persists beyond this period right through the history of Chartism. Continually, the Chartists, as much as the unionists, mistake their desires for facts. They believe that the intensity of their wish in some way must bring their hopes to achievement. The result of this mass hysteria is most admirably expressed by a trade unionist writing in 1841.

"We were present," he wrote, "at many of the meetings of the Grand National Consolidated Trade Union, and have a distinct recollection of the excitement that prevailed in them— of the apparent determination to carry out its principles in opposition to every obstacle—of the enthusiasm exhibited by many of the speakers—of the noisy approbation of the meeting —the loud cries of 'hear, hear,' 'bravo,' 'hurrah,' 'union for ever,' etc. . . . A little molehill obstructed their onward progress; and rather than commence the labour of removing so puny an obstacle, they chose to turn back, each taking his own path, regardless of the safety or the interests of his neighbour. It was painful to see the deep mortification of the generals and leaders of this quickly inflated army, when left deserted and alone in the field."

CHAPTER XXIII

THE NEW POOR LAW AND THE RISE OF CHARTISM

THE fantasies which filled the heads of the working class in these years contrast sharply with the realist acts and policies of its chief opponent, the merchant and employing class. The process of changing the constitution and face of England to its own benefit at the expense of both the old Tory oligarchy and where necessary the working class went on slowly but calmly and irrevocably. After the Reform Act of 1832 the most important immediate step was the reform of the municipalities, achieved for Scotland in 1833 and for England and Wales in 1835. These two Acts quietly extinguished the existing municipalities—there were 246 incorporated towns in England, nearly all grossly corrupt and exclusive bodies—and replaced them gradually (except in the City of London) by town, city or borough councils, elected on a standard franchise which admitted the whole middle class without distinction of religion. Over the whole island a considerable tribe of Anglicans and Tories were ultimately removed from profitable positions in favour of councillors who were as often as not Dissenting shop-keepers, and who put a stop to the irregular and wasteful expenditure by which their predecessors had often enriched themselves. But it must be remembered that this reform was wholly negative in character. Waste and exclusivism were ended, but no positive municipal activities, such as a modern Socialist expects, were made possible. The Councils, even supposing by a freak they had had the will, were not granted the powers. All that they could do, for the most part, was to organize the police and administer the existing municipal property. Special Acts, expensive and slowly passed through Parliament, were necessary for other activities. Health work, street cleaning, water-supply, and such matters, where they were attempted at all, had, up to 1835, been usually entrusted to bodies of Special Commissioners, set up by special Acts, and often with powers which overlapped or conflicted with those of older manorial bodies, as at Manchester, or with those of the corporations. These Special Commissions were open to Dissenters, as they were not covered by the Test and Corporation Acts; and this enabled them to draw on a much wider body of leading citizens. Sometimes the Commissioners were elected: sometimes nominated and recruiting themselves by co-option. Gradually in the decades following 1835, their duties were generally taken over by the Councils, though there was often a prolonged struggle before this was achieved. In towns which had no pre-1835 Corporations, there were similar struggles before the older type of authority gave way to the new. For a time the new broom swept hard, clearing away numberless venerable corruptions and abuses. But the victory was not complete. By the middle of the century, abuses were creeping back in new forms; and many of the borough councils were again being accused of jobbery, nepotism and minor corrupt practices.

A similar but slower and less thorough cleaning-up process took place among the sinecurists and pensioners. A certain number of the worst scandals were quietly and separately ended and no new ones were permitted. An upward limit was put to the amount of money available, and a committee of enquiry in 1837 led to the ending of some more of the more outrageous sinecures. Money and trust funds, however, already diverted were not recovered. The administration of a Vestries Act, already secured in 1831, enforced on the Church of England administration the same compromise—past corruption and waste were forgotten on condition that moderation and comparative honesty were observed in the future.

These measures were blows against the old Conservative Party: the new Poor Law of 1834 was an attack upon the working class which was far more bitterly resented. The new governing class disapproved on both moral and economic grounds of the existing Poor Law. Out-relief should never, it was considered, be given to able-bodied males; and when work-house relief was given it should be given only on such terms that life on relief should be more unpleasant than the most unpleasant way of earning a living outside. How dreadful a principle this was can only be appreciated by those who have considered what life could be for a working man in the '30's and '40's. Perhaps even contemporary opinion might have hesitated had it not been pricked on by a rather disingenuous report in 1834 from the Commissioners appointed to inquire into the administration of the Poor Law. Recklessly generalizing from certain improvident authorities it said that "in far the greatest number of work houses" (a notable exaggeration) the able-bodied were kept "in sluggish sensual indolence" (an even more remarkable hyperbole). It was true that some disorder had marked the administration of the old poor law, in both parish poorhouses and municipal work-houses. The conditions in Oxford were reputed to be ribaldly medieval, and to result in "internal bastardy." It was, by sleight of hand, assumed that these conditions were typical, and the public approbation was desired for the contrasting model establishment at Southwell, set up by Sir George

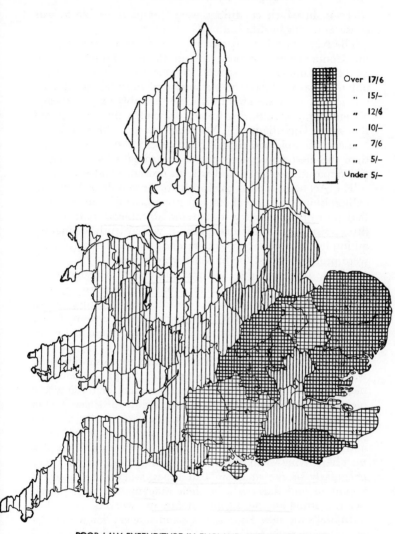

Over 17/6
  ,, 15/-
  ,, 12/6
  ,, 10/-
  ,, 7/6
  ,, 5/-
Under 5/-

POOR LAW EXPENDITURE IN ENGLAND AND WALES IN 1834,
PER HEAD OF POPULATION, BY COUNTIES

Nicholls, in which conditions were "as disagreeable as was consistent with health."

The New Poor Law, passed in 1834 under the influence of the Commissioners' report, set up three Commissioners to establish "union" workhouses by means of a compulsory union of parishes for that purpose, and in order to "deter" applicants who were presumed to be probably only work-shy, to enforce the following main principles through elected Boards of Guardians: (i) No relief except within a work-house to the able-bodied; (ii) Such relief to be "less eligible" than the most unpleasant means of earning a living outside; (iii) Separation of man and wife to prevent child-bearing.

The Act was applied forthwith to the South of England, extinguishing the Speenhamland system, which had reduced that part of the country to extreme abjectness. It met with little resistance. In the first place, it was in truth wiping out an intolerable nuisance; in the second, the years 1834 to 1836 were prosperous and the harvests were good.

When, however, the Act was applied to the industrial workers in the developing factory and mining areas, none of these palliating conditions was there to help. In these areas, it is broadly true to say that the Speenhamland system of poor relief had never been in force. That is to say, there had never been any system of subsidizing wages regularly out of the poor rates. The old Poor Law had served here not to subsidize the wages of the employed, but to provide a form of unemploy-ment relief both for the wholly workless and for those whose piece-work earnings fell in slack times below the sheer level of subsistence. This last condition applied especially to such groups as the handloom-weavers, who were being forced more and more into the position of marginal workers, able to pick up a bare living when trade was good, but employed only very irregularly or not at all in bad times, when the employers sought to find full work for their machines in the factories before putting any out to the "domestic" workers.

In 1836 the new Poor Law Commissioners, known every-where among the workers as "The Three Bashaws [Pashas] of Somerset House," had already accomplished the first part of their task, by enforcing the new Poor Law principles all over the South of England. They were now ready to turn their attention to the industrial areas, in which, though the Speenhamland system did not exist in the same form, they saw a "laxity" in the granting of relief to the distressed of which they disapproved almost as much.

The approved unpleasantness of relief was to be secured by offering it only in the workhouse—the hated "Bastille," as the poor soon learned to call it—and in addition keeping those who accepted the "workhouse test" in a contrite frame of mind by means of a low diet, a severe discipline, and a rigid segregation of the sexes which separated man and wife. Malthusian fears about the pressure of population on the means of subsistence were invoked to justify this final savagery; and the working man who sought the inhospitable shelter of the new "Bastilles" was admonished that, since he had demonstrated his incapacity by coming to the Poor Law for support, he had no right to father children with mouths to feed, who would impose burdens on the public purse. Few of the perorations of Feargus O'Connor, the famous Chartist orator, evoked more delight than his description of how he would treat Lord Chancellor Brougham and his wife on their arrival at the workhouse door: "I shall be sorry for Lady Brougham. I know no harm of her. But I would have no pity for him: 'No, no, Harry,' I will say to him, 'you may not go with my lady; this is the way for you; otherwise you might breed.'"

William Cobbett and a tiny band of left-wing Radicals and old-fashioned Tories fought side by side in vain against the Bill. Their opponents, even the most fanatical, were not inhuman monsters, but rather ruthless logicians, who believed that in the end their strong medicine would benefit the sufferers. Edwin Chadwick and his friends, who set out to administer the new Poor Law with a mercilessness which provoked widespread revolt, were the very same persons who were in the forefront in exposing the social abuses of the time, and calling on the State to intervene in order to remove them. If Chadwick, as Secretary to the Poor Law Commissioners, made himself rightly the best-hated man in England, the same Chadwick, as author of the great reports on the *Sanitary Condition of the Labouring Population* (1842) and on the *Health of Towns* (1844), set going the agitation which, aided by the cholera epidemics of 1831 and 1848, led up to the Public Health Act of 1848, and thus laid the foundations of modern sanitary legislation.

Edwin Chadwick was a logical follower of Jeremy Bentham, seeking, according to his lights, to promote the greatest happiness of the greatest number. For Chadwick believed that the effect of the Speenhamland system, and of the lax Poor Law administration generally, had been to keep down the level of wages and increase working-class misery, and that, when once the poor were prevented from relying on the poor rates for support, and compelled to depend on their own resources for earning a living, wages would be bound to rise, and the labourer to fare better by his own exertions than he could ever hope to fare at the public expense.

In this, Chadwick and the advocates of the new Poor Law were broadly right, as far as their case referred to the areas in which wages had been regularly subsidized out of the rates. In these areas, after a brief interval of acute misery, wages did rise; and the labourers in the countryside were on the whole soon rather better off for the change. But in thinking of the Speenhamland system and of the agricultural labourers, Chadwick and Nassau Senior forgot, or ignored, the fact that in the industrial districts the old Poor Law served quite a different purpose—that of relieving unemployment due to the fluctuations of trade, and also that of preserving from literal starvation the handloom-weavers and other domestic producers whom the factory system was throwing rapidly upon the industrial scrap-heap. The removal of outdoor relief could not help unemployed factory workers or miners to find employment when the times were bad: nor could it do anything at all to raise the wages of the miserable handloom-weavers. If the New Poor Law had been first introduced into the industrial areas at a time when trade was good, it might have encountered relatively little resistance. But the boom ended in 1835—depression in the factory areas became severe in 1836; and in 1837, the year of its introduction into the Northern Counties, there was a commercial crisis which sent hosts of unemployed factory workers, as well as handloom-weavers, clamouring to the parish officers for relief. Deep depression continued till 1842, but Chadwick and his friends were much too logical philanthropists to hesitate in applying their principles. They went straight ahead; and, in doing so, they turned discontent into a mass movement of revolt.

The resistance of the employed and unemployed was often stiffened by an unexpected assistance from the employers. John Fielden of Todmorden prevented the Act being applied at all in his district so long as he lived: over great areas of the North it was held up for some years. The Commissioners had to watch for their opportunity and cajole and persuade local authorities to build "Bastilles" whenever a calm period permitted it, but their progress was very slow. The chief organizers of resistance were the bailiff Richard Oastler, who professed himself a Tory, and the Reverend J. R. Stephens, a Methodist minister, both of whom explicitly advocated resistance by violence. "If the musket," said Stephens, "and the pistol, the sword and the pike are of no avail, let the woman take the scissors, the child, the pin or the needle. If all fails, the firebrand—ay, the firebrand, the firebrand, I repeat."

Such advice, delivered to mass meetings all over the North, had considerable effect in deterring the Poor Law Commissioners, and even more in deterring the local Guardians. But the rank and file of the movement, their leaders, their language and their methods, were all taken up in a larger agitation, to which they gave strength rather than wisdom.

This movement, beginning from London, was given the general name of Chartism. Its origin was as follows.

Although the abandonment of the persecution of Carlile had meant that the more violent ill-treatment of the propagandists had ceased, nevertheless, the Radical Press was far from free. Continually Hetherington, Cleave and other pertinacious publishers of the "unstamped" were arrested and fined, and the circulation of their papers impeded. In 1833 there were eight unstamped Radical weekly papers in London with considerable circulations:

The Gauntlet, R. Carlile	about	22,000
Poor Man's Guardian, H. Hetherington	,,	16,000
The Destructive and Poor Man's Conservative, J. Bronterre O'Brien	,,	8,000

The Working Man's Friend, Jas. Watson	about	7,000
The Man, R. E. Lee	,,	7,000
The Crisis, R. Owen	,,	5,000
The Reformer	,,	5,000

These figures, which come from a hostile source, may be exaggerated. But they omit some papers, including Cobbett's widely read *Register*, which was at that time stamped, i.e. paid tax. Three years later all but the first two journals had been put out of existence, and their place not adequately taken by other papers. A number of the soberer and more pertinacious working-class Radicals of London met together to found an organization to succour and pay the fines for the printers and editors. Among them were Henry Hetherington, James Watson, John Cleave, John Gast and William Lovett, all skilled craftsmen and dependable and earnest men. Out of their consultations rose, on 16 June 1836, the "London Workingmen's Association for Benefiting Politically Socially and Morally the Useful Classes," soon naturally abbreviated to the L.W.M.A. It kept in close touch with about a dozen sympathetic Radical M.P.s, including Daniel O'Connell (Cobbett and Hunt both died in 1835), and tried to find a common programme for all the disappointed democrats. It attracted public support by championing the French-Canadian ucing against the British Government, and even more by prodrevolt early in 1837 a Petition to the House of Commons including all the "Six Points" which were afterwards the provisions of the Charter. These six points were: Universal male suffrage, equal electoral districts, annual Parliaments, payment of members, secret ballot, and no property qualification for M.P.s. So exactly did these correspond to the public wishes that when "missionaries" were sent out to advocate them they were soon able to report the foundation or affiliation of over a hundred societies in other parts of the kingdom, including one at Newport, Monmouth, which was in due course to make its parents sorry it had ever been born.

Not every man was welcomed into the Association. G. J. Harney, a young man who dreamed of pikes and saw himself as the English Marat, was compelled to resign, consoling himself with forming a rival "Democratic Association," and the bar was also up against Feargus O'Connor, a powerful Irish orator and squireen, one-time Irish M.P. and follower of O'Connell, who went North and induced some supporters to help him to start a new paper called *The Northern Star*. But murmurers such as these were unnoticed amid the general applause: the affiliated societies rose to one hundred and fifty and the only other Radical society of importance in the kingdom, the Birmingham Political Union, signified its adhesion. With a prestige remaining from the Reform Bill days and the rich banker Thomas Attwood as leader, it completed the army of supporters, and in 1838, when Lovett drafted the six points into a formal Bill and called it the "People's Charter," the enthusiasm was enormous. The Chartist Movement was formally launched at a vast meeting at Newhall Hill, Birmingham, on 6 August 1838, at which representatives of every school of thought spoke in harmony.

The harmony was on the surface alone. The speakers were agreed upon the necessity for the Charter and no more. They were not agreed upon the means of attaining it. The L.W.M.A. and the Birmingham men intended to rely upon "moral force"—upon petitions, meetings, resolutions and education; Harney and unnumbered others chiefly from the North upon "physical force," including insurrection. O'Connor, whose *Northern Star* was rapidly gaining readers, used physical force as a threat ("peaceably if we may, forcibly if we must") but never came to the point of countenancing it in fact. The division between the two schools was not one bridgeable by argument; it was a class division. The "moral force" men were middle-class supporters and skilled artisans, who had leisure and security enough to reflect. The "physical force" men, except for some of the leaders, were the more miserable masses of the North and Wales, whose sufferings made them impatient and who were unable to judge the forces against them.

Nor were they agreed upon the manner in which the Charter should be used to end poverty. Many Socialists—that is to say, Owenites—were scattered among their ranks, but their views were not generally accepted, while their movement officially held aloof. O'Connor believed in small peasant holdings. Lovett put his trust in education. Bronterre O'Brien, a theorist who through O'Connor's admiration for a while held a dominating position, borrowed *en bloc* from Babeuf a scheme for a State-supported Socialist community. Harney's views scarcely went beyond the need for a terror. Attwood, whose theories have been unjustly decried, wanted the abandonment of the gold standard, which being inelastic was unsuitable to a growing industrial society, and its replacement by a paper-money currency.

It was curious that it should be the last-named who produced for the movement a programme whose incendiary character he cannot fully have realized. It was this: A petition, drafted by his colleague, R. K. Douglas, for the enactment of the Charter should be as widely signed as possible. A Convention (a menacing word) should be elected to present it to the House of Commons and urge it on M.P.s by all the methods of moral force. Should these fail, a general strike of a month, called a Sacred Month, should be called to force surrender.

Here was a programme on which all could unite delightedly. Enormous meetings held by torchlight on moors and waste spaces outside the big towns welcomed the orators. The more violent their sentiments the more the audiences cheered: pikes were brandished and the fiercest resolutions carried. O'Connor became the most influential speaker, and his *Northern Star* the most influential paper. Before long the groups round Lovett and Attwood were seriously alarmed at the anger they had unleashed. They made attempts to destroy O'Connor's influence, but failed; and when the fifty-three delegates to the Convention met in London on 4 February 1839 (the same day as Parliament and the first national Anti-Corn Law League Conference) they did so in an atmosphere of frenzied excitement. Over £2,700 had been collected as "National Rent"—mostly in sixpences—to pay expenses, and some opponents as well as supporters looked on the Convention as potentially the new Government. O'Connor in the *Northern Star* begged his readers' pardon for having so underestimated its powers "as to have postponed the coming of Universal Suffrage to the 29th of September. Bailie Craig [a leading Scottish

Chartist], has given the Queen a *month* and three days' grace, and it can be done."

Such extreme high spirits came down considerably even in the first few days. The Birmingham delegates and Lovett, the secretary, drew the Convention's attention to the real weakness of its support in the country. The Petition as yet had been signed by no more than 600,000 persons, and the "constituents" who had elected the delegates consisted of excited mass meetings which were wholly incapable of supporting the Convention in "ulterior measures" if the Petition was rejected. Feargus O'Connor and the more extreme wing were stimulated by these criticisms to greater propaganda activity: the Petition began to be signed on a larger scale, and meetings were adjured to prepare themselves (and in reply promised that they would) for every action, including strike, boycott and insurrection. O'Connor's violent language caused the Birmingham men pusillanimously to leave the Convention one by one rather than fight him. The Chartist movement began already to fall under his domination. He boasted in April that he had himself made the reputation of Stephens, Oastler, John Frost of Newport, Peter Bussey, Dr. M'Douall and a number of other leaders. The average circulation per week of his *Northern Star* was now 32,692: its price was 4½d., the profits were considerable, and as the vast majority of copies were taken in by beerhouses or other places where they were read by the customers, its effective circulation must have been enormous.

Little brains though this bull-necked and noisy giant possessed, he had instinctive cunning, and his suggestions were far from being as imbecile as his opponents believed. He was partly responsible for the decision to have nothing to do with the Anti-Corn Law League, in which he fitly represented the hatred of the Chartists against the employers who financed that body. His suggestions had something to do with the decision to transfer the Convention to Birmingham on May 13. A political crisis had enforced a delay in presenting the Petition: since "ulterior measures" had to be concerted in the event of its refusal, there was a good tactical reason for doing this in a town whose governors had till recently been prominent Chartists. Lovett and Harney, in unexpected alliance, then united in passing the "eight questions of the Convention," an interrogatory to be administered to all Chartist meetings up to July 1. It was now clear that the Petition would be refused, and the audiences were asked if they would start a run on the banks, if they would carry out a "Sacred Month," if they would boycott hostile dealers and newspapers, and if they had armed themselves.

Both the Convention and the Government were seriously preparing for a conflict. What seemed a rehearsal for it took place on July 4. Chartist speakers were steadily defying the Birmingham magistrates' ban on meetings in the Bull Ring. On this day the Mayor imported sixty of the new London police and set them on the crowd, on which they tried their new tactics. The Chartists, however, fought back, and the police were actually driven off until soldiers were brought in to aid them. Later in the same evening there was a fresh affray, in which the authorities again came off second-best; but in the end, as was inevitable, the city remained in their control. The Convention issued a furious placard denouncing the behaviour of its one-time allies, and for signing it Lovett was arrested and put in prison.

While his sobering but uninspired influence was removed, the Petition, with 1,280,000 signatures, was debated on July 12 in Parliament and rejected. Attwood, in a careful speech, made the poverty of the working class his theme in proposing it; Lord John Russell, in opposing for the Government, declared that the Charter would mean the confiscation of all property. On receiving the news of the rejection, the Convention called the Sacred Month for August 12.

The vote brought even the Harneys up against realities. They had no organization behind them, their followers did not yet compose the majority of the people, and could not come out for a month on strike if they did (especially during a heavy trade depression), they had no money to cause a run on the banks, and even the advocates of insurrection realized that most of them had no arms. Napier, the general commanding, an able soldier who sympathized with the Chartists while despising their chiefs, privately gave a display of artillery force to the Manchester leaders, and sent to others a brief account of what exactly a revolt would entail, and how he proposed to deal with it. The exhibition and lecture cooled their heads suddenly. The Convention, after dismal debates lasting ten days, cancelled the order for the Sacred Month and adjourned till the end of August, having destroyed its influence. August 12 passed by with only a few riots: many leaders were arrested and sentenced. Lovett, who made a good appearance in the dock, and Stephens, who cut a poor figure, were among those sent to serve their sentences in jail. "Moral force" had met with complete ill success.

What the moral force men had failed to do, the physical force men now decided to attempt. The darkness which covered their actions has only recently and partially been lifted. David Urquhart claimed that the Tsar of Russia was responsible: more recently it had even been doubted whether there was a genuinely insurrectionary plot at all. But Zephaniah Williams's confession details a "plan to overthrow the present government and establish a Republic," based upon not wholly absurd calculations of the relative number of soldiers and of armed Chartists in South Wales, and the arms procured or procurable from the ironworks and powder magazines which could be seized. Many details, however, are still missing. An insurrectionary committee of five survived the Convention, consisting certainly of John Frost of Newport, and Peter Bussey of Bradford, and probably of Robert Lowery, Dr. John Taylor and one other unknown. A national conference was held at Heckmondwike, and lesser organizing conferences elsewhere, where difficulties were met with such as that presented by Dr. Price of Llantrissant, the commander in Merthyr and district, who declined to move his men unless he was provided with a list of a thousand soldiers to be executed. Beniowski, a Pole who had instructed numbers of Chartists in street-fighting, was eliminated from the area where the revolt was to start on the ground of unreliability: "the Pole," wrote Dr. Taylor, "has not gone to Wales, but a much honester man." The signal for the insurrection was to be given by the capture of Newport in Monmouth by the Chartists of that district, headed by John Frost, a draper, ex-mayor and Radical politician of long standing.

It appears that wind of this came to O'Connor and that he made creditable efforts to dissuade the leaders. Early in October he urgently warned the physical force men through the *Northern Star* of police spies: "I caution you against those who give exaggerated accounts of the spirit of one locality to the people of another. Some missionaries speak of London and its forwardness; without any disparagement I say 'Come and see.'" There are circumstantial stories of his sending an agent, George White, to hold back Lancashire, and another to Wales, Charles Jones, to whom Frost is said to have answered: "I might as well blow my brains out as try to hold back the Monmouth lodges now."

The plot moved unarrestably forward. Frost fixed the night of November 3–4 for the capture of Newport and the release from Monmouth prison of Henry Vincent, the most brilliant orator of the London Working Men's Association, who had built up a great influence in South Wales and the Bristol area. Frost's detachment, like the rest nearly completely made up of miners, assembled at Blackwood on the Rhymney, his lieutenant Zephaniah Williams's at Nantyglo, and his other lieutenant William Jones's at Pontypool. All were to meet at Risca; but the rain and storm of the night, and the inexperience of the leaders, prevented them from keeping the rendezvous. At last, when a grey and wet dawn had fully broken, Frost set off without the others—Williams being but a quarter of an hour behind, and Jones nowhere near. By now the authorities were fully warned, and when the disorderly army swept into the square opposite the Westgate Hotel, it ran straight into a trap. The battle was short and sharp. Frost's force was some four thousand, though it was utterly untrained; the soldiers numbered some thirty with an uncertain addition of timorous special constables. But behind the hotel shutters they were untouchable, while the Chartists in the square were without shelter from their volleys. Every shot told; some Chartists endeavoured to storm the front door, and repeatedly broke into the passage but "faltered when they encountered their own dead." In quite a short while the army broke and fled, leaving behind it dead or dying estimated variously at between eleven and fifty-three. In its rout it swept away Williams's column; Jones heard of the disaster by messenger and dismissed his men.

The Yorkshire Chartists, despite this news, endeavoured to proceed with their revolt, but Bussey hid behind flour sacks in his own loft to avoid leading them. There was nothing left for the Chartists to do but to endeavour to save Frost, Williams and Jones, who were under arrest with many of their followers. The most skilled counsel were hired, but were unable to avert a sentence of death for the three leaders. Their followers pleaded guilty on the understanding that their lives would be spared. But the same sentence was pronounced, and after a minute of horrified silence "almost with one voice the prisoners exclaimed: 'We've been sold.'" The three leaders in prison contemplated suicide, from which they were deterred, as they believed, by the intervention of their God. However, against the wishes of Lord Melbourne, their sentences were commuted to transportation and those of the others to lesser penalties; but this success was all. O'Connor, Bronterre O'Brien and every other known Chartist leader soon joined the others in prison on short sentences: in 1840 the movement was leaderless and defeated.

A less discouragement than this had extinguished the Consolidated Union, but the Chartists had more staying power. Though their leaders were in prison, the conditions there were not yet so bad as in the twentieth century, and they were able to put down the result of their reflections on paper and even to send them out on occasion. A number of schemes appeared in the Chartist Press in that year, all with the intention of stiffening the Chartist ranks by setting up a permanent organization. Lovett's plan, smuggled out to Francis Place, was for a network of schools to be paid for by the signatories to the Petition: it was wholly unlikely to satisfy Chartist aspirations even if the financial provisions had not been preposterous. Opinion was in favour of a strictly political organization, and later in the year the "National Charter Association" was organized. It enrolled members very slowly: by the end of 1841 it had only 13,000 members in 282 localities, and on 19 February 1842, it had 40,060 members; in the summer it seems to have had 48,000 members in 400 localities, which was probably its peak

figure. These figures, however, are not important: the
members were only the "shock troops"; evidence was shortly
forthcoming that to find the number of supporters and sympathizers the figures must be multiplied by nearly a hundred.
O'Connor, through the *Northern Star*, had a dominating influence on the Executive, of which he was not a member;
but it is wrong to consider that Executive as null. Dr. Peter
M'Douall, a serious revolutionary, worked hard· at a new
policy of organizing Chartist trade societies. The existing
Unions, remembering 1834, were cautious in the extreme, and
he found that he had to organize separate bodies. Their use
remained for the minute obscure; at first the Association's
efforts were largely confined to putting up dummy Chartist
candidates at elections or by-elections, and persecuting the
Anti-Corn Law League by attending its meetings and moving
and often carrying amendments in favour of the Charter. It
was also decided to present yet another petition, and in the
winter of 1841 signatures began to be busily collected.

O'Connor's dominance was resented by others than Lovett
—O'Brien now quarrelled with him—and he expressed it by
means which a wiser or saner man would have avoided. He
even wrote a poem which he expected Lovett to recite at a
banquet to celebrate his release, of which the seventh verse
ran as follows:

> *O'Connor is our chosen chief,*
> *He's champion of the Charter;*
> *Our Saviour suffered like a thief*
> *Because he preached the Charter.*

He addressed his followers as "Imperial Chartists!" and before
long was to write open letters to the *Northern Star* beginning:
"To the Working Classes: My Dear Children——." Natural
irritation at this arrogance caused a number of the Chartist
leaders to consider an alliance with their class enemies. Under
O'Connor's direction the working class as a whole had opposed
the Anti-Corn Law League steadily. Chartist speakers had not
denied, in general, that the repeal of the Corn Laws would
benefit momentarily the town working class. But they said,
with great truth. that the Anti-Corn Law Leaguers and their

supporters were precisely the manufacturers whose greed and cruelty made their lives intolerable. They said that the moment the Corn Laws were repealed the manufacturers would cut wages down by an amount exactly corresponding to the fall in the price of bread, pointing out that by current economics this would be regarded as justifiable and even inevitable. Generally, too, they added that no salutary action, such as repealing the Corn Laws, would in fact be carried by a middle-class Parliament.

Acutely perceiving the class nature of the disagreement, a Birmingham Quaker merchant and Chartist in principle, Joseph Sturge, held back certain colleagues after the League Conference of 1841 and in alliance with them issued, under the title *Reconciliation between the Middle and Labouring Classes*, a plea for the organization of "Complete Suffrage Associations," which should combine opposition to the Corn Laws with strictly legal agitation for extension of the suffrage. In the early months of 1842 the plan attracted the support of a large number of Chartists, including Lovett himself: O'Connor's opposition was ineffective, although in his reply he astutely distinguished between the "*middle*" class or "shopocracy," i.e. employers and traders, and the "*middling*" class, or brain workers, whose support he declared he would welcome. Not until the end of the year was the new organization disrupted. At its December Conference Sturge's followers declined to accept the Charter; Lovett and O'Connor, for the last time speaking on the same side, insisted on its adoption and split the organization in two by carrying their motion.

But far more exciting events had occurred before then. The Petition, in the first place, had been presented. It was blunter and more effectively phrased than its predecessor, it was signed by 3,317,702 persons and was over six miles long. Broken up on the floor of the House (for it was too large to enter whole) it made the room look "as if it had been snowing paper." It was, of course, rejected, by 287 votes to 49. But the number of signatures stimulated Chartists to wild hopes. Their leader was most ecstatic of all; one can almost watch the illusions growing and flowering in his mind. "We are 4,000,000, ay, and more," O'Connor wrote in the *Northern Star*. ". . . How proud was I to call you 2,000,000 just twelve months ago . . . and how doubly proud must I now be to call you 4,800,000!''

Four million men, or men who think they are four million—out of a total population of less than nineteen millions in Great Britain (including women and children)—are not likely to remain quiet under such an insult as the rejection of the petition. Accident, and the labours of Dr. M'Douall, gave them the opportunity for their next move. In the second week in August a casual strike in Ashton-under-Lyne was turned by the strikers into a strike for the Charter. Immediately the cry was taken up: Manchester came out, and from there the strike radiated over Lancashire, Yorkshire, Cheshire, the Potteries, Warwickshire and into Wales. The Scottish miners came out: "The trades of Great Britain," said the delegates' manifesto, "carried the Reform Bill. The trades of Great Britain shall carry the Charter." The Executive of the Association hurried to Manchester; Campbell, the secretary, as he first saw the smokeless chimneys of the city from the train cried out with an oath: "Not a single mill at work! Something must come out of this, and something serious too."

While the strikers were marching from town to town, knocking out the boiler-plugs to prevent working, even if the employees wished it, the Charter Association debated its action frantically. Thomas Cooper, a Leicester Chartist, demanded that the strike be adopted and extended, in the hope that it might become an insurrection. O'Connor opposed an insurrection. Hill, till then the editor of the *Northern Star*, even opposed the strike. Ultimately the strike was enthusiastically supported. O'Connor publicly took an odd line: he said the strike had been arranged by the Anti-Corn Law League. "They have gotten the people out! How will they get them in again?" "I would never have counselled the present strike, but as we have been assailed in our peaceful position you have no alternative but to bow or to resist the tyrant's will," he added. Suddenly, a week later, August 27, when trades as far north as Aberdeen were considering joining the strike, he swung round. He denounced the strike in the *Star*, and declared he would stop it. It had failed in Manchester; it was bound to be defeated; it was an Anti-Corn Law plot. The effect of this was to shatter a movement that was already weakening at the centre. The strike ended as soon as the *Northern Star* was put on sale. Fifteen hundred persons were arrested and 79 transported to Australia.

CHAPTER XXIV

THE HUNGRY 'FORTIES

SOME such startling defeat of the Chartists was inevitable, even if the leadership had been wiser. The enemy, the capitalist class, which the Chartists were attacking, was enormously stronger than they believed. It was nothing like the feeble landowners who had surrounded George IV. So far from being in decay, it had during this period and, the immediately subsequent years, begun to use fully its economic powers of expansion for the first time, and had provided itself with legal instruments which enabled its progress to astonish the world.

The first of these, in its own opinion, though not perhaps in that of after years, was the Bank Charter Act of 1844. Under it the Bank of England assumed for the first time the full responsibilities of a "Central Bank" entrusted with the function of managing the currency on behalf of the State, and also of serving as a "lender of the last resort" to which the world of finance would henceforth look for security—relying upon it to use all its arts of monetary management to prevent crises, and, if a crisis nevertheless arose, to come to the assistance of the private bankers and merchants with timely accommodation.

Under this Act, Peel supposed that he had once and for all removed the danger of inflation, by limiting to a quite small sum the Bank's power to create money by printing notes apart from notes actually backed by gold in the Bank's possession. Against full gold backing, the Bank was to be allowed to issue notes without limit; but its fiduciary issue against a backing of Government securities was to be restricted to £14,000,000; with a further provision that no new note-issuing banks were to be set up, and that the existing banks of note issue were to be limited to the amounts actually then in existence, and even so that any bank of issue was to lose its note-making privilege if it amalgamated with another bank—two-thirds of its lost issue then being added to the Bank of England's permitted fiduciary issue, and the rest lapsing once and for all.

While the Bank Charter Act was designed to lay sound monetary foundations for the new capitalist era, the legalization of joint stock enterprise in the field of ordinary productive industry was a recognition that the needs of the factory system for large accumulations of capital could no longer be met under the old system of purely personal business ownership through private firms and partnerships. In the first year of Queen Victoria's reign a tentative step had already been taken towards the more general recognition of the joint stock system, by an Act which allowed the Crown, by letters patent, to grant to trading companies the privileges of incorporation, including, where this was thought desirable, limited liability for the shareholders. But this had been a special privilege, not meant to be widely granted; and the Act of 1844 was of quite a different sort. For now, for the first time, it was open to any business having, or desiring to have, a considerable capital and a considerable body of shareholders, to register itself as a joint stock company, and therewith to acquire, not indeed the privilege of limited liability (for that was withheld for another eleven years) but the right to sue and be sued in its registered name, and to act as a corporate body through its officers and directors.

In order to understand the meaning of this development it is necessary to go back to what was said in a previous chapter about the development of the forms of business enterprise. Up to 1825 the formation of joint stock companies, except by means of separate private Acts of Parliament, was prohibited by law. This did not prevent Parliament from incorporating any companies it chose; but in fact the creation of such bodies was practically limited to the transport services and to public utility undertakings for the supply of gas or water, or for carrying on insurance. The Act did not prevent many bodies called "companies" from being formed; but they remained in the eyes of the law simply unlimited partnerships without any corporate personality of their own. The Act of 1825, which removed the positive prohibition of joint stock companies, made little change in the situation; for in practice the Act of prohibition had not been enforced. The Act of 1837, which enabled the Crown by letters patent to establish companies and grant rights of incorporation, including limited liability, was designed to prevent the expenditure of time on numerous private Acts, and also to reduce the expenses of incorporation, but not to introduce any new principle—for it was not contemplated that its privileges would be widely extended to ordinary trading concerns. Nor, in fact, were they: indeed, most companies between 1837 and 1844 continued either to operate without legal protection, or to seek private Acts, because only an Act of Parliament could confer "rights against the public," such as the right compulsorily to acquire land, or to dig up the streets for placing mains for gas or water.

But by 1844 the situation had greatly changed because of the advent of the railways, and of railway investment on the grand scale. Railway companies, because they needed special powers of land acquisition and policing and of making public regulations binding on the users of their service, had to get their powers directly from Parliament by means of private Acts; and these powers and privileges included limited liability for the railway shareholders. Under these circumstances, with Parliament setting up railway companies right and left, railway enterprise was placed in a position of great advantage in comparison with other forms of business in raising the capital which it called for, because it could offer the attraction of limited liability, whereas most other forms of business enterprise could not. Accordingly, factory owners and mine owners began to complain that the railways were absorbing nearly all the available supplies of capital, and that manufacturers were placed at a disadvantage which stood seriously in the way of economic progress. They wanted equal rights with the railways to appeal for capital from the investing public.

The Companies Act of 1844 was designed to go some of the way—but only a part of the way—towards meeting this claim. It was made easy to form trading companies, and to appeal to investors for capital; but the crowning privilege of limited liability was refused. For it was still widely felt to be immoral for an ordinary commercial business to be carried on under conditions which might allow the "partners" in it to escape paying its debts. The trading or manufacturing company was still regarded only as an enlarged partnership, in which the responsibility of the partners must be several as well as joint. In the case of railways and other public utility concerns, Parliament was able to feel differently, largely for historical reasons. The railways were the successors of the canals, which were in turn the successors of the Turnpike Trusts. The gas and water companies were the successors of the bodies of Local Commissioners which had been set up in large numbers during the eighteenth and early nineteenth centuries for the purpose of supplying a town with water, or lighting or watching or paving its streets. But neither Turnpike Trusts nor Local Commissioners had ever been regarded as businesses, whose members ought to be individually liable for the corporate debts. They had been treated as analogous rather to municipal corporations, or colleges, or charitable foundations; and these upon the grant of a charter of incorporation became at once legal entities quite distinct from the members who actually administered them from time to time.

The railways and gas and water companies thus won the rights of limited liability without a struggle, as a by-product of incorporation by Act of Parliament. They were thought of as exceptional, chartered institutions, standing apart from the general mass of private business enterprises. Parliament, in 1844, still sought to keep up this distinction. But the logic of events compelled it to recognize and regulate joint stock companies in the field of productive enterprise.

There was, however, no rush to form joint stock companies after the Act of 1844, or after its amendment in 1847, when the advantages of limited liability were still refused. The history of joint stock enterprise and of the investment market continued, until well after the middle of the century, to be mainly concerned with the development of the railways and of locomotion by steam power.

The earliest "rail-ways" date back a long time before the advent of the age of steam. They were simply track-ways, designed to afford smoother passage for horse-drawn wheeled traffic, and used mainly for the cartage of coal and other minerals from mine or quarry to the nearest navigable water. Track-ways of this sort were made in plenty in the eighteenth century in the colliery areas; and the first public companies formed by Act of Parliament for the conduct of "rail-ways" were for enterprises of this type, to be open to all comers on payment of a toll. On these early rail-ways the user commonly provided his own vehicle and means of traction, simply paying a toll for the use of the "way"; but in some cases the promoting company also acted as a common carrier, and had its own horse-drawn vehicles plying along the track. All these early enterprises were designed primarily for goods rather than passengers; and even after the advent of steam power it was some time before there was a full appreciation of the possibilities of passenger traffic.

Between 1801 and 1824 no less than 37 private Acts of Parliament authorizing the construction of railways were passed into law; and at least one Act was passed in every year during this period. Then came a sudden increase—from 3 Acts in 1824 to 9 in 1825 and 11 in 1826. This figure was not reached again till 1833; and then the number of Acts again rose rapidly. There were 14 in 1834, 19 in 1835, 35 in 1836, and 42 in 1837—the period of the first "railway mania." After that the numbers again fell, averaging about 23 from 1838 to 1843 during the period of general economic depression. Then came the second "railway mania," with 48 Acts in 1844 and 120 in 1845, when the capital authorized for new railway undertakings reached nearly £60,000,000 in one year, as against a previous high record of under £23,000,000 in 1836. For the successive five-year periods beginning in 1826, the capital authorized for railways was roughly £4,000,000, £15,000,000, £48,000,000 and £87,000,000—a total of over £153,000,000, and a yearly average of £7,672,000.

These sums far exceeded any which had previously been raised by way of public investment. That they could be raised, and in addition very large sums provided for industrial development in mining and manufactures, shows clearly how rapidly wealth was accumulating in the hands of the richer classes; for clearly the bulk of the new investment must have come out of the profits of industry and commerce. It is a sign of this that the bulk of the capital for the railways was raised not in London but locally, in the centres which the railways were to serve; for most of the early railways were built in independent and often unconnected sections by companies of promoters who appealed for financial support largely on the ground of the service which would be done to a particular town or district or local industry by giving it quicker and cheaper access to a wide market for its products, or a cheaper supply of essential raw materials.

London did, indeed, play its part in financing the railways; but it was not an overwhelming part. It must, however, be realized that, with the cessation of war borrowing, large amounts of annual savings which had previously been taken up by the Government became available for private investment. In the years immediately after 1815 the London financiers lent large sums to foreign Governments which needed financial resources in order to establish their position. There followed in 1824 and 1825 a second wave of overseas investment, this time directed largely to America, including both the United States and the newly "liberated" Republics of Central and South America. In both these waves of foreign investment there was much mismanagement—as in the Greek loan of 1826; and a number of the issues were plainly fraudulent. Often only a fraction of the issued capital ever reached the borrowing country; and some of the loans involved heavy losses to the subscribers.

After the boom and crisis of 1825, the centre of speculation shifted nearer home; and in the 'thirties and 'forties the worst speculative excesses occurred in connection with investments in railways, and in certain forms of mining enterprise, such as the Cornish tin-mines. The railways, indeed, overshadowed all other forms of investment; and for one railway that was built in fact there were at least a dozen projects launched by competing groups of promoters. This speculative competition involved great waste; and for other reasons besides, the British railways cost an exorbitant sum to build. The expenses of getting a private Bill through Parliament were usually very high. The Parliamentary expenses of promoting the Great

PRINCIPAL ENGLISH RAILWAYS IN 1846

Western Railway amounted to £89,000, of the Northern and Eastern Railway to £74,000, of the London and Birmingham to £73,000, and of the South-Eastern to £82,000. But even more serious was the high cost of construction, swollen chiefly by the necessity of paying extravagant prices for land in order to buy off the opposition of landowners, who might otherwise easily bring about the defeat of a railway Bill in either the House of Commons or the House of Lords. By these means railway-building feathered the landlords' nests; and in consequence the railway companies were driven to exact high charges in order to earn a dividend on their inflated capital.

Nevertheless, subscribers rushed to purchase railway shares, which offered the then unusual attraction to the speculator of a possible high return combined with a risk limited to the amount of the capital subscribed. The age of railway investment did not indeed really set in until 1836—eleven years after the opening of the Stockton and Darlington Railway, which was the first to make more than experimental use of steam locomotives. Even the Stockton and Darlington at first made only a limited use of locomotives for power, employing haulage by stationary engines over a part of its route, and horse-traction as well as steam for its own vehicles, in addition to allowing access to horse-drawn vehicles belonging to private users. Clear demonstration of the advantages of the locomotive was not given until 1829, when George Stephenson's *Rocket* carried off the prize at the Rainhill trial, and determined that the Liverpool and Manchester Railway, opened in 1830 under powers obtained from Parliament in 1826, should use locomotives exclusively. Even after 1830 new railways continued for some years to be made for horse-drawn vehicles only, and stationary engines, with rope-haulage, continued in use for inclines. But the spectacular success of the Liverpool and Manchester Railway in lowering costs and increasing the speed of goods traffic, as well as in attracting passengers, before long finally settled the issue in favour of the locomotive, and therewith completed the conversion of the railway from a track-way open to private vehicles into a service of public transport operated by the companies themselves. The private railway truck survived—and survives even to-day—especially for coal;

but the locomotives, the passenger coaches, and most of the rolling stock for goods, except coal, soon came to be owned by the railways.

In 1836, when the first "mania" for railway investment set in, most of the existing railways were quite short local lines, either linking together two or three neighbouring towns, or joining mines or ironworks to a nearby port or river or canal. The most important lines already open were the Stockton and Darlington (essential for the Durham coalfield) and the Liverpool and Manchester, which provided the cotton industry with an improved means of communication with overseas markets and sources of supply, and in addition enabled passengers to travel easily between Liverpool and Manchester, the centres respectively of the trade in imported raw cotton and in manufactured cotton goods. A cross-country line from Newcastle to Carlisle was nearly finished, and there was a line from Selby to Leeds. London had made a beginning, with dockland lines from London Bridge to Greenwich and from Fenchurch Street to Blackwall. There were groups of local lines in the Durham coalfield, in Lancashire, and round Glasgow and Edinburgh, but elsewhere only scattered small railways of purely local importance.

This situation was rapidly altered during the next few years. In 1837 the Londoner could get by railway only as far as Tring in Hertfordshire. In 1838 he could get to Birmingham, and thence on by other lines to Warrington, Manchester, Liverpool, Preston and Derby, as well as to Maidenhead on the Great Western. In 1839 he could also get to Nottingham by a roundabout route, to Basingstoke, as far as Twyford on the Great Western, and by other lines to Croydon and Romford. In 1840 he could get to Leicester, to Nottingham by a more direct route, to Southampton, to Swindon on the Great Western, to Brentwood and Broxbourne towards the Eastern Counties, and in the North as far as Lancaster and Fleetwood, as well as to Leeds and Sheffield and Hull by other lines, and via Chester to Birkenhead. In 1841 he could also get to Brighton, to Bristol, and beyond Bristol to Bridgwater, and in the North to York. In 1842 new lines had linked him to Stockport and Oldham in the North, to Taunton in the West, and nearer London to Ashford in Kent and Bishop's Stortford in Herts. In 1843 the Kent line reached Folkestone, and the Eastern Counties line Colchester; and in 1844 the Londoner's range was widened in the West to Exeter and Gloucester, in Kent to Dover and Maidstone, in the Midlands to Leamington and Oxford, and in the North to Gateshead, just across the river from Newcastle, whence he could proceed by rail to Carlisle. Newcastle itself could not be reached directly till the opening of Robert Stephenson's Tyne Bridge in 1850.

Meanwhile, in the North, a traveller could get from Manchester to Leeds and thence to Hull by 1841, and also from Leeds via York nearly but not quite to Darlington and the Durham lines. By 1840, he could get from Birmingham to Lancashire or to Cheltenham and Gloucester, or via Derby to Sheffield, York and Darlington, or via Rugby or Derby to Leicester and Nottingham, as well as to London. There was still no through communication from England to either Wales or Scotland, or to Devonshire beyond Exeter or to Cornwall, and not a single mile of railway existed in either Lincolnshire or East Anglia or North Wales. But by 1844 lines were under construction or had been sanctioned westwards to Plymouth, northwards from Lancaster to Carlisle and from Darlington to Gateshead, in the East to Norwich and Yarmouth and via Colchester to Ipswich, along the South Coast from Chichester to St. Leonards via Brighton, across country from Norwich and Ely via Peterborough to Rugby, in the North-West from Chester to Holyhead and from Carlisle to Whitehaven, and in Scotland southwards from Glasgow and Edinburgh to Berwick on the Border—to say nothing of a host of supplementary local lines and extensions.

In London, the great terminus stations were becoming defined. London Bridge dates from 1836, Euston from 1838, Paddington from 1841, Waterloo from 1844, Bishopsgate (later moved to Liverpool Street) from the same year, and King's Cross from 1850. The Metropolitan, first designed to link up the main line stations in North London, was authorized in 1853.

The coming of the railways made a profound difference, far beyond that made by the canals, to the economic "shape" of

England. It opened up the interior, independently of the waterways, to heavy as well as light industries; and it made internal migration, as well as travel for business or pleasure, immensely easier than before. Moreover, the actual processes of railway-building exerted a far-reaching social influence. The migratory railway labourers, called "navvies," or navigators, by analogy from the canal era, brought strange ways and strange tidings to the villages through which the railways passed, and left a deposit of settlers along their routes. Workers whose range of movement had been confined to the distance that a man could travel on foot, under constant threat of being removed under the Settlement Acts back to his parish of origin, lest he should become chargeable to the local Poor Law authorities, found their power to move suddenly expanded; and this helped to people the growing factory and mining areas with recruits from much further afield. In 1843 there were 2,000 miles of railway lines: in 1850 there were 6,621. In 1843 they carried 23,000,000 passengers: in 1850 the numbers had risen to 73,000,000. The great age of the commercial traveller was beginning: the consolidation of local lines into through systems of communication was being seriously taken in hand.

The advent of the railways was of special importance to the part of the country lying north of a line which ran roughly from Liverpool and Manchester in the west through Leeds and Bradford to York and the Humber. For, with a very few exceptions—the most notable being the devious canal from Liverpool to Leeds via Skipton—this northern area had not been opened up at all by canals and was almost devoid of navigable rivers. The country was too hilly for successful canal-making, and the rivers flowed too swiftly down from the hills and were too rocky to be open to any sort of navigation except very near the coast. Accordingly, the north-eastern area, where the most developed coal-fields of England lay, had to wait for the railway age before it could be linked with the rest of the country except by road and sea. The railways there served two purposes. First, they opened up to sea communication the coal-fields lying further from the coast; and thereafter they connected Newcastle and the north-eastern coal and iron fields by land with Leeds and Sheffield, and enabled them to export their manufactured products through Liverpool across the Atlantic. What the canals were to Birmingham and the Midlands the railways became to the industrial area of the North-East. Cumberland profited less, for its coal-fields lay quite near to the sea, and communication by water with Liverpool remained easier and cheaper for its industrialists than the land route, even after the railway had been extended north through Preston and Lancaster to Carlisle and the West of Scotland.

Between 1832 and 1850 the value of British exports rose from £36,000,000 to £71,000,000, and the quantity more than doubled. Shipping tonnage rose from 2,262,000 to 3,565,000, and the number of seamen employed from 138,000 to 193,000. Shipping clearances from British ports rose from under 3,000,000 tons to nearly 7,500,000. The tonnage of pig-iron produced rose from 700,000 to 2,250,000, and of coal from about 26,000,000 tons to about 60,000,000. The quantity of cotton consumed increased from 259,000,000 lbs. to 588,000,000 lbs., and the value of exports of cotton goods from £17,000,000 to £28,000,000. The number of workers in textile factories rose from 340,000 in 1835 to 570,000 in 1850. Population, for Great Britain, increased from 16,261,000 in 1831 to 20,816,000 in 1851.

How, during this period of exceedingly rapid capitalist expansion, did the working classes fare? The evidence is irresistible that they fared very ill. In the cotton factories of Lancashire and Cheshire, for example, Mr. G. H. Wood has estimated the average weekly wage at 9s. 9d. in 1833, 10s. in 1836, 9s. 7d. in 1840, 10s. 1d. in 1845, and 9s. 6d. in 1850. The compositor's wage in both London and Manchester was the same in 1850 as in 1832. Male woollen weavers in Huddersfield averaged 20s. a week in 1832, and 21s. in 1850. London shipwrights got 36s. at both dates. Carpenters in Newcastle rose meanwhile from 18s. to 20s., and builders' labourers in London also from 18s. to 20s., while builders' labourers in Glasgow rose from 10s. to 12s. Scottish cotton workers' average earnings fell from 8s. to 7s. 5d., and Lancashire cotton-spinners' from 25s. 9d. to 21s. 9d. The ironfounders' average wages, over all districts, rose from 25s. 6d. to 27s. 6d., and mechanics' wages

in Manchester from 27s. to 30s. Mr. Wood's general wage
indices, taking 1832 as 100, show increases by 1850, in engineering to 104, in shipbuilding to 106, in building to 109,
and in the Huddersfield woollen industry to 105. In printing
the wage level remained unchanged, except for levelling

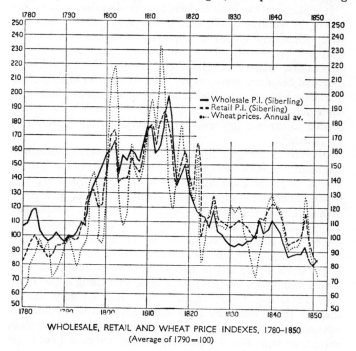

WHOLESALE, RETAIL AND WHEAT PRICE INDEXES, 1780–1850
(Average of 1790 = 100)

up in a few low-wage areas; and in cotton it dropped by
7 per cent.

These figures refer to money-wages, and do not take account
of changes in the cost of living, which underwent over the
period between 1832 and 1850 two contrary movements.
Taking the average of 1828 to 1832 as a basis, the cost of living,
as measured by Silberling's index, dropped 2 per cent in
1833–7, rose 8 per cent above the basis in 1838–42, and then
fell to 6 per cent below the basis in the next five-year period,

and to 17 per cent below in 1848–50. Wheat prices, which for the worse-paid sections of the working class probably still presented a fairer picture, averaged 63s. 2d. a quarter in 1828–32, 48s. 7d. in 1833–7, 64s. 8d. in 1838–42, 55s. 5d. in 1843–7, and 42s. 10d. in 1848–52.

It is plain, on the basis of these figures, that the worst sufferings of the working classes were in the years between 1838 and 1842, when widespread unemployment existed side by side with low wages. In the main factory areas, especially in Lancashire, wages were definitely lower in this period than they had been ten years before, whereas the cost of living was markedly higher. The Poor Law, in the meantime, had been made far more deterrent and severe. No more than this is needed to explain the mass hunger-revolt of the Chartists in the North.

Deficient as the wage-figures are, certain general conclusions can be drawn with a fair degree of confidence. In the 'forties, miners' wages had fallen, sharply in Scotland, less sharply in Northumberland and Durham. Builders' wages had risen, perhaps on the average by 8 per cent since 1832. Mechanics' wages had risen less, by about 4 per cent. In the factory areas, wages had remained stationary in Yorkshire and actually fallen in Lancashire. Skilled artisans in London had kept their wages unchanged; but in the smaller towns there had been some levelling up. Agricultural wages, after rising in the South after 1834, had begun again to fall, and fell very sharply through the 'forties. By 1850 falling prices had substantially advanced the real wages of most sections of the working class, except the agricultural labourers; but this benefit did not begin to be felt until after 1842.

It seems clear in the light of these facts that the distribution of the national income must have been changing greatly to the advantage of the richer classes. The income tax, at 7d. in the pound, yielded more in 1850 than in 1843, despite the sharp fall in prices. The rich could spare huge sums for investment in railways, mines, factories, gasworks and other enterprises, and could at the same time expand their standard of living. The main brunt of business depression was borne by the workers.

Richard Pilling, a leader of the working men sentenced for the 1842 strike, told the court: "I have seen in the factory in which I worked wives and mothers working from morning to night with only one meal; and a child brought to suck at them thrice a day. I have seen fathers of families coming in the morning and working till night and having only one meal, or two at the farthest extent. This was the state we were in at the time of the strike." He was recounting nothing exceptional; but he was talking of those who were employed, who had wages. The unemployed, scarcely employed and destitute were throughout this period enormous in numbers: on 25 March 1842, the paupers numbered 1,427,187, and on the same date in 1845, 1,539,490. There was also a class slowly dying—whose earnings were nominally their own choice, as they were by a fiction regarded as their own masters, the handloom-weavers. In 1838, when 12s. was a common wage for woollen weavers in factories, outdoor masters on the hand-loom earned commonly 8s. a week and journeymen 6s., while the cotton handloom-weavers averaged 1d. an hour as late as 1840. Such conditions explain the abysmal poverty, oriental in character, in the worst parts of the new cities. It was, for example, shown at a meeting in Leeds in October 1841, that there were then 19,936 individuals in the city with only $11\frac{1}{4}d.$ a week per head to live on.

It must be remembered that the worsening of conditions of both employed and unemployed workers was increased by a circumstance which, though it is of the gravest importance, is seldom allowed for in economic calculations. Britain had changed over from a rural to an urban civilization. In 1790 the country labourers had been about double the town labourers in numbers; in 1840 the reverse was true. Specific figures may make the meaning of this more clear. The census figures for the population of certain typical towns are as follows:

	1801	1831	1861
Manchester and Salford	90,000	237,000	400,000
Leeds	53,000	123,000	172,000
Bradford	13,000	44,000	104,000
Bolton	18,000	42,000	61,000
Blackburn	12,000	27,000	65,000

Now twelve insanitary houses on a hillside may be a picturesque village, but twelve hundred are a grave nuisance and twelve thousand a pest and horror. The window-tax, which caused only one-seventh or less of British houses to have enough light to pay the tax, was a nuisance in eighteenth-century England; in nineteenth-century towns it was a major affliction, though no change had in theory been made for the worse. Streets largely remained uncleaned; where street-cleansing Acts applied frequently only the main streets were cleaned. Picturesque courts in small towns became squalid and filthy slums in large cities. Dung, which was still regarded as a marketable produce, when left to decay in the streets of Lancashire towns, led to results which it is not suitable to describe: when it was turned into the sewers and thus into the rivers or canals, the revolting consequences were merely spread more widely. Drains of any kind, indeed, were presumed to be no more necessary than they had been fifty years before. There were many towns like Tranent, which the 1842 Commission found had for its chief drainage a water-course which frequently flooded the main road and the "lower class of houses." Its paving was shoddy and collapsed, it was not repaired, and on dark nights the citizens frequently fell into it. The contents of the rivers round about Manchester were thus described some years later: "The compound thus formed, to be perfectly appreciated, must be seen and smelt. Being by causes presently to be named rendered almost stagnant, and the liquids which are poured into it from the manufactories on the banks of the stream being usually warm, it is in the most favourable condition for continued putrefactive fermentation. Every now and then large bubbles rise which bursting give off noxious gases and diffuse over the surface solid particles which in one of the rivers, the Medlock, at times form a crust so thick that small birds have been seen to walk upon it."

The art of medicine had greatly advanced in the eighteenth and early nineteenth centuries. Theory indeed had not made a great leap forward comparable to Harvey's discovery, but practice had been enormously advanced. John Hunter's example in surgery had been slowly spread all over the island;

obstetrics had vastly improved; auscultation and the use of the thermometer, two unparalleledly important clinical devices, now came into general use. But the greater portion of the benefits that the people should have gained from this was withheld by the conditions under which they were forced to live. Death rates did indeed decrease, but not so fast as they should have done, and visitations of epidemics such as cholera were frequent. Doctors were scarce in the poorer areas, and those who practised there were rarely the better qualified practitioners.

If the traveller whom we have imagined visiting the country in 1746 had returned a hundred years later, he would no doubt have been astonished by the mechanical inventions, but also deeply shocked at their results. No care was taken of the mass of the population, not even of its children. In any large block of tenements, stated the Glasgow superintendent of police in 1842: "I should be able to find a thousand children who have no name whatever, or only nicknames, like dogs." In Edinburgh the usual answer to: "When were you last washed?" was "When I was last in prison"; in Dumfries (where one person out of every eleven died of cholera) there were twelve bakers' shops and seventy-nine whisky shops.

Nothing, indeed, would have discomposed an eighteenth-century traveller more than the deliberate refusal of any form of recreation except alcohol to the working class. No public free libraries existed before 1845. Public open spaces were not provided or were sold on the flimsiest grounds. Sport was made more and more impossible as the towns extended. Playhouses were of course denounced as immoral, and widely successful attempts were made to close every garden, museum or other place of recreation not a beer-house, on Sundays, the only day when the working class could patronize them. The Anglican Church connived at this, but the driving force was Nonconformist. Wesley had rejoiced that his Methodists had abstained from "reading plays, romances or books of humour, from singing innocent songs or talking in a gay diverting manner." This ignoble rule was enforced and extended as far as the power of what O'Connor called the "shopocracy" could carry it. Dissenters, generally regarded as Radicals, turned Roebuck and other of their most ardent defenders out of their Parliamentary seats in 1837 for declining to support a Sabbatarian campaign.

Not unnaturally, in such a régime the arts which made life pleasant declined and disappeared. Painting and music touched a new low level of vulgarity; architecture destroyed city after city and covered the face of Britain with bestial ugliness which probably can never be wholly undone. Only literature survived.

Even education, in which the "shopocracy" at least professed an interest, was but little improved. The percentage of illiterates was 41·6 in 1839 (men 33·7 and women 49·5) and it remained virtually unchanged until 1846 and probably later. Indeed, there is reason to argue that the educational position of the working class was actually worsened, by a foolish "discovery" which was widely adopted at this period. The old dame and parish schools had frequently been bad, but they were also sometimes good, though always unpretentious. But the systems of Bell and Lancaster, which their propounders said were "with great propriety" called "the STEAM ENGINE OF THE MORAL WORLD," annihilated any possibility of education. The device merely consisted of teaching blocks of information, generally in the form of answers to a series of questions, to a group of "monitors," who then taught them to another group of children, and so forth. So knowledge was "multiplied"; if an ill-disposed examiner asked the questions in the wrong order, the sham was disastrously exposed. Fortunately this rarely happened.

It is a notable example of the gullibility of the historian that this probably retrograde step is still frequently referred to as an advance. Mr. and Mrs. Hammond have disinterred specimens of the catechisms inflicted upon the children. One must suffice:

Monitor: You read in the lesson *The enamel is disposed in crescent-shaped ridges.* What is the enamel?
Boy: The hard shining part of the tooth.
Monitor: What part of our tooth is it?
Boy: The covering of that part that is out of the jawbone.

Monitor: What do you mean by disposed?
Boy: Placed.
Monitor: The root?
Boy: "Pono," I place.
Monitor: What is crescent-shaped?
Boy: Shaped like the moon before it is a half-moon.
Monitor: Draw a crescent. *Boy draws it on the blackboard.*
Monitor: What is the root of the word?
Boy: "Cresco," I grow.
Etc., etc.

This is a specimen of an intelligent and untheological ques-
tionnaire: its value to exhausted factory children can be
imagined. How far this "discovery" was in fact universally
applied we can only conjecture: there is some reason to hope
that its practitioners were less senseless than its propounders.

One further worsening of conditions remains to be noticed,
though it cannot be estimated. Decaying, damaged and adul-
terated food is a plague of town civilization. Communities
which live in close touch with farming areas are served with
fresher food and are more skilled in detecting fraud and
deception. Systematic adulteration of food seems to have
developed during this period on a large scale. No real regulations existed to prevent it and the system of "fair competition"
encouraged it. Dr. Wakley, in the *Lancet*, began to expose
individual instances at the end of the period. But its extent can
only be conjectured, for the evil was not seriously investigated
until thirty years later.

CHAPTER XXV

THE CORN LAWS AND THE CHARTIST DECLINE

To a people so distressed, permanent quiet was impossible.
Not even the defeat of 1842 on top of that of 1839 could
permanently depress Chartism. A number of the Chartist
supporters indeed transferred their allegiance to other allied

causes. But some portion held together. Better trade came in 1843—accompanied by a considerable revival of Trade Union activity—and remained till 1846, when it was shattered by the effects of the Scotch and Irish famines; this recovery accounted for some weakening in the Chartist energy. A more potent cause was probably discouragement at past defeats and distrust of the leadership, now completely in O'Connor's hands.

The faithful Chartists nevertheless held a fresh Convention in 1845, which decided to make yet another attempt to achieve economic equality in a legal manner. It sponsored a "Chartist Land Co-operative Society" which should use Chartist subscriptions to settle workers on the land; from the profits of these settlers and the mortgaging of their land more farms should be bought, and so on indefinitely. In 1847 this body was reconstituted as the "National Land Company"; 42,000 persons contributed to it and raised £80,000. An estate was purchased at Heronsgate in Hertfordshire (where there is still a public-house called *The Land of Liberty*), opened, and renamed O'Connorville; another settlement was started at Charterville, near Witney, in Oxfordshire. At the General Election of 1847, when the pinch of the Irish famine had begun to be felt, a Chartist, J. H. Parry, polled 1,648 votes at Norwich, nearly putting out the Marquis of Douro, and O'Connor was actually elected for Nottingham, though after he had taken his seat he spoke chiefly on Irish affairs.

But these were deceptive appearances of strength. The circulation of the *Northern Star* fell from 13,580 in 1841 to 12,500 in 1842 and 9,350 in 1843. Next year it was moved to London and became the *Northern Star and National Trades Journal* in an endeavour to secure a Trade Union circulation. Vainly, for the *Northern Star* was suffering in the Press world what the Chartists were suffering in the political. It was unable to overcome the competition of Radical rivals which were better run and were polite to its principles while treating its tactics with derision. *The News of the World* and *Lloyd's Weekly News* both surpassed it journalistically, while the *Weekly Dispatch*, which had over 66,000 circulation in 1842, drove O'Connor to fury. "You unmitigated ass! You sainted fool! You canonized ape! You nincompoop!" he wrote of it and to it.

Some Chartist strength, of necessity, went to the longest established rival advocates of social reform. Robert Owen's followers were busy throughout these years carrying on their propaganda in Halls of Science, often built and owned by themselves. An account survives of a typical meeting of one of their societies, apparently called: "The Institution of the Intelligent and Well-Disposed of the Working Classes for the Removal of Ignorance and Poverty by means of Education and Employment," and held in the Tivoli Gardens at Norwood. "The Socialists proved to be persons whose appearance and manners did not render them in the slightest degree remarkable, and their founder, a little benevolent-looking, quiet-mannered gentleman in an ordinary suit of black. A short address was delivered by the philanthropist, and dancing on the lawn began, concluding when darkness began to settle on the pleasant scene, and gave the necessary background for the pyrotechnic display, the culminating effect of which was the motto in letters of fire: 'Each for all and all for each.' " But the energies of Owen's followers were increasingly diverted by him from these innocuous activities to running the largest and most ambitious of his projects, the "Home Colony of Associated Industry," Harmony Hall at Queenwood, in Hampshire. It was conceived on a grandiose scale, and Owen could not raise enough funds to meet the deficit incurred. In 1845 it collapsed, and the Owenite movement followed. Owen himself continued to lecture for another thirteen years till his death in 1858, but though he had audiences he had no support. Thirty years later, in the late 'seventies, the observer quoted above wrote with perfect truth: "The system which he advocated has no longer an exponent either in the Press or in the lecture hall."

More popular energy, naturally, went to support agitations which had greater chances of success than Chartism than to one which had less. The organizations which benefited most by the diversion of energy from O'Connor were the Anti-Corn Law League, the Ten Hours Committees, and especially, during the period of trade activity in the middle 'forties, the Trade Union movement.

The Anti-Corn Law League had been founded in 1838 and

in its earlier years had been seriously hampered by Chartist assertions that the real object of its supporters was to reduce wages by the amount that corn prices would fall. This argument was weak in that it conceded implicitly that by itself Repeal would be a good thing; at a greatly advertised debate Feargus O'Connor was even in his followers' opinion utterly defeated by the League speaker on these grounds. Organizers and speakers such as Cobden and Bright were far more competent than the disorderly Chartist enthusiasts: the volume of support for repeal in popular circles grew steadily larger from about 1840 onwards. Though to ascribe the strike of 1842 to the League was grotesque, it is very probable that then or soon after the League had as many followers as the Charter, if not more. Moderate democrats such as Ebenezer Elliott, the writer of *God Save the People*, had indeed transferred to it their whole energies.

But the repeal of the duties was not directly due to working-class agitation. The manufacturing interest was the most powerful driving force. There can be no reasonable doubt that the despairing anger of the repeated Chartist attacks made many of the ruling class consider that some genuine relief must be given to the working class, and to that extent the impulse behind the agitation was working-class. But the effective voice of England was, in Parliament or outside, that of the middle class; and it was the rapidly growing conviction of this body that the duties were a grave and vexatious hindrance to prosperity which ultimately induced Peel to yield.

The wheat prices from 1835 to the year of the famines showed how the cost of living was artificially held up. In 1835 wheat averaged 39s. 4d. a quarter. In the following seven years the average prices were 48s. 6d., 55s. 10d., 64s. 7d., 70s. 8d., 66s. 4d., 64s. 4d., and 57s. 3d. In 1843, 1844 and 1845 prices fell a little to 50s. 1d., 51s. 3d. and 50s. 10d., but they rose again to 54s. 8d. in 1846. In that year the duties were repealed, but the repeal was not to come into effect till 1 February 1849. But though the fall of the blow was suspended, the effect was nevertheless to override the interests of the landlord class in favour of the employers, and (to some extent at least) in favour of the working class. During the years of suspense the prices were 69s. 9d. in 1847, and 50s. 6d. in 1848. Then prices fell sharply, to 44s. 3d. in 1849 and 40s. 3d. in 1850. In 1851 the average price was actually as low as 38s. 6d.

This fall in prices was accompanied by a large increase in wheat imports. In the years 1829 to 1831 bad harvests had been met by large imports of wheat, despite the tax, at an average rate of not much less than 2,000,000 quarters a year. Then from 1832 to 1837 imports fell very low, on account of good harvests, and averaged less than 300,000 quarters. In the bad years from 1838 to 1842 imports again rose sharply, to an average of 2,500,000 quarters annually. From 1843 to 1845 they were only a little over 1,000,000 quarters, rising to 2,344,000 in 1846, and 4,465,000 in 1847. Over the next five years, from 1848 to 1852, they remained at this high level, averaging 4,400,000 quarters. From that time onwards imports continued to rise, but not rapidly until the 'sixties, the average for 1853–7 being still under 5,000,000 quarters. Meanwhile, wheat prices had again risen sharply, despite the repeal of the Corn Laws, from an average of 42s. 10d. in 1848–52 to one of 65s. 2d. in 1853–7. But the story of that great rise in the general level of prices belongs to our next period. For the time being, there is no doubt that the repeal of the Corn Laws was accompanied by considerable gains in real wages to the working class.

The success of the Ten Hours movement was even less disputably a gain to the working class. The restriction of hours to ten, or indeed to any figure at all, was angrily opposed by the millowners, and by apparent Radicals such as John Bright himself. The most eminent economists, headed by Nassau Senior, proved to their own satisfaction that all profits were made "in the last hour," and that the adoption of this proposal would immediately extinguish the whole of British industry. The movement, as has been explained, nominally demanded the banning only of women's and children's labour after ten hours, knowing that to keep the mills open without them would be unprofitable. It was conducted strictly on parliamentary lines: its selected representative was Lord Ashley, an evangelical Tory, afterwards Lord Shaftesbury, but at this time still in the Commons with a courtesy title only. Committees of operatives and some enlightened masters in the towns provided him and his few assistants with material and instructions he conducted the actual parliamentary agitation with patience and skill. He was no democrat. In his opinion Socialism and Chartism were "the two great demons in morals and politics". he was in no other way an enlightened or tolerant man, but his immense kindness and undefeated persistence in relieving misery made him perhaps the noblest figure of the nineteenth century, and his very faults—his pride and his narrow religion—assisted him in the Parliaments of these years. He had no doubt that even the smallest incidents of his career were directed by his Deity: "Thank God a thousand times for His mercy and goodness!" he wrote when Black Rod arrived at a convenient moment for him.

Largely by his skill, a Bill was passed in 1842 wiping out women's underground labour in the mines and appointing inspectors of mines—a provision of profound importance for the future—and another in 1844 making factory inspection more adequate, bringing silk mills under control, and limiting the hours of women and young persons to twelve a day. His triumph was complete in 1847, when the Act instituting the Ten Hours limitation in textile factories was finally carried. At the moment of success he was by an accident out of Parliament and the bill was introduced by John Fielden, but it was universally recognized by the working class that success was due more to him than to any other one man, and the towns of England rang with their expressions of gratitude.

Before long—in 1850—an ingenious judge, Baron Parke, acting, as the Attorney-General said, "not according to law but on policy," managed to defeat the purpose of the law by permitting the relay system. The Act had said that the protected women and children should work ten hours, calculated from the time of their beginning work, but it had not said ten *continuous* hours, or the same ten hours. By bringing them in in relays, standing some off for one period during the day and others at another, the factories could be run as far into the night as the employers chose, and the protection of the men was torn from them. The decision was a shabby lawyer's trick; but it was valid, and to secure an Act to annul the relay system Shaftesbury on his own authority gave consent to an increase of hours to ten and a half. Forthwith, forgetting their previous adulation, the committees and their followers covered him with insults and vituperation which were, at the least, excessive. The amending Act was passed in 1850, and he withdrew himself to other spheres where, as saviour of climbing boy-sweeps, patron of ragged schools and protector of lunatics, his autocratic decisions would not be questioned. The clear ten hours was not secured till 1874.

A further advantage that the working class secured was the relaxation of some of the rigours of the administration of the Poor Law. The punitive character of this law was not altered —indeed, has not yet disappeared—but its application was made milder. No one was more successful in exposing the results than Dr. Wakley, the Radical coroner, who in West Middlesex held inquests even on paupers. In 1839 he enforced the exhumation of Thomas Austin, a pauper who had fallen into the Hendon workhouse copper, been scalded to death and quietly buried. The jury censured the workhouse authorities; the workhouse master from his place in court sneeringly replied: "The jury have found a verdict, but they have not identified the body." "If this is not," said Wakley, "the body of the man who was killed in your vat, pray, sir, how many paupers have you boiled?"

The Hoo Union workhouse master was punished for stripping young girls and beating them indecently, and his action declared illegal; in 1847 the Andover scandal overturned the Poor Law Commissioners themselves. The Andover paupers were employed in bone-crushing: they were so ill-fed that they fought each other for the putrid gristle adhering to the horses' bones. A parliamentary enquiry followed: the exposure of the personal squabbles as well as of the meannesses of the Commissioners shocked a not-too-squeamish House and they were removed from office. Their place was taken by a regular ministerial Board which relaxed a number of their more malicious regulations; but the law, as administered by middle-class Guardians, could not even so be described as humane.

These three great advantages—the repeal of the Corn Laws,

the Ten Hours Act, and the softening of the Poor Law—were secured under the pressure of the torchlight meetings, the riots, insurrectionary plots and strikes of Chartism. To that extent Chartism was not a failure, but it was already clear to many that it would not receive its Six Points. A keen observer might have seen growing up under its shadow the organizations which were to take, in fact, its place. The Trade Unions, firstly, were reviving. Martin Jude, leading the miners of the North-East Coast, acting on a Yorkshire proposal, was successful for a while in organizing a National Union, which was powerful from 1841 to 1847, and paid W. P. Roberts, an able, bullying lawyer, connected also with O'Connor's Land Scheme, £1,000 a year to fight every possible case in the courts. These were mostly brought under the Master and Servant Acts, for breach of contract or leaving work unfinished, and the resistance was unexpectedly successful. Though the National Union broke up after an unsuccessful strike in 1847, local sections remained intact. Local engineering societies, headed by the Journeymen Steam Engine Makers' Society—soon to become the nucleus for the more famous Amalgamated Society of Engineers—grew active and sponsored a number of forward movements in particular districts for shorter hours, higher wages and the abolition of the hated piece-work system. There was similar activity in many towns in the building trades; and the printers and certain other groups were also improving their organization.

Indeed, in 1845, just before trade took its downward plunge, the Sheffield Trade Unionists, under the leadership of John Drury and in close association with John Normansell of the Yorkshire miners, called together the first national Trade Union Conference that had met since the collapse of 1834, and launched a new body designed as the successor to John Doherty's National Association of 1830 and Robert Owen's Grand National Consolidated Trades Union. More exactly, the Conference launched two bodies. The National Association of United Trades for the Protection of Labour was to unite as many societies as agreed to join for concerted resistance to wage-reduction—each separate society being left to push its claims for improved conditions without financial aid from tne central body. This Association was also to represent the claims of the workers before Parliament and the public, and to act as a general co-ordinating body. At the same time, the National United Trades Association for the Employment of Labour was to revive the idea of "Union Shops" and Co-operative Production, dormant since 1834, and was to aid the members' wage-struggles by means of collective self-employment, with a view to the ultimate supersession of the capitalist system of competition.

These two organizations, launched with a great flourish, sought both to revive the ideals and to profit by the errors of the earlier experiments in "General Unions." The Association for the Protection of Labour was designed to be not an inclusive Union of all trades, but a federation of societies which would retain their independence and their separate funds, while subscribing to and receiving help from the central body. In order to avoid risking the general funds of the movement in the fortunes of co-operative production, the Association for the Employment of Labour was to be kept distinct from it, though the two meant to work together closely under a common leadership. Thomas Slingsby Duncombe, a Radical M.P., who was sympathetic to Chartism and to working-class claims, was persuaded to become President of both bodies; and the Sheffield craftsmen and Yorkshire miners put their best efforts into making them a success.

But hardly had the new movement begun to take shape when the serious economic recession of 1846–7 set in. Successful strikes at once gave place to lock-outs in which the Trade Unions vainly sought to resist attempts to reduce wages and worsen conditions of labour. The National Association for the Employment of Labour had to be given up, though this was done by nominally merging it in the twin Association. As the funds of the Protection Association became exhausted and levies were called for in order to replenish them, many societies which had joined the movement at the outset fell away; and no success was achieved in bringing in the larger societies which had failed to join. Nevertheless, the Association did not disappear, even when it was subjected to an ordeal akin to the Dorchester labourers' case which had done so much towards destroying the Grand National Union in the previous decade.

In 1847 John Drury and two other Sheffield Trade Union leaders were arrested on a charge of inciting their followers to destroy machinery. The only evidence against them came from two informers, both with criminal records behind them; but the prisoners were convicted and sentenced to ten years' transportation. The National Association, already hard pressed for money, had to devote its energies to the defence of its leaders; and, on appeal, the convictions were quashed on a technical point. But this was not the end. Drury and his associates were promptly re-arrested on a second charge, and again threatened with conviction. A second time the Association took up the case, and after a year's agitation, finally secured their release. But the struggle, and the temporary incapacitation of some of its principal leaders, had weakened it almost to exhaustion.

It is interesting to find that in the course of this double struggle against economic recession and legal persecution, the Association for the Protection of Labour seriously considered the launching of a Trade Union political party. The debates on this matter at its conferences revealed strong differences of opinion. While some of the delegates argued that only political action would enable the workers to get their economic grievances redressed, a rival faction held that any introduction of politics into the Trade Unions would fatally destroy working-class industrial solidarity, and lead to the disruption of the movement. In the end, after Drury's release and the revival of trade had relaxed the immediate pressure, the project of Trade Union political action was abandoned—to be taken up by Ernest Jones in his attempts to revive the decaying fortunes of Chartism in the early 'fifties. But the Protection Association deserves to be remembered as the first body to suggest the creation of a working-class party resting primarily on Trade Union support.

After these troubles, the Association continued to exist, and to do useful work within a limited sphere. Connected with it was the "Redemptionist" movement, established at Leeds in 1846, largely on Owenite foundations. The Societies for the

Redemption of Labour set out, with subscriptions collected at the rate of a penny a week, to found Co-operative Societies and workshops which they hoped would gradually displace capitalism by peaceful means. The movement spread to Lancashire and Cheshire, Norwich, London and other areas, and conducted for some years a colony in Wales, with small factories as well as a farm. Its members took a leading part in forming the Leeds Co-operative Society, which became one of the most successful in the country, and they worked in with the Christian Socialists in the Co-operative ventures of the early 'fifties. We may also record here, though it takes us beyond the strict limits of this chapter, that the Protection Association was primarily responsible for the movement which resulted in the legalization of peaceful picketing under the Combinations of Workmen Act of 1859 (often called the "Molestation" Act). It also kept up a steady pressure for the recognition of Trade Unions, both by employers and by the law. In its later phases it became much more moderate, and devoted itself largely to the attempt to promote schemes of conciliation and arbitration. It finally expired only in the 'sixties, and soon after its demise some of its demands found very imperfect embodiment in the Conciliation Act of 1867. But before that time it had been, in effect, superseded in 1866 by the United Kingdom Alliance of Organized Trades, launched like itself at Sheffield by a national conference of Trade Union delegates as the immediate predecessor of the Trades Union Congress which exists to-day.

Less noticed, but as significant, was the opening in 1844 in Toad Lane, in the textile town of Rochdale, of a shop by a small number of workmen calling themselves the Equitable Pioneers. Their shop succeeded where other Owenite ventures failed: indeed, it flourished, and was before long being imitated. From it derives, demonstrably, the great Co-operative Movement of to-day. The principle which saved the Rochdale Society was "dividend on purchases" as well as interest on share capital: the Pioneers sold their goods at market prices and returned their surplus to members in direct proportion to each member's expenditure at the shop. They were encouraged, if they would, to reinvest their "divi" at interest; however, the full results of this device belong to a later chapter. The advance of Co-operation was yet to come; for the minute Chartism overshadowed everything else.

The reason for the last revival of Chartism, which took place in 1848, was partly economic. No doubt, nearly all large political movements arise ultimately from economic conditions, but only one as incoherent and unaware of its objects as Chartism moves so directly as economic conditions move. It was almost as exact as a barometer. Like the high waves of 1839 and 1842, the 1848 uprising was the result of a trade depression. In 1847 a great commercial crisis, following on the good trade of 1846, had increased suddenly the number of the unemployed. Both 1847 and 1848 were years of deep trade depression (but prices were not, as they had been before, rising). In 1849 revival started, and Chartism began to weaken; in 1850 prosperity was general, and Chartism collapsed.

The sea began to rise in 1847: the election of O'Connor for Nottingham was in itself a sign of the coming storm. But it was alien example that raised Chartist hopes and discontents to a height that they had not reached since 1842. In February 1848, without any warning whatsoever, the French King was driven from his throne by the Paris populace, and a Republic proclaimed. The effect of this was as if someone had put a match to a series of Chinese crackers. One by one the royalties of Europe were brought low by popular insurrections. The small German royalties, headed by the Elector of Hesse, were the first to be compelled to grant Constitutions, all of which were similar to the Charter. Almost at the same time the kingdoms and duchies of Italy began to go up in smoke: the inhabitants of Milan, in five days of fighting, drove out a fully equipped Austrian garrison. Next, the King of Prussia was forced to grant a similar constitution, and to stand bareheaded, with crocodile tears pouring into his handkerchief, while the funeral of revolutionary dead passed before his balcony. Before the sensation this caused had abated, an even more surprising collapse was reported. A royal house far more anciently established, far less subjected to popular violence than the English, yielded before "the mob": the Emperor of Austria accepted the National Guard forced on him, and Metternich fled to England. After that, the coercion and ultimate expulsion of the Pope seemed almost of secondary importance.

Under the influence of such news, the Chartists lost whatever balance they had retained. A new petition was promptly drafted, a National Assembly called to present it, and O'Connor drafted a constitution of the British Republic, with himself as President. A mass meeting was called for April 10 to present the petition. It was to meet on Kennington Common and march to Parliament: in the opinion of a badly frightened governing class, this meant that April 10 was the day of the revolution.

The Chartists were not the only persons to believe that the year 1848 was one in which everything was possible. The spring and summer were filled with a hullabaloo of excited proposals. Sects which had been almost forgotten rose to a great importance and then vanished, including the Concordium, a Socialist society, under a "Pater"—William Oldham —who disapproved of marriage. Its members insisted on a diet of "unfired" foods and cold water and on the absolute minimum of clothing, which did not include shoes or stockings. The editor of their principal paper, J. E. Duncan, was arrested and imprisoned for causing a disturbance in Bishopsgate by persistently reciting his own poetry. But the rigours of English February and March by a natural but extreme reaction caused them to decide to emigrate to Venezuela and remove themselves from the scene with a suddenness and completeness never before equalled by a political organization.

The Reverend Mr. Barmby—the title is more than suspect— ran a general Communist paper, which was for a while successful in concentrating the energies of the Utopians, but he weighted the news too much in favour of his "Communist Church," and it disappeared. A more important religious movement was that of the Christian Socialists, who endeavoured to turn the Chartist and Socialist enthusiasm to the benefit of the Church. Their chief men—Charles Kingsley, E. V. Neale, F. D. Maurice, J. M. Ludlow—were or became eminent in other spheres. Momentarily they founded numerous small co-operative producing societies which all came to a speedy end, and whose principles were expounded in a manner far from comprehensible to the average working man. "To call men to repentance first of all, and then also, as it seems to me, to give them the opportunity of showing their repentance and bringing forth fruits of it. This is my idea of a Tailors' Association," wrote Maurice. Repentance was also needed on the Christian as well as on the working-class side. "We have used the Bible as if it were a mere special constable's handbook, an opium dose for keeping beasts of burden patient while they are being overloaded," wrote Kingsley, so sending on its travels a phrase which was to end up on the walls of the Red Square in Moscow in 1917.

For Maurice, the Church was a visible society ordained by Christ for the bringing about of the Kingdom of God. This Kingdom was at all times more truly real, more genuine, than the "kingdoms of this age" because it existed in the Divine mind. Baptism took the individual from his natural barren state of selfishness and made him part of the visible fellowship of the children of God. Partial apostasy from this fellowship of local congregations could blur but could not destroy the effects of baptism; Maurice's chief interest in the new co-operative societies was that they might counter this partial apostasy which he saw all around him.

The events of 1848 seemed to him a direct manifestation of Divine power. He echoed the Abbé Lamennais: "Cannot you feel the breath of God?" "Do you really think," he wrote, "that the invasion of Palestine by Sennacherib was a greater event than the overthrowing of nearly all the greatest powers, civil and ecclesiastical, in Christendom?" Ludlow was equally exalted, but more practical; his insistence on working-class self-government and the practical details of workshop management seemed to Maurice unwise and more than a little worldly. Considerable trade union support was gained by him, Neale, Thomas Hughes and a few others, especially from the engineers. The societies that they started carried on, in most cases, till 1851 or even a little later.

Their efforts ended thereafter in a failure as complete as the Concordium's; but the after-effects were considerable. Their invaluable aid to the nascent Co-operative movement, especially in securing the Act of 1852, will be mentioned later. Together with Radical dissenting ministers they were responsible for preventing that hostility between the organized working class and organized religion which became universal on the Continent. There was, henceforward, always a small percentage of parsons with a genuine sympathy with Socialism and the misery of the working class, whose influence prevented the Church and the Chapels being counted wholly as enemies; similarly a strain of religiosity and pietism ran powerfully in the Labour movement and was later to be an effective obstacle to the spread of Marxian philosophy.

But this was in the future: momentarily the Chartist excitement had to flare itself out. O'Connor was nearly delirious: the Petition had four million signatures, it had five million, it had six million. Victory was practically secured; "France is a Republic!" cried Ernest Jones. When April 10 came, the Duke of Wellington had packed London with troops and special police. The Kennington Common meeting was proscribed, but was held nevertheless. The common was packed —the attendance may have been 25,000 or 125,000, for the reporters estimated it according to their politics. As soon as he arrived, O'Connor was sent for by the police at the Horns Inn. He came out again with a compromise. The meeting should be allowed, but the procession to Parliament abandoned. The Petition was taken there in a cab.

When it arrived the signatures were hurriedly counted, and were announced to be slightly less than two million. O'Connor attempted to fight the chairman of the reporting committee, but abandoned for three months any attempt to move for a debate. The Chartist Convention (a forerunner of the projected National Assembly) debated irresolutely the question of armed insurrection, and gave way on May 1 to the Assembly without having made a decision. The man to whom they looked for guidance, O'Connor, was unable to give it. His Land Company, and the Bank he had founded in connection with it, were in grave difficulties, and even in the ordinary affairs of life he seemed to suffer from an incoherence. His two chief lieutenants, who had echoed his boasts, Harney and Ernest Jones, were dejected and unable to take up the reins.

The Assembly, as in 1839, fell under the control of revolutionaries when the reformers had failed. It reconstituted the National Charter Association on a basis of "classes" of ten "wards" of ten men with a hierarchy of commanders, and elected an executive headed by Dr. M'Douall. But the disagreements which had been produced paralysed the Assembly and it dissolved before the month was out. The more determined Chartists went on with their preparations for rebellion. A National Guard was instituted as a result of a local Lancashire and Yorkshire Conference. Three thousand were reported drilling at Wilsden, under a black flag. At Bingley and Bradford there were strong detachments, the latter of which beat the police in a straight fight, killing one and wounding others, but retreated before the military. Similar events occurred at Ashton-under-Lyne and Liverpool; there is evidence of other armed Chartist forces at Leicester, Aberdeen and Glasgow. Spies—Ball at Liverpool; Flynn, Shepherd and Emmet at York Assizes—were responsible for many arrests, though the warrant issued by an innocent magistrate for "Wat Tyler" could not be executed. But the centre of the insurrection was to be London: Blackaby, the blacksmith who was Chartist chief in Croydon, arranged to hold as many police as possible by uproar in the suburbs, while M'Douall marched on Whit Monday from Bishop Bonner's Fields on to Whitehall. Blackaby carried out his part, but the secret was out and the exits from the Fields were heavily garrisoned. Rain fell without ceasing, and the Chartists were relieved to obey M'Douall's signal to go home.

But they believed themselves to be 80,000 organized in London; they were in touch with the Irish revolutionaries, and were unwilling to go down without a fight. Cuffay, a mulatto appointed a Commissioner by the Executive, took charge of the London area, and with six others—Ritchie, Lacey, Fay, Rose, Mullins and Johnson—reorganized the revolt for August 15. Ritchie had a corps of "luminaries"—alleged experts in starting fires—and Johnson a method of making caltrops to break cavalry charges. The headquarters were in Orange Street (now Parton Street, Red Lion Square) and on the appointed day numerous bands of armed men were scattered about Bloomsbury. The largest number were at Seven Dials, with pickaxes to break up the pavements for barricades. The plan may sound preposterous, in view of the later prosperity of Victoria's reign, but it was in just such a way that the recently successful revolution in Paris had started.

The Chartists had, however, no opportunity to try their strength. The authorities in their alarm had fallen to the devices of Sidmouth and Castlereagh. "Johnson," whose real name was Powell, was a spy and provocator. He had reported the whole plan (much of which he had concocted); and the whole revolutionary executive except Rose was arrested at its headquarters on the morning of the insurrection day. Cuffay, Fay, Lacey, Ritchie and the Irish envoy Darling, were sentenced on Johnson's evidence to transportation for life: Mullins and a number of others to lesser sentences. The cases were, if anything, more sensational than those of Frost, Jones and Williams in 1839; but no agitation for their reprieve followed. The Chartists were becoming disheartened. Their discouragement was increased by the news that the Land Company was bankrupt. The House of Commons had appointed a Committee to inquire into it. It found that it was in such distress through mismanagement that it must be wound up, but added that O'Connor had made no money from it: he had indeed lost over £3,000 through it. O'Connor trumpeted this vindication loudly, not realizing his honesty was saved at the expense of his intelligence.

The other surviving leaders—Jones, when released from prison, O'Brien, who returned to active propaganda as O'Connor's prestige declined, Harney, G. W. M. Reynolds, who founded the journal that bears his name—became in their propaganda more definitely Socialist in the modern sense. Jones's publications and speeches excited the admiration of Marx and Engels. O'Brien produced a sensible scheme for the nationalization of the chief industries. Harney wrote in his *Red Republican*: "Every proletarian who does not see and feel that he belongs to an enslaved and degraded class is a *fool*."

The new tone of their propaganda was mainly due to foreign influence. The last years of Chartism established a link between British and foreign workers which has never since been totally broken. Ernest Jones in 1846 had attended at Brussels, as a Chartist delegate, a meeting of the short-lived International Democratic Committee. One of the Chartist "shadow" candidates of 1847, Dr. Epps, had stood as representing the Fraternal Democrats, another short-lived international body. While the growing colony of foreign workers in England impressed the Chartists by their clarity of thought, the Chartists impressed them by their apparent power. Even the most intelligent, Marx and Engels, for years expected that a turn of the wheel would bring back the tense excitement of 1848, this time with a clearer revolutionary intention. For the collapse which occurred was not so clear to the contemporary observer as it is now: Ernest Jones indeed, the last to despair, carried on his agitation under the Chartist banner until 1858—at the end, almost alone.

For the energy of the leaders, and of their diminishing following, depended on foreign example as well as foreign precept. And foreign example was failing. Mostly gloriously, but sometimes ingloriously, the Continental revolutions ended in defeat. Mazzini was driven from Rome, Manin from Venice, Kossuth from Hungary. The German revolutionaries were crushed with ease and a Bonaparte reigned in Paris.

Fewer and fewer Chartists voted in Executive elections. Many of them emigrated: in 1830 the emigration figures had probably been 60,000, and from 1847 to 1849 they averaged over 250,000 a year. The leaders cancelled one another out in bitter personal squabbles: the most famous was to be seen early in the mornings wandering about Covent Garden, "a huge, white-headed, vacuous-eyed man, looking at the fruits and flowers, occasionally taking up a flower, smelling at it, and putting it down with a smile of infantile satisfaction." In 1852, O'Connor was mercifully, but too late, taken to an asylum.

In that year there was a further split in the Chartist ranks. A majority of the Chartist Executive favoured an attempt to secure an alliance with the middle-class Radicals: Ernest Jones and two others resigned, and at a conference held under their auspices in Manchester later in the year a new Executive of three full-time members (Jones, R. G. Gammage and John Finlan) was elected. Meanwhile the *Northern Star* passed finally out of existence, its place being taken for a time by Jones's *People's Paper*, which was fortunate to rise in 1854 to a circulation of three or four thousand.

In 1855 O'Connor died. Some fifty thousand persons followed his hearse to Kensal Green, and stood motionless in the rain while a Chartist named William Jones pronounced the funeral oration both of his leader and of his movement:

"He was unguarded in his confidences and often deceived, unthinking in his generosity and often imposed upon. He was unbounded in his desire for the public good and sometimes miscalculated the means necessary for success in an over-anxiety to succeed."

These were the kindest things that could be said if truth were to be respected, and with small changes were true of the Chartists as a whole. After the mourners had dispersed, no Chartist meeting of any size was ever held again. In a generation's time the word Chartist was already beginning to be forgotten.

THE GREAT VICTORIAN AGE

CHAPTER XXVI

THE GREAT EXHIBITION

THE era that lies between 1850 and 1875—or let us say between the Great Exhibition of 1851 and the proclamation of Queen Victoria as Empress of India in 1876—has been called, not inaptly, the "Golden Age" of British capitalism. It was indeed for the British people an age of miracles. At the turning-point of the nineteenth century, Great Britain was still but at the beginning of her industrial expansion. The country had been covered with a network of railways; and travellers came from all over the world to visit the wonders of the new industrialism of Lancashire, the Black Country, and the coal-fields and ironworks of the North-East Coast and the Clyde. But marvellous as the developments of 1850 seemed to contemporary observers, most of them were still on a small scale. The railways were still only at the beginning of that process of consolidation which was to link up the innumerable local companies into a few nationally organized systems. Within the next twenty-five years railway mileage was to increase one and a half times, railway receipts nearly fourfold, and the number of railway passengers nearly sevenfold. By sea, steam-shipping was to rise from under 200,000 tons to over 2,000,000 tons, and outward clearances of all types of sea-going vessels were to increase threefold. Coal production and pig-iron production were both to be much more than doubled; and the output of steel was to rise from a negligible quantity to about 700,000 tons a year, which amounted to a veritable economic revolution, though it seems but little beside the 13,000,000 tons of to-day. The developed industrialism of the 1870's, though itself but a pygmy beside the industrialism of the twentieth

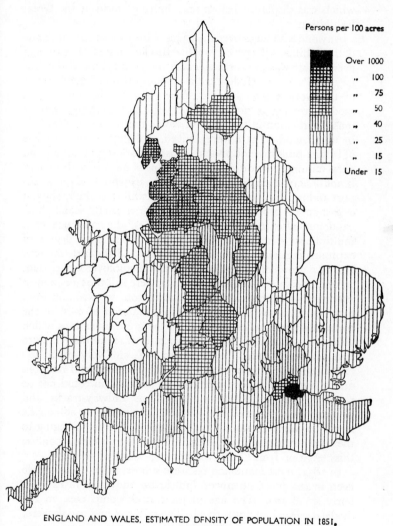

Persons per 100 acres

Over 1000
„ 100
„ 75
„ 50
„ 40
„ 25
„ 15
Under 15

ENGLAND AND WALES, ESTIMATED DENSITY OF POPULATION IN 1851,
BY COUNTIES

century, was a very giant in comparison with the industrialism which was displayed before an admiring world at the Great Exhibition.

Any one who turns over the pages of the monstrous catalogue of the exhibits will speedily realize this for himself. For though every effort was put forth to make the grand show at the new Crystal Palace in Hyde Park a demonstration of the wonders of the world's foremost industrial country, the effect, to a modern reader, is rather one of petty craftsmanship than of mass production in the sense in which the phrase was later to be understood. There were, indeed, real engineering wonders of bridge-building, locomotive construction, shipbuilding, and deep mining to be displayed, by means of models or drawings, if not of actual examples. But with the exception of the transport and mining industries most of the exhibits strongly suggest a system of production still on quite a small scale. The catalogue also suggests, in most trades, the existence of a multiplicity of small firms rather than of any high degree of capitalist concentration. The workshop and the little factory, run by a group of partners or by a single employer rather than by an impersonal joint stock concern, were still the rule in most branches of production. Brittle cast-iron, or wrought-iron, and not steel, was still the principal material of most of the metal-using industries. Not one of the great inventions which were to revolutionize the basic processes of metal manufacture had yet been made. In 1850 steel was still very much too expensive to be employed except for cutting tools and weapons and a few other special purposes for which iron could not be made to serve. Machines, as well as railway-tracks and bridges, were made of iron—where they were not still made largely of wood or stone. We may rank 1850 as belonging to the "Iron Age"; but, if we do, we must by no means confuse this "Age of Iron" with the coming "Age of Steel."

In 1851, most manufactures were still on a fairly small scale even in the more advanced industries, and most firms were fairly small too. The age of joint stock companies, in the modern sense, had not arrived. The railways and canals were, indeed, from the very beginning joint stock concerns, with large numbers of shareholders; and so were the gas and water companies, as well as the insurance companies and some, but by no means all, of the banks. But in industry, even if firms very often included the word "Co." in their trade names, the typical business was still the private firm or partnership, working under conditions of unlimited liability. Even when manufacturing businesses had a large number of shareholders, as occurred quite commonly in the textile trades, liability was usually unlimited; for until 1855 the privilege of limited liability could be secured only by incorporation under an Act of Parliament, or by special grant of privilege under the Companies Acts—and such grants were made only in quite exceptional cases. There were, indeed, still many persons who regarded limited liability as a disreputable subterfuge for evading the payment of debts, and the struggles of a section of the manufacturing interest to secure its general extension to large-scale manufacture did not enjoy united support among the manufacturers themselves. Only in 1855 did Parliament legalize the extension of the privilege of limited liability to the general run of joint stock companies in manufacturing industry; and not until some time after the consolidating Companies Act of 1862 did the practice of applying for it become at all widespread. Moreover, long after the 'sixties most small manufacturing businesses and a good many large ones, as well as practically all distributing and most merchant concerns, continued to be conducted as private firms; and it was still regarded as potentially dishonest for a business which was in effect a partnership to register itself as a company with the object of limiting the liability of its owners.

Industries carried on under these conditions were naturally competitive to a very high degree. The host of small firms competed eagerly one with another to enlarge their markets; for though total demand was increasing very fast, this did not prevent keen competition where each separate employer was seeking to expand his scale of operations in order to become wealthier and to attract more capital to his firm. Moreover, the competitive system was stimulated by the forms of economic organization. It was uncommon in the majority of trades for manufacturers to have any direct contact with the final buyers of their products. For the most part they sold to merchants, who often helped to provide capital for manufacturers whose goods were in constant demand. The merchants had almost exclusive control of foreign trade, above all in the textile industries, which exported a high proportion of their total product; but the merchant also played a very large part in controlling the course of home trade.

These merchants, each dealing with a number of different manufacturers, played one producer off against another in terms of both cheapness and quality, or type, of product. They competed also among themselves; for though the merchant often specialized in a particular market, he was usually in direct rivalry with a number of other specialists in the same field. In foreign trade especially, one merchant was continually trying to undercut another in order to capture trade; and this competition kept down the prices paid to the manufacturers—for, at any rate in the trades catering for large-scale consumption, the extension of foreign markets depended greatly on the cheapness of British goods. Competing merchants and competing manufacturers between them were constantly cutting prices to fine margins; and the high profits which they made were due much more to rapidly increasing turnover than to a wide margin on each particular commodity. Great Britain was leading the world in cheapness as well as in the productive technique which made this cheapness possible. But of course the effect was to make employers very reluctant to raise wages and so increase their costs; for, in the absence of well-established standard rates of wages and organized methods of collective bargaining, they could seldom feel at all sure that their competitors would have to pay the same wages as they. Trade Unions, where they existed, were still for the most part local: there was no system of national wage-determination over whole trades, and in fact wages and conditions varied widely not only from place to place, but also from firm to firm within the same district.

This competition to make goods cheap was not due mainly to fear of rival manufacturers abroad. Prices were cut, not for the fear of foreign producers, but mainly in order to enlarge the total market. Price-cutting, however, applied a good deal less to capital goods such as machinery than to goods designed for the consumers' market; for in this case the demand was a good deal less responsive to lower prices, and the promoters of capital investment abroad were often the same people as hoped to make a profit by the sale of capital goods. The British railway engineer or rail-maker wanted a high price for his wares; and he was able to command a high price by taking part in the financing and controlling of the concerns which bought them. These lines of British business were much less competitive, and on a larger scale, than the typical manufactures of finished goods for consumption; and they lent themselves much more readily to numerous forms of price-fixing and partial monopoly.

Accordingly, while the general run of manufacturers made money fast because of the endless expansiveness of the market, even though they competed eagerly one with another in cutting prices, the exporters and manufacturers of capital goods were mostly in a position to take advantage of their monopoly of the supply of such things so as to extract a surplus profit. This surplus, moreover, went largely into the further accumulation of capital; for, though the larger industrialists were expanding their standards of consumption and rising by thousands into the ranks of the gentry, their incomes grew a good deal more rapidly than their expenditure on luxuries, and what they did not spend in this way they put back into their businesses to earn yet more surplus profits.

Industry, indeed, for some time after 1850, was still being financed largely out of the profits of its owners. This did not apply to railway undertakings, or to such public utility services as the supply of gas and water; nor was it nearly universal in the coal and heavy metal industries, which were expanding very fast indeed. But in most industries the small size of the typical factory made private accumulation, with some help from the banks, adequate for the financing of development. Even in 1870 the average cotton factory employed fewer than 180 workers, and the average woollen mill or silk works not more than 70. The average establishment making machinery had only 85 workers, and even the average ironworks only 209. On the other hand, already the average shipyard employed nearly 600 people; and the average ironworks in South Wales—where concentration was greatest —about 650. In other manufacturing industries the large factory might have from 100 to 150 employees; but the general run of factories using power—that is to say, excluding work-shops—cannot have averaged more than 50 workers at the outside.

Limited liability, conceded in 1855, was made easier and systematized in the Companies Act of 1862. Nevertheless, in manufacturing industries the growth of joint stock enterprise was slow until the great boom of the early 'seventies; and even then the textile trades were but little affected by it, except in the Oldham area, where there occurred a rapid growth of limited companies financed largely by working-class share-holders—especially workers in the cotton industry itself. The metal trades, operating on a larger scale, began to make use of joint stock and limited liability in the 'sixties; but even in their case middle-sized firms did not adopt the new system until the 'seventies, or even the 'eighties.

This slowness to change had various causes. It arose in part from the continued suspicion in which limited liability was held—a suspicion kept alive by the numerous exposures of fraudulent company promoters which took place in the finan-cial crises of 1857, 1866 and 1873. It was partly due to the prevalence of high profits, which enabled businesses to finance expansions without needing to appeal to the investing public for funds. It was partly a product of sheer conservatism, and partly of a strongly individualistic desire among self-made men to keep their businesses in their own hands. The pressure of falling prices, trade depression and intensified competition was needed to induce many owners even of large firms to unload a part of their risks on the general body of investors.

Thus, at any rate up to the early 'seventies, the typical industrial employer was still an individual, or at most a small group of partners. Where the joint stock system was adopted, for manufacture, this was far less often for the creation of a new business than for the conversion of one that was already in being as a private firm.

Nevertheless, joint stock enterprise was spreading; for, apart from its extension into manufacturing industries, the capital embarked in railways, gasworks, waterworks, insurance companies and other service undertakings was increasing very fast; and there was a rapid growth in the 'sixties of "finance companies," designed chiefly to push British investment abroad in order to provide work, and profits, for the makers of railway material and other capital goods. It was in the 'sixties that the "company promoter" and the "financial agent" became familiar figures of city finance.

It is a curious reflection that the new finance took its models to a quite considerable extent from France, where there had been from the 'fifties, under the Second Empire, a feverish crusade for economic development. British finance companies modelled themselves on the *Crédit Foncier* and *Crédit Mobilier* of Paris; but, unlike their prototypes, they devoted themselves principally to foreign investment, because the structure of British industry and banking offered them relatively few opportunities at home. French finance did indeed at one point invade England, when in 1855 a group of French capitalists conceived the notion of unifying the London omnibus services, and founded the *Compagnie Generale des Omnibus de Londres*—the parent of the London General Omnibus Company and of the London Passenger Transport Board. But such cases were rare. Foreign capital seldom came to England, except for banking and financial operations; whereas British capital spread itself out over the whole world in an increasing stream of investment in railways, public utilities, public loans and, later, manufacturing industries of many sorts and kinds.

British industry was greatly helped to finance itself by the development of the banks. Joint stock banking had already established itself side by side with private banking well before 1850; and Peel's Bank Charter Act of 1844 had put the Bank of England in a commanding position. One effect of Peel's Act was to make bank-notes relatively unimportant. By strictly limiting the number of notes that could be issued without a pound for pound gold backing, and by confining the privilege of note-issue to banks which had possessed it before 1844, Peel in effect laid down that any future expansion of the currency must take the form either of gold or of notes fully backed with gold. The issue of additional uncovered notes had indeed to be authorized in the crises of 1847 and 1857, but only for very brief periods. From 1844 to 1914 Great Britain remained, practically without interruption, under a very stringent form of gold standard.

The effects of this would have been very different if it had not been for the Californian and Australian gold discoveries of 1849 and 1851. Already in the 'forties the rising output of Russian gold had done something to increase the monetary supply. But in the 'fifties the annual addition to the gold stock became immensely greater, and most of the new gold was applied to monetary rather than industrial uses. This helped to bring about the sharp rise in prices during the early 'fifties, and long after that to prevent prices from falling as productive efficiency increased. In the 'sixties gold production began to slacken off, and more gold came to be absorbed by industry— a clear sign of advancing wealth and luxury among the richer classes. But by this time the use of cheques was widespread, and the banking system had advanced a long way with economies in the employment of gold.

Up to the middle 'fifties, even the London clearing banks were in the h1bit of settling balances in notes, and not by cheques upon the Bank of England. This was changed about 1853; and throughout the 'fifties the use of cheques for ordinary commercial purposes was spreading fast. This change in money-using habits had probably quite as much influence as the increased supply of gold in maintaining prices, despite the falling real costs of production.

CHAPTER XXVII

THE FRUITS OF FREE TRADE

BY 1860 Gladstone had completed Peel's work, and Free Trade was to all intents and purposes in full operation. All restrictions on exports had been abolished, and on imports there remained only a few duties of quite minor importance, apart from those which were offset by a corresponding excise on home products. The Navigation Laws and the Usury Laws had been repealed. *Laissez-faire* had reached in Great Britain the culminating point; and Cobden's French Treaty of 1860 seemed to promise the advent of more liberal commercial policies in continental Europe. For, where Britain seemed so plainly prosperous under Free Trade, other countries felt an instinctive wish to follow suit. Friedrich List and the "National" economists of his school might tell them that Great Britain had built up her prosperity under a system of protection, and had knocked the props away from her industries only when they were strong enough to stand up without them. Such economists might urge their own countries first to develop their "infant" industries behind tariff walls, and to adopt Free Trade only when they had caught up with Great Britain in efficiency. Their arguments carried little weight, for the time being, except in the United States, where it was already being urged that a tariff was necessary for the protection of the high American standard of life. Elsewhere the simpler argument that freer trade was paying Great Britain, and would therefore pay her neighbours, seemed to be gaining ground. It needed the falling prices and the depression of the middle and later 'seventies to provoke any strong general reaction towards a protectionist policy.

In the third quarter of the nineteenth century British foreign trade grew extraordinarily fast. In the boom of 1872–3 exports were nearly four times as great in value, and imports nearly three times as great, as in 1850. Even when allowance has been made for a rise of wholesale prices by about one-third, the increase remains enormous.

British exports went, in rapidly growing quantities, to every corner of the earth. The United States, both in 1850 and in the 'seventies, was Great Britain's largest market, despite the already rising American tariff; for consumption there was advancing too fast for the swiftly developing home industries to meet the demand. India, where the native textile industry had been ruined by Lancashire's competition, absorbed a rapidly increasing quantity of cotton goods and other British products; and in the early 'seventies the German market expanded extraordinarily under the double influence of rapid

internal development and the spending of the French indemnity after the war of 1870. The Australian market also
grew very fast, especially in the 'fifties, after the gold discoveries; and British exports to France increased considerably
after the Cobden Treaty of 1860.

Despite the rise of the coal and metal-working industries,
textile goods continued in the 'seventies to occupy easily the
leading place among British exports. Cotton goods accounted
for almost a third of total exports, and woollen goods came
second in value, still ahead of exports of iron and steel, even
during the boom in capital exports in the early 'seventies.
But coal exports rose fivefold in value between 1850 and 1872,
and exports of machinery fourfold; and over the same period
exports of iron and steel increased by well over 250 per cent.
Meanwhile, imports of wheat had more than doubled in
quantity, and the bill for imported meat had risen more than
eightfold. There were also very large advances in the imports
of butter, cheese, eggs, fruit, tea and sugar—all significant
indications of a rising standard of life.

Naturally, this great increase in foreign trade involved
a corresponding expansion of shipping. During the third
quarter of the nineteenth century British shipping underwent
many vicissitudes. The period was one of double transformation—steam gradually ousting sail, and iron wood. In the
'forties the British mercantile marine had already been growing
fast, and between 1850 and 1875 total tonnage was nearly
doubled. Steam tonnage was not listed separately till 1853,
when it was about 250,000. By 1875 it was approaching
2,000,000; but there were still over 2,000,000 tons of sailing
ships in service under the British flag.

Nor did iron at all quickly take the place of timber as a
material for shipbuilding. The 'fifties and 'sixties were still a
great time for the building of wooden clippers; and although
iron steamers began to be built in the later 'fifties, there were
not very many of them till the next decade. Until the new
material had made its way, shipbuilding remained keenly
competitive between British and foreign shipyards, including
those of Canada as well as of the United States. Indeed, in the
Atlantic trade the American- and Colonial-built vessels were

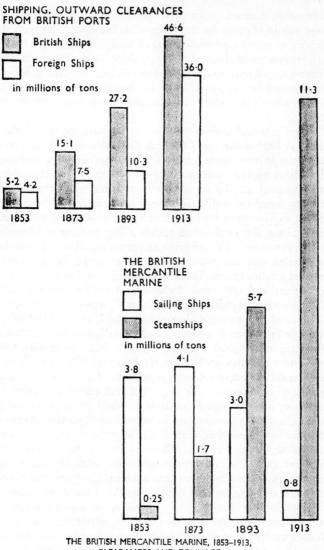

SHIPPING. OUTWARD CLEARANCES
FROM BRITISH PORTS

British Ships

Foreign Ships

in millions of tons

5·2 4·2
1853

15·1 7·5
1873

27·2 10·3
1893

46·6 36·0
1913

11·3

THE BRITISH
MERCANTILE
MARINE

Sailing Ships

Steamships

in millions of tons

3·8 0·25
1853

4·1 1·7
1873

3·0 5·7
1893

0·8
1913

THE BRITISH MERCANTILE MARINE, 1853–1913,
CLEARANCES AND TONNAGE

commonly deemed better than the British, whose chief advantage was in clippers for the trade with the East. But with the victory of steam and iron—and, of course, later steel—British predominance in shipbuilding and shipping was assured. The Americans almost abandoned shipbuilding after the interruption caused by the Civil War. In the 'seventies two-thirds of the vessels clearing from British ports were under the British flag.

Regular shipping lines, such as the Cunard, the Royal Mail, and the Peninsular and Oriental, had been already in active existence in the 'forties; with the coming of steam and iron their hold on the trade routes grew stronger. But the sailing tramp vessel was by no means ousted; for while the regular lines creamed the traffic along the principal routes, there was a steady expansion of trade with new and developing areas, and even along the established routes a big residue of irregular traffic remained. For all types of vessels together, the number of seamen rose less rapidly than the tonnage, for steamships needed smaller crews. In addition, each vessel did more work; for steam and improved docks and harbours made possible both speedier voyages and a quicker "turn-round" in port.

Meanwhile, on the railways, the first heroic period of the struggle for power was over. The Midland, London and North Western, and Great Western systems had come fully into existence; and though George Hudson had fallen from power and repute, much of his work remained. The State had set up a Railway Commission in 1846, but had omitted to endow it with any adequate powers. It was abolished in 1851; and in 1853 Cardwell's Committee, in reporting upon the process of railway amalgamation, regarded it as probably desirable from the standpoint of technical efficiency, but as involving dangers of monopoly. The railway companies were urged to enter into joint working arrangements that would not require parliamentary sanction. In general Parliament throughout the 'fifties set its face against major amalgamations, as distinct from the absorption of smaller lines by the more important companies. But an exception was made; for the North Eastern Railway was allowed to acquire what was in effect a regional monopoly over a large area. Parliament hovered between conflicting policies in its handling of railway problems; but on the whole throughout the 'fifties the advocates of unrestricted competition had their way.

In the 'sixties there was a change, and the amalgamation movement was resumed. There was at this time much discussion, led by Walter Bagehot, of the desirability of railway nationalization, which was seriously considered by the Royal Commission of 1865. But despite Bagehot's advocacy nothing was done; and in the 'seventies parliamentary opinion turned round again, and brought the amalgamation movement once more to a stand. But these fluctuations of policy did not check the rate of growth, though by the 'sixties the emphasis had shifted from the building of primary main lines to the linking up of the various systems by cross-country lines, the opening up of the remoter districts, and the improvement of railway transport in and around London. As we have seen, total mileage rose fast. In 1850, Great Britain had about 6,000 miles of railway open for traffic. By 1875 there were 14,500 miles. In the meantime, gross receipts rose from about £12,000,000 in 1850 to £58,000,000 in 1875. The British railways carried 68,000,000 or so of passengers in 1850, and no less than 490,000,000 a quarter of a century later.

Roads—though much less attention was being paid to them, for it was the common view that railways were destined to supersede them except for local traffic—were also being gradually improved. Statute labour had been replaced finally by local rates in 1835 as the means of providing for the maintenance of highways not under the charge of Turnpike Trusts; but nothing had been done at that time to create outside the towns any highway authority larger than the individual parish. When, however, local Boards of Health or other sanitary authorities were set up for urban districts under the Public Health Acts of 1848 and 1858, highway maintenance was entrusted to them as one of their sanitary powers; and in the corporate towns the corporation was the responsible highway authority. In 1862 an attempt was made, in the Highway Districts Act, to induce parishes outside the urban areas to combine for the purpose of maintaining and improving the roads. But this Act never worked, and in the rural areas the

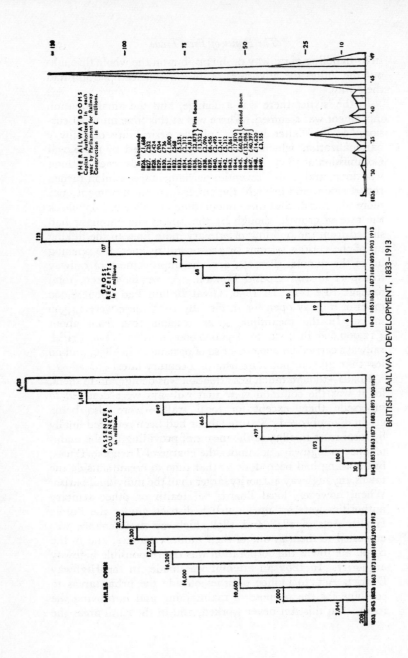

BRITISH RAILWAY DEVELOPMENT, 1833–1913

parish remained responsible until the establishment of Rural Sanitary District Councils (in effect, the Poor Law Guardians under another name) by the Public Health Acts of 1872 and 1875.

Long before this the Turnpike Trusts had been dying out fast. Their powers under their separate private Acts had only been granted for a fixed term of years; and when they applied for renewals Parliament, from the 'sixties onwards, usually disallowed their claims. This was done under strong pressure from public opinion; for the turnpikes remained unpopular to the last, and the growth of local government bodies capable of taking over control removed the principal argument for their continuance. They perished first of all in the urban areas, and then more gradually in the countryside, where a few lingered on into the 'nineties. The majority were gone by 1885, if not sooner.

Industry, meanwhile, was undergoing a transformation dependent largely on the new developments in metal-working and in the making of machines. Joseph Whitworth had begun in the 'thirties his great work of devising gauges and instruments of precision for the testing and making of guns, rifles, and of every type of productive machine. The display of his achievements ranked as one of the principal glories of the Great Exhibition of 1851. Armstrong had assumed control of the Elswick factory in 1847. But Whitworth's inventions could not fructify on a large scale until the advent of reasonably cheap and reliable steel; and that was not available till after Bessemer's new process of steel-making had come in the later 'fifties. The Siemens-Martin open-hearth process followed in the 'sixties, providing a cheap supply of "mild" steel as a material for plates and boilers, and thereby helping on the revolution in shipbuilding by making possible the transition from iron to steel as a material for ocean-going vessels. In the 'seventies came the further discoveries of Gilchrist Thomas, which brought the phosphoric ores of Lorraine into use and so helped to raise up powerful new competitors for British industry.

The Gilchrist Thomas inventions fall beyond the period discussed in this section. But Bessemer and Siemens fall well within it; and their discoveries caused an almost complete transformation of the British metal-working industries. The old iron-puddling districts, such as Staffordshire, lost their predominance, which passed to areas which were better suited, on account of the character of their deposits of ore, to the production of steel by the new methods. In 1855 the three leading iron-making areas were South Wales, Staffordshire and Scotland. By 1875 Staffordshire had sunk to the fourth, and South Wales to the fifth place; and the North-East Coast was easily first, followed by Scotland and the Cumberland and Lancashire areas. Ten years after that, the North-East still led easily, and the North-West had risen to second place, leaving Scotland well behind. By that time the Welsh output was again rising fast, but Staffordshire had fallen yet further down the list, while the ancient iron industry of Shropshire had shrunk into insignificance in comparison with its newer rivals.

The market for the rapidly rising supplies of iron and steel was partly at home—for railway construction and maintenance, shipbuilding, machine-making and public works of many kinds. But British steel was also sold abroad to an increasing extent; for as railways were built in more and more countries the foreign demand for railway material expanded at a prodigious rate. With this expansion went a rapid increase in overseas investment of British capital. No one knows at all accurately how much British money had been invested abroad before 1850. Estimates vary widely, from £200,000,000 to £250,000,000 at the lower to as much as £400,000,000 at the higher end of the scale. But it is undoubted that foreign investment went on at an unprecedented rate during the next twenty-five years, and that by 1875 there was at least £1,200,000,000 of British capital invested abroad, chiefly in railways or in Government bonds. This process reached its peak in the early 'seventies, when foreign investment was proceeding at the rate of well over £40,000,000 a year. In 1872 it is believed that over £56,000,000 of money was loaned or invested by British capitalists outside the country; and, as we have seen, most of this money went directly into the purchase of British goods. There was a corresponding rise in the net earnings of the British mercantile marine, which doubled between the early 'fifties and the early 'seventies. The visible "adverse" balance of imports over exports also doubled—to £70,000,000—between the early 'fifties and 1874; but there was no difficulty in meeting the bill out of the high earnings of British vessels and the income from overseas investment, and still leaving a large annual surplus for additional investment abroad.

Agriculture, meanwhile, by no means bore out the dismal prophecies of the landlords and farmers in 1846. Land prices and agricultural rents are as good indications as can be got of the general level of farming prosperity; and by both these tests agriculture was much more prosperous in 1875 than in 1846. Other forms of property had doubtless risen more rapidly; for there had been an immense amount of factory- and house-building, railway and other utility service construction, and so on. But, even if farmers and landlords received a diminishing proportion of the total national income, they had certainly nothing to grumble at in the absolute amount of their returns.

Yet food prices had been for the most part at a low level. Between 1846 and 1849 Sauerbeck's index of wholesale food prices had fallen by no less than 25 per cent. Thereafter the general rise in prices brought an increase; but in the middle 'sixties the index of food prices was still about 12 per cent below the level of the middle 'forties. Even in the boom of the early 'seventies food rose in price a good deal less than most industrial goods.

How, then, is the continued prosperity of farmers and land-lords—but not, be it noted, of the agricultural labourers—to be explained? The answer is twofold. It was due partly to a rise in the efficiency of production, and partly to a great expansion in the demand for the most highly priced foodstuffs, such as meat. Despite the abandonment of protection there was no decline, up to the middle 'seventies, in the area under arable cultivation. On the contrary, this area increased—to the accompaniment of a much more rapid expansion of the area used for pasture. So far from land being thrown out of cultivation, uncultivated land was brought into use. The farmer prospered because he was able to adapt himself to the changed balance of cultivation that the repeal of the Corn Laws had made remunerative in face of a growing population, which was also getting richer year by year. The farmer in 1875 used a good deal less labour for each unit of output than he had used thirty years before; and the migration from the country to the towns remained unchecked. But less labour meant higher profits; and the farmers, adapting themselves to the supplying of rising needs, were able to compete advantageously with foodstuffs produced under the very different conditions of the New World. The slump in farming came not before but after 1875; and even then for some time meat prices kept up well amid the general decline of values.

Even before the advent of Arch's Agricultural Labourers' Union in the 'seventies, rural wages had moved up to some extent—from an average of about 9*s.* 6*d.* a week in 1850 to one of 12*s.* in 1870. But the village labourer remained much worse paid than the general run of urban craftsmen. The falling demand for agricultural labour made it possible to keep down wages, especially in areas remote from factory or mining employment. Labourers near the growing industrial areas did better, for they had a way of escape. But from the purely rural areas escape was still very difficult indeed. It might often be easier to emigrate to Canada or the United States than to move over a long distance in Great Britain looking for work.

In 1851 about 18 per cent of the occupied population of England was engaged in agriculture: in 1871 only 11 per cent. Factory trades occupied 27 per cent in 1851, and 35 per cent in 1871. The proportion engaged in commerce rose from $4\frac{1}{2}$ to nearly $5\frac{1}{2}$ per cent. But much more startling was the increase in the proportion classified as following a "professional" occupation, which rose from under $2\frac{1}{2}$ to $4\frac{1}{2}$ per cent during these twenty years. In absolute figures, the 1851 Census showed for England a total of 272,000 professional workers, whereas by 1871 the number recorded was 684,000. The English middle class was being multiplied at an extraordinary rate; and the increase in the number of well-to-do employers was carrying with it a still greater increase in doctors, teachers and other classes of professional workers.

Meanwhile, the number of agricultural workers in England

and Wales fell from 2,029,000 to 1,657,000; while the number of domestic servants leapt up from about 900,000 to 1,500,000. Naturally, these changes in occupations were accompanied by a large geographical shift of population. Between 1851 and 1871 the total population of England and Wales rose by nearly 27 per cent. But, whereas Durham and Glamorgan both increased the number of their inhabitants by over 70 per cent, and Middlesex and Surrey, taken together, and also Staffordshire by more than 40 per cent, the population of Norfolk actually decreased, and in such rural counties as Wiltshire, Somerset and Cornwall, there was hardly any change. Meanwhile, the population of Lancashire and the West Riding rose by nearly 40 per cent.

The towns, especially in the manufacturing areas, grew very greatly. But in this case the growth is less easy to measure, because already the urban population was spreading itself out into suburbs beyond the municipal boundaries. Thus, while Manchester's population rose by 16 per cent, that of Salford, virtually part of the same town, nearly doubled, and the combined rate of increase for the two boroughs was 30 per cent. Sheffield, swollen by the rapid development of the metal trades, increased by no less than 78 per cent, even within its municipal boundaries. Within corresponding limits, Leeds was increased by 50 per cent, Birmingham by 48 per cent, Hull by 43 per cent and Liverpool by 31 per cent. For the reasons given, all these figures considerably under-represent the real increases of the urban populations.

In 1871 London, within the area then administered by the Metropolitan Board of Works, which coincides with the present London County Council area, had already a population of 3,261,000, as compared with 2,363,000 for the same area in 1851—an increase of about 38 per cent. Meanwhile, the City had fallen from 128,000 to 75,000, whereas the population of the suburbs outside the administrative area had risen from 318,000 to 624,000: so that the total population of Greater London had grown from 2,681,000 to 3,886,000—a rise of 45 per cent. No other city, without its suburbs, had reached 500,000 in 1871, but Liverpool had just under that number, and Glasgow over 400,000, while Manchester, Birmingham and Leeds had each over 250,000 inhabitants, and Sheffield nearly 250,000. Thus London, the industrial North and the South Wales mining area were rising in populousness much faster than the rest of the country. The proportion of urban to rural population was increasing rapidly, though the numbers outside towns were being kept up by the development of the coalfields.

CHAPTER XXVIII

WAGES, PRICES AND CLASSES

DURING the quarter of a century reviewed in this chapter there occurred two marked economic crises—in 1857 and 1866. The first of these crises followed on a financial panic in the United States, then in the full flood of development. The collapse of American banks and of the American market brought important business houses and banks in Liverpool and Glasgow to ruin; and the iron trades, largely dependent on exports to the United States, were seriously dislocated, and their condition in turn forced banks in Staffordshire and on the Tyne to close their doors. The crisis, spreading over Europe, also bankrupted a number of exporters engaged in the German trade. The Bank Charter Act had to be suspended, as it had been in 1847. But the financial difficulties were quickly sur-mounted, and by 1859 industry generally was again in a prosperous condition.

The financial collapse of 1866, serious as it appeared at the time, was in reality a much less grave affair. It was a purely internal crisis, following upon a series of fairly prosperous years —for the troubles of Lancashire during the cotton famine caused by the American Civil War did not extend to the rest of the country: indeed, some industries, such as the woollen trades, prospered as a result of Lancashire's difficulties. The 1866 crisis was financial and not industrial. It was due mainly to unsound speculation, which led to a widespread collapse of confidence when the famous financial house of Overend and Gurney failed for more than £5,000,000. The effects of this failure were aggravated by the war scare in Europe, which was making money tight, and causing withdrawals of foreign funds from London. But when once the bubble of speculation had been pricked, and a considerable number of joint stock companies had followed Overend and Gurney into liquidation, the Bank of England soon recovered control of the situation. The Bank Act was again suspended; but the power to issue additional notes without gold backing was never actually used. The financial crisis was soon over; and by 1869 the whole country was back in a condition of high prosperity.

Apart from these two crises, both mainly financial in character, the period between 1850 and 1875 was one of rapid and nearly continuous economic advance. There was practically uninterrupted industrial prosperity from 1850 to 1856, and again from 1859 to 1866. After 1869 began the great boom which, reaching its peak in 1872–3, lasted until 1874—after which came the downward slide towards the deep depression of 1879. In a period of a quarter of a century there were only five bad years, as far as trade was concerned, except in Lancashire; and there were two periods of remarkably sustained boom, in the early 'fifties and the early 'seventies.

Both these periods of boom were accompanied by a sharp rise in prices. Between 1850 and 1857 wholesale prices rose by more than one-third, largely as a result of the increased credit made possible by the influx of Californian and Australian gold. The 1857 crisis brought them down sharply, to less than 20 per cent above the level of 1850; but by 1864 they were back again at the 1857 level, and in the boom of the early 'seventies they rose still higher—to 44 per cent above the prices of 1850. Then began the long fall of prices which lasted until 1896—but that belongs to a later chapter.

Rising prices, in face of rapidly increasing prosperity, clearly demand an explanation. As the costs of production fall with the growth of technical efficiency, it is natural to expect prices to fall with them. If they rise instead, the probability is that the rise is to be explained by the course of monetary events. But, as we have seen, between 1850 and 1875 there occurred not only the huge influx of new gold, but also changes in banking methods which made possible great economies in the use of currency, or in other words the creation of a much larger volume of credit on a given basis of gold. In the 1850's the supply of new gold from the mines was four times as great as it had been in the 'forties; and in the 'forties, on account of the increased Russian output, it was twice as large as in the 'thirties. In the 'sixties there was a slight fall in output, and more of the new gold was used in industry, instead of being added to the monetary supply. This checked the rise in prices; but the economy in the use of gold through the cheque system continued, so that in the early 'seventies it was possible to finance a hugely increased volume of transactions without any fall in prices—and indeed, to the accompaniment of a rise. Thereafter the supply of new gold declined further, until the advent of South African gold in the 1890's; but even at its lowest, in the early 'eighties, the world production of new gold was more than three times as large as it had been before the Californian and Australian discoveries.

While prices in general were mounting under the influence of a larger gold supply and an expanding volume of credit, the cost of living rose less rapidly than the general level of wholesale prices. According to Mr. G. H. Wood's cost of living index, retail prices rose by only a quarter in the early 'fifties, whereas wholesale prices rose by a third. Thereafter the gap widened further. In 1864 wholesale prices in general were 36 per cent higher than in 1850, and wholesale food prices 17 per cent higher. But the cost of living, as measured by Mr. Wood, had increased by only 6 per cent. After the crisis of 1866 retail prices went up again to over 20 per cent above the 1850 level, and this occurred again in the boom of 1873. But these years were exceptional. In 1870–1 and again in 1875–7 retail prices showed only about half as much increase over 1850 as wholesale prices in general.

This meant, of course, that comparatively modest wage-increases were enough to secure a rise in the standard of living. According to Mr. Wood's index, money-wages rose on the average by about a quarter between 1850 and 1865. Thereafter came a more rapid increase, temporarily interrupted by the crisis of 1866. By 1870, Mr. Wood holds, money-wages had risen by a third as compared with 1850; and by 1874, when the peak was reached, by more than one-half. This means that in terms of real wages—that is, of purchasing power—for workers in full employment, there was a rise above the level of 1850 of 17 per cent in 1865, of 18 per cent in 1870, and in 1874–5 of at least one-third.

This advance in real wages was not due to a cheapening of wheat, which was actually a good deal dearer in the 'sixties and early 'seventies than it had been round about 1850. What appears to have taken place, both for wheat and for other consumers' goods, is a narrowing of the gap between wholesale and retail prices, due partly to improved transport and distributive services, and partly to keen competition between traders for enlarged custom in an expanding market.

It is not possible to give any complete picture of the actual changes in working-class standards of living between 1850 and 1875; but a comparison between the figures of consumption per head of certain foodstuffs in the early 'sixties and the early 'seventies gives a clear impression of a substantially improving standard of life. Over this period, consumption per head of cereals went up very little—by about 3 per cent. But meat consumption per head rose by over 10 per cent, that of tea by over 60 per cent, and that of sugar by 75 per cent. Tobacco consumption also increased, by about 18 per cent per head of population. Nor should it be omitted that the consumption of spirits rose by over one-third per head, and that of wine by about two-thirds. For beer there are unfortunately no figures available.

These particulars, except those which relate to wines and spirits, tell us little about the change in the distribution of incomes. It is, however, important to know not only how much per head was consumed on the average, but also who consumed it. We have, indeed, evidence in the figures already given of a considerable rise in real wages. But it has to be borne in mind that the available wage-figures relate chiefly to skilled workers, and that there is comparatively little information about the fortunes of the unskilled. The skilled craftsmen worked for the most part at standard wage-rates, established either by custom or by collective bargaining; and their wages are therefore comparatively easy to ascertain. Moreover, between 1850 and

1875, with the growth of Trade Unionism among the skilled workers, standard rates came into being for a considerable number of additional trades, and there was a greater tendency towards uniformity of wages for men working under similar conditions in the same area. Unskilled workers, on the other hand, were hardly touched by Trade Unionism between the collapse of the Grand National in 1834 and the sudden growth of new Unions in the early 'seventies; and this latter movement did not last long enough or establish itself firmly enough to secure and maintain recognized standard rates of wages for the main body of unapprenticed workers.

Bearing these limitations in mind, we can get some sort of idea of the movement of wages among the more skilled types of workers in particular industries. Builders' wages seem to have risen above the level of 1850 by rather over 30 per cent in 1870, and by about 40 per cent in 1875. Engineers and shipbuilders, on the other hand, raised their rates on the average by only about 16 per cent up to 1870, and 30 per cent up to 1875. In both these groups the struggles of the early 'seventies resulted in a substantial reduction of the working day, the engineers winning the Nine Hours Day after the North-East Coast strike of 1872, and the builders speedily following their lead in a series of local movements up and down the country. In the cotton trades wages rose a good deal faster, by well over one-third before 1870, and by two-thirds before 1875. For the woollen trades figures are scantier, and standard rates were less generally observed; but it seems probable that the average rise was about 25 per cent by 1870, and 33 per cent five years later. Printers' wages rose much less, from a higher initial level: the total rise up to 1875 was hardly more than 20 per cent.

There remain two groups, the miners and the agricultural labourers, whose fortunes during the period are of special interest. Agricultural wages had fallen substantially in the 'forties, whereas on the whole the skilled craftsmen had secured advances. By 1860 the agricultural labourers were getting on the average rather over 20 per cent increases over the wages of 1850, and by 1870 nearly 30 per cent. Then came the great movement of reorganization headed by Joseph Arch; and by

1875 average wages were about 55 per cent above the 1850 level—to fall back to about 45 per cent over it before 1880, under the impact of the depression of the later 'seventies.

The miners also went through a period of rapid unionization. Jude's national organization had virtually disappeared by 1850; and Alexander Macdonald's crusade for a new National Association, beginning in the late 'fifties, achieved large-scale results only after 1863. Miners, like agricultural labourers, had suffered wage-reductions in the later 'forties. In 1860 they averaged about 14 per cent more than in 1850, or 10 per cent or so more than in 1840; and even in 1870 they were still getting only about 20 per cent more than in 1850. But between 1870 and 1875, thanks partly to Union organization and partly to the great boom in the heavy industries, their wages rose on the average by about two-thirds over the level of 1850. Thereafter the slump brought their earnings tumbling fastest of all; and by 1880 they were on the average distinctly lower than in 1870. For wages formed so large a part of the cost of coal production that Macdonald's powerful Trade Unions were quite unable to resist the attacks which the coalowners launched promptly upon the coming of the great depression.

These particulars, scanty as they are, are enough to show that there were large variations in the fortunes of the workers in different industries during the period under review. On the whole, it seems probable that the skilled workers, aided by the growth of organization, improved their position a good deal more than the less skilled: so that the average figures, based chiefly on particulars for the skilled trades, tend to exaggerate the general improvement. But as against this it must be borne in mind that there was a considerable increase in the relative numbers of skilled craftsmen, and that allowance has to be made for a steady movement of workers from worse- to better-paid trades. There are, however, no means of measuring at all accurately the extent of this movement, or its effects on the level of earnings for the working class as a whole.

In 1867 Dudley Baxter published a book in which he made an approximate attempt to estimate the size and distribution of the national income. For this purpose he attempted to classify all recipients of incomes into a small number of groups or classes; and his estimates give a useful picture of the class-stratification of society in mid-Victorian England. The figures are for England and Wales only; and they cover rather fewer than ten million persons in receipt of incomes. About eleven million other persons, who were not receiving independent incomes of their own, are excluded from the classification.

Here are Baxter's groups:

Class	Income p.a.	Number of Recipients	
Upper Class	Over £5,000	7,500	49,500
Upper Middle Class ..	£1,000–£5,000	42,000	
Middle Class	£300–£1,000	150,000	150,000
Lower Middle Class ..	£100–£300	850,000	1,853,500
Lower Middle Class ..	Under £100	1,003,000	
Skilled Labour Class ..	—	1,123,000	7,785,000
Less Skilled Labour Class ..	—	3,819,000	
Agricultural Workers and Unskilled Labour Class[1] ..	—	2,843,000	

It is to be observed that this classification of Baxter's includes among the "lower middle classes" all the non-manual workers, irrespective of the size of their incomes. The groups, of course, include non-adult earners as well as adults, but exclude all persons not in receipt of personal incomes.

At the same time as Baxter was making his estimates, the economist, Leone Levi, was preparing, at the request of Michael Bass, the brewer M.P., who helped to found the first railway workers' Trade Union, an elaborate estimate of the level of money wages in the United Kingdom as a whole. Levi arrived at the conclusion that in the middle 'sixties the average income for a working-class *family* was about 31s. in England and Wales, 28s. in Scotland and 23s. 6d. in Ireland. Unfortunately, most of his figures lump Ireland in with Great Britain, and thus bring down the average. For the whole United Kingdom he estimated the average earnings of adult male workers at 19s. a week, and of adult women at 11s. For workers under twenty years of age his estimates were, for males, 7s. 3d., and for females, 7s. 10d., this latter figure being raised by the large numbers of young women earning relatively high wages in the textile trades. Levi's general average per

---

[1] Of whom about 1,000,000 were agricultural workers.

worker was 14s. 5d. a week. As to hours of labour he records as follows:

"The workmen usually labour six days in the week, and each day the hours of labour are from six to six in the factories, and from eight to eight in other occupations, with one hour and a half for meals, and shorter hours on Saturday. But in many occupations longer hours prevail, whilst in some even Sunday work is to a certain extent carried on. A movement has commenced in Lancashire for reducing the hours of labour from ten and a half to eight hours a day, or forty-eight hours per week."

As we have seen in an earlier section, the workers in the textile factories, after a long struggle, had won the "Ten Hours Day" in 1847. To this the Factory Act of 1850, by ordering the mills to be closed at two o'clock on Saturdays, added the weekly half-holiday; but the working week remained at sixty hours, on the basis of a normal day of ten and a half hours. No further concession was secured by the textile operatives till 1874, when the standard weekly hours were reduced to fifty-six and a half, making a real ten hours day except on Saturdays. There had been a number of Factory Acts between 1850 and 1874; but their main purpose had been to extend the system of regulation to additional trades, and not to improve the conditions of workers whose employment was already under control. Bleaching and dyeing works had been included under the Factory Acts in 1860, lace works in 1861, and calendering and finishing works in 1863–4. Up to this point the Acts had applied only to textile factories; but in 1864 a number of new trades, including pottery works, were included; and in 1867 the system was at last made generally applicable to all factories employing more than fifty workers, and at the same time "workshops"—that is, any workplaces in which manufacture was carried on with fewer than fifty employees—were placed under the supervision of the local authorities. This latter extension in fact meant little; for few local authorities were prepared to take such duties seriousiy. But the dual system continued until 1878, when the Factory and Workshops Acts were consolidated under a single system of State inspection.

Some sort of control over factory conditions had thus been established for nearly all manufacturing industries by 1867. In the meantime the miners also had been pressing for protection. Lord Shaftesbury's Act of 1842 had prohibited the employment of women and children underground. In 1850, after a series of appalling colliery disasters, Parliament was induced to pass the Coal Mines Inspection Act, providing for the State inspection of mines on the lines already introduced for textile factories, and laying down minimum requirements in respect of lighting and ventilation. A second Act followed in 1855, amplifying the safety provisions; and under this Act the first code of "General Rules" for collieries was drawn up. Next came the important Coal Mines Regulation Act of 1860, laying down new General Rules, prohibiting the employment of boys under twelve years of age (or ten years if they could produce a certificate of education), and granting in form the miners' demand for the right to appoint "checkweighmen" to check the weights of coal credited to them by the colliery weighmen as a basis for reckoning their piece-work earnings. But this last concession, valuable as it was to prove later on, was rendered useless in many pits because the owners were left free to discharge any checkweighman who made himself a nuisance to them.

Throughout the 'sixties the miners, under Macdonald's leadership, were continually agitating for better legal protection; and they secured a good deal of what they had claimed in the Coal Mines Act of 1872—accompanied by a companion Act regulating conditions in metalliferous mining. Under this Act checkweighmen were to some extent protected against dismissal, though they could still be chosen only from among men actually employed in the colliery concerned. At the same time colliery managers were compelled to carry State certificates of technical competence. It was laid down that the deputy overseers must carry out a daily inspection of each pit in order to test the safety of the working conditions; and miners were given the statutory right to appoint from their own ranks inspectors who were to be entitled to visit any district of the pit in order to check the adequacy of the safety precautions taken by the management. This Act again followed a series of colliery disasters, to which much attention had been paid in the newspapers. But accidents continued despite the improved provisions; for in the slump of the later 'seventies there was a general attempt to speed up production at the cost of safety in order to offset the fall in coal prices.

The other group of workers upon whose grievances public attention became fixed during the early 'seventies was the merchant service. In 1873 Samuel Plimsoll's campaign on behalf of the seamen, who were compelled to work under terribly crowded and insanitary conditions in vessels which the owners were under no legal obligation to keep seaworthy, produced its first effect in a temporary Act of Parliament which imposed special regulations pending the results of a further inquiry. In 1876 this Act was replaced by a permanent measure, the Merchant Shipping Act, imposing a limit on the weight of cargo which vessels were to be allowed to carry—the Plimsoll "load line"—and laying down rules governing the conditions under which seamen were to be engaged and accommodated on board ship. Plimsoll published his famous book, *Our Seamen*, in 1873, and distributed copies at the Trades Union Congress of that year, in an attempt to enlist Trade Union support. But the seamen, though Plimsoll's agitation secured a large measure of Trade Union backing, remained unorganized until Havelock Wilson set to work in the 'eighties to create a Union for them in face of the determined opposition of the powerful Shipping Federation.

Hours of labour, by Leone Levi's testimony, remained at ten and a half or more in 1867, even in the organized trades. The effective introduction of the ten hours day in the factories in 1874 came only after the engineers on the North-East Coast had taken matters into their own hands and struck successfully —without the backing of the official Trade Union leaders—for the Nine Hours Day. Moreover, the success on the North-East Coast had been speedily followed by the concession of the nine hours day to engineers in many other areas; and the builders had largely secured equivalent concessions, though in their case the conditions of work resulted in settlements which offset longer hours in summer by a working week of forty-eight hours during the winter months.

CHAPTER XXIX

SOCIAL CHANGES AND LEGISLATION

W E have seen in an earlier section how the repeated outbreaks of cholera and the chronic prevalence of disease in the
industrial areas led in 1848 to the establishment of a General
Board of Health, with Edwin Chadwick as its principal
executive officer. This measure, despite the admitted gravity
of the problems with which it was designed to deal, was passed
with extreme reluctance, on the ground of its tendency to
restrict the autonomy of the authorities responsible for local
government—the municipal corporations (or, sometimes, *ad
hoc* statutory bodies), in the towns, and the county justices in
the rural areas. All the arguments against bureaucratic
centralization which had been invoked against the Poor Law
Board were advanced anew against the General Board of
Health; and only the heavy, recurrent mortality from
cholera, among the rich as well as the poor, sufficed to get
Parliament to acquiesce. Even these fears did not persuade
it to give the Board powers extending beyond five years,
during which it was hoped that the cholera danger would
have been averted with success, so that the Board could be
wound up.

Under the Act of 1848 municipal councils, where they were
willing so to do, had been permitted to assume the functions
of local Boards of Health, responsible for the improvement of
sanitary services within their areas. Elsewhere the central
Board was empowered to authorize the establishment of new
ad hoc bodies, modelled largely on the Boards of Guardians set
up under the Poor Law Amendment Act of 1834. All local
Boards of Health were to be subject to inspection by the officers
of the General Board, and their members were to be elected
on the basis of a differential franchise under which plural
votes were accorded to the richer ratepayers.

Under stress of the fear created by the cholera epidemic,
numerous local Boards of Health were set up under the Act of

1848, and many municipal corporations assumed sanitary functions. But as soon as the danger seemed to be over Parliament begin to repent of its concession to bureaucracy. In 1854, when the Act fell due for renewal, Edwin Chadwick was retired upon pension, and the General Board was reconstructed with much narrower powers than had been conferred upon it under stress of emergency. Up to 1858 its reduced functions were annually confirmed; but under the Act of that year the General Board was dissolved altogether, and its remaining duties were distributed between the Home Office and the Privy Council. The local Boards of Health set up under the Act of 1848 were, however, allowed to remain in being; and power was given to them, as well as to the municipal corporations, to "adopt" by resolution the powers embodied in the various "Clauses" Acts which had been passed, chiefly in the later 'forties, for the regulation of public utility services, such as the supply of gas and water.

Thereafter nothing was done towards coping with the public health problem over the whole country until 1872. Meanwhile, under the Metropolis Management Act of 1855, main drainage in the London area had been placed under the control of a single body, the Metropolitan Board of Works, of which the area was the same as that which is now administered by the London County Council. Gradually, over the next twenty years or so, additional powers were conferred upon the Board; but Greater London remained a chaos of separate local authorities, each exercising for most purposes unqualified jurisdiction over the tiny area it was held to represent.

The 1860's, up to the Reform Act of 1867, were for the most part barren of legislation in the matter of public health. There were special Acts in 1863 and 1864 for the relief of distress caused in Lancashire by the Cotton Famine; a number of minor Acts extended the functions of the Metropolitan Board of Works; and the London Fire Brigade was set up in 1865. There were also Acts amending the Law of Settlement, Acts regulating public-houses, and Acts providing for the better maintenance of the roads, both in London and elsewhere. But there were no major changes in local government until after the appointment, in 1868, of a Royal Commission to report on the sanitary problem as a whole. Thereafter came the establishment of the Local Government Board in 1871, and the Public Health Act of 1872.

Under the Act of 1871 the Poor Law Board which had been set up in 1834 was turned into a Local Government Board, with sanitary as well as poor law functions, and became a regular Civil Service department under the auspices of a responsible Cabinet Minister. This was a prelude to the Act of 1872, which consolidated urban local government in the hands of the municipal councils, gave the Local Government Board power to order the establishment of a local sanitary authority in any urban area where none was in effective existence, and virtually converted the Boards of Guardians in the various Poor Law Unions in the country areas into rural sanitary authorities. This Act, consolidated and amended by the Public Health Act of 1875, finally equipped every area in the country, rural as well as urban, with some sort of local authority responsible for sanitary measures under the general supervision of a central government department. But the constitution of this department on the basis of the Poor Law Board, and the use made of the Poor Law Guardians in constituting the rural sanitary authorities, left this important new sphere of government activity under the continuing influence of poor law methods and habits of mind, which were not easily to be shaken off. Some part at least of the improving health of the public was due to the decline in food adulteration. The protagonists in this, after Dr. Wakley, were Dr. Arthur Hassall and later Dr. John Postgate. The *Lancet* for years printed the names and addresses of tradesmen, with the adulterations for which they were responsible. The more sensational of these included alum in bread and red and white lead in sugar-confectionery; and the paper's solitary but damaging guerrilla war in 1860 forced the passing of an Adulteration Act empowering local authorities to appoint analysts. But most authorities refused to do so, a flaw which made equally ineffective an Amending Act of 1872. The Sale of Food and Drugs Act in 1875 at last made the appointment of analysts and the prosecution of offenders compulsory, and, despite skilled and prolonged litigation, the grosser and more dangerous frauds began to be stamped out. But misdescription of foods and false claims on labels and advertisements were not generally prevented until the Ministry of Food used its wartime powers from 1940 onwards.

Meanwhile the State had been very tentatively entering upon another new sphere of activity intimately connected with the health of the public. In 1847 the Society for Improving the Dwellings of the Labouring Classes had set out on a campaign for better houses and the establishment of model lodging-houses for the homeless poor. In 1851 Shaftesbury succeeded in passing an Act which not only provided for the inspection of private lodging-houses but also gave local bodies power—which was seldom used—to erect lodging-houses of their own. Further legislation strengthening the original Act followed in 1853 and 1855; and in the early 'sixties progressive municipalities, such as Liverpool and Glasgow, secured under private Acts special power to clear or improve insanitary areas and to provide alternative accommodation. These purely local measures led up to the Torrens Act of 1868, under which local authorities were empowered, but not required, to take steps for the demolition of insanitary dwellings and the improvement of slum areas. Wider powers were given under the Cross Act of 1875, which enabled local authorities to acquire and clear whole districts, and to build dwellings for the rehousing of the slum-dwellers. Broadly, the Torrens Act and the subsequent amending measures were used in dealing with individual dwellings deemed unfit for habitation, and the Cross Acts for slum-clearance in a wider sense. But these Acts were but slowly adopted by the local authorities, with which the initiative lay. There was no widespread public intervention in housing until after the Housing of the Working Classes Act of 1890. Moreover, until 1885 the powers accorded to municipal councils under the Cross and Torrens Acts were not extended to the councils of the new urban sanitary districts.

The remaining sphere in which State action was extended during the period covered by this section is education. As we have seen, the first State grants in aid of school building had been made in 1833 by the first Reformed Parliament. These grants were distributed through the two voluntary societies which were endeavouring in their several ways to provide for the education of the poor—Dr. Bell's National Society under strict Church of England auspices, and the undenominational British and Foreign Schools Society, to which the various sects of Dissenters gave their support. In 1839 the distribution of the State's educational grants had been entrusted to a special central body set up for the purpose—the Privy Council's Committee on Education. Under the auspices of this body Parliament continued up to 1860 to vote increasing annual grants for educational purposes, including the training of teachers, and a system of inspection of schools was slowly developed. The grants rose under this system from a mere £30,000 in 1839 to £150,000 in 1851, and to £663,000 in 1858, when a Royal Commission under the Duke of Newcastle was appointed to inquire into the whole question of public educational policy.

Long before this it had become evident that the principal obstacle to the development of any general system of public education was the religious quarrel. Churchmen claimed education as falling within the spiritual province of the Established Church, whereas most Dissenters demanded an undenominational system, and there were many who favoured completely secular education. This religious controversy led the Newcastle Commission to reject the idea of compulsory education under public control, and to advance instead a proposal for County Boards, to be appointed by the justices at Quarter Sessions, and to be empowered to levy an educational rate, which they would then distribute in grants between the rival voluntary societies. The Newcastle Commission, however, is best remembered as the inspirer of the new system of "payment by results," which was instituted under the revised Educational Code of 1862. It had been alleged that under existing conditions public money was being grievously wasted upon inefficient schooling; and the Commission proposed to remedy this by making all grants to schools subject to a searching test by examination of every child in attendance.

The application of the revised Educational Code was followed by a sharp fall in the State grant, which declined from £813,000 in 1861 to £637,000 in 1865. Educationists fought

hard against the new system; and some modifications of it
were introduced in 1867. But it was not wholly abolished
until 1904.

Meanwhile, the demand for more comprehensive State aid
continued to gain ground; and at last, in 1870, the Forster
Education Act became law. Forster, in introducing it, carefully disclaimed any intention of superseding the voluntary
system. The State, he said, should come in only in order to fill
up gaps which the voluntary system had left unfilled. With
this end in view, School Boards elected by the ratepayers were
to be set up in areas in which there was found to be a deficiency of school accommodation, and these Boards were to be
responsible within their areas for ensuring that there should
be a sufficiency of school places for all children.

Board schools were thus set up under the Act of 1870 side by
side with the existing voluntary schools. There followed an
energetic contest between the two types; for Churchmen,
hostile to the undenominational education provided in Board
Schools, hastened to set up additional voluntary schools
wherever they could, in the hope of keeping as many areas as
possible free from School Boards. But the new system went
ahead rapidly, especially in the urban areas; and by 1876
School Boards existed in areas having a total population of
twelve and a half millions.

At this stage a further advance was made. The Act of 1870
had not made education compulsory, though it had empowered
the local School Boards, where they existed, to apply compulsion by by-laws, if they so desired. The Act of 1876 introduced compulsory education up to the age of twelve, but with
provision for exemptions at an earlier age. In order to enforce
attendance, School Attendance Committees were to be set up
in areas where no School Boards were in being. Elementary
education thus became general, but not free. Fees were
actually retained until 1891, and even thereafter for elementary schools providing "higher grade" education. Meanwhile
the Science and Art Department, set up originally in the early
'fifties under the Board of Trade, developed gradually a system
of grants in aid of technical and art classes up and down the
country, and thus helped to prepare the way for the growth

both of post-primary education and of the newer Universities and Municipal Technical Colleges of to-day.

Thus the State at length took over the major part of the responsibility for the elementary education of the poor. There s no doubt that this would have taken place much earlier, and much more completely when it did take place, but for the religious controversy. Long before Robert Lowe proclaimed, on the morrow of the second Reform Act, the need for the governing classes to "educate their masters," the necessity at the very least for the general diffusion of the three R's existed by virtue of the very character of the new civilization of the machine age. Industry needed operatives who were able to read its rules and regulations, and an increasing supply of skilled workers able to work to drawings and to write at any rate a simple sentence. Commerce needed a rapidly growing army of clerks, book-keepers, shop assistants, touts and commercial travellers. The State needed more Civil Servants and local government employees for the developing tasks of public administration. The growing professions needed more skilled helpers. And, apart from all this, the *paperasserie* of the new world of machine production and parliamentary government made illiteracy more and more a nuisance which had to be put down.

But the Church would not surrender without a struggle its claim to control the education of the poor—or even that of the rich, for religious tests in the Universities were not abolished until 1871. All through the nineteenth century the battle raged over education between Churchmen and Dissenters— with the Roman Catholics coming in as a third party in the later phases of the struggle. The State pushed away the problem as long as it could by paying subsidies to the rival societies founded on the principles of Dr. Bell and Joseph Lancaster. But with the growth of industry and commerce it became steadily more urgent; and at length something had to be done in areas in which there was an intolerable shortage of schools. Even then the Church was left in possession of a considerable part of the field; for whereas education in the industrial districts, except in a few Roman Catholic areas, passed for the most part fairly rapidly into the hands of the new School

Boards, Church schools remained firmly entrenched in the rural areas and in many of the smaller towns. Moreover, in the new State schools the religious problem had to be dealt with by the unsatisfactory compromise of the "Cowper-Temple" clause, under which denominational religious teaching was forbidden in Board schools, though not in the "voluntary" schools provided by religious bodies. It was, however, provided that no child should be compelled to attend religious instruction in any State-aided school against the parents' wishes. Under this dual arrangement there grew up in the Board schools a curious system of undenominational Protestant education, which in the main holds the field even to-day. The advocates of secular education were too few to stand up against the united hostility of Churchmen and devout Dissenters.

Public elementary education came at last; and the Dissenters of the British and Foreign Schools Society handed over their schools to the new Boards. But the State remained until 1902 outside the sphere of secondary education, though measures were taken to reorganize and re-equip many of the old Grammar Schools which had fallen into decay, and there was also an active movement for the foundation of new "public" schools for the children of wealthy or well-to-do parents. The poor got their elementary schooling; but the caste system in English education remained, and was even intensified as a result of the Public Schools Act of 1864 and the Endowed Schools Acts of 1869 and 1874.

The years immediately after the second Reform Act brought, in addition to the reform of the educational system, the reorganization of the Civil Service and of the Army. In the Civil Service the old methods of nomination and patronage were replaced by the Benthamite method of recruitment by competitive examination, which had been extensively applied earlier, on the basis of Lord Macaulay's famous Report, to the Service in India. The system of qualifying examinations for entrants to the Home Civil Service had in fact been introduced in 1855; but not until 1870 was open competitive examination established as the principle of recruitment. Army reorganization, beginning in 1871, was greatly influenced by the success of Prussia in the Franco–Prussian War; but Great Britain, unlike most of the European Powers, did not adopt the model of a conscript army based on universal liability to military service.

The law, as well as the armed forces and the departments of State, underwent a drastic overhauling, in the course of which some of the worst abuses pilloried by Dickens in his novels were removed. The Judicature Act of 1873 reformed the High Courts of Justice on lines better suited to modern needs; and a number of other Acts both modernized various aspects of the criminal law and simplified the working of County Courts and magistrates' courts of summary jurisdiction.

In general, the period between the Great Exhibition and the boom of the early 'seventies was one of extraordinarily rapid and almost uninterrupted economic advance. In the sphere of political opinion it was a time of transition from Cobden and the Free Traders to a new age of Imperialistic expansion. Goldwin Smith's *The Empire*, published in book form in 1863, aptly summarized the Cobdenite view of Empire. The author proposed colonial "emancipation" at the earliest possible moment. He regarded colonies as useless burdens upon Great Britain and as involving a perpetual danger of war. But even in 1863 this view did not pass unchallenged. Goldwin Smith was furiously assailed by *The Times*, and a lively controversy followed.

Goldwin Smith's book was almost the last popular manifesto of the anti-Imperialists. By 1875 the opposing view had triumphed, and the nations of Europe were well set upon the race to partition out the still undivided territories of Africa. Sir Charles Dilke, whose *Greater Britain* appeared in 1869, dreamed for a time of a reunion of the "Anglo-Saxon" race —Great Britain, the Colonies and the United States—into a political combination powerful enough to dominate world affairs, and assume the "White Man's Burden" by colonizing the empty places of the earth. Before long that vision of "reunion" faded; but Dilke and many others continued to believe in the colonizing mission of the Anglo-Saxon peoples. The story of the new Imperialism belongs, however, more properly to a later section.

CHAPTER XXX

NEW UNIONISM AND CO-OPERATION

FROM 1850 to 1875 the Trade Union movement, which, if we except the Co-operative stores, was the only part of the working-class movement which maintained a successful existence, was wholly remodelled by what to-day would be called a youth movement. It was the younger generation, reacting against their disastrous Chartist and Owenite elders, who laid rough hands upon the existing Unions and founded others upon new principles. But this youth movement was one whose objectives little suggested young and hot blood: it was a revolt in favour of prudence, respectability, financial stability and reasonableness, and against pugnacity, imagination and any personal indulgence.

To be calm, prudent, temperate and enlightened—the qualities their seniors seemed most notably to lack—was the younger unionists' object: to succeed in it was to approximate more nearly to the ideal working man of the Victorian Age, in the minds of both employer and employed. To some extent, the adoption of this aim was due to deliberate propaganda or education of the workers by the class above. The Society for the Diffusion of Useful Knowledge, whose moving spirits had been Lord Brougham and Charles Knight, had ceased its activity about 1847, but, as is always the case, the full results of its educational work only appeared some ten years later. Its publications had circulated in millions, and it had many imitators. It provided clear instruction, in simple concise language, on every subject which an intelligent man desirous of improving himself or his position could wish to study— mathematics, engineering, biology, history, philosophy, literature. It issued encyclopædias in penny parts and editions of the classics at a low price. It paid especially attention to the working man, and its booklets, *The Results of Machinery, the Workingman's Companion, the Workingman's Year Book*, issued in the 'thirties, were no less persuasively written than its other publications. The working man, it preached, had a commodity to sell like anyone else—his labour—and his only way to prosperity was to raise its price. This he could do individually by improving his skill as a craftsman, saving his money, working hard and living temperately. By this means he would himself become an article of rare value and his price would rise: his fellows, by doing the same, would increase the general wealth and keep goods in rapid circulation. Universal abundance would result, except, of course, for the idle, turbulent or debauched. Friendly societies were prudent and laudable institutions; Trade Unions, by calling strikes and violently stopping the wheels of industry, merely spread desolation and despair.

Other publications put the same arguments more bluntly. *Songs for English Workmen to Sing*, by E.B., published in 1867, contained among other verses one which was before long famous:

> *Work, boys, work and be contented*
> *So long as you've enough to buy a meal;*
> *The man, you may rely,*
> *Will be wealthy by and by*
> *If he'll only put his shoulder to the wheel.*

From 1850, John Cassell's manuals and magazines became phenomenally popular, the *Workingman's Friend* (1850), *Cassell's Popular Educator* (1852) and *Cassell's Magazine* (1852) mingled useful information with articles on the beauties of Nature, the wonders of science, the curious customs of foreigners and the delights of literature. Cassell induced a surprising number of working men, duly rewarded with small prizes, to contribute to his papers articles on all manner of subjects, from bee-keeping to poetry and from the virtues of temperance to the principles of political economy.

Cassell, like others, started as a temperance reformer. From the 'thirties there had been in Great Britain a growing temperance movement, which, beginning in the main as a crusade against spirit-drinking only (sometimes even encouraging the use of beer and cider), passed over, largely under American influence, to complete teetotalism. Among the foremost of the teetotal crusaders were Joseph Livesey of Preston, an Anti-Corn Law leaguer and active on the fringes of "moral force" Chartism, and John Finch, who, after serving for a time as Governor of Queenwood, attempted in the 'forties to organize the Liverpool dock labourers into teetotal clubs, and was then and later a leading advocate of Co-operative Production. In the declining years of Chartism, "Temperance Chartism" developed as a distinct movement, attracting many of the more moderate supporters of the Charter away from O'Connor and Ernest Jones into the safer paths of moral reform and social uplift.

These varied forms of propaganda, growing voices since their first widely diffused expression in the eighteen-thirties, had by the 'fifties begun to drown the Chartist or Socialist opposition. Economic circumstances made it possible for the craftsmen to consider them: the experience of the last twenty years seemed to enforce them: it is not surprising that even the Trade Union leaders accepted them in their main outlines. The Amalgamated Society of Carpenters and Joiners at its foundation announced that its members aspired to "become respectful and respected." The *Flint Glass-Makers' Magazine* in its first number told its readers to "get knowledge . . . get intelligence instead of alcohol—it is sweeter and more lasting." "On the 20th of September, 1860," wrote Patrick Kenney, recording an attempt to extend the new principles to builders' labourers, "I left off buying beer and took to buying books to improve my mind." The new Unions, which frequently had "Amalgamated" in their names and were sometimes referred to in bulk as the "Amalgamated Unions," were to be stable and firm-rooted bodies, confined to skilled craftsmen of sober and prudent habits. They almost always had high subscriptions—of round about 1s. a week—and a series of "friendly benefits," such as unemployment, superannuation, sickness, accident and death allowances. Plans for Socialist communities, sympathetic strikes or political turmoil were proscribed: the new generation held firmly to all the tenets of Victorian liberalism. The relation between employer and employed was regarded as permanent; in that case, it was demonstrable that labour was a commodity. A commodity rises in price if the supply of it is limited. It was very difficult to limit the supply of labour as a whole, though certain Unions made a gesture by starting an emigration fund, whose influence on wages and conditions was infinitesimal. But few of the members of the Unions thought of "labour" as a whole, or were interested in raising its price. What they wanted to push up was the price of their own craft's labour; as they were all skilled men, this was most easily done by barring the entry of all unapprenticed or insufficiently skilled men. The new skilled trades of ironfounders, boilermakers or engineers joined with older skilled building craftsmen in insisting on apprenticeship and restricted overtime. Strikes the new unionists avoided whenever possible, denouncing them repeatedly in Union journals. To enforce the alternative of negotiation, and to enable the careful financial provisions to work, the autonomy of the "lodges" or local branches had often to be ended, and authority concentrated in the Executive Committee, responsible to an annual conference or to the membership as a whole. Also, to administer the new Unions skilled secretaries were required, and for the first time Trade Union officials appear as a caste.

One of the earlier methods of social reform continued to recommend itself to the new generation—co-operative workshops and factories. The engineers, whose constitution will be described shortly, voted no less than £10,000 to this object, and helped to start several such enterprises, of which one, the Southwark Working Engineers' Association under John Musto, survived till 1854. Though for financial reasons these societies did not last, the hope of salvation through "self-employment in associative workshops" lingered on for many years and in the 'eighties was still to be found among the nominal objectives of some unions.

The financial condition of the skilled workers made it possible for the new Unions to take root, and by 1860 the British scene began to take on the appearance which it was to retain with little change for half a century. Strongly rooted Unions appeared in many industries and in nearly every craft, united locally in Trades Councils but otherwise separated and more than a little cautious of one another. The most famous and richest was also the earliest, the Amalgamated Society of Engineers—A.S.E.—constituted in January 1851 with William Allan as secretary, by an amalgamation of several smaller societies with the Journeymen Steam Engine Makers. By October of that year it had 11,000 members paying a shilling a week, constituting an income no Union had ever before dreamt of. It was subjected to a severe attack the next year, by the Lancashire and London employers, who locked out its members (on questions of piecework and overtime); it was defeated and nevertheless emerged unbroken. The "Document" was presented; its members signed it and ignored it, as a promise extracted by *force majeure*. Ten years after its constitution its funds were £73,000. An even more overwhelming evidence of its substantiality was given in 1859 when, in sympathy with the London builders locked out that year, it astounded the country by presenting the workers' funds with £1,000 a week for three weeks.

So surprising a subscription not only assisted to defeat the employers, but caused a widespread attempt in the building trades immediately afterwards to imitate the engineers. The most famous case was the Amalgamated Society of Carpenters and Joiners (A.S.C.J.—Robert Applegarth, secretary), which repeated the Engineers' successes and their failures. But the "London Order" of Bricklayers (O.B.S.—Edwin Coulson, secretary) also reorganized themselves on the same principles; so too did the Plasterers, and less successful Unions were started for painters and builders' labourers. Older societies such as the Ironfounders (Daniel Guile, secretary) modified their constitutions and policies to conform with the new fashion.

It so happened that all the general secretaries mentioned above had their offices in London, where they formed a group to which the Webbs have given the name of the "Junta." (At the time they were known as the "Clique.") They were administrators rather than speakers, but for orators they had willing assistants in George Odger, a shoemaker, George Howell, a bricklayer, Robert Danter, the president of the Engineers, and many others. They were all members of the London Trades Council, which consequently, for some eleven years after its foundation in 1860, became a body of great weight.

Trades Councils are the Union equivalent of town councils: they are made up of the delegates of the Unions or branches of Unions in a given town. They had existed before: a "Metropolitan Trades Union" had been active in 1818 and again in the later 'twenties and early 'thirties. Temporary committees were often formed to support a strike or a particular claim. But the earliest to have had a continuous history of any length seems to have been the Aberdeen Delegated Committee of Sympathy, of 1846. Only about 1860 were permanent organizations, mostly still existing, formed in most of the large towns, and by that time the process of cutting down the power of the local branches and absorbing local independent Unions was well under way. As a result, the Trades Councils never had the powers that they were expected to have. That London's for a short while was influential was due to the fact that so many secretaries of national Unions sat for about ten years on its benches. It mediated between quarrelling Unions and gave or withheld "credentials" to trades on strike enabling them to raise subscriptions throughout the country. The withholding of credentials might well mean the loss of the dispute, and was a weapon which was used firmly to promote the new ideas. If the strikers had declined unconditional arbitration or behaved in the Council's opinion disrespectfully to the employers, they were liable to be told, as were the South Staffordshire puddlers in 1866, to mend their manners or to go back home.

A student who kept his eye on London alone might easily imagine that the Junta swiftly made itself the dictator of the Union world, and that the older, more disorderly Unions rapidly faded away. This did not happen; better times were, as always, propitious to Trade Union growth and outside London new Unions arose, or old Unions were revived, generally before the new ideas had attained to influence. Nor were the principles outlined above accepted invariably as a whole. They were, after all, not in logic inevitably dependent on one another; centralized funds need not mean pacifism, pacifism might be independent of high friendly benefits. The

Amalgamated Association of Miners derived its name from its centralized funds, but its policy was very bellicose. The North-East Lancashire Weavers' Association, though conciliatory in policy, saw no reason to centralize its friendly benefits. Even the industries where craft differences were most marked did not immediately fall under the domination of the new ideas. In the building trades the older Unions' aggregate membership certainly outnumbered the newer until .well after 1870, and generally the older Unions were not broken or forced to reform until the big depression that started in 1875 enforced the sermons of the Junta.

Provincial Unions were sometimes hostile, sometimes indifferent to the Junta's policy. The Stonemasons, whose organization and policy were radically opposed to it, were indeed patronizing; Richard Harnott, their venerated and autocratic Corresponding Secretary, told his members to "instruct any joiners" with whom they worked to join Applegarth's promising little society. The writing on the wall is clear enough to a later generation; but Belshazzar could not yet read it. Initial indifference, however, tended to pass into hostility and before long there was at times open conflict.

Among the important provincial Unions was one, John Kane's Amalgamated Ironworkers' Association (1868), which was clearly an "amalgamated" Union. But other rising Unions were but slightly affected by the new ideas. The Weavers' Unions remained local with the exception of the North-East Lancashire Weavers' Association (1858) already mentioned, while the Amalgamated Association of Cotton Spinners (1853—rising to considerable membership in 1869) had strictly circumscribed powers which made it in financial matters not much more than a federation of district Unions. Its policy, however, was conciliatory and, in natural sequence to the Ten Hours Committees, directed largely to parliamentary agitation.

The chief single agent in the revival of mining trade unionism was Alexander Macdonald. The collapse of Martin Jude's National Association had meant the disappearance of national Trade Unionism, and of most effective protection for the workers; but it had not, at any rate in some coal-fields, meant the extinction of the local lodges. Thus Macdonald, when he crossed the border in 1856 as the emissary of the small Scottish Miners' Association, had an easier task than appeared. He had not to create Trade Unionism where none existed, but to persuade lodges already feeling the swell of the tide to unite with other lodges. The resultant National Miners' Union was, not unexpectedly, far from a highly centralized body: it was federal in character, it was pacific without enforcing the Junta's uncompromising pacifism, and attached great importance to bringing pressure on Parliament. In both these ways it offended critics, and in 1869 a conference that it called to organize Lancashire decided instead to form an Amalgamated Association of Miners which should have both centralized funds and a fighting industrial policy. In 1873 these two Unions had 123,000 and 99,000 members respectively.

Such Unions could not be propagandists of the new ideas, and the enemies of the Junta could appeal to them with some hopes as to a jury to render a verdict against the odious behaviour of the new model Unions. The chief resistance to the Junta appeared in the building trades: Thomas Connolly, President of the Stonemasons, and George Potter, member of an old-fashioned carpenters' club, organized in London itself a sort of counter-attack. Potter was a member of the London Trades Council and also editor of the only national Labour journal, *The Beehive*, a weekly founded in 1862. He was the most serious opponent of the Junta, and the only one with a London reputation. But it would be a grave mistake to attribute to him Socialist views, or a class-struggle philosophy. He and his supporters, when cross-questioned, adopted the same political views as the Junta.

The beginnings of class-conscious Socialism which had appeared among the later Chartists had utterly faded away; Owenism had died before its founder; Christian Socialism had only had a shadowy existence. The old-fashioned unionist in fact merely preferred industrial conflict to industrial peace because he had never thought about the matter, and preferred slack organizations without centralized friendly benefits and run by the local lodges because he was used to carrying on his business in public-houses. It is difficult to campaign for such a programme; it is no wonder that Potter was reduced to personal vituperation, at which his antagonists were fully his equals.

The dissension between the two principles interfered with Labour unity throughout the kingdom, and is preserved to-day in the convention which makes the Trades Union Congress of 1868 the first which is "recognized" in official numbering, just as kings are left unnumbered before 1066. It would be more reasonable to begin in 1864, with the national Trade Union Conference summoned by Alexander Campbell, then secretary of the Glasgow Trades Council, at the instance of Alexander MacDonald, to consider the oppression caused by the Master and Servant Acts. This the Junta attended, but, disliking the policies of the northern Unions, henceforward withdrew and concentrated its influence on the Conference of Amalgamated Trades (founded in 1867), summoned for a purpose which will shortly be described, and entirely under its direction. A second Trade Union Conference met at Sheffield in 1866 and launched the United Kingdom Alliance of Organized Trades —an attempt to link together the better organized Unions for mutual support in strikes and lock-outs and thus to revive one of the two wings of the defunct National Association of 1845 (see page 316). This body continued to exist and to hold conferences in the North of England during the next few years, and even discussed the launching of a Trade Union Labour Party; but it never became widely representative. The Junta boycotted it from the start, and did not even reply to a request from its sponsors that the London Trades Council should convene in 1867 a further general Trade Union Conference to follow up that held at Sheffield the previous year. Potter was delighted to step into their place and call it for them through his recently founded London Working Men's Association. Thirty-three Unions attended, including a half-dozen of some weight. Its proceedings greatly annoyed the Junta. The next conference (1868, Manchester) is the first "official" conference, and the next (Birmingham, 1869) appointed the first "Parliamentary Committee," which was for many years the only central organization of the Trade Union movement.

In that year the only active and persistent enemy of the

Junta gave up his campaign. Potter had the sympathy of many northern leaders in his criticisms of the Junta's policy and even more of its personnel. But this indulgent kindness was of no sufficient help to him. *The Beehive* circulated but little outside London, and in London the Junta's influence had driven it very low. He came to his enemies for funds to save the paper: they agreed on condition that he accepted a Unitarian clergyman, the Rev. Henry Solly, once a Chartist and now organizer of working-men's clubs, as superior editor. Henceforward, the solitary Labour journal was a supporter of the Junta: henceforward, too, the Junta was able to co-operate with, and more and more influence, the northern Unions. It reversed its previous attitude to the Trades Union Congress, and in 1871 its close adherent, Odger, replaced Potter as secretary; and during the legal struggles of that and succeeding years, the northern Unions as a whole contentedly co-operated with it.

This unity came none too soon. During the 'sixties a sudden attack was made on the whole existence of trade unionism, partly by Parliament, partly by the judiciary. In the year 1866 the explosion of a tin of gunpowder in the house of a Sheffield non-unionist gave rise to a local agitation against the Union clubs. The Sheffield police were unable to trace the culprits; the local Union leaders professed themselves anxious to aid the investigation demanded by the employers; the London Trades Council sent down a commission of inquiry. Applegarth, with incautious zeal, relying upon this commission's favourable report, suggested an inquiry to the Home Secretary. To his dismay, the Government adopted the suggestion in a far larger way than he had wished, appointing in February 1867 a Royal Commission to inquire not only into the outrage but into Trade Unions as a whole; to his greater dismay, Broadhead, a Sheffield unionist, and others confessed soon after to a series of unionist violences and actual murders, and crimes as bad or worse were proved against certain Manchester brickmakers' clubs. The circumstances of the disclosures were often so melodramatic that even the friends of Trade Unionism might well have been pardoned for withdrawing their support. James Hallam, a Union saw-grinder, pressed by Mr. Overend, the examiner, to declare whether he was or was not in possession of a pistol the night when Linley, an "unfair" employer, was shot, sweated in the witness-box and seemed unable to speak.

"Say yes or no."

After an internal struggle Hallam said: "Yes, I was."

' "Where did you get that pistol?"

'No answer, the witness looking fixedly at Mr. Overend and apparently struggling with a sensation in the throat' (continues a contemporary report).

' "Now, I ask for what purpose did you buy that pistol?"

'No answer.

'The witness shook from head to foot.' He staggered up to Mr. Overend and whispered something inaudible to the Commissioner, to which Overend answered testily: "Oh, we'll give you the indemnity if you tell the truth."

Nevertheless, the prisoner fainted in court and was unconscious for a quarter of an hour, returning to his wits to "snatch at his throat" and then collapsing again. Led back into court, he admitted in a feeble voice that he had secured the pistol to shoot Linley, which in the end he had compelled a man named Crookes to do for him.

Crookes took his place in the box, Broadhead with bowed head calling to him through the fingers of his hands: "Tell the truth, Sam. Everything." Crookes, in reply, stated that he had been paid £20 by Broadhead for the assassination.

In the same year as these disclosures were made, the Court of Queen's Bench, dealing with an appeal brought by the Boilermakers' Society, declared that though Trade Unions were, since 1824, no longer forbidden by the law, they were nevertheless associations "in restraint of trade" and so could not be allowed to sue for the recovery of funds appropriated by dishonest officials, though they had been doing this under the Friendly Societies Act since 1855. This was the once famous case of *Hornby v. Close*.

The double threat was firstly to all funds of the new Unions, secondly, through the Commission, to their very existence. The passing, on the initiative largely of Alexander Campbell of the Glasgow Trades Council, of an Act in 1867 removing some of the grosser injustices of the existing Master and Servant law was of great importance to the miners; for they especially had been subjected to constant persecution under the old law. But it was poor comfort to the general body of Trade Unionists that a "servant" should be no longer arbitrarily imprisoned before trial and then sent back to jail for the offence of breaking his contract, if the organizations which made it possible for him to resist oppression were to be outlawed. Moreover, even after the Act of 1867, a workman could still be imprisoned and not merely fined for "aggravated" breach of contract—it was left to the courts to decide which; an employer could only be forced to pay damages (if any).

To parry the stab, the Junta called in 1867—the year in which working men in the towns first got votes—the "Conference of Amalgamated Trades" mentioned earlier. Except for the Ten Hours Committees of the textile workers, it was the first consistent attempt by working men at parliamentary agitation since the days of Francis Place, and it was signally successful. With the aid of friendly middle-class M.P.s and lawyers, chiefly of the "Positivist" sect which adopted Comte's theories, and with help from the Christian Socialists, some temporary protection was achieved. Gurney's Act of 1868 incidentally allowed the prosecution of defaulting officials, and a temporary Act of 1869 permitted civil actions for the recovery of funds. The evidence before the Commission was skilfully marshalled and skilfully questioned. It turned very largely upon the structure of the new Unions; the employers were tempted into attacking the actuarial basis of the funds; the Trade Union witnesses replied; and soon, so far from outlawing the Unions, the Commission was absorbed in calculations about the prudence of their financial commitments. In the end public excitement subsided, and no final action, favourable or unfavourable, was taken by Parliament till 1871. But for their new status as voters, the Unionists would have fared far worse.

The new Trade Unions were not the only mechanisms constructed by the workers in these years to make their lives more comfortable and secure. Of nearly equal importance, in contemporary eyes, were the working men's clubs and the Co-operative shops. It is a sign of the extreme narrowness and monotony to which working-class life had been reduced in the vast Victorian slum cities that the formation of the bare and beery working men's clubs that still in some places exist to-day should have been regarded as a major event. But so it was; a meeting house other than the public house, for rest, talk and even reading, was at length provided, and seemed like the return of civilization. At the commencement under the guidance of the Rev. Mr. Solly, the object of the new clubs was purely educational and beer was forbidden. The first club seems to have come into existence in 1852—Brougham's and Birkbeck's "Mechanics' Institutes" of the 1820's and onwards having turned very largely to technical education—and was the Clare Market "Colonnade Club." Three years later this was followed by "Bastard's Club" of Charlton Marshall in Dorset (named after its founder, not its members). But not until Solly formed the "Working Men's Club and Institute Union" in 1862 did the clubs become widespread. He drew subscriptions even from aristocratic sources, with the energy of fanaticism. "This is Henry Solly, my dear," said Fawcett, the blind Postmaster-General, introducing the missionary to his wife, "who believes that Heaven consists of working men's clubs." He extracted cheques from business men and dukes: Queen Victoria presented a consignment of autographed copies of *The Early Years of the Prince Consort*. The working men, however, received these gifts with Israelitish cunning; they spoiled the aristocracy of their subscriptions, restored beer to the amenities of the clubs, and refrained from paying their own dues to the centre. In one year the subscriptions of all the local clubs only reached the sum of 17s. 6d. Not for many years did they consent to make any considerable contributions to the Union.

But the clubs were, in the long run, less important than the shops. The Rochdale "Equitable Pioneers" had founded their Co-operative shop in Toad Lane in 1844, twenty-eight men with a capital of twenty-eight pounds. Innumerable Co-operative stores had preceded them, and had mostly failed: the derision with which they were greeted when they took down the shutters had some excuse. The device which enabled them to survive was the combination of fixed interest on share and loan capital with dividends to members in proportion to the amount of their purchases. Earlier societies (for example, Meltham Mills, and some of the Owenite Societies in London, as well as some Scottish Societies) had paid dividends on purchases long before 1844, and other Societies had allowed interest on share capital. But the combination of the two had probably not been tried before; and it worked. Of the two, the dividend on purchases was the more important. Five per cent a year or even more, upon the small investment that he could make, was insufficient to retain the interest of the average working man. Why should he remember to deal at one particular store for the sake of half a crown or five shillings at Christmas? He should, in theory, have received some benefit in reduced prices; but alert shopkeepers were prepared to cut prices for a while to put a dangerous rival out of business. Once the Co-operative store was deserted, prices would go back to normal. But a dividend on purchases meant that each time a member went out of his way to deal at his shop he received a pecuniary reward. To pay the "divi" at all, credit trading had to be forbidden, and thus the "Co-ops" were confined to the better-paid and more regularly employed workers. Rochdale's first year was fortunate: the 28 members became 74, the £28 became £181. The turnover was £710 and the profits £22. Thenceforward the society's growth was steady: in 1875 its members numbered 8,415, its funds £225,682, its turnover £305,657, and its profits £48,212.

The greatest single benefit that the "Co-ops" brought to their members was pure food. The 'sixties and 'seventies were the happiest years for the sand-in-the-sugar grocer and other adulterators, whose early activities have been mentioned in a previous chapter. But the Co-ops had no more reason to poison than they had to cheat their members, and the difference between good and fresh bacon, flour, cheese, tea, bread, sugar and butter, and faked or stale substitutes was something of immediately understood importance to every working-class woman, though it cannot be evaluated in wage-tables.

Parliament, so suspicious towards Trade Unions, looked indulgently upon the Co-operatives, largely because of

Christian Socialist influence. The Industrial and Provident Societies Act of 1852 gave them the privileges of friendly societies—the right to vest their funds in trustees, to prosecute their officers for malversation, to own property, the even more valuable privilege of trading with others than their own members. An amending Act in 1855 accidentally removed the permission to spend money on education, but this was restored in 1862, and the amount which any member might invest in his society was raised from £100 to £200. The severest test which the Co-ops had to face came in 1861 and following years, when Lancashire, where they were strongest, was half-ruined by the American Civil War. But while private shops were driven out of business left and right, hardly any Co-operatives of importance were forced to close down.

In the late 'sixties there occurred an astonishing revival of the movement for Co-operative Production, which had largely disappeared after the failure of the Societies started by the Redemptionists and Christian Socialists in the late 'forties and early 'fifties. Glasgow and Newcastle-on-Tyne were its two main centres; but it was also strong in the textile areas of Lancashire, in the West Riding, and in nearly all the English coal-fields. The miners' unions of Durham, Northumberland, Yorkshire and the Midlands embarked large sums in the purchase and development of Co-operative collieries; the Trade Unions as well as the Co-operative Stores in the North-East entrusted their funds to the Industrial Bank founded by Dr. J. H. Rutherford, who used it to support the Co-operative Ouseburn Engine Works on the Tyne and various other productive ventures. The Co-operative Wholesale Society advanced considerable sums to support a number of these projects, and then drew back. Meanwhile in Lancashire Trade Unions and consumers' Co-operative Societies participated in starting a series of Co-operative textile mills, some on a genuinely Co-operative basis, but others in the form of "Working-class Limiteds," registered under the Companies Acts and differing from ordinary joint stock companies only in the large number of factory workers who held their shares.

This vogue of Co-operative Production lasted right through

the great industrial boom of the early 'seventies. The Ouse-burn Engine Works flourished through the period of the Nine Hours struggle on the Tyne; and the Co-operative collieries profited by the sharp rise in coal prices which accompanied the boom. Then the ensuing slump brought increasing diffi-culties. Reckless financing of Co-operative enterprises brought the Industrial Bank to collapse in 1875; and the Ouseburn Works went down with it. The Co-operative collieries began to make serious losses, and went into liquidation as the miners' unions, hard hit by the slump, cut off supplies. Many, though not all, of the textile concerns lost their Co-operative character. By the end of the 'seventies this third wave of Co-operative Production had spent its force. The surviving Producers' Societies (among which the Co-operative Printing Society, founded in Manchester as early as 1860, deserves special men-tion) consolidated their position by building up regular markets in the consumers' Co-operative movement.

Meanwhile, consumers' Co-operation had come practically undamaged through this period of varying fortunes. In 1863, Abraham Greenwood, William Cooper, and other leaders of the Rochdale Society, after long efforts, persuaded a number of the Lancashire Societies, with a few elsewhere, to join together in forming the North of England Co-operative Wholesale Society, which paid dividends on purchases to its member-societies, just as these in turn paid dividends to their individual members. From Lancashire the new body gradually spread, first to Yorkshire and then by stages over the rest of England and Wales; and a separate, but allied, Scottish Co-operative Wholesale Society followed in 1868–9. The membership of the constituent Societies of the English C.W.S. in the first year was 18,337, and sales amounted to £51,858. By 1875 membership was 241,129 and capital £360,527, and sales had risen to £2,247,000. Moreover, in 1873 the C.W.S. had begun to set up its own productive factories—a policy in which the Scottish C.W.S. showed even greater enterprise. Total sales by Co-operative Societies of all types increased over the same period from about £2 millions to over £18 millions. In 1869 began the regular series of annual Co-opera-tive Congresses which has continued ever since, and from the second Congress sprang the Co-operative Central Board, which developed into the Co-operative Union, the co-ordinating body for propaganda and education. The first Central Board had sixteen London members—four sympathetic Liberal M.P.s, Lloyd Jones the one-time Owenite, two members of the Junta, two Christian Socialists, a few middle-class sympathizers, and two men, E. O. Greening and G. J. Holyoake, who, whatever their past, could best be described as Co-operators pure and simple. The fifteen provincial delegates, headed by Abraham Greenwood of Rochdale, were all Co-operators of the same kind. As time went on this last element prevailed. Middle-class sympathizers were less needed, and so less influential, though Neale became secretary to the Co-operative Union in 1873 and spent his life in its service. Necessarily and naturally, men who were chiefly occupied in the practical details of successful commercial trading came to the top, and the belief that the movement would peacefully put an end to the competitive system, while never formally abandoned, became more and more a pious hope which clearly had no relation to everyday affairs.

CHAPTER XXXI

THE FIRST INTERNATIONAL— REPUBLICANISM AND REFORM

WHILE such advances were being made in the economic world, parallel political victories were being secured. The defeat of the attack on the Unions already described was not by any means all, or even the most spectacular, of the successes. The political advancement of the working class was partly the work of a general Radical agitation, whose greatest success was the granting of the franchise to the town workers in 1867, partly also the work of specifically working-class organizations. The endeavours of the last-named were almost wholly confined to securing a better legal position for the Unions and sending a small number of working men to Parliament.

But before these are described notice must be taken of one political activity which in view of the general opinions of the working-class leaders can only be described as eccentric. Sporadic but not infrequent communications had in the past been held with foreign workers: out of these, by a process whose exact nature is still disputed, came a meeting in St. Martin's Hall, Long Acre, London, on 28 September 1864, which led to the founding of the First International, officially called the International Working Men's Association. Among the initial supporters were such antagonistic characters as Robert Applegarth, Karl Marx and Giuseppe Mazzini. But Mazzini withdrew, Marx was prevented by illness and poverty (though he and Engels had drafted the Rules and Address) from taking a directing part for the first two years, and the English Trade Unionists were left in control. Their object was to extend the benefits of British trade unionism to the Continent, which had previously known only the tedious alternation of tyranny and revolution. They observed with pleasure the appearance under their guidance of trade societies in France, Belgium, Switzerland and Germany, and later (or so they believed) in Spain, Italy, Holland, Denmark, Portugal and North America. They perceived in the International a useful means of discouraging foreign blacklegs, but their attention was soon turned to home affairs and they let the International fall more and more under the influence of Marx. He was occupied in imposing a policy of revolutionary Socialism on it, against the endeavours of Bakunin to make it Anarchist. The opinions of both sides, indeed the whole world in which such opinions could be held at all, were in the last degree foreign to the Junta. On the fall of the Commune of Paris, the International published Marx's *The Civil War in France*, over the signatures of the whole General Council, and men like Lucraft and Odger found to their horror that they were signing a defence of an attempt by working men to destroy a government by violence. They resigned in indignation, and severed their connection with the International. Their resignation, followed soon after by Applegarth's, ended the influence of that body in England. It had formed about twenty branches in Britain, and these attempted to form a British Labour

Party, but only one (Woolwich) appears to have survived the year 1873.

Even the more romantic Radicals, who sympathized with the Paris Commune, had little knowledge of and less sympathy with the Socialist programme of Marx and the International. *The Workman's Magazine* of 1873, Henry Solly's influential paper, in its Utopia called *England in 2085*, provides as an economic measure only the nationalization of a few remaining railways after a bloody conflict between King and Republic arising from the cruelties of the Marquess of Salisbury: indeed, the most notable differences between the old and the ideal societies are the total abandonment of smoking, the almost total abandonment of drinking, and the invention of a side-saddle for bicycles, enabling young ladies to use those machines without impropriety.

When men in their dreams of the future reached no further than this, the "wild and extravagant" hopes of Owen and O'Connor had indeed been forgotten. The working people of Britain may be said not to have despaired, but to have abandoned their hopes. Their placidity and acquiescence alarmed even those who had been most harassed by their previous activity. "Have they no Spartacus among them to head a revolt of the slave class against their political tormentors?" wrote Cobden in 1861, complaining of their meekness under taunts and insults. "I suppose it is the reaction from the follies of Chartism that keeps them so quiet." It was too late to call back Chartist ghosts: what portion of the working class still retained political interests had definitely determined to accept the lead of the Free Traders and Manchester Radicals whom the Chartists had most detested. And as these Radicals were strict parliamentarians, the history of working-class progress has now in part to be traced in parliamentary politics; as they were by no means sharply separated from the groups nearest to them, it is impossible to draw the clear dividing line which makes the task of the historian of Chartism so easy. In political matters the views and policies of Robert Applegarth, the Trade Union leader, differed hardly at all from those of Mr. Edmond Beales, the lawyer who led the National Reform League. Mr. Beales agreed on most subjects with Mr. Bright, the famous

Free Trade orator and pacifist. Mr. Bright followed with confidence and trust the guidance of Mr. Gladstone: Mr. Gladstone had served honourably, happily and successfully under Lord Palmerston. All the world remarked how thin was the dividing line between Palmerston and the tolerant head of the Conservative Party, Lord Derby. And Lord Derby was the trusted leader of Colonel Sibthorp, a Conservative so extreme that he endeavoured to prevent the holding of the Great Exhibition, lest it attract from all the world "Red Republicans, pickpockets and whoremongers," three overlapping classes of which he believed foreigners almost wholly to consist. Individuals in this long unbroken chain might break away in pursuit of some extravagant policy, Dilke into Republicanism, or Disraeli into Tory democracy, but these were personal aberrations and are no signs of general division. Politically, all previous dividing lines had become blurred.

This process was notably assisted by the character of the politician whose power was greatest immediately after the collapse of Chartism. Lord Palmerston was not a Liberal; he was a Whig. He had no sympathy with social reforms at home, though he was prepared to support them if they were of a trivial character (and no other reforms were likely to be proposed). But just as he considered the condition of England to be ideally satisfactory, so he despised or pitied those countries which had not achieved it. Revolutionaries and Radicals in foreign lands received his vigorous and indiscreet applause. When the Austrian General, Haynau, torturer of the Hungarian rebels, visited Barclay and Perkins's brewery and was set upon by the indignant draymen and whipped till he hid in the dustbin of the George Inn on Bankside, Lord Palmerston wrote words of delighted approval which were spread about with discreet indiscretion. When Kossuth or Garibaldi visited England, all the world knew that it was only official etiquette that prevented the Prime Minister or Foreign Secretary, whichever he might be, from joining in the vehement addresses and congratulatory banquets. If, as in the case of Denmark or Poland, his enthusiasm encouraged the resisters of oppression only to their own ruin, he was doing no more than his supporters desired, for they too only wished to approve verbally of foreign Radicals and not to risk the life of a single British soldier in their support.

Now, the longest-lived of the Chartist sentiments was their interest in foreign affairs. After they had despaired of success in England, they were still convinced that the revolution would shortly be victorious abroad. Anyone who turns over the remaining advanced journals of the late 'forties and early 'fifties will find that the eyes of the editors are constantly on the ends of the earth: more space is given to foreign affairs than to home: the enemy of the paper is no longer the "shopocrat," the sweater or the Tory landlord, it is Napoleon III or Radetsky. Even when Palmerston's irruptions ought least to have pleased the Radicals, accident put him right in their eyes: he was temporarily expelled from office in 1852 for too hastily recognizing the Empire declared by Napoleon III, the enemy of all freedom. But his dismissal was known to be the work of Prince Albert, and in detestation of the German would-be autocrat, Palmerston's exact offence was forgotten. In 1850 his bullying of Greece in defence of the baseless claims of the utterly disreputable Don Pacifico was the rankest imperialism; but he secured the cheers of the democrats and turned the ignobility of his protégé into a virtue by declaring that it was his policy to secure to even the poorest and humblest British subject the majestic protection of the British fleet.

The early years of his predominance, therefore, were admirably calculated to lull into their final sleep the remaining energies of the remaining Chartists or Radicals. Once this was done, public attention was continually distracted by a series of exciting external events, from Canton to Ashanti, some directly provoked by the Government or its officials, some, like the Crimean War or the Indian Mutiny, wholly unexpected. At home the story was one of rapid expansion. Two commercial crises, in 1857 and 1866, only momentarily interfered with the phenomenal increase of industrial enterprises. The period was one of dramatic changes—enormous increases of wealth and sensational downfalls. The atmosphere was as hectic as New York's in the days of Harriman and Jay Gould, and equally unfavourable to the growth of a serious reform or Labour movement. The most casual inspection of contemporary journals provides many examples. Soon after the surprising rise and fall of George Hudson, the railway magnate, some of his feats were reproduced by the financier, John Sadleir, the M.P. who headed the group called the Pope's Brass Band in the House of Commons. His downfall and death were near in time to the more important fraudulent collapse of the Royal British Bank, which spread enormous devastation after stimulating feverish activity. This preceded slightly the exposure of the Secretary of the Crystal Palace Company, William Robson, who was discovered to have issued and sold so many non-existent bonds that he was about to purchase Kenilworth Castle when arrested. In such a whirl of unsound and insane projects conservative financial opinion consoled itself that a relic of common sense caused the repudiation of the two most impracticable projects mooted about 1856—Mr. Field's plan for an Atlantic cable (constructed ten years later) and M. de Lesseps's for a Suez Canal. Even more absurd was held to be the programme of women's enfranchisement put forward after 1857. A group of middle-class ladies with an office in Langham Place, London, and a newly founded *Englishwoman's Journal*, advocated the rights of women to take up any employment they chose in industry, to retain their property even after marriage, and even to vote. Rather timidly, and to the accompaniment of ridicule in the press, ladies addressed drawing-room meetings and eventually even larger ones. From 1865 the movement had the powerful patronage of John Stuart Mill; and though this brought it nowhere near to success, it did bring it consideration and serious discussion.

Nothing but the most trifling reforms could be secured in such a period. Lord John Russell twice—in 1852 and in 1854 —brought forward very modest Reform Bills and had to abandon them in face of the universal apathy. A divorce Act of 1857 put an end to the rather indecent debates on private "divorce bills" and the very indecent cases in the courts once known as Doctors' Commons, and extended the privilege of divorce to persons of moderate incomes. Transportation was abolished the same year, owing to the Colonies' protest and not to reforming zeal. A Mr. Salomons, by taking his seat when elected and refusing to leave the House until expelled by force, made it fairly sure that Jews would be shortly given the right to sit in Parliament. But this reform, which was enacted in 1858, was due to a one-year Conservative Government. Indeed, this Government was the first to raise some hopes of reforms of importance. In addition to relieving the Jews it abolished the East India Company and put an end to the property qualification for Members of Parliament. This was he smallest and least important of the Chartist demands (for the qualification had been repeatedly evaded), but its granting was significant. The Government was defeated on a Bill for an ineffective franchise reform in 1859.

Now for the first time since the collapse of 1848 an active popular campaign began for the enfranchisement of the people. Its leader was John Bright, the famous Free Trader. Like his predecessors of 1832 he was often vague about the exact amount of enfranchisement that he proposed, but the terms of his speeches, and the response they secured, suggested to all that it was the Charter without the name that he was demanding. But his use of "reform" may be compared with "the people" in the mouth of Brougham, who said: "By the people I mean the middle class, the wealth and intelligence of the country, the glory of the British name." Bright at least did believe in manhood suffrage as a theory, though he was prepared to compromise, as earnestly as he believed in Free Trade, where he was far less willing to compromise, and as earnestly too as he believed (being an employer) that Factory Acts were disastrous. It was a mark of the new passivity of the working class that the great majority of it was willing to accept such a leader and to believe, with him, that the victory of Gladstone and Palmerston at this election (1859), which he largely secured, would mean a great instalment of reform.

The movement as a whole was committed to parliamentary methods and it had not allowed for the slowness and tortuousness of parliamentarism. Reforms were certainly begun by the new Government. A treaty with France for almost-free trade was concluded by Cobden's agency in 1860; the paper duty was lowered drastically enough to permit of a real popular Press. But when the Reform Bill appeared in 1860, its provisions were far less Radical than Bright had hoped. It was mangled in its passage through the Commons, and in the Lords the Premier, Palmerston, secured its defeat by merely showing he considered it a Bill of no importance. It was now clear that however earnestly reformers might intrigue in the lobbies, or agitate outside, they could have no success until Palmerston was dead.

He died in 1865: the next year Russell and Gladstone presented a new Reform Bill. Once again it was inadequate; once again it was defeated. A Conservative Government took the place of the Liberals, held an election, but returned without a firm majority. Thereupon followed one of the most contorted and unexpected portions of parliamentary history, ending in the enfranchisement of a considerable part of the British working class by the party which was controlled by its most resolute and natural enemies. This could, of course, only be done because it was obvious to all that the articulate section of the working class had abandoned its revolutionary aspirations and could safely be trusted with the vote. It was universally believed that a large measure of enfranchisement was bound to come before long. The only question unsettled was, which party should have the credit of carrying the reform: Disraeli, the most cunning of all Victorian politicans, slipped in first and secured it both at the time and in history books for the less probable party.

However, there was more to it than a supremely ingenious lobby trick. Considerable indignation—not a Chartist rage, but disappointment and annoyance—was caused by the expulsion of the Liberal Government on the question of reform. The National Reform League, already existent and with considerable Trade Union support, sprang into renewed activity under the direction of Edmond Beales. With it were the National Reform Union, of both working and middle-class membership, covering mostly Lancashire and Yorkshire, and the Northern Reform Union on the North-East coast, led by Joseph Cowen and strongly backed by the miners. Bright's propagandist tour was repeated by many other speakers on a far greater scale, and this time the organizers did not hold meetings only, but processions whose effect was far greater.

They were not, as in Chartist days, torchlight riots, but quiet and disciplined marches, and it was noticed with surprise that some of them consisted exclusively of members of Trade Unions behind their banners. "great in numbers and most imposing in their silent united strength." The most remarked of all these, and one which by universal account had a profound influence on the Government, was a march upon Hyde Park in the summer of 1866. The gates of Hyde Park were closed arbitrarily—and, in the common belief, illegally—by the police. Beales, at the head of the demonstrators, made a formal protest and retired to hold a meeting in Trafalgar Square. Others were less patient: they pushed down the railings and stormed the Park.

It was under such pressure that Disraeli introduced his Bill. As first drafted, it did not show a great advance, and had the further disadvantage of creating educational, "savings bank" and other fancy franchises. It was consistently amended until the point was reached when all who paid rates were to be granted the vote in towns. However, those who did not directly pay their rates, but paid them through the landlords (the so-called Compound Householders), were excluded, and they constituted two-thirds of the householders rated under £10. At this point Gladstone proposed to relax his pressure on the Government: he suggested that a line should be drawn above which all ratepayers, direct or indirect, should have the vote. While his voice was sounding his followers accepted his views, but afterwards a group meeting in the tea-room of the Commons daringly decided to insist on plain household suffrage. This Tea-Room Party, as it was called, held to its proposition despite strong abuse: Disraeli—possibly not un-amused at Gladstone's predicament—unexpectedly accepted it, and in 1867 the great majority of the urban working men of Great Britain were granted the vote. J. S. Mill proposed to give women the vote also, and found seventy-three supporters: no one proposed to enfranchise the farm labourer.

The newly enfranchised voters did not show the gratitude that the Conservative Party may have expected. The Liberals were triumphantly successful at the election of 1868, and for the first time a representative of the extreme Left of the day—

CP: O

the free competition "Manchester men"—was in the Cabinet (Bright). The reward that the Trade Unionists received will be described later; meanwhile, it should be noted that certain indubitable advantages were secured. The Torrens Housing Act has already been referred to. The new telegraph system was nationalized in 1869. The Ballot, an important Chartist demand, was decreed in 1872. Cross's Housing Act in 1875 made slum clearance possible, and other Acts which were landmarks were the Mines Regulation Acts of 1872, Plimsoll's Merchant Shipping Act of 1875, which will be referred to again, and the Public Health Act of 1875 which has already been described. Even more valuable, a national system of elementary education, voluntary as yet, with elected School Boards, on which women could serve, was founded in 1870 and schools began to be built forthwith.

But that year and the next few years saw, not perhaps unnaturally, the Left which had entered the Government outbid by a yet more uncompromising section. Republicanism, partly under the influence of the expulsion of Napoleon III, now became a powerful movement. Charles Bradlaugh, the militant atheist, was its chief London representative; Joseph Chamberlain, the municipal Radical, its Birmingham leader; its national leader was unquestionably Sir Charles Dilke. Nor had they any doubts of their success: "the Republic must come," wrote Chamberlain to Dilke in 1871, "and at the rate at which we are moving it will come in our generation." Prince Albert had been feared for his ambitions; Victoria was disliked for her parsimony and refusal to perform her ceremonial duties. "Citizen Dilke" stumped the country, rousing hysterical applause, and Conservative politicians were thankful that the Prince of Wales fell seriously ill and a counter-sentiment could be invoked. In 1872, when Dilke brought up in Parliament a motion criticizing the Crown, he was listened to in silence, but his followers were not. Auberon Herbert's speech was the signal for a tumult, a yelling riot in which members hurled abuse and insults, and some imitated the squawking of a cock, a device which, according to interested observers, had not been used in the Commons since the later years of George IV. But a large proportion of the House, though perhaps not the cock-crowers, were currently believed to be as Republican as Dilke, and merely not to consider the problem one of immediate urgency.

Republicanism itself hardly provided a social programme. *The Republican* attacked fiercely the cost of the Crown, and of recent wars, costing £1,913,000,000 and in its opinion chiefly fomented by dynastic ambitions. But the use to which it suggested that the sums saved might be put is unexpected to a modern reader. It was to "build and fill with objects of art and interest" 1,530 reproductions of the Crystal Palace at Sydenham. However, Dilke and Bradlaugh's "Land and Labour League" was able to fill the gap. "Henry Georgism," as it was later called, made an alliance with Republicanism. The League's principal aims were the nationalization of the land, the compulsory cultivation of unused land, the establishment of "home colonies" for this purpose, no other tax being levied than property tax for secular education, and—almost as an afterthought—shorter hours in industry. Its spokesmen publicly derided the Trade Union leaders—"George P. P. P. P. Potter, the Applegarths, Howells & Co."—as "the abandoned tools of commercial philanthropy."

Despite Dilke's tours and despite the foundation of numerous Republican clubs in the country, the Republican agitation faded away in the late 'seventies. The cause cannot have been Dilke's sudden political extinction by a quite unusually scandalous divorce case: such an event can extinguish a man but not a movement. Nor was it a revival of Royal popularity: it was not until after the Jubilee that Queen Victoria is shown, by a study of the Press, to have become generally liked. As late as 1885 the paper most far removed from Labour sympathies—*Town Talk*, the paper for Piccadilly johnnies and the forerunner of the *Pink'Un*—published a savage mock "programme for the Jubilee" beginning "The Queen will come to London and stop a whole week; her Majesty will spend five shillings with two London tradesmen" and ending with a procession closed by "10,000 children who have had no meat for a year," "100 workmen who have been sent to prison for being poor," and "Prince Lagerbeer of Stunkenstein, in his carriage and four, accompanied by his English princess, fed and clothed and housed by the English ratepayers." The reason for the slow abandonment of anti-Royal agitation was the reason which moved the M.P.s who failed to rally to Dilke in the parliamentary riot. As she grew older, Victoria seemed to grow more innocuous. She did not interfere, as far as the public knew, in running the country as Albert might have done and William had done: if she had the will, she did not have the abilities. The Crown remained a nuisance, an expense and an undemocratic institution, no doubt, but it was not a danger.

CHAPTER XXXII

THE TRADE UNION ACTS—THE NINE HOURS MOVEMENT—JOSEPH ARCH

DURING this whole period, "Labour candidatures" for Parliament are intermittently reported. They were "Labour" only in the sense that the candidates were or had been "labouring men" and trade unionists. Their programmes were always Liberal or Radical: they were not always to the Left of middle-class members of their party, and were distinguished by their origin rather than by their programme. They had indeed a direct if thin connecting line with Chartism. The last conference which took the name "Chartist" was an insignificant meeting held in 1858 under the influence of Ernest Jones. Jones himself stood for Nottingham in 1857 and 1859; where O'Connor had polled 1,257 of the smaller electorate of 1847 he polled first 614 and then 151. William Newton, of the A.S.E., had stood as a Chartist in 1852 for the Tower Hamlets, the famous Radical seat in East London which has now disappeared. Holyoake offered himself there as a Radical in 1857, but never reached the poll.

Ernest Jones had become reconciled to collaboration with the middle-class Radicals. In 1861 he settled down in Manchester, and began building up a new Radical movement to work for franchise reform. Abel Heywood, the Owenite and Chartist bookseller, stood for Manchester as a Radical in 1859 and 1865—on the second occasion in conjunction with Jacob Bright. After the Reform Act of 1867 Jones himself appeared as a third-party Radical candidate, polling over 10,000 votes against 13,500 for the lowest successful candidate (Jacob Bright). In 1869 Jones died, and almost the last link between Chartism and the new working-class Radicalism was snapped.

Only after the extension of the franchise in 1867 was it possible to present working-class candidates seriously. In February 1866, George Potter had founded a new London Working Men's Association, which devoted itself to promoting the candidatures of workingmen. At the 1868 election six such candidates were nominated and three even went to the polls—W. R. Cremer at Warwick, George Howell at Aylesbury, and E. O. Greening at Halifax. Newton, as an independent, again tried Tower Hamlets. None were successful, though they stood as Liberals or Radicals, and were strictly moderate in their demands. To ask for "exceptional laws" for the benefit of the workers, said the Association, would mark its members as "foolish and irrational visionaries." It merely desired that a number of workmen should be included in Parliament, so that that body should become truly representative of all classes. When, in 1869, Potter's society vanished into a new "Labour Representation League" the same mildness remained. The *Beehive* announced that the proposed M.P.s' duty would be to "diminish the growing passion for mere sensual indulgence." Certain Conservative organs, such as the *Law Times*, actually supported the League's demands, in the fairly clear but insulting belief that working-class M.P.s would be easier to handle than their middle-class leaders.

The new League ran George Odger as candidate for Southwark in 1870, unsuccessfully, but in the same year elected Benjamin Lucraft for Finsbury in the first School Board elections—a success received with a delight which to-day seems a little disproportionate. The League was not to achieve its larger ambition, by the election of two real workingmen M.P.s, until the year 1874, after which effort it languished, and within a few years expired. And this success was not due to its own energies so much as to the progress of the Trade Union parliamentary agitation.

In 1871, when the Sheffield outrages of 1866 were partly forgotten, the Gladstone Government decided to regularize the whole position of Trade Unions. Its project, put out early in the year, did not please the unionists, but despite a good deal of wire-pulling its main outlines were unchanged when it passed into law the same year, as two contemporaneous Acts, a Trade Union Act and a Criminal Law Amendment Act. The first Act gave Unions adequate legal status: no Union could be regarded as criminal because "in restraint of trade," any Union whose rules were not criminal could be registered, registration gave protection to the funds without (it seemed) enabling a Union to be sued at law or interfering in its internal affairs. So far, so good: the Conference of Amalgamated Trades dissolved. But this was not because no tasks remained. Age and changes of occupation were breaking up the Junta. Applegarth retired, and his Union's headquarters were moved to Manchester. Allan was near his death; Odger was a politician; Howell had already quarrelled with Coulson. The conduct of a campaign of protest against the second Act fell naturally into the hands of the whole body of Trade Union leaders at the Trades Union Congress. For the second Act— the Criminal Law Amendment Act—provoked nation-wide anger. It did not, perhaps, invent any new crimes (though by repealing the Trade Union Act of 1859 it removed the legalization of picketing) but it codified and made more specific certain recent anti-Union decisions, and since (under Liberal Governments) the employers had provided batch after batch of magistrates these were not few. All the vague phrases of the old Combination Laws about "molestation," "obstruction," "intimidation" and so forth were revived; and "persistently following" a person and "watching" premises were also declared crimes. In fact, it was clear that with the usual prejudices of the Bench this would mean that the mere announcement of a strike by two Trade Unionists to the workers entering a factory might lead to imprisonment. Judges held that unfriendly looks, or the presence of strikers in large numbers, constituted "intimidation": even the mere posting-up of a strike notice had been held to be intimidation of employers. Men were at that moment in prison for the mere act of striking and urging others to strike; but till then it had been in doubt whether these sentences were legal or due only to the spite of particular magistrates. The Trade Unionists became the more anxious the more they studied the Act, but the Government rejected all their protests. In 1872, secure in the new Act, Lord Justice Brett sent the London gas-stokers' leaders to prison for a year for merely preparing to strike, holding this to be a conspiracy to molest the employers. The Home Secretary declined to modify the sentence: by a back way the Combination Acts appeared to have returned.

Mr. Gladstone met appeals for redress with his well-known obstinacy, and when a General Election came in 1874, the Trade Union leaders took the painful and dramatic decision of opposing the Liberal Government. Trade Union candidates were to be run where possible, even if the Conservatives were let in: where no such thing was possible, anti-Labour Liberals were to be opposed, even to the extent of voting for Conservatives. There were other factors, including great resentment of the publicans at the Licensing Act, making for the defeat of the Government; the disapproval of the Trade Unions was only one of the reasons for Mr. Gladstone's *débâcle*. But the Trade Union leaders felt themselves to be past-masters of political strategy when the Government crashed, and the new Conservative majority duly fulfilled its part of the tacit bargain.

The Criminal Law Amendment Act was repealed, and replaced by a new law—the Conspiracy and Protection of Property Act of 1875. This, despite its forbidding title, made substantial concessions to the Trade Unions. Peaceful picketing was expressly legalized, though within narrower limits than under the Act of 1859—for the right of "peaceful persuasion" was not regained by the Unions until 1906—and it was definitely laid down that no act done in contemplation or furtherance of a trade dispute was to be punishable as a conspiracy simply because it was done "in combination," i.e. by more than one person. At the same time the offences which had been listed under the Act of 1871 were more narrowly and exactly defined, so that freedom of strike action was effectively increased. Moreover, a second Act of 1875—the Employers and Workmen Act—carried much further the process of making "master" and "servant" equal parties at law to a purely civil contract. After 1875 breach of contract became in general a purely civil matter, which could give rise to a claim for damages, but not to imprisonment or fine. The Government, however, insisted on keeping, in the Conspiracy and Protection of Property Act, the power to fine or imprison workers whose breach of contract was calculated to cause loss of life or damage to valuable property, or an interruption of the supply of gas and water. It also passed a Factory Act for a 56½-hour week demanded by the cotton workers.

The Parliament that passed these satisfactory measures contained two members of the working class. Thomas Burt sat for Morpeth, Alexander Macdonald for Stafford. Both were miners; Macdonald was secretary of the National Union of Miners and a more independent M.P. than Burt, who consistently voted with the Liberal Party.

Very important, if little advertised, gains were made for women in the late 'sixties and early 'seventies. In 1869 they received, if ratepayers, the municipal franchise, and they were made eligible for School Boards in 1870, while the education they supervised was supplied to girls as well as boys. A very few well-to-do young women could attend at Girton College from 1869 and at Newnham from 1871. A daring attempt, organized by Miss Sophia Jex-Blake, to secure for women medical degrees at Edinburgh lasted from 1869 to 1873. Male medical students hooted and pestered the girls, and drove sheep into the lectures they attended; after allowing them to take the course the Senate withheld the degrees from them and the right to practise was, oddly enough, secured more quietly in 1875 by the King's and Queen's College of Physicians in Ireland agreeing to grant degrees. Other universities, beginning with London, followed its example.

No lack of publicity attended the efforts of Mrs. Josephine Butler in her attempt to repeal the Contagious Diseases Acts. These Acts provided that women in certain areas were, on police accusation, liable to be declared common prostitutes and thereupon forced to submit to periodical medical examination for venereal disease. Protests had been made in the past, but until Mrs. Butler appealed to workingmen in 1870 (starting at a big railwaymen's meeting in Crewe) they had attracted little attention. The indecency of women discussing such a subject at all shocked even some of the feminists; but Mrs. Butler and her colleagues carried the subject down to Colchester, where the Government candidate, Sir Henry Storks, was an ardent advocate of the Acts. More ardent than well advised, indeed, for he expressed the view that the wives of private soldiers ought to be subjected to a similar régime; and Mrs. Butler had the pleasure of seeing him soundly defeated. Despite this success, however, the Acts remained in force till 1883.

Not much more success was gained in the most important field—the campaign for the parliamentary vote. The quiet campaign started under Mill's patronage moved on until in 1870 a general bill drafted by Dr. Pankhurst passed its second reading by 124 to 91. But at that juncture Mr. Gladstone put an end to the women's hopes. "It would be a very great mistake to carry this Bill into law," he said severely, giving no further reasons for what seemed to himself evident. Though in 1885 a bill was allowed to go to a second reading, it was clear that no further advance would be allowed while Mr. Gladstone's influence remained paramount.

The years 1871 to 1875 were years of great prosperity, and the Union members, despite the pacific exhortations of their leaders, wished to derive some immediate benefits. The biggest trade movement that had shaken England for some years started in 1871 in the engineering shops on the North-East Coast. A strike for a nine-hour day—one hour less than in the famous Textile Act of 1847—lasted for five months and ended in success. But this was not due to any support from the Amalgamated Society of Engineers: it openly lamented the strike and refused to provide funds for any but its own members. Indeed, its supineness was the cause of dissident engineering Unions being formed, of which the most notable was the Patternmakers (1872). But it was only carrying to an extreme the principles which directed many of its fellow

Unions. Their three guiding principles were now: (1) to wage merciless war upon intruders into the craft, whether general labourers or other craftsmen; (ii) always to come to agreements with employers and deny any class struggle in action or theory; (iii) to keep up high contributions for the purposes of friendly benefits. These principles impressed themselves deeply upon contemporary working-class opinion: transplanted to America by emigration they ruled the early years of the American Federation of Labour and in that extensive soil exuberated into an astonishing forest. In Britain they were rapidly turning the Amalgamated Societies into rich friendly societies with dormant Trade Union rules. But this development was never accepted wholly without demur. The success on the North-East Coast led to an outburst of strikes for the Nine Hours all over the country, into which the Amalgamated Societies were swept willy-nilly; and the result was frequently success. The miners, never acquiescent except in the North-East, also took sporadic action, of which the most notable instance was a big South Wales strike. This was conducted by the Amalgamated Miners' Association for a 10 per cent rise in wages, and ended in general success.

This last victory marked the emergence of a class of workers who had been among the most oppressed and isolated for years. Living in their own villages, subjected to an unusually tyrannous and autocratic class of employers, the miners had in Scotland been relieved from legal serfdom only at the very end of the eighteenth century, and their Unions had everywhere been repressed with exceptional violence and efficiency. They were wild and terrifying in their appearance and even in their language: the arrival of Burt, their Morpeth M.P., in Parliament was expected with considerable apprehension, and celebrated by a local bard with a poem declaring:

> *Wey, lads, aw just think hoo the biggins will stare*
> *When into St. Stephens's a howkie goes there.*

An 1860 Act had given them the right to elect "checkweighmen" (to check the weight of the coal that each man hewed and loaded, on which his earnings depended) and so to prevent the commonest theft practised by the employers. But the Act was consistently evaded, and only the rising strength of the Unions enabled it to be applied; indeed, it was estimated that twenty years passed before it was generally obeyed. Miners were even omitted from the voting registers of parliamentary boroughs after the Act of 1867, on the ground that they did not pay rent for their cottages. A Miners' Franchise Union was now (1872) formed and was successful in its agitation in 1874. In this year the Trades Union Congress at Sheffield claimed the astonishing total of 1,100,000 members.

Among these members were some belonging to a class even more oppressed than the miners. Not only in upper-class circles had it begun to be believed that the horrors with which Lord Shaftesbury had shocked earlier Parliaments had passed away. The explosion (there is no other word) of Trade Unionism among the agricultural labourers in 1872 showed that in the rural districts these conditions still remained. "Let anyone" wrote a friendly observer "picture to himself a poorly fed, half-clad and wholly ignorant family of eight or nine, including say two grown young women and two grown young men, who habitually slept in one room and in not a few instances in one bed. Let him think of all this and imagine what the worst consequence must be, and his imagination will probably have fallen far short of the fearful reality." By those who cared to know, these facts could have been ascertained at any moment; but scarcely anyone cared to know, until in February 1872, Joseph Arch, a Warwickshire farm-labourer of genius, started a Union for his fellow-labourers which spread with the rapidity of a heath-fire. By the end of the year it had 100,000 members, and 50,000 were organized in other Unions. Throughout the year, and the next, increases of wages were secured with comparative ease. But the rage which this invasion of the dominions of Conservative squires excited was something far more dangerous than the indignation of the urban employers. The Church, which in the towns had learned to observe some decorum and diplomacy, here became openly partisan. The parsons, encouraged by their superiors—one bishop urged that Union organizers should be thrown into the horse-ponds—made common cause with the squires and farmers. A bare handful followed Canon Girdlestone in his support of the union. Surprise as well as anger moved the rest, as if the dumb had spoken and the crippled walked, at "meetings of rural labourers—meetings positively where men made speeches." The forces opposed to the workers, despite the instant aid of Trade Unionists such as Odger and Potter, and Radicals like Dilke and Herbert, were too powerful. As soon as farm-produce prices began to fall in 1874, lock-outs were enforced by the farmers and wages fell again, though not to the previous level. Before long the Union was broken, and though Arch was later (1885) elected to Parliament the labourers had returned to their age-old submissiveness.

But this defeat was almost the only one of importance. At the opening of the year 1875 the Trade Unionists of Britain had reached a height of prosperity they had never attained before. Their organizations had, as for example by the foundation of the Amalgamated Society of Railway Servants in 1871, entered trades which had seemed absolutely closed. Their members were prosperous as never before, and for the most part assumed that their well-being would go on increasing. They had, with insufficient consideration, frequently accepted sliding-scale agreements by which wages depended on prices, but if, as they and most of the official economists on whom they relied assumed, prosperity was going on indefinitely, the dangers in such agreements were purely theoretical.

IMPERIALISM AND SOCIALISM

CHAPTER XXXIII

IMPERIALISM AND THE RADICALS

THE closing quarter of the nineteenth century opened symbolically with the proclamation of Queen Victoria as Empress of India (1876) and ended with the South African War. Between 1875 and 1900 the total area of the British Empire was increased by not far short of 5,000,000 square miles, containing a population of at least 90,000,000. In other words in the space of twenty-five years the British governing class added to the Empire territories forty times as large as Great Britain, and with a population more than twice as large. In all, by 1900 Great Britain was the centre of an Empire ruling over 13,000,000 square miles of subject territory, inhabited by nearly 370,000,000 persons, of whom nearly 300,000,000 were to be found in India alone.

These facts sufficiently stamp the period as one of intensive imperialist expansion. It is, above all else, the period of the partition of the African continent between the European Powers, of the clash of rival Imperialisms both in Africa and in the Far East, and of active foreign investment both in areas politically annexed to the various Empires and in countries, such as China and the South American Republics, which, without political annexation, were scrambled for as spheres of economic influence and brought by the loan of capital and the development of economic enterprise within the business orbits of the leading industrial Powers.

For Great Britain, though first in the field and in by far the most favourable position for the acquisition of political and economic empire, was by no means alone in the quest. Between 1884 and 1900 France annexed 3,500,000 square miles—not counting the vast area of the Sahara—with nearly 40,000,000 inhabitants. Germany, under the new Empire, got 1,000,000 square miles and 17,000,000 subjects, mainly in Africa. Belgium, in the Congo, obtained nearly 1,000,000 square miles and 30,000,000 people. Portugal expanded her African possessions by 800,000 square miles and 9,000,000 inhabitants. Russia opened up Siberia, subdued Bokhara, Khiva and other Asiatic States, and proceeded to the military occupation of Manchuria. Even the United States, as the outcome of the Spanish–American War, had become by 1900 an imperialist Power, holding Porto Rico, Cuba and the Philippine Islands, controlling the Caribbean Sea, and contending with the European countries for spheres of influence and economic penetration in China and Latin America.

Even before 1875, as we have seen, the British capitalist had come to have his eyes upon the ends of the earth; for foreign investment had already reached gigantic proportions in the boom of the early 'seventies. But after 1875 the current set less towards the United States, though that developing country still continued to absorb foreign capital right up to 1914, and more towards areas which could be brought under effective political or at least economic control. The "surplus" capital, which flowed out in an abundant stream from Great Britain, was directed increasingly towards "the Empire," or towards areas which could be brought within the British "sphere of influence." The traditional Cobdenite attitude, which regarded colonies as a nuisance and a source of loss, and looked forward to their dropping off "like ripe plums" as soon as they became capable of managing their own affairs, went clean out of fashion. Imperial possessions came to be valued, not only as markets, but also increasingly as sources of supply, whence raw materials essential to the higher forms of economic development could be obtained on preferential terms. The older generation had regarded the example of British–American trade as demonstrating the fact that mutual exchange could develop to the full without the need for any imperial tie. But the younger generation of capitalists saw things differently; for it was coming to think in terms of raw materials to be derived from the opening up of tropical countries, and of profits

from investment in "uncivilized" areas where foreign property
needed the safeguard of the strong hand of imperialist intervention. It was one thing to lend money to the United States,
or Germany, or to any country possessing a soundly capitalist
government imbued with the principles of orthodox finance.
It was quite another to risk capital in opening up the interior
of Africa or of China, where the principles of Capitalism were
unrecognized, and States comparable with those of Western
Europe and North America did not exist. In less developed
areas, it was held, "trade followed the flag"; and the conclusion was drawn that it would pay to plant the flag of empire
on every unappropriated spot of the earth's surface.

At home, the period opened with a heavy slump and a fierce
attack upon labour conditions. The pride of place which the
Trade Union workers had assumed by the year 1875 was
quickly threatened. That year began a five-year period of
slump in which a great many hard-won advantages were lost.
The "sliding scales" in the mining, iron and steel trades
operated swiftly and in the wrong direction. It is arguable,
no doubt, that the scales merely recorded reductions which
would have been enforced anyway. Certainly the Unions in
other trades which attempted resistance, such as the Operative
Stonemasons, were entirely unsuccessful and in addition
severely damaged themselves. However, it is at least some
advantage to the employers to secure reductions automatically
and without conflict: these reductions may be larger, and more
cheaply gained, than those that they would have secured
without such agreement.

A shrinking labour market meant fewer jobs, fewer jobs
meant a fiercer struggle for those that existed. "Demarcation
disputes," no new phenomenon, now spread and became of
the first importance. A "demarcation dispute" is a quarrel
between rival craft unions as to whose members shall be
entitled to perform a particular type of work: the immediate
enemy in such a dispute is not the employer but fellow-
members of the working class. A dispute arising from an
attempt by a skilled Union to keep out unskilled or semi-
skilled workers is not technically "demarcation," but is similar
in character. The engineering, building and shipbuilding

trades were the most fruitful fields for both types of dispute: the Union of Platers' Helpers complained that the Boilermakers had attempted to stamp it out of existence, and the Plumbers were in continual dispute with no less than five other crafts.

Such fierce dissensions destroyed what little remnants of class solidarity existed. The Trades Councils, as well as the Trades Union Congress, were reduced to semi-impotence when their chief constituents were so frequently not on speaking terms. Proposals for federation of Unions in particular trades, or even for a universal federation, were made in 1875, 1879 and 1882, but were all completely ineffective. The Unions remained isolated, except for the annual meetings of Congress, and showed their fighting spirit almost wholly against one another and not against the employers.

But though the five years (from 1875 to 1880) are years of defeat, disaster and dissension, they are not years of complete ruin. The Unions were not shattered into tiny fragments as they had been in 1834. They lost members (generally, but not always) and their members' wages were much worsened. The old-fashioned Unions, such as the General Union of Carpenters, which had declined to accept the Junta's office methods and efficiency, were battered into insignificance. The Unions of the worse-paid workers (and of the miners) suffered more than the skilled craftsmen's Unions. But in general the structure of the Trade Union movement emerged undamaged. No improvement in structure, no acceptance of common direction, nor any other modification resulted from the lessons of the slump. But also no irreparable damage was done.

Such advances as were made were won in the political field. The examples of Burt and Macdonald were followed. Other seats were contested by the Trade Unionists (in all cases as Liberals) and isolated successes were secured until in 1886 (to anticipate slightly) there were ten Trade Unionists in the House, supported by T. R. Threlfall's Labour Electoral Association and headed by the stonemason, Henry Broadhurst, who was in that year given by Mr. Gladstone an unprecedented honour. He was made an Under-Secretary of State, he was invited to stay at the Palace, and the Prince of Wales poked his bedroom fire. The solemnity with which, in his memoirs, he records this has its ridiculous side (though his phraseology is never so servile as that of some recent Labour leaders' memoirs), but neither to him nor to his followers was it ridiculous at the time. It was a sign that their essential desires were being fulfilled. A man who had worked with his hands at building the Houses of Parliament could sit therein as a minister and be entertained by royalty. The Junta, and these its successors, had set before themselves the object of removing from the statute-book all laws which treated, directly or inferentially, the workers as an inferior class. The exaltation of Broadhurst was a proof that they had succeeded.

The first Acts of the Conservative Government in 1875 and 1876 had essentially finished their work. Besides those mentioned already, these Acts included a great co-ordinating Public Health Act and the establishment of compulsory education. The items which now remained upon the programme of the Parliamentary Committee of the Trades Union Congress were not of importance comparable to the complete freedom of the workers in the industrial field. The most important were the codification of the criminal law (still not achieved) and the reform of the jury system. (This also has not been achieved. To this day, juries are not drawn from the working class, and the administration of justice bears clear marks of this fact.) On social questions they had very little to say—very little more than to express approval of small holdings and easy methods of house purchase. They wished for a bill granting workmen's compensation without the limitations attaching to the common law principle of employers' liability, which involved proving that the employer was personally at fault and was further limited by the doctrine of "common employment," excluding liability for accidents due to the negligence of a fellow-employee. This latter defect was remedied in 1880; but for workmen's compensation proper the Trade Unions had to wait until 1896. Finally, in the electoral field, they wanted the town franchise to be extended to the country seats; but so mild were their desires even here that in 1882 and 1883 the Trades Union Congress rejected as inopportune resolutions in favour of universal suffrage.

It is not surprising, therefore, that the most representative leaders of the British working class are in this period to be found outside the ranks of the Trade Union leaders. Indeed, at this time the Trade Unionists counted for very little in political history compared with the Radicals. The Radicals were not only in closer touch with the mass of the people; they were more energetic, more aware of realities, and with a more intelligent programme. (As early as 1869 Engels, surveying the once famous by-election at Southwark, had hoped that Bradlaugh would stand against George Odger, the Trade Unionist, and beat him.) Chamberlain and Dilke, since pure Republicanism seemed to have lost its appeal, had gradually adopted a social policy which harmonized with Liberal principles but had an embryo of Socialism in it. Chamberlain was Mayor of Birmingham in 1873, 1874 and 1875, and under his impetus the City Corporation entered on a career of what later would have been called "municipal Socialism." Gasworks, waterworks and a sewage farm were purchased; slums were pulled down and "artisans' dwellings" were put up. There were free libraries and art galleries. In January 1875, Chamberlain was largely responsible for the calling of a conference of municipal authorities which, though it dealt mainly with sanitation, gave gratifying general support to his ideas.

By now the Radicals were generally regarded as a distinct section of the Liberal Party—the working-class section. Their leaders might not be workers (though Bradlaugh had been a private in the army) but the Radical clubs were almost always mainly working-class in membership. It was a recognized technique for them to use their position within the great Liberal Party to secure advantages over their middle-class allies. Professor Beesly, the Positivist whose assistance had been of inestimable value to the Junta in the 'sixties, wrote a letter in 1880 to F. W. Soutter (who was endeavouring to increase working-class influence on the occasion of another Southwark by-election), which shows this process in operation:

"I think your idea of calling a Radical meeting in support of Rogers and Cohen is a good one. You would thus preserve your independent action and show you had decided as a body to support the present candidates while at the same time not amalgamating with the middle-class organization. You would then be free and prepared when an election comes to act with that organization or not, according as it behaves."

Chamberlain and his colleagues were adepts at making the Liberal Party behave. What appeared to be their greatest success came in 1877. It was the organization of a federation of local Liberal Associations, which subscribed to the "Birmingham Plan" and became the formidable National Liberal Federation, with Schnadhorst as organizer. Bradlaugh's influence brought in the London Radical clubs. The new Federation was largely responsible for the Liberal victory at the General Election in 1880, and in the end Gladstone had to find places in his ministry for both Chamberlain and Dilke. Dilke before long saw his career end in the divorce court, but Chamberlain and Bradlaugh remained as leaders.

Bradlaugh was elected M.P. in 1880, and was prevented from taking his seat because he was an atheist. He was forcibly ejected amid scenes that recalled the removal of Wilkes. He was re-elected in 1881, 1882 and 1884; the House of Commons did not indeed seat a Luttrell in his place, but in every other way it imitated its eighteenth-century forebears' obstinacy. But in 1886 he was allowed to affirm and to take his seat, and a further advance of Radicalism was confirmed thereby.

In 1881 an Electric Lighting Bill was passed which gave a further instalment of municipal Socialism by empowering town councils to supply electricity without a special Act. Other Acts sponsored by Chamberlain were passed to favour the small employer against the great; the bankruptcy laws were reformed in 1883; and the Patent Act was passed. Next year a Reform Act made law another great section of the old Chartist demands—the county franchise was made the same as the town, and the farm labourers were thus enfranchised as well as those miners who had been left outside before. In June 1885, Parliamentary seats were redistributed, many half-rotten seats being destroyed, and the same year Chamberlain put out an "unauthorized programme" which excited enormous popular enthusiasm. It went to the extreme limits to which Radicalism could go without becoming Socialism. Chamberlain's argument, which reads in parts like a revival of Paine's programme in his *Rights of Man*, ran as follows:

Private property having, by the development of industry, taken the place of communal ownership, the owners of it owed a "ransom" which they should be made to pay. What should that ransom consist of? Of raising the condition of the "lower orders," of free education, good housing, fair rents, compulsory powers for the municipalities to buy land at a fair price, payment of M.P.s, the abolition of plural voting, Church disestablishment, security of tenure for farmers, and the revision of the system of taxation. To this Jesse Collings, his close ally, added the scheme for smallholdings which achieved temporary fame as "three acres and a cow." Before this, Henry George had toured Britain in 1882 and 1884. His *Progress and Poverty* had been published in 1879, selling (according to supporters) about 100,000 copies in three years. Its basis was the "single tax" on land values, which he believed would be a final solution to all economic difficulties. Land, in his doctrine, belonged of right to the whole people of the country, and alienations made in one generation could not bind the next. Private occupancy and use of land were necessary, and the land must continue to be allocated to the individuals who would pay the highest rent for any given parcel. But this rent should be paid to the community, no more being left to landlords than would induce them to continue to collect it and act as land agents. Since the total of rents, even thus diminished, was always far more than enough to meet the expenses of any Government that existed in Henry George's day, all other taxes on manufactures, imports, exports, documents, buildings, personal property and so on would vanish. Nothing made by man would be taxed and universal free trade would be rapidly established.

After the Reform Acts of 1884 and 1885 had enfranchised the main body of the workers living outside the parliamentary boroughs and had redistributed seats so as to give effect to the changed balance of the electorate, Joseph Chamberlain anticipated the rapid success of his new "Radical Programme," which he claimed, should be henceforward the programme of the Liberal Party. "At last," he wrote, "the majority of the nation will be represented by a majority in the House of Commons, and ideas and wants and claims which have hitherto been ignored in legislation will find a voice in Parliament, and will compel the attention of statesmen. Radicalism, which has been the creed of the most numerous section of the Liberal Party outside the House of Commons, will henceforward be a powerful factor inside the walls of the popular Chamber. The stage of agitation has passed, and the time for action has come." And the programme itself proclaimed that Socialism was "not a stigma, but a modern tendency, pressing for recognition," and that "the path of legislative progress in England has been for years, and must continue to be, distinctly Socialistic." It clearly indicated that the continuance of the monarchy must be subject to the good behaviour of the monarch as a mere figurehead for an essentially democratic government.

It is significant that, almost simultaneously with Chamberlain's "Radical Programme," there appeared under the title, *The New Liberal Programme*, a collective volume to which a number of Trade Union Members of Parliament contributed their views. George Howell, Thomas Burt and Ben Pickard all set down their ideas; but not one of them had a single measure of an even remotely socialistic character to suggest. They did not even propose any sort of industrial legislation; their contributions, apart from vague phrases about Radicalism and democracy, were concerned with Home Rule for Ireland, smallholdings for agricultural workers, temperance reform, and similar proposals which, however estimable, in no way marked them off as representatives of the working class. Their views were not in advance of Chamberlain's; they were an immense way behind.

What is here of importance is that the imperialist Radicalism of Chamberlain and his group represented the extremity of the divorce between Radicalism in home affairs and opposition to the advance of economic imperialism in the world as a whole. The domestic Radical programme, like the Fabian programme of a few years later, rested on the assumption that home and foreign affairs had in practice very little connection. At home, the task of the Radicals was to promote a more even distribution of wealth; but the wealth that was to be redistributed was taken for granted, without any examination of its sources. It was regarded, in effect, as natural and assured that Great Britain, as the leader of world industrialism, should go on getting richer and richer, and should devote her surplus capital resources to the exploitation of the less developed regions of the world, drawing therefrom an increasing tribute which Radical legislation would proceed to redistribute by means of taxation more equitably between the rich and the poor in Great Britain.

Even in home affairs there was, of course, no questioning of the fundamentals of Capitalism. The Chamberlainites did indeed develop, especially in Birmingham, a "gas and water Socialism" based on the public ownership of essential utility services. But they had no thought of nationalizing the general run of productive industries. Outside the sphere of "municipal Socialism," they meant by "socialistic legislation" not the extension of public ownership but only heavier taxation of the rich and a greater care by the State for the development of social services.

The Radicalism of 1885 did, however, seem to contemporary opinion very radical indeed. The extension of the electorate under the Reform Act of 1884 added over two-thirds to the number of voters. In Great Britain in 1866 the total electorate had been only 1,200,000. It was 2,250,000 in 1869, and had grown by 700,000 more by 1883. In 1886, after the new Acts, it was 5,000,000; and democracy seemed to have been secured at last—even though the population of Britain numbered 31,400,000, so that many men, as well as all women, were still excluded from the right to vote. What had happened in effect was that the franchise had ceased at last, in the counties as well as in the boroughs, to be a class-privilege; and accordingly there seemed to be substance in the view that for the future Parliament would have to govern the country with an eye to the interests and wishes of the majority of the people.

In fact, however, Chamberlain's Radical Programme came to nothing. The General Election of 1885 had been handsomely won by the Liberals; but in the following year Gladstone resigned when his Home Rule Bill was defeated on a second reading, and appealed to the electors. The result was a victory for the Conservatives, reinforced by the Liberal

Unionists who had refused to stomach Irish Home Rule, among whom was Chamberlain himself. From 1886 to 1892 the Conservatives were in power, and coercion in Ireland for the most part elbowed social reform out of the way of parliamentary attention. The Conservatives did indeed reform Local Government in 1888, setting up elected County Councils to replace the nominated justices in the administration of county affairs; and they went a long way towards abolishing "payment by results," whereby grants from the State depended on individual examination, in the elementary schools, and, in 1891, made elementary education generally free of school fees. The School Boards, though nominally confined to elementary education, were in practice allowed some latitude in providing for education of a higher type; and secondary education was also aided through the grants for classes in science and art made through the Science and Art Department. There was also a steady, though not spectacular, growth of technical education. They did also pass the Housing Act of 1890, under which the powers of local authorities, both to clear insanitary dwellings and to provide houses, were considerably extended; and they did provide an almost abortive Allotments Act in 1887. But these measures fell far behind the Radical demands; and in the great working-class agitations of the 'eighties the Trade Unions and the unemployed had to fight their own battles, without the backing of either of the great parties. Gladstone had never understood or sympathized with the economic claims of the workers; and in his old age he was almost exclusively occupied with the question of Home Rule.

During these years of opposition the Radicals were struggling inside the Liberal Party, in the hope of bringing it over bodily to their own point of view. But Chamberlain, their outstanding propagandist, had already deserted them over Home Rule, and become in effect the leader of Liberal Unionism. In 1895 he was to become a member of a Conservative Cabinet. Deprived of his driving force, the Radicals could do but little. They secured in 1892 the adoption by the Liberals of the "Newcastle Programme," which included some very Radical political demands, such as "one man one vote," and the "ending or mending" of the House of Lords, triennial parliaments and payment of members, but was weak and ambiguous in its economic proposals. It promised amendment of the land laws, compulsory acquisition of land for allotments and for other public purposes, employers' liability for industrial accidents, and very vaguely some limitation in excessive hours of labour. But it was very much in the nature of a compromise; and when the Liberals came back to office in 1892, no spate of social legislation followed. Sir William Harcourt introduced graduated death duties on large estates in the Budget of 1894; and a Factory Act limiting overtime for young persons, and laying down regulations for statutory holidays and for precautions in dangerous trades, followed in 1895. But Home Rule still dominated the situation as long as Gladstone remained; and when, after the overwhelming defeat of his Home Rule Bill in the House of Lords, Rosebery succeeded him in 1894, the Government was too weak to do more than stagger on towards defeat. In 1895 the Conservatives came back, to remain in office for no less than ten years. Workmen's Compensation, on a basis wide enough to cover accidents for which the employer could not be held to blame, was left over to be conceded by the new Conservative Government in 1896.

CHAPTER XXXIV

THE REVIVAL OF SOCIALISM—
THE SOCIAL DEMOCRATIC FEDERATION

THE decline of the Radicals was not due to the misadventures or treacheries of a few leaders, or to the intrigues of even such an organizer of genius as Schnadhorst. It was due in part to the faults of the programme itself. The fallacies of Henry George's programme are obvious, though this is not the place to expose them; and the levying of "ransom" on capitalists is possible only so long as they are willing and able to pay it. But it was due also to the emergence of a new movement which demanded and promised a great deal more than the Radicals had ever done—the Socialist movement. And the spread of this movement coincided, in time, with the irruption of the unskilled into the quiet circle of skilled Trade Unionism, and was indeed in certain aspects the same event.

The Socialist movement can be shown to have sprung directly out of the Radical movement. The Democratic Federation was founded on 8 June 1881, it was intended to be based on Radical working-men's clubs, and its principles were purely Radical: the only Socialist item among them was the nationalization of the land. Though Hyndman's *England for All* was published in the same month, the Federation did not take the name "Social Democratic Federation" (S.D.F.) till August 1884. It dominated English Socialism from its inception. The Guild of St. Matthew, a Christian Socialist body (using those adjectives in their literal sense and not the Continental political sense) was of small weight. The Fabian Society, founded in 1884, was non-revolutionary and specifically abandoned such general principles as the abolition of the wage-system or the right to the whole produce of labour. It fairly soon worked out a practical rival policy of its own, but it was almost wholly a middle-class body and its period of power was to begin in the next decade. The S.D.F. outshone it for years. The Federation was the first Socialist political body to exist in Britain, and the first Socialist organization of any size since the disappearance of Owenism. Its inspiration was Marx's, relayed through his most eminent English pupil, H. M. Hyndman. In appearance, the conditions were favourable for the production of the same phenomenon as was produced sooner or later in Germany, France, Italy, Spain, Austria, Hungary, Holland, Denmark, Norway, Sweden, and even Russia—the organization of a great Marxist-Socialist party, to which there might or might not be rivals and opposition, but which it was impossible not to recognize as a mass organ of the working class. In addition, the two inspirers lived in London, and the movement developed under their eyes.

Yet Britain was the one European industrial country where this failed to happen. For that there were two reasons, one of major and one of minor importance. The minor reason was that Marx and Engels refused their support and advice to the

Marxist party. In no other country did this occur, and the cause was mainly personal. *England For All* was in part an exposition of Marx's views, but Hyndman had not acknowledged Marx by name. He had merely referred to "the work of a great thinker and original writer, which will . . . mostly be inaccessible to the majority of my countrymen." Marx was ill, ageing and over-sensitive; Hyndman was tactless in himself as well as in his writings. Marx took the words as a deliberate slight, and he and Engels broke off relations with Hyndman and the S.D.F. In 1893, Engels went so far as to patronize the wholly un-Marxist I.L.P. and to endorse Aveling's action in sitting on the executive as a Marxist representative.

But if conditions had been ready for a great Marxist success, it is hardly likely that personal squabbles would have stood in the way for long. And in everybody's belief conditions were more than favourable. Hyndman fixed 1889, the centenary of the French Revolution, as the date for the commencement of "the complete international Social Revolution." H. H. Champion, a colleague of his with military training, spent months drilling the unemployed. R. B. Cunninghame Graham (a crofters' M.P. and Scots laird), and William Morris the poet, actually headed an attack, a few years later, on the police in Trafalgar Square. Marx and Engels themselves were inclined to believe that the Social Revolution, whose false dawn they had so often saluted, was at last really rising upon the horizon.

They were all mistaken, but before the reasons for their mistake can be understood it is necessary briefly to explain what was the Marxist doctrine spread among the English workers in the 'eighties. Marxism falls most conveniently into three parts. There is, firstly, the "Dialectic," a philosophical system which can, for our present purposes, be left aside, as it had at that time no influence on the British working class, and was understood, or even regarded, by very few even of the propagandists. The operative parts of Marxism for the S.D.F. were the Labour Theory of Value and the Materialist Conception of History. The Labour Theory of Value was a system of economics which appeared to show that the existing economic system was rapidly and inevitably proceeding to its own destruction. Briefly summarized, it is as follows.

All economic value is created by labour. Capital, which is the stored-up product of labour, creates no value: it merely transfers to finished commodities the labour-value of which it is the embodiment. But the labourers, though they create all the value, receive back only a part of it—only as much as is necessary for their subsistence, that is, for the maintenance of the requisite supply of labourers of different types and degrees of skill. The rest of the value created by labour becomes *surplus value*, and is appropriated by the capitalists, who thus, by virtue of their monopoly of ownership of the means of production, seize for themselves the benefits resulting from the increasing productivity of labour. This happens because the labourers, deprived of independent access to the means of production, are forced to sell their labour-power to the capitalists at a valuation determined in the same way as other commodity values—by the amount of labour required to produce it, or in other words its necessary subsistence cost.

As capitalism develops, more and more capital is needed to set a labourer to work. The "composition of capital" changes, as between *constant capital* and *variable capital*. By "variable capital" Marx means the sums expended on the employment of labour, and by "constant capital" all other capital. Marx uses these terms because he holds that the entire surplus value is attributable to the variable capital, which thus varies in amount as a result of the productive process, whereas all other capital remains constant in amount and merely transfers its value to the final product unchanged.

As variable capital becomes a smaller proportion of the total capital employed, the rate of surplus value, calculated upon the entire capital, tends to fall, since surplus value arises solely from the variable part of the capital. This tendency involves a falling rate of profit, which the capitalists are constantly endeavouring to counteract. They attempt this both by a lengthening of the duration of the working day, and by increasing the intensity of labour within each working hour; whereas the workers struggle to reduce the hours of labour and to check its intensification. Capitalists, in order to increase productivity, are continually impelled to introduce fresh labour-saving devices, although these involve a continual increase in the proportion of constant to variable capital. The workmen, tied down to subsistence wages by the law of capitalist production, receive a steadily diminishing proportion of the total product. The mass of surplus value and of profit goes on increasing even though the *rate*, calculated on the volume of capital, falls off. In this sense the workers are subject to a law of increasing misery, in that the proportion which they receive of the total value which they create continually declines. In addition to this, Marx believed that the absolute position of the artisans and lower middle classes would get worse, as the increasing concentration of capital flung down more of them into the ranks of the proletariat. He did not—and probably could not, at the time—realize the extent to which capitalist development would create a new middle class of salaried workers or afford opportunities for an increase in many kinds of professional and service employment.

This maldistribution of the product of industry connotes a very high and increasing rate of *capitalist accumulation*. The capitalists, receiving more surplus value than they wish to spend upon their own consumption, invest at a pace which is continually threatening to outrun the demand for finished commodities, since this demand is restricted by the limited consuming power at the command of the workers, who form the great majority of the population. Whenever capitalist accumulation results in a supply of goods largely in excess of the quantity that can be sold at remunerative prices, there ensues a *capitalist crisis*, which can be disposed of only by writing off a considerable fraction of the accumulated capital as lost. The process then begins over again; but in Marx's view capitalist crises tend to become increasingly severe. This is the case, not only because the tendency to over-accumulation is cumulative, but also because the entry of fresh national groups of capitalists into the field of developed capitalist production deprives capitalism of the means of dumping its surplus commodities upon the undeveloped parts of the world—to the ruin of native industries and standards of living. Capitalism becomes increasingly competitive, as between rival national groups, even while within each country competition is being more and more limited by the swallowing up of the smaller capitalists and the concentration of power in the hands of those who are able to organize production on the grand scale. Out of these international capitalist rivalries develops economic imperialism, leading inevitably to world war, and in the end to the collapse of capitalist production by its own unstable weight. Herein lie the growing contradictions of capitalism— its tendency to defeat itself by producing more than it allows society the means of consuming, and its tendency, by filling up the world with rival capitalist groups, to destroy its power to get rid abroad of the surplus products which cannot be consumed at home.

Based upon the Theory of Value was the inspiring philosophy which directed the new revolutionaries, the Materialist Conception of History. In one aspect, this can be regarded as a development of the Owenite thesis that "Man's character is formed for and not by him." The general shape of men's thinking, Marx held, is conditioned by the underlying economic circumstances of each historical epoch. Men's *ideas* did not make the broad movement of history: it would be truer to say that history shaped men's ideas.

The superstructure of morality and ideas—the "ideology" of human beings—was a reflection of their economic relations. Human history, so regarded, fell into certain obvious periods, to which Marx gave the name of the Asiatic, the ancient, the feudal and the bourgeois. Each of these depended upon certain forms of property-relation, and the destruction of each one was due to these forms of property-relation becoming fetters upon production. Consequently, each rising class had had to burst its bonds; it had had to fight the existing owners of the means of production; all history till now had been a history of class struggles.

The most revolutionary class in the past had been the bourgeoisie; it had transformed the whole of the earth and rescued millions from "the idiocy of rural life." But like its predecessors it had produced its own grave-diggers; it had thrown great masses of expropriated labourers together into factories, and at the same time as this army grew greater and more organized the capitalist system advanced toward economic collapse. When the proletarian victory was complete, there would be no other submerged class to challenge it; the long tale of class struggles would end, and "human history would begin."

Now whether or no this prophecy was wholly exact, this is not the place to determine; but what is certain is that neither Marx nor Engels had a true appreciation of the time that would be required for the process to work itself out. They continually antedated the revolution. Once they had, as they believed, grasped and explained the process by which the working class would oust its exploiters, they expected the operation to begin forthwith. Modern psychology did not exist, and though Engels in his *Feuerbach* allowed that existing ideologies might delay the operation of economic forces, neither of them realized how slowly men's minds could react to changed circumstances. They continually believed the revolution to be round the corner. In 1849 they were young, and might have been excused the illusions of youth, but in 1858 Marx had written to Engels "on the Continent the revolution is imminent and will also immediately assume a Socialist character." In 1859, when there was scarcely a Chartist to be found surviving, Marx was expecting an immediate Chartist victory: "I have broken with Ernest Jones," he wrote. "He has disorganized the Chartist Party. . . . Imagine an army whose general goes over to the enemy on the day of battle." (Ernest Jones's fault was that he had shared a platform with some Radicals of the Bright type.) In 1867, when the International appeared strong, Marx wrote to Engels: "In the next revolution, which is perhaps nearer than it seems, we (i.e. you and I) have this powerful machinery *in our hands*."

Despite, therefore, their contempt for Hyndman and his colleagues, they were prepared to expect the Revolution in England in the 'eighties. In 1886, James Mawdsley, the leader of the Lancashire cotton operatives, told the International Trades Union Congress that he "did not understand their Socialism; he had not studied it as perhaps he ought to have done. The workmen of England," the report continues, "were not so advanced as the workmen of the Continent. Nevertheless, they possessed at least one clear conception; they realized that the actual producers did not obtain their share of the wealth they created." Here, less hopeful observers than the Marxists might have concluded, was a clear example of the working-class leader who was gradually realizing the truth of the Marxist position and would shortly align himself and his followers on the proletarian side of the class war.

But no such thing resulted. The Cotton Unions remained for another half-century as cautious and inert as they had been. Mawdsley, so far from becoming a Socialist leader, stayed not even a Liberal; in 1906 he stood for Parliament as a Conservative. The solid Unions built by the Junta, with their membership of Victorian Liberals, were not shaken by a logical demonstration of the fact of the class war, or changed in their habits by the changing economic circumstances of the era of imperialism. The obstacles to the advance of revolutionary Socialism appeared momentarily to be swamped in the swirl of the 'eighties, but they were too deeply bedded to be moved by a sudden flood.

The flood, though, was impressive for a time. A short revival of trade between 1881 and 1883 faded away, leaving a savage depression that dragged down wages and seemed to make the strongest Unions worthless. The tonnage of ships built in these years (quoted by the Webbs) shows the trend in a highly marked form:

1883	..	..	..	..	1,250,000 tons
1884	..	..	..	..	750,000 „
1885	..	..	..	..	540,000 „
1886	..	..	..	..	473,000 „

Parliamentary investigations reinforced these figures by horrible disclosures. There was a Royal Commission on the Housing of the Poor, and one on the Depression of Trade; a Select Committee of the House of Lords on the Poor Law and another on the Sweating System. The S.D.F. sprang into enormous temporary importance. It had been checked at the opening of its career by a quarrel between Morris and Hyndman. Morris, Walter Crane, Belfort Bax, Eleanor Marx and some others seceded to form the Socialist League, a short-lived body whose only abiding influence was in the Clyde area.

(In 1889 it was captured by the Anarchists, the parliamentary Socialists having left it: William Morris was removed from the editorship of its organ, the *Commonweal*, an action which put an end to any importance it might have had.) Hyndman, Champion, John Burns and Harry Quelch were left to run the S.D.F. They organized and even drilled the unemployed. The victims of the depression were being left to the mercies of Victorian charity when in January 1886 a procession in which Hyndman and Burns were concerned was turned aside by the police and consoled itself by shattering the windows of the Pall Mall clubs. The Lord Mayor's relief fund leapt in the next few days from £30,000 to £79,000. Hyndman and Burns were prosecuted in April and after a sensational speech by the latter (reprinted as *The Man with the Red Flag*) were acquitted. In November 1887, Cunninghame Graham and Burns vainly attempted to storm Trafalgar Square against the police at the head of the unemployed; Alfred Linnell, the first English Socialist martyr, died of injuries received from the police in the conflict.

> They will not learn: they have no ears to hearken.
> They turn their faces from the eyes of fate,
> Their gay-lit halls shut out the skies that darken,
> But lo! this dead man knocking at the gate.
> *Not one, not one, nor thousands must they slay,*
> *But one and all, if they would dusk the day.*

wrote William Morris. But his warning was without basis: the revolution was not at hand. The S.D.F. had in 1885 made a trial of popular feeling at a tribunal more sober than a packed crowd in Trafalgar Square; it had fought elections, and that it had taken Tory money was not a sufficient explanation of the disastrous poll of its candidates, falling as low as 32 in Kennington. There was no rooted popular support for revolutionary politics. When trade revived in 1888 and 1889 the influence of the S.D.F. rapidly fell away.

But this did not mean the disappearance of British Socialism; it meant the emergence of a Socialism of distinctively British type—based, that is, on the contemporary conditions and states of mind of the British workers and their middle-class allies.

British Socialism, as a practical force, took shape in Fabianism and in Keir Hardie's essentially empirical and non-doctrinaire movement for independent Labour representation. Proclaiming a Socialist system as their objective, both the Fabian Society and the Independent Labour Party set out in practice to get, not Socialism, but social changes pointing in a Socialist direction. James Keir Hardie, a miner and organizer of the Ayrshire miners, graduated out of Liberalism and concentrated his practical propaganda largely upon the minimum wage, the legal limitation of hours of labour, and the "Right to Work." The Fabians, led by Sidney Webb and Bernard Shaw, gave full support to these working-class demands, and added to them projects for the gradual transformation of the police State of capitalism into the welfare State which, in order to ensure to the people the means of decent living, would find itself compelled to take the ownership and control of the means of production into public hands. Fabianism was the new Benthamism, seeking the "greatest happiness of the greatest number," not by means of *laissez-faire*, but through the collective control of the economic forces of society, and regarding Socialism as simply the logical consummation of a progressive policy of social reform.

Socialism of this sort was so directly based on British conditions as to have about it, inevitably, very little that was international, beyond a general sympathy with the parallel aspirations of the workers in other countries. It had assuredly no thought of world-revolution. It was definitely reformist, permeative, evolutionary—seeking to get its way by logic rather than by main force, and welcoming the conversion of any of its opponents to some particular reform which it favoured. It envisaged Socialism as a heap of reforms to be built by the droppings of a host of successive swallows who would in the end make a Socialist summer; and in this spirit it managed to express an essentially Socialist philosophy in terms of immediate proposals which made a strong appeal to many reformers who were by no means Socialists. The Fabians were pleased at this: they declared their policy to be one of "permeation"—that is, of getting Liberals and Tories to take up Socialist ideas without understanding their Socialist

CP: P

implications. It has, of course, to be borne in mind that the Fabians took this line at a time when there was no Labour Party, and when the only chance of getting a reform carried out was to get one or other of the traditional parties to take it up.

Of course, this attitude, plain enough in Fabianism (for example, when the Fabians, for the most part, supported the South African War), was much less plain in the Independent Labour Party; for Keir Hardie and his followers had in them a spirit of insurgency which made them instinctively take sides with the Left both at home and abroad. But in practical demands the I.L.P. and the Fabians were not far apart; and even in attitude, as Keir Hardie aged, they tended to come closer together. The I.L.P. under J. R. MacDonald and Philip Snowden became as evolutionary and gradualist as the Fabian Society itself; and MacDonald, in his *Socialism and Society* and other writings, produced an evolutionary theory of Socialism which went far beyond the sweet reasonableness of *Fabian Essays*.

Thus, even though the I.L.P. took up the cudgels against imperialism as expressed in the South African War, Socialism in Great Britain counted for very little as an anti-imperialist force. Nor was this wholly because it was not strong enough to count. Many of the Fabians, especially Bernard Shaw, were not without a touch of the imperialist spirit. Shaw, for example, intensely disliked small nations and backward peoples as obstacles to the onward march of civilization, and was inclined to regard the British Empire—despite the rude things he often said about it—as a potentially civilizing force; while the Fabian love of order and competent administration made many of the Fabian leaders exceedingly impatient of anarchic "Leftism" in all its forms.

Moreover, Imperialism, though it was in due course to become identified with the Conservative Party, had, at the outset, some of its outstanding supporters well on the Left. Dilke and Chamberlain were Radicals who combined the demand for a domestic policy of radical reforms with a deep belief in the civilizing mission of the "Anglo-Saxon race." Dilke, as we have seen, had begun, in *Greater Britain*, with dreams of "Republican reunion" of Great Britain and the United States into a single Power strong enough to guide the whole world along the paths of righteousness, and to administer a decisive checkmate to the Russian powers of darkness, which seemed to him to represent the one grave threat to the onward march of humanity. This dream of reunion faded soon; but there remained the belief that Great Britain and her white colonies might, on terms of close amity with their "cousins" in America, advance the cause of civilization over all the world.

CHAPTER XXXV

THE DOCK STRIKE AND THE INDEPENDENT LABOUR PARTY

THE place of the political revolutionary movement was taken instantly by an even more impressive upheaval, whose leaders were for the most part the same persons. The unskilled and semi-skilled workers, whom Trade Unionism had for years forgotten, rose up in revolt. They formed Unions which not only had temporary successes, but remained as permanent parts of British society. They brought to the attention of the public, and of the later historian, a whole section of humanity which had been forgotten. In this history stress has been laid on the real monetary advantages which many Victorian workers had secured. They were no longer the famished and savage ghosts of Chartist days; they were skilled craftsmen of sober appearance and often (as John Burns gibed) with gold alberts across reasonably expansive black waistcoats. Even more stress was laid upon them in contemporary accounts. Ragged schools and religious charities would take care of the incurably shiftless; the rest of the industrious population wa presumed to be continually on the up-grade. Charles Booth's investigation into *Life and Labour in London* (begun in order to refute S.D.F. propaganda) and the great dock strike of 1889 showed up enormous stagnant pools of misery and degradation which society and the Trade Union leaders had both forgotten. When Robert Lowe, as Chancellor of the Exchequer, proposed a tax upon matches which would have thrown a number of East End women out of work, Westminster was invaded by a "deputation" of filthy and haggard harridans whom the London which saw them for the first time considered to be only half human. When Burns spoke upon Tower Hill to his dockers only a small part of his speeches was devoted to Union demands: a large section was turned to urging them to behave as human beings—not to beat their wives, not to fight one another savagely, not to drink themselves stupid at the first opportunity. The most oppressed and unhappiest of human beings, those who were nearest to the animal, now had recovered their humanity and demanded their rights. They naturally took as leaders those who were most fiercely in opposition to respectable society; they were not (though the mistake was natural) for that convinced Socialists.

The storm broke, with the sudden violence of a thunderstorm, in August 1889. But there had been premonitory rumbles. The rule of the Parliamentary Committee, headed by Broadhurst, had been repeatedly challenged at Trades Union Congresses by delegates who demanded, with varying degrees of vehemence, the class-war policy outlined by the S.D.F. The Parliamentary Committee resisted mild and extreme resolutions alike, if they were unpalatable to orthodox Liberalism, and if it was defeated did not adopt the new proposals, but merely dropped the old from its own platform. Nationalization of the land was first proposed in 1879, and defeated. A legal eight-hour day was actually carried (in a very thin house) in 1883, but laid aside. The Parliamentary Committee was generally victorious, but its critics' ranks were continually increased. Keir Hardie was the most feared among them; but the two most extreme delegates were members of the arch-reactionary Union, the model creation of the Junta, the Amalgamated Society of Engineers. Their names were Tom Mann and John Burns, and they both belonged to the S.D.F. At the Dundee Congress (1889) it looked momentarily as though Broadhurst might sustain a defeat, but his enemies had made the error of attacking him personally and spitefully, with charges of corruption which were not generally believed, and they were heavily defeated, polling only eleven votes.

More serious events than resolutions occurred outside the Congress. The sliding scales, which had worked so disastrously after 1875, had nowhere pressed more hardly, or been more faithfully observed, than in coal-mining. The National Union of Miners, or what was left of it, was now controlled by the Durham and Northumberland Societies, whose leaders, true to the Liberal policy of the Junta, were pretty steady in their support of sliding scales and opposed even a legal eight-hour day (which might have worsened the conditions of the most influential section, the hewers). Other mining areas, more weakly organized, heartily disagreed, and in 1888 they formally broke away and created the Miners' Federation of Great Britain.

Nearly all observers, and the Socialists themselves, had assumed the revolutionary supporters would be recruited among the organized and intelligent working class. The S.D.F., it is true, till 1897 proclaimed that the existing Unions were too hopelessly involved in the capitalist system to be of use to Socialists; but their members as much as other propagandists believed that Union members, or likely Union members, were their best "prospects."

The first sign of a move by others came in July 1888, when Mrs. Besant, who was abandoning at once her Radicalism and her friend Bradlaugh, accidentally brought about seven hundred London match girls out on strike. She had written a fierce denunciation of the conditions under which the women worked, not thinking that they possessed the power to defend themselves; to her surprise they read her article and struck. With Herbert Burrows, she was able to raise about £400 for them and win their battle.

This was only a spark; the blaze was to come. One more flash occurred before it. In August 1889, the London gas-workers, hastily organized by Mann, Burns and Will Thorne—a gas-worker—presented a demand for the eight-hour day. After a few days, to the universal surprise, the companies agreed without a struggle. But the agreement brought no general calm. The atmosphere was electric. The weather was stiflingly

hot; there was heat in men's minds as well as in the air.
A small dispute would be enough to cause a grand explosion;
the small dispute came on 13 August, 1889. A few labourers
at the South-West India Dock struck work over a trivial dispute. Tom Mann and John Burns, already agitators-of-all-
work, were called in to assist; Ben Tillett, a teetotal labourer
who had founded two years before a tiny "Tea Workers' and
General Labourers' Union," was the chief organizer from the
ranks. The secretaries of the Stevedores' and Lightermen's
Unions, the aristocrats of the docks, also assisted. On Monday
the 19th meetings were held outside the East India Dock gates
at which it was announced by the organizers that a Dockers'
Union had been formed. From those meetings, like water from
a burst pipe, the strikers flowed from dock to dock, bringing
their fellow-workers out. By the next day, for the first time
since 1797, the Port of London was closed. As far away as
Tilbury, twenty miles off, Harry Orbell kept his fellow-dockers
on strike as if he were defending an isolated fortress.

The same Monday Burns took the most dramatic step to
victory, one which was possibly in the end the chief single
cause of success. Conspicuous with his black beard and white
straw hat, he led a great procession of the striking dockers
round the City of London. There were forty-one banners,
some no more than red rags on poles, but some stranger.
There were stinking onions, old fish-heads, and indescribable
pieces of meat stuck on spikes, to show the City magnates what
the dockers had to live on. Each day the processions were
repeated, growing larger and larger, and commonly ending
in Hyde Park.

The demands of the dockers were meagre enough. They
were for a minimum wage of sixpence an hour, the abolition
of contract work (the source of the worst sweating) and some
minor reforms. The dock companies refused even to discuss
them, being confident that creatures so degraded as the
labourers had no staying power and would rapidly be defeated.
No organization was behind the strikers. The leaders had to
improvise a system of relief for tens of thousands, as well as to
organize pickets and run the strike. Wade's Arms, the public
house which was their centre, was pandemonium from morning

till night. Only the subscriptions brought in by Burns's demonstrative processions prevented the strikers giving way from sheer starvation.

A fortnight passed, and the end seemed to be near. The strike committee's minutes of Thursday 29th say: "Information received that at present finances were running short. Resolved: that a notice be posted outside that no further relief can be given this day." As a last desperate resort the leaders decided to call a general strike for Monday. There was little likelihood, London organization being what it was, that the call would be answered. But what else was to be done? Starvation was very near, and a reckless last throw seemed better than ignoble defeat.

Upon the very night that this decision was taken, a meeting was held on the other side of the world which was to make it unnecessary. It was on the day of the general strike manifesto that the first gathering of the Brisbane wharf labourers was held to consider sending aid to London. The sudden rush of generous sympathy which then swept Australia defies explanation. Even the middle class was drawn in. The banks remitted money without charge. The Postmaster-General sent cables free. The Salvation Army sent the profits on the *War Cry*. Football clubs telegraphed their gate-money. Every Union sent donations, commonly in three figures. The subscriptions began to arrive in London, first in single amounts, and then in a growing shower like a hailstorm, until the Australian gifts reached the fantastic sum of £30,000.

It is difficult to say who were more astonished, the dockers or the dock companies. The whole aspect of the battle was changed. The desperate general strike manifesto was cancelled. Relief was properly organized. Blacklegs were pulled out and loafers bribed with food tickets to stay away. The companies for the first time became nervous. They issued a furious attack on the police. They had been hoping for a struggle between the police and the strikers in which batons would break down the labourers' enthusiasm; and they were foolish enough to let their disappointment be seen. Burns had wisely kept carefully on the right side of the Metropolitan Police, and had organized his processions in obedience to their advice. Superintendent Forster's helmet next to Burns's white straw at the head of the marchers was an infuriating spectacle to the company directors.

On September 5th, under pressure from a mediating committee headed by the Lord Mayor, they began at last to yield. Complicated negotiations resulted, and the Lord Mayor and others withdrew; but the Roman Catholic Cardinal Manning persisted. Terms were outlined which gave the dockers nearly all they required: Burns, on Tower Hill on September 9th, reminded a huge audience of how the garrison at Lucknow strained its eyes for the silver shine of the relieving bayonets. "This, lads, is the Lucknow of Labour, and I myself, looking to the horizon, can see a silver gleam—not of bayonets to be imbrued in a brother's blood, but the gleam of the full round orb of the dockers' tanner." As was expected, the next night at Kirby Street Catholic School the Cardinal brought to the Strike Committee official terms granting practically all their demands. The audience was so wrought up that many believed, as he raised his hand in blessing, that a brilliant light played round the Madonna and Child above his head. But more serious impulses than fairy lights moved the strike committee. They had gained practically all their demands, and on September 16th the dockers victoriously marched back to work, having won the first and biggest victory of their history.

They had won victories for a great many other workers besides themselves. Their own Dockers' Union was now not only a big organization in London but shortly organized a number of the other principal ports, and where it did not extend independent Unions were formed such as the National Union of Dock Labourers in the North. The Gas-workers' Union spread to the provinces; the agricultural labourers' Union again numbered many thousands; the General Railway Workers' Union, as rival to the Amalgamated Society of Railway Servants, enrolled thousands of unskilled railway workers; the National Amalgamated Sailors and Firemen's Union, two years old and small, shot up to a membership of 65,000. The General Union of Textile Workers (woollen workers), insignificant since its foundation in 1882, sprang into power in Yorkshire and was actually strengthened by the

big unsuccessful Manningham strike in 1890. The Webbs'
History of Trade Unionism gives figures of surprising increases
even in the older Unions. Eleven shipbuilding and metal
Unions saw their membership rise from 115,000 in 1888 to
145,000 in 1890. Ten building Unions rose from 57,000 to
80,000. The Boot and Shoe Operatives rose from 11,000 in
1888 to over 17,000 in 1891; the Amalgamated Society of
Railway Servants from 12,000 to 30,000. The new Miners'
Federation increased from 36,000 members to 147,000. The
craft Unions even made some concessions to the new spirit of
solidarity. The A.S.E. opened its ranks to other crafts, and
a Federation of Engineering and Shipbuilding Trades was
formed. But it remained weak, and the other crafts mostly
stayed outside the Amalgamated Society of Engineers.

The same year, 1889, was marked by an advance which was
small at the time, but very significant for the future—the
beginning of an understanding between the women's movement and Trade Unionism. The middle-class ladies running
the *Englishwoman's Journal* were immensely ignorant of all
trades outside those of the needlewomen and governesses whom
they chiefly had to protect, and of clerking and serving in shops,
into which they hoped to introduce more and more women.
They had no connection whatever with the women textile
workers, nor much more with chainmakers, pithead women,
and other trades; even nursing was practically the preserve of
the autocratic and terrifying Miss Nightingale. Their endeavours, therefore, looked to Trade Unionists suspiciously like
an attempt to flood industry with underpaid and unorganizable
labour. So little were they aware of realities that they induced
Henry Fawcett to attempt repeatedly to repeal the Ten Hours
Act on the ground that its provisions were an infringement of
women's liberties. The only early feminist who had any
knowledge of Trade Union problems, Mrs. Emma Paterson,
nevertheless endeavoured to secure the support of the Trades
Union Congress for the repeal: she gained the votes of the two
other women delegates only (1877). But the speech of
Broadhurst as spokesman for the Parliamentary Committee
showed that the Trade Unionists had as long a journey to
travel as the feminists. "It is natural," he said, "for ladies to

be impatient of restraint at any time . . . [but it is] the duty of
men and husbands to bring about a condition of things when
their wives should be in their proper sphere at home instead
of being dragged into competition of livelihood with the great
and strong men of the world."

But in 1889 the great and strong men of the world at last
concluded that they had better assist their sisters to protect
themselves. Mrs. Paterson's tiny Women's Protective and
Provident League was officially adopted and patronized; its
title was changed to the Women's Trade Union League, and a
large number of existing Trade Unions became affiliated and
some even passed members across into it. More and more,
instead of fighting to expel women from industry, Union
branches would turn to the League to organize these new
competitors. ("Please send an organizer to this town as we
have decided that if the women here cannot be organized they
must be exterminated," said a letter for years piously preserved
at the League headquarters.) The hoped-for rush of new
members did not come, partly because of a decline in trade,
but partly also because of the continued intractability of
women workers; but a steady increase did result, and from
now on women everywhere, and not merely in the textile
trades, were a recognized part of the Trade Union movement,
and their interests were more and more protected and considered in industrial negotiation. Mrs. Paterson was dead, but
her place was taken by a younger generation of no less patient
and indomitable organizers, among whom the best-known
name was perhaps Mary Macarthur (wife of W. C. Anderson).

At the Liverpool Trades Union Congress of 1890 Burns and
Mann overturned with ease the "old gang" which had
defeated them at Dundee the year before. Broadhurst, disavowed by his own Union, resigned the Secretaryship. The
Eight Hours Bill was approved by 193 votes to 155. Sixty
resolutions were passed by the Congress, and of these forty-five
were sponsored by the Socialists, being, according to Burns,
"nothing more nor less than direct appeals to the State and
municipalities of this country to do for the workman what
trade unionism, 'old' and 'new,' has proved itself incapable of
doing." The resolutions were indeed pure State Socialism,

and in essence were a long distance away from the revolution-ism of the S.D.F., a fact which Burns and Mann implicitly recognized by resigning from the latter body.

For the victory of the unskilled workers did not lead to an increase in revolutionary feeling. The time (if there had ever been one) to dream of a revolutionary *coup* on the Continental model and a Commune of London, had passed with the revival of trade in 1888. The extinction of revolutionary hopes passed unnoticed in the rejoicings over the dockers' victory. But in the years after 1889 it became rapidly clearer that the energies of the Socialists were being directed to constitutional State Socialism, and that the means they had chosen were the slow ones of municipal and parliamentary electioneering. Three parliamentary seats were secured in 1892, but though these were greeted with wide rejoicing it was obvious to anyone who did some calculation of how long it would take those three to become a majority that the revolution had receded to a great distance. As in the first years of the 'eighties the policy of the extreme Left had been dominated by Hyndman and Cham-pion, and in the late 'eighties by Burns and Mann, in the 'nineties it was dominated by Keir Hardie.

Hardie had only slowly emancipated himself from Liberalism. He published in Scotland in 1887 and 1888 *The Miner*, a small but passionate sheet in defence of his fellow-workers, in which he undertook his own education as well as theirs. The second volume is more consistently Socialist than the first, but even while he was writing it he was standing as a candidate for Mid-Lanark, and hoping for Liberal adoption. In August of the same year, however, he became convinced that the Liberal Party would do nothing for the workers, and on the 25th took part in forming the Scottish Labour Party, becoming secretary himself while R. B. Cunninghame Graham was President. The programme adopted was still semi-Liberal; its chief Socialist demands were the nationalization of the railways and national banks. This was, however, Hardie's more or less con-scious policy. He wished to bring the working class first to the decision to insist on independent Labour representation, and from that to trust to the experience of facts and the educa-tional power of propaganda to get them to adopt Socialism.

Though Scotland was before any others with its Labour Party, the first independent Labour M.P.s did not sit for Scottish seats. The election of 1892 found the new party unprepared, and the only three seats that were won by independent Labour men were Battersea (John Burns), Middlesbrough (J. Havelock Wilson, the sailors' leader), and South West Ham (Keir Hardie). But this success stimulated wide hopes, which were further supported by an appearance of general Socialist unity. Morris's Socialist League had in effect disappeared. Champion, the most militant member of the S.D.F., had campaigned for Keir Hardie in a previous by-election. The Fabian Society had issued a manifesto supporting the candidatures. A newcomer of journalistic genius, Robert Blatchford, editing *The Clarion*, which he had started in 1892, expressed the same views in more vehement and popular language. All was set fair, in appearance, for the inauguration of a united Socialist constitutional party.

A hundred and twenty delegates met to that end at Bradford on 13 and 14 January 1893, under the chairmanship of Keir Hardie. Five delegates attended from the S.D.F. Dr. Aveling carried, in some sort, the blessing of Friedrich Engels personally. Robert Blatchford was present. G. Bernard Shaw and eleven other delegates represented the Fabian Society, which had greatly but silently increased its influence since its foundation. It had published *Fabian Essays* and forty-four pamphlets, all of a strictly practical character, dealing with the facts of modern industrial life and the use that could be made by Socialists of the existing municipal and parliamentary powers. Its influence was wholly anti-revolutionary and was extended by imitative societies springing up in the provinces, of which there were at one time as many as ninety. Its pamphlets were still mostly unsigned, but its guiding philosophers were already Bernard Shaw and Sidney Webb. The rest of the delegates were from the Scottish Labour Party, various local Labour Associations and a few Trade Union branches. It was the wish of this group of delegates that decided the general form of the decisions taken at Bradford. The Fabian Society decided that permeation was better done from outside the new body (though most of its local groups joined it), the S.D.F. refused to join it because it was not revolutionary. Blatchford left a little later. The conference, abandoned to the guidance of Hardie and his collaborators, formed an Independent Labour Party (I.L.P.—the name Socialist Labour Party was rejected) for the purpose of running independent Labour candidates. Its primary object was to be the "collective ownership and control of the means of production, distribution and exchange." That is, it was a Socialist Party whose object was to coax into supporting it workers who already recognized themselves as "Labour," in particular the Trade Unionists.

The formation of the party greatly increased the influence of Socialism in Britain. It held out the hopes of practical action to a great number of workers who were unable or unwilling to practise the subtle permeation of the Fabians, and considered the strict revolutionism of the S.D.F. futile. Branches were formed all over the country and staffed by enthusiastic propagandists. The next conference, just a year later, listed 280 of them, and Tom Mann was secretary. But it did not unite the Socialist movement. The abstentions of Bradford were repeated outside. In Parliament only one of the three M.P.s supported its programme—Keir Hardie. Havelock Wilson was only nominally an Independent Labour man. His Labour interests were confined solely to organizing the sailors; in the early years of the Union he did good work, but once the Union was established he abandoned any but respectable activities, and before long had acquired for himself a more disagreeable reputation than any contemporary British Trade Union leader. John Burns was already moving rapidly from his original S.D.F. position. Fabian propaganda, and the progressive programme of the new L.C.C., had greatly impressed him. Keir Hardie twice offered to serve under him in a two-man party of relentless opposition to the capitalist system, but both times Burns evaded answering. Later on he was to become a Liberal Cabinet Minister.

The Socialists had therefore to be defended at Westminster single-handedly by Keir Hardie; his championship, partly to his own surprise, was unexpectedly sensational. He was escorted to Parliament by his constituents in a charabanc on which was playing a quite small brass band. He himself wore a cloth cap. The clothing was natural to him, and so too to his supporters were the chara' and the musicians. But the violent, snobbish and vulgar uproar which was made about this in the West End and the Press turned it into a political demonstration. In February 1893 he opposed the address to the Throne, moving an amendment demanding that the Government pay attention to the condition of the unemployed, of whom, he said, no less than 1,300,000 were even then in receipt of relief or Trade Union out-of-work pay. The indignation that this excited was far outpassed by the hatred which he aroused next year. "I've been in a wild beast show at feeding-time," wrote the reporter of the West Ham local paper. "I've been at a football match when a referee gave a wrong decision. I've been at rowdy meetings of the Shoreditch Vestry and the West Ham Corporation, but in all my natural I've never witnessed a scene like this."

The occasion of this "scene" was somewhat complex. On 23 June 1894, the Duchess of York had a baby. On the same day a mining disaster at Cilfynydd killed no less than 260 workers. The next day the French President, M. Carnot, was assassinated. On the 25th, Sir William Harcourt, on behalf of the Government, moved that condolences be sent to France over the last event. Hardie rose to ask whether some official regrets should not also be sent to those bereaved by the Cilfynydd disaster. "Oh, no," replied Sir William airily, "I can dispose of that now by saying that the House does sympathize with these poor people." The fury with which this casual remark filled Hardie was genuinely incomprehensible to the rest of the House, used only to the Broadhurst type of working man. He revenged himself the only way he could see, by opposing the vote of congratulation to the Queen upon the birth of the child to the Duchess of York, and this was the intervention responsible for the scene described above.

Such explosions did not discourage the I.L.P.; they filled it with good heart. When a general election came next year (1895) it put forward twenty-eight candidates. But not one was returned, and Keir Hardie lost his seat. The mass of the British working class was not Socialist or prepared for Socialist tactics. It had been turbulent and angry for the moment, but easily sank back into apathy. The I.L.P. fell into a period of decline. The propaganda of its individual members, of the *Clarion* "vanners," of the S.D.F. members, and in their own way of the Fabians, went on; but prospects were much bleaker and speakers were more discouraged. The I.L.P. was only rescued from its decay by the miners' strike in South Wales in 1898, lasting six months. Though it ended in failure, it convinced the miners that the I.L.P. was their champion, and Keir Hardie was soon provided at Merthyr with a parliamentary seat which he held for the rest of his life. The party was now being led by a group of men who marked on it their particular philosophy—Hardie, J. Ramsay MacDonald, Philip Snowden, Bruce Glasier, F. W. Jowett and a few others —and in 1899, when the Fabians trimmed, it scored a temporary unpopularity by opposing the Boer War.

There was not much to record outside the political world. The Co-operative movement continued to prosper. Its trade, its membership and reserves expanded steadily. 1880 membership: 600,000; 1900: 1,780,000. 1880 share capital: £2,246,000; 1900: £23,256,000. The management committees with certain exceptions became more and more "practical" in their attitude. References were punctiliously made at annual meetings to Co-operative principles, but their application to day-to-day routine became less and less obvious. Societies came more and more to resemble ordinary trading concerns whose internal arrangements were slightly different from those of limited companies; they were almost wholly neglected by Socialist propagandists and theorists.

The older Unions remained impervious to the new Socialist propaganda, contesting it with the invincible weapon of apathy. Their calm was made more secure by an amendment of Standing Orders at the Trades Union Congress of 1895 which excluded from Congress all but actual workers at a trade or full-time officials, thus expelling at once Hardie, Burns and Broadhurst. Socialist resolutions were nevertheless still put forward at Congress, and in the annual general meetings of particular Unions, but even if carried they were likely to be ineffective, for so few of the rank and file voted either way.

The reforms of the Junta in the 1860's and later were now having full effect. In the earlier Trade Unions the Lodge had been everything, the centre nothing. The Lodge conducted strikes, held the funds, negotiated with the masters, administered funeral, sickness and unemployment benefit, and in consultation with other lodges controlled the society; the central office had no powers. Now the lodges' powers had been withdrawn from them one by one. Strikes were severely discouraged, and when permitted were conducted and settled by the head office. In most Unions friendly benefits were centralized. Elaborate rule books laid down the only permissible expenditure or action in almost every conceivable circumstance. Many branches (the word "lodge" was dying with the old form of organization) had no funds of their own at all. In such circumstances the members saw no reason to attend branch meetings. Attendances dropped to phenomenally low levels—2 and 3 per cent. A 10 per cent attendance was considered good; a 25 per cent one was a mass meeting. The members were still convinced of the usefulness of their Union, but they took less and less part in running it. This was true even in the 'nineties, when industrial disputes were continually exploding. Just before a strike members would roll up to branch meetings, and during it they would attend *en masse*, rather than hang round the streets; but at other times most of them would never come.

Yet there were conflicts enough to have deserved their attention. Trade fell off in 1891; the new Unions lost members heavily and the employers attacked wages. In 1893 there was a big Lancashire cotton strike, lasting nearly five months and ending unfavourably for the workers, though it resulted in the negotiation of the Brooklands Agreement, which regulated the spinning section of the industry without dispute for about twenty years. In the same year the Miners' Federation of Great Britain was involved in its first strike of size. Although the Federation did not cover all Britain by any means, 400,000 men were brought out; the strike did not prevent a reduction of wages but did secure the practical acceptance of a minimum wage in the areas involved. At Featherstone two miners were shot dead by soldiers, a piece of brutality long remembered against the Home Secretary, Asquith. The Scottish miners struck the next year, without success, but the Scottish Miners' Federation was reorganized as a result of the struggle. The South Wales miners came out in 1898 and were beaten in a fierce struggle; it resulted again in a reorganization of their Federation, which forthwith joined the Miners' Federation of Great Britain. By 1900 the Miners' Federation of Great Britain covered all the coal-fields except the North-East Coast: Northumberland and Durham only joined in 1908. In 1897 the Amalgamated Society of Engineers was defeated in a gigantic lock-out, involving about 50,000 workers. This dispute was the first to raise directly the question of "managerial functions"—an issue which to-day would be described as "workers' control."

Two considerable apparent successes were gained by the Socialists in the 'nineties. The division between political and industrial revolutionaries had not yet been devised to make argument clearer and action more difficult. The *Clarion* propagandists, political revolutionaries, threw themselves in the middle 'nineties upon the Trades Union Congress as naturally as Burns and Mann of the S.D.F. had earlier turned to organizing the unskilled. Their object was to unite all the Unions into one big fighting federation—an earlier form of the "One Big Union" propaganda. So effective was their advocacy of the "*Clarion* scheme" that the Parliamentary Committee was forced, in appearance at least, to bow to their wishes and in 1897 put out officially a Trades Union Congress scheme for a General Federation of Trade Unions, which was submitted to the member-unions for their approval. Its powers were far more limited than in the *Clarion* scheme, but it would have been a considerable step forward. But a resolution, and even a draft constitution, were far different from action. The officials who had reluctantly drafted this scheme viewed their own product with suspicion: it was sent out to the vote of the membership very often with chilling comments that ensured its rejection. Only two really big Unions, the Engineers (86,000) and the Gasworkers (50,000), joined it when it was launched. Though others came in later—mostly not to stay—it could never offer any important advantage to a large union. A strike by, say, the miners would have bankrupted it within a fortnight. It thus settled down as a useful but unimportant body which pooled the funds of minor Unions and acted as a sort of mutual insurance corporation, nor did it change from this even though its membership in time rose above a million.

Greater real success appeared to attend a strictly political victory of the Socialists. The Trades Union Congress of 1899, after years of ineffective debate, passed a resolution drafted in the I.L.P. office and ordering the Parliamentary Committee to call a special conference of all working-class organizations to secure Labour representation in Parliament. The conference met in February 1900; once again there was the appearance of universal unity. The Trade Union leaders sat with the I.L.P., the S.D.F. delegates, the Fabians, Keir Hardie and John Burns. A "Labour Representation Committee" was formed, which was at once colloquially called "the Labour Party." J. Ramsay MacDonald was elected secretary and carried out the policy of recruiting Trade Union branches to the support of the idea of independent Labour candidates, with rapid success in the next twelve months. Burns was now opposing: "I am getting tired of working-class boots, working-class brains, working-class houses and working-class margarine," he said. "I believe the time has arrived when we should not be prisoners to class prejudice." The S.D.F. objected from the other side and shortly afterwards left; it denounced the new body as in no way consciously Socialist and as a result likely to be an obstacle and not an aid to Socialism. But at the minute its Cassandra cries were disregarded; the spirit of unity seemed to brood victoriously over all, and under its influence Keir Hardie called (though in vain) upon John Morley to lead the new party at the forthcoming election.

CHAPTER XXXVI

WAGES IN THE "GREAT DEPRESSION"— THE EXPORT OF CAPITAL

FROM the middle 'seventies to the middle 'nineties there was an almost continuous fall in prices. Between 1873 and 1896 wholesale prices, measured by Sauerbeck's index, fell by 45 per cent; and the cost of living went down by nearly one-third. This decline was not quite uninterrupted; for the

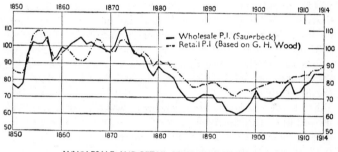

WHOLESALE AND RETAIL PRICE INDEXES, 1850–1914
Average of 1867–77 = 100

general trend was deflected at times by the upward and downward movements of economic activity. There were crisis years in 1879 and 1886, and, less seriously, in 1893. In 1879 unemployment reached a peak of nearly 12 per cent among the Trade Unions making returns, and in 1886 it again exceeded 10 per cent. On the other hand, in the slump of 1893 it did not reach 8 per cent. In the best years—1882, 1889–90 and 1899—it was barely above 2 per cent, a minimum which was not to be reached again until 1913.

With prices falling at such a rate, the employed workers had only to avoid wage-reductions in order to secure a steady improvement in their real standards of living. Actually, between 1873 and 1896, when prices touched bottom, average money-wages over all trades rose a little—perhaps by 5 per cent. This meant, in view of the fall in retail prices, a rise in real wage-rates of 35 to 40 per cent. At the least, the purchasing power of the average skilled worker in full employment increased by one-third. Moreover, many of the less skilled workers, at any rate after 1889, shared in this increase, leaving behind only the utterly unorganized strata at the bottom of the social system—the depressed classes whose appalling conditions Booth's famous *Survey* did so much to bring to light.

The figures of consumption confirm the evidence of the figures of wages and prices. Per head of population, the consumption of bread stood practically still; but meat consumption rose from about 110 lb. a year in the middle 'seventies to nearly 130 lb. twenty years later. The consumption of tea increased from 4½ lb. to nearly 6 lb., and that of sugar from about 60 lb. to well over 80 lb. The consumption of tobacco also rose appreciably, and from the 'eighties onwards there was also a rise in the consumption of beer, offset by some fall in spirit-drinking, which seems to have reached its maximum in the 'seventies.

From 1896 onwards the price-trend was reversed, and prices moved upwards, slowly for a year or two and then very rapidly during the South African War. But up to 1900 wages kept pace with this increase—or rather the organized workers, after a small initial set-back, were able in 1899 and 1900 to gain wage-advances which more than cancelled the rise in living costs. In 1900, according to Mr. Wood's figures, money wage-rates were 15–16 per cent higher than they had been in 1873, and their purchasing power was 42–43 per cent higher.

There is, then, no doubt that over the last quarter of the nineteenth century the *absolute* living standards of the working classes considerably improved. The advance was, indeed, very uneven between trade and trade. In the Lancashire cotton industry, and indeed, almost generally in the textile trades, money-wages were actually lower in 1900 than in the early 'seventies—largely as a result of intensified competition, but also for want of militancy in the textile Trade Unions. In the coal industry generally wage-rates rose by about 12 per cent, but there was a decline in some of the coal-fields. In Durham, for example, the day rate for coal-hewers was 7*s*. 6*d*. a shift in 1874, and less than 6*s*. in 1900. The main advances had been in districts which had emancipated themselves, under the leadership of the Miners' Federation, from the evil influence of the sliding scale. In the building trades money-wages had risen, on the average, by well over 20 per cent, or about 1½*d*. per hour in the skilled crafts. In engineering the average rise was only about 12 per cent; but there were great local differences, some districts, such as the Clyde, having very greatly improved their position, whereas others had stood practically still. The range of increases was from 2*s*. to as much as 7*s*. a week in standard rates. In 1900 a skilled fitter or turner got 38*s*. in London, and 36*s*. in most other large towns, and an ironfounder 42*s*. and 40*s*. A London compositor on time rates got 38*s*., which was in fact the commonest rate for a highly skilled London craftsman. In agriculture, over the country as a whole, average weekly wages rose by about 1*s*. between 1874 and 1900—from 14*s*. to 15*s*.; but this followed on a rise from about 12*s*., under Joseph Arch's leadership, in the early 'seventies.

In general, with the growth of collective bargaining, there was a tendency towards greater uniformity of wage-rates in the skilled trades. This had both good and bad sides. There was some levelling-up in the worst-paid areas, such as the Clyde; but the areas in which wages had been relatively high found it harder to secure advances, now that employers as well as workers were combined over a wider front. The growing keenness of competition, both at home and abroad, made employers scrutinize more closely the relative wages in different areas. If the builders did best of all in securing advances, that was due partly to the immunity of their industry from foreign competition, and partly to the great activity of the constructional trades; but it may have been due in part to the fact that they bargained much more locally than most of the big industries.

Absolutely, real wages rose. But what of their relation to the share of the national income accruing to the richer classes? Professor Bowley has estimated that between 1880 and 1900 the distribution of the national income between wages and other forms of income changed very little. Income from the land fell off, for both landlords and farmers; but income from house property increased a great deal. So, of course, did profits and interest derived from industry—by as much as 40 per cent, if no allowance is made for the growth of population. Actually the gross amounts brought under review for Income Tax under Schedule D (mainly profits) rose from £173,000,000 in 1867 to £267,000,000 in 1875. This latter total was reached again in 1882, after the intervening slump, and by 1896 the total had reached £352,000,000, and by 1900 no less than £466,000,000. Even when allowance has been made for changes in classification and assessment, these figures show that there was a very remarkable upswing of profits before 1896, and a tremendous rise in the closing years of the century.

In general, however, thanks mainly to falling prices, the wage-earners up to 1900 did succeed in maintaining their proportionate share in the national income, as well as in bettering their actual conditions of life. The drop in real wages and in the workers' share came only in the period of rising prices after 1900.

Between 1875 and the end of the century industrial production continued its rapid advance. In only one year (1890) between 1874 and 1896 did British exports exceed the money value reached in the boom of 1872-3. But in terms of quantity they increased over the period by about two-thirds. Net imports, meanwhile, rose by over 20 per cent in money value, and considerably more than doubled in quantity. Imports of wheat doubled in amount; butter imports doubled in value, in spite of falling prices. Meat imports rose in value from £13,000,000 to £47,000,000, and fresh fruit imports from £1,000,000 to over £7,000,000. In face of a fall in wholesale food prices by one-third, these figures mean an even bigger rise in the quantities available for consumption.

British agriculture, as we have seen, remained prosperous up to the 'seventies, despite the influx of foreign corn. But, with wheat imports doubling, and consumption per head remaining practically unchanged, the period after 1875 involved a rapid decline in arable farming. Farmers made good for the time being by shifting over, wherever they could, from arable to pasture. But they soon had to face the competition of foreign meat and butter, as well as of foreign wheat. From the 'eighties refrigeration developed fast, and New

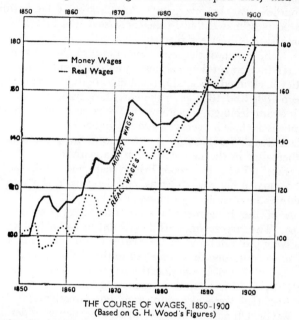

THE COURSE OF WAGES, 1850-1900
(Based on G. H. Wood's Figures)

Zealand, Australia and the Argentine became important suppliers of food for the British market. Net imports of all goods from Australia and New Zealand rose from £18,000,000 in 1874 to £35,000,000 in 1900. Those from the Argentine, almost negligible up to about 1890, increased from £2,000,000 in 1889 to £13,000,000 in 1900. For most sections of the British moneyed class, falling prices were more than offset by the rise in production. But it was not so for the farmers and landlords. In agriculture the so-called "Great Depression" was real.

Even if, in general, the distribution of returns between wages and other forms of income was not much altered, the absolute rise in the wealth of the industrial and financial capitalists was very great. They had enough both to expand their standards of living at a great rate, and to accumulate capital on the grand scale. Of this capital, a high proportion flowed out into foreign investment, in search of the higher profits and rates of interest that could be looked for in the less developed countries. This outflow was, however, very variable from time to time. It has been estimated that in the early 'seventies British long-time investment overseas reached a rate of over £60,000,000 a year. The slump of the later 'seventies brought the volume of foreign investment down almost to nothing; and then in the 'eighties it climbed up again, reaching about the same level between 1885 and 1890 as in the early 'seventies. From that peak it again declined, though not to the same extent. For the 'nineties as a whole it averaged about £30,000,000 a year. The South African War brought it down to about £20,000,000; and thereafter in the new century it leapt ahead at a prodigious rate. Even by 1900 British capitalists had about £1,700,000,000 invested overseas, and drew upon this sum an annual tribute of at least £100,000,000.

Most of the investment abroad after 1875 was outside Europe. The largest amounts flowed out to India (especially for railway building) and to the British Dominions. But very large sums continued to be invested in the United States, and in the latter part of the period the Argentine was opened up mainly by British capital. Brazil and other countries of Latin America were also important borrowers; and in the East, Egypt, China and latterly Japan absorbed considerable amounts of British capital.

These changes in the character of investment were important; for they helped the flow of the imperialist tide. Previously, British capital had gone largely to foreign countries with settled governments with which it was not open to Great Britain to interfere. But by 1875 such countries as France and Belgium were beginning to repay what they had borrowed; and as British investors fought shy of the capital markets of Russia and other needy and backward European countries, the main investments were placed, except in the case of the United States, in areas which were either subject to British political control or unable to claim equal status with Great Britain. In these circumstances, a new intimacy sprang up between the financiers concerned with overseas investment and the politicians to whom they looked to safeguard the interests of British capital. Foreign investment was no longer a means of helping Frenchmen or Americans to buy railways or machinery which they would take over and work for themselves, paying back the loan in due course out of the profits of the undertaking. More and more it came to involve the permanent ownership and management by British companies and investment agencies of industrial undertakings carried on abroad; so that the British investors acquired a permanent interest in the preservation of order and the protection of property rights in the areas in which their money was being used. Political interference went hand in hand with economic penetration; and the rivalry for colonies became inextricably mixed up with the rivalries of the various national investing groups.

For Great Britain was no longer in effect the only country interested in foreign investment. The French had also become great investors, with a big annual surplus to lend abroad; and both the United States and Germany lent as well as borrowed, though on balance they borrowed more than they lent.

More important, however, than the competitive lending of capital was the competitive supply of exports from these countries. The German output of steel rose from about 300,000 tons a year in the early 'seventies to over 6,000,000 tons in 1900, when the British output was under 5,000,000 tons. American output rose even more—from under 200,000 tons to 10,000,000. Most of the steel made in these countries was indeed consumed at home; and even in 1900 British iron and steel exports exceeded those of Germany and the United States together. But it must not be forgotten that the home markets of these and other advancing countries had been largely closed to the British exporters.

For tariffs had been rising fast. In 1902 the Board of Trade calculated that the average import duty on British goods exported to the United States amounted to 73 per cent of their value. France imposed an average duty of 34 per cent, and Germany of 25 per cent. On the other hand Australia and South Africa were still at the low level of an average 6 per cent duty New Zealand at 9 per cent, and even Canada at only 16 per cent. The movement towards lower tariffs in Europe which had followed the victory of Free Trade in Great Britain had been utterly reversed under the new conditions of rapid industrialization in Germany and elsewhere. Tariffs had risen, and were continuing to rise. Protection was beginning to be talked of again in Great Britain, though Joseph Chamberlain's crusade for tariffs and imperial preference was not launched until the new century.

There was, indeed, up to 1900 more talk of Imperial Federation than of Imperial Preference. The first Colonial Conference had met in 1887, the year of the Queen's Jubilee; and out of it the Imperial Conference was being gradually developed. The Imperial Federation League had been founded in 1884; and till its break-up in 1893 it conducted an active campaign in favour of Empire unity. But when Chamberlain, presiding over the Colonial Conference of 1897, tried to persuade the Colonial Governments to set up some sort of nucleus for a federal council of the self-governing Empire, it was at once made plain that the Colonies would have none of it. They wanted freedom to go their own ways: they would accept no imperial organ that might be used to commit them to the policy of Great Britain. Nor, though they wanted Imperial Preference, would they have anything to do with Chamberlain's notion of an Imperial Customs Union, based on Empire Free Trade. They wanted preference in the British market; and though Great Britain, as a free trade country, was not ready to give it to them, there were other concessions, such as preferential terms for borrowing in the London capital market, which could be accorded in exchange for preference to British goods in Empire markets. Canada actually made a beginning of Empire preference in 1897, after trade treaties which prevented it had been denounced. But the main developments in this field came after 1900, though the establishment of imperial penny postage in 1898 may be noted as a milestone on the road.

Meanwhile, Great Britain had followed up Disraeli's purchase of the Khedive's shares in the Suez Canal in 1875 with the effective occupation of Egypt, complemented in 1898 by the final conquest of the Sudan. In tropical Africa, one territory after another had been annexed, or taken under British "protection." The existence of the two independent Boer Republics in South Africa became more and more intolerable to the imperialist mind. Great Britain had actually annexed the Transvaal in 1877—only to let it go three years later. But that had been before the great gold discoveries of 1888, which within a few years raised South Africa to the first place as a producer of gold, and in less than a decade doubled the annual world output. The Jameson Raid of 1895 failed, and was disowned. But war had to come before long. It came, in 1899; and in the following year the Conservative Party was able to claim the annexation of the Boer Republics and to win the "Khaki Election" in Great Britain. Imperialism, fairly in the saddle since Gladstone's withdrawal, had come home in a canter. The newly formed Labour Representation Committee could win only two seats in the new Parliament. Even the "Lib–Labs" were reduced to eight. Will Thorne, Snowden, MacDonald and George Lansbury were all among the defeated candidates.

BEFORE THE FIRST WORLD WAR

CHAPTER XXXVII

EDWARDIAN BRITAIN

THE period from 1900 to 1914 is like the two first acts of a play whose third act was never written. The historian can trace the breaking-up of the Victorian age, its castes, taboos, commercial methods and social habits, and the development, isolated or allied, of various movements of revolt. But when the struggle develops and it seems that some sort of denouement must come, the action is violently and suddenly stopped. Within a day almost—a week at the longest—in August 1914, the whole of men's previous preoccupations and thoughts was wiped out. The suffragette movement, industrial unionism, even for a while the Irish question, suddenly became of infinitely small importance. For months or years they were forgotten; some never revived, and those that did appeared in very different forms.

It would be very rash to assume that these discontents would have secured in the end the victory that at one time seemed promised to them. But of their general character there is little doubt; they were all directed to the moral and economic destruction of Victorian capitalism. About 1875 British society had been so universally under the rule of one idea, so completely moulded into one admired form of organization, that we must probably go back to the Roman Empire to find an equally contented unanimity. Victorian society was one of a very high degree of political liberty. Speech and political thought were freer than they had ever been before, or are to-day; economically, the individual was almost entirely free —at least, of any legal restraints. Extensions of State authority, such as Factory Acts, were only admitted as exceptions, after

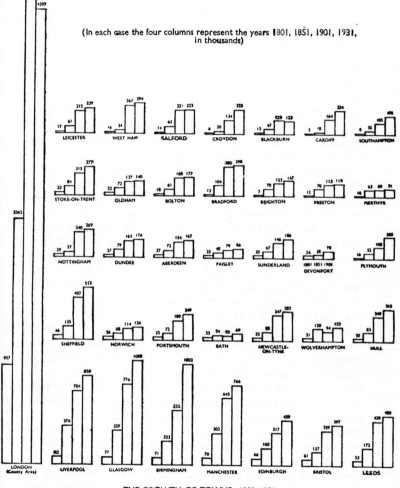

(In each case the four columns represent the years 1801, 1851, 1901, 1931, in thousands)

THE GROWTH OF TOWNS, 1801-1931

prolonged agitation and with the greatest reluctance; even Co-operation was only encouraged if it involved no form of coercion or pressure. (Economic coercion of the average worker by the power of capital was not recognized, though it undoubtedly existed.) This libertarian State was cemented by a strict uniformity of belief and action in other spheres than those of economics and politics. Family discipline, the authority of the father, almost compulsory church or chapel-going, strict sexual rules, the discouragement of any form of amusement that could not be proved to be educational or edifying—all this and much more provided what later years would call an "ideology" which was historically if not logically entwined with economic and political Victorianism. It was nearly as strong in the "lower orders" and aristocracy as in the rapidly increasing middle class. Support both for it and for English political liberty was provided by the general belief that through their joint existence the community was becoming continuously richer and more powerful.

The end of the century, the death of the Queen, and the humiliations of the Boer War shook this placid certainty, but only because it had been disturbed by continuous attacks beforehand. We have already described in detail the political and economic dissent, and can only refer briefly to the more ideological attacks. A number of distinguished men had preached or practised very effectively against typical Victorian beliefs and behaviour; they include such ill-assorted names as Huxley, Arnold and Oscar Wilde, Ruskin, Bradlaugh and the Prince of Wales. Huxley destroyed the foundations of religious belief in the minds of an enormous number of thinking men; Bradlaugh, with a courage which can only be appreciated by those who have read an account of his missionary tours, carried the same scepticism out to the general people. Arnold and Ruskin enlarged the sphere of this spirit of inquiry; they encouraged more humane and rational behaviour or belief in social fields and in culture. Wilde and the other artists of the *Yellow Book* period were shriller and far more embracing in their condemnation of middle-class standards. The Prince of Wales (Edward VII) had not the mentality of a reformer, but in a snobbish country like England his position made his every

action of disproportionate importance. The sight of a man
who was shortly to be the most exalted person in the land
openly playing cards for money, answering disagreeable
questions in the divorce courts, and consorting with Jews,
impelled a great number of unthinking people a long way
along the path of tolerance.

The connection between freer social customs and political
revolt was obscurely felt. "Advanced" political circles were
more inclined than others to make excuses for Wilde when he
was convicted of homosexuality; Wilde wrote *The Soul of Man
under Socialism*. The alliance became clearer when the suffrage
movement, intended only as a protest against sex tyranny,
threw into bright relief the horrors of sweating and slum life,
or when Syndicalism, an anti-parliamentary revolutionary
movement, incorporated into its philosophy a general attack
on "capitalist morality."

The Edwardian age thus seemed to be an age of ever-
increasing liberty. Political liberty—"civil liberty" in the
common sense—had previously been immense; it was hardly
at all interfered with during this period. One serious instance
occurred, but only one. In 1912, Fred Crowsley, a railwayman, Guy Bowman, B. E. and C. E. Buck, the printers, and
Tom Mann were sentenced to various terms of imprisonment,
up to nine months, for circulating a "Don't Shoot" leaflet
containing the words:

"You are Workingmen's Sons.
When We go on Strike to better Our lot which is the lot
also of Your Fathers, Mothers, Brothers and Sisters, *You* are
called upon by your Officers to *Murder Us*.
Don't do it. . . .
Don't you know that when you are out of the colours, and
become a 'Civy' again, that You, like Us, may be on strike,
and You, like Us, be liable to be Murdered by other soldiers.
Boys, Don't Do It.
'Thou shalt not kill,' says the Book.
Don't forget that!
It does not say, 'unless you have a uniform on.'
No! *Murder is Murder*. . . .

Think things out and refuse any longer to Murder Your Kindred. Help Us to win back Britain for the British and the World for the Workers."

The inclusion of the printers was a peculiar piece of malice, and the contemporary Conservative encouragement to officers to forget their oaths and duty over the Home Rule Bill remained unpunished. All that can be urged in mitigation is that the leaflet was exceptionally telling, its detail well calculated, and its object very alarming; more important is that this piece of persecution remained isolated.

Social liberty began greatly to increase; the liberation of the younger generation from family and religious restraints was only surpassed by the first effects of the suffrage movement, in which half of the human race began to escape for the first time from personal tutelage. The sense of safety which the Victorian age had produced was as yet unshaken, and the inevitable progress in which everyone believed seemed only to have been turned into better channels than that of merely increasing wealth.

But the manifestations of the new liberties were in places disquieting. The new democracy showed preferences which had not been anticipated. These fifteen years witnessed the partial extinction of the existing sober and honest provincial Press, and its replacement by a new kind of centralized London journalism which was disliked by the older Conservatives almost as much as by Liberals and Socialists. Alfred Harmsworth started his *Daily Mail* in 1896, but it was only after 1900 that it rose to great importance. Serious matter was banished from its columns—thoughtful leaders, long Parliamentary reports, connected accounts of conditions at home or abroad or underwritten and restrained news were equally forbidden. Their places were taken by news items which were disconnected, short, sensational, inaccurate, and in one famous case (during the Boxer expedition of 1900) mere fabrications. In policy the *Daily Mail* favoured a violent and bellicose patriotism. In most, if not all, of these features it was imitated by a newly founded *Daily Express*, and an altered *Daily News* the equally popular *Daily Mirror* and *Daily Sketch* made even fewer demands on their readers' intelligence. Similar irresponsibility, as it was commonly and politely called, appeared also in ranks which were supposed to be the guardians of the Constitution; the Curragh incident and the arming of the Ulster Volunteers were little less than a calculated threat of mutiny and insurrection under the protection of the Conservative Party.

The earliest, however, of such unconstitutional actions was taken by a body of people of far different complexion. One of the most beneficial acts of the earliest years of the century was the Education Act of 1902, which for the first time gave to the mass of the people some possibility of an education extending beyond the three Rs and a little undenominational religion. But in putting the "voluntary" (mainly Church of England) schools on the rates, it revived the religious sectarianism which had for so many years already impeded education. The Nonconformists, considering that their rivals had secured undue advantage, made an organized attempt to wreck the Act by refusing to pay their rates. In view of later history, the spectacle of "Dr. John Clifford forcibly having his teapot sold" suggests a very mild martyrdom, and the selfishness of all religious factions seems more noticeable than their devotion; but at the time the events seemed immensely sensational, and the protesting Nonconformists were considered (according to the observer's politics) either to be bravely suffering unexampled persecution, or to be wantonly embarking on a career of reckless illegality.

This excited period commenced very calmly. Between 1900 and 1909 the tendency of the previous century had been reversed. Real wages—that is to say, not money-wages but the value of money-wages compared with prices—went down, as will be shown later. In the earlier part of this period, too, there were no Liberal social reforms to compensate for this plain loss. One would expect the working class through its Unions to react vigorously, and enforce, or try to enforce, increased wages by continual strikes. There is nothing of the sort to record. The Unions were too inefficiently organized, too competitive and quarrelsome, and too apathetically led to take any forward steps; and there does not even appear to

CP: Q

have been much pressure from the rank and file. The impotence of the Unions was increased by a successful raid from the other side. In 1900 a number of railwaymen employed by the Taff Vale Railway Company in South Wales struck without the approval of their Union, the Amalgamated Society of Railway Servants. When the Company brought in blacklegs, however, the Society gave strike pay to the men who were out and sent down its General Secretary to support them. But railway companies were the most obstinate enemies of Trade Unionism among all employers; the Manager of the Taff Vale had thought of a new device. He sued the Society for the loss which the Company sustained through the strike, carried the case to the Lords, and secured a verdict of £23,000 in damages. The total cost to the Society was £50,000.

This decision undid a great deal of the good done by the Acts of 1871 and 1875. It meant that henceforward a Union was liable to be mulcted in damages, without any ascertainable limits, for losses caused by a strike in which it participated. The most routine-minded and orthodoxly Liberal Trade Union officer could not fail to see how disastrous the decision was. Any strike, even if successful, might ruin the Union which ran it. There could be no means, moreover, of countering this amazing decision by industrial action; political action was the only method. The activities of the Labour Representation Committee, which to many Trade Union officers had seemed superfluous if not dangerous, became suddenly important. A great deal of support which was neither disinterested nor genuinely converted suddenly appeared for the Labour Party.

The 1900 general election had given the Conservatives a large majority; the Liberals suffered heavily and with them the "Lib-Labs." There were only six of the latter left; there was John Burns, whose position was already becoming uncertain. The Labour Representation Committee had put up fifteen cand dates, but only two were successful—Keir Hardie at Merthyr and Richard Bell at Derby. But they were shortly joined by others. David Shackleton won Clitheroe in 1902; Will Crooks Woolwich, and Arthur Henderson Barnard Castle in 1903. The Miners' Federation of Great Britain started a separate fund in 1901 for its own candidates. But no real progress could be made towards annulling the Taff Vale Judgment until the Government was overturned; and the thin Labour ranks were further depleted by Richard Bell passing across to the Liberals in 1904.

The Conservative Government, however, was manufacturing its own ruin. To contemporary observers the fault was chiefly in Balfour's inertia, but it lay deeper than that. The rivalry of other capitalist countries and the increasing importance of colonies and dominions as both markets and sources of raw material made it highly likely that sooner or later the British capitalist class would abandon its free trade policy in order to tie these dependencies more closely to themselves. Chamberlain's explosive and unexpected Tariff Reform crusade, which he left the Cabinet to conduct, was not merely an electoral tactic; it was an intelligent anticipation of what were soon to be the real needs of British employers.

The Colonial Conference of 1902 had convinced him, as Colonial Secretary, that his dream of Empire could never be realized while Great Britain remained a free trade country. On this issue, in 1903, he seceded from the Government, and set out, much to the annoyance of the Conservative Old Guard, to win over the rank and file of the Conservative Party to the cause of Tariff Reform. What Chamberlain wanted was mainly not protection for the British industrialist, but Imperial Preference; but his crusade speedily turned into a campaign for securing the British capitalist against foreign competition. Though Chamberlain admired Germany, and had struggled hard to improve Anglo-German relations, his tariff movement did much to stimulate anti-German feeling; for any British protective tariff would be necessarily directed largely against imports from Germany. But, when he began it, he did not foresee that consequence. It was not aimed against any country in particular. He wanted Empire unity for its own sake, and for the consolidation of British economic supremacy and the power of exploitation which he believed a united Empire would involve.

But while Chamberlain, now outside the Government, was converting the Conservative Associations and the manufacturers to Tariff Reform, the forces in Europe were already aligning themselves for the coming struggle for power. In both France and Great Britain there was growing fear of Germany's rapidly increasing naval and military strength. In 1904 the Government not only instituted the Committee of Imperial Defence, but entered into that Anglo-French Convention which speedily became an Entente plainly directed against potential German aggression. The first Morocco crisis followed in 1905, when Germany staked out her claim to interfere in the dealings of the Mediterranean Powers in Northern Africa. She dared to do this, because Russia, France's ally, defeated by Japan and in the throes of internal revolution, was in no state to interfere. But the effect was to bring Great Britain, determined to keep the Germans out of the Mediterranean, into much closer relations with France. In effect the Morocco crisis of 1905 lined up Great Britain on the anti-German side, and so prepared the way for the Great War. Military conversations between French and British military authorities began soon after it, sanctioned by the Liberal Government which the crushing defeat of the Conservatives had meanwhile brought to power.

Before this Chamberlain, by 1905, had converted the bulk of the Conservative Party to his new gospel, and had forced the quite unconverted Balfour to give him virtually a free hand at the General Election. But he had not converted the electorate. Since 1896 the price-trend had been reversed, and the cost of living had been rising rapidly enough for the poorer classes to feel the pinch. The well-to-do persons who controlled the Conservative machine remained unmoved by the new trend; but the majority of the voters were by no means disposed to give Chamberlain and the Tories a free hand to tax their food and other necessaries in the interests either of Empire unity or of industries which seemed to be doing very well as they were. The working classes, indeed, had a further reason for rejecting Chamberlain's blandishments; for the Taff Vale Judgment of 1901 had so paralysed Trade Union action that, despite the high profits which were being made, they were powerless to strike for higher wages. Real wages had been falling; and they looked like falling faster if the Conservatives got back to power. For certainly a Conservative

Government would do nothing to reverse the Taff Vale decision and give back to the Trade Unions the rights which the House of Lords had taken away. The Liberals, on the other hand, were ready to promise redress: if the Liberals got back to office not only would the "big loaf" be saved from the Imperialists, but in addition Labour would stand a good chance of getting back the right to strike, and thus of raising wages as well as keeping up their purchasing power.

It would be too much to say that the Conservatives lost the 1906 election solely on the issue of Tariff Reform; for, even apart from that, the voters were tired of them, and ready for a change. But the fear of the "little loaf," and the urgency of the Trade Union demand for the reversal of the Taff Vale decision, turned what would otherwise have been an ordinary swing of the pendulum into a knock-out blow. The Tories were not wiped out; for without an awakening of the country-side that could not happen. But they came as near to it as seemed to make no matter. The Liberals came back with a majority of 220 over the Conservatives and of 84 over all other parties combined.

Sir Henry Campbell-Bannerman, whose Radicalism was distrusted by important men of his own party such as Grey and Asquith, became Prime Minister, the pro-Boer Lloyd George was (after 1908) Chancellor of the Exchequer, and the once-revolutionary John Burns was President of the Local Government Board. Twenty-nine Labour Representation Committee candidates were successful, fourteen miners' M.P.s were separately returned, and there were about a dozen old-style "Lib–Labs." The first two sections combined, upon a decision of the Miners' Federation, in 1909, but before then the miners' M.P.s had been generally reckoned as part of the Labour forces, and a first victory of considerable importance had been secured. The new Government had attempted to temporize over the annulment of the Taff Vale decision, but to its discomfort member after member from its own benches rose to explain that he had only been elected upon the specific promise of legislation to cancel that decision. The promises had to be fulfilled forthwith, and the power of the new group was signally advertised.

It was indeed estimated far too high. The public—that is to say, persons interested in politics and not supporters or students of the Labour movement—obtained its ideas of the new party from recollections of the explosions of the 'eighties, from Conservative election speeches, from accounts of or chance encounters with I.L.P. or S.D.F. speakers, and perhaps also from some guilty promptings of its own conscience, for a robust satisfaction with great individual riches and extreme poverty had died with the Victorian age. Many people who might have known better assumed that thirty odd M.P.s—the numbers, with the miners' M.P.s, soon reached over forty —had been sent to Westminster by an indignant proletariat to demand retribution and recompense; and that considerable concessions might be necessary to appease them. The 1903 conference of the new party had given countenance to this theory by forbidding candidates to be connected with any other party, even the Liberals. But this apparent intransigence bore different aspects to the two halves of the movement. The Socialists welcomed it as a declaration of principle; the Union leaders saw in it merely a tactical move and a suitable reply to the Taff Vale provocation.

For the project of converting the Trade Unions to a militant Socialist policy had really made but small advances: indeed, a reverse action seemed sometimes to have taken place. The new M.P.s were none the less Liberals for having taken a strange name, and the Union leaders were frequently openly hostile to their Socialist allies. "We shall no longer allow the tail to wag the dog," a carpenters' delegate assured the Trade Union Congress in 1902, "we shall wag our own tails"; the intention if not the phrase was continually repeated. Keir Hardie, opposed by too many established Union officers, gave way as leader of the party to James Ramsay MacDonald, who had had no insurgent past in industrial affairs, and was more skilled in reconciling opposites. He had a natural skill in parliamentary tactics, and had evolved a theory of evolutionary Socialism, expressed in biological metaphors which satisfied I.L.P. supporters, while his conviction that circumstances required an inflexible support of the Liberals reassured the Trade Unionists.

Their own supporters realized the extreme mildness of the Labour M.P.s sooner than the Liberals did. *Justice* (the S.D.F. paper) and *The Clarion* were not read by Liberals, but they were by Labour supporters, and their exposure of the enormous distance that separated the Party's activities from Socialist hopes was largely responsible for a sensational by-election at Colne Valley in 1908, when a young man named Victor Grayson carried the seat on a programme of uncompromising Socialism.

By 1911 (to anticipate slightly) the annoyance with the party direction had grown so strong that the S.D.F. united with a number of angry I.L.P. branches and *Clarion* supporters to form a new party to supplant it, the British Socialist Party (B.S.P.). The new party, however, made no progress for all its high hopes, for it took over from the S.D.F. both its established "impossibilist" policy and its autocratic leader, Hyndman.

CHAPTER XXXVIII

LABOUR AND LLOYD GEORGE

BROADLY speaking, up to 1910, everything, from the Liberal as well as the Labour standpoint, appeared to be going reasonably well. In foreign affairs the Moroccan question seemed to have been fairly well settled at the Algeciras Conference of 1906; and the disturbances in south-eastern Europe following on the Turkish Revolution of 1908 and the annexation of Bosnia and Herzegovina by Austria-Hungary had been got over, if not gloriously, at any rate without a European war. The South African question had been settled by the British South Africa Act of 1909, on lines which seemed to most Liberals eminently satisfactory; for the party which had made such a song between 1903 and 1906 about Chinese labour on the Rand remained quite oblivious of the fact that it had handed over the African majority of the population of the new Union of South Africa to unrestricted exploitation by the now reconciled Dutch and British settlers. In India, a very tiny step towards the concession of local self-government had been taken by the India Councils Act of 1909 (the "Morley-Minto" Reforms). In home affairs, a good beginning had been made with social legislation. Medical inspection of school-children had been instituted in 1907, and the employment of children outside school hours regulated in 1908; and in addition a concession had been made to the Labour Party in allowing the passage of the Education (Provision of Meals) Act of 1906, under which local authorities were allowed, though not required, to make a start with school-feeding in necessitous districts. The miners, under the Coal Mines Act of 1908, had been granted a nominal eight-hour day, though in effect the actual working day still averaged half an hour more. A first attack on the sweating evil had been delivered in the Trade Boards Act of 1909, under which a legal minimum wage had been instituted by way of experiment in a small number of exceptionally ill-paid women's trades. Labour Exchanges had been set up all over the country under an Act of the same year. A new Housing and Town Planning Act, giving greatly enlarged powers to the local authorities both to demolish slum areas and insanitary dwellings and to build new houses, and in addition introducing at least the thin end of the wedge of town planning, had been passed, also in 1909; and it was not yet seen that the measure would be utterly wrecked in action by John Burns's unsatisfactory administration at the Local Government Board. Most important of all, non-contributory Old Age Pensions had been instituted in 1908; and small and subject to a Means Test though the pensions were, they represented a new and vitally important use of the power of taxation for the definite redistribution of income.

So far, so good. The Labour Party might demand more than the Liberals were giving it; but it was undoubtedly getting more than most of its members had expected them to give. It was the contented ally of the Liberal majority, kissing the hand that fed it with these rare and refreshing fruits. To be sure, the Trade Unions were not quite so well content; for despite the restoration of the right to strike wages lagged farther and farther behind rising prices. There was growing discontent among the railwaymen, who were finding that the s/ttlement which Lloyd George had persuaded them to accept in 1907, when they had pressed their first All Grades Movement to the point of threatening a national strike, afforded the railway companies every possible opportunity for evasion. The railwaymen wanted recognition for their Unions; but this the companies still utterly refused to concede. The miners too were growing restless despite the concession of the eight-hour day—or even in part because of it; for the owners in certain areas had met the shortening of the working day by introducing the three-shift system, against which there were numerous unofficial strikes. But apart from this grievance, the miners had plenty more. There were strikes against non-unionism, especially in South Wales; and the entire Miners' Federation was getting in motion with its further demand for a guaranteed minimum wage.

But in 1909 the labour unrest, though it was growing, had not yet become serious enough to shake the complacency either of the Government or of the Labour M.P.s. The Government at any rate had other things which worried it a good deal more. To begin with, it was already wondering what to do about the House of Lords.

The Lords, unwilling to antagonize the working classes but determined to assert their right to act as the permanent Conservative brake upon a Liberal House of Commons, had prudently let the Trade Disputes Act of 1906 pass without amendment, even though they must have found it a hard morsel to swallow. Nor had they rejected any of the Government's measures of specifically industrial reform, or even the Old Age Pensions Bill, with its underlying implications of redistributive taxation. But in the interests of the Church they had killed Augustine Birrell's Education Bill, and in the interests of the brewers and the "right to get drunk" they had flung out the Liberal Licensing Bill. Both these rejections naturally infuriated the Nonconformists, who rallied more and more behind Lloyd George in readiness to hit back when the chance came. A Plural Voting Bill had gone the same way; for its enactment would obviously have damaged the electoral prospects of the Tory Party.

These activities of the House of Lords confronted the Liberals with a problem. To many of the more reactionary Liberals the existence of the Lords' veto was very welcome; for it presented them with a powerful argument against their more Radical colleagues. It would never do, they said, for the Government to be too advanced; for that would only mean that the Lords would reject its measures. Its proper course was to keep just within what the Lords would let through without provoking a dangerous constitutional crisis.

This was all very well from the standpoint of those Liberals who merely wished to have their own party in office and to maintain Free Trade, and felt no interest in social reform or in far-reaching changes of any sort. But it did not at all suit the Radicals, who wanted a fight with the Lords for its own sake, or the Nonconformists, who found their pet Bills singled out for rejection. Nor did it at all suit the Irish; for if there was one thing certain it was that the House of Lords, except under direct coercion, would never accept Home Rule. But the Irish, as long as the Liberals were in a majority over all other parties, had no power to force the issue; and it suited the lukewarm Home Rulers among the Liberals very nicely to be able to tell the Irish leader Redmond that they were very sorry, but he would have to wait.

In 1909, then, the Liberals were wondering what to do next. They could not remain entirely passive while the House of Lords, having tasted blood, rejected more and more of their Bills. The moderates would have liked to come to a private arrangement with the Tories, under which the Lords would be allowed to kill a Bill every now and then, on condition that they did not do it too often, or so as to make it impossible for the Government to remain in power. But the Tories would not play the game. Most of them were eagerly urging the Lords to do their worst, in the belief that, if the Government could be forced to an election on some such issue as that of the right to get drunk, the electors could be relied on to drive it helter-skelter from office in defence of their traditional liberties. The Empire *versus* Mr. Stiggins would make, they thought, an admirable election cry.

Lloyd George, on the other hand, was well aware that

it would make a very bad one for the Liberal Party. And, as Chancellor of the Exchequer, he was able, in 1909, to force the Cabinet's hand. The famous "Land Tax" Budget of that year was meant to force a constitutional crisis. Lloyd George not only proposed to hit the titled landowners where it would hurt them most: he also put forward in defence of his proposals all his powers of invective. Without the stimulus of Lloyd George's oratory the Lords would almost certainly have hesitated to reject a Money Bill; for the exclusive control of finance by the House of Commons was definitely a part of Great Britain's unwritten constitution. But Lloyd George could be very provoking; and at Limehouse and a dozen other places he put forth all his powers in order to lure the Lords to their destruction. They responded by rejecting his Budget, and Asquith and the Liberal moderates, much to their chagrin, found themselves under the unavoidable necessity of playing Lloyd George's game, and setting out to wreck the British Constitution in a way that they did not at all desire. For they saw that, if they were beaten by the House of Lords, that would mean the eclipse of the Liberal Party; whereas, if they won, Radicalism would be immensely strengthened, and they would find themselves compelled to carry out their election promises to the Irish and the workers, and no longer able to argue that in doing nothing they were merely yielding to *force majeure*.

It was all very unpleasant for Asquith, who had succeeded Campbell-Bannerman as Prime Minister on his death in 1908; but he was left with no alternative. From 1909 to 1911 the unhappy battle was fought out. The Liberal moderates obtained the consolation prize of a preamble to the Parliament Bill in which the Government announced its intention of reforming the constitution of the Second Chamber; and this, they faintly hoped, would enable them later on to interpose fresh obstacles in the way of parliamentary democracy. But until that could be done (and it remains undone to-day) the frightened Liberal right wing found itself committed to a constitution under which a mere majority of the electors, mostly poor people, could pass what Bills they liked simply by returning M.P.s who would vote for the Bills in three successive sessions.

Nor was that all; for now the Liberal Government would have to give Ireland Home Rule, not merely because Home Rule had been promised, but because it could no longer do without the Irish votes in the House of Commons. The two General Elections of 1910—for in face of the King's reluctance to coerce the Lords by the threat of creating peers, it had taken two General Elections to get the Parliament Act on the Statute Book—had so reduced the Liberals' strength that they now only equalled the Conservatives in number, with eighty-four Irishmen and forty-two Labour members to hold the balance of power. Home Rule would have to be granted; and who could tell to what horrid complications the attempt to apply it would give rise? Moreover, who could tell what price the Labour Party, as well as the Irish, might not exact for their support?

It seemed, then, in 1911, that the Radicals had triumphed over the Liberal reactionaries, and that the country was in for a period of advanced Radical legislation. But the actual outcome was very different from this. The Irish demanded Home Rule, and as long as they saw a chance of getting it from the Liberals they could be relied on to keep the Government in office without insisting on anything besides. The Labour Party, for its part, could not outvote the Liberals if the Irish backed them; but, apart from this, there was something else that kept them tied securely to the Government's coat-tails. For in 1909 the House of Lords, undeterred by the reversal of the Taff Vale Judgment of 1901, had delivered a second judicial decision which struck at the very foundations on which the Labour Party rested. The House of Lords—that is, of course, the judicial tribunal called by that name, and not the legislative chamber—had declared in the Osborne Judgment (so named after W. V. Osborne, a branch secretary of the Railway Servants, who brought the case in the first instance), that it was *ultra vires* and unlawful for any Trade Union to expend any money at all on returning members to Parliament, or indeed, on any political object whatsoever.

Now, what the House of Lords declares to be the law *is* the law, until an Act of Parliament alters it. The fact that Trade Unions had been freely spending money on political objects ever since they had created the Labour Representation League in 1869, and sporadically long before that, could make no difference. From the moment when the House of Lords gave its decision, no Trade Union could lawfully contribute a penny to the Labour Party's finances, or spend a penny in helping any of its members to get elected to a public body, or in maintaining him when he had been elected. The Labour M.P.s saw themselves salary-less, unable to meet their election expenses, threatened with absolute expulsion from political life unless they could repeat their success over Taff Vale, and persuade the Liberal Government to pass a further Act reversing the effects of the Osborne Judgment.

Somehow, by begging, borrowing and scraping, the Labour Party managed to get through the two General Elections of 1910 with its representation practically unchanged. The Miners' Federation, which had stood aloof in 1906, having joined it under pressure of the threat to working-class political action, it came back nominally stronger than before—with forty members in January, and forty-two in December 1910, as against twenty-nine, exclusive of the miners, in 1906. But actually the working-class strength in Parliament remained almost the same; for even if further seats could have been won with more candidates and better organization, there was no money available for financing a forward drive.

The Labour Party, then, came back in 1910 clamouring for the immediate reversal of the Osborne Judgment. But the Liberals were in no hurry; for as long as the judgment remained in effect the Labour Party dared not risk turning them out. Something, however, had to be done at once if the unfortunate Labour M.P.s were not to starve or be forced to resign their seats. The answer was found in giving all M.P.s a salary at once. Payment of members, granted in 1911 at the rate of £400 a year, saved the Labour M.P.s from destitution and earned their gratitude. But for the reversal of the Osborne Judgment they could be made to wait, voting meanwhile in support of their Liberal paymasters. Not until 1913 did the Trade Union (Amendment) Act legalize political action by the Trade Unions; and even then the Labour Party had to be satisfied with much less than it had claimed. Trade Unions were allowed to spend money on political objects only if they first took a ballot of their members and secured a majority in favour, and then passed a special set of rules under which any member could claim exemption from political payments without suffering any disability in respect of his rights of union membership. Moreover, all political payments were to be made out of a special fund; and the general funds of the Unions could not be applied to any political purpose.

Even this, however, was conceded only after two years' delay; and the Labour Party had spent these two years obediently voting for Liberal measures. But these measures, so far from taking on a more truly radical character after the victory over the House of Lords, subtly changed their direction, and became essentially conservative—in the sense that they were designed to conserve the existing economic order against socialistic attack. The new spirit was manifested very clearly in the great National Insurance Act of 1911, which was to a large extent deliberately copied from Bismarck's German social legislation. In 1908, Old Age Pensions had been granted on a non-contributory basis, and financed out of general taxation. But now health and unemployment were to be dealt with in such a way that most of the cost of the new service would fall, not on the general body of taxpayers, but on the workers themselves. Each workman, and each employer, was to pay a weekly contribution into a national health insurance fund, to which the State was also to give a relatively small subsidy. Nominally, the workmen were to pay less than half the cost of the benefits they were to receive; but it was not difficult to see that the employers' contribution also would tend to come out of wages—for it would form a part of the cost of employing labour, and would be taken into account when wage bargains were being struck. A similar system of unemployment insurance was to be introduced experimentally for a few selected industries, with the idea that it could be extended later on when there had been time to see how it would work. In the meantime, small subsidies were to be paid in any industry to those Trade Unions which provided unemployment benefits of their own—that is, chiefly to the skilled workers; for the less-skilled workers could not afford high enough contributions to provide unemployment benefits, and would therefore get no share in the subsidies.

By this Act Lloyd George, following Bismarck's example, introduced into Great Britain the device—so greatly extended since by Liberals and Conservatives alike—of paying for social reform mainly out of the pockets of the poor. For redistributive taxation falling chiefly on the richer classes he successfully substituted a lateral redistribution, whereby the healthy and the employed workers were made to contribute towards the needs of the sick and the workless. And in doing this, he spiked the Socialist guns. Almost insurmountable obstacles were put in the way of the creation of a State Medical Service; and the Labour Party's Right to Work Bill, with its demand for full maintenance at Trade Union wages in default of work, was ruled out of practical politics.

The National Insurance Act was an answer, and politically an effective answer, to the Minority Report of the Poor Law Commission, which, appointed under the Conservatives, only finished its labours in 1909. On one main issue the Majority and the Minority of the Commission agreed. They both held that the Poor Law, as it stood, was obsolete, and that the *ad hoc* Boards of Guardians ought to be abolished and their functions handed over to the town and county councils, as had actually been done in the case of the *ad hoc* School Boards in 1902. But the Minority Report—the work chiefly of the Webbs—went much further than this, proposing a complete break-up of the Poor Law, and the institution under the local authorities of a complete public health service, without any taint of pauperism, and therewith of a complete system of provision for the unemployed, based on the "right to work."

The Insurance Act was Lloyd George's essentially conservative answer to these demands. Not only did he institute the contributory system: he also firmly entrenched it against attack by handing over the administration of health insurance to a list of "Approved Societies"—friendly societies and insurance companies in the main, but also Trade Unions, where they chose to set up special machinery for the purpose—and by instituting the system of "panel practice," whereby the medical profession, which used its chance to drive a remarkably hard financial bargain, came to regard the insurance system as its guarantee against nationalization through a State Medical Service. Similarly, by allowing the Trade Unions to administer unemployment insurance, Lloyd George bought off their opposition and secured himself against their pressing demand for a non-contributory system of public maintenance of the unemployed.

It was all very cleverly done; and in doing it Lloyd George successfully dished the Socialists. For, though a small minority of Socialists, reinforced by Hilaire Belloc, denounced the contributory system as an attempt, imitated from bureaucratic Germany, to introduce the "servile state," the majority of the Trade Union leaders took a quite different view. Attracted by the powers accorded to the Trade Unions to administer both health and unemployment insurance, they regarded the Bill with favour, as giving to Trade Unionism a new recognition at the hands of the State, and a new opportunity of extending its membership and influence.

Thus the Labour Party, with the exception of a few convinced Socialists, so far from fighting the Insurance Bill, supported it, and ranged itself more decisively than before on the side of the Liberal Government. In the same year, the Cabinet made a further bid for the backing of the Unions by passing the Coal Mines Regulation Act, which did something to stiffen up safety provisions; and in the same session the Shops Act was passed in a sadly mutilated form, providing for regular meal-times and weekly half-holidays, but leaving the major question of working hours untouched.

But with 1911 the output of social legislation, good and bad together, abruptly ceased. Parliament became too fully occupied with the Irish question to have time to spare for major social measures, even if there had been any which the Cabinet really wished to pass into law. Parliamentary attention was shared between Ireland, militant suffrage and the growing menace of European war. Meanwhile, in the country, labour unrest increased apace. There were great strikes in 1911 and 1912, and a host of smaller disputes in one trade after another in 1913. The unrest continued into 1914, and on the eve of the outbreak of war the new Triple Alliance of Miners, Railwaymen and Transport Workers was just setting about its preparations for the biggest strike of all. Ulster was threatening civil war, and the British Army rebellion. Suffragettes were destroying property wholesale in a desperate attempt to assert the claims of women against man-made law and order. More and more evidently, the Government was ceasing to govern, and parliamentary institutions were falling into disrepute. The spirit of revolt was spreading from one section of the people to another, and manifesting itself in a demand for new leadership and a new philosophy of life. One after another the old leaders were made to look ridiculous. The hesitant Balfour had been thrust out of the Tory leadership in 1911 in favour of the fire-eating Presbyterian, Bonar Law. Redmond was losing his hold in Ireland, in face of the rise of the National Volunteers, Sinn Fein, and the Irish Labour movement led by James Connolly and James Larkin. Mrs. Fawcett had been pushed into the background of the suffrage movement by the Pankhursts, with their militant policy of violence and destruction. And, in the world of labour, while the Parliamentary Labour Party continued to vote placidly for the Liberals, the Trade Union leaders had lost their grip on the rank and file, and spent their time alternately denouncing unauthorized strikes and reluctantly conducting them.

A recent writer has given to his history of these years before the outbreak of the First World War, a significant title—*The Strange Death of Liberal England*. Others have regarded the year 1914 as marking, for all Europe and perhaps for all the world, the end of "the Liberal experiment." What is meant by Liberalism in this connection cannot be quite simply said; for it involves at least two separate things. Economically, it involves a system in which the State stands as far as possible outside the field of industry and trade, confining itself to the police protection of property rights, and, apart from that, leaving things to be settled by private contracts. Free Trade is only one manifestation of this attitude, albeit the most prominent. For Free Trade among the nations is only the logical corollary of free enterprise within each nation, regarded as the one way of ensuring the maximum total production of wealth. This freedom, said the Liberals, conveniently ignoring the unequal distribution of property rights, will ensure to each man what he is worth as a producer, and therewith to the whole community the largest possible output of wealth and— since everyone will be free to spend his income as he chooses —of welfare as well as wealth. And the old-style Radical was ready to assent, with only one qualification, which was that the inheritors of unearned wealth must be taxed and deprived of special privileges and the door of opportunity opened more equally to all comers.

This was one aspect of pre-war Liberalism. But there was another. The Liberal believed in government by persuasion and not by force, and in the duty of magistrates to be tolerant, and of minorities, when they were tolerated, to give way. He believed in parliamentary institutions, in representative government, and in the party system as a means of both canalizing and in the last resort compromising political differences. It would be much too much to say that he believed in democracy, even in a purely political sense; for most Liberals, fully as much as most Conservatives, drew in their minds a sharp distinction between those who were fit to govern and those who had merely a claim to vote, and even the right to vote was still denied by many Liberals to all women and to some adult men. Nor did the Liberal faith involve a belief in the virtues of exclusive government by a popular chamber, even if it consisted mainly of persons qualified for active, and not merely for passive, citizenship. They held to the monarchy and most of them, even if they disliked the House of Lords, wanted some sort of Second Chamber, less democratically chosen and composed than the Commons, with the mission of stopping unduly hasty innovation. What they did believe in was not democracy but consent to do nothing except in order and without violence, and an acceptance of Parliament as it actually existed as the necessary instrument of change.

Politics could work on the basis of this set of beliefs as long as no body of persons large enough or influential enough to resist the ordinary police methods of coercion wanted with real passion anything which they could not hope to win in a reasonable time, or to retain, if they had it already, by parliamentary means. What happened in the years immediately before 1914 was that not one powerful group, but several at the same time, found Parliament standing with apparent immobility in the way of things which they wanted much too strongly to be prepared to give them up without a struggle. They felt too seriously about these claims to be limited by the traditional rules of the game. Before the impact of these forces Liberal parliamentarism found itself helpless and afraid. It could not see its way to granting what the protestants wanted without undermining the foundations of the social system and provoking violent reactions on the part of those who wanted the very opposite. But equally it could not see its way to resisting the demands except by force; and it was well aware of the danger that, if it resorted to force against force, it might speedily cease to be Liberalism, and forfeit its claim to govern. For, if Liberalism started suppressing the Left, it would be attempting to carry out a policy which Toryism could carry out much better. It would be ground to powder between Toryism and the new Radicalism, which would inevitably pass under Socialist leadership.

What needs explaining is why simultaneously so many groups, whose grievances and aspirations were not after all new, began about 1910 to demand what they wanted in a violent fashion that had been well-nigh forgotten in British political life. It is easy enough to explain this, up to a point. The Irish had grown tired of waiting for Home Rule, and the women of a constitutional agitation which seemed to bring them no nearer the vote. The Trade Unionists had grown tired of a parade of social reforms which did not prevent the purchasing power of their wages from falling year after year. The Tories, untrue to the principles of political compromise which they had lauded while in office, had egged on the House of Lords to unconstitutional action against the declared will of the electors and the traditional rights of the House of Commons. The law, acting through the House of Lords in its judicial capacity, had shown itself so monstrously unfair to the Trade Unions as to destroy all respect for its sanctions.

All this is true, as far as it goes. But it does not sufficiently explain what happened. The deeper truth has to be stated in terms of a changing world situation. Parliaments, everywhere

where they held real power, were coming up against problems which could not be solved by the traditional parliamentary methods. The assumption which lay behind the Liberal attitude was that everything that was necessary could be accomplished by slow, cumulative changes, none big enough by itself to shock any large body of its opponents into positive revolt, and all together not amounting to any alteration in the fundamental character of the social and economic system. But for a variety of reasons this attitude was rapidly becoming untenable.

This was not at all because the advocates of change were for the most part by any means exacting in their claims. On the contrary, they demanded very little. The Irish Home Rulers would have been content with an Irish Parliament which would not have been very much more than a glorified County Council, empowered to manage purely local affairs under the continued sovereignty of the British Parliament. Most suffragettes would have been quite ready to accept a Bill which would have left the great majority of women— indeed, nearly all working-women—without the vote. And the Trade Unionists would have been satisfied, all but an insignificant minority of them, with a quite small rise in real wages, such as capitalism seemed as if it could easily afford to grant out of its rapidly increasing profits.

But not one of these essentially moderate demands was conceded. The Liberals played at Peep-Bo with the advocates of women's suffrage, alternately raising hopes with promises and slipping dexterously out of their fulfilment. Some of them feared that the women would vote for the Tories, and others that the admission of women to the franchise would undermine the respect of men for parliamentary government. Yet others simply disliked the idea of change, especially now that the existing electorate had thrice returned a Liberal Government to office. As for Ireland, Home Rule was all very well in theory; but it looked very different when it came to drawing up an acceptable Bill. For the Irish Nationalists would not agree to exclude Ulster; and Ulster had already made plain its extreme aversion to being governed under the orders of the "Pope of Rome." Moreover, the Tories, defeated over the

House of Lords, were looking round for a new instrument through which they could re-assert their indefeasible right, in office or out of it, to decide how the country should be governed; and now that the Irish Nationalists were in a position to force the Government's hands, they saw their chance in egging on the Ulstermen to rebellion, just as they had previously egged on the peers to veto Lloyd George's Budget. Finally, as to Labour, the capitalists said they were very sorry, but in the face of growingly intense world competition for trade, they simply could not afford to raise anybody's wages, at any rate as long as Free Trade continued to leave British industry at the mercy of foreign "dumping."

Accordingly, one after another, the petitioners for change were sent away empty-handed. With traditional British aplomb—for even Irish members of the British Parliament were apt to imbibe the British spirit—they went away quietly, to explain to their followers how undeniably difficult everything after all was. But their followers were not so ready to follow them as they had been; for the Liberal victory of 1906 had aroused great and insistent hopes. Much to Mrs. Fawcett's horror, Mrs. Pankhurst, who had launched her Women's Social and Political Union as far back as 1903, and had actually made her first essays in militancy in 1905, suddenly became a power, commanding a fanatical body of followers. Sir Edward Carson, though he hailed from Southern Ireland, made himself the uncrowned king of Ulster with his Ulster Unionist Council of 1911 and his Ulster Covenant of 1912; and John Redmond was alarmed to find his followers begin drilling in imitation of the Northerners instead of putting their trust in the good faith and constitutional authority of the British Parliament. Even more were Ramsay MacDonald and the Trade Union leaders scandalized when Trade Unionists came pouring out on strike without Trade Union authority and often in breach of agreement, and when Tom Mann and other left-wingers began preaching the gospel of "Direct Action," and telling the workers that nothing real would ever be done for them until they took their courage in both hands and did things for themselves.

Why did the politicians and the capitalists fail, at this stage, to make the moderate concessions which would still have quelled the unrest? In the main, they failed because they really felt that the system could not afford to make them. Thus, to take first the case of the capitalists confronted with the workers' claims for higher wages, it was true that foreign competition had grown more intense, and that British exports were being sold abroad at a narrower margin of profit. This did not prevent the British capitalist class from making in the aggregate much bigger profits than ever before; for they were selling more goods, and reaping a rapidly increasing harvest from the investments of British capital abroad. But they did feel that, if they had to pay more in wages, Germany and America would make heavy inroads on their markets; and Liberal apologists agreed with them that a rise in wage-costs in Great Britain would provoke a flight of capital to lands where labour could be exploited with less hindrance. Actually, the capitalist class was investing its profits abroad rather than at home at a very rapidly increasing rate; and this was widely held to show that British wages were in fact too high, and that the rise in prices which was lowering real wages was really a blessing in disguise.

On the other hand, what the workers saw, more and more clearly, was that capitalist incomes were increasing fast, even while the purchasing power of their wages was going down, and that Liberal social reform, especially since Lloyd George had hit on the device of making the workers pay for it, was doing nothing to arrest this process. Their simple view was that, as the power to produce wealth grew greater, the standard of living ought to rise with it. They still held mostly to Free Trade, for it seemed a queer way of improving their lot to send the cost of living up still faster by tariff reform. But, if Free Trade maximized wealth, as the Liberals maintained, the workers wanted their share, and they did not appear to be getting it, or the Labour Party to be helping them to get it. Hence the revulsion against Labour politics, and the resort to direct action by one body of Trade Unionists after another.

Irish Home Rule was, of course, on a different footing; but here too there were economic forces at work. The opposition to Irish self-government was strengthened by the fear that, if it came to war between Germany and Great Britain, a half-free Ireland might range itself dangerously on the German side. The struggle between Great Britain and Germany was at bottom largely economic. It was a contest for world economic supremacy and colonial empire. Ireland became a pawn in the game. Great Britain might lose the Irish market: Great Britain might lose Ireland itself, and find German naval bases interposed between her shores and the countries from which she must draw the food to supply her people. Even the most moderate measure of Home Rule began to look too dangerous when politicians considered to what it might lead in the end.

Liberalism had reached an impasse. Having gone a long way towards clearing the House of Lords out of its path, it dared not advance along the road which had been laid open. But equally it could not retrace its steps. It was penned up helplessly in a narrow space, from which it could find no exit that it dared attempt. It was reduced to feeble efforts at compromise, varied only by pitiable simulations of a firmness which was entirely alien to its character.

The militant suffragettes, as the most unpopular of its adversaries, fared worst at its hands. They were beaten and bludgeoned, forcibly fed in prison with almost Hitlerian barbarity, alternately released and re-arrested under the "Cat and Mouse" Act of 1913 when these brutalities failed to quell the movement. The militant suffrage movement was largely psychopathic; but it would hardly have happened, or at any rate have survived the first reprisals, had it not found the world in a ferment, and the parliamentarians already with the utmost plainness on the run.

In their defiance of the rights of property, and in the sheer lust for destruction which came upon them, the militant suffragettes far outran even the most extreme Syndicalists and apostles of Labour revolt. Indeed the workers, all through the strike movements of 1911 and the following years, remained remarkably law-abiding. Only once, at Liverpool in 1911, in the course of the local transport strike which was the prelude to the national railway stoppage, was there any considerable rioting, though there were a number of small scrimmages with

the police in the mining areas of South Wales. Strong words
were used in plenty; but the strikers were not violent in deed.
At the most, they tried to stop blacklegs from working: they set
fire to no pillar-boxes and burnt no churches—or even factories
—after the fashion of the suffragettes. They simply refused to
return to work until something had been done to set right their
more pressing grievances.

Doubtless, this was partly due to the fact that the Trade
Unions, however much many of their leaders disliked the wave
of strikes, were usually compelled to take charge of them when
they had actually broken out. The national railway strike of
1911 began unofficially; but it was speedily made official. The
national mining strike of 1912 was official from the outset, and
so were the strikes in the cotton industry in 1910 and 1911.
But there was another reason for the law-abidingness of the
strikers. The suffragettes were a tiny minority of women,
taking violent action without reference to the opinion of the
majority. But a strike cannot succeed without majority support. It has to carry the moderates as well as the extremists.
It therefore takes quite extraordinary provocation to induce
a body of strikers to resort to violence. Blacklegging under
police protection may do it now and then, or so extreme a
measure as the refusal of the bare right of combination. But
usually strikes are tame enough, unless the strikers are driven
past all bearing.

Ireland also was much less violent than the suffragettes.
There, rival armies of Ulstermen and Nationalists drilled
enthusiastically; but even in Ulster, where the two were mixed
up together, they did not come to fighting in earnest. Indeed,
right up to 1914 it remained a matter of doubt how far the
threatened Ulster resistance was mere bluff. If Parliament
passed a Home Rule Act, would Ulster really declare civil war?

By 1914 probably Sir Edward Carson and the rest of the
Ulster leaders had talked themselves into a mood in which
they would really have resisted Home Rule by force, if any
attempt had been made to impose it. But it is improbable that
they, and still more improbable that Bonar Law and the
British Conservatives, were really serious in threatening civil
war at the beginning of the Home Rule controversy. It is far

likelier that they believed the Liberal Government, known to
be both timid and lukewarm about the Irish claims, would
yield to their bluster, at any rate to the point of excluding
the Protestant counties. In that event, the onus of resistance
would be transferred to the Irish Nationalists, and Home Rule
would be either dropped altogether, or carried in a form
which would alienate the Nationalists from the Liberals. But
Redmond could not agree to partition without losing control
of his followers, and the Liberals could not govern Great
Britain without the Irish vote. Partition, therefore, could not
be proposed until the eleventh hour, when the Liberals were
already between the devil and the deep sea.

In the end, Ulster's will to resist was not put to the proof.
What defeated the Home Rule Bill was not an Ulster rebellion,
but mutiny in the British Army. No one, to be sure, consulted
the common soldiers about their willingness to coerce Ulster:
it was a body of officers, overwhelmingly Tory in politics,
who, encouraged thereto by extraordinary folly at the War
Office, announced their refusal to obey orders, and their
intention of resigning their commissions sooner than take up
arms against the Ulster "loyalists." The "Curragh Incident"
of March 1914 finally destroyed what was left of the Government's prestige, and incidentally played its part in settling the
date of the European War. After it, no one was surprised when
the Ulstermen were allowed to run in unmolested at Larne
a large supply of guns and ammunition for the volunteers,
whereas an attempt by the Nationalists to run a counter-
supply at Howth promptly brought British soldiers upon the
scene, and led to an affray in which several Irishmen lost their
lives. Ulster, aided and abetted by the Tory Party, had
successfully threatened rebellion. A considerable body of
officers, encouraged by a high War Office official and serving
soldier, had mutinied against the Government. Coming on
top of suffragette outrages and widespread strikes which the
Government was powerless to settle or to repress, the Irish
events of 1914 had reduced the Liberal Party to the last gasp.
The great Liberal experiment, begun so glamorously with the
electoral victory of 1906, was ending in ignominious rout.
Only the outbreak of the Great War could have sufficed to give

the Government a reprieve. The day of parliamentary Liberalism, or at any rate of the Liberal Party, was definitely done.

All this time the threat of war had been hanging over the Government, in addition to its domestic troubles. In July 1911, by way of retort to French military operations in Morocco, the German Government had dispatched the warship *Panther*, to seize the Moroccan port of Agadir. For a full month Europe seemed on the brink of war; but then, faced with the certainty that Great Britain and France would act together, the Germans gave way, and the war danger again receded for a time. But the Italians seized their chance, by way of "compensation" for the French occupation of Morocco, to declare war on Turkey and lay hands on Tripoli; and Turkey's defeat at the hands of Italy led on directly to the Balkan Wars of 1912–13, which in turn led on to the Austro-Serbian conflict and to the Great War of 1914.

This is not the place for any full consideration of the factors which went to the making of the Great War. We are concerned here to notice only the extent to which almost continuous tension in international relations affected and conditioned the course of events at home. The national railway strike of 1911 was settled largely by urging upon both sides that its continuance might easily cause war; for the crisis following upon the Agadir incident was at its height when the strike occurred. Some part of the Government's extraordinary pusillanimity in humbling the Ulster revolt must be attributed to the fear that civil war in Ireland would probably mean world war as well. But to recognize this is only to throw into stronger relief the unparliamentary conduct of the British Tories; for they at any rate were not at all deterred from promoting rebellion and mutiny at home by the thought of international consequences. So set were the Tories on defeating the Government that they hesitated at nothing. But when one of the two great parties between which the only choice of government lay had ceased to play the parliamentary game, and was ready to appeal to force even against the verdict of the electorate, parliamentary Liberalism had become unworkable. Its forms might indeed precariously remain; but its spirit was dead. For it takes both sides to play the Liberal game successfully.

CHAPTER XXXIX

SYNDICALISM AND SUFFRAGE

WITHIN the ranks of the working class, unparliamentary action remained an aspiration. No actual revolutionary movement took place; the destructive tendencies of Direct Actionists were expressed solely in strikes and sabotage. Its development was, however, sufficiently disconcerting. A new group of devoted agitators, expounding a new theory, provided a philosophy and a programme of tactics which were with good reason far more alarming to the employing class than the decorous and hypothetical Socialism of the Labour M.P.s.

The new philosophy was called Syndicalism or industrial unionism, two names with much the same meaning, but the first indicating a French inspiration and the second an American. The French influence, perhaps, was philosophically greater, for it was derived from a thought-out system whose ablest exponent was Sorel. Practically the American influence was greater, for it was based on the solid advantages of industrial unionism. The basis of the whole movement was certainly best expressed in the famous Preamble of the I.W.W. (the American "Industrial Workers of the World"):

"The working class and the employing class have nothing in common. There can be no peace so long as hunger and want are found among millions of working people and the few, who make up the employing class, have all the good things of life. . . . These conditions can be changed and the interest of the working class upheld only by an organization formed in such a way that all its members in any one industry, or in all industries if necessary, cease work whenever a strike or lockout is on in any department, thus making an injury to one an injury to all. Instead of the Conservative motto: 'A fair day's wage for a fair day's work,' we must inscribe on our banner the revolutionary watchword: 'Abolition of the wage system' . . . By organizing industrially we are forming the structure of the new society within the shell of the old."

The I.W.W., whose period of power lies between 1903 and 1913, was a magnificently heroic union whose violent conflicts with a singularly brutal employing class make an epic history very far removed from the peaceful British record. The boycott, the sympathetic strike, no peace with the employers, the smashing of the old reactionary Unions, the breaking of all agreements when convenient, the forcing of non-unionists out of existence, the use of sabotage—all of these principles were taken over in theory from the I.W.W., but their application was much milder and the enemies were far less savage. More French, possibly, was the provision that no officials should be re-eligible (so that rank and file control might be certain), no friendly benefit funds allowed, no political activities permitted, and the private soldiers appealed to directly not to shoot their fellow-workers in civil troubles. The French leaders had systematized a whole philosophy which declared that bourgeois morality and ethics were false and an instrument of class oppression, and had prescribed a programme of revolution by incessant strikes which would end in a "social general strike" to put an end to the capitalist system by the local Unions taking over each its appropriate industry in its locality and creating a federation of autonomous industrial republics. In certain French circles it was held that the general strike would never really happen and was only an "energizing myth"; but such artificial mystery-making was never imported into Britain. The syndicalist belief in the general strike was entirely genuine.

But the new movement was not wholly foreign in origin, though the return of its most able propagandist, Tom Mann, from abroad in 1910 underlined its imported character. French and American Syndicalism derived mostly from Proudhon and Bakunin, but a Marxist form was already present in Britain. The Socialist Labour Party (S.L.P.) founded in 1903 was strictly orthodox Marxist, as its inspirer the American Daniel De Leon required. "He held the materialist conception of history, the class war, and even the iron law of wages to need as little defence as the multiplication table." Translated into immediate policy, the S.L.P. doctrine meant a policy of industrial class war similar to that of the

I.W.W., but under the direction of a strictly disciplined and uncompromising political party. The S.L.P. never had more than a few hundred members, mostly in Glasgow, but these members were picked men, distinguished by fanaticism, energy, and skill in industrial conflict, and right up to 1920, when the better part of the party joined the Communists, they wielded an influence out of all proportion to their numbers.

Another powerful influence was educational in origin. In the 'seventies, the University Extension Movement had attempted to carry the message of academic culture to the working classes and Extension Centres had been founded in many of the larger towns. Several of these served as the basis for Colleges which grew later into Universities; but in general the movement soon lost its working-class appeal and became predominantly middle-class. In the 'seventies and 'eighties progressive University teachers had attempted to persuade the Co-operative Movement seriously to take up adult education; but this attempt also petered out, and presently the way was clear for a fresh campaign.

Ruskin College had been founded in 1899, for the purpose of extending the benefits of an Oxford education to members of the working class. The Workers' Educational Association (W.E.A.) was founded in 1903 with the object of setting up classes for working people in every locality where University talent was available. Ruskin College owed its finances to private benefaction; the Association before long was able to draw fairly freely upon help from the Universities, supplemented later by financial aid from the Board of Education and the local educational authorities. The general satisfaction with which the work of both bodies was received was broken in 1906 by the news of acute dissension within Ruskin College. A revolt of students occurred, patronized by the Principal himself, Dennis Hird; the revolt was not against conditions but against the character of the teaching, which the students claimed was merely a disguised propaganda in favour of the capitalist system. Specifically, they demanded that the College abandon teaching Jevons's economics and replace it by Marx's. Disagreement became more and more violent until in 1909 an actual split occurred. The Principal and the rebellious students set up a Central Labour College, which was shortly after removed to London and financially supported by the South Wales Miners' Federation and the new National Union of Railwaymen. The organization which had supported and organized the secession took—from a De Leon pamphlet drawing a simple parallel from Roman history—the name "Plebs League," and before long began to organize classes, mostly taken by ex-Labour College students, up and down the country. This brought it in due course into collision with the W.E.A., but the fiercest conflict between the two was to come after 1918. The League never made anti-Parliamentarism one of its formal principles, but its members were convinced that the revolution would come through the uncompromising direct action of industrial Unions, and that the Labour Party was a feeble and timorous body.

In every industry Syndicalists preached the same gospel. Tom Mann the engineer, Guy Bowman the journalist, George Hicks and J. V. Wills the bricklayers, John Hamilton the mason, W. H. Mainwaring, Noah Ablett and A. J. Cook the miners, W. W. Craik the railwayman, A. A. Purcell (furnishing trades), E. J. B. Allen (Gasworkers), and many others collaborated in working out plans for reconditioning the Trade Union movement. The Industrial Syndicalist Education League, launched at a conference held in November 1910, assembled 200 delegates representing 60,000 workers. Both before and after this a stream of pamphlets was issued, many written by Tom Mann alone but the most famous, *The Miners' Next Step*, by A. J. Cook and others. Nearly all appealed to what was the most incontestable point in Syndicalist propaganda—the abject inefficiency of the Trade Unions as they stood. There were no less than 1,168 Unions in Great Britain in 1909 (with 2,369,000 members); in the opinion of the Syndicalists no more than fourteen were needed. Even on the railways, where it should have been simple to organize the workers into one block against their peculiarly tyrannous employers, there were five strictly railway Unions, frequently on bad terms with one another, and forty-seven more competing for members in the railway engineering and carriage shops.

Mining appeared less confused, but the Miners' Federation of Great Britain was no more than a Federation, embracing many local Unions and Federations, which had their own funds and only too often wanted to have their own policy. The textile Unions were so complicatedly organized that it would need a chapter to describe them fully. In the engineering and ship-building trades the Unions were so many and so overlapping that the industry was chronically racked by vicious inter-union disputes which left the workers with no funds or fighting spirit to use against their employers. But the nadir was probably reached in the building trade, where there were nineteen major Unions and an uncounted number of trivial or local societies. They were divided by craft and by region; the United Operative Plumbers recorded without dissatisfaction that they had permanent disputes with no less than five other crafts, not counting their local dispute with the Scottish plumbers.

Such hopeless confusion could have been overcome only by effective unity between all the officials of the competing bodies, and their earnest co-operation in campaigns against the employers. No such thing occurred. The officials were mostly ageing and inert men, attached to routine and precedent. They generally shared their more reactionary members' jea-lousy of other craftsmen or of unskilled labourers. They had a human dislike to the prospect of losing their jobs by the amal-gamation of craft Unions into industrial Unions, and they frequently were honestly convinced that the Syndicalist pro-paganda was immoral and destructive. They carried on a tenacious and obstructive fight against the industrial unionists in every trade.

Not only the Syndicalists, but the suffragists, the Irish Nationalists, and the "distributists" led by Belloc and Chesterton, had from 1912 on a more powerful ally than any revolutionary movement had ever had. After a short run in 1911 as a printers' strike sheet, the *Daily Herald* started in April 1912 as a daily paper devoted to the revolutionary Labour cause. Its first editors were Seed, Rowland Kenney, Charles Lapworth and then, at the end of 1913, George Lans-bury, who occupied the editorial chair for ten years. Its first

issues had to handle the *Titanic* disaster; it at once made its
class viewpoint clear. It picked out the fact that many more
first-class passengers were saved than third. "They have paid
30 per cent to their shareholders and they have sacrificed 51
per cent of the steerage children," it said of the White Star
line. In May 1912 it said of strikes: "We have considered the
matter. We have considered every phase of it and we say:
'Prepare your organization and then strike.' STRIKE AND
STRIKE HARD." Its chief object of derision was the I.L.P.,
which, under the guidance of Philip Snowden and Ramsay
MacDonald, was with some difficulty holding the Socialists of
Great Britain firmly attached to the Liberal Government.
Will Dyson's cartoons, with a power and ferocity entirely new
to British politics, were the most effective vehicle of this mock-
ing; G. K. Chesterton's special articles were wittier but hardly
less destructive. After the Trades Union Congress withdrew
its support in October 1912, to sponsor a mild and moderate
rival called the *Daily Citizen*, personal attacks were included.
"Mr. MacDonald," wrote Chesterton, "has no position, high
or low, in any of the three dimensions of the universe. It would
not have made the slightest difference for good or ill, to the
future of anything or anybody, if the tiger had eaten him.
There would have been a Liberal member for Leicester
instead, who would have made the same speeches, given
exactly the same votes; and, if he were the usual successful
soapboiler, would have eclipsed Mr. MacDonald in everything
except good looks."

The revolutionaries were at the same time conducting a war
and reconstructing their war machine. Every big strike was
a victory for them; so was every reform in Union structure.
In both spheres they achieved some remarkable successes.
Britain had probably never seen such a storm of strikes as
broke over the country from 1910 onwards. Clouds had been
gathering before; the Amalgamated Society of Railway Servants had threatened to take the offensive in 1907, and the
situation had been sufficiently serious for Lloyd George to
enforce a compromise which instituted Conciliation Boards on
the railways. The next year he ended an obstinate strike of
shipyard engineers involving thirty thousand employees. But

neither he, nor the overworked civil servant, George Askwith, could cope with the outburst when it came.

There had been considerable wage losses in 1908, and in 1909 the first attempts were made to reverse them. These were chiefly local mining strikes and might well have been dismissed as not significant. On the last day of the year, the day before the Coal Mines Act was due to be applied, the Northumberland and Durham miners' leaders agreed to a system of three shifts a day, to which the colliers objected, as depriving them of much of the benefit of an eight-hour day. Defying their leaders—a notable point—about a third of the miners on the North-East Coast went out on an unofficial strike which lasted till April 1910. But it was not successful; neither was one on the North-Eastern Railway. The restiveness of the workers, indeed, was elsewhere anticipated by the bellicoseness of the employers; in October 1910 the Federation of Master Cotton Spinners locked out 102,000 workers because of a local dispute over the victimization of a grinder named Howe, and the month before the shipyard employers locked out all members of the Boilermakers' Society on questions of interpretation of a previous agreement. Both these lockouts ended in compromise. In South Wales, continual disputes at the collieries of the Cambrian Combine led to a general miners' strike—not officially supported—for a minimum wage. This, too, was unsuccessful, but it started more serious things. In January 1911, the Miners' Federation of Great Britain declared in favour of action to enforce a minimum wage. A big strike was obviously looming.

Before it could come, the thunderstorm broke elsewhere. The National Sailors' and Firemen's Union called its members out on strike: Southampton, Goole and Hull were the first to come out, but soon the whole island was tied up. When the ship-owners tried to use blacklegs the carters and other dockworkers struck in support. The employers were angry, but unprepared. In port after port they climbed down and granted the sailors large increases in wages. The sailors' victory had started the dockers off. For years dock organization had remained at the point reached in 1889, but only the year before industrial unionist pressure had brought the

CP : R

various Unions together in a Transport Workers' Federation. This now did excellent service in co-ordinating and supporting a series of local strikes, beginning with the Manchester stevedores and carters, and culminating in the great London dock strike of August 1911. Everywhere the strikers were victorious and considerable monetary gains resulted. Most sensational of all was the Liverpool strike in the same month. Every form of transport, railways included, was struck and for some days the city was in a state of siege. A Government Commission alone persuaded the strikers back to work, the Corporation proving oddly enough the most obstinate among the employers. The Liverpool railwaymen's example infected their fellows elsewhere; local strikes began to occur, and on August 17, rather hurriedly putting themselves at the head of a movement which was proceeding forward without them, a joint Committee of the four railway unions called a national strike. The stoppage was not complete, but the railways were badly disorganized, and the Government hurriedly patched up a settlement pending the report of a Royal Commission. The report, in December, gave the Unions some of their demands, not including that of recognition by the companies, but including a greatly improved Conciliation Scheme. This scheme allowed union officials to become secretaries to the Conciliation Boards and soon the whole machinery was safely in their hands.

The Syndicalists were soon to be able to point out that governments as well as employers could be coerced by strong strike action. At the beginning of December the Miners' Federation Conference formally demanded a national minimum wage, and in January 1912 its members voted 445,801 to 115,721 in favour of striking to secure it. The Government intervened with a plan for district negotiations to secure to all miners "power to earn a reasonable minimum wage." This plan was wrecked by the coal-owners of Scotland and South Wales, and on the first of March there began the biggest strike Britain had ever seen, "about a million" being involved according to the Board of Trade. The strength of the men was obvious, and on the 19th the Government introduced a Minimum Wage Bill, by which twenty-two district boards of workers and employers, with a chairman either agreed on by both parties or appointed by the Board of Trade, should fix legally compulsory minimum wages. This the Miners' executive accepted, though the poll showed 244,011 Noes to 201,013 Yeses, since the majority was obviously too small to justify a prolonged struggle for a nationally fixed minimum.

The only important counter-attack came from the London dock employers. The newly formed Port of London Authority had as chairman the grocer Hudson Kearley, who had been ennobled as Lord Devonport, and who deeply resented not finding among the dockers the submissiveness that he expected from his unfortunate shop-assistants. But his own venom, though Labour propagandists fixed upon it, was merely characteristic of his type and indeed of a vast number of company directors. Far more than their financial loss, they resented the ending of their autocracy; it was indiscipline, the self-assertion of those born to be subordinate, that provoked their most implacable resentment. A chance dispute gave the dock authorities their opportunity in the summer of 1912; ignoring the proposals of the Government as well as the Transport Workers' Federation, Lord Devonport announced their intention of refusing to take part in any joint body or recognize the Federation. The struggle was bitter; it was on this occasion that Ben Tillett on Tower Hill led the dockers in the famous prayer: "God strike Lord Devonport dead." The resentment of the old-fashioned Union leaders against the Syndicalists now came into the open; J. H. Thomas, a powerful railwaymen's leader, for the first time intervened against fellow-unionists during a strike, by publicly attacking and "deprecating" the methods of the Federation. The Federation, overestimating its power and forgetting it was a Federation and not a Union, called a national provincial strike in support of London. It was not obeyed, and in August the strike ended in defeat.

A smaller, but most significant strike, ended in partial victory. Driver Knox, of the North-Eastern Railway, one day drank too much while off duty; the company thereupon reduced him in rank. Six thousand fellow-employees forthwith struck work, as a protest against this impertinence. The newspapers featured this strike, with unusual unfairness, as one "for the right to get drunk," but the strikers successfully destroyed the employers' claim to interfere with an employee's life out of working hours. Driver Knox was reinstated, though his supporters accepted a fine for striking without giving notice.

Mostly, these conflicts went on without State interference. The "Don't Shoot" prosecution has already been quoted, and in Llanelly during the railway strike two men were shot dead by the military. But apart from these two incidents no use was made of the State power; mediation was all that was offered. Far more violence was shown to the militant suffragettes. Their attack was more violent; they smashed windows, fired pillar-boxes, slashed pictures, threw things at M.P.s and even burned down churches and houses; in reply they were treated with great roughness by policemen and worse by crowds. They were kicked and beaten; their hair was pulled and their clothes half-torn off; hatpins were pushed into them, they were knocked down and trampled upon. In prison they were "forcibly fed" as a reply to their hunger-strikes; great suffering was caused by this operation, which sounds far milder than it is. The Government increased this by the "Cat and Mouse" Act, which empowered it to release prisoners when starvation or forcible feeding had reduced them to a dangerous state of illness, re-arrest them when recovered, release them again when they had been reduced again to collapse, and so on.

These spectacular conflicts came as the result of suddenly exhausted patience. After Mr. Gladstone's influence had been removed, a Bill for woman suffrage on which great hopes were pinned was successfully carried to a second reading by a Mr. Faithfull Begg in 1897, only to be talked out as a great jest by Mr. Labouchere, who delivered an enormous speech on verminous persons. Numerous societies continued to agitate peacefully, and from that year on the National Union of Women's Suffrage Societies, led by Mrs Fawcett, co-ordinated their actions. But their appeals were ignored; from 1903 Mrs. Pankhurst and her daughters Christabel and Sylvia, with Mr. and Mrs. Pethick Lawrence, founded the Women's Social and Political Union, to take more active measures—though in fact for some years these consisted in little more than persistently asking questions at Liberal meetings and holding up small banners inscribed VOTES FOR WOMEN.

Discouraged by their small success, the suffragists had their hopes revived by the Liberal victory of 1906. That year saw the development out of the Women's Trade Union League, an organizing and propagandist body, of the National Federation of Women Workers, a regular Trade Union, with branches and all the usual powers. It was a far more valuable and powerful body than its predecessor, but the excellent work that it did was underestimated by the political feminists, the majority of whose leaders, being middle-class, remained almost as isolated from and ignorant of labour problems as the Victorian ladies.

They expected, rashly in view of previous Liberal history, that the various platonic promises made to them during the election would be fulfilled. Sir Henry Campbell-Bannerman informed them almost at once that though there were four hundred members pledged to support women's suffrage the Cabinet and the Party were divided and he could do nothing. "Go on pestering," he said; his successor deeply regretted that advice. From 1906 onwards the impatience of the women took more and more vivid forms. The National Union of Women's Suffrage Societies, organizing the great majority of supporters, kept within legal limits, though its ever more numerous speakers dealt very unsparingly with the cowardice and evasiveness of the Liberal leaders. But they were before long eclipsed in the newspapers by the "Suffragettes" (their own members were called "Suffragists") members of the Women's Social and Political Union, which now became almost military in its discipline: as repression increased so did the hysterical devotion of its members. They acted upon the principle that destruction and lawbreaking were the only methods of securing attention and ultimate success, and that it was for that reason a good thing to slash pictures in the National Gallery, burn houses, set fire to pillar-boxes, smash windows, chain themselves to Ministers' doorsteps, interrupt meetings, and slap policemen's faces. The suffragists claimed that by these tactics they outraged public opinion; the suffragettes answered that only after they started had the demand for votes for women received any serious attention

In the autumn of 1911 the Liberals at last appeared to be about to fulfil their promises. Every parliamentary delay having been exhausted, Asquith announced that a Reform Bill would be presented, extending and making more democratic the franchise, and to this amendments providing for women's suffrage could be moved, and the question thus at last be voted upon. But when, after unendurable delays, Sir Edward Grey rose in January 1913 to move the first amendment the Speaker indicated that it or any similar one would be out of order, and that a new Bill (which everyone knew to be out of the question) must be brought in if the question was to be dealt with.

Convinced that they had been victims of a particularly shabby trick, both suffragists and suffragettes broke out into fresh agitation. Yet the strength of the latter was beginning to wane under the strain. Their numbers were dwindling and their leaders divided. First Mrs. Despard and then Mr. and Mrs. Pethick Lawrence had parted company with the Pankhursts. Christabel had gone to Paris, whence she directed the campaign, in a manner which called forth the criticism of others than anti-suffragists. Sylvia, disapproved of by the rest of the family for Socialist tendencies and her pre-occupation with the socially uninfluential East End women, saw her influence restricted to that part of London only. Mrs. Pankhurst remained in the fighting line with unquenchable courage, but under the Cat and Mouse Act it looked for a time as if she might pay the price of her life.

On Derby Day, 1913, Emily Davidson, a suffragette, threw herself in front of the King's horse and died next day. The sacrifice sobered the anti-suffragists and silenced for a while the vulgar writers in the Press, but it brought the vote no nearer. It seemed, in the summer of 1914, as if the cause had been momentarily defeated. The energies of both suffragists and suffragettes were slackening. Both groups had learnt that their only reliable friends were the Labour Left wing, the *Daily Herald* writers and readers, and the I.L.P. members. Most of their leaders accepted this as a mere temporary alliance and remained conservative in their outlook, wanting only one political change, and satisfied otherwise with the social hierarchy. But a large and intelligent minority had realized that the granting of the vote was only one step on the road to social justice for both men and women.

The Syndicalists, however, unlike the suffragettes, had been able to continue in the belief that they could effectively ignore the State. In 1912 they secured an exemplary victory in the construction of a new model union, whose constitution was as skilful and justly admired as the A.S.E.'s sixty years before. The National Union of Railwaymen was formed by the Amalgamated Society of Railway Servants (132,000 members), the General Railway Workers' Union (20,000) and the United Signalmen and Pointsmen (4,000); the Locomotive Engineers and Firemen (A.S.L.E.F.) held aloof as did the Railway Clerks' Association (R.C.A.). A two-thirds majority vote was necessary to make fusion legal (under the Act of 1876) and to secure this took six months (January–June 1912). The supreme power in this industrial Union was the Annual General Meeting, elected geographically. But a wise provision for watching over craft interests was contained in the method of electing the Executive Committee of twenty-four, chosen by the single transferable vote from six electoral districts, which were themselves subdivided into four "electoral departments" —(1) Locomotive department; (2) traffic department; (3) goods and cartage; (4) engineering shops and permanent way. The Executive Committee was divided into sub-committees representing the four departments. The mere fact of unification caused union membership to leap in eighteen months from 150,000 to 300,000. The local branches of the N.U.R., moreover, brought liberty into small and tyrannized country towns; N.U.R. district councils or branches often provided propagandists or even secretaries for political or industrial organizations whose other members dared not show themselves.

The next year, 1913, the Cotton Spinners' Amalgamation terminated the Brooklands Agreement by which the industry had been regulated for twenty years. But this news, which would once have astounded the industrial world, was eclipsed by a struggle which technically belongs to Irish history but must be briefly mentioned here. The Irish Transport and General Workers' Union, under the leadership of James Connolly, a first-rate organizer and Socialist theorist, and

James Larkin, an orator and mass-leader of genius, had been carrying out on the Dublin employers the Syndicalist principles of steady warfare. At last William Martin Murphy, the most powerful employer, headed a determined attempt to reply by smashing the Union. The struggle was bitter, and its effects in England were immense. The official leaders of British Trade Unionism were by now fierce enemies of the new ideas; they detested Larkin particularly for his principles and his immense oratorical power. But the hideous conditions of the Dublin slums, and the passionate feelings of their own rank and file, drove them forward; grudgingly and reluctantly they were compelled to aid, and the Co-ops. even sent a food ship on behalf of the Trades Union Congress. The Dublin conflict ended in apparent defeat—though the result is better described as a draw—but while it lasted it had united the "rebels" of every kind.

The Labour world was shocked in October by what was probably the worst mining disaster for a century. Four hundred and thirty-nine lives were lost in a violent explosion at Senghenydd in South Wales. Serious breaches of the Coal Mines Act were proved; the manager's fine was nominal. *Miners' Lives at* $1\frac{1}{4}d.$ *each* ran the newspaper headlines. Everything, now, was interpreted in terms of the class war; there were very few who knew the words, but a great many who believed that *la lutte finale* of the "International" was really at hand. Trade Union membership in 1914 nearly reached four millions; but something better encouraged the rebels. One million three hundred and fifty thousand of these millions had been united in a powerful industrial alliance to wage war upon the capitalists in the most vital trades. The great model Union, the N.U.R., the fighting Transport Workers' Federation, and the Miners' Federation of Great Britain agreed in principle in April upon a Triple Industrial Alliance, whose object was plainly and simply to arrange for concerted strikes, and from whose counsels the despised craft Unions were effectively barred—indeed the secretary of the Locomotive Engineers found the conference door literally shut in his face.

In many circles, with either hope or fear, it was believed that all that remained to be settled was the date when this formidable force would deliver its "straight left to the chin of Fat"; a good many believed that autumn would see the monster Triple Alliance strike. June saw the organizing conference; the officers of the new body were eventually: Robert Smillie (Miners), chairman; Harry Gosling (Transport), vice-chairman; J. H. Thomas (N.U.R.) treasurer; Thomas Ashton (Miners), secretary. The first two alone were convinced adherents of the new policy; J. H. Thomas was already known as its most convinced opponent, and Ashton was an elderly official of the old school. But this oddity was not remarked upon generally.

In another trade into which they had flung all their strength the industrial unionists were less successful. Their repeated efforts to induce the numerous quarrelling building Unions to amalgamate were consistently defeated by the hostility of the officials. It became clear that while the two-thirds vote was legally necessary, the officials could prevent indefinitely the fusion of even the most obviously overlapping Unions; and in this trade they did. The votes of their members were in the case of every Union in favour of amalgamation (scheme of October 1912) but with a remarkable arrogance the officials with the almost solitary exception of the Bricklayers' continued to fight against it. In January 1914, their London members were locked out by the employers: the struggle was notably prolonged, but the conditions were worsened by the distrust between the strikers and their leaders. In July the united front was broken by pure craft sectarianism; the masons, having secured terms suitable to themselves, simply walked back into the yards.

Exasperated by this end to four years of ceaseless work, the industrial unionists took a step which in every other trade had been rejected as imprudent. At a conference held in Birmingham on August 2 and 3, they formed a rival union, the Building Workers' Industrial Union, constructed upon completely revolutionary principles, and intended to replace the existing unions. True, it had very few members, but it was hoped that the great surge of industrial unionist feeling would soon sweep the masses in.

No such thing was to happen. The delegates had not, it is

fairly safe to assume, paid more attention than anyone else to news items announcing the murder of an archduke of whom they had never heard in a town whose name they could not pronounce. It is certain that they were immensely astonished to read in their papers, on the journey home, that Great Britain had declared war on Germany.

CHAPTER XL

LIFE AND WAGES BEFORE 1914

IN one sense, the years of the twentieth century which preceded the outbreak of the first World War were, for Great Britain, a period of remarkable progress and prosperity. Despite the rapid growth of industrial production in other countries, British exports were increasing at a tremendous pace. Net imports were also rising fast, but not so fast as exports; and in consequence the visible adverse balance of trade was actually smaller in 1913 than it had been in the later 'nineties. Over this period the money value of British exports was more than doubled; and even if allowance is made for the rise in prices by nearly a third between 1896 and 1913 the expansion remains remarkable enough. Net imports, meanwhile, rose by well over 50 per cent in value between the later 'nineties and 1913.

The rapid growth of exports was not confined to any one market, though it was somewhat greater in the case of the Empire than in the rest of the world. In 1896 Empire countries took 35 per cent of all British exports, and in 1913 they took 37 per cent. Exports to Canada, then expanding at an extraordinary pace in production and population, grew more than fourfold in value over these seventeen years. Exports to India and to New Zealand more than doubled: exports to Australia nearly doubled. But as against this there was a threefold growth in exports to the Argentine; and France, Holland, Russia, Italy, China and Japan, as well as a number of less important markets, paid more than twice as much in

1913 for their imports from Great Britain as they had paid in 1896. Even the United States, despite the high tariff wall and the growth of domestic production, paid over 40 per cent more. Nor did Germany cease buying British goods. Indeed, British exports to Germany nearly doubled in value between 1896 and 1913. But in this case there was a significant change in the character of the trade. To a quite substantial extent the Germans stopped buying British manufactures and took to buying British coal instead.

Now, a situation in which exports are expanding more rapidly than imports, in a country which is already a large creditor on account of its past investments of capital abroad, can mean only one thing—that the rich are getting the lion's share of the increasing wealth. For Great Britain, at any rate, under the conditions existing during this period, a rise in the standard of living necessarily meant a rapid increase in imports; for with population still growing fast, a substantial increase was needed in order to prevent the standard from actually falling. But there can be no doubt that the standard was falling. Between the later 'nineties, when the cost of living began to rise, and about 1910, when the great labour unrest set in, home consumption of wheat per head of population remained stationary, and home consumption of both meat and sugar declined. There was a great fall in the consumption of both beer and spirits; but it does not appear that this was offset by a rise in the consumption of food. According to Mr. G. H. Wood's calculations, average real wage-rates were 4 per cent lower in 1910 than they had been in 1896; and even in 1914 the purchasing power of 1896 had not been regained. Between 1899 and 1913 real wages had actually declined by about 10 per cent. Wages were reckoned as having constituted in 1880 about 41 or 42 per cent of the national income: in 1913 they were only 35 or 36 per cent. Doubtless, some part of this decrease was due to the increased numbers of salary-earners and professionals; but even so there is a large fall left unaccounted for.

Some part of the failure of the workers to get their share in the benefits of increasing production is attributable to the Taff Vale Judgment, which, as we have seen, paralysed Trade

Union action from 1901 to 1906. But even when the Trade Disputes Act had given the Unions back the right to strike, the forward movement hung fire. Money-wages rose between 1906 and 1907; but the two following years were a period of moderate industrial depression. The percentage of Trade Unionists out of work rose from under 4 per cent in 1906 and 1907 to nearly 8 per cent in 1908 and 1909. Wage-rates fell back by an average of 2 per cent, to a level barely higher than that of 1906, though in the meantime the cost of living had risen by a further 6 per cent. The labour unrest of 1910 and the following years had behind it the full force of the bread-and-butter argument.

Meanwhile, profits soared. Gross assessments to Income Tax under Schedule D (Profits and Interest) rose by 55 per cent between 1899 and 1913. The pace of the accumulation of capital out of profits became swift beyond all precedent. But for the most part the new capital did not flow into British industry. It was invested to an increasing extent abroad, in the British Dominions or in foreign countries—where even higher profits than at home could be secured by the opening-up of new areas or the exploitation of cheap labour. The output of wheat in Canada was more than four times as great in 1911 as in 1901; and by 1915 it was seven times as great. Production expanded immensely in the Argentine, Australia and New Zealand. Total British investments overseas had probably amounted to about £2,000,000,000 in 1900. By 1907 they had reached £3,000,000,000, and by 1914, £4,000,000,000. According to Mr. C. K. Hobson, British overseas investments had averaged about £24,000,000 a year between 1894 and 1904. In the years 1910 to 1913 they reached an annual average of about £185,000,000. By 1913 they were bringing in to the British investing classes a net annual income of about £200,000,000, of which nearly all was being promptly re-invested abroad—for the excess of imports over exports of commodities was being met out of the profits drawn from overseas by British ship-owners and financiers in return for their current services to world commerce.

The British investor, in putting his money abroad rather than at home, was of course prompted by the incentive of higher profits. Immediately, his loans of capital created a large part of the demand for British exports. Indeed, his investments of capital *were* the exports which persons in other countries bought with the borrowed money. It could thus be argued that overseas investment was an indispensable factor in creating the demand for exports, and thus providing employment for British labour. So indeed it was, as matters stood; for plainly overseas purchasers could not have bought the exports unless British capitalists had lent them the money. But to a considerable extent the goods which were thus loaned by Great Britain to other countries were capital equipment, which raised up new competitors against the British labourer. The immediate effect was to alter the proportions of British workers engaged in making different kinds of goods. Coal, iron and steel and machinery together accounted for 23 percent of British exports in 1896, and for 27 per cent in 1913. Cotton and woollen goods sank meanwhile from 39 per cent to 31 per cent. Great Britain was fast equipping less developed countries with instruments of production which would enable their cheaper labour to be used in competition with that of the British workers.

This tendency was of course to some extent inevitable; for it was impossible for Great Britain to retain permanently her monopolistic position as the workshop of the world. But it was immensely speeded up by the outpouring of British capital; for it mattered nothing to the investor where he made his profit. Capital, unlike labour, could move freely across national frontiers. The British owners of capital could enjoy the profits of exploiting Indian, Chinese or Argentinian labour, just as easily as those to be derived from exploiting labour at home.

In two distinct but related ways, this extended competition in the labour market was disadvantageous to the majority of British workers. It simultaneously put up the price of capital, i.e. the rate of interest, in Great Britain, and caused the British exporter to cut his prices in order to compete with the products of the newer countries. But, when prices had to be cut in face of rising interest rates, there was only one resource left. Wage-costs had to come down. Where this could be secured by advancing mechanization, wage-rates might remain intact;

but, even so, there would usually be a substitution of cheaper for dearer kinds of labour, and often an intensification of the pace of work. Where, on the other hand, it was harder to improve the methods of production, the obvious resource was to reduce wages, or at the very least to refuse to increase them as the cost of living rose. The alternative of lowering interest rates was not open, as the offer of lower interest at home would simply have diverted still more capital abroad.

This is the economic explanation of the curious phenomenon of falling real wages side by side with rapidly advancing trade and capitalist prosperity. The workmen, even with the aid of their Trade Unions, could not meet their employers on equal terms, because they were face to face with a capitalism that could invoke against them the unorganized labour and the unexploited resources of the less developed parts of the world.

If, under these circumstances, real wages did not fall faster than they actually did, the reason was twofold. The British consumers were still getting the benefit of Free Trade, which enabled them to buy in the cheapest market; and the immensely rapid economic expansion of such countries as Canada and the Argentine resulted in a rising demand for British-manufactured goods for consumption as well as investment. In the cotton industry, the number of looms in Great Britain rose by nearly a quarter between 1900 and 1914. Lancashire was already beginning to lose a part of its older markets to new competitors; but new markets were developing, albeit at cut prices, more than enough to offset the loss. The British workers were finding it difficult to get better wages, in face of foreign competition; but they were not yet finding it difficult to get work, as long as they were prepared to work at wages which represented a declining purchasing power.

There was, however, a second factor, besides that of foreign investment and the development of competitive production abroad, which was threatening the continued advance of British exports. Over the world as a whole tariffs were rising fast. In the United States a new era of high protectionism had begun with the McKinley Tariff of 1890; and, after a brief return to somewhat lower duties in 1894, rates went up higher than ever under the Dingley Tariff of 1897. France had resorted to a high tariff in 1892, and thereafter continued to raise her rates. Germany remained under a low-tariff system until 1902, but thereafter rapidly raised her duties against manufactured imports, while lowering other duties in order to cheapen raw materials for her rising industries. By 1904 the average duty levied on British manufactures exported to Germany was 25 per cent *ad valorem*. To France it was 34 per cent, to the United States 72 per cent, and to Russia actually 130 per cent. On the other hand the Dominions were still under a low-tariff régime. British-manufactured exports to Canada paid on the average 17 per cent *ad valorem*, to New Zealand 9 per cent, to Australia and South Africa only 6 per cent. India had still no tariff autonomy.

In the Dominions, the system of tariff preference to British goods had already begun. Canada had started it by way of retaliation against the American tariff of 1897; and New Zealand and South Africa followed suit in 1903, and Australia in 1908. Great Britain, as long as Free Trade remained, could not reciprocate in kind, despite Joseph Chamberlain's desires. But in 1897 Great Britain had denounced all commercial treaties with foreign countries which prevented the grant of imperial preference; and in 1900 the Colonial Stocks Act, by granting trustee status to the public loans of the Dominions, enabled them to borrow at specially low interest rates in the British money market, and thus gave them a *quid pro quo* for tariff preference. In addition, British shipping subsidies were so applied as to foster Empire trade: bounty-fed foreign sugar was excluded for the benefit of the West Indian producers; and capital works were speeded up in the Colonies under the Colonial Development Act of 1899. Thus a beginning was made with imperial economic development, even though the electorate resolutely turned its back on Tariff Reform.

It is sometimes argued that, even if real wages appeared to be falling when they were measured in terms of wage-rates and retail prices, the fall in the standard of living was illusory, because the workers were getting in new social services more than they were losing in wages. It is true that in 1913 British Government expenditure was double what it had been in the early 'nineties. In 1895 it exceeded £100,000,000 for the first

time. Thereafter it rose sharply to £205,000,000 in 1901, at
the height of the South African War. In 1905, before the
Liberals took office, it was down again to £150,000,000; but
by 1914 it had mounted once more to £197,000,000, and had
thus doubled in less than twenty years.

Of this increase in expenditure the fighting services had
absorbed a substantial part. The army cost £18,000,000 in
1895, and £29,000,000 in 1905. The Liberals made no further
increase before the war; but naval expenditure is a different
matter. The navy cost less than £20,000,000 in 1895,
£33,000,000 in 1905, and more than £50,000,000 in 1914.
Thus, the fighting services together claimed twice as much in
1914 as they had done two decades earlier. This was the effect
of the naval race with Germany, in face of which all the
Liberal pledges of retrenchment were swept away. Between
1905 and 1914 expenditure on the fighting services went up
by £18,000,000.

This leaves roughly £30,000,000 for all other services. The
cost of the civil services, excluding the Post Office but including the expenses of tax collection, had risen from £22,500,000
in 1895 to £31,500,000 in 1905. In 1914 it reached
£61,500,000. Of this increase of £30,000,000 under the
Liberals about £24,500,000 can be attributed to the social
services in the widest sense. The Education estimates went up
by nearly £4,000,000, largely on account of rising population.
Nearly £21,000,000 was due to the new services—Old Age
Pensions, Labour Exchanges, and State grants in aid of Health
and Unemployment Insurance. This sum, equal to rather
under 1 per cent of the national income as it stood in 1913,
broadly represents the Liberal contribution to redistribution
through taxation. Even if all of it had gone to the wage-earners
it would have represented only about a 3 per cent rise in wages.

It is true that there had been, over the same period, an
increase in the sums levied in local rates, which had risen from
about £42,000,000 in 1895 to £67,000,000 in 1905 and
£82,000,000 in 1913, for the United Kingdom as a whole.
These increases meant some advance in local services; but the
unfair incidence of rates makes it impossible to regard this as
representing an equitable redistribution of wealth. As for the

National Debt, it was much the same in 1895 and in 1913, the big increase due to the South African War having been cancelled by subsequent repayments. The actual debt charge was somewhat smaller in 1913 than it had been in 1895; but as against this the costs of government had increased to a more than corresponding extent.

It is evident, then, that the Liberal achievement in redistributing income, though it seemed dreadfully confiscatory to the Tories of the time, was in fact quite inconsiderable in comparison with the forces making the other way. It is the plain truth that, in the new century, the long-sustained tendency for the standards of living of the people to rise seemed to have been decisively checked; and neither political action nor industrial action had by 1914 succeeded in remedying the workers' grievance. Nevertheless, industrial action had made the better showing; for whereas real wages had fallen until the great labour unrest began, by 1914 the workers had got back some of what they had lost, and were back in purchasing power about where they had been in 1906, though they were still well below the standards of 1900.

THE FIRST WORLD WAR

CHAPTER XLI

1914–18

THE British nation was wholly unprepared for war. Continental quarrels had never been real to the average Englishman, and his inapprehension of the crisis was increased by a peculiar circumstance. War became inevitable over a bank holiday, while no ordinary man was considering it. The *Daily Mail* had indeed been announcing it, but even for its readers the "German war" was a half-real threat, like universal ruin from Free Trade, or universal robbery as a result of Lloyd George's speeches. On Saturday, August 1, the average man went on his holidays, knowing and caring very little about foreign affairs. *John Bull*, then under Horatio Bottomley's control, was screaming "To Hell with Servia!"; a few people noticed it. When he returned to work on Tuesday morning the decision had been taken; at eleven o'clock that night Britain was at war with Germany.

The Labour movement was the only power which had made any attempt to hold back the catastrophe, and it had been ineffective. Some few people (but mostly those who did not know it well) had pinned their hopes upon the Labour Party's membership of the International Socialist Bureau, which it had joined in 1903. But this International, dating itself from two rival congresses held in 1889, was nothing like Marx's International Workingmen's Association; that had been a centralized body with a General Council controlling national sections. The intervening years, with the development of Socialism nationally, made the Second International only a loose federation of national Socialist Parties. Though it acted as a tribunal to which differences could be referred, which could issue bulletins and make declarations of principle, its disciplinary powers were very small. It had only had a Central Bureau since 1900. Nor had the still more shadowy International Federation of Trade Unions any more effective power. The French Trade Unionists had endeavoured to induce it to sanction the policy of a general strike against war, which it had referred to the political International for discussion. A decision was to have been made at the 1914 International Socialist Congress, which was never held.

Meanwhile, the only valid resolution on war was that passed at Stuttgart in 1907, and again at Copenhagen in 1910. It was drafted by Jean Jaurès.

"If war threatens to break out it is the duty of the working class in the countries concerned and of their parliamentary representatives, with the help of the International Socialist Bureau as a means of co-ordinating their action, to use every effort to prevent war by all the means which seem to them most appropriate, having regard to the sharpness of the class-war and to the general political situation.

"Should war nevertheless break out, their duty is to intervene to bring it promptly to an end, and with all their energies to use the political and economic crisis created by the war to rouse the populace from its slumbers, and to hasten the fall of capitalist domination."

This amounted to an instruction to endeavour to prevent war, and in the event of failure to use the opportunity for revolution. The second part of the resolution was carried out by nobody outside Russia; indeed, Lenin and Trotsky and their followers always claimed that they were merely obeying literally the decision of the International. But a sustained effort was made to carry out the first part.

The International Socialist Bureau itself, on the eve of the assassination of Jaurès in Paris, met and issued an emphatic declaration against war; on August 1 the British section met and issued a manifesto of its own, signed by Keir Hardie and Arthur Henderson on behalf of all the affiliated bodies. This document vehemently denounced any attempt to bring Great Britain into war on the side of Russia, and called upon the workers to stand firmly for peace, and to refuse to allow the Government to commit the country to war. All over Europe the Socialist movements of the various countries were making similar protests, and holding demonstrations against the participation of their Governments in the threatened conflict.

But the Stuttgart resolution, while it had been very definite about the duty of the workers to prevent war, had been very indefinite about the methods which they were to adopt. When the Governments held on their way towards war despite the workers' protests, the apparent solidarity of world Socialism speedily disappeared. In Great Britain, France and Germany alike, though not in Tsarist Russia, the majority of the leaders of the Socialist and Trade Union movements, faced with the fact of war, rallied to the support of their respective Governments, and were soon voting for war credits in their Parliaments, helping in recruiting for the army and the war services, and in one way or another proclaiming their solidarity with the "nation" in its hour of crisis. They mostly continued for a time to denounce the machinations of imperialist diplomacy which had caused the conflict, and to demand a speedy peace on terms which would enable the peoples of Europe to live together in friendship. But at the same time they were unable to contemplate any action which might help to bring about the defeat of their own nations.

Thus, while the German Socialists proclaimed a holy crusade against Tsarist reaction, French and British Socialists denounced German militarism; and each group saw in the situation imperative reasons for the victory of its own side. Accordingly, so far from attempting, when war had actually broken out, to carry into effect the second part of the Stuttgart resolution, the majority of the Socialist and Trade Union leaders took active steps to damp down industrial conflict, and to induce their followers to co-operate whole-heartedly in the prosecution of the war.

No body in Britain, on the outbreak of war, was sufficiently hardy to oppose it. Some dissented from the eagerness of the official leaders to support it; that was all. In the Labour Party itself, Ramsay MacDonald, who had strongly asserted the responsibility of both sides for the outbreak of war, was compelled to resign the leadership, in which Arthur Henderson succeeded him. MacDonald, however, could not be described as "anti-war." He asserted, as strongly as the majority, that the war, once embarked on, must be won; and he supported, in September, the recruiting campaign launched by the Government with Conservative and official Labour support. So too did most of the other I.L.P. leaders—Snowden and Jowett almost alone excepted. Keir Hardie wrote in the *Merthyr Pioneer* on August 14: "A nation at war must be united. . . . With the boom of the enemy's guns within earshot the lads who have gone forth to fight their country's battles must not be disheartened by any discordant note at home." Even the *Daily Herald* seemed content to lament the disaster. The *Clarion* turned violently militarist overnight, and its cir-culation collapsed from 90,000 to 10,000; the *Clarion* move-ment was the first war casualty. (It was shortly followed by the *Daily Citizen*, which vanished completely; the *Daily Herald* became a weekly.) Hyndman for a short while committed the British Socialist Party to supporting the war; but before long the majority expelled him. He formed, with a very few col-leagues, the National Socialist Party, a rabid anti-German organization. Only with the winter did a definite opposition to the war begin to crystallize. The first *Herald* article demand-ing its end appeared on 19 December 1914; thereafter the *Herald* was the most powerful anti-war journal, though it was soon joined by the *Call* (Hyndman by legal action wresting from the British Socialist Party the hallowed title of *Justice*), the *Labour Leader* (I.L.P.) and the Glasgow *Forward*. Hardie now gave his whole-hearted support to the pacifists; but he was already ill, and died broken-hearted in 1915. His seat at Merthyr was captured by a ranting anti-German Trade Union leader, C. B. Stanton, of a type which was to become very familiar before the war was over.

The Trade Union movement, with much less apparent dissension, followed on the outbreak of war the same line as the Labour Party. The Trades Union Congress which was to have met at the beginning of September was postponed and, in the event, not held at all; and the leaders of the Congress and the General Federation of Trade Unions joined with the

Labour Party in proclaiming an "Industrial Truce." Even before this, most of the strikes which had been in progress when war broke out had been promptly settled; and Trade Unions which had been on the point of launching big demands for improved wages and conditions had decided to postpone their claims until the war was over—for at that time nearly everyone still expected that it would be over quite soon, and hardly anyone anticipated the economic consequences—high prices, extra demand for labour of every sort, huge profits in almost every industry—to which it was soon to give rise. The Trade Unions had no idea that their declaration of an Industrial Truce meant putting off their claims for more than a few months; and they were still under the belief that the war would so upset the world economically as to cause acute unemployment rather than the shortage of labour which was speedily to arise.

The response was not, of course, unanimous. There were from the first anti-war groups based on the "rank-and-file" movements of the years of unrest just before 1914. There were local anti-war Trade Unionists, especially on the Clyde and in South Wales. But they were not strong enough to carry with them a single national Trade Union of any standing.

For the one exception—the new-born Building Workers' Industrial Union—could hardly count as a Union of standing. And its voice was very quickly stifled. It had by its foundation merely drained the rebel members out of every Union in the industry, leaving the reactionary officials in complete control. Emergency or no emergency, these took their opportunity. The B.W.I.U. members were struck against, by orders, wherever they appeared: a silent but bitter struggle lasted a few months, and at the end the new Union had been battered into total insignificance. The tactic of dual unionism, of founding a rival, true-red Union, had led to utter disaster, and the lesson was remembered in later years.

When the Trade Unions had declared their truce, the few strikes that still continued were speedily settled. The Liverpool dockers, the builders in several areas, and the agricultural labourers in Essex settled their differences for the time being, and went back to work. In Scotland, the mine-owners withdrew a wage demand which had been on the point of throwing the coal-field idle, and might have involved the miners in other districts as well. The railway Unions postponed their new All-Grades Programme. In the latter months of 1914 strikes fell away almost to nothing. On August 24 the "Industrial Truce" was formally proclaimed, not by agreement with the employers, but by the one-sided declaration of the Trade Union and Labour Party leaders.

Before this, on August 5, all the leading working-class bodies had met in hastily summoned conference, and agreed to set up a new body to deal with the economic problems created by the war. This body, the War Emergency Workers' National Committee, did not deal with matters of political policy, or with strictly Trade Union affairs. Its function was to safeguard working-class interests in such matters as the relief of unemployment, the supply and prices of food and other necessaries of life, house-rents, and other matters of social policy. At this early stage, the effect of the crisis was to dislocate industry and to give rise to widespread unemployment in trades not directly related to war needs; and the first problems with which the new Committee had to deal were mainly those of relief, both for workers who had lost their jobs and for dependants of men who had enlisted or been recalled to the colours. The Government at first attempted to deal with the problem of relief along voluntary lines, creating a National Relief Fund to which Trade Unions as well as individuals and business firms were invited to subscribe, and setting up for its administration a great number of Local Relief Committees in loose connection with the Local Authorities. The working of this system speedily gave rise to many protests. The conditions on which relief was granted differed from area to area according to the composition and spirit of the Local Committees; and the Government assiduously preached economy in the use of the Fund. Many of the Committees refused relief except in kind, and instituted inquisitions that were keenly resented into the family circumstances of the applicants. The Trade Unions found themselves paying weekly contributions into a fund upon which their workless members could draw only upon terms which they regarded as unfair and degrading. Before long the South Wales Miners and some other bodies announced that they would cease making payments to the fund unless their grievances were redressed; and the Government, very unwillingly, was compelled to allow the Trade Unions to administer payments to their own members in certain cases, with a subsidy from the fund varying with the size of the levies which the Unions themselves had imposed.

This was the first small sign that war conditions were to bring the Trade Unions a new recognition at the hands of the State. But before long the problem of relieving unemployment almost disappeared in face of the very rapid rise in the demand for labour. The drain of workers for military service left in the essential industries gaps which had to be filled; and the surplus labour from the industries which had been hit by the war was rapidly transferred to those which had to be expanded in order to meet war needs. It began to be realized that both the probable duration of the war and the supply of ammunition and equipment that would be needed had been grossly underestimated; and by October or November the employers in the war industries were crying out loudly for an increased labour force, and were eagerly recruiting not only men from other trades but also women for jobs which until then had been regarded as suitable only for male workers. The "dilution of labour," as it was soon to be called, was already beginning.

We have no space to describe, except in the merest outline, the successive stages by which the "dilution of labour" was introduced and extended. It began, here and there, as contractors working for the Government sought to increase output by taking on any sort of additional labour they could get. This immediately brought protests from the craft Unions, which regarded their exclusive right to work on certain machines and processes as indispensable to the maintenance of their standards of life. The newcomers were at first mainly men, drawn into the engineering industry from other occupations; but before long women were being introduced on the lighter machines, especially for the making of shells, fuses and cartridge-cases. As early as November 1914 a serious dispute arose at Crayford, where the skilled engineers refused to set up machines to be operated by female labour. This matter was patched up by a local agreement; but trouble soon began in many other places, and in December the Engineering Employers' Federation came forward with a national demand that all Trade Union rules which they regarded as hindering the output of munitions should be abolished.

To this demand for a holocaust of all their cherished rules and customs the Trade Unions naturally refused to agree. Nor were they more accommodating when the War Office joined in on the side of the employers and Government orators and journalists began denouncing the unpatriotic conduct of the Trade Unions in impeding the prosecution of the war. At this stage the Unions proposed that the War Office, instead of attacking them, should take steps to extend its list of contractors to include, besides the regular armament firms, other engineering works, many of which were working short time. But the employers persisted in their demands; and after a number of abortive conferences between them and the Unions the Government stepped in, and appointed an official body, the Committee on Production, to make a full report.

The establishment of the Committee on Production was the first step towards that comprehensive system of State control of war industries which was developed under the Munitions of War and Defence of the Realm Acts. Almost at once it was given power to act as well as to report. It began with a series of proposals which concluded with the suggestion that all strikes and lock-outs in the war industries should cease, and that all disputes which the parties could not settle between themselves should be submitted to Government arbitration. It further recommended that the Trade Unions should agree, in order to speed up the output of shells and fuses, to a suspension of their regulations and to the employment of female labour, in return for guarantees from the employers that piece-work prices would not be reduced and that the suspension would be strictly limited to the war period. Every Government contractor who desired to take advantage of the suspension was to be called upon to give a written guarantee both that the suspension of Trade Union rules should not prejudice the Unions after the war, and that preference for employment would then be given to men who had been employed by them before dilution began.

The Government acted on these proposals. It authorized the Committee on Production itself to act as an arbitration tribunal, and it put pressure on the Unions to agree to the measures of dilution which the Committee had recommended —measures which in a further report the Committee had widened to include not only the production of shells and fuses, but all types of munition work on which semi-skilled or unskilled labour could be employed. The Unions accepted the proposals relating to shells and fuses; but the Government had by this time decided to arm itself with compulsory powers. Under the Defence of the Realm Act of March 1915 it assumed authority to commandeer any factory required for war work, and to issue orders to the workers employed.

Immediately after the passing of this Act, the Government called a conference representative of the entire Trade Union movement, with the object of securing complete endorsement of the proposals of the Committee on Production. At the Treasury Conference (17 March 1915) the Union representatives, after considerable discussion, accepted the First Treasury Agreement, pledging the Unions, specifically in the war industries and more generally over the entire field, to give up the strike weapon for the war period, and to accept Government arbitration upon all disputes. It further pledged them to accept a "relaxation," though not a complete suspension, of Trade Union rules and customs. In return for this all Government contractors were to pledge themselves not to use the introduction of semi-skilled or unskilled labour as a means of reducing wages, to keep a record of all changes made, not to allow the suspension of any rule or custom to prejudice the Unions in resuming and maintaining it after the war, and to give priority in post-war employment to pre-war employees.

The Trade Unions at the Treasury Conference thus signed away, for the war period, the right to strike, and agreed to dilution. But the Union principally affected by dilution and most able to stand in its way refused to accept the agreement. The Amalgamated Society of Engineers insisted that, since dilution and compulsory arbitration under war conditions would present the employers with huge profits and prevent the Unions from pressing for their share, they could accept these sacrifices only if the Government would pledge itself to limit profits "with a view to ensuring that the benefit resulting from the relaxation of trade restrictions or practices shall accrue to the State."

The Treasury Agreement was nearly useless without the engineers; for if they persisted in rejecting it the Government and the employers knew very well that the leaders of the other Unions would not be able to hold their members to the bargain. Accordingly, a week later, at a second Treasury Conference with the A.S.E. alone, the Government gave way. Under the Second Treasury Agreement (25 March 1915), the Government pledged itself not only to limit profits in the munitions industries, but also to use its influence, where dilution was introduced, "to secure the restoration of previous conditions in every case after the war." Having secured these additional promises, together with some others which more narrowly defined the scope of the relaxation of Trade Union practices, the A.S.E. signed the Second Treasury Agreement, and thus accepted both Government arbitration and the dilution of labour on all types of war work.

The next step was to provide machinery for giving practical effect to the bargain between the Government and the Trade Unions—a bargain which Lloyd George described as "the great charter for Labour—opening up a great new chapter in the history of Labour in its relations with the State." At the outset, the Government's intention seems in fact to have been that the control of the new arrangements for speeding up the output of munitions should be in the hands of joint bodies in each area, representing the Trade Unions, the employers, and the State. In accordance with this view it began to set up in the big engineering centres a series of Local Armaments Committees constituted in this way; and these committees set to work to arrange for the conversion of factories to meet war needs, for the further dilution of labour, and even for the establishment of new National Factories under their direct control. There seemed for a month or two to be some meaning in Lloyd George's assertion that Trade Unionism was being given for the first time real recognition of its claim to a share in the "control of industry."

This phase, however, did not last long. The employers had no love for "joint control" and from May onwards the functions and powers of the Armaments Committees were steadily whittled away. It had already been decided that the war-time organization of industry was to assume a very different form. Before the autumn was out the last of the Local Armaments Committees had been thrown on the scrapheap.

The new system of direct Government control, without Trade Union participation, was ushered in by the establishment, in June 1915, of the Ministry of Munitions, with Lloyd George at its head. The Munitions of War Act, passed in July 1915, gave the new system a definite form. It set up a new category of "controlled establishments," under the orders of the Ministry, and subject to the limitation of profits which had been promised; and therewith it gave compulsory force to the concessions which the Trade Unions had made. Strikes were forbidden by law and compulsory arbitration was established in all industries concerned with war work. The acceptance of dilution was made legally binding; and the section of the Act dealing with the suspension of Trade Union rules went immensely further than the conditional "relaxation" to which the Unions had agreed in March.

Nor was this all. The Act gave legal force to the system of enrolment of War Munition Volunteers, who could be moved from factory to factory under the orders of the Government; and at the same time it instituted a system of "Leaving Certificates," whereby no workman engaged on munition work could move to another job without a certificate of release from his former employer. To administer this system the Act set up a network of Local Munitions Tribunals of a quasi-judicial character, with power both to hear appeals against the refusal of employers to grant certificates, and to impose fines upon workmen who attempted to resort to strike action to maintain any rule or practice which the Government wished to suspend, or were guilty of other offences which were held to hinder the output of munitions.

As against all this, the Unions, thanks to the insistence of the A.S.E., had gained the legal limitation of profits. This, however, did not in practice amount to much; for the limitation was only on *excess* profits above the pre-war level, and the pre-war standards were so defined, by allowing firms to select their most profitable years to form the basis for an average, that munition firms were able not only to make but also to retain very high profits in spite of the Government's promise. There was no such drastic restriction on profits as there was during the Second World War; and, as prices also were much less strictly controlled, huge war fortunes were made even by firms which kept well within the terms of the law. The limitation of profits and the excess profits duty subsequently levied on industries generally were largely a pretence; for firms were allowed to inflate prices to such an extent that after paying 60 per cent of their "excess profits" in tax, they had more left than they could have hoped to make if there had been no tax on profits, but prices had been kept under reasonably effective control. This aspect of war finance was infinitely better managed in the second World War than in the first.

In face of widespread profiteering, it is not surprising that the penal provisions of the Munitions Act gave rise to lively complaints. The Leaving Certificates interfered greatly with the opportunities for men of special skill to secure higher wages in view of the scarcity of labour; while the general prohibition of strike action and the enforcement of arbitration left the Government, through the tribunals which it set up, to fix wages as it pleased, though it was now virtually the employer as well as the arbitrator. Moreover, opportunity was taken to strengthen further the Government's powers under the Defence of the Realm Acts to issue orders as to the work that was to be done; and the Munitions Tribunals, consisting of a lawyer aided by employers' and workers' assessors, were authorized to punish workers under this head as well.

Nevertheless, the Trade Unions accepted these drastic provisions. The Miners' Federation, indeed, objected to compulsory arbitration, and demanded that the Act should not be applied to the coal mines. But in view of the acquiescence of the rest of the Unions mainly concerned, the Miners' protest

was disregarded. Actually, the first dispute proclaimed **unlaw-**
ful was the South Wales Miners' strike of July 1915.

Having thus taken compulsory powers, the Government
went on apace with the extension of the dilution of labour.
The provisions of the first Treasury Agreement, though they
had been appended as a Schedule to the Munitions of War Act
(those of the second Treasury Agreement being significantly
left out), were generally disregarded by employers; and the
new labour was taken on in many cases at rates immensely
lower than those previously paid for work of the same kind.
Women especially were engaged in very large numbers at
wages not above 15*s.* a week. The Trade Unions launched
strong protests against these wages; and in the autumn the
Government was induced to issue circulars recommending
higher wages, including a minimum of £1 a week for women
engaged on "men's work." Workers, men or women, employed in skilled jobs were to receive the standard Trade
Union time rates for the job, but not necessarily the same
piece-work conditions or bonuses. These concessions would
have gone some way to meet the workers' grievances if they
had been enforced. But they were not made legally binding;
and many firms took no notice of them. When the Government put forward big additional schemes of dilution, the
A.S.E. refused its co-operation unless the recommended wages
and conditions were generally enforced. The Government,
while advising employers to comply with the scales, refused to
apply compulsion; and workshop unrest developed apace.
The answer of the Government was to introduce an amending
Bill giving it wider powers both to enforce dilution and to
compel employers to observe the rates and conditions which
it prescribed.

Quite apart from the question of wages, the Munitions of
War Act was already giving rise to numerous further troubles.
Hardly had the Act been passed when the first really big war-
time strike broke out. The South Wales Miners, in dispute
with their employers over the terms of the new wage agreement
which was to replace that which had just expired, came out on
strike; and the Government promptly proclaimed the strike
illegal under the Act.

In order to understand this development, it is necessary to retrace our steps and to consider the course of wages and prices since August 1914. On the outbreak of war the cost of food rose sharply to about 15 or 16 per cent above pre-war level. Thereafter there was a slight fall; but by October the rise was beginning again, and by February 1915 food prices were up by 25 per cent. By the beginning of July they had risen by well over a third. By this time other prices, and also house-rents, were being sharply raised as well. Consequently, unless wages were substantially increased, there was bound to be a severe fall in working-class standards of living.

The War Emergency Workers' National Committee, from its inception in August 1914, was continually pressing the Government to adopt measures to prevent this rise in prices; but in face of the extreme dislike of the Liberal Government for any form of State control nothing was done. Wages, however, remained practically stationary; and the result was a rapidly growing discontent. By February 1915 things had gone so far that the railway workers, then an exceptionally ill-paid group, were compelled to take action. The railway companies, under pressure, thereupon agreed to grant a "war bonus" of 3s. a week to men earning less than 30s., and of 2s. to men earning over 30s. a week.

These advances, apart from the fact that they were granted only in the form of a "bonus," were inadequate to meet the rise in prices, even at the time when they were granted; and the railway Unions were strongly criticized by other groups for accepting such terms, which were speedily made a precedent in other cases. But at any rate from this time onwards wage advances, usually in the form of "war bonuses," were granted in a large number of trades, though almost always on a scale which left real wages well below the pre-war level.

In March the Miners' Federation entered the field, demanding a national advance to meet the rise in prices. The mine-owners attempted to insist on separate negotiations in each district; but the threat of a national miners' strike compelled the Government to intervene and insist on the owners meeting the Federation in national conference. The conference, however, broke down, and the Government then took matters into its own hands. The demand for a national advance was not granted; but varying advances were conceded in each area, and the edge was thus taken off the growing unrest.

It happened, however, that at this time the miners all over the country, in accordance with a national decision taken before the war, were terminating their existing agreements with the owners and negotiating for new agreements based on a common set of principles laid down at their "Scarborough Conference." In most districts some sort of new agreement was finally reached; but in South Wales the two sides arrived at a complete deadlock and, as we have seen, in defiance of the newly passed Munitions Act, the South Wales Miners' Federation called a strike of the entire coal-field.

Under the Act the strikers were liable to fine and imprisonment for what they had done. But the Navy depended on South Wales coal; and there was in fact no way of coercing about 200,000 men who were prepared to yield neither to threats from the Government nor to the denunciations of the Press. Instead of setting the law in motion, Lloyd George and Runciman hurried to South Wales; and the strike was promptly settled on terms which met most of the miners' demands. It was thus promptly shown that the outlawry of strikes, while it might be effective against small groups, could not be successfully enforced against any big Trade Union whose members were engaged in essential war work.

However, the example of the South Wales Miners was not followed elsewhere. Most of the Trade Union leaders were ardent supporters of the war, and were not prepared to resort to strike action even if the Government refused to redress their grievances. Nevertheless, the success of the South Wales strike did cause wages in other trades to be advanced more rapidly than before; for the Government and the employers were alarmed at the possibility that, unless the fall in real wages were arrested, the Trade Union leaders might be unable to hold their followers in check.

The South Wales Miners' strike was not, indeed, the first war-time strike of importance, though it was the first in which the numbers ran into hundreds of thousands. As early as February 1915 the Clyde engineering shops had been brought to a stand by a widespread unofficial strike, called in defiance of the national officials of the Unions concerned. At the time of the outbreak of war the Clyde engineers had been bound down by a three-year agreement which was due to expire at the beginning of 1915. This had prevented them from securing the advances which had accrued to most other groups between 1912 and 1914; and they had been long preparing to demand a substantial advance. But, when the time arrived, the employers argued that the men ought to wait until the war was over before pressing their major demands, and to rest content meanwhile with a merely nominal increase.

Protracted negotiations followed, the employers using every device to delay matters. At length the Clyde workers' patience gave out, and an unofficial strike began. To conduct it, the workers created a Central Withdrawal of Labour Committee. The Government issued orders to the men to resume work at once; but at this time the Munitions Act had not been passed, and not even in theory were any legal means of coercion available. The strikers defied the order; but the Executive Council of the Amalgamated Society of Engineers hurried to Glasgow, and finally succeeded in getting work resumed on a promise of arbitration—which resulted in an award falling a long way behind what the men had claimed.

In getting work resumed on these terms, the A.S.E. leaders seemed to have got the better of the unofficial Withdrawal of Labour Committee. But this body, though it was not able to carry on the strike, was by no means done with. It decided, instead of disbanding, to become a permanent organization representing the rank and file; and under its new name, as the Clyde Workers' Committee, it played a very important part. throughout the rest of the war period.

The Trade Union leaders, as we have seen, by giving up the right to strike and undertaking to co-operate, on terms, with the Government and the employers in extending the dilution of labour, had given up their power to conduct a militant policy for raising wages or defending Trade Union claims. Half-instinctively, first on the Clyde and then in other areas, the workers in the munitions industries began to create for themselves an alternative kind of protective organization

CP : S

There had existed for a very long time in many engineering works a minor type of Trade Union delegate, called a "shop steward," whose duty it was to act as a recruiting agent for the Union, to take periodical "shows" of Union cards of membership, and to report to the District Committee on the state of organization in his particular shop or factory. These shop stewards had no negotiating powers, and were usually not recognized, even if they were tolerated, by the employers.

But now, under the peculiar war-time conditions, the shop stewards acquired a new importance. Chosen by the men in the shops, and untrammelled by the agreements made by the Trade Union leaders, they could do things which were now outside the leaders' power. Moreover, as the question of dilution began to assume importance, new issues kept on cropping up almost daily, needing to be argued out and if possible settled upon the spot, and in any event far too numerous for the small number of full-time Trade Union officials to attend to. In these circumstances, the shop stewards found themselves compelled, as the men's representatives in the shops, to assume negotiating functions; and although at the outset each steward represented only his own Union, it was inevitable that the stewards from different Unions should take to acting together on matters of common concern. Then, as the number of dilutees increased, they too began to appoint stewards of their own, often without the endorsement of any particular Trade Union; and gradually there sprang up, side by side with the official shop stewards and sometimes indistinguishable from them, unofficial stewards who simply represented the men in a particular trade or workshop, and owed no formal allegiance to any higher Trade Union authority. In one establishment after another the shop stewards, official and unofficial, continued to form Shop Stewards' or Workshop Committees; and upon these bodies, more and more, the effective detailed handling of the problems of dilution devolved.

The Clyde Central Withdrawal of Labour Committee was in effect a gathering of leading shop stewards from a number of establishments, under the guidance of a small group of left-wing Socialists belonging to the Socialist Labour Party on the extreme Left, or to the I.L.P., a good deal less to the Left. This group set out from the first to make the Clyde strike the starting-point for a militant movement organized on an inclusive industrial basis, cutting right across craft Union divisions, and representing skilled and less skilled workers alike. The dilution question was soon to present it with just the opportunity that it desired.

For the Government, needing simultaneously a larger supply of men for the armed forces and a larger output of munitions, proceeded in the autumn of 1915 to intensify its efforts to substitute less skilled and female labour for that of skilled men. With this object it established, in January 1916, while the struggle over the amendment of the Munitions Act was in full swing, two special Dilution Commissions, one for the Tyne and one for the Clyde area. The Tyne Commission was relatively inactive; but on the Clyde the Commissioners' efforts to speed up dilution aroused an immediate storm. To the annoyance of the Trade Union leaders the Commissioners, in their progress from factory to factory in order to draw up schemes of dilution, recognized and negotiated with the Shop Stewards' Committees; but they refused to recognize the Clyde Workers' Committee and dealt, on matters relating to the area as a whole, with the official Trade Union organizations.

The Commissioners had not gone far with their work when there broke out a serious strike at Parkhead Forge, over the question of the right of the convener of shop stewards, David Kirkwood, to go from one workshop to another within the establishment as the workmen's representative. This strike, under the leadership of the Clyde Workers' Committee, speedily spread to other factories; and the Government decided to take drastic action against the leaders of the militant movement. In March 1916 a number of the most prominent Clyde left-wingers were arrested under the Defence of the Realm Act without charge or warrant, and simply deported out of the district and forbidden to return. They were not kept in prison, but were allowed to find work in other towns at a distance, where their influence was not expected to count.

This action did in fact strike a severe blow at the militant movement; for the leaders who had been deported were not easy to replace. Gradually some of them were allowed to return, on giving an undertaking to take part in no further strikes during the war; but the rest, who held out for unconditional return, were not allowed back until May 1917.

While, as far as the Clyde was concerned, the Government might regard its "firmness" as having succeeded, the influence of the Clyde Workers' Committee had, before this set-back, spread to many other areas. Workers' Committees on similar lines had been set up in a large number of engineering centres; and "rank and file" movements were developing on the railways and in a number of other industries. These movements, at the outset almost wholly economic in purpose, were soon to take on a secondary political character as the hopes of a speedy peace died away and as the Government in its need for men turned from the voluntary system to military conscription.

Compulsory military service was introduced, for single men only, in March 1916; but despite all promises to the contrary it was extended to married men only two months later. These developments, for which the ground had been carefully prepared by earlier measures, caused a deep upset in the Labour world, Trade Unionists and Socialists protesting that there could be no case for applying conscription to men unless it were applied to property also, and expressing their fears that military conscription would in fact involve "industrial conscription" as well. From the very beginning of the war, as we have seen, Labour leaders had taken an active part in the recruiting campaigns under the voluntary system. In July 1915 they acquiesced in the National Registration Act, which set up a complete register of the population, on an absolute pledge that it should not be used for the purpose of conscription. In October 1915 they gave full support to the "Derby Scheme," under which men who were needed for work at home, as well as others, were invited to "attest" for potential service in the armed forces. This was in fact the thin end of the conscription wedge; for by this time nearly everyone who felt any disposition to join the Army had done so, and those who "attested" under pressure tended to favour conscription all round in the hope of reducing their own chances of being called upon to serve.

When at the beginning of 1916 the Government produced its Conscription Bill, the Labour Party and the Trade Unions opposed it; but a special Labour Conference decided to offer no further opposition, beyond protest, if it became law. The Labour movement thus acquiesced in military compulsion, only declaring that it ought to be accompanied by the "conscription of wealth," and that any attempt to apply "industrial conscription" would be resisted.

It was, however, inevitable that the power vested in the Government to call up anyone it chose for military service should have a profound influence on conditions in the workshops. The further dilution and substitution of women and unfit persons could be extended, the more men of military age could be released for the Army. This gave the workers who remained a second motive, besides their insistence on their Trade Union rights, for standing out against workshop changes. Moreover, the longer the war lasted and the more bitter and destructive it became, the more men would be needed, and the more unfit men would be sent back to release yet more fit men for the front. On the other hand, the employer's power to certify that a man could be spared gave him a new disciplinary power over the workers; and there was always suspicion that a man who made himself awkward in the workshop would speedily find himself called up for service. Finally, as the war dragged on, the workshops became fuller of unfit men who had been sent back from the Army without being released from it, and were liable to be called up at any time if they were thought fit for further service.

These conditions, though some of them increased the difficulties of workshop opposition, gave those who remained in the workshops a strong motive for greater solidarity, as a protection against intimidation. They knew that the Government could ill afford to face a serious strike, even though the shortage of munitions became less acute as the war went on. But, side by side with these selfish motives, there were others. At all events after the rejection of the German peace overtures in December 1916, and still more after the first Russian Revolution of 1917, anti-war feeling was developing apace. There was growing suspicion of British and Allied war aims.

In May 1915 the Labour Party had agreed to take a small place in a Coalition Government under Asquith, with Henderson as its principal representative. When Lloyd George overthrew Asquith in December 1916, and formed a new coalition, there was much more difference inside the Labour Party, especially as the crisis coincided in time with the German offer of peace and with President Wilson's Peace Note to the belligerent countries. Persuaded by the promise of stronger State control of industry, of a tight hand on food prices and coal, of the establishment of a Ministry of Labour, and of the drawing up of ambitious plans of post-war social reform, the Labour Party took a larger part in the new coalition, but with more dissentients than before.

The Trade Unions, meanwhile, continued their official support of the Government and of the war; and the shop stewards' movement, under the combined pressure of increasing dilution, military conscription, and anti-war feeling, took on a more revolutionary temper which had little in common with the attitude of any of the main contending groups inside the Labour Party.

The political doubters from Henderson and MacDonald leftwards had no real desire for a Socialist revolution; they merely wanted to bring the war to an end, and varied among themselves only as to the amount of concessions they would make to Germany and the vehemence with which they demanded peace in speech or writing. More and more the I.L.P. became a peace party; its ranks were heavily diluted by pure pacifists, often of middle-class origin and with little knowledge of what they meant by Socialism. But the division between pacifist and revolutionary was obscured while the war lasted; the *Herald* and the *Labour Leader* spoke for both and were supported by both; in June 1917 a large but irregularly called conference was held at Leeds, at which MacDonald and Snowden supported a resolution—which was passed with enthusiasm—calling for Workers' and Soldiers' Councils in Britain. (It must of course be remembered that at this time the Soviets were not under Bolshevik control, but even after the November revolution the two wings—pacifists and revolutionaries—kept up an uneasy alliance.)

But the effect of the Leeds Conference was as nothing compared with what was to come. The Russian Socialists of every complexion were tired of the war, and the government of their country was more and more falling into their hands. Eminent right-wing Socialists from the Allied countries—Arthur Henderson from England, Cachin and Frossard from France—were sent to recall them from their deplorable endeavours to end the war, and returned abruptly converted to the Russian view. Henderson, who was a member of the War Cabinet, came back convinced that it was necessary to hold a full conference of the International, including the Germans, at Stockholm, as demanded by the "Dutch–Scandinavian Committee" (the sole remaining fragment of the old Bureau) and the Petrograd Soviet. Such a conference meant in effect an attempt to secure peace by direct communication between the workers of the warring countries; only those who remember the vitiated atmosphere of the war can realize the immense relief caused by the Labour Party Conference when it adopted the proposal on 10 August 1917, by 1,840,000 to 550,000 votes. Immediately afterwards Henderson was forced out of the War Cabinet, and nearly the whole Press followed the Premier's signal for a violent attack on him and the new policy. The war party in the Labour Party revived, led most actively by Will Thorne of the Gasworkers and Havelock Wilson of the Sailors and Firemen, the latter now a raging anti-German as a result of U-boat warfare. Propagandists of the British Empire Union toured the Trade Union centres denouncing the very idea of a negotiated peace; it was hoped that at the adjourned conference meeting on 21 August the decision would be reversed. The Miners' Federation delegates, controlling a block of 600,000 votes, decided by a 3 per cent majority to cross to the "patriotic" side; the fire-eating delegates arrived with Union Jacks concealed in their pockets and waistcoats, to be waved when the pro-Germans were crushed and "Rule Britannia" sung. The flags were thrust back and "Rule Britannia" drowned under the "Red Flag" when the original decision was reaffirmed, though by only a 3,000 majority. But the shift had been enough to make the Government feel safe in refusing passports to Stockholm. The Stockholm Conference was prevented; the war proceeded to its end. Arthur Henderson and his colleagues had to be content with the summoning of an inter-Allied Labour conference which met in February 1918 and made a declaration on war aims and peace terms which, though not free of imperialist ideas, was far in advance of anything their Governments would agree to.

Yet "Stockholm" had released men's minds; to work for peace and even to oppose the war became a task in which men now knew they had many allies. The Irish revolt of Easter week 1916 had had no effect upon the Labour movement. Even the appeals of the Russian Soviets had been lackadaisically received till Henderson had brought them straight to the Party Conference. Now there was a certain and steadily growing anti-war movement.

This is not to say that in industry even the shop stewards were mostly either pacifists or revolutionary Socialists. Far from it. Most of them were ordinary rank-and-file Trade Unionists who were very sick of being badgered and overworked, very unwilling to be sent to fight in a quarrel which had lost all its meaning, and very conscious of getting no lead at all from their official leaders. What happened was not that most of the shop stewards became revolutionaries, but that the changing conditions threw to the head of the movement a larger proportion of left-wing Socialists to whom the actuality of revolution in Russia made it seem a more real possibility at home.

After the Clyde strike and deportations of March 1916, things seemed for a time to be settling down. It took time for the workers to adjust themselves to the new situation created by the advent of compulsory military service. Even the introduction of a "Substitution Scheme" in September, designed to release workers from the less essential industries for labour on munitions, and the extended "Dilution Scheme" which followed hard upon it, were applied without widespread opposition. On top of that came, after the formation of the Lloyd George Government, the "National Service Scheme" under Neville Chamberlain, heralding a fresh drive for men now that the German peace overtures had been definitely pushed aside.

From that point industrial troubles became again more

serious. There were strikes in March 1917, at Barrow and on
the Tyne, arising largely out of the skilled men's dissatisfaction
at the fact that they were able to earn in many cases much less
than unskilled men engaged on repetition work. In the following month, in connection with a fresh drive, this time based
on the need for more skilled craftsmen in the Army, the
Government abolished the "Trade Card Scheme," under
which the Amalgamated Society of Engineers and certain
other Unions had been allowed to issue their own certificates
of exemption from military service to fully skilled workers.
Hard upon this, but only in part arising out of it, came in
May the most widespread strike movement of the whole war
period. In one centre after another the munition workers,
proclaiming an endless variety of grievances from place to
place, came out on strike unofficially, under the leadership of
the shop stewards' movement.

The dilution of labour to which the Trade Unions had
agreed in 1915 had been confined strictly to war work—understood as meaning work on war supplies made at the Government's order. But as the pressure on man-power increased,
more and more attempts were being made to apply the same
measures to "commercial work," to which the special limitations of profits under the Munitions Act did not apply—though
of course the general Excess Profits Duty imposed on all businesses in 1915 did apply. The Trade Unions strongly resisted
this extension, and up to the autumn of 1916 it was not officially pressed. By the amending Munitions Act of 1916 the
Munitions Tribunals had been to some extent reformed. Their
power to imprison had been taken away, and an Appeal
Tribunal had been set up to revise contested local decisions.
The Unions' grievances concerning wages had been partly met
by the taking of power to enforce by order the wage-rates for
women and men "dilutees," and by the setting up of two
standing Special Arbitration Tribunals to deal with disputes
concerning their application. But the Unions complained,
not only that the conditions thus laid down were very imper-
fectly observed, but also that employers were illegitimately
taking advantage of the Unions' acceptance of dilution on
war work to apply it to other work as well.

The Government, as early as September 1916, asked the Unions to accept this extension in order to release more skilled labour for essential work. Then, however, the change of Government for some time held matters up; and only in March 1917 was it again seriously pressed. In that month Dr. Addison, the Minister of Munitions, introduced a new amending Munitions Bill which had as its principal object the compulsory extension of dilution to commercial work. The Unions strongly objected; and the agitation against the Bill coincided with the "Man-Power" crisis of April and the withdrawal of the "Trade Card" scheme. In the midst of this agitation a Lancashire firm, which refused to recognize Trade Unions at all, suddenly applied dilution to their commercial production, and, when a number of their skilled employees refused, discharged them in a body, upon which the military authorities promptly seized them for the army. A big sympathetic strike was at once threatened, and the men won their case.

But there were plenty of similar troubles elsewhere; and in May the strike movement spread like wildfire. The Government met it by arresting a number of rank-and-file leaders; but the strikers refused to return to work until a guarantee had been given that all their grievances would be promptly and fully investigated. Accordingly, in June the Government appointed a body of Commissioners on Labour Unrest who were to divide into panels and conduct a series of local inquiries into the causes of the late troubles. But at the same time the demand for commercial dilution was still pressed; and at length the Executive of the A.S.E. agreed to take a ballot upon the question and recommended their members to accept, under safeguards promised by the Government.

The members of the A.S.E., however, decisively refused to agree to commercial dilution; and the reports of the Commissioners showed the existence of widespread unrest based on manifest grievances. Churchill, succeeding Addison as Minister of Munitions, not only dropped the proposal to extend dilution, but also took powers, in the re-draft of the Munitions Bill, to abolish "Leaving Certificates," which were shown to have been at the bottom of a good deal of the trouble.

The abolition of Leaving Certificates did not, however, restore the full mobility of labour. A new Order under the Defence of the Realm Act made it unlawful for men working on munitions to transfer to other types of work, though they could now move from one munitions factory to another. Moreover, a second Order remained in force, preventing any employer from seeking to attract labour by offering higher pay, or bringing workers from a distance except through the machinery of the Labour Exchanges.

One of the most serious grievances disclosed by the Commissioners on Labour Unrest had been the relative underpayment of highly skilled workers. Less skilled men and women, engaged on repetition work, could be speeded up to very high rates of output, which in some cases brought in very large earnings. But highly skilled work could not be speeded up in this way; and consequently the most skilled men were often earning less than some of the unskilled dilutees. In order to redress the balance, Churchill granted, in October 1917, a bonus of 12½ per cent on total earnings to certain classes of fully skilled time-workers engaged on munitions.

This well-meant concession led to endless confusion. The Order in its original form excluded many highly skilled men who had as good a claim as those to whom the bonus was given. The Ministry was at once bombarded with applications for inclusion; and gradually by concessions to one group after another the bonus was extended to all time-workers classified as skilled. There was, however, no clear line of division between the lower ranks of the skilled men and the upper ranks of those graded as less skilled; and a second bombardment set in from these grades. After some weeks of confusion, the Government gave way, and the bonus was made payable to all time-workers on munitions, irrespective of skill. The original purpose was thus entirely defeated, and it was converted into an ordinary wage-increase.

It still, however, excluded workers on piece-work or other systems of payment by results; and these sections now began in their turn to bombard the Ministry. Finally, in January 1918 a bonus of 7½ per cent was conceded to piece-workers, and the unfortunate episode was at an end. What happened in effect was that a general wage-advance was granted in an unusual form, and other piecemeal methods had to be used for raising again the wages of a limited number of highly skilled men.

Before the war, wages in the engineering and kindred trades were fixed locally. Each area had its own district rate, agreed upon by the local employers' association and the Trade Unions. There was a procedure whereby, if agreement could not be reached locally, the matter was referred to a national conference between the Trade Unions concerned and the Engineering Employers' Federation. Failing agreement there, the workers were free to strike locally, or the employers to lock them out.

When arbitration was established under the Treasury Agreement, this machinery was preserved; but failure to agree was followed by reference of the dispute to the Committee on Production. For some time this method was maintained, each separate locality making its own wage demands. But early in 1917 a new system was established. In view of the rising cost of living, the arguments advanced for wage-increases were much the same over the whole country; and the Trade Unions, without giving up their right to make local claims on special grounds, agreed in general to put forward uniform national applications for the whole country, these to be referred at once for settlement by the Committee on Production, which thus became the general wage-fixing authority for workers engaged on munitions work. Up to April 1917 the war advances had varied from district to district, but had not fallen below 7s. a week on pre-war rates. By the end of 1917 the Committee on Production had granted another 13s. But thereafter no further advance was given until August 1918. In fact, the 12½ and 7½ per cent bonuses had been offset by the refusal to grant additional advances in the ordinary form. In August 1918 a further 3s. 6d. was granted, bringing the total war advances up to 23s. 6d., excluding the bonus, on pre-war rates of from 30s. to 37s. for skilled workers, but often as little as 20s. or even 18s. for unskilled male workers.

Up to the Munitions Act of 1917, these arbitration awards applied only to firms which were members of the Employers'

Federation, and endless separate negotiations were needed in order to get them adopted by non-federated firms. But power was taken under the Act of 1917 to issue Orders applying the awards of the Committee on Production to all firms; and the State thus came by Order to prescribe directly the standard wages throughout the munitions industries. We shall see later that this system of State wage-regulation was gradually abolished after the war.

When the "May" strikes of 1917 were over, things settled down for a time. The Lloyd George Government had set up a Food Control Organization under Lord Devonport in December 1916. But this had been thoroughly inefficient, and food shortage and food profiteering had been among the important grievances laid bare by the strikes. In June 1917 Lord Rhondda was appointed Food Controller, with J. R. Clynes as his assistant; and a new spirit of efficiency at once appeared at the Ministry of Food. Unrestricted naval warfare was making serious inroads on the tonnage available for transport; and the entry of the United States into the war meant additional demands for ships to transport American troops and supplies. "Standard bread" had been introduced in January; and now additional steps were taken to economize supplies and to check the rise in prices. Food prices had risen above the pre-war level by 18 per cent at the beginning of 1915, by 45 per cent a year later, and by 87 per cent at the beginning of 1917. By the end of June 1917 the rise was 104 per cent; but thereafter it was checked for a time. It was only 106 per cent at the end of the year, and 110 per cent at the end of June 1918. Thereafter the control lost its hold, and by November 1918 food prices were 133 per cent above the pre-war level, and the cost of living as a whole had risen by about 125 per cent. But for a time the new methods of the Food Ministry were effective both in checking the rise in prices, and in preventing really serious shortage even in face of the submarine campaign.

There was, however, enough fear of shortage to cause strong measures to be taken both to speed up shipbuilding and to ration the available tonnage with increasing strictness, and also to increase food production at home. Under the Corn

Production Act of August 1917 the State guaranteed the
farmers very remunerative prices for their output and compelled them in return, under Labour pressure, to grant the
agricultural workers a minimum wage. A National Agricultural Wages Board was set up, with power to fix wages for each
area, on the advice of local Wages Committees representing
the farmers and labourers, subject to an overriding minimum
of 25*s*. a week—as against the 30*s*. demanded by the Labour
Party and the Trade Unions. This Act produced a great
growth of Trade Unionism among agricultural workers.

Very few of these Trade Union recruits were gained from
female land workers, but these were already of great importance. By the next year there were nearly 400,000 women
working on the land—18,000 whole-time in the Land Army
and 300,000 part-time, in addition to the normal 80,000. It
seemed in parts of the countryside that there was no one
working except old men, German prisoners, and land-girls
in breeches.

The war had been the great liberator for women. There
had been a short sharp struggle within the Suffragists' ranks.
Some endeavoured to uphold the view that women should
take no part in war, and that their task was to seek peace and
prevent slaughter. But they were swept aside as old-fashioned
or unpatriotic; in 1915 half the Executive and a number of
officers of the National Union of Women's Suffrage Societies
resigned in protest against the bellicose policy of Mrs. Fawcett
and thereafter the way was clear. Suffrage memoirs and histories still reflect the glee with which the Suffragists saw the
prospects opening before them. Some nursing, some giving
of white feathers, were all that had been permitted to them
before; now, from 1915 onwards, they were to be munition
workers, land workers, car drivers, tram conductors, sweeps,
bakers, all known kinds of factory workers—in fact everything
except miners and builders. Though they were not allowed to
fight in the trenches they came as near to it as possible; they
put on uniform, submitted to military discipline and as
"Waacs" and "Wrens" and "Wrafs"—Army, Navy and Air
Force auxiliaries—150,000 of them "did their bit" (though
less than 10 per cent got to France). Conscription for males

(it was never applied to women) began officially on 2 March 1916, but pressure almost as strong had preceded it. ("Will you mırch too or wait till March 2?" the posters had asked.) An unprecendent shift in the population was taking place. First in thousands and then in tens and hundreds of thousands young and not-so-young women voluntarily entered industry or agriculture, "substituting" themselves for men who were taken into the armed forces. "The success and popularity of substitution grew steadily from the summer of 1915 onwards, and by the middle of 1916 there was a universal chorus of praise for the women," writes Mrs. R. Strachey (*The Cause*, p. 344).

The breaking of innumerable local tyrannies that this meant can only be imagined by a later generation. In health first: the hobble skirts, the tight lacing, the lack of exercise which had for long kept the female sex subject to "vapours," fainting, and apparent incapacity for connected effort or connected thought, disappeared not to return. In domestic liberty: the decrees of unnumbered mothers and fathers forbidding association with boys, staying out late, meeting vulgar friends, travelling alone or unchaperoned, or working away from home, were not only broken but denounced by authority as unpatriotic. "There are still," said Walter Long, a steel-plated Conservative, "places where women believe their place is the home; that idea must be met and combated." In financial liberty: many wives of respectable working men, and even more of shiftless labourers, found for the first time in their lives what it was to receive every week without fail a regular wage or pension, which they could expend sensibly for themselves and their children. Many more unmarried girls found themselves unexpectedly earning wages which seemed fantastically high, given apparently absolute personal freedom, and publicly praised and flattered for doing work which two years before they would have given their eyes to be allowed to touch. In morals: when Ronald McNeill, M.P., announced (mistakenly) that a vast crop of war-babies was about to appear round every camp, he did so not to enforce rebuke and punishment, but to demand official relief and countenance for those who had too ardently consoled their warriors. The unanswerable arguments of army health statistics compelled universal military instruction in the avoidance of venereal disease by a means which was also the earliest effective contraceptive; the knowledge did not remain confined to the male sex.

The new women workers, however little they reflected, had to doubt whether the life which their mothers had led, or been expected to lead, of secure affection and obedience to one man, father of their many children, was either possible or desirable. Their potential husbands were being methodically and indifferently killed off in Flanders or in the Near East; they did not know, nor did their rulers, whether the war and the strange unnatural society which it required would end this year, next year, some time or never. Everything was temporary and uncertain; life itself was uncertain, their lovers were temporary gentlemen, their own liberty was unreliable and conditional.

But not until years later was the full extent of the change realized. No one could fail to see that enormous numbers of men were being massacred and that this must have some temporary effect on the population. The excess of births over deaths per thousand of the population in England and Wales, which in 1914 had been at the rather low figure of 9·8, fell in 1915 to 6·1, rallied slightly to 6·7 next year, fell to 3·6 in 1917 and to 0·4 in 1918. But even those who most lamented it tended to assume, consciously or unconsciously, that this heavy loss was the total loss, a final figure, and that the population would, as it had before in history, renew itself in time by natural processes, only missing in one generation a million or so valuable lives. They were confirmed in this belief by the "baby boom" which followed the Armistice, in which the excess of births rose to 13·1 (1920) and 10·3 (1921). For years birth-control propagandists were able to use arguments derived from the probable pressure of a growing population upon natural resources without being laughed at.

But not merely did many potential fathers never return from the war, those that did had smaller families or none at all. The war ended the Victorian family. Up to its outbreak the average annual increase of the population, calculated in ten-year periods from official figures, had fluctuated round 1 per cent. After it, the figure fell to less than half, and did not rise again.

Average Annual Increase per cent in Population in Great Britain

1871–81 ..	1·3
1881–91 ..	1·06
1891–1901	1·13
1901–11 ..	0·98
1911–21 ..	0·46
1921–31 ..	0·46
1931–38 ..	0·44

Britain had not been so deeply wounded as France. But the injury was of the same type. Families were going to become smaller. The population would become older—the elderly would be many and the young rare. In due course, it might be, the population would actually decline, absolutely and in relation to the world around.

Meanwhile, to women, carrying on the work of the nation, growing its food, and changing its morals and ideas, the longed-for gift of the vote could not be denied. Once they had flooded into industry the principle was accepted by all but the most reactionary. The Representation of the People Act in February 1918, without agitation and with but little dissent, gave all women over thirty the vote, and extended the local government franchise to the same class (women householders had had it since 1869). It was expected widely that female voting privileges would be made the same as male immediately after the next election, but so little did the women "stick together" once the suffrage agitation had died away that this amendment was not secured till 1928.

The balance between men and women in the country was not merely temporarily altered; it was changed for years to come, and it was certain that men could never take all the places occupied by women. Too many would not return. The old Regular Army was more or less destroyed in 1914; its ranks were replaced by Kitchener's Army, whose first hundred thousand was secured in that autumn and whose numbers soon reached a million—the largest volunteer expeditionary force ever sent out by Britain or perhaps by any country, consisting of the best, in body and spirit, of their generation and, at that date, recruited wholly by enthusiasm and conviction and scarcely at all by open or veiled compulsion. "On the Somme, in 1916," writes John Brophy, "this first national army was so desperately, stupidly, and callously misused that it was broken at its first encounter with the enemy. After the Somme, Kitchener's Army ceased to exist and the British Expeditionary Force was made up of battalions and batteries in which professional soldiers, territorials, volunteers, middle-aged conscripts and boys called to serve on their eighteenth birthday were all mixed and the traditions of units were forgotten." The next year, under the same generals, a similar senseless massacre was carried on for months round Passchen-daele. By the end of the war over nine hundred thousand were dead and over two million wounded.

War enthusiasm waned, after such grotesque follies, even in the Army; indeed, war hysteria and savagery were the marks of civilians and of those who had not yet gone out. But though many of the troops longed for the war to end, despised the politicians who would "never sheathe the sword," and even took part in a serious mutiny at Etaples, they had little or no sympathy with the pacifists at home. The papers they read were *John Bull*, the *Daily Mail*, and similar journals; they generally accepted these papers' pictures of South Wales miners and Clyde engineers as well-fed slackers skulking in safe jobs. There was an almost complete lack of understanding between the workers in uniform and those out of it.

More and more drastic powers were used as the war went on to deal with civilian disaffected persons. Under the Defence of the Realm Act Orders in Council could be issued forbidding almost any activity that the Government considered harmful; new crimes could be created overnight. In addition to "Dora," the Military Service Acts were used, not only in the war industries, to break or prevent strikes; tramway-men, printers, farm labourers and jute-workers within six months of March 1916 found strikes either prevented or broken by a threat of calling up the discontented workers. The Acts were administered by a network of local and appeal tribunals (and one Central Tribunal) which had power to award exemption from service on the ground of conscience, of personal hardship, or of indispensability. These exemptions were regularly revised as the demands of the Army increased; the process, by a metaphor drawn from lice, was known as "combing out." They were granted capriciously after such questions as (at Whitechapel): "Has your sister's young man attested?" and under the eye of a Military Representative who not uncommonly dominated the tribunal himself. The greatest suffering was probably caused to the owners of one-man businesses; a study of tribunal records shows a quite surprising number of these which would be forced to close down or be taken over by multiple firms. More publicity was received by the conscientious objectors: 8,806 courts martial were held on those who were refused exemption and still maintained their principles. About 5,000 were either sent to prison or set to work under various schemes; an uncertain number were "on the run" to the end of the war.

There were very few things which could not, under "Dora," be regarded as spreading false news or taking action likely to discourage recruiting. Any discussion of the way in which the war came that did not cast the whole blame on Germany, such as was continually attempted by the Union of Democratic Control under the leadership of E. D. Morel, was liable to come under the second category; a facetious statement like: "We shall see the Germans in the Mile End Road yet," came under the first, as an East London man named Hawkins found at the cost of £100. Bertrand Russell was fined the same amount for pacifist propaganda. John Maclean, who was more dangerous because he spoke in Glasgow to working men, was sent to prison for three years. A Mr. E. Parker was punished for saying the King was "a bloody German"; it was more serious that in the case of J. M. Williams and others the possession of written matter which, if published, would be a contravention of "Dora" was held as much an offence as the actual publication. Domiciliary visits, and the searching of homes by force, now became a regular feature of police procedure; large numbers of convictions were thereafter secured on the basis of the possession by the raided persons of old "no-conscription" leaflets and other matter. The importation of books was for the first time subject to censorship:

W. H. Mainwaring was forbidden to receive a parcel of
C. H. Kerr books from Chicago, including one called *The
Germs of Mind in Plants*, though it is true that this particular
work was at last admitted after the matter had been raised
in the House of Commons. Letters were opened and read—
P. Kearne, an old soldier of Edgware, was fined £100 for
a garrulous letter about Hendon aerodrome, though it was
never delivered and it was agreed that the writer was an ardent
patriot. Rounding-up (so called by a metaphor derived from
cattle) was practised: the police would block the exits to
parks, picture palaces or restaurants, corral all the men, force
them to show their papers, and take those who could not to
the police station, where they would either be drafted into the
Army or released according to the evidence they could produce.
Despite Habeas Corpus, deportation and internment without
trial were not infrequent; but as (apart from the munitions
cases already mentioned) this weapon was used largely against
persons genuinely suspected of aiding the Germans, no widespread protest was made. Meetings could be prohibited by
the police without the right of appeal; where they were held,
volunteer mobs would sometimes wreck them and attack the
speakers. The police, as at a famous meeting in the Southgate
Brotherhood Church and an attempted I.L.P. conference at
the Essex Hall, withheld their protection in the fairly clear
belief that dissentients deserved all they got. National papers,
such as the *Daily Express*, approved this, and local papers
incited to the mauling or mobbing of "C.O.s."

Plays such as Miles Malleson's *D Company* and *Black 'Ell*
were forbidden to circulate; books and pamphlets were seized.
Newspapers were from the beginning subject to a censorship
which concerned itself mostly but by no means wholly with
war news. Left-wing papers were, of course, the most frequent
victims of official attentions, but not the only ones. *Britannia*,
organ of the ex-militant suffragettes, and the *Globe*, a powerful
London evening paper, were both suppressed for an hysterical
campaign charging the Government with being in league with
the Germans. The latter paper stated (in September 1916)
that Lord Kitchener had resigned in disgust; it was allowed
to reappear after a fortnight; but its circulation was ruined

and it soon expired, a warning to all inclined to insubordination.

Many of the devices of the age of Sidmouth and Castlereagh had already been revived. Democrats suspected that the only remaining step had been taken when on 7 March, 1917, *The Times* reported that a middle-aged pacifist lady in Derby, Mrs. Wheeldon, with her two daughters, Hetty Wheeldon and Mrs. Mason, and her son-in-law Arthur Mason (a chemist), had been put on trial on a charge based on a government agent's evidence of conspiring to murder Lloyd George and Arthur Henderson by pricking them somehow with a needle dipped in a rare South American poison. This story did not seem preposterous to a nation which was prepared to credit the insanities of the "Black Book" case, though the only independent evidence consisted of a letter from Mason to Mrs. Wheeldon enclosing certain poisons. These were intended, the defence insisted, to kill dogs guarding a concentration camp in which were imprisoned conscientious objectors whom Mrs. Wheeldon wished to help to escape, a plan suggested to her by Alec Gordon, a government agent posing as a "C.O." This man, originally sent down to Derby by his superior, H. J. W. Booth, had called Booth in and introduced him as "Comrade Bert" of the I.W.W., a C.O. "on the run." The two, according to the defence, had formed this plan with the Wheeldon and Mason family; their own version (or that of one, for Gordon did not appear in court) was that they were horrified spectators at the concoction of a complex plot to blow or throw needles poisoned with curare at Messrs. George and Henderson. The jury believed them: Mrs. Wheeldon and Mr. and Mrs. Mason were sentenced to ten, seven and five years in prison respectively, Hetty Wheeldon being acquitted.

The end of 1917 and beginning of 1918 saw the loss of another chance of peace and the worsening of war conditions. The Russians from November on had been negotiating for peace at Brest-Litovsk; but the Allies had ignored their appeals to join in. Their appeal to the German workers produced widespread strikes in January 1918, but the Allied governments, confiding in American aid, would only accept a complete German surrender. In March the Russians signed the peace treaty, the German workers were brought to heel again, and a German offensive began which seemed to suggest that the Allied politicians had been wrong in their calculations. Ludendorff, quicker to learn than his Allied rivals, had evolved a new system of attack which the British and French seemed unable to resist. Throughout March and April the news from the front was in the last degree alarming; the troops were pushed back nearly to the 1914 line.

At home food shortage became serious. The submarine war now had its effect: rationing, which had been extended from sugar to other foods in February, was made more stringent. Though the countryside, the small towns, and the richer classes were not inconvenienced, the beginnings of a shortage of fats and sugar were observable in the cities. Meatless days were enforced, and there was a great lack of beer. The military service age was raised to fifty and a fresh and most severe "comb-out" was instituted.

But by May the German offensive had been held, and the tide was turning. The submarine danger had been lessened by the blocking of Zeebrugge and Ostend; the Americans were reaching France in increasing numbers. The war was entering on its final phase of dogged German resistance to now inevitable defeat.

These changed conditions enabled the Government to give more of its attention to what was to happen when the war was over. The Whitley Reports, dealing with the future relations of employers and workers, had been published in 1917, but can best be discussed in dealing with the post-war period. In August 1918 Parliament passed a new Education Act, removing school exemptions under fourteen and considerably extending the public provision for higher education, and a Trade Boards Act, under which the protection of a legal minimum wage could be extended to any trade in which serious underpayment was held to exist. Numerous Government Committees were at work under a special Ministry of Reconstruction drawing up plans for the period after the war. There was an immense outpouring of talk about the new "spirit of the trenches" and the new heaven and earth which would be brought into being by the collaboration of all classes in the post-war effort. Little enough was to come of all this prophesying; but for the time being it served to some extent to check the growth of unrest.

Meanwhile, in the world of labour, the relaxation of the tension of March and April 1918 was followed by a fresh outbreak of unrest. At the beginning of July the Ministry of Munitions made an attempt to compel a number of employers to release further skilled workers; and about the same time many employers, especially in the Midlands, entered into a private arrangement under which they virtually reimposed the "leaving certificate" system by refusing to engage any man who had left the employment of any other of their number. In protest against these moves, a series of strikes broke out in July at Coventry and elsewhere. The strikers returned on a promise that their grievances should be rectified; and an official enquiry subsequently condemned the "embargo" system.

In August there were more strikes—one in the transport service on the question of equal pay for men and women, and even a sudden strike of the London police, who demanded the recognition of their Union. This latter greatly alarmed the authorities, and they made haste to improve police pay; but they refused to recognize the Union, only promising to set up a Police Representative Board under official auspices to consider grievances in the Force. An unofficial railway strike followed in September, by way of protest against the settlement of wages made by the Union leaders; and unrest flared up again in the South Wales coal-field and the Lancashire cotton industry. But thereafter the collapse first of Austrian and then of German resistance caused a lull, and the Unions began to prepare their programmes with a view to the impending period of "Reconstruction."

Right up to November 1918 the Labour Party continued to be represented in the Coalition Government. But in effect in the later stages of the war the Labour Ministers (G. N. Barnes, John Hodge, J. R. Clynes, G. H. Roberts and a few others in minor posts) represented very little except themselves. Arthur Henderson, after his withdrawal, had set to work to reorganize the Labour Party machine with a view to its effectiveness after the war; and from the moment when the Party formulated its own statement of War Aims in December 1917, it stood more and more for an independent policy. In the early months of 1918 the Party, hitherto simply an alliance between the Trade Unions and the Socialist Societies, of which the I.L.P. was very much the most important, adopted a new constitution, embodying a far-reaching change of structure. In future the Party proposed to set up in every constituency a Local Labour Party, with individual as well as affiliated members. Proclaiming itself the party of "the workers by hand and brain," it issued in June 1918, under the title *Labour and the New Social Order*, a revised statement of its policy committing it more definitely than ever before to evolutionary Socialism; and on this basis it set to work to enlist the support of sections of the electorate whom it had previously done nothing to enrol. The Labour Party, in face of the divisions of Liberalism, which was hopelessly split between the followers of Asquith and Lloyd George, was staking out its claim to be regarded as His Majesty's Opposition, and as the alternative Government to that of Lloyd George.

As soon as the Armistice was signed (11 November 1918), and it became plain that the Government meant to force an immediate election, the Labour Party was compelled to clear up the ambiguity of its position. At a special conference in the same month it decided to withdraw the remaining Labour Ministers from the Government, and to fight the election as a completely independent party.

BETWEEN THE WARS

CHAPTER XLII

REVOLUTION AND THE "DOLE"

NOVEMBER 11, 1918, at eleven o'clock in the morning, a grey but clear day. Maroons banged to announce the war was over. In a few minutes the streets were full of shouting people. Public-houses were broken into, and drunk dry of their small stocks of beer. Buses, taxis, even the official motor-cars were seized and forced to career round the streets, packed with shouting and singing people, waving flags, kissing strangers, laughing and crying, drunk not with drink but with relief and thankfulness. No work was done that day: rejoicing went on far into the night.

By that part of the nation which was in arms in France or elsewhere the news was received at first more phlegmatically. "At about 10.45 a.m. we were in action against the Germans east of Mons, and one of our troops had just charged some German machine-guns. A private soldier came galloping towards us; he was much excited, had lost his cap and could not stop his horse. As he passed he shouted: 'The war's over! The war's over!' We thought, undoubtedly, the poor fellow was suffering from shell-shock. Soon after an official message came. . . . Out came the inevitable cigarette, but there was no cheering, or wild exuberance of feelings." So run some reminiscences in the *Army Quarterly* quoted by Guy Chapman in his *Vain Glory*; he adds his own recollection: "We took over our billets and listlessly devoured a meal. In an effort to cure our apathy, the little American doctor from Vermont who had joined us a fortnight earlier broke his invincible teetotalism, drank half a bottle of whisky and danced a cachuca. We looked at his antics with dull eyes and at last put him to bed."

But relief and even gratitude, though never so unquestioned a gratitude as at home, before long possessed the army too. On the surface, indeed, it seemed that contentment and delight had seized all the nation, and with the perfect instinct of the

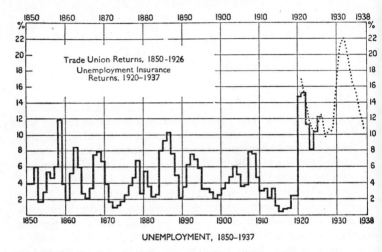

Trade Union Returns, 1850-1926
Unemployment Insurance
Returns, 1920-1937

UNEMPLOYMENT, 1850-1937

electioneer Lloyd George instantaneously arranged for the greatest of all khaki elections, held in December 1918. His coalition, the precursor of a later "National Government" and containing Conservatives, Liberals, and even a few who called themselves "Labour," secured a tremendous victory, carrying about 530 seats while Labour had only about 60 and Asquith's independent Liberals 29. A chorus of praise surrounded the Government; the rosiest promises, including the once-famed "homes fit for heroes," scintillated out from Lloyd George like a halo; even the Labour opposition (the Liberals remained the "official" opposition) could not forbear to cheer. The accident of electoral choices had deprived the Labour M.P.s of their natural leaders, Left, Right or Centre. Ramsay MacDonald, Arthur Henderson, George Lansbury and all the pre-war figures of eminence had been defeated. The leadership fell upon an unskilful miners' official, W. Adamson, later succeeded by J. R. Clynes, who had been a minister to the very end in Lloyd George's War Cabinet and was divided by the very narrowest line from his old chief. The Party as a whole might demand vigorous and semi-revolutionary opposition; the M.P.s were unwilling or unable to provide it. The Labour Party Executive condemned the Versailles Treaty, for example, but the condemnation was inadequately echoed in the Commons. When Lloyd George officially brought back this fatal document to the Parliament the mass of the Labour M.P.s joined in the wild and hysterical welcome. A few—Ben Spoor, Will Thorne and others—sat down while the others stood up to cheer and shout; the contemptuous glances they received turned to rage when one, Neil Maclean, was hardy enough to continue sitting through the "God Save the King" that followed. Too many of the Party were elderly Trade Union officials; and so far from opposing the Government, many were soon more occupied in opposing their own members, "deprecating extremism" and damping down the revolutionary spirit.

For the cheering and hysteria were the cheering and hysteria of only a part of the nation. Some, probably the majority, were willing to celebrate the end of the war by a great orgy of "Hun-hating" and revenge. They were content to entrust their fate to men like Sir Eric Geddes, First Lord of the Admiralty, who promised to squeeze Germany till the pips squeaked. The defeated enemy was to be stripped and starved; he would pay for everything; everyone should have a great deal of money, even enough to satisfy the "hard-faced men" who now ruled the nation. Others, war-weary or touched with revolutionary feeling, hated the war-Government, the profiteers, the yellow journalists more fiercely than they hated the Germans. They were determined at the least to get the country that they had fought for, and to force the construction of a just new world in fact and not merely in politicians' speeches. Almost immediately after the election fierce conflict began between the Government on the one hand and the soldiers and workers on the other. In a less acute form, the same revolutionary fever which burned in every European country burned for a while in Britain. The Labour M.P.s were useless for its purpose; it had to express itself outside Parliament.

The Government was still possessed of great coercive war-time powers. (The war was not allowed to end officially till August 1921.) It used them as much as it dared. But it was by no means certain of its implements. The London police had actually come out on strike, successfully, in August 1918, and it was scared. One of its earliest preoccupations was to break up the Police and Prison Officers' Union. It drafted in an army expert, Sir W. Macready, and in August 1919, though the country was still convulsed with strikes, rushed through a Bill forbidding Trade Unionism in the police, although it promised the constables certain rights of appeal and consultation within the force. The police of London (and some in Liverpool) alone answered the Union's strike call, and the Union was broken.

The military were even less amenable. "Soldiers' Councils" were actually reported from Egypt, and insubordination and mutiny were frequent at home. 10,000 mutinied on January 6 at Folkestone, 2,000 at Dover, and some 60,000 at various other camps: on that day and the next three days lorry-loads of angry mutineers descended on Whitehall, forcing high officials to interview them, impartially asking advice of Lansbury and Bottomley, but getting little satisfaction. Intermittent riots continued well into the summer. Five were killed and twenty-one wounded in one at Kinmel Park, where the Red Flag was raised, the "Tin Town" at Witley was burned down, Epsom Police Station stormed and the Station Sergeant killed.

These violences looked like being repeated in civil life. Strikes in the Yorkshire mines, on the North-East Coast, and in London tubes were fairly peaceful. But in January and February 1919 the Clyde and Belfast engineers came out, defying their Unions, in strikes for a forty and forty-four hour week respectively. They were defeated, because with the end of the war the shop stewards had overnight lost their importance and the centre of power had returned to the Union headquarters. But during the strikes' progress what were almost pitched battles with the police occurred in Glasgow, the workers, under the leadership of E. Shinwell, David Kirkwood, W. Gallacher and others, standing up with surprising vigour to police batoning. More serious strikes were looming, of which incomparably the biggest was a coal strike.

The Government was for all its glory in a tantalizing position. It had no idea of the real economic outlook. Its members, and the war-rich who supported it, saw an apparently limitless prospect of profits. The world was starving for British products; by July 1919 household coal was being forced up to 19s. a ton above the 1914 prices, and much higher prices were being charged for coal exported to needy Europe. The British employers exploited these momentarily insatiable markets as selfishly and foolishly as Allied politicians carved up Europe and divided up colonies. Money seemed inexhaustible; the silliest hopes occupied the minds of men who believed themselves above all practical. But in the sky of their delighted anticipation appeared one black and recurring cloud—what they called "Bolshevism." Lenin and Trotsky, despite repeated announcements of their fall, remained established in Russia. Endeavours to imitate their horrifying policy of confiscating property and putting an end to rich men as a class were repeatedly made in the west. They had been momentarily successful in Hungary and Bavaria; the condition of Italy was very alarming. Now the same ideas appeared in Great Britain.

Unable momentarily to use force, the Government used deception. Once the Army had been demobilized the most immediate danger would be over. The civilian workers must be cajoled into quietness until this was done and until the most immediate markets had been supplied and strikes were no longer an appalling financial disaster. The motions, therefore, were gone through of applying a great "Reconstruction Programme," very little of which was ever allowed to be put into practice.

Some Acts had been passed in the last months of the war, when they may have still seemed hypothetical dangers to their natural opponents. The operation of these was not wholly an illusory benefit. The Representation of the People Act has been already mentioned. The "Whitley Committee" (named from its chairman, the then Speaker) had since 1917 been issuing reports, adopted by the Government. These led to a stronger Trade Boards Act (1918) permitting the Ministry of Labour to set up Boards wherever wages were sweated or Unions weak, to the constitution of a number of Joint Industrial ("Whitley") Councils and of a voluntary State arbitration court, to the legalization of "Courts of Enquiry" appointed by the Ministry of Labour if arbitration was refused, and finally to the extension of the Whitley principle of workers' representation to Government offices—perhaps the only unquestionable advantage remaining from 1919.

Throughout the year the Labour threat was held off by a Wages (Temporary Regulation) Act which forbade any reductions; State control in the coalmines was not ended till the April of 1921; an "out-of-work donation" scheme was established on a temporary basis. Wide promises were made over housing; an Act to which Dr. Christopher Addison's name was attached was passed and from its provisions much was expected; but no allowance was made for the great shortage of builders, and so far from preventing profiteering its terms seemed almost to encourage the great rise in costs which made it useless within a year. Rent restrictions were maintained. The Fisher Education Act was already on the Statute Book and much was made of it. It stopped exemptions under fourteen, and allowed the local authorities to raise the school-leaving age to fifteen, though hardly any of them did. But reasons were found continually to adjourn its application till 1921, when it was in part incorporated into a new Act. Restoration of Trade Union conditions was carried through without much trouble, but it applied only to existing factories which had been engaged in war work; and even in these, the employer, when he had once restored the old practices, was free to abrogate them again as soon as he felt strong enough to defy the Trade Unions.

These were small toys; the great deception was more elaborately staged. It had two parts, the Sankey Commission and the National Industrial Conference. The Sankey Commission dealt with the miners; the Conference with all the rest of the Trade Union movement except the Engineers and the Railwaymen and Transport Workers, who like the Miners, declined to attend it.

The miners were demanding not only wage-increases, but complete public ownership and workers' control of the industry. They refused the Government's wage-offer on February 12, and prepared to strike. This could not be allowed: there was a heavy shortage of coal and it was unlikely that armed forces would have consented to be used in the pits. It was not impossible that the Government would be openly and soundly beaten—forced in the flush of its triumph to nationalize the largest single industry on terms more or less laid down by the workers. Instant action had to be taken: the Government appealed to the miners to hold their hands a very short time while investigation was made. The Miners' Federation was to be allowed, on its peremptory insistence, to approve six of the investigating Commission's thirteen members; the chairman selected was Mr. Justice Sankey, an intelligent and sympathetic lawyer; the Commission must report by March 20; the Government pledged itself in advance to accept its report. The Federation agreed; but promises by Lloyd George were already somewhat suspect in Labour circles, and after the interim report on the 20th had conceded wage-increases, promised a seven-hour day, later to become six, and condemned "the present system of ownership," the miners began to hesitate again. But Bonar Law's personal honour was regarded as intact, and the doubts of the miners were ended by a letter to their secretary, Frank Hodges, in which he said:

Dear Sir,

. . . I have pleasure in confirming, as I understand you wish me to do, my statement that the Government are prepared to carry out in the spirit and in the letter the recommendations of Sir John Sankey's report.

Yours faithfully,
A. Bonar Law.

The National Industrial Conference met on February 27; the employers' representatives were amiable, almost ingratiating. Both sides discussed far-reaching plans for the regulation of industry, the improvement of conditions, and the establishment of such reforms as the universal forty-eight hour week. The acute might have commented that the employers were more eager to vote for requests to the Government to initiate reforms than to concede improved conditions themselves. Nevertheless, the first report of the conference, including the forty-eight hour week, was accepted "in principle" by the Government on May 1. It only gradually became clear that the Government had no intention of doing anything whatever about the reports submitted. It even failed to enforce the forty-eight hour week. The employers' delegates' tone hardened. They had formed themselves, with the consent of the Federation of British Industries, into the National Confederation of Employers' Organizations, which undertook to "handle" labour questions from the general capitalist standpoint. Their strength was therefore considerably increased, but the main reason for intransigence was that before the end of 1919 the danger-point for capitalism was passed. The experience of the Labour side in the end also led indirectly to some improvement in organization. But the Labour delegates were very slow to see the truth; they held on until Midsummer 1921, when the Conference had amply succeeded in its task of holding the Trade Unions amused by vain discussions until the risk was over. Some, indeed, of the Trade Union leaders were simple-minded enough to expect gratitude for assisting in this. T. E. Naylor, of the London Compositors, in 1922, begged the Government to remember that the Trade Unions had prevented "the revolution which would undoubtedly have broken out."

The awakening of the miners was swifter and ruder. An interim report from the Sankey Commission had duly appeared on 20 March 1919, as has been said, and in April it resumed its sessions to deal with the wider problem. Sensational propaganda filled the papers as Robert Smillie, for the miners, cross-examined peers and other royalty owners on what work they did for the large sums they drew. In June the final reports were issued: the majority of the members reported in favour of nationalization. The six members approved by the Miners' Federation also demanded a share in control. Five employers opposed; a sixth, Sir Arthur Duckham, produced a scheme of his own.

Even the most cynical gasped when the Government

announced their decision to ignore the report because of the disagreements shown, and to take up the Duckham scheme, watered down. No person was prepared to approve of this and the Government abandoned it in October, with the air of good men frustrated by senseless obstinacy. The miners turned to the Trades Union Congress (not, it was noted, to the Triple Alliance); Congress voted for a political campaign, not a strike, and so shelved the matter.

In September the Government and its allies—for at this time at any rate the employers and the Government acted as allies—felt that the time had come for a counter-offensive. Churchill, before the 1918 election, had announced the nationalization of the railways. This pledge, too, had been forgotten, and the railwaymen had not even been able to secure the wage-increases they wanted. Indeed, Sir Eric Geddes now on behalf of the Government put out a "definitive offer" of a sliding scale which involved exceedingly low minimum rates. On the 26th all the railwaymen came out: the service practically ceased till October 5. The Government went into battle with glee, urging the public on against the "Anarchists" in terms they had previously used against the Germans. Their calculations of public mentality were wrong; a well organized publicity service provided by the Labour Research Department, supported by threats by the printers to refuse to print the worst type of anti-Labour propaganda, completed their defeat. Both sides spent large sums on advertising, but in the end the Government came off second-best; the strike had secured improved scales of wages and a national grading of railway workers.

The Labour movement was still in a very aggressive mood. The Labour Party Conference, to the distress of its leaders, had voted in principle, in a debate on the Russian war, in favour of "direct action" for political ends; and a motion to join the new Third International had received a respectable number of votes. The Trades Union Congress censured its own Parliamentary Committee for inertia in failing to call a special Congress to deal with the crisis. In addition, the circumstances of the railway strike had called attention to the need for a more effective executive for the Trade Union movement as a whole. In December 1919, it was decided in principle to establish a "general staff" for the Trade Unions, in place of the Parliamentary Committee and the various *ad hoc* bodies which had sprung up to supply the need.

All through 1919 and 1920 active reorganization was proceeding in the Trade Union world. The A.S.E. became in 1920 the Amalgamated Engineering Union, taking in a number of smaller societies. The National Federation of Building Trades Operatives, which had been formed in 1918 to link up the various craft Unions, strengthened its hold, and became an effective negotiating body. The Transport Workers' Federation discussed plans of amalgamation, though these did not become effective till 1921, when most of its constituent Unions joined forces in the Transport and General Workers' Union. Other amalgamations, made somewhat easier by the Trade Union Amalgamation Act of 1917, included the fusion of two bricklayers' and one masons' Union to form the Amalgamated Union of Building Trade Workers, the merging of several societies to create the National Union of Foundry Workers, and the absorption of the National Federation of Women Workers, the Municipal Employees' Association, and a number of other Unions into the Gasworkers, which became the National Union of General and Municipal Workers. A little later, the Transport and General Workers' took over the Workers' Union, leaving only two societies catering for general workers, instead of seven or eight.

Through 1919 and 1920 the total Trade Union membership rose with extraordinary speed. It was 6,500,000 at the beginning of 1919 and 8,334,000 by the end of 1920, as against 4,145,000 in 1914. Co-operative membership rose from 3,000,000 in 1914 to 4,500,000 in 1920. Moreover, the General Election defeat of 1918 gave place in November 1919 to large successes at the Municipal Elections. The Labour Party won control of a number of towns, and large gains nearly everywhere; most observers were too elated to draw any warning from the lowness of the polls. At the Dockers' Inquiry early in 1920, at which Ernest Bevin gained his name of the Dockers' K.C. for his able conduct of his members' case, the tide still seemed to be flowing strongly in favour of Labour. The dockers gained not only substantial wage advances, but also a strong recommendation in favour of decasualization—though this ultimately was for the most part not carried into effect.

The Labour movement was, however, no longer exclusively interested in home events. Before 1914 trade unionists and politicians had alike been indifferent to foreign affairs; only a few eccentrics were even well informed upon the subject, and the average party member was as little interested in the Empire as a mid-Victorian Liberal. The disaster of war had ended that indifference. No resolutions commanded more attention than those on external affairs. Nor did any command greater unanimity, for they were usually an effective compromise between those who still remembered the strategic problems of the war and those who burned with revolutionary ardour. The programme adopted for India unequivocally condemned the autocratic régime which led to the Amritsar massacre and equally plainly demanded self-government for India, but it added the hope that conciliation would retain India for the Empire. The programme for Ireland—adopted after a special Commission of Inquiry had been sent out— declared that the British Army should be withdrawn and an Irish Constituent Assembly called, whose decisions should be final provided they prevented "Ireland becoming a military or naval menace to Britain" (a proviso forgotten by 1938). On Russian policy all were agreed: interference must cease. For the Government was running two illicit wars—one in Ireland against Sinn Fein, one in North Russia against the Soviets. Both were unpopular, but Labour opposition was keener to the latter. In July of 1920 the Congress voted for a general strike to end both wars. Almost at once it was asked to carry out or to eat its words. Part of the Allied attack had been an invasion of Russia by the Poles, who had penetrated the country beyond Kiev. The Russian Red Army, newly organized by Trotsky and commanded by Tukhachevsky, eventually first checked and then drove them back in headlong rout. It seemed that they would soon be expelled from Warsaw and the Red Army would reach the borders of distressed and oppressed Germany. No one could say what would happen then. The British and French Governments decided to act. An ultimatum was sent to the Russians, but their advance continued. Lloyd George and the French Premier, Millerand, went into conference at Lympne to arrange aid for the Poles. Sir Henry Wilson and Marshal Foch were called into consultation: war on a large scale was clearly being planned.

The Labour Party Executive and the Parliamentary Committee of the Trades Union Congress acted swiftly. A "Council of Action" was summoned from the constituent bodies of both, to arrange for an immediate strike to stop the war. So general was the opposition to the Government's policy that it was clear as soon as the threat was made that it would be implemented and that it would be effective. Overnight Lloyd George's tone changed to one of scolding assertion that war had never entered his mind. Pilsudski's genius and French aid saved Warsaw; Britain was not in the war and before long the British troops in North Russia came home. The Irish war continued.

The Trades Union Congress of September 1920 passed a scheme for a "General Council," to be elected by the whole Congress from nominees put forward by the Unions in the various groups into which it was subdivided. This, it was hoped, would secure at once general unity and sectional representation; the first elections were to take place next year. A Communist Party was formed in August 1920, with ten thousand members drawn mostly from the dissolved British Socialist Party, Sylvia Pankhurst's east-end Workers' Socialist Federation, and part of the Socialist Labour Party. It met with sympathy and good wishes far beyond its ranks. A strike of miners, involving a million or so men, ended in October in a temporary advance of wages, but also in considerable discrediting of the Triple Alliance, which failed to function.

Indeed, through most of 1920 wages were rising fast. Nor is this surprising, when the general character of the period is taken into account. For the year was, from the capitalist point of view, one of prodigious—even insane—boom. By 1918 wholesale prices had averaged about 135 per cent above the pre-war level: in 1920 they averaged 207 per cent above it, and at the peak in May 1920 over 225 per cent. At such prices, any fool could make profits; and capitalist profits rose to quite extraordinary heights. Moreover, there developed in the early part of the year an almost incredible speculative mania. On the assumption that the vast profits which could be made for the moment (because devastated areas and industries in need of reconstruction must have supplies at any price) were to continue indefinitely, businesses were re-capitalized right and left at absurdly inflated values, and a gullible public was persuaded to buy shares in new companies floated to take over existing concerns on terms which could not possibly pay the buyers. Many capitalists sold their businesses under these absurdly advantageous conditions, and retired with huge fortunes on the proceeds. Others, after making a fortune, themselves got caught up in the speculative mania, and lost it by falling into the very trap which they had laid for the purchasers of their own businesses. Great captains of industry developed megalomania, and began buying up competing businesses at prices which were sheerly absurd. When the public could not be persuaded to supply enough money for these adventures, the capitalists went to the banks and borrowed it—so that, when the slump came, the banks became the real owners of a huge number of businesses which had borrowed money they could not possibly repay.

This speculative mania assumed the most dangerous forms in the textile and metal industries. It was no uncommon thing for a spinning-mill to be bought up and refloated at six times its previous capitalization; and the big armament firms were not far behind.

Under these conditions of colossal current profits and absurd expectations of profits to come, it was not difficult for many Trade Unions to secure advances in wages. At the end of 1918 the average level of wages was about 95–100 per cent above the level of 1914. At the end of 1919 it was up to 115–120 per cent, and by the end of 1920 to 170–180 per cent. Meanwhile the cost of living rose from 120 per cent above the 1914 level at the end of 1918, and 125 per cent at the end of 1919, to 176 per cent in November 1920, when it reached the peak. Thus, nearly all that the workers gained was wiped out by the rise in prices. Nevertheless, the Trade Unions had a sense of gaining victories all along the line, and were quite unprepared for the dramatic reversal of fortune which was soon to come.

In face of this sensational rise in prices, the Government had to give at any rate some appearance of trying to control the course of events. The Profiteering Act, first passed in August 1919, when war-time food controls had been largely removed, was intended to remain in force for only six months—to tide over the "return to normal conditions" then supposed to be imminent. But actually it had to be renewed until May 1921 (by which time prices were tumbling of themselves). The Act, however, was almost entirely ineffective. The real causes of high prices lay in the world market and in the great capitalist producing and trading concerns. But the Act penalized in effect only the retailers, and of these chiefly the smaller and less alert.

Momentarily, Labour still seemed victorious; but the clouds were massing. A temporary system of non-contributory "donation" benefits had tided over the period of demobilization of soldiers and munition workers; and thereafter the boom of the latter part of 1919 and the early months of 1920 had kept unemployment at a low level for a time. But in the latter part of 1920 conditions began to worsen rapidly; and the count of the unemployed under the new Insurance Scheme, in December 1920, showed the unexpected total of 858,000 out of work. In January 1921 the total rose to 1,213,000. By March it was well over 1,500,000; and the scheme was subjected to a serious financial strain. Up to November 1920, unemployment insurance applied only to a few selected trades. About 3,000,000 workers were insured under Part II of the National Insurance Act of 1911, and about another 1,000,000 under the Munition Workers' Insurance Act of 1916. The new Act, which came into force in November 1920, brought in about 8,000,000 additional workers, and thus covered the greater part of the wage-earning population. Every male adult worker had to pay 4*d.* a week, and his employer the same amount; and to this the State added 2*d.* a week. For women and for juveniles there were lower rates of contributions. Benefits were at the rate of 15*s.* a week for men, 12*s*. for women, and half-rates for juveniles, but benefit could be drawn only for fifteen weeks in any year, and only for one week for every six weeks' contributions actually paid.

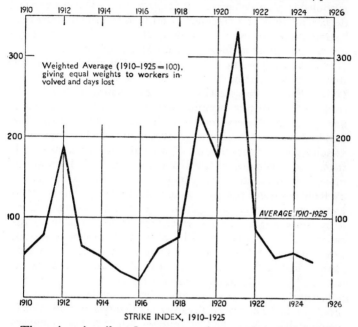

Weighted Average (1910–1925 = 100), giving equal weights to workers involved and days lost

AVERAGE 1910–1925

STRIKE INDEX, 1910–1925

The miners' strike of 1920 came just at the turning-point from illusory prosperity to acknowledged depression. Coal prices, after the reductions at the end of 1919, had soared to prodigious heights in 1920; and they remained high, and demand brisk, at the time of the strike. But the slump was just coming; and the miners were put off with a purely temporary advance, linked to the output of coal, which was about to fall off sharply as demand collapsed. Moreover, the Government seized the occasion of the Triple Alliance's abortive threat to strike in the miners' support to carry into law a new oppressive measure—the Emergency Powers Act of 1920. This Act was intended, despite a prohibition of "industrial conscription," to make it possible for the Government legally to break any large

strike which should extensively (in the words of the Act) interfere with "the supply and distribution of food, water, fuel or
light, or with the means of locomotion." The Act was
muddled in phraseology, but it empowered the Government to
declare a "state of emergency" and then to issue undescribed
"regulations" whose breach might be punished by anything
up to three months' imprisonment and £100 fine.

Here was a portent of bad weather, but the sun was still
shining in one part of the labour world at least. The building
Unions had resisted the Government's attempts to flood their
trade with ex-service labour. Houses were still badly needed
and practically every man was in work. The hopes of a
hundred years before seemed to have returned when the papers
announced the formation of a National Building Guild, with
the support of many of the Unions and the collaboration of
many existing local guilds. Its philosophy was not provided
by Robert Owen, but by a group of "Guild Socialists" who
had come into prominence during the War and shortly before
it by producing a formula which seemed to reconcile Syndicalist and State Socialist. The State, they proposed, should
own industry, while the Trade Unions in each industry, transformed into a "Guild," should run it. Their insistence on
workers' control in any scheme for the conduct of socialized
industries was the most incontestably valuable part of their
propaganda. They were already in difficulties. Some of their
members had joined the Communists, others Major Douglas's
Credit Scheme adherents; the Guild was their expiring effort. It
had some months of dizzy success. But Government aid under
the Addison Act was withdrawn; the Guild had no capital
resources and borrowed recklessly; it had far too many workers
on its pay-roll; it could not cut wage-rates like the jerry-
builder; it fell with a resounding crash, and dragged down
with it local guilds whose finances had not really been unsound.

Both in this period of high revolutionary hopes and in that
of angry disillusionment which was to follow, the intellectual
activity of the British Labour movement had been more feverish
than at any time except perhaps in 1912 and 1913. The Left-
wing papers rose to a high peak of circulation—the *Communist*

reached 60,000, the *Labour Leader* probably exceeded it. The *Daily Herald* with a circulation between 200,000 and 300,000 consistently supported Left-wing ideas, printed news that no one else would carry, and was responsible for spreading, and sometimes initiating, almost all the effective movements for Labour militancy and reform. In education a violent battle started. Both the Workers' Educational Association and the Plebs League had found their activities partially held up by the War; now they restarted with renewed enthusiasm and came at once into head-on collision. The W.E.A., drawing its funds partly from voluntary contributions and partly from the Universities, the Board of Education and Local Education Authorities, which were in turn assisted by State grants, continued to work in close partnership with the extra-mural sections of the Universities, under a system of joint committees composed half of university teachers and half of W.E.A. and Trade Union and Co-operative representatives; but in addition it ran many classes on its own, or in association with the Co-operatives or the Trade Unions associated with it through the Workers' Educational Trade Union Committee. Its work covered, not only the social studies, over which the conflict chiefly arose, but also philosophy, literature, psychology, science and many other less directly controversial subjects. It claimed in its teaching to avoid propaganda, and expected its tutors not to make up the students' minds for them, but to help them to make up their own in the light of the facts. The Plebs League, its antagonist, was no longer a mainly syndicalist body; time had made its changes here too. But it remained revolutionary; its finances were exclusively of working-class origin and its teaching was Marxist. It made no claim to cover the wide field of the W.E.A.; its chief subjects were philosophy, history, economics and economic geography, on which it issued text-books of an uncompromising kind. Where it extended its work to other fields, as (for example) to English, it did so only to assist in its main task, of providing a number of picked workers with the information and training to enable them to lead their fellow workers in the class struggle. For this they needed not only to be able to conduct union business and propaganda generally, but to see through to the truth about existing class relations and economic structure—a truth which they believed W.E.A. lecturers persistently obscured. A teacher did not leave his class to make up its mind on whether two and two made four, and to the League the truths of Marxism seemed equally self-evident to all but humbugs. The Central Labour College in London had to be closed owing to internal disorders, but the organization of classes up and down the country (soon united in the National Council of Labour Colleges) brought about a fight with the W.E.A. in every large-sized town or Union. Many sleepy Trades Councils and Labour Parties were astonished by a violent conflict between rival W.E.A. and "Plebs" propagandists, and gained the erroneous idea that a course of lectures would be as exciting as a free fight. Later, the National Council was to grow into a large organization, with big subscriptions from national unions; in due course it consumed its parent, the Plebs League, and the warfare with the W.E.A. sank back into a desultory sniping. For the moment, however, there was an active intellectual battle.

But the after-war summer was over. The insatiable markets were satiated: the idiocies of the Versailles Treaty were destroying any hopes of prosperity in Europe: the hashish dreams of the new rich vanished and left a headache. British capitalism fell into an abyss. In November 1919 there had been 353,000 ex-soldiers unemployed and the nation had been scandalized. By March 1921 the registered unemployed numbered 1,664,000; and in May the coal stoppage had brought the total to over 2,500,000, exclusive of the miners themselves. Even at the end of the year, when the miners were back at work, unemployment was barely under 2,000,000. It then fell gradually, to 1,400,000 at the end of 1922, and about 1,200,000 a year later. Until 1939 it hardly ever fell below a million.

Neither the Lloyd George Government nor the official Labour movement had any remedy for this colossal disaster. The Government merely cut expenditure wildly, throwing more and more men on to the labour market, closing down valuable and employment-giving public works, and backing to the limit the employers' attack on wages. The official Trade

Union and Labour leadership was deeply distrustful of its own left wing, afraid of revolution, and in principle unwilling to use extra-Parliamentary pressure to enforce even the limited programmes which it had; it was thus reduced to little more than official speeches of regret. The I.L.P. still looked to the next election and the installation of parliamentary Socialism as the remedy. The Communist Party had still no considerable membership among the organized working class.

But the last-named rapidly gained support from a group which the official leaders neglected. The unemployed were largely ex-soldiers, and after a short while of drawing their official unemployment relief many of them were thrown back on to parish relief and the Guardians, who as often as not were as unfriendly, unctuous and self-righteous as those of 1834, setting intentionally disgusting and useless tasks, such as stone-breaking. This, to men who had been promised an England fit for heroes, was too much. Sporadic violence resulted. Soon the unemployed began to march in fours, to hold up shopping throughfares and frighten rich women and their chauffeurs, to lock up and scare the worst sort of Boards of Guardians. Some I.L.P.'ers, some local Labour Parties assisted them; but the bulk of those who threw their energies into their protection were Communists. In the autumn of 1921 the Party founded the "National Unemployed Workers' Committee Movement"; and the pressure was soon greatly increased.

The provisions of the Unemployment Insurance Acts were being continually altered throughout this period, improved when Parliament was alarmed at the menace, and worsened when it considered the cost. Benefits were raised early in 1921, and the rules as to the period of benefit were temporarily relaxed. Then, later on the same year, as prices fell and unemployment rose still further, benefits were reduced and contributions increased, in a desperate attempt to make the fund balance. In November 1921, in view of the widespread distress, dependants' allowances had to be grafted on to the scheme. By April 1922 the insured man's contribution had been raised to 9*d*. a week, and the employer's to 10*d*.—the State adding 6¾*d*.

At the same date was introduced the distinction—to be a

source of great trouble—between "covenanted" benefit, to
which an insured worker was entitled of right for a limited
period, and "uncovenanted benefit," which was payable for
further periods only at the discretion of the Ministry of Labour.
This was given the insolent nickname of the "dole," and many
people believed, or affected to believe, that all the payments
were mere charitable relief. The Government further introduced the iniquitous system known as the "gap," whereby
any worker who had drawn "uncovenanted benefit" for five
weeks could get nothing for the next five weeks, and so on in
alternate periods. Thus, the unemployed were driven at five-
weekly intervals to and fro between the Labour Exchange and
the Guardians. This led to so much unrest that later in the
year the "gap" had to be reduced to a week. But in 1923 it
was put back to three weeks after twelve weeks of "uncovenanted benefit"; and there it stayed until the Labour
Government abolished the "gap" altogether in the following
year.

Before the strength of the unemployed had reached its
height, the employed workers had fought their battle and lost
it. The Government passed the mines back to private control
at the end of March 1921: the owners had already announced
cuts in wages. The miners refused the terms, were locked out
and appealed to the other members of the Triple Alliance, the
Railwaymen (N.U.R.) and Transport Workers (T.W.F.; the
new Transport Workers' Union had not yet been formed).
These, after negotiations proved vain, voted on April 8 to
strike on the 15th; the Trades Union Congress and the Labour
Party pledged support. On the evening of the 14th, at a meeting in the House of Commons, Frank Hodges, the miners'
secretary, made an incautious speech in which he seemed to
agree to a compromise on wages without a National Wages
Board; though this interpretation of his speech was repudiated
it gave the railwaymen's and the transport workers' leaders,
Thomas, Cramp, Bevin and Williams, the opportunity they
were anxious to find of withdrawing the strike order, which
they did by telegraph on the next day, "Black Friday." There
were various excuses offered for this—the Triple Alliance had
not been intended for sympathetic strikes but for a joint

presentation of programmes, it had not been used except for propaganda purposes recently and might have been regarded as moribund, it was not clear how the miners could ever return the transport workers' assistance, and so forth. But for the world at large it was no more than a failure in solidarity. The words of the *Daily Herald* were widely echoed: "Yesterday was the heaviest defeat that has befallen the Labour movement within the memory of man. It is no use trying to minimize it. It is no use pretending that it is other than it is. We on this paper have said throughout that if the organized workers would stand together they would win. They have not stood together, and they have reaped the reward."

The rank-and-file members of the Unions concerned bore little responsibility for the disaster; indeed, later history seems to show that many felt an acute sense of shame. The *Daily Herald* sponsored a "Save the Miners' Children" fund; it raised no less than £86,000; and large donations came from other, mainly Labour, sources. But it would not do; the miners fought on through the summer to defeat. It is uncertain whether resistance would have saved the workers on Black Friday; it is certain that by their retreat the leaders had given the signal for general disaster. Trade Union membership pitched downwards: by 1925 three million members had been lost. Co-operative trade did not fall more heavily than private trade—possibly less—but several of the smaller societies put themselves into the hands of a C.W.S. manager to avoid bankruptcy. Wages fell universally; in the spring of 1922 the richest Union in the world, the Amalgamated Engineering Union, with no fewer than forty-seven minor engineering Unions around it (so foolishly organized was the industry) was faced with a lock-out which it fought till its funds were exhausted, without any success. The *Daily Herald*'s readers had no spare pennies to support it; circulation fell and by mid-1922 it was in danger of ceasing to appear. The hostility between the unemployed and the Labour leaders grew sharper. Almost the sole action which united the two was taken by the Poplar Councillors headed by George Lansbury, who refused to pay the contributions required by the London County Council until the wealthy West End boroughs took a fairer share of the burden of relieving the stricken East End. Persisting in their illegal action, they were sent *en bloc* to prison, where they remained contumacious until the Government and the Council gave way. But this success meant no reconciliation: the official Party leaders, London and national, hastily dissociated themselves from "Poplarism."

The Lloyd George Coalition Government was behaving with a recklessness which was both frivolous and ferocious. It was using "a strong hand" in India, and deporting and jailing Egyptian nationalists. It was wrecking the Irish countryside with a Black and Tan terror. Traditional English liberties were overridden by the police, who raided houses and seized property—generally without redress, provided the victims were Irish or Communist. The offices of the Communist Party were stripped as if locusts had been there, even watches and fountain-pens being carried off. Prosecutions were begun and sentences secured, for nothing worse than class-war Socialist speeches, a thing scarcely known since 1886. Mounted police rode down the unemployed, often batoning them severely, as at Sunderland and Dundee in September 1921, and, before a larger and more powerful audience, in Trafalgar Square in October.

But these extravagances were drawing to an end. Many outside the Labour ranks were shocked at the brutality shown to the unemployed: the second Hunger March on its arrival in London was escorted by sympathizers whose presence deterred the police from any excesses such as those which had welcomed the first. The Recorder of Liverpool from his place on the Bench publicly rebuked the local police for their violence. The Hunger Marchers themselves were never violent: they paraded in military formation, it is true, and in considerable numbers, but they wrecked no buildings and seized no food; their banners were as often Union Jacks as Red Flags; as a marching song they preferred, for both sentiments and tune, "Colonel Bogey" to the "International." The relatively prosperous parts of the country were brought by them to a sense of their duty; all over the island relief conditions were markedly improved and the "dole" was more widely given. It was commonly said that in the winter of 1921 and 1922 the "dole" saved Britain from revolution.

The conservative capitalist and the conservative Labour leader were both, consciously or unconsciously, beginning to look back to a period of peace before the war, of two-party government, prosperity and calm progress. Circumstances enabled them both to take some steps towards their ideal. The repeated industrial defeats took the heart out of the Union members; Left policies and candidates received fewer and fewer votes. The "Red International of Labour Unions" (a Trade Union subsidiary of the Communist International) opened a British Bureau, whose sole important success was a vote of adhesion from the South Wales Miners' Federation. In other countries, the new Communist policy and the resistance to it of the existing Labour leaders led to splits which mortally injured the Trade Unions; in Britain the only instance of such a split on any considerable scale occurred much later, mostly in Fife, in the mining industry, in 1927 and 1928, under very great provocation. The lesson of Syndicalist days had not been forgotten; however provoked they were the rebels scarcely ever founded rival "red" Unions.

The newly constituted General Council of the Trades Union Congress consisted almost wholly of known "moderates." The Labour Party reaffirmed the exclusion of the Communist Party, and a "Trade Union group" of M.P.s showed revived hostility to the I.L.P. In May 1922, the *Daily Herald* was compelled to come to the General Council and the Labour Party for financial aid: criticism and independent comment now ceased. In November the paper was actually taken over by the Trades Union Congress.

On the capitalist side more and more people were desiring a return to what they believed to be normality. The Irish war had ended in British defeat, and the application of the "axe" in February 1922 had met the most urgent demands for State economy. When Lloyd George, still thinking in terms of war finance and war hysteria, nearly broke the links binding the Empire in an attempt to resume war with Turkey, it was decided that he must go. A meeting of Conservative politicians at the Carlton Club decided the matter; in October 1922 he was toppled from the Premiership with surprising ease. A General Election followed, in which an unhyphenated Conservative Party faced a constitutional Labour Party; in the void between, isolated and many-named Liberals whirled confusedly in eccentric and conflicting orbits like asteroids. The election returned Bonar Law with a comfortable majority; the Labour numbers rose from 75 to 142, which was the more pleasing as the municipal elections had just removed most of the 1919 gains. The new M.P.s selected Ramsay MacDonald as their leader; some, remembering his war and forgetting his pre-war record, supported him as a "left-winger," some merely because the time was overdue for a competent parliamentary leadership. The second group, and not the first, were justified by results.

There was still, as ever, more agreement on foreign than on home affairs. All sections of the Labour movement, and many Liberals, could see the disastrous effects of the continuation of the policy of violence that had started at Versailles. In 1923, to enforce the payment of "reparations" which they were themselves soon to admit were impracticable, the French invaded the Ruhr, the great industrial region in the west of Germany. While the Conservative press cried: "Hats off to France!" the Transport Workers sent an investigating committee to the Ruhr which brought back alarming news. All savings, all security, family life itself were being destroyed by the inflation which was the Germans' only reply to the Poincaré incursion. The Printers' Union, it noted, which had had reserves of £600,000, found them reduced in value to £48. Tillett, the committee's leader, warned his hearers of the effect on the despairing masses in words which seemed to presage Nazism: "The occupation of the Ruhr has renewed into incipient life the madness of the Monarchy; it has substituted a capitalist madness more brutal and dangerous."

But that was abroad; at home, throughout 1923 it might really have seemed that the quiet days of Edward VII were back again, with MacDonald instead of Asquith leading the more progressive of the two great parties. Britain was entering on a short period of relative prosperity and calm. The unemployed were not re-employed, but became apathetic or reconciled to their lot. The Communist Party lost influence and members, its papers lost circulation, the new policy of

"Bolshevization" (by which its members became rigidly disciplined and formed secret groups of "nuclei" to control other Labour bodies) caused fierce anatagonisms between it and other Labour organizations. Some of the Labour members went a very long way in their admiration of the restored tranquillity: "I love the Empire!" exclaimed J. H. Thomas on the day when the imperial tariff decisions were announced at the Empire Conference of October 1923, and his sentiments were echoed by J. R. Clynes, Ben Tillett and even Fred Bramley, Secretary of the Trades Union Congress. Not all, indeed, shared in this satisfaction: July had seen a big but short-lived London dock strike in defiance of the Union, and a group of I.L.P. members, mostly from the Clyde, systematically opposed MacDonald's extreme Parliamentary correctitude, and acted as uncompromising advocates of Socialism and a class-war policy.

In November Baldwin, who had succeeded to Bonar Law on his death, went to the country: Labour secured 192 seats, and, if Asquith's 157 Liberals were to support it, had a majority over the 258 Tories. Asquith decided to do so, and after weeks of hesitation and conflicting rumours, the dearest hopes of many Socialists were fulfilled early in 1924 when the King sent for Ramsay MacDonald and invited him to form a Government. Acceptance seemed a dangerous step; the Liberal veto would act as an automatic check; but, as MacDonald said, "Whoever has power has opportunity"; and in the spirit of that epigram the Labour Party and the T.U.C. authorized him to accept office.

CHAPTER XLIII

THE FIRST LABOUR GOVERNMENT

THE newspapers since 1918 had intermittently discussed the question "Can Labour Govern?"—always on the assumption that the question was very hypothetical and generally implying the answer, "No." The prospect of an actual Labour Govern-

ment was viewed with considerable trepidation in Conserva-
tive-minded circles, from Buckingham Palace downwards, and
to the last many hoped that Asquith would flinch from his
decision to permit this dangerous experiment. It seemed as if
the Labour movement, too, shared these doubts. MacDonald's
Government did not even consist wholly of members of the
Labour Party. One of the chief law officers, H. P. Macmillan
(later Lord Macmillan) Lord Advocate for Scotland, was not
a member of the Labour Party and did not even join it on
taking office. Lord Chelmsford, sent to the Admiralty after
(it was generally believed) a violent protest by the senior
officers against any Socialist appointment, did not belong to
the Party either. John Wheatley, the Clyde M.P., who
became Minister of Health, was the sole left-wing member of
the Cabinet, and even he soon disappointed many supporters
by his refusal, as a Catholic, to permit birth-control instruction
at centres under his control. Very great power proved to be
concentrated in the hands of the Prime Minister, who also took
the Foreign Office, and rapidly moved towards conservatism
in policy and in social relations. His chief advisers—for there
was a sort of unofficial inner Cabinet before long—were all of
the right wing—J. H. Thomas, Colonial Secretary, a skilled
Trade Union negotiator who did not profess to be a
Socialist; Philip Snowden, at the Exchequer, earlier a rigid
State Socialist but already fast regressing past Single Tax
into pure Free Trade and "sound finance"; J. R. Clynes,
Lord Privy Seal; and Arthur Henderson, who at the
Home Office had little chance to show the qualities,
especially strict loyalty to the Party programme, which
were later to rally such strong Labour support to him.
An excellent innovation was the appointment of a woman,
Miss Margaret Bondfield, as Parliamentary Secretary to
the Ministry of Labour, but her bureaucratic attitude
quickly created wide discontent not only among the unemployed, but among her own supporters in the Commons.
Such a team was but ill-equipped for the quick daring
use of executive power which the phrase "opportunity is
power" suggested.

But, to a considerable degree, economic circumstances were

favourable. Conditions were improving after the great deflation of the preceding years; France was obviously wearying of the virulent anti-German policy which had led up to the occupation of the Ruhr, and was on the point of installing a left-wing Government; the conditions were ripe for a more realistic treatment of the Reparations problem, and for an attempt at reconciliation in Europe. At home, there was room for substantial social reforms without much risk of upsetting the economic system or provoking capitalist sabotage. The political conditions, which made Labour dependent for all its measures on a large amount of Liberal support, precluded any attempt to apply a real Socialist policy—unless the Government decided to provoke immediate defeat on a decisive issue, and appeal again to the electorate on the strength of its challenge. But this course, if it was considered at all, was rejected out of hand. The first Labour Government set itself to the task of governing with the aid of Liberal votes, and attempted nothing for which it could not reasonably expect Liberal backing.

Half-way through the year, fortune favoured it again. M. Herriot took office in France, at the head of a Radical Government, returned partly by Socialist electoral support. The first chance presented itself of a progressive policy conducted in unity by the French and British Governments. To Ramsay MacDonald fell the task of satisfying—or of disappointing—the hopes of European appeasement.

Before this, the Government had clearly marked out the line which it proposed to follow in home affairs. By far its most important achievements were the Wheatley Housing Act and the changes introduced into the unemployment insurance system. After the suspension of the Addison housing scheme there had been an interval, during which house-building seriously declined. Then, in 1923, had come the Chamberlain Housing Act, deliberately designed to encourage the private builders as against municipal enterprise. It was plain that this Act would not provide houses at prices which the bulk of working-class tenants could afford to pay. Indeed, the Chamberlain scheme provided few houses that could be rented at all. Most of the houses built under it were for sale—at prices which were only within the reach of middle-class families, or at most of a small sprinkling of the best-paid workers. The Wheatley scheme was designed to meet the needs of working-class tenants, by offering to the local authorities higher subsidies for the building of houses to be let at limited rents. It was highly effective, though its results were not seen till the Government responsible for it had fallen from office, and the succeeding Government had effectively wound it up. The total number of houses built rose from 93,000 in 1923–4 to 261,000 in 1927–8; and in all well over 500,000 houses were built under the Wheatley scheme alone.

In order to make possible this great increase in building activity, it was necessary to negotiate a treaty with the building Trade Unions for the augmentation of the supply of skilled labour. Previous attempts to do this had broken down because the previous Governments had been ready to guarantee neither the maintenance of Trade Union wages and conditions, nor the continuance of building at a high level over a period of years. Without these guarantees, the building operatives naturally refused to accept schemes of "dilution" which threatened both to destroy their standard rates and to confront them with a serious over-supply of labour as soon as housing activity slackened off. Wheatley's "treaty" included these guarantees; and the Trade Unions accepted the necessary accession of workers to the building trades under special schemes of shortened apprenticeship and "up-grading" of less skilled operatives.

The Wheatley plan had another side; for it was plain that a rapid expansion of house-building would mean a sharp rise in the price of materials unless measures were taken to control the price-rings which dominated the supplying trades. Accordingly, the Labour Government introduced, in addition to its Housing Bill, a second measure establishing a system of control over the prices of building materials. But this measure could not be passed into law before its untimely fall from office.

Next in importance to the Wheatley Housing Act was the amendment of the unemployment insurance scheme. Under the scheme as it existed at the end of 1923, though the "gap" had been reduced, a sharp distinction was drawn between

"covenanted" benefit, which the insured worker had a right
to claim for a limited period dependent on the contributions
he had paid, and "uncovenanted" benefit, which could be
granted for further periods at the sole discretion of the Ministry
of Labour. Tom Shaw's new Unemployment Insurance Act
swept away this distinction, and made "uncovenanted" as
well as "covenanted" benefit a continuous legal right.

In addition to these major social measures the Government
instituted a number of others. It restored to the agricultural
workers the legal minimum wage which had been taken away
in 1921: it raised the rate of old-age pensions; and it reversed
the previous policy of "economy" at the expense of the educational and other social services. Snowden, in his Budget,
delighted the Liberals by sweeping away the McKenna duties
on imported motor-cars, and making other changes in the
direction of a complete return to Free Trade.

Internationally, the new Government seemed to make good
beginnings and then fear to continue on the same lines—as if,
critics commented, its original impulse on Socialist lines was
steadily weakened as its members were subjected to official
influence and forgot the atmosphere of Trades Union Congresses and Labour Party Conferences. It immediately
recognized Soviet Russia, and opened negotiations for a trade
and general treaty; but the negotiations were enormously
long-drawn-out, and the appointment of an ambassador in
Moscow mysteriously delayed. It reduced armament expenditure and stopped the building of a naval base at Singapore.
But it started the building of five new cruisers. It co-operated
with M. Herriot in an attempt to put Reparations on a sane
basis, but the "Dawes Plan" which resulted was only a degree
less crazy than its predecessors.

The greatest and most courageous advance might have been
marked by the Geneva Protocol, agreed between the Labour
Government and M. Herriot's Radical Government in France.
It provided for the assumption of a definite obligation by the
signatories to apply "sanctions"—that is, to use their armies
and navies to enforce the decisions of the League. It accepted
the principle of compulsory arbitration, and arranged for a
general reduction of armaments. In short, it would have

provided the League with the armed force denied it at Versailles; it might have made a future war impossible, as its supporters hoped. But, though it was not to come into force until thirteen States (to include three out of the four great powers) had signed it, its opponents clamoured that it would "hawk the British navy round the Seven Seas" and the ensuing government gleefully destroyed it.

In India, Egypt and Iraq, where it had been hoped that the new Government would show a new liberal spirit and initiate real steps towards self-government, nothing whatever was done.

Here was a good deal less than the active Labour supporters in the country had confidently expected; for it included no step towards the reorganization of the coal-mines or any other basic industry, and no measure at all that could be described as in any sense socialistic, even in tendency. There was, moreover, considerable discontent at the Government's failure to give any effective support to the workers' demands for higher wages and improved conditions. The Washington Forty-eight Hours Convention—the first and principal reform put forward by the new International Labour Organization founded after the war—remained unratified; and the Trade Unions were for the most part left to fight their own battles without Government help.

Reviving trade, and the presence of a Labour Government in office combined to make 1924 a year of considerable industrial disturbance. At the beginning of the year there was a railway strike, conducted by the Associated Society of Locomotive Engineers and Firemen, for better terms than had been accepted by the N.U.R. In this dispute, with N.U.R. members continuing at work, and the Government even making plans to use the Emergency Powers Act, if necessary, in order to secure the maintenance of the railway services, the cleavage between the Labour leadership and the left wing was already plain. There followed, in swift succession, a dockers' strike in February, a tram and omnibus strike in March, a shipyard lock-out in April and a threatened miners' strike in May. In June the workers on the London tube railways came out, and in July the builders.

These disputes were signs of the upward trend of economic activity. The strike of the locomotive men against the unfavourable award of the National Railway Wages Board ended in defeat, in face of the hostility of the N.U.R. But both the dockers and the road transport workers were able to gain substantial advances. The miners also secured, without a stoppage of work, a temporarily favourable settlement; for the closing of the German mines owing to the occupation of the Ruhr had caused for the time being a boom in the British coal industry. But the wage-increases granted to the miners were secured only for one year; and before that year ended the boom was over. The settlement of 1924 prepared the way for the renewed conflict of 1925–6: the Labour Government made no attempt to grapple with the fundamental problem of reorganizing the industry.

Following upon this equivocal victory came the defeat of the strike on the tube railways in June, and a compromise in the building struggle of July. The first-named was a very brief outburst; but Labour opinion was considerably alarmed by the behaviour of the Prime Minister, who spoke like any Conservative of protecting blacklegs, issued a proclamation of a "State of Emergency" under the Emergency Powers Act and appointed Colonel Wedgwood Chief Civil Commissioner under it. Fortunately the strike ended almost at once. Over the year as a whole, wage-rates rose a little on the average, whereas they had been falling rapidly ever since 1920. But the rise was small—not much more than enough to balance the rise in the cost of living during the year.

In this sequence of wage disputes, the Government in general stood aside, and left the Trade Unions and the employers to settle matters in accordance with the balance of economic forces. The existence of a Labour Government was probably helpful to the Unions, in that it made the employers more disposed to compromise. But even that is doubtful. Wages would almost certainly have risen to some extent in 1924, even if the Conservative Government had remained in office.

Up to October, however, the Labour Government, even if its achievements had not been very striking and even if it had done nothing to bring Socialism nearer, had committed no positive sins: there was nothing up to this point to suggest the follies and mismanagements that were soon to come. MacDonald, even if he had done little, had at any rate satisfied his own ambition of looking and sounding like a Prime Minister, and had thus helped to demonstrate, for the moment, that Labour was "fit to govern" after all. But it soon began to appear that MacDonald's ambition was not merely to look like a statesman of the traditional type, but also to behave like one. Compelled by the pressure of Labour opinion to recognize the Soviet Union and to institute negotiations for an Anglo-Russian treaty, he had abated nothing of his hatred of Communism, or of his determination to dissociate his party from all taint of Communist associations. It might be necessary to enter into relations with the Russian Communists as a Government; but that seemed to MacDonald all the more reason for stamping hard on the propaganda of Communism in Great Britain. The launching by the Communist Party of an oddly named "Minority Movement" in August, with the powerful support of Tom Mann and intended to control the Trade Union movement, seemed to him and his colleagues a piece of impertinent arrogance made possible only by considerable Russian subventions. The initial support which it received, which was not inconsiderable, was due not to Communist convictions but to acute disappointment with the Government; but that was no less an offence to MacDonald.

His Attorney-General, Sir Patrick Hastings, whether of his own volition or urged on, presented him in October with a court case which relieved his feelings. He prosecuted J. R. Campbell, Editor of the Communist *Workers' Weekly*, for a "don't shoot" article. This, though the article was probably illegal, was a folly; the Labour rank and file had not sent its Government to Westminster to attack free speech. The indignation in Labour circles was such that the suit had to be withdrawn, an admission of folly. No defence of the withdrawal was attempted in Parliament against the Conservative attack, except some sentimentalizing over Campbell's warwound and military medal, an admission of weakness. It would not do, and after a defeat in Parliament, MacDonald dissolved it on October 9.

This was a bad enough case for the Labour candidates to fight on, and he proceeded to make it worse. A document called the "Red Letter" was produced and printed in the *Daily Mail* and elsewhere. It purported to be a letter from Zinoviev, Chairman of the Communist International, instructing the British Communist Party on ways of controlling the Labour movement. Much energy was spent later by Labour investigators on showing it to be a forgery, which it quite probably was; but it contained very little that was not a paraphrase or quotation of what Zinoviev or other Communist International officials had said at one time or another. What was serious was that the Foreign Office, MacDonald's own department, took it at face value and published it together with an angry note of protest to the Russian Government. MacDonald did not repudiate this action, and his supporters, till now eagerly defending the proposed Russian treaty, found themselves deserted by their chief. The electoral results were what might be expected: the Labour Party lost 42 seats out of 192, the Liberals 119 out of 158, and the Conservatives gained 152. Baldwin immediately took MacDonald's place as Premier.

MacDonald had done his party considerable injury. He had made a rather poor show in office, getting worse and not better as he went on, he had disappointed Labour hopes in very important respects, and he had lost office and the election by behaviour which at the kindest could only be described as exceptionally unintelligent. Criticism was publicly expressed, even in the *Daily Herald*. But after it he retained his position and authority unimpaired. Partly, this was due to his personality: no one, who has not watched it, can have any idea of the peculiar power which that organ voice and handsome figure, without the true eloquence of Lloyd George or the intellectual content of Gladstone, could exercise over a Labour audience. Partly, it was because he had no serious rival: the elderly Trade Union officials who surrounded him were as reactionary as himself and without his charm and apparent fervour, and no younger leaders had risen to an eminence sufficient to challenge him. But mostly it was because the opposition was disunited and had neither programme nor rallying-ground. The Communist Party could not provide them, as it had built a high wall between itself and the rest of the Labour movement by its policy of "Bolshevization," which called for the formation of secret "nuclei" to control other working-class organizations, and pointed to ordinary Socialist and Labour Parties and Unions as "social fascists" and the worst enemies of the workers. The Trade Union malcontents tended to fall back on a virtual Syndicalism, relying on industrial action and Union reform, and treating their political colleagues with contempt. The politicians were still mostly organized in the I.L.P., which was MacDonald's own sponsor: though its discontent with his behaviour was obvious, he retained sufficient influence to prevent the Party as a whole forming a centre of opposition to him. Until the various opponents could find a common point of unity his reign would go on.

CHAPTER XLIV

THE GENERAL STRIKE AND AFTER

LESS than a month after the fall of the Labour Government, a first step was taken in opposition to the clique who had led to defeat. The British Labour movement has continually swung to and fro between the attractions of political and industrial action. It was natural now to turn to the newly organized General Council of the Trades Union Congress, which had never yet had an opportunity to show what it could do. It was in the mood to exercise its powers, and Fred Bramley, who had succeeded the aged C. W. Bowerman às Secretary, was showing energy and competence unsuspected when he had been an officer of the small Furnishing Trades Association. He was ably supported by a Left triumvirate who gained temporary fame, A. B. Swales of the Engineers, A. A. Purcell of the Furnishing Trades and George Hicks of the A.U.B.T.W. (Bricklayers). The Miners' Secretary, A. J. Cook, though not a member of the Council, wielded enormous influence by his passionate oratory. Words poured from him in a flood: the most powerful speaker in the Labour movement since Tom Mann, he swayed his audiences not by studied eloquence or by argument, but by his own flaming conviction and patent devotion. The Council's first step was peculiarly offensive to the politicians: it was to form a joint committee with the All-Russian Council of Trades Unions with the object of uniting the Labour movements of the whole world, beginning with the International Federation of Trade Unions.

The I.L.P., torn by unwillingness to reject its most eminent member and by deep discontent with his policy, drew up and later adopted a programme for "Socialism in Our Time," which MacDonald and his colleagues regarded as chimerical, but which rallied ardent support from its members. It evaded continually, however, passing resolutions which would mean a direct break with him, and, when forced to a decision, still voted for him.

The most powerful single group, straddling both "industrials" and "politicals," was that around George Lansbury, who in 1925 finally left the tamed *Daily Herald* and founded a weekly of his own—*Lansbury's Labour Weekly*. The group supporting this organ, which reached at one time 170,000 circulation, was responsible for a great number of the "rebel" plans and policies which were taken up and tried out between 1924 and 1926, the most elaborate of which was actually drafted in official headquarters by the Chief Woman Officer of the Labour Party, Dr. Marion Phillips, and other discontented colleagues.

The conflict with the Government and the employers came, as it was almost bound to come, in the coal industry. The coal-owners, notable even among post-war British capitalists for their inert stupidity, had made no plans whatever for the disappearance of the temporary boom due to the Ruhr adventure of the French. They demanded in 1925, when bad times had come, their usual remedy of heavy cuts in wages and a lengthening of hours. The miners, not yet wholly recovered from their ferocious struggle of four years before, appealed to the General Council. This time they were answered. Their argument that the attack on them was but a prelude to a general attack was endorsed by the Premier, who told them that the return to the gold standard meant that "all workers in this country have got to take reductions in wages." The railway and transport Unions met the General Council and pledged themselves to support it, and orders were issued for the complete stoppage of all movements of coal on July 31, to be followed, if need be, by a sympathetic strike.

The Government was unprepared: it had been over-contemptuous of the Labour movement. Baldwin, on the crucial day, called "Red Friday" by the Labour Press, promised a nine months' subsidy to the coal-owners mainly to support wages, and to enable—ostensibly—a Royal Commission under Sir Herbert Samuel to arrange reorganization of the industry. Amid the rash rejoicing that this decision caused this statement was taken at face value: more cynical warnings that the time would merely be spent in organizing to smash both miners and General Council passed unheeded.

But there were sufficient indications that these were right. After the temporary prosperity of 1924 a steady decline had set in. The Chancellor, Winston Churchill, with the approval of the City and the Treasury, had put British currency back on the gold standard at the pre-War level. This was equivalent to an automatic tax on every export. Markets shrank and profits fell; with them wages. It was not surprising that the Government was far less occupied with the proceedings of the Samuel Commission than with governmental plans to break the General Council if it repeated its threat in nine months' time. Large reserves of coal were piled up. An elaborate organization was set up, divided into ten areas, under Civil Commissioners, like Napoleonic prefects, who would be entitled to "give decisions on behalf of the government." Ex-viceroys and ex-admirals were put at the head of a voluntary strike-breaking organization, called the Organization for the Maintenance of Supplies, which was to provide these divisional generals with troops. All the machinery was ready by April 1926, to move on receipt of the one telegraphed word: "Action."

On the Labour side a mixture of inopportune pacifism and over-confidence had produced an exactly opposite result. No organization, local or national, to carry out a General Strike was countenanced, let alone started. For example, proposals for Workers' Defence Corps were rejected in alarm. The personnel of the General Council also changed. J. H. Thomas resumed the seat he had vacated to join the Labour Government. Arthur Pugh, a steel-trade right-winger, followed Swales as President. Death had already removed Fred Bramley from the secretaryship; he had been replaced by the electrician, W. M. Citrine, once a left-winger, but now moving as steadily to the right as Bramley had moved the other way. The Council, indeed, re-affirmed its support of the miners, but many of its members had reached the conclusion that a fall in wages was inevitable. The knowledge of this had a grave effect upon the miners' executive: they voted when the crisis was obviously near at hand (in April 1926), not as before to put their case in the hands of the Council unreservedly, but only subject to "consultation" with themselves, modified later to the more exact condition that the miners' slogan of "not a penny off the pay, not a minute on the day" should be agreed to—a condition which was never formally accepted.

Despite all the omens, the Labour leaders were surprised when the conflict actually came. The subsidy ended, the owners demanded their wage-cuts, the Government refused assistance. The Labour leaders, in Thomas's words, "begged and pleaded . . . almost grovelling." But the Government had decided, and behind Baldwin were Winston Churchill, Sir W. Joynson Hicks and Lord Birkenhead (F. E. Smith), spoiling for a fight. On Friday, the last day of April 1926, the lock-out notices went into effect. On Saturday, the most sensational of all May Days, the Council reported the facts to a specially summoned conference of Trade Union executives and asked for a mandate to call a general strike. The answer was given by roll-call, Union by Union, and the final figures were: Against 49,911; Awaiting instructions, 319,000; For 3,653,529. A wave of enthusiasm swept round the conference and out into the world beyond. Ernest Bevin spoke of the "magnificent generation" that had "placed its all upon the altar"; "How proud I am to be a part of this great movement," exclaimed John Bromley; Ramsay MacDonald joined in tumultuous singing of the "Red Flag."

Strike notices were not to take effect until midnight of Monday, May 3; in the meantime the Council anxiously resumed negotiations with the Government. Late on Sunday night it believed it had reached a basis, which "might involve some reduction in wages": about half-past eleven it was engaged in a room in Downing Street in endeavouring to persuade the miners to agree, when the Prime Minister sent for it. Headed by Arthur Pugh and J. H. Thomas, the members entered Baldwin's room: "Gentlemen," he said, "I am sorry to say our efforts for peace are unavailing. Something has happened at the *Daily Mail* and the Cabinet has empowered me to hand you this letter. . . ." As Thomas read it, he added: "And now we ask immediately for a repudiation of this action." The letter referred to an unauthorized lightning strike by machine-men on the *Daily Mail*, who had refused to print an exceptionally violent leading article attacking the Labour side. Thomas immediately disowned the action, and the Negotiating Committee withdrew, drafted a formal repudiation and sent a deputation downstairs to present it. The deputation found the Prime Minister's room empty and dark. A servant informed them that everybody had gone to bed and they had better go home. The Government had decided on war.

It was probable that it considered it was doing little more than calling a bluff. Judging the Labour movement from the Union officials and professional politicians they met at Westminster, the more bellicose Conservatives felt that it could be dealt with easily. A few men, no doubt, in some industries would come out and there would be some dislocation, which could be dealt with by the Commissioners and the Organization for the Maintenance of Supplies. Within a day or two the Council would be shattered and a recurrent menace and nuisance be finally ended. Nothing but a belated firmness was needed for a smashing and final victory over working-class organizations.

Neither they nor their opponents had any idea of what was really going to happen. The General Council had drawn up a plan for calling out industries in sections. The first and most powerful battalions, to come out on Monday, were: All transport workers of every kind, sea, land or air. The whole

•

printing trade. Iron and steel workers. Metal workers and chemical workers. Building workers, except for hospital and housing work. Electrical and gas workers supplying power for industry (not light). Sanitary services were to be continued, and health and food services not interfered with. Other Unions might be called upon later; instructions in each case would be sent out by the Unions concerned. Of those called upon, Havelock Wilson had already announced that his Sailors' and Firemen's Union would refuse to obey; he succeeded in preventing the members coming out except on the North-East Coast, in Lancashire, and on the south side of the Thames.

But his was the only exception of importance in all Britain. When the bells rang at midnight on Monday over the silent cities, they announced the beginning of a stillness which nobody had ever known before in English history. The Council had said that all activities should cease, in the trades that it named, and cease they did. There were no trains, no bus services, no trams, no papers, no building, no power. In a strike 100 per cent is an unobtainable figure, generally: there are always a few blacklegs hanging about, one or two safety or maintenance men, or a little pocketful of unorganized workers in some forgotten corner or craft. But even this ideal 100 per cent was frequently achieved. Unions like the Railway Clerks' Association—black-coated, of recent date, and doubtful spirit —in most cases came out as loyally as modern fighting Unions like the National Union of Railwaymen or ancient and obstinate craft societies like the London Compositors. Whatever plans there may have been for mining, railway or other services by the famed "Organization" under the Commissioners broke down at once; the Commissioners had to do the best they could either by negotiation with the strikers, or by a scratch service of middle-class volunteer drivers.

The T.U.C. permitted foodstuffs to pass, and others to move by "permit from the T.U.C.," brightly placarded in black on yellow. But no effective direction was given to local strike committees from headquarters, no scheme of organization for councils of action or strike committees sent out, no clear instructions issued even on how to deal with the Co-ops

Too few of the General Council were of an age or resolution to cope with the immense problem they had set themselves: the work fell on a small handful of men who were soon overworked and exhausted. Initiative returned to the localities and the local Trade Union and Labour officers rose splendidly to the occasion. It was for many a dazzling revelation of the workers' real power. As lapsed members and "nons" joined up, drawn at last by the sight of real action by the Unions, employers were more and more forced to come to the strike headquarters as real centres of authority, "begging for permission to do certain things. . . . 'Please can I move a quantity of coal from such and such a place?' or 'Please can my transport workers move certain foodstuffs in this or that direction?'" "I thought," wrote an Ashton committeeman, "of the many occasions when I had been turned empty away from the door of some workshop in a weary struggle to get the means to purchase the essentials of life for self and dependants. I thought of the many occasions I had been called upon to meet these people in the never-ending struggle to obtain decent conditions for those around me, and its consequent result in my joining the ranks of the unemployed. . . . The only tactic practised by some of them was bullying, and that was no use in a situation such as this; some tried persuasion, referring to us as *Mr. Chairman and Gentlemen*, but only a rigid examination of the stern facts of the case moved our actions. The cap-in-hand position reversed."

Headquarters aid and instruction were intermittent. The service of dispatch-riders gave some regular information. The Government published, from the *Morning Post* offices and in the coldly provocative tone of that paper, an unscrupulous *British Gazette*; the T.U.C. replied with a *British Worker* couched in deliberately moderate tones. Great dailies produced with extreme difficulty single sheets a few inches square, which circulated for a few miles round their offices. The British Broadcasting Corporation was a more dangerous enemy: under Government direction the stations broadcast false news of "returns to work" on a large scale. Labour headquarters at the beginning telephoned corrections, but abandoned this on finding that they were never used. All about the country cyclostyled and printed strike bulletins—over one hundred are known to have existed and probably many have not been preserved—endeavoured, with general success, to counter this propaganda, by direct contradiction or by mockery ("THE STRIKE IS OVER" announced Kensington, "only 400,000 N.U.R. men are now on strike plus 1,000,000 miners and 2,000,000 others. But three trains are running in Manchester and there is a five-minute service every two hours on the tubes. . . . Sir John Simon says the General Strike is illegal. The 3,000,000 strikers are advised to keep in hiding, preferably in the park behind Bangor Street, where they will not be discovered").

Headquarters refused, for tactical reasons, a subscription offered by the Russian Trade Union Council. It discovered, by the 7th of May, that the permit system was being misused and withdrew it. It issued orders to refrain from any provocative action or conflict with the police. On May 11 it called out its second line—shipyard workers and engineers. All its orders were scrupulously obeyed. But the actual direction of the strike fell on local officers and organizations. Some of these, even in nine days, began to achieve remarkable elaborateness and efficiency, with local sub-committees, and sports, food, workers' defence, intelligence, communications, prisoners' aid, mass picketing and other branches. As the strike had turned into a struggle with the Government, so they were developing into organs of government themselves. As far as can be judged (reports are fallible) there is no reasonable doubt that the efficiency and effectiveness of the strike were steadily increasing up to the very end; strain there undoubtedly was and in isolated sections, as of the tramwaymen in the Scottish industrial belt, evidences of weakening could be found; but against this is to be set a vast pile of reports which say the strike had just got into its stride. It is certain that when the news of the calling off came it was received with universal anger, as from an army which felt itself to be victorious.

For the enthusiasm of the rank and file had no reflection at headquarters. Muddle and fear reigned there. Fear among many Council members who dreaded the strike weapon they had chosen and wanted only to lay it down; muddle between

CP : U

the miners and the Council itself. The two mining members, incredible though it may seem, absented themselves throughout the whole period: Richards was unwell (though not seriously ill) and Smillie went home to Larkhall and stayed there. Communications were made from time to time to Miners' Secretary Cook or President Herbert Smith; but in general the Negotiating Committee of the Council went on its way alone. It was alarmed and anxious: an appeal for a compromise by the Archbishop of Canterbury was suppressed for days by the Cabinet diehards, and it seemed that it might be in for a fight to the finish. A way out seemed to eager eyes to be provided by Sir Herbert Samuel, Chairman of the Coal Commission, who saw Baldwin and then produced a Memorandum on the reorganization of the coal industry, somewhat more favourable to the workers than the Commission's Report. The Council decided the plan was acceptable, and summoned the Miners to agree to it, though it contravened their "not a penny, not a minute" motto. Now was shown the worst consequence of unpreparedness. The miners and the Council quarrelled because no terms of alliance had been agreed on. The Council claimed that having once called on the mass of the Unions to aid them the miners must obey the same discipline as the rest: if the Council felt that the rank and file had been used to the limit and the miners should make some concession, they must do so. They must not ask their fellow-workers to remain on strike on their behalf indefinitely, till every detail was settled to their own satisfaction. Such an argument was unanswerable: the miners did not attempt to answer it. They evaded by pointing to an equally undeniable truth—that Sir Herbert Samuel stated expressly that he had no authority whatever to say that his terms would be accepted by the Government. The Memorandum was no more than a statement of his opinion, though no doubt members of the General Council hoped that a united "acceptance" of it would somehow compel the Government into applying it. No one can test that hope now. What happened was that the Miners refused the memorandum and the next day, Wednesday, 12 May 1926, about noon, the Council, headed by Chairman Pugh and Secretary Citrine, waited on Baldwin,

and the former made a statement which seems not to have been quite clear. "That is, the General Strike is to be called off forthwith?" asked the Premier. "Forthwith. That means immediately," assented Pugh: he and others made some attempts to persuade the Cabinet into at least some verbal concession, Thomas pointing out that he and his colleagues had done "the big thing" and Bevin pleading that it "took a little courage." The Premier only replied that no doubt both he and they had work to get on with; and so it was all over.

Over for the leaders, perhaps, but not for the rank and file. These had somehow to be induced to accept the decision and the news. The Council took the bold course of declaring by implication and when necessary by outright statement that the Memorandum was an authorized document and the "terms of peace." Momentarily it was believed: some local councils even issued "victory bulletins" in good faith. But the falsehood would not stand: Baldwin exulted about "unconditional surrender" on the wireless, and even the *British Worker* carried Samuel's written statement: "I have made it clear to your committee from the outset that I have been acting entirely on my own initiative, have received no authority from the Government, and can give no assurances on their behalf." The employers in rail and road transport and printing, taking their cue, disclosed plans for wage-reductions, hours increases, "open shops" or victimizations. This very haste undid them. The strike was unbroken, and the strikers (except for the shipyard and engineering workers, so frivolously called out when the end was already clear), could defend themselves. The newspapers did not appear, nor did the trams, trains or buses run until the proposals were withdrawn and conditions little if at all worsened.

The miners fought on and in November had to accept defeat. Nothing whatever had been secured by the greatest effort the British workers had ever made.

In a political democracy, a Government which leads its country to unexampled defeat is likely at the least to be expelled from office never to return. The Trade Union leaders were more fortunate. While the long-drawn miners' struggle **was on,** criticism was suspended by a compact between both sides. The Council did not report to the recalled Conference of Executives until January of the next year, 1927. By that time passions had cooled down and the criticism of the workers had expressed itself otherwise. Too many of them had "voted with their feet," as Lenin said of the Russian Army deserters. Trade Union membership fell by over half a million; the same General Council members and miners' leaders were left at the head of these diminished battalions, but they could never call upon the same loyalty and sacrifice again.

Making the best of a bad job, they cancelled the Russian alliance, tried to conciliate the victorious employers, and took part in the "Mond–Turner conversations," which led to a draft scheme for a joint council of workers and employers. Ben Turner, the venerable textile leader, was official spokesman for the Trade Unions, but Sir Alfred Mond, the chemical magnate, was not authorized by any corresponding employers' organization, and no results followed, though it may be the conversations adjourned any general assault by the employers. Nor did much more result from a whirlwind campaign by A. J. Cook and James Maxton—after Wheatley's death the leader of the I.L.P. rebels—to rally the left wing. The chief event to record was the considered harvesting of victory by the Conservative Party: the Trade Disputes and Trade Unions Act of 1927 combined astutely prudence with revenge. Trade Union subscriptions to the Labour Party were not forbidden, but each Union member had now to request to make them (instead of a request to be excused being necessary). The Party would not be stamped out, but it might be crippled. Civil Servants were not forbidden Trade Unionism, but their Trade Unions must leave the Congress and Labour Party, and have no relations with other Unions outside the service. Local authorities were forbidden to make a rule of employing only Trade Unionists. General strikes and most (not all) sympathetic strikes were forbidden under clauses of the widest and loosest drafting. Severe penalties were prescribed for these and fresh restrictions on picketing enacted.

Nor were the unemployed forgotten. The Government administratively worsened their condition by wholesale deprivals of benefit on the ground that applicants were "not genuinely seeking work." No work was there: though dividends were going up, unemployment was scarcely at all better. The instruction to "go and look for work" was little more than a spiteful insult: but little money was saved by these tactics, though the suffering and humiliation caused were unmeasured.

It was, indeed, this tactic more than any other single thing which led to a Labour victory at the election of 1929. There were 287 Labour members and 59 Liberals, who together formed a majority against the Conservative and others' 296. Ramsay MacDonald came back as Prime Minister, once again dependent on Liberal votes.

CHAPTER XLV

THE SECOND LABOUR GOVERNMENT

IT is undeniable that the Labour Government which held office from 1929 to 1931 suffered from very bad luck. The second Labour Cabinet was formed under circumstances which were generally believed to hold out the prospect of advancing business prosperity in the world as a whole. The great American boom was in full swing, and Europe, reconstructed largely with the aid of American capital, seemed at last to be well on the way to recovery from the effects of war. Unemployment in Great Britain remained serious, and certain industries and areas were badly depressed. But in general profits were high, and there appeared to be every possibility of carrying through large measures of social reform and of reducing unemployment by public works and schemes of economic development and reorganization without causing any crisis likely to lead to a collapse of the profit-making system.

The Labour Party and the Liberals who then followed Lloyd George had both fought the General Election of 1929 largely on the issue of unemployment, promising ambitious measures of economic advance designed both to increase employment and to promote productive efficiency. The Labour Govern-

ment therefore seemed assured of Liberal backing for this part
of its programme, and also for a good many of its projects of
social reform. Like its predecessor of 1924, it was of course
dependent on the Liberals for its majority in the House of
Commons; and it was faced with an overwhelmingly Conservative House of Lords which had power under the Parliament Act of 1911 to delay for three years the enactment of
any measure (except one of finance) which it disliked. Nevertheless, in view of Liberal promises and the favourable economic
situation, the new Government's opportunities looked good.

Long before MacDonald brought about the fall of his own
Cabinet in September 1931, this situation had changed
radically for the worse. The American collapse began as early
as 1929, with the crisis on Wall Street in September; and thereafter the United States slid down gradually into worse and
worse panic and depression. In Europe, the unsound financial
situation which had been built up largely with American
capital threatened to topple as the Americans not only ceased
to lend, but scrambled to withdraw their existing investments
in order to meet losses incurred at home. British financiers,
also deeply involved in Germany and elsewhere, lent heavily
to Continental banks and traders in a desperate attempt to
avert collapse. The gravity of the situation remained concealed from the general public through 1930, and even through
the early months of 1931. But when, in 1931, European banks
and great industrial concerns began collapsing right and left,
it became obvious that Great Britain too was faced with a
serious financial crisis, aggravated by the great destruction of
purchasing power in the Dominions and other primary producing countries—Britain's best markets—which had followed
on the cessation of American buying. Unemployment, which
had been rising fast in 1930, soared in 1931 to an intolerable
height—so that the effects of the Government's small efforts
to provide employment by public works and development
schemes were completely obscured. The Government was
attacked by its own supporters for failing to cope with the
problem; and it was simultaneously blamed by the capitalists
for causing the depression through lavish expenditure and
economic ineptitude.

In effect, the financial interests found in the crisis of 1931 the opportunity not merely of getting rid of a Government they disliked, but also of discrediting the Labour Party and bringing the entire working-class movement into disrepute. To handle the world crisis of capitalism, the British capitalists wanted a Government in which they could feel full confidence—confidence that it would put first and foremost the interests of capitalism, which they of course identified in their own minds with the interests of the country. They were no longer prepared to give a weak Labour administration rope: they wanted a Government of their own, and wanted it quickly, in order that it might deal with the developing world crisis. MacDonald proved himself an instrument well suited to their purpose; for without his change of sides the Conservatives could never have swept the country. As "Nationals" they could appeal to all classes—to all who had taken fright at the crisis, and were fearful for their jobs or their small savings, as well as to the property-owners and the financial interests generally. The "National" Government won in 1931 its resounding victory; and Labour was swept away into the dustbin as a broken plate.

But before we consider what happened in the crisis of 1931 let us pause to look back upon the actual record of the second MacDonald Government. What had it actually done; and what had it left undone of the things it ought to have done?

Its constitution was wiser than that of the first Labour Government. None but Party members were included. MacDonald did not try to hold the office of Foreign Secretary as well as Premier. He left it to Arthur Henderson, who made himself an international reputation. A woman was raised to Cabinet rank—but she was Margaret Bondfield, still at the Ministry of Labour and still of the same mind in policy. Two known left-wingers were included in the Cabinet, but in posts where practically no administrative functions existed— Tom Johnston as Lord Privy Seal with no department at all, George Lansbury as First Commissioner of Works with a small department which he managed to make momentarily appear important. Sir Oswald Mosley (then claiming to be a left-wing Socialist) was Chancellor of the Duchy of

Lancaster, with merely vestigial functions. Lansbury and Mosley were supposed to form, with J. H. Thomas, a Committee on Unemployment, but it depended on the last named and was wholly ineffective.

The Government's programme had been conceived in the conditions of 1929—conditions of evanescent opportunity. As the situation changed between 1929 and 1931, no new programme for dealing with the changing conditions was ever worked out. All that happened was that the Government, finding more and more difficulty in carrying its original projects into effect, abandoned, modified or postponed them one after another, while it sought with growing weakness of will for any agreement among its own members concerning the measures that ought to be taken in order to deal with the threat to British stability. As exports fell off with the decline of purchasing power abroad, imports grew fast—for foreign exporters, desperate for ready cash, dumped goods at any price they could get into the world's greatest open market. A cry went up from British industrialists and farmers that they could not employ labour unless they were protected from the flood of cheap imports. The balance of payments turned sharply against Great Britain, and the Bank of England found itself steadily losing gold—with the knowledge that unless this loss was checked it might at any time provoke a flight from the pound which would make it impossible to maintain the gold standard, so precariously and foolishly restored in 1925.

The Government put up a stronger resistance to criticism from the Left than from the Right. Sir O. Mosley resigned his post upon the refusal of the Cabinet to adopt a memorandum on unemployment which he had presented, and at the 1930 Party Conference he very nearly carried a resolution compelling its publication and circularization. He was able to organize a mass of left-wing discontent, and, early in 1931, with the assistance of John Strachey and a few others, chiefly Labour M.P.s, organized a "New Party" for "action." This was commonly still regarded as a left-wing movement, though it appealed to all parties and contained one Ulster Conservative M.P. Eventually, slowly losing its Labour supporters, it ended as a pure Fascist movement.

On the Government's right the financiers clamoured for drastic retrenchment in public expenditure by cutting down the social services and especially by reducing benefits to the unemployed and depriving as many as possible of them of any sort of dole. They demanded that any domestic sacrifice necessary for the maintenance of the gold standard and the profit system should be made—by the poor. Supported by Chancellor Snowden, a whole-hearted convert to "sound finance," they badgered Ramsay MacDonald with their prophecies of disaster, until he came to believe with them that the one thing needful for economic salvation was that the Government should enjoy the fullest confidence of the capitalist class.

If there had been no world crisis, the achievements of the second Labour Government might have made in history a respectable, though by no means a brilliant, showing. In the course of 1929–31 they substantially reduced the hardships in unemployment insurance, by removing the provision which allowed applicants for benefit to be arbitrarily disqualified on the ground that they were "not genuinely seeking work." They extended the contributory pensions scheme (started in 1925 by the Conservatives) to about three hundred thousand persons previously excluded from it, passed an important Act for the improvement of mental hospitals, and set on foot a big housing and slum-clearance scheme under the Housing Act of 1930. They extended the Export Credits scheme to the Soviet Union, and made loans and grants more easily available both at home by the Development Act and in the Colonies by the Colonial Development Act. They passed a Land Utilization Act for State demonstration farms and land settlement (but the clause providing for the State farms was struck out by the House of Lords), and the first Agricultural Marketing Act, setting up Marketing Boards for agricultural products. They instituted a system of public regulation of road transport under the Transport Act of 1930, and set on foot a scheme, subsequently enacted in a mutilated form by the National Government, for a London Passenger Transport Board. They carried the Coal Mines Act of 1930, but in a form which, though it reduced miners' hours from eight to seven and a half, preserved all the features of capitalist monopoly without safeguards for effective reorganization of the industry—for these too the House of Lords mutilated into impotence. They gave improved grants for school-building, afforestation, road-making and a number of other services.

Therewith the Labour Government attempted certain other things—an Education Bill raising the school age to fifteen, a Bill ratifying the Washington Forty-eight Hours Convention, a Representation of the People Bill further democratizing electoral methods and introducing the alternative vote, a Consumers' Council Bill directed against profiteering, an extension of Trade Boards to the distributive trades and a measure repealing the obnoxious Trade Union Act of 1927. But all these measures were either destroyed or mutilated by the House of Lords, or held up or spoilt by the Liberals in the House of Commons. The Liberals, for example, were responsible for the failure to repeal the Trade Union Act.

Moreover, internationally the Government had an excellent record. It signed on behalf of Great Britain both the Optional Clause of the League Covenant, providing for reference of all international disputes of a legal character to the Hague Court, and the General Act, providing for arbitration in disputes not amenable to legal decision. It did its best to institute a Tariff Truce, to get a settlement of the Reparations question on lines tolerable to Germany and to set the Disarmament Conference to work on an effective basis. It caused Lord Irwin, the Viceroy (later, Lord Halifax), to make his famous declaration promising India ultimately Dominion status, and it made some attempt to settle the India question at the Round Table Conference—-though meanwhile it continued the repressive policies of previous Governments in India.

The sum-total of these achievements and attempts would, had the times been normal, have been a respectable record for a Government inheriting the attitudes and ideas of the Liberal Governments of 1906–14. It would have been a record entirely devoid of any attempt to introduce Socialism, or fundamentally to transform the economic system—tasks which Mac-Donald and most of his colleagues ruled out as impracticable for a "minority Government." But, within these limits, the excellence of the Government's foreign policy, under Arthur Henderson's direction, would have atoned for the modesty of its domestic accomplishments.

The times, however, were far from normal; and in facing an abnormal and difficult situation, MacDonald and his colleagues showed themselves utterly incompetent. In 1931 only boldness could have saved them; but they chose the defeatist course of wavering whenever any powerful vested interest criticized their doings. They were induced by clamour to pass an Anomalies Act which became, in the hands of the National Government, a powerful instrument for depriving unemployed workers of benefit; and they were guilty of the lunacy—or worse—of appointing a committee of their political opponents —the notorious "May" Economy Committee—to pronounce judgment on their financial policy. This folly was, indeed, largely responsible for their fall; for the financial interests seized their opportunity. The May Committee produced an alarmist and grossly exaggerated report on the state of the finances, and so precipitated the threatened run on the pound. And, when the crisis was thus provoked, the Government, instead of standing up to the financiers, fell into feckless argumentation among themselves, most of them, it seems clear, with barely a glimmering of knowledge of what the trouble was all about, and the outstanding leaders—MacDonald and Snowden—already determined to betray their followers, and go over openly to the capitalist side.

The exact method of the split is vehemently disputed. The Labour Cabinet was still discussing the outrush of gold and the "threat to the pound," under the influence of the deliberately exaggerated menaces of Philip Snowden, when it came. They had agreed to enormous concessions but jibbed (it is stated) at plucking the unemployed. Then it was shot at them that arrangements had already been made, with the King's consent but clearly on MacDonald's initiative, for the formation of a "National Government" of Labour, Conservatives and Liberals, with Baldwin as Vice-Premier. The Cabinet voted against this; MacDonald resigned with it and constructed his National Government immediately; and some, though not most, of his colleagues went with him to their appointed places.

MacDonald, Snowden, Thomas and Lord Sankey were in the new Cabinet.

The Government almost at once called a General Election to save the country and to save the pound. Their opponents were in no sort of state to resist them: their three most famous leaders were leading the campaign against them, and their remaining leaders discredited by compromises and association with very much the same policy as they were now denouncing. Snowden provided the most effective weapon in a broadcast endorsing Lord Runciman's assertion that the Labour Party would rob the Post Office Savings Bank if it returned to power. The result was a fall of the Labour vote to the still respectable figure of 6,648,000, and the swelling of the Conservative vote to the figure of 11,800,000, the total "National" votes being 14,500,000. All the unattached voters, and some who had never voted before, went "National": Labour seats safe for twenty years were lost; every ex-Cabinet Minister lost his seat except George Lansbury: only 49 Labour M.P.s returned to Westminster, while the Conservatives had 417, the rest being various kinds of Liberals (Samuelites, Simonites, or members of the Lloyd George family) and "MacDonald Labourites." The defeat of the industrial army had been followed by an equal catastrophe to the politicals.

CHAPTER XLVI

THE CLOSING YEARS

THE world economic crisis, heralded by the Wall Street crash of 1929 and definitely begun by the financial collapse in Austria and Germany in the summer of 1931, did more to Great Britain than break up a feeble Labour Government and drive the British currency off the gold standard. It developed, in the two following years, into a severe and prolonged depression which sapped the strength of Trade Unionism, without ever becoming quite deep enough to provoke extremes of revolutionary feeling. In the early months of 1929 unemployment had been round about 1,250,000. A year later it was round about 1,750,000, and in the early months of 1931 about 2,600,000. By September 1931, in the midst of the crisis, it was nearly 2,900,000, and there, or thereabouts, it remained until the later months of 1933, when it began slowly falling. Not until July 1935 did it fall below 2,000,000: but thereafter the fall continued, and in the summer of 1937 the recorded totals were under 1,500,000.

Thus, the Labour movement from the onset of the crisis had to face several years of continuously and seriously adverse conditions.

It was indeed, surprising, in face of the crushing election defeat and the manifest bewilderment of the leaders who remained within the Labour ranks, that there was no real split in the party. When it came to the point, the instinctive solidarity of the organized working class asserted itself. The Labour machine was not broken—hardly a local Labour Party suffered any serious cleavage. The only break of importance was the secession of the I.L.P. It had before now carried indiscipline to the verge of a breach, demanding (and more or less exercising without being granted) the right to act as a separate party and vote according to conscience in the House of Commons. The new leader of the Labour Party, George Lansbury, made all the concessions which were in his power to induce the handful of I.L.P. Members of Parliament, now nearly all Clyde men and led by Maxton, to continue within the ranks, but the I.L.P. leaders were convinced that the Labour Party was thoroughly counter-revolutionary and that to accept its discipline would be treachery. Early in 1932 its leaders broke away. Their party was split by this decision: a minority both of M.P.s and rank-and-file members stayed with the Labour Party, the latter forming in Scotland the "Scottish Socialist Party" and in England joining with the members of a propaganda group called the Society for Socialist Inquiry and Propaganda, the Socialist League. But apart from this, Labour organization remained almost intact: what was lost was prestige among the general body of electors. And from such a loss recovery was bound to take a substantial time, even if the subsequent leadership were of the best.

While the Labour Party was being thus battered into impotence, the Trade Unions were suffering under the impact of the economic crisis. Trade Union membership, which had been 5,500,000 in 1925 before the General Strike, fell to under 5,000,000 in 1927. In 1932 and 1933 it was well under 4,500,000—whereafter there was a slow recovery as trade revived. For the time being the Trade Unions could only hang on as best they could, avoiding disputes wherever possible and making practically no attempt to extend their organization to new groups or industries. The employers were in a highly favourable position; but for the most part they did not launch any onslaught on the rights of combination, or even attempt big changes in wages or hours of work. Between 1930 and 1933 money-wages fell, on the average, by about 5 per cent; but the sharp fall in world prices caused their purchasing power to rise, so that in 1933 even the reduced money-wage would buy about 11 per cent more goods than the higher wage of 1929-30. This, of course, applies only to workers who were able to remain in regular jobs. The millions who suffered from intermittent employment, as well as the actually unemployed, found their purchasing power curtailed despite the lower prices. The unemployed were penalized by the imposition of a stringent Family Means Test, as soon as they had been "on the dole" beyond a short period of "standard benefit" under the Unemployment Insurance Scheme. This Means Test was bitterly resented in the depressed areas, which felt it most because they contained the majority of those who had been out of work for long periods. There were disturbances in the depressed areas, reminiscent of the troubles of 1921 and 1922: there were renewed Hunger Marches, chiefly under Communist leadership. The Communist Party gained recruits, especially in the coal-fields and other distressed industrial centres. But what were these unfortunates to do? Isolated in these derelict towns and villages, they could not by demonstration or riot make any impression on the Government away in London; and in the rest of the country, in view of the fall in prices, the distress was not widespread enough to cause any general movement of revolt.

In fact, the employers were wise, in face of the quietism of the Trade Unions, to refrain from any mass attack that might have provoked them into activity. There was no real point in cutting wages when much the same effect on costs could be produced more easily by allowing the pound sterling to

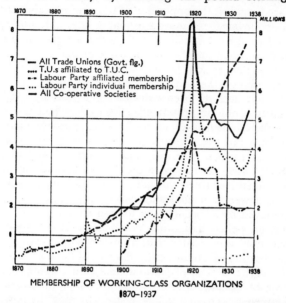

MEMBERSHIP OF WORKING-CLASS ORGANIZATIONS
1870–1937

depreciate in value, or alternatively in many industries the new protective tariff, introduced in 1931–2 under cover of the crisis, would enable them to exclude foreign competition. A Conservative Government securely in power—for from the first the "National Government" was in effect simply Conservative—suited them much better than any attempt to introduce Fascist methods. As long as Labour would stay quiet in defeat, there seemed to be no need to hammer it very hard. It was more advantageous to let the moderate Trade Unions alone—with the Act of 1927 to fall back upon for knocking them down if need arose—and to concentrate for the time being on repressing the minority of Communists and extremists.

Trade Unionism, through this period, became more and more inclined to seek an accommodation with capitalism, and to repudiate and where possible discipline the extremists in its own ranks. The Labour Party, on the other hand, under the impulse of defeat and resentment at its betrayal, moved for a time towards the Left. The Leicester Conference of 1932 declared, against the opposition of the platform, that the next Labour Government must nationalize the joint stock banks as well as the Bank of England, and must set out upon an immediate programme of constructive Socialism.

The parliamentary leader, Lansbury, was one who had always been on the Left, and the party as a whole felt that if defeated it had yet been defeated for a resistance of which Socialists could be proud: even its leaders had saved their souls, though some had taken the latest possible moment of salvation. But the leftward swing had no great momentum and could not last. The industrial pacifism of the Unions was bound to have its influence on the party, and the Labour Party executive, since the fall of MacDonald, possessed far greater power than the leader, who was soon, in any case, to be removed by a dispute over foreign affairs.

Foreign policy had, until now, provided a subject upon which unity was greater than anywhere else. Except for the isolated group of Communists who still, though less assuredly, depicted the League of Nations, in Lenin's terms, as a conspiracy of bandits, all the working-class organizations and spokesmen agreed on a policy of strengthening the power and authority of the League, and reducing by general agreement the armaments of individual powers. Whether this policy logically involved war against an aggressor was a question which was avoided by pointing out what was true enough at the time and for some few years to come—that the power already in League members' hands was so overwhelming that, if they resolutely supported the League, war would not occur. In 1931, when Japan invaded Manchuria, attacking a fellow member of the League, a manifesto on the policy Britain should follow was signed with equal conviction by George Lansbury for the parliamentary party, John Bromley for the Trades Union Congress and George Lathan for the Labour Party. It asked the Government to arrange through the League for the calling home of all Ambassadors from

Tokio, and, should this have no effect, for the application of "measures of financial and economic constraint" in agreement with the United States. (The Government, which had already put its foot on the road which led to Munich, declined to find time to receive a deputation to present this plan; Mr. Amery issued a public defence of Japan; what tentative approaches may have come from the United States Secretary of State, Mr. Stimson, were rebuffed.)

Until Hitler took power in Germany in January 1933, this policy could be maintained. No insoluble problems seemed to have arisen. Japanese aggression, though lamentable, seemed no new phenomenon, merely a recurrence of an age-old imperialism, which could be checked if the Powers chose. Since the Conference of Ambassadors and the mere appearance of a British squadron had turned Mussolini out of Corfu, Italian Fascism had been internationally very well behaved. Its propagandists declared Fascism was "not an article for export" and Italy supported the League more consistently than many democratic powers. It was not immediately realized that the Nazi victory had entirely changed the situation. True, Socialists of all kinds had for fifteen years warned the governing classes in their countries that they were sowing the seeds of future wars by wrecking European economy and driving Germany to despair; but in Britain at least they were reluctant to believe that the seed was growing before their eyes, into a tree which would shortly overshadow their lives. Many still continued to urge remedies which, valid before, were meaningless after the Nazis were fixed in power. As refugees streamed out of Germany, a realization of the truth began to filter through with them. It is a slow process, however, for a great democratic movement to change its mind: the *Queen Mary* cannot swing round in a pond.

Not, indeed, that anyone failed to understand that the stamping out of existence of what had been the greatest Socialist movement in the world was a disaster. But the immediate deduction drawn by the leaders of the British Labour movement was chiefly that they must dissociate themselves more sharply from the Communists. Treating the Nazi régime not as a threat from abroad, but as a warning of what might happen at home, they threw a great deal of the blame upon the Communists. Slurring over the record of compromise by the German Social Democrats, they concentrated their eyes upon the Communist collaboration with the Nazis in the Berlin tram strike, their ferocious attacks on the Social Democrats as "social fascists," and other actions which, they held, had so split the German workers as to render them defenceless. Not only did the Communists seem to them no better than wreckers, but Communist propaganda appeared likely to terrify the middle class, at present quiescent, and drive it into supporting a Fascist movement in Britain. It would, at the least, make impossible a reversal of the 1931 election. It seemed to be, therefore, essential both to bar the door to any Communist irruption, and to concentrate on moderate and "gradualist" proposals which would not alarm the middle class. This policy seemed to have earned a dividend in 1934, when Labour captured the London County Council and started under Herbert Morrison's leadership on a wide policy of reform and a long reign of power.

The Communists also were changing their policy. The new programme of co-operation with anyone who appeared willing to resist Fascism, which internationally had its most famous example in the Stalin–Laval pact, in Britain led to repeated attempts to enter the Labour Party, either directly or via controlled organizations, and to secure positions of power in the unions and other bodies. Disproportionate energy and time were spent upon the wrangles over this infiltration: it bulked far larger than it deserved in the thought and writings of the time.

The first internal conflict, however, came over the question of peace and war. In 1935, a year which in some ways was to be a turning-point in British history, the League of Nations Union published the figures of its "Peace Ballot." It had polled no less than 11,500,000 votes, and, of these, eleven millions supported the League. 10,500,000 were in favour of universal disarmament. Only 6,500,000 voted in favour of "military sanctions" to support the League. Almost forthwith the first major attack on the League followed: in October 1935 Italy invaded Abyssinia.

This was a crisis which forced the Labour movement to a decision. Till now it had condemned Fascism vigorously, but had otherwise followed its traditional policy. Votes against armament estimates could be regarded as only the usual parliamentary means of expressing no confidence in the Government's policy, but such actions as dissolving the O.T.C.s in L.C.C. schools could not. At the Labour Party Conference of 1935 the parliamentary leader, George Lansbury, forced the issue. Support of "military sanctions", he said, was support of war; and to that he and his colleagues were resolutely opposed. He received but little support—one big textile union, the small Socialist League (which, through Sir Stafford Cripps, restated the old Socialist policy of fighting in a class and not in a national war), and a few scattered votes. The overwhelming mass of the conference voted in favour of supporting the League, up to and including war. Though the opposition was probably larger than its vote of 200,000 suggested, the decision was undoubtedly that of the workers as a whole. George Lansbury, the rejected leader, withdrew from any active participation in the party activities and turned his attention to a remarkable series of journeys about the world, endeavouring to call the attention of potentates and peoples to the economic causes of the world war he saw looming—a gallant and hopeless one-man endeavour to push back the wheel of history.

A more subtle politician had been watching the conference. Immediately the vote was recorded, Stanley Baldwin (the Conservative leader who had replaced the ailing MacDonald) called for a general election. The Conference had endorsed what he claimed to be his own policy; J. L. Garvin, editor of the *Observer*, provided him with the necessary slogan—that the Labour Party wished Britain to be the policeman of the world, deprived of his helmet and truncheon. He himself promised resolute support of the League, and a certainty of peace. On this slogan was elected the House of Commons which was still sitting ten years later. In it the Labour Party secured 154 seats. This was indeed three times what it had secured in 1931, but in 1929 it had had 287. The Government, and the House's majority, were overwhelmingly Conservative. There was a sprinkling of "National Liberals" and even

"National Labourites"; and for electoral purposes the label "National Government" was retained.

In the same year, 1935, took place two events, little noticed at the time, which foreshadowed a profound change in public thought. The Left Book Club was founded, and the first Penguin Books were published. Both of these speedily found imitators, none of which were as successful. The Left Book Club, an enterprise of Mr. Victor Gollancz, rose to have 50,000 members, most of whom received one and sometimes more large books of Socialist propaganda a month. Some of these may have been shallow, some no doubt were sold but unread, some were criticized as following blindly official Communist policy; but the majority were books of value and depth, likely not to cause momentary excitement so much as to make solid converts. The Penguin Books, and their subsidiaries the Pelicans and Penguin Specials, had no direct political bias: indeed, Mr. Allen Lane, their producer, sought anxiously for Right wing books to balance the Left Specials which alone it seemed possible to find, but with very infrequent success. The total number of books issued must have been astronomical: members of the working and middle classes who had never bought books before were buying vast quantities of the best and newest literature, including social, historical, and scientific works mostly by Left-wing experts, and directly political studies. Other less widespread publications helped—*Fact* booklets, pamphlets from the reviving Fabian Society, and the books of Messrs. Allen and Unwin, Secker and Warburg, George Routledge and Co.'s Labour Book Service, etc. A vast shift of public opinion was on the way, and showed itself even in the columns of such papers as *Picture Post* or, oddly enough, in the writing of detective stories, where the curious observer could note the gradual eclipse of the aristocratic hero by a more proletarian policeman, or even a romantic adventurer who sympathized with the Republic in Spain.

For the next year saw an event which divided Britain more deeply than it had ever before been divided on a question of foreign policy. Mussolini's invasion of Abyssinia had been wholly successful: despite the support of forty-two nations, the

British and French Governments failed to bring any support to the assaulted League member. This success emboldened what now called itself "The Axis": by arrangement with it, a disappointed Spanish General, Francisco Franco, concocted with others a plot which burst in July 1936. It came within an inch of success: the feeble Spanish Republican Government was utterly unprepared for the treachery, and the half of Spain which was rescued was only saved by spontaneously formed workers' committees, led mostly by Socialists, syndicalists and anarchists. Franco was able to continue his campaign by using Moors, and later a great many Italian and some German soldiers and airmen, as well as German equipment. The French and British Governments broke their treaty or Covenant obligations and refused arms to the Spanish Government.

Momentarily the official British Labour movement, pressed by the French which was deeply tinged with pacifism, favoured non-intervention; but it reversed its vote after hearing a Spanish delegation at the next conference and realizing the facts of the war. Unofficially, there was no hesitation. Support for the Spanish Republic was immediate and generous. Very early on recruiting started for the International Brigade which stopped the Franco Fascists on the Jarama: a moving article by the highly respected Socialist journalist, H. N. Brailsford, in the *News Chronicle* was responsible for its first big send off. The Communist Party regained power and prestige by its share in raising the Brigade, but the Brigade was careful to make clear it was not a Communist force: its battalions were named after Garibaldi, Abraham Lincoln, or, in one case, after C. R. Attlee, who had succeeded George Lansbury in the Parliamentary leadership.

The Government, before long, forbade recruiting for the Brigade, and took part in the formation of a Non-Intervention Committee on which were represented the chief European powers, including those responsible for Franco's rebellion. Its effect was to prevent arms reaching the legal Government, while both arms and men were steadily supplied to the rebels, by Germany and Italy. So weak, at this time, was the Axis still that, when a decision was taken, by the Noyon convention, to put down "piracy," that particular form of mainly Italian attack on Spain ceased at once. Nevertheless, the British Government (whose lead was followed by the French and also by the Americans) persisted in this policy of assistance to the Fascists, despite repeated exposure of the facts, and the withdrawal from the Committee of Russia, which thereafter sent limited supplies to the Republic. This policy, so contrary to Britain's obvious interests, was assumed by the Left to be due mainly to class motives. Franco's supporters were the narrow class of rich men whom Chamberlain's supporters knew and liked: his opponents were the Socialists and trade unionists whom they hated. The war in Spain was the same class war as was being fought at home.

While certain sections of the working class might reasonably be contented with the moderate policy officially advocated in the years up to about 1937, there were many who could not be. As will be shown later, real wages of those employed had been rising in the early 'thirties, owing to a price fall greater than wage reductions. Life was something easier for those who lived in the lucky areas, such as the London suburbs, where new light industries were allowed to pile themselves up without regard to convenience, health, town planning or even elementary military safety. Even in such areas there remained black patches of squalor and misery which were only exposed by the mass evacuation of children in 1939. But these were the lucky areas. In others, first called "Depressed" and then "Special" areas, misery now seemed perpetual. The worst areas were a great belt across industrial Scotland, the whole area of the North-East coast, and practically all of South Wales. There were other isolated areas of extreme wretchedness, such as parts of Cumberland, or the city of Dundee, which had depended mainly on the jute trade and seemed on its way to become a "ghost town." In these places not only were there men who had never worked for years, there was good reason to believe that they would never work again. Pit after pit was closed, shipyard after shipyard, factory after factory, and the best endeavours of the more enlightened employers, the "rationalizers," was not to re-open them but rather to close more. In these areas, the human decay was as serious as the material. The effects of idleness, poverty and the "dole" as sole income alarmed every grade of social worker from archbishops downwards: an investigation by the Pilgrim Trust reached the conclusion that hundreds of thousands of adults were beyond reclamation. Even the strongest based protections built for themselves by the workers of these areas, the unions, began to crumble under a régime where servility was often the only hope of securing a job. From 1933 onwards, for example, South Wales coalowners began an attempt to break down the Miners' Federation by a company union sardonically called "The South Wales Miners' Industrial Union": it secured a foothold in places where once it would have seemed impossible.

In such circumstances, home and foreign, anger was bound to break out. Of the attempts to "ginger up" the Labour movement, the most important was the "United Front" which started as an alliance between the Socialist League, the I.L.P. and the Communists. The campaign, whose most popular speaker was Sir Stafford Cripps, met with immediate success. "Circles" of the Left Book Club were swung into its support: many local Labour parties, chafing under the trade union block vote at conferences as well as the uninspired timidity of "Transport House" generally, loudly applauded its speakers and voted in support. Not an inconsiderable number of the most active workers in the provinces wondered whether they would not be better advised to quit their old-established organizations and work for this new programme. But the alliance soon ran into trouble. There was before long dissension between the Communist Party and its allies, particularly the I.L.P. The I.L.P., by now an uncompromising class-war Socialist body, of small membership outside Glasgow, was defending principles which the Communists were now denouncing as "Trotskyist." Following the new Moscow policy of close alliance with all nominally democratic parties, and of throwing aside programmes which might antagonize them, the Communists were more eager to co-operate with Liberals than with I.L.P.ers. What started as a difference of opinion grew into a far deeper division as the "Trotsky trials" in Russia led to the conviction of thousands of the older stalwarts of the Revolution. What the truth behind the trials was it is not even now easy to say; there is no doubt of the effect in confusing and dividing the forces of the British "left," and weakening the United Front propagandists.

On its side, the Labour Party took vigorous action against what it regarded as a threat to its unity and influence. It had in 1936, decisively refused an application by the Communist Party to affiliate to it. It had condemned the whole "United Front" agitation. It not merely distrusted the allies, Communist or Liberal, proposed to it; it charged many United Frontsmen with illogicality over armaments. Sir Stafford Cripps, demanding resistance to Nazism, had called rearmament "tomfoolery." "To say we must oppose the arms programme because we distrust the present Government," replied John Marchbanks, the railwaymen's general secretary, "is balderdash, and dangerous balderdash at that."

For its discontented local parties the Party granted a concession at its 1937 conference: they were given seven seats instead of five upon the Executive, and the Trade Unions were not to vote in the selection of these representatives. This placated many of them and there was no split.

This conference also voted resolutions which indicated a serious attempt to arrest the rapid steps by which the "National Government" was leading the world first to Munich and then to war. Conservative spokesmen were still claiming that the Party was opposing rearmament, and were spreading the rumour that it was only too glad to be out of office and leave these difficulties to Mr. Chamberlain. In answer, the resolutions committed the Party to "fully equipping" the country for defence, and specifically to continuing rearmament, and demanded to be allowed to form a new Government. The conference adopted a "Short Programme" which, though its proposals were moderate and limited, was a more immediately practical programme than others which had preceded it, after *Labour and the New Social Order* had been published in 1918. It read less stirringly than *For Socialism and Peace*, adopted in 1934, but it consisted of proposals which a Labour Government would have to carry out in the first few years of office or be convicted of bad faith. Equipped with these decisions, the Labour Party felt it could deal drastically with its dissidents.

The United Front was formally condemned; as a propaganda, it did in fact vanish. Two of its constituents dropped out: the Socialist League had already dissolved and the I.L.P. declined to take part in the agitation which succeeded it. For, although any hope of final success ended when the Labour Party decided to walk alone, the agitation was in effect continued under another name, the "Popular Front." The Communist Party and its "fellow-travellers," Sir Stafford Cripps and his not inconsiderable following within the Labour Party, a number of local Liberals and members of the Co-operative Party supplied its strength. But the Labour Party refused equally firmly to accept the Popular Front, and at the beginning of 1939 expelled Sir Stafford Cripps and certain of his colleagues for refusing to abandon it.

No opportunity thus was to be given for any political change: but none of those who voted for the 1937 resolutions suspected that the Parliament whose actions so alarmed them would not face the electors until after the final disaster had come.

Nor was there much more opportunity for economic change. The provision of work was still regarded as a matter for the employers, and the National Governments made only a few half-hearted attempts to reduce unemployment by instituting public works or by subsidizing a few trades which were in special difficulties. Economists were, indeed, for the most part gradually becoming converts to the notion, once the monopoly of Socialists with their slogan of "the right to work," that it was the State's business to ensure that employment should be available for all who needed it. But this idea, energetically advocated by J. M. Keynes, met with dogged resistance in the minds of the politicians and civil servants. The Treasury set its face against public works designed to increase employment, on the absurd ground that any rise in the volume of public "investment" would necessarily involve an equal fall in private "investment," and would thus leave total employment unchanged; and both Treasury officials and politicians continued to insist on the indispensability of a balanced budget, even at the cost of making unemployment worse.

Of course, one reason why there was strong opposition to public works and to the acceptance by Governments of any responsibility for maintaining the level of employment was the fear, among the defenders of "private enterprise," that these things would lead to increased public economic activity and to an invasion by the State of the fields traditionally reserved for profit-making. Some small extensions of public enterprise did occur between the wars, not chiefly for the purpose of diminishing unemployment but rather because it became plain that there was no other way of securing efficient service. The London Passenger Transport Board, under an Act originally promoted by the second Labour Government but made law under its successor, took over the passenger transport services of the metropolitan area; and the building of the electricity "Grid" for main-line transmission of electric power was entrusted, also by a Conservative Government, to a Central Electricity Board publicly appointed and raising its capital in the form of bonds carrying no control over its working. The importance of these developments lay less in what they actually accomplished than in their setting up a new model for publicly administered concerns. This new model, usually called the "Public Corporation," provided a form of public management which did not mean putting socialized industries or services under the bureaucratic control of Government departments or of the Treasury, but equipped them with a more businesslike and flexible form of management, and, thus met the objection felt by so many people to socialization on the score of bureaucracy. There were differences of opinion about the forms which such Corporations should take, and in particular about workers' representation on them; but in general both the Labour Party and the Trade Unions favoured the method of the Public Corporation as against civil service control. Socialist programmes of nationalization were re-cast so as to provide for the taking over of the industries affected by them by Public Corporations responsible to the Government and linked together by a general planning authority acting directly under the Cabinet.

Socialization in this form was no more pleasing to most advocates of capitalist enterprise than in any other. Indeed, the appearance of this kind of public enterprise even tended to stiffen the capitalist resistance. The mines were not taken over, despite the obvious inefficiency of their conduct under the colliery owners. The iron and steel industry, in order to save it from its difficulties, was converted not into a Public Corporation but into a private monopoly licensed to exploit the public. It was, however, well understood that the State, if it were once to assume the responsibility for the level of employment, could hardly avoid assuming therewith a large measure of responsibility for ensuring the efficiency of industry: and all who wanted to avoid such State intervention in the affairs of profit-making naturally fought against the measures which alone could have cured the severe unemployment of the years between the wars.

Eventually, however, expenditure on rearmament began to bring life back to parts of the "special areas." The sums voted by Parliament from 1937 onwards seemed, at the time, inconceivably large; and a great part went eventually to the coal and metal industries, the most depressed. Nor were British Government orders all: British industry had already been equipping the Nazis' forces and continued, to the end, enthusiastically to send out essential raw materials for the *Wehrmacht* and *Luftwaffe*: indeed, when Sir Thomas Inskip was appointed to co-ordinate the Government's programme it was announced that his care would be not to disturb unnecessarily existing channels of trade. The vast stagnant pools of unemployment were disturbed and partly drained by the new orders. The shipyards closed by the owners' reorganization were by no means all restored—some were irrecoverable—but pits were reopened, and engineers and steelworkers found jobs again. Company unions withered as the workers found they could choose without fear of the sack. Trade union membership began to climb again; at the end of 1938 it had passed six millions. Efforts, not without success, were made to extend trade unionism in the most dangerously neglected areas—the mass-production industries and the distributive trades, with their high proportion of unskilled and female labour. As profits rose, wage increases were granted, often by negotiation and without a strike. Strikes did indeed, occur: in many cases leading to trade union recognition for the first time or, as in the case of engineering apprentices, to recognition of the right to speak for a class previously unrepresented. But the division between Left and Right here also did its work: the London busmen's strike, for example, though duly called by Ernest Bevin's Transport and General Workers' Union, was settled over the heads of the busmen's committee, which was dismissed by the Union, and some of its members expelled for acting under Communist influence. A rival union, patronized by W. J. Brown of the Civil Service Clerical Association, was founded in protest.

The history of Britain between 1931 and 1939 presented most of the features of the history of the Continental countries which fell victims to Fascism, but always in a much less marked degree. Disputes over Communism, and between Left and Right, racked the working-class organizations, but did not split them, as in Germany. Pacifism had its supporters, but it did not half-paralyse the Labour Party, as it did the French Socialist Party. Members of the governing class visited Germany and Italy, and slavered their admiration; but few fell to the level of the Petainists. Britain was also to have a Fascist movement, but on a small and manageable scale.

In 1934, 1935 and 1936 the British Union of Fascists, with Sir Oswald Mosley as leader, sprang out of insignificance. Lavishly supplied with money, complete with blackshirt army, anti-semitic propaganda, and other dangerous and brutal devices of Continental Fascism, it had some appeal for the idle, reckless, venal, savage or despairing of all classes—including some of the working class. Violent assaults were made on opponents, or even peaceful questioners, and that in the most public places, as at Olympia in June 1934, or the Albert Hall in March 1936. Police protection could rarely be secured: in the latter case, indeed, the police who failed to intervene were occupied in charging and batoning a peaceful anti-Fascist meeting not far away in Thurloe Square. An apparent check was given to the Fascist movement in 1936 by the passing of the Public Order Act, forbidding the wearing of uniforms by private armies. But experience of the Act showed that it had other uses. For another of the marked characteristics of this period was a steady invasion of the civil liberties of the individual: though the spectacle of the parades of bravoes in their black shirts was ended by this Act, the extensive powers of prohibition or forcible closing of meetings or processions were used more widely against critics of the Government policy, who had no strong Trade Union behind them. The Government had also armed itself with exceptional powers by passing, in 1934, the Incitement to Disaffection Act which made it an offence to possess any document the circulation of which to members of the forces would have been an offence if it had been so circulated. It was also able to use the ample but partly dormant powers of the Official Secrets Act as revised in 1920, and the Trade Unions Act of 1927, with the all-embracing Emergency Powers Act of 1920 in reserve at need. Suppression of criticism, raiding of union halls and even dances, and so forth, were both more easy and more frequent. Attacks were rarely made on official Labour organizations, but left-wing Socialists and Communists were regarded as fair game.

Moreover, possibly under impulse from above, the behaviour of the police in many districts became noticeably worse. Individuals were manhandled, anti-Fascist crowds attacked, and cases fabricated. A newly founded organization, the National Council of Civil Liberties, under the chairmanship of Henry Nevinson and with a diligent and fearless secretary in Ronald Kidd, found its attention almost wholly occupied in contesting or exposing cases of police interference with liberty.

Compared with what has occurred since and was occurring even then on the Continent—compared even with the régime of Pitt and Castlereagh—the invasions of private liberty seem small and unimportant. So, in themselves, they were. What was not unimportant was that the current of history had changed. For slightly over a hundred years progress had been in the direction of increased personal and civil liberty. Now the reverse was true; civil and personal liberty, so far from being extended, was cautiously and continually diminished.

Personal liberty had declined also in ways for which the State was not responsible. Judicial interpretation of the law of civil libel, over a period of years, had so restricted editors that the freedom of personal comment of Cobbett's *Political*

Register seems unbelievable to one who reads it to-day. Printers and distributors were mulcted in "damages" (though plaintiffs were rarely required to prove damage) and thus were compelled to constitute themselves amateur censors: insurance against libel could usually only be secured by signing over to the insurance company the right to compromise any action. In this period damages were granted to a singer whose singing was adversely criticized by a critic, and to a littérateur whose book received an unfavourable review. Late in 1937 the Duke of Windsor was granted agreed damages which were not disclosed for a discussion of the circumstances of his abdication: till then, it had been assumed that the courts would sustain discussions in good faith of questions of political importance.

In the inter-war period two new inventions had risen to rival the Press as means of discussion and communication. To neither of them did the principle of free speech apply. The British Broadcasting Corporation was set up in 1926 under a Government Charter renewed in 1936. As the years passed on, its programmes showed more and more the impress of its Director-General (till 1938 Sir J. C. W. Reith, later Lord Reith). Its influence was undoubtedly educative, especially in music: the technical progress made, as for example in television, was far from negligible. But nothing in its Charter required it to provide a channel for free opinion; and it did not. Apart from its strong, one-sided intervention in the General Strike of 1926, it continually played for what the authorities regarded as safety. A critic who mentioned Joyce's *Ulysses* and a commentator on foreign affairs whose views were not wholly orthodox were both equally smartly shown the door: before long the texts of all broadcasts were censored by the Corporation beforehand.

The first World War had caused Hollywood to become the centre of the film industry, and the majority of films shown in Britain were fairly rigorously censored before arrival by the activities of the Hays office. Nevertheless, a further censorship was imposed. Under an Act of 1909, intended to prevent fires, local authorities were empowered to make regulations for cinemas. By a wide but unchallenged interpretation of this, local authorities assumed the power of censorship which they delegated to a private "British Board of Film Censors," set up by the trade and not subject to public control or inquiry. Its first head was T. P. O'Connor, the Roman Catholic M.P., its second Edward Shortt, Lloyd George's Home Secretary in the 'twenties, its third Lord Tyrrell, a Roman Catholic peer. Occasionally some of its bans, such as that on the anti-Fascist film *Professor Mamlock*, were reversed by the Labour London County Council; but for the most part its vetoes were universally obeyed.

But after 1937 there were few whose minds were turned to local and domestic tyrannies. The shadow of advancing Nazism darkened the whole scene. None of the public knew what use had been made of the considerable sums voted for defence, and how inadequate for their task British defences really were. Disquiet centred upon the Government tenderness to the Axis aggressions, which amounted almost to indulgence. China, Abyssinia, Albania, Spain and Austria formed a terrifying list of countries entitled to British aid under treaty or the Covenant which had been allowed, or actively helped, to fall under partial or total Axis control. The German army and air force, and even the navy, had been rebuilt with British materials. Possible Allies had been repelled: the League was a ruin and Russia was held at arm's length. It seemed, in the autumn of 1938 when Germany manufactured a crisis over Czechoslovakia, that a new war might be breaking out with Britain half-armed and almost without Allies. This is not a history of the British governing class, and there is no place to discuss the process by which Mr. Chamberlain averted war and handed over yet one more country to Hitler; nor how later a guarantee was given to Poland and Rumania, and a belated approach to Russia bungled. A small part of the Conservative Party, whose spokesman was Winston Churchill, now shared the alarm of the opposition: though there was no formal collaboration, there were individual communications, and in time there might have been a closer co-operation. But time was not allowed, and the Conservative majority was immovable.

In August 1939 Hitler attacked Poland. He may have counted on a fresh repetition of the now familiar surrender by Britain;

ᶦf so, he was not alone. "I speak what is in my heart at this moment," said Arthur Greenwood for the Labour Party on September 2, "I am gravely disturbed. An act of aggression took place thirty-eight hours ago. The moment that act of aggression took place, one of the most important treaties of modern times automatically came into operation. There may be reasons why instant action was not taken . . . but there are many of us on all sides of this House who view with the gravest concern the fact that hours went by and news came of bombing and news to-day of an intensification of it; and I wonder how long we are prepared to vacillate."

When it was clear that a decision had been taken to resist Nazism, and that war was inevitable, there was no doubt or hesitation in any part of the people of Britain.

BRITAIN IN 1939

CHAPTER XLVII

BRITISH IMPERIALISM
IN THE TWENTIETH CENTURY

WE began this book with an attempt to describe Great Britain as it was two centuries ago, when the population was probably about 8,000,000, and no town except London and Bristol had more than 50,000 inhabitants. We do not propose to repeat the device of sending an imaginary traveller journeying round the country to-day; for the understanding of modern Britain depends at least as much on knowing the rest of the world as on visualizing the internal condition of the country. We propose, therefore, to give our closing survey a different form, and to begin by looking at Great Britain, not merely as the home of 46,000,000 people, but as the capital of an Empire of well over 500,000,000. We propose, moreover, to make this survey an account of Great Britain as it was before the outbreak of war in 1939. It would be of small profit to present a picture of the abnormalities of the British economic situation during the war years; and the time has not yet come for an objective appraisal of the position of Great Britain in the economy of nations after the second World War.

Take any map that shows the great trade routes of the world, and you see at once how many of them converge upon Great Britain. Across the North Atlantic to Canada and the United States, further south by the West Indies to the Panama Canal and the west coast of the Americas, and further south again to the Guianas, Brazil, Argentina and round the tip of the Continent, British ships ply ceaselessly, carrying the goods of many nations. Another route goes past Spain and West Africa down to the Cape, whence ships can voyage right to

CP: X

Australia across the empty southern sea. But most important of all, in relation to Great Britain's imperial position, is the Mediterranean route, through the Suez Canal to Britain's Indian Empire and to the Far East, and to Australia and New Zealand. If we seek an analogy to the roads and rivers and

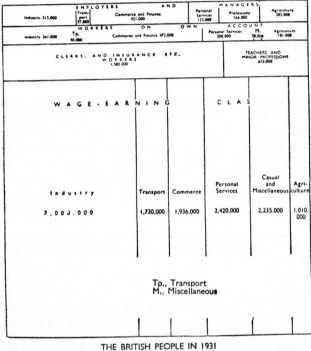

THE BRITISH PEOPLE IN 1931
(occupied population only. Approximate distribution by classes and occupations)

canals of eighteenth-century England, we must find it above all else in these great ocean routes.

For the outstanding fact of Britain of 1939 was its dependence on the rest of the world. In 1746 this island, though even then the richer classes drew large advantages from foreign trade, could have been cut off from all the rest of the world without disaster. But the Britain of 1939, if it had been cut off even for a short time, would have starved. Only about one-third of the total food supply was by this time produced at home. Two-thirds were imported, either from the British Colonies and Dominions, which now provided the larger share, or from foreign countries. Moreover, British industry depended not only on overseas markets for coal and manufactured goods, but also on supplies of raw materials as well as foodstuffs from overseas. On the average of the three years 1936–8 British imports of foodstuffs, drink and tobacco cost £430,000,000 and imports of raw materials about £270,000,000, or, after deducting re-exports not worked up in the country, £237,000,000: and in addition most of the £220,000,000 of imported manufactures were in fact half-finished goods destined for further treatment in British factories.

This dependence on the outside world conditioned the entire British system. It exposed Great Britain to immense danger in time of war, unless British naval supremacy sufficed to keep the sea-routes effectively open in face of air and submarine attack. Great Britain must have either peace, or supremacy at sea, or the people could not be kept alive. Great Britain must have foreign trade, both to get the means of buying food, and to keep the people employed in the great industries which depended either on exports or on imported materials. Self-sufficiency, or some approach to it, might be possible for the Soviet Union, with its vast diversity and extent. It might be possible for the United States, though not without great dislocation. Even Germany showed, under the Nazis, that it was possible to go some way towards it, though not without substantial sacrifices in standards of welfare or the imposition of drastic controls on every aspect of the national economic life. But for Great Britain self-sufficiency, or any substantial decrease of dependence on the rest of the world, simply could not be contemplated. It would mean ruin, starvation, a complete reconstruction of the entire way of living—and a population cut down even more drastically than it was in process of being cut down by the decline in fertility.

Everybody in Great Britain knew this. It affected the entire British people's view of life. It explained the hold of imperialism upon the mind of the people; it explained the Labour Party's difficulties in formulating a Socialist policy towards the

Empire. In a world securely at peace, the British people might live well by bartering its products for those of other countries, and not concern itself about empire, or the security of trade-routes, or naval strength. But in a world threatened by war it could not. It must keep thinking about its next meal—about the assurance that food imports would continue to reach its harbours.

As long as the world, or most of it, remained at peace, there was no difficulty about food, or about imports of materials for British industry. The producers of these goods in other countries were eager to sell, and Great Britain was for them a vitally important market. Moreover, Great Britain could afford to buy, not only by offering exports in exchange, but also because British capitalists owned vast investments abroad, on which foreigners had to pay them interest or dividends, and because British shipping still did much carrying of goods for foreigners, who had to pay for the service, though the British proportion of the world's carrying trade had never recovered the level at which it stood before 1914. The sums derived from these sources—Britain's "invisible exports" as they are called—could be used to pay for imports. On the average of the three years 1936–8 British net imports were valued at about £866,000,000 and British net exports at £478,000,000 (these figures exclude about £66,000,000 of re-exports, which of course do not affect the balance). The difference was made up by the "invisible exports" without which it would have been impossible to go on importing on anything like the same scale. Great Britain was, in fact, still a great "creditor country"; and a large proportion of British foreign investments was in the British Empire. That, too, helps to explain the tenacity of British imperialism.

But it involved a further dependence. Men could not help wondering, in view of the unsettled state of the world between the wars, what would happen if the British debtors overseas were to refuse to go on paying the British capitalists? It would have been impossible under the prevailing conditions to increase current exports nearly enough to meet the loss. Imports would have had to be drastically cut down—to what could still be paid for with exports and out of the earnings of

British shipping, which were themselves by no means what they had been. The British standard of living would have suffered a catastrophic fall.

This was none the less true, though these foreign investments belonged to British capitalists and not to the British workers. For the capitalists bought the goods from abroad, and then sold them to the workers—after taking their toll of profit, of course. The workers got the money to buy them from their wages; and, if these were spent largely on imported goods, there was the less left to spend on home products. Home industry was therefore diverted to producing luxury goods for the rich to buy and to the making of such exports as a world given over to Protectionism could be induced to admit.

Actually, in the inter-war world, imports—and especially imported foodstuffs—were usually cheap in relation to other goods. They became very cheap during the years of world crisis after 1929, when the food producers found themselves with vast stocks, which they had to sell off at any price. That was why, during these years, the standard of living in Great Britain—except for the two millions or so who were unemployed and the millions more who were on short time—actually rose instead of falling. Wholesale food prices came tumbling down, and retail prices had to come down after them—though not so far. Real wages, for workers in full employment, rose by 10 per cent or more between 1929 and 1933—thereafter first to fall slightly as prices rose again with partial world economic recovery, and then to remain fairly stable up to the outbreak of war in 1939. This one fact largely explains why, except in the depressed areas, the world slump caused much less hardship in Great Britain than in most other countries. Food was cheap; and owing to British investments abroad there was no need to restrict food purchases when exports fell off. It was actually possible to buy more, with less money.

What happened during these years was, in effect, that the British capitalists stopped making new investments abroad. Up to the slump only a part of the return on capital and shipping from overseas was spent on imports; the rest was invested, so that the total British holdings of capital overseas increased year by year. They fell indeed between 1914 and 1918, when money holdings were sold to Americans in order to pay for war supplies. But after 1918 the process of foreign investment by British capitalists started again, though it never reached the heights attained before the first World War. It continued up to the world slump, and then it ceased. Nor was it ever renewed up to 1939: on the contrary, in the later 'thirties Great Britain, once the world's chief producer of exported capital, became a re-importer, as investments which fell due for repayment at maturity went unrenewed. In 1939 the tribute British capitalists drew from foreign countries was used in buying imports. Nor did this tribute suffice to cover the need. There was an annual deficit of £50,000,000 or £60,000,000 on the current balance of payments. Not merely the income from British overseas investments but the gradual using up of the capital appeared to have become a necessary constituent of the British standard of life.

This change was the outcome not merely of the world slump, but of the changed situation of British industry in the world. In the nineteenth century British industry was supreme. It could pick and choose its markets, lend promising countries (from the standpoint of profit-making) the money for economic development, and then get its money back by selling them railway rails and engines, power plant, and a thousand other things. It had, till late in the century, no serious rivals in the markets of the world. Accordingly, British industry specialized on producing for the world market. The British cotton, woollen and worsted, coal, steel, engineering and shipbuilding industries were all developed on a far larger scale than was needed for supplying the population at home. The cotton industry exported more than four-fifths of its total product, the woollen industry more than half, the machinery trades much the same proportion, and even the coal industry over a quarter.

As we have seen, for a long time before 1914 the British industrialists had met with growing competition; above all from Germany, and in American markets from the United States. But up to 1914 there appeared to be room for all, in a rapidly developing world market sustained by loans from the richer countries. British exports in 1913 were larger than they had ever been. British capitalism was booming, even if the workers were not getting their share. But after 1918 British exports never regained their old prosperity. This was largely because, during the War, British industry had been too busy making war supplies to keep up exports to other countries, which were therefore compelled to look elsewhere, or to turn to and supply their own needs.

In particular there was a huge development of textile production in India and the Far East, not only in modern factories, but also, in India and China, by the revival of domestic weaving. Japan leapt right to the front as a producer, first of cheap textiles, and soon of all manner of manufactured goods for the world market. The Japanese capitalists, strongly organized and protected by the State, used cheap factory labour upon the most modern machines and a highly efficient selling system, which was in strong contrast to Lancashire's obsolete methods, to defeat their rivals. The trade in cheap cotton goods was largely lost by Lancashire to the Far Eastern producers, never to be regained. By 1930 Lancashire's exports of cotton piece-goods were only about one-third of the exports of 1913. They sank even lower in the 'thirties.

Moreover, countries which had set out during the War to build up industries of their own to replace imports from Great Britain were not prepared after 1918 to go back to the old conditions. The post-war world, even before the great slump, was very much more protectionist than the world of 1913. There were tariffs everywhere, except in Great Britain and Holland; and year by year tariffs rose higher, at any rate in relation to current prices, despite all attempts to bring them down by means of World Economic Conferences and the like. Great Britain had to readjust its economic system to a smaller proportion of exports; and persistent unemployment in the exporting industries was one of the results. Throughout the whole inter-war period registered unemployment in Great Britain never sank appreciably below a million. In most years, even before 1931, it was a good deal more.

Nevertheless, Great Britain remained, and remained up to 1939, a very wealthy country. Its workers were highly skilled and productive, its capital equipment (despite some black spots of obsolescence) on the whole abundant and not obviously inefficient; its financial organization was still notably strong and expert in extracting profits from money-lending to the rest of the world, and its capitalists, as we have seen, were still able to levy a large tribute on account of their investments overseas. The serious weaknesses which formed the other side of this picture were, first, a failure to devise effective means of organizing the sale of exports, secondly, a tendency on the part of many industries, including some of the most important, to resort to policies of restricted output and high prices instead of going all out to lower costs of production in order to enlarge the market, and thirdly, a certain slackness and discouragement which infected the attitudes not only of business men but even more of those responsible for the direction of high economic and political policy. From the standpoint of profit-making, there was nothing very much amiss with British industry except in the depressed industries and areas, whose condition had been largely made up for by the growth elsewhere of new industries and services catering mainly for the home market. But, from the standpoint of the export trades and of the consuming public, there was a good deal amiss; and British industrialism was notably lacking in the enterprise and adaptability which had been its outstanding characteristics in the nineteenth century.

Moreover, the position of British industry, and of British capitalism, had grown very much more precarious than it used to be. Already the "invisible exports" were being consumed in buying imports, and were not enough to bridge the gap. What was to happen if either exports of British goods fell off still further, or overseas peoples got tired of paying tribute to British capitalists, and wiped off their foreign debts, as Russia had done after the Revolution of 1917? How, if that happened, could imports be paid for, or the standard of living be maintained? Or, if it could not, how would the working-class movement react when it began seriously to fall? Or, again, what would be the consequence of another war?

The effect of these uncertainties was to drive British capitalism into seeking closer economic alliances with countries which could be persuaded to go on buying British goods. The downfall of Free Trade in 1931–2 was hastened by the economic crisis; but it would have come without it. The return to Protectionism was due fundamentally to the desire of British capitalists both to keep the home market to themselves as an offset against the loss of foreign sales, and to strike a bargain with the countries of the Empire—and to a smaller extent with other countries—for preferential treatment of British goods. Empire markets, already, since Chamberlain's day, sheltered to some extent by preferential tariffs, shrank less in the inter-war years than most foreign markets, in which no similar advantage could be claimed. But the question soon arose whether the Dominions would go on admitting British goods on favoured terms unless they were given reciprocal advantages? British capitalists feared not; and at Ottawa in 1932 the Dominions profited by their fears to strike a very satisfactory bargain for themselves.

Thus, between the wars, British imperialism became more important than ever to British capitalism. But there were hungry eyes on the British Empire—the hungrier because the victors of 1918 had despoiled the vanquished of their colonial territories. The Empire became a source of weakness as well as strength; for it now involved the perpetual menace of war. Nor could it be exploited with the old freedom. The Dominions used the opportunity of the first World War to complete their political emancipation; even in India tariff autonomy had to be granted in view of the strong demands of Indian capitalism, which could use Indian nationalism to browbeat Great Britain into concessions. The Colonial Empire remained; but there two difficulties arose. The traditional British policy in the Colonies had been that of the Open Door; the attempt to convert them into preserves for British manufacturers caused international complications and provoked widespread unrest among the colonial peoples.

Imperialism, in its developing phases—such as the phase through which it was passing in Japan before 1939—is essentially expansionist and aggressive. But British imperialism in the inter-war period was long past this stage of evolution. It was pacific, intent on holding its past conquests and not on making new ones, and consciously intent to maintain peace because war threatened its very existence. Who could suppose that at the end of another world war, whatever its outcome, Great Britain would still be able to govern India, or be still in receipt of tribute from nearly all the world? British capitalists were very well aware that they stood only to lose from the entanglement of Great Britain in a new world war; and they were ready to tolerate a good many blows to British prestige sooner than become involved in one. This alone can explain the course of British foreign policy in face of the rise of Fascism in Europe and of aggressive imperialism in Japan. The governing groups in Great Britain dared not risk war, if they could avoid it by any means short of a surrender of really essential interests. And they were prepared to let go things which they would have treated unhesitatingly as vital at any time before Rome and Berlin had gone into partnership to blackmail them.

In face of the decline in British exports and in investment overseas, British industry was compelled to concentrate to an increasing extent on the home market—a tendency both leading to and accentuated by the abandonment of Free Trade. The greatly increased technical efficiency of industry and the advance of mass-production methods on the one hand and the relative cheapening of essential foodstuffs on the other co-operated to make possible a big development of new types of demand—for goods just above the level of necessaries, but capable of being greatly cheapened as output is increased. In 1924 it took 203,000 workers in the motor industry to produce 147,000 cars; in 1936 only 314,000 workers were able to produce 461,000. Gramophones, wireless-sets, artificial silk goods, and many other "consumers' goods" of semi-luxury type were sold in rapidly growing quantities, and there was at the same time a greatly increased demand for "services," resulting in the multiplication of restaurants, cinemas and other places of amusement, laundries, swimming-pools, and so on. The growth of urban populations and the spread of suburbs over much larger areas, especially in the south of England, increased the demand both for shopping-centres and for means of public transport.

Thus there was in pre-war Britain an illusory appearance of increasing prosperity for large sections of the population, existing side by side with a decline in the older staple industries and the stagnation of areas which had once been great centres of highly developed production. These paradoxes could exist because Great Britain was in a position not only to draw tribute in the form of interest and dividends from the rest of the world, but also, by selling off old overseas investments and repatriating the proceeds, to carry a deficit on the current balance of payments over a long period of years. There was nothing alarming in an annual repatriation of capital at the rate of £50,000,000 or £60,000,000 a year when British overseas investments were still reckoned in thousands of millions. There was disquietude no doubt at the growth of the "adverse balance," and orthodox financiers were upset about it; but it involved no immediate threat to the British standard of living. For such a threat to develop in any immediate sense, there had to be a much larger loss of income from overseas than was involved in meeting the current deficit. This loss, of course, was actually incurred after 1939, but we are not dealing in this chapter with the effects of the second World War on Great Britain's economic position and prospects.

CHAPTER XLVIII

POPULATION AND ECONOMIC STRUCTURE

THE consequence of these developments was a remarkable change in the make-up of the industrial system. This can be seen at a glance from the change in the distribution of the insured population in Great Britain in recent years. Between 1923 and 1937—the last "normal" pre-war year—the number of insured workers rose by about 2,200,000. Over the same period the number of workers in the distributive trades alone increased by 807,000, and the numbers engaged in public and private "services," as distinct from productive industries, by 560,000. Building and the construction of public works (largely roads) absorbed 485,000 additional workers, and transport 119,000. As against these increases, all forms of mining and manufacture together had only 219,000 more workers in 1937 than in 1923; and even these totals include those who were unemployed. The number of miners actually fell by 374,000; and the more depressed sections of the textile and metal industries had 437,000 fewer insured workers in 1937 than in 1923. These figures again include the unemployed.

Let us put the situation in another way. In 1923, out of every 100 insured workers, approximately 51 were in manufacturing industries and 12 in mines; 7 were builders; 20 were engaged in distribution, commerce and transport; and 10 were in the "services," public and private. In 1937 the numbers in manufacture had fallen to 47, and in mines to 7; builders had increased to 10, workers in distribution, commerce and transport to 24, and workers in the "services" to 12.

Or take the wide category of all "occupied persons," including employers, managers, "independent" workers, and workers in uninsured occupations, among whom domestic servants form the largest group. In 1939, out of about 23,000,000 "occupied" persons, about 9,500,000 were in manufacturing industries, 1,100,000 in mining and quarrying, 1,000,000 in agriculture and forestry, 70,000 in fishing—making in all 11,700,000 in "productive" industries in the widest sense. About 1,500,000 were in transport and communications, about 3,700,000 in distribution, commerce and finance, about 2,900,000 in personal, mainly domestic, service, and about 3,200,000 in other "non-productive" services, including public administration, the professions, and the armed forces. Thus, "services," as a whole, accounted for about 11,300,000, or 49 per cent of the total, and "productive" for 51 per cent. Nearly half the occupied population of Great Britain was in "services" as against "productive" industries. In fact, many more were not directly "producing"; for transport workers, clerks, and other persons attached to "productive" industries we have counted in with the industries in connection with which they worked.

These changes are commonly regarded as signs of a rising

standard of living; and so, to a certain extent, they were. The growth of productivity in many consumers' trades allowed those who were able to find employment to improve their living conditions; and the cheapness of imports had a similar effect. But the correlative of this shift in industry was the existence of a mass of destitution in the areas given over to the occupations which were declining. London and Birmingham may have prospered; but there were years upon years of misery for the unwanted miners of South Wales and Durham, the shipbuilders of the Clyde and Tyne, the cotton operatives of Lancashire, and other groups dependent largely on export or on the "heavy" industries. In 1936 and 1937 intensive rearmament did something to tip the balance back in favour of the depressed areas. But even at the end of 1937—the most prosperous of pre-war years—the unemployment percentage was 21 in Wales, 16 in the Northern region, and 14½ in Scotland, as against 7 in the Midlands and only 6 in Greater London.

In effect, there appeared in inter-War Britain a new "submerged tenth." The dire poverty of the less-skilled workers in many parts of the country was to some extent diminished, though the Social Surveys of London, Liverpool, and other towns round about 1929 showed that there remained perhaps 10 per cent of the urban population below the "poverty line," even outside the depressed areas. But after the War there appeared, side by side with the "old poor," a "new poor" consisting largely not of "casuals" or unskilled labourers, but of skilled workers whose skill had been made useless by the processes of industrial change. These unfortunates were not numerous enough—though there were at least half a million of them, *plus* their dependants—to insist on their wrongs being redressed. They were crowded in certain parts of the country where neither had the well-to-do to live among them nor the more fortunate workers in the other areas to be made daily conscious of their plight by actual contact. What was the use of rioting in South Wales, or of making orderly demonstrations? Who would take notice of them? And when the unemployed of the distressed districts tried "hunger marching" on London the leaders of Trade Unionism and of the Labour

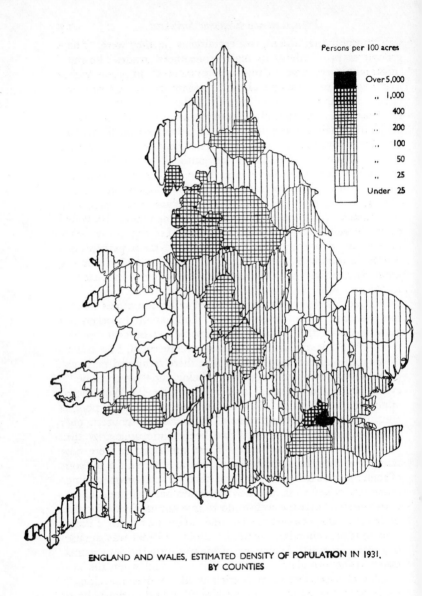

Persons per 100 acres

Over 5,000
„ 1,000
„ 400
„ 200
„ 100
„ 50
„ 25
Under 25

ENGLAND AND WALES, ESTIMATED DENSITY OF POPULATION IN 1931,
BY COUNTIES

Party disavowed them, and the police stood ready, at the Government's orders, to prevent them from making "scenes." Sometimes they were prevented from moving by the threat of having their unemployment benefit or relief payments stopped if they did.

Inevitably, the shift in industry weakened Trade Unionism, which had its strongholds chiefly in the old skilled trades and in the depressed areas. The Trades Union Congress had 6,500,000 affiliated members in 1920, and only 3,300,000 in 1934, whereafter membership rose slowly as trade revived, but was still under 5,000,000 in 1939. The workers in the growing trades were much more difficult to organize than miners, or cotton operatives, or engineers. The proportion of skilled manual workers was much smaller; the new trades employed many more women, most of whom expected to retire on marriage, and many more merely dexterous machine-minders, who could shift with relative ease from one occupation to another. The old-style skilled craftsman had taken five or seven years to learn his trade as an apprentice; and he had remained in it for life. The new trades could be learnt in a few hours or days; and it was easy for workers who left one mechanized occupation to pick up another.

Where these conditions prevailed, the tight bond of common craftsmanship did not exist to hold the workers together. If one factory was bad, they did not so much put up a collective fight to improve matters, as try individually to find better jobs. Many employers in the new industries were able to ban Trade Unions altogether, or to refuse to recognize any rights of collective bargaining. Moreover, employment grew most rapidly of all among shop assistants, hotel and restaurant workers, and other "black-coat" groups in which Trade Unionism had always been weak or even non-existent. There was unrest, especially in those mass-production factories where the workers were driven at a hotter and hotter pace by big firms determined to cut costs in order to reach a wider market. But the unrest remained spasmodic, and for the most part unorganized and unled.

The changed tempo of highly mechanized production fell with especial severity on the older workers—above all on

those who had been long unemployed. The young, entering
industry for the first time, could learn to stand the pace; the
older men often could not adapt themselves, especially where
they had to shift into totally new occupations, and unlearn the
skill of years. They found jobs, where they found them at all,
only to lose them. They were flung aside by thousands as
useless—to live a bare and dispirited existence upon the
"dole." At the other extreme were young workers who, growing up in a time of slump and in a depressed area, remained
unemployed through the formative years of life, and learnt
the habit of doing nothing, so that they were rejected as
"unemployable" even when trade improved. Among both
young and old there was a disastrous and inhuman waste of
capacity for service, and a vast infliction of unmerited misery.

This deplorable state of affairs was accepted with quite
amazing complacency in official quarters. Governments made
no attempt to remedy it by any fundamental attack on the
problem of unemployment; for trade depressions were still
widely regarded as "acts of God," and Governments accepted
no responsibility for maintaining the national income. Only
Socialists proclaimed the "right to work": only a few non-
socialist economists had begun to preach the Keynesian
doctrine of "full employment."

Yet Britain—the greater part of it—was getting richer, in
spite of the appalling waste of productive power. So fast did
the process of production advance where it was not held up
by the influence of restrictive monopolies; so fast did new
"labour-saving" industries arise to replace the old. The main
body of the employed workers did not revolt; for the most part
it left the workers in the depressed industries to fight their own
battles, or gave them but sporadic help.

Napoleon is said to have called Great Britain "a nation of
shopkeepers"; by 1939 it seemed to be turning into a nation of
shop assistants, clerks, waiters, and machine attendants. But
this meant the sacrifice of the very qualities which had given
the country its pre-eminence in industry. More and more during the nineteenth century Great Britain had become a
country of skilled workers, renowned all over the world for the
high quality of their products. The newer industrial nations

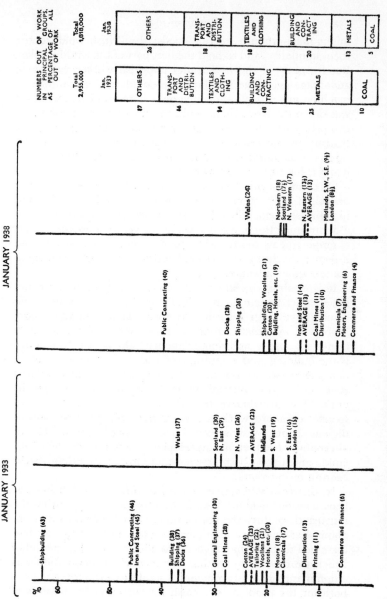

UNEMPLOYMENT. Distribution by Regions and Principal Occupations in January 1933, at the bottom of the slump, and in January 1938

might mass-produce inferior goods; the British would outdo them in quality, and so hold the best part of the world market. But in many of the new trades a British worker was at no advantage over others; a Japanese could tend an automatic machine just as well—and live on a handful of rice while he was doing it. How, then, could the British workman hope to compete with him? Market after market was lost; and the British capitalist answer was protection, which would at any rate save the home market, and perhaps a part of the Empire market, for British-made wares.

Of course, British supremacy did not disappear in every branch of production. There was still a quality market, and in it British goods still held a high place. But this market was a diminishing fraction of the whole. Over an increasing range of employments the British advantage was disappearing; and it seemed likely to be narrowed still more as mass production made further advances.

It is doubtful if, after 1931, any boom in industry could have reduced unemployment in Great Britain to a scale which would have been regarded as tolerable a generation ago. Moreover, were there not limits to the power of the distributive trades to absorb additional labour? On account of active house-building and migration of populations to new areas, new shops had been opened much faster than old ones had been shut down. But this process seemed to be reaching its limit. The distributive trades had, by 1937, almost ceased to take on more workers; and house-building, after a pro-digious boom, was already being slowed down. Unless alternative occupations developed apace, would not un-employment soon become even more formidable than it had been in recent years?

In this connection there comes in a factor which has not been considered so far—the factor of population. During the nineteenth century the population of Great Britain rose from about 10,000,000 to about 37,000,000; and by 1939 it had increased to more than 46,000,000. Throughout the period of which we have been writing, the increase in population was a dominant factor. It provided a naturally expanding market both for the products of British industry and for imports of foodstuffs and raw materials from the countries which bought British exports and received investments from British capitalists, in order to develop their production for the British market. But this tendency was very near to its end: there were few things more certain in 1946 than that in a short time the population of Great Britain would become static, and thereafter would, for some time at least, decline. The first striking warning of this change came during the first World War. Before that time the average annual increase of the population had been about 1 per cent; after it, as we have noticed already, it fell to half that amount. A more exact method of charting the growth or decline of the population is to observe what is called the "net reproduction rate." The figure 1, in this method of calculation, indicates that the population promises to remain steady—that the coming generation is likely to equal in numbers the passing generation unless female fertility rises or falls. According to Mr. David Glass, this figure in the 'eighties and 'nineties had been 1·5 and 1·4, in round figures. That is, there was a marked and regular rise. In the 1930's it fluctuated between 0·8 and 0·75; there was a continual deficiency. Though there was a small rise just before the second World War broke out, it was too slight, and had lasted too short a while, for anyone to be sure that it was a significant rise. There can be little doubt that the second World War will eventually (despite a much-publicized crop of "Bevin babies") be found to have caused a further decline. The population of England and Wales in 1939 was about 41,500,000. This figure was likely to increase for some short while, for the offspring of more prolific generations was in 1946 still with us. But the smaller generation, the generation of little families, was growing up to take their place; however successful plans to revive the population might ultimately be, nothing could now make that generation larger. It was almost certain that by 1951 the population would be something like two millions less than it was twenty years before. In these circumstances, the British market can expand only if the standard of living rises faster than the total population declines. This is already a potent factor in discouraging **the investment** of capital in the Dominions and other food-producing countries; for will a declining population be ready to absorb larger supplies? And it also discourages the expansion of industry at home; for the fewer customers there are, the more difficult it is to improve productive efficiency.

It is, of course, impossible to predict with any confidence how large the population of Great Britain will be in a hundred, or even in fifty years' time. Population forecasts can always be upset by changes in fertility. But for some decades it is possible to make fairly confident estimates on the basis of the existing trends; and hardly anyone believes that the birth rate, which has been falling rapidly in recent years, will rise much in the near future, even if it does not fall further still. It is, to say the least, highly probable that in twenty years' time the population will not exceed 40,000,000.

But what matters is not only the total number of the people, but also the age-distribution. A rapidly falling birth-rate—especially when the death-rate is also falling, though much more slowly—involves a decrease in the proportion of children, and an increase in the proportion of older people. Even by 1941 there were nearly two million fewer children under fifteen, and nearly one million more persons over 65 than in 1931. The change had not greatly affected the number of persons of working age (15–65); indeed, there were rather more of them in 1941 than there were in 1931. But the working population had to support more old people retired from industry on the one hand, and fewer children on the other. The average family was getting smaller, and the number living on savings, old-age pensions or other kinds of allowance, considerably greater.

Consider first the political and then the economic implications of this change, which is already well advanced. Great Britain will have, for some time at any rate, an ageing electorate—and the old are not as a rule venturesome or forward in demanding change. It has always been a charge against parliamentary democracy—and against democratic procedure generally—that it has tended to encourage government by the elderly. But may not this characteristic become even more pronounced if the electors themselves include a growing proportion of elderly people?

Economically, the changing age-composition of the population is also important. Although it will not for some time after the war affect seriously the total number of workers available for employment, it was in 1946 reducing—and likely to go on reducing, even apart from any further raising of the school-leaving age—the supply of juvenile labour, and at the same time increasing the proportion of comparatively elderly workers. Juvenile labour will tend to become scarce, and therefore to command a higher wage. But the present tendency of industry, with its growing use of mechanical processes, is to use more juveniles and to discharge the older workers, who are less adaptable to changing techniques and to modern methods of "speeding-up." What, then, was likely to happen? Would employers adapt their ways, so as to make a greater use of older labour; or would they try to reduce their total demand for workers by still greater mechanization? If, as seemed probable, they attempted the latter method, more drastic measures than would otherwise be necessary would have to be applied to ensure full employment; and failing such measures, there would be more "non-producers" to be maintained out of the product of a reduced number of productive workers; such a situation would inevitably tend to drag down the standard of life—unless the economic system were so altered that capitalism was no longer allowed to call the tune to which the people danced.

It is no part of our purpose to venture into prophecy. We mention these tendencies only because they are already powerfully at work. The Britain we have been describing in the foregoing chapters has been, with all its defects and inhumanities, a "progressive" country—advancing almost continuously in wealth and population. It has been a country of many children and young people—a country in which consuming power has expanded steadily with rising population, even apart from any improvement in the standard of life. But in the Britain of to-day and to-morrow the expansion of industry is bound to depend, not on the number of mouths to be fed and bodies to be clothed, but on rising standards of nutrition and material welfare. This difference colours the entire outlook; it shifts the emphasis from easy profits based on an automatically expanding market to the necessity of making deliberate provision for improved standards of consumption unless production is to decline.

Population trends are important in many other ways. In 1851 approximately half the population of England and Wales lived in urban, and half in rural, areas. By 1901 three-quarters of the population were in towns, and by 1939 more than four-fifths. Six great urban centres in Great Britain, with their immediately surrounding satellite towns, contained one-third of the total population. Greater London alone included one-fifth of all the inhabitants of England and Wales. Cities—and especially great cities with their spreading suburbs—were absorbing more and more people, while the rural areas were being steadily depopulated.

Moreover, population was shifting in a reverse direction from its movement in the Industrial Revolution. The nineteenth century created an industrial system based on coal and iron, and population moved into the Northern counties, South Wales, and the industrial belt of Scotland. But nowadays coal and iron play a much smaller part in settling the location of industry. Electricity or sometimes gas replaces coal as a direct source of power; and the developing trades making finished goods for consumption are attracted rather to ports and to markets—above all, cumulatively, to where the richest aggregations of consumers are to be found. First jobs and then population desert the coal-fields and the older textile areas, and pile up in Greater London, in the Southern counties, and in the Midland area around Birmingham. Between 1921 and 1934 the population of London and the South-East rose by nearly 14 per cent, whereas the population of South Wales fell by 5 per cent. That of the Midlands rose by more than 7 per cent as against 2½ per cent in Lancashire and only 1 per cent in Scotland. This made the Britain of 1939 a good deal more like the Britain of 1746 than it was like, say, the Britain of 1850. But there was a great difference. Population had moved south again; but in 1939 most of it lived and worked in great towns and not in villages.

These towns, moreover, were spreading further and further beyond their older boundaries. The nineteenth century packed its town dwellers into a scanty space. It wasted no money on gardens, and little enough on parks or open spaces, for the "industrious classes." As long as towns remain quite small, and the country is within easy reach, this lack is serious only in its sanitary aspects or to the garden-lover. But, as towns grow, urban congestion comes to matter in other ways as well. The urban slum-dweller—and even the respectable inhabitant of a "good working-class quarter"—is cut right off from access to the green fields, save for a rare excursion involving cost which can ill be met. The towns soon cease to know the country, and come to regard it as something foreign. On its side, the country has always so regarded the town.

But the very pressure of urban congestion and the growth of site values near the centres of huge towns force removal further out. Towns have to spread over larger areas; and improved housing standards lead to increasing decentralization. The outstanding characteristic of inter-war building, both public and private, was the suburban extension of urban areas. Houses were built fewer to the acre, with more garden space and more parks and open spaces. The suburbanites, except in London, were again getting nearer to the country— but at the same time further from the places where they were employed.

This growth of suburbs, however, was largely for the comparatively well-to-do. The private builder did not find it worth his while as a rule to build for the general run of insured workers; and even on municipal estates rents were usually too high for any but the best-paid sections of the working classes. Slum-dwellers, removed by clearance schemes to suburban districts, often drifted back to increase congestion in the remaining slums, because they found the costs of living in the new houses too much for them. Costs of travel to and from work were a formidable expense; and the additional costs of keeping up appearances in a "Council house" were often beyond the means of the labourer. He must live near his work, and he prefers to live where there is a spirit of human "give and take"—so that one family helps another, and is helped in its turn, over lean weeks. The cleared slum-dweller was apt to find the Council estate a bleak and unfriendly place, after the comradeship in poverty of the tenement. The suburbanites often constituted a labour aristocracy of black-coats and superior skilled artisans. The families further down the social scale still crowded together in the older dwellings. The poor still used second-hand houses, even if they were no longer mainly clothed in second-hand garments.

Thus, the growth of towns, in the form which it took after 1918, was part of the process of creating an "aristocracy of labour." The development of suburban housing fitted in with the increase in the proportion of "blackcoats" in the working population as a whole. The worker might get nearer to the green fields again—if he were well enough off to afford the costs of suburban living. But the more the better-paid workers moved into the new suburbs, the more they became differentiated from the poorer sections of the working class.

The Building Society was a well-known Victorian institution; and even in the Victorian age its name had become a misnomer. For the Building Society never builds; it merely advances money to enable its clients to buy their houses on the hire-purchase system. In 1913 there were well over fifteen hundred Building Societies, and between them they lent during the year about £9,000,000. In 1935 there were under a thousand Societies; but they lent over £130,000,000. The Building Society had become, from a position of comparative unimportance, the foremost investment agency in Great Britain. By the end of 1939 the British public owed the Building Societies £700,000,000, and in 1938 the Societies made £137,000,000 of new mortgage advances.

This was an immensely significant social phenomenon. In 1939 the "blackcoats" and the top layer of the manual working class, as well as the middle classes, largely bought their houses, instead of renting them. They became house-owners, or part house-owners, not from any passion for ownership, but because they had to. Houses to rent were not to be had, save for a small minority. Consequently the savings of these classes went largely into house-purchase—on highly unfavourable terms. For the Building Societies not only charged high rates of interest (which incidentally made them excellent investments for the middle classes), but advanced only a proportion of the value of each house, so that, if values were to fall, the house-buyers would have to stand the loss, whereas the Societies would be covered to the full. A substantial fall in house values would sweep away a very large proportion of the savings of the "blackcoats" and the better-off manual workers who were buying their houses on the instalment plan.

These "house-owners," however, had a stake in the country —even if the stake was not really their own. The Building Society was a safeguard against revolution; it gave a section of the employed workers a sense of ownership. This factor came powerfully into play in the General Election of 1931, when every effort was made to scare the respectable people into a belief that their savings were insecure. It might be still more powerful in the future; for the sum owed to Building Societies was nearly doubled between 1931 and 1939.

It is true that the very growth of Building Societies was a sign of rising standards of living; for only the comparatively well-to-do workers could afford to buy houses, even on the instalment plan. But it was a sign rather of differentiation among the employed than of any general advance. The Building Societies grew most in the relatively prosperous South, where the proportion of non-manual workers was largest, and where industry had been immune from the extremes of depression. The workers in the depressed areas could not afford to buy their houses; more often they failed to keep the ownership of houses which they had bought, or begun to buy, in more prosperous times.

CHAPTER XLIX

WAGES IN BRITAIN BETWEEN THE WARS

THE standards of living of the people can be measured either absolutely or relatively—by reference to some standard of human needs, or by comparison between different dates. When the comparative method is used, the practice is to estimate the average money-wages at certain periods, and to relate these to changes in the cost of living, so as to arrive at an estimate of average "real wages." We have made comparisons of this sort at a number of stages in the course of our survey; and these have shown that over the greater part of the nineteenth century real wages rose almost continuously, but that there was a serious setback round about 1900, so that real wages were actually lower in 1914 than they had been when the century began. We have now to take 1914 as our starting-point, and try to see what happened to wages after that date.

During the first World War, as we have seen, wages rose, but lagged for most of the period behind the rise in prices. By the end of 1918 money-wages were approximately double what they had been in August 1914; but the cost of living had risen, according to the official estimate, by 120 per cent, so that wages were still well behind. By the end of 1920, however, wage-rates had advanced to about 175 per cent above the pre-war level, while the cost of living, at its peak point in November, was up by 176 per cent. The two figures thus approximately balanced, though of course some bodies of workers had received advances above and others below the general average. Plainly, then, up to the end of the post-war boom, the workers had made, in terms of real wages, no improvement on their pre-war standards, and nothing had been done to fill up the arrears of wage-improvement which had accumulated between 1900 and 1914.

After 1920 prices fell rapidly in the post-war deflation. On the average of the year 1924, which the Ministry of Labour takes as the standard for later calculations, the cost of living was 75 per cent above that of August 1914. Average wage-rates were from 70 to 75 per cent above that level (the Ministry did not venture on a more exact estimate). Thus, real wages were, if anything, rather lower than before the War.

From 1924 onwards changes in money-wages were relatively small. By the end of 1929 they had fallen further, on the average, by about 1½ per cent, and by 1933, at the bottom of the world slump, the fall had reached 6 per cent. Thereafter money-wages again rose slowly, reaching by the middle of 1937 about the same level as in 1924, or perhaps a little more. But over this period there had been a considerable change in prices. Between 1924 and 1929 the cost of living fell from 75 to 64 per cent above the 1914 level, or by more than 6 per cent. There had been at last a small rise in real wages— between 4 and 5 per cent. From 1929 to 1933 the cost of living fell by $14\frac{1}{2}$ per cent, whereas money-wages fell by only $4\frac{1}{2}$ per cent. Thus, real wages again rose—for those workers who were still able to keep in regular employment in spite of the depression—by about 11 or 12 per cent. But after 1933 the cost of living again advanced, as the world gradually picked up after the great slump. By August 1939 the cost of living was about 11 per cent lower than it had been in 1924, whereas wage-rates were about a few per cent higher. In effect, from 1924 to 1939 real wages had risen by about 15 per cent.

It has, of course, to be remembered throughout that all these calculations are based on comparing the official estimates of the cost of living with the available particulars of *rates* of wages. They take no account of overtime or of piecework earnings above the standard rates on the one hand, or of unemployment and underemployment on the other. They tell us nothing about the total wage-bill of the country, or about the aggregate of working-class purchasing power. They show only the changes in the purchasing power of those workers who, either at time rates of wages or at standardized piece-work earnings, were able to maintain a constant level of employment at the dates compared. Nor, even within these limits, does a general average measure adequately the fortunes of the workers; for it is cold comfort to those whose wages have fallen to be told that workers in other industries have received an advance. We have, therefore, before we can pass any judgment on the fortunes of the people since the War, to take some account of the incidence of both short time and unemployment and to consider, if we can, both the changes in earnings as well as wage-rates and the relative movements of wages in a few of the principal trades.

First, unemployment. In the industries for which figures are available, unemployment in the ten years before the first World War averaged rather over $4\frac{1}{2}$ per cent. Between 1921 and 1926, on a comparable basis, it averaged 12 per cent. These figures are based on Trade Union returns; but for the inter-war period we have also the returns of unemployment among workers under the insurance scheme. For the years 1920–6 these are fractionally higher than the Trade Union returns, but not enough to invalidate comparison. They work out at 12·2 per cent. From 1927 to 1929 unemployment among insured workers averaged about 10 per cent. Thereafter, in the world slump, it rose to 22 per cent in 1933, and then fell to 12 per cent in 1936. In November 1937, despite the boom in certain industries—especially those engaged in rearmament—it was still over 10 per cent, whereas before the War unemployment fell in prosperous years to 2 or 3 per cent. In the course of 1938 it rose to more than 12 per cent; and in January 1939 the unemployment total again exceeded two millions. Over the whole post-war period after 1920, it seemed as if about 10 per cent were the irreducible minimum.

This obviously involved a big reduction in the total earnings of the workers, and, for the post-war period as a whole, meant that up to 1924 real wages, for the entire working class, were appreciably below the pre-war level. At the bottom of the world slump in 1933, though wage-rates were 11 or 12 per cent better in purchasing power than in 1929, there were 22 or 23 per cent of the workers unemployed. Total working-class purchasing power, excluding the "dole," had remained almost unaltered.

Perhaps the best idea of the levels of money-wages can be got from the following table, based mainly on the Ministry of Labour's inquiry into weekly earnings in the single month, October 1938. This inquiry did not cover all trades, and we have space to give only a few representative averages, supplemented, where necessary, from other official sources.

AVERAGE WEEKLY EARNINGS, OCTOBER 1938

s. d.	Men over 21	Women over 18	All Workers
83 0	Printing, Paper and Bookbinding, Motor and Aircraft Manufacture		
80 0	Iron and Steel Manufacture		

AVERAGE WEEKLY EARNINGS, OCTOBER 1938—*contd.*

s. d.	Men over 21	Women over 18	All Workers
73 6	General Engineering		
73 0			Iron and Steel Manufacture
71 0	Transport and Storage		
70 6			Motor Engineering
67 6			Transport and Storage
66 6	Woodworking		
66 0	Building and Contracting. Food, Drink and Tobacco		
65 0	Clothing		
63 0	Public Utility Services		
61 0			Building and Contracting
60 6			General Engineering
59 6			Public Utility Services
57 6	Woollen and Worsted		
56 0			Coal Mining (5 shifts)
55 6			Paper, Printing and Bookbinding. Chemical Trades
52 6			Woodworking
51 0	Cotton		
47 0			Food, Drink and Tobacco
40 0		Motor Engineering	
39 0			Woollen and Worsted
36 6		Transport and Storage	
35 6			Cotton. Clothing Trades
34 0		Paper, Printing and Bookbinding	
33 6		Woodworking. Food, Drink and Tobacco	
33 0		Clothing Trades	
32 0		General Engineering. Miscellaneous Metal Trades	
31 6		Cotton	
31 0		Woollen and Worsted	
28 0		Artificial Silk. Public Utility Services	

It will be seen that, in the autumn of 1938, men over twenty-one averaged from over £4 in the printing and kindred trades to just over £2 10s. in the cotton industry, and that in a number of fairly typical industries, men's earnings averaged from £3 to £3 10s. a week. Women over eighteen ranged from £2 in the motor trade to less than 30s., with a predominant average of from 32s. to 33s. For all workers, including juveniles as well as men and women, the range was from 73s. in the manufacture of iron and steel—an almost wholly male occupation—to 35s. 6d. in the depressed cotton industry. It is notable that coal-mining, which also employs almost exclusively men and boys, comes low down on the list, with an average of only 56s. a week, based on the working of five shifts a week, or on the known figures of earnings averaged over the year.

We may say then, very broadly, that in 1938 the average adult workman was earning from 60s. to 70s. a week, and that the average woman was earning somewhere about 33s. or 34s. Of course, some highly skilled workers got more. In 1936 the linotype operator in London had a jobbing rate of 96s. a week, the London skilled engineer got 68s., and the London tram-driver 71s. to 80s. But such rates were exceptional, and only for London; the comparable rates for Manchester were 86s., 63s. and 60s. to 66s. Less skilled men got a good deal less than the average. Thus, in London engineering labourers averaged 50s. 3d., and labourers employed by local authorities 58s. 8d.; and in Manchester the corresponding wages were 45s. to 47s. and 52s. 9d. Smaller towns had substantially lower rates.

What relation do such wages, even when they can be earned regularly, bear to the "poverty line"? Seebohm Rowntree published in 1937 a rewritten version of his book, *The Human Needs of Labour*. Using the minimum standard of nutrition laid down by the British Medical Association, and making allowance for other factors in the cost of living, he arrived at a *minimum* family budget for a man, wife and three children, of 53s. a week. This is made up of 20s. 6d. for food, 9s. 6d. for rent, 8s. for clothing, 4s. 4d. for fuel and light, 1s. 8d. for household sundries, and 9s. for miscellaneous expenses, including insurances and Trade Union contributions. For a single woman living alone he arrived at a figure of 30s. 9d. These figures are averages, and obviously do not cover the higher costs of rent and travelling in such a place as London. On the other hand, Rowntree laid down, for rural areas, a family minimum of 41s., which compared very unfavourably with the actual rates fixed by the Agricultural Wages Board; for these were in most counties from 31s. to 33s., but ran as low as 28s. 6d. in some parts of Wales.

It is apparent that, on Rowntree's standard, a high proportion of the workers in cotton and coal-mining, and of less-skilled workers in most industries, fell below the *minimum* wage necessary for decent maintenance. So did many of the women workers, including those in the cotton trade and in the public utility services. Yet the Rowntree standard was meant to be a minimum, and it is certain that where earnings fell below it there would be actual going short of the necessaries of life—for people will not, even if they could in theory, lop off all expenses that are not sheer necessities before they cut down their purchases of food.

There were published in the inter-war period a number of Social Surveys of particular towns—London, Liverpool, Southampton and others—in which an attempt was made to ascertain the proportion of the people who were living below the "poverty line." In the Merseyside Survey it was found that nearly a third of the working-class population fell below the Rowntree "line." But most of the social investigators used a poverty line much below Rowntree's—a standard by which practically all sundry expenditures were excluded, and the entire income was assumed to be spent with the fullest economy on the physical necessaries of life. In London in 1929, on a standard of 39s. a week per family, there were found to be from 10 to 12 per cent of all working-class households below the "line." For other towns percentages were estimated as follows (though not for the same dates, or on a fully comparable basis): Merseyside, 17 per cent; Southampton, 20 per cent; Sheffield, 15½ per cent. But even these figures do not tell the whole story; for households below the "poverty line" are very apt to be those with the largest number of children; so that a considerably larger fraction of the child population was plainly going short of the sheer necessaries of healthy living.

Working on a quite different basis—that of average food consumption in families at different income levels—Sir John Orr estimated in 1936 that about half the population was too poor to afford an adequate all-round diet, and that nearly one-third suffered from serious dietetic deficiencies. His calculations showed 30s. a week income per head as necessary for full, and 20s. for reasonable, sufficiency, and at least 15s. per head for even tolerable sufficiency. But nearly a third of the total population, including the well-to-do, had to live on less than 15s. per head.

Of course, it can be answered that these deficiencies in diet have always existed, and that they were probably less serious in 1939 than at any previous date. But that does not alter the fact that they were still serious—and increasingly so if they are considered in relation to the world's capacity to produce. Poverty, in the sense of actual malnutrition, had probably diminished since 1929, in view of the lower price of food; but it is none the less a fact that, even outside the depressed areas, from 20 to 30 per cent of the working class were still living in 1939 below the Rowntree minimum.

It is true that, in certain other respects, besides wages, the conditions of employment had changed to the workers' advantage. In 1918 and 1919 the forty-eight hour week was successfully established as a maximum in most of the organized industries, though much longer hours continued to be worked in many unorganized occupations. The engineers secured a forty-seven hour week, and the builders, on the average of summer and winter, one of about forty-four to forty-five hours. The miners won a seven-hour day (*plus* on the average half an hour for winding time) in 1919; but this was filched from them after the struggle of 1926, when the eight-hour day was reintroduced. From 1930 they worked seven and a half hours (plus the winding time). Except in the case of miners, there had been up to 1937 few changes in working hours since 1919, except in factories which introduced the shift system. In October 1935 it was only in the building trades that any large proportion of the workers were found to be working less than forty-four hours a week—and that was because the survey was made during the winter. In 1939 average hours in most industries were still forty-seven or forty-eight a week. Nor had many industries succeeded in gaining the valuable concession won by the railwaymen after the War—a "guaranteed week," or in other words a guarantee of full employment during the week. In most trades, workmen still lost wages for any part of the week for which the employer did not need their services.

In 1939 the Trade Unions were pressing, not very hopefully, for the forty-hour week, which the French and American workers had to a large extent already secured. With much more immediate hope they were demanding the statutory right to "holidays with pay"—a benefit already secured in some form in 1938 under collective agreement by nearly eight million wage-earners in various trades. On the other hand, successive Governments had still refused, right up to 1939, to ratify even the Forty-eight Hours Convention adopted by the International Labour Organization in 1919—much more so the Forty Hours Convention of 1936-7. In that year, the Holidays with Pay Act enabled Trade Boards and other statutory wage-fixing bodies to make holidays with pay compulsory in the trades under their jurisdiction, but embodied no general enforcement of the reform. Holidays with pay were, however, conceded before the outbreak of war in a number of additional industries; and the movement showed signs of becoming general in the better organized trades even without further legislation. It would obviously require legislation to extend it to the mass of small and unorganized firms.

CHAPTER L

CAPITALIST ORGANIZATION

PROFESSOR BOWLEY has estimated that the national income in Great Britain and Northern Ireland amounted to about £2,022,000,000 in 1911, and to about £4,203,000,000 in 1924. Taking the change in the purchasing power of money at a price rise of about 90 per cent, he reached the conclusion that *real* home-produced income *per head* had hardly changed, and that total income per head had actually fallen by something up to 5 per cent, on account of the fall in the yield from foreign investments. Between 1924 and 1934 he estimated that total national income fell by about 5 per cent, whereas population rose by about 4 per cent. This fall, of course, reflects the effects of the world slump. Professor Bowley has suggested that by 1937 the national income *per head* was roughly back at the 1924 level in money, but that the cost of living had fallen since 1924 by about 20 per cent.

On this showing there was, up to 1924, clearly no possibility of an advance in real wages save at the expense of other forms of income. But the possibility of an improvement did appear, apart from a fall in other incomes, after 1924, on account of the fall in prices during the slump. This tallies with the actual course of real wages, as we have set it out earlier in this section. It is not easy, under the capitalist system, for the workers to raise their real wages at the expense of profits. But where falling prices in the world as a whole raise British purchasing power over food imports the workers can raise their real wages at the expense, not of the British capitalists, but largely of the primary producers in other countries. The same effect can be secured, though usually to a smaller extent, by improvements in efficiency which lower the cost of production. Both between 1875 and 1896 and between 1929 and 1937, the workers owed their rising *real* wage-rates mainly to falling world prices. And on both occasions the fall in prices meant more unemployment as well as more purchasing power for those in regular work.

Of the total income of the British people, rich and poor, how much went in the 1930's to different groups and classes? According to estimates made for many different dates, the wage-bill tends to remain a fairly constant proportion of the national income. It has been put at $38\frac{1}{2}$ per cent for 1911, $39\frac{1}{2}$ per cent for 1924, 37 per cent for 1929 and $40\frac{1}{2}$ per cent for 1931—the two latter figures connoting abnormally high and low levels for profits, first in the boom and then in the slump. For 1938 it has been put, officially, at $37\frac{1}{2}$ per cent. Profits and interest together with rent—that is, incomes from property—have been estimated at roughly 51 per cent in 1911, 40 per cent in 1924, 42 per cent in 1929, and 36 per cent in 1931 and 37 per cent in 1938. But these figures are misleading, unless they are taken in conjunction with the rise in incomes from salaries—from 10½ per cent of the total in 1911 to 20½ per cent in 1924, 21 per cent on 1929, 23½ per cent in 1931 and 24 per cent in 1938. For this extraordinary advance in salaries is to a large extent the result of the growth of joint-stock organization, which transforms private profit-makers, at any rate as to part of their incomes, into salaried directors and managers. On any showing the greater part of the apparent fall in the income of the profit-makers is illusory; they are merely receiving their profits in another form. Doubtless, a substantial part of the increase in salaries is due to the growing numbers of smaller-salary earners; but it is quite impossible to say how much.

That there had been no material change in the distribution of incomes to the benefit of the poor is shown clearly by the statistics of inheritance, and also by estimates of the distribution of the national income, irrespective of the forms in which it is paid, between different income groups. In the 1930's only one person out of every three who died after reaching twenty-five years of age left property worth as much as £100; and even of those who did leave over £100, nearly two-thirds had less than £1,000 to leave. A mere 6½ per cent of those with over £100 left over two-thirds of the total property passing at death, whereas nearly two-thirds of them left only 7 per cent of the property. Nor had these proportions changed appreciably in recent years; they were much the same in 1938–9 as ten years before.

In 1929, out of nearly 19,000,000 persons who had incomes of their own, over 11,500,000 got less than £125 a year, and under 310,000 had over £1,000 a year. One and a half per cent of those in receipt of incomes got 22½ per cent of the total income; and at the other end of the scale 88 per cent of the recipients got only 58 per cent of the income. The class system persisted unchanged, despite the complaints of high taxation made by the rich. Redistributive taxation had done singularly little to affect the extremes of wealth and poverty.

And, since the imposition of the tariff in 1931–2, the tax system had again become more regressive; for taxes on consumption hit the poor harder than the rich.

Precisely corresponding figures are not available for later years, but it is officially estimated that in 1938 the national income was distributed by size-groups in the following way:

MONEY INCOME BY SIZES, 1938

	No. of Incomes thousands	Aggregate Income £ millions	Per Cent of Total
Under £250 ..	—	2,681	53·2
£250—£500 ..	1,745	595	11·8
£500—£1,000	500	350	6·9
£1,000—£2,000	195	270	5·4
£2,000—£10,000	97	360	7·1
Over £10,000 ..	8	170	3·4
Incomes of corporate bodies[1]	—	612	12·1

Thus, just before the second World War, the rich—those with over £2,000 a year—were getting directly 10½ per cent of the national income, besides what accrued to them by way of company reserves, whereas the middle classes—with from £500 to £2,000—were getting nearly 12½ per cent, plus some share in the "corporate" income. These figures take no account of taxation, either direct or indirect. Colin Clark has estimated that the net effect of taxation in 1935–6 was to redistribute about £91 millions from the richer to the poorer classes, after debiting the costs of government to the former.

Capitalism went on its way. But, since 1914, the structure of British capitalism had undergone many important changes. There were powerful capitalist trusts and combines long before the first World War—armament rings, shipping rings, "gentlemen's agreements" in the steel and many other trades, the thread combine, the tobacco combine, and so on. But war conditions immensely increased their numbers and their strength. Whenever an industry passed under any sort of State control—and most did before the first World War was over—there arose a collective body to deal with the Government on behalf of the employers as a group. After the War,

[1] Company reserves, incomes of Trusts, Charities, Schools, Colleges, Hospitals and other institutions.

when State control disappeared, combination usually did not. Moreover, whereas there had been a habit, up to 1914, of looking askance at trusts and rings, as methods of exploiting the consumers, after 1918 there was a growing tendency to encourage them, as means of bringing about the "rationalization" of industry. Large-scale production, standardization and specialization were held to be essential to productive efficiency; and it was argued that, under the more intense world competition, it was indispensable that there should exist powerful bodies able to bargain with foreign interests as the spokesmen of entire industries. The temporary "anti-profiteering" legislation passed during the post-war boom in prices was speedily allowed to lapse. In one case after another, Governments set to work to persuade the capitalists to re-organize their industries in great inclusive associations, and even, as in the coal industry in 1930 (under a Labour Government!) compelled minorities to come in. After 1931 the steel industry was given a tariff only when it had promised to combine into a great federation, which was thereafter a powerful factor in holding up prices. The Agricultural Marketing Schemes represented a similar tendency. Competition went out of fashion, with Governments as well as with employers. Huge combines, regulating prices and output and negotiating with similar combines abroad, became the typical business units of the inter-war world. Banking went the same way, with the integration of most of the joint-stock banks to form the "Big Five," which thereafter worked closely together and followed, in effect, a single credit policy over the whole range of industry.

Combination of this type had not, indeed, in 1939 yet covered all industries. Despite many schemes, it had never been successfully introduced into most of the textile trades, though a renewed attempt to apply it to the cotton industry was being made in 1939. Nor did it dominate certain of the newer industries. The motor-car business remained highly competitive; and so did many of the smaller metal trades and the miscellaneous factory industries. Distribution remained unrationalized, despite the growth of large concerns such as Woolworths and the great department stores. So did building. But the first Lord Melchett (Sir Alfred Mond) had very thoroughly rationalized the chemical trades in Imperial Chemical Industries; and the makers of heavy electrical equipment were in a close and powerful federation. The main-line railways were working closely together since their amalgamation by the State in 1921 into four great companies; on the roads there had been a great movement towards combination in passenger transport, but goods transport remained highly competitive despite attempts at "rationalization."

Apart from combinations covering entire industries, or large sections of them, there had been in many branches of production a great increase in the size of the bigger firms. The period immediately after the War was notable for intense activity by large companies in buying up smaller businesses, often at grossly inflated prices. Characteristic of these years was a tendency towards "vertical" as well as "horizontal" combination—that is, towards the acquisition by a single controlling group of plants engaged in successive processes, sometimes reaching right from the supply of raw materials to the marketing of finished goods. Indeed, in some instances —e.g. Lever Brothers and Vickers-Armstrong—combinations went much further than this, and great firms acquired hosts of businesses related in the most diverse ways to their original activities. Lever Brothers, beginning with soap-making, at one time included under their control firms engaged in African trading, shipping, sweet manufacturing, whale fishing, fish retailing, and a large number of other trades. But it was gradually realized that this type of "concern" was uneconomic, because it demanded a knowledge of too many different techniques and was unwieldy and difficult to control. Many of the great amalgamated "concerns" were subsequently redivided into more manageable units; but even so the scale of operations of the bigger businesses remained much larger in general than before 1914. Moreover, there was in certain industries, notably coal-mining during the depression, a considerable amount both of amalgamation into larger units and of buying-up of companies which got into difficulties by the more prosperous great concerns, such as Powell Duffryn in South Wales.

The adoption of a tariff in 1931–2 inevitably fostered combination; for when imports were made subject to duties (and sometimes to a quota system as well) there was a plain inducement to the home producers to enter into mutual agreements for the regulation of prices. The growing use of branded "proprietary" articles further encouraged a tendency to enter into agreements regulating the discounts to be allowed to traders and the terms of sale. This led to conflicts with the Co-operative movement, as the producers of proprietary goods for sale at fixed prices objected to the payment of "dividends on purchase" as violating fixed-price agreements, and sometimes withheld supplies from the Co-operative stores.

Thus in very many ways capitalism between the wars was unlike the system which existed up to 1914. Relations between Big Business and the State became much closer. Business men looked increasingly to the State to drive hard bargains for them with foreign countries (as when the Swedes were compelled to buy half their coal imports from Great Britain) and even to subsidize them when they got into difficulties. Sugar-beet factories, coal-mines, tramp shipping, livestock production, wheat growing and the production of oil from coal were all subsidized in various ways, at either the taxpayers' or the consumers' expense. Big Business had become more vocal in Parliament, and more closely integrated as a whole both for pressing its commercial policies upon the Government and for resisting working-class demands. The Federation of British Industries, formed during the first World War, united most big firms and associations in the manufacturing industries for the furtherance of capitalist economic policies; and the National Conferation of Employers' Organizations, formed in 1919 to unify the employers' group at the National Industrial Conference, developed into an inclusive combine of capitalists corresponding to the Trades Union Congress on the Labour side.

Financially, the consolidation of capitalist interests had advanced by 1939 even further than the structure of industry itself would suggest. There had been a very great development of "holding" companies, which existed only to hold the shares, and therewith the control, of a number of nominally independent businesses; and the big firms had thrown off "subsidiary" companies in very large numbers. These subsidiaries, being in form usually "private companies," were under no compulsion to publish balance sheets or to disclose the same particulars about their working as companies whose shares were more widely held; and this meant that the balance sheets of the big concerns had become less and less informative —even though since 1928 there had been compulsion to disclose the general position of subsidiaries as a group, but without disclosing the affairs of any one of them separately. The "pyramiding" of finance through holding and subsidiary companies and the purchasing of an "interest" in nominally separate concerns enabled the big capitalists to wield control over much larger amounts of capital than they themselves possessed; and the smaller investors, who usually spread their risks by holding small amounts in a number of different concerns, had in effect no control at all over the use that was made of their money. To a small extent, this loss of control had been offset by the growth of Investment Trusts, which received the money of the small investor and spread his risks for him by placing their funds in a large number of undertakings. But, even though the Trusts were supposed to act as watchdogs for the smaller investors, their directors formed, in effect, a part of the narrow financial oligarchy which held the dictatorship of high business affairs.

Meanwhile, in the City, the stock-market gamblers pursued their accustomed course. But the uncertainty of the entire world outlook put a greater premium than ever on short views and caused stock-market values to fluctuate wildly without any real cause. The reluctance after 1929 to take the risks of long-term investment caused a piling-up of short-term funds in the world's money markets; and these, flitting from one centre to another in search of safety or profit, put large liquid resources from time to time at the disposal of the gamblers— until these resources were suddenly withdrawn with catastrophic effects. Production became the helpless victim of high finance; and the financiers themselves oscillated between extremes of optimism and panic which alike prevented the steady development of the world's productive power.

Yet, for all that was amiss, a traveller who visited Great Britain in 1939—say, an American bent on combining business with pleasure, and visiting the industrial centres, as well as the places of beauty or historic interest—would have got in general a strong impression of stability and indeed of prosperity as well. If he had found his way to certain parts of South Wales or industrial Cumberland, or to a few other specially depressed areas, he would indeed have seen the plain evidences of industrial decay. But on the surface the effects of depression did not show greatly even in Lancashire; and the Clyde and the North-East Coast were for the moment more active than they had been for a long time, because of rearmament. All over the South of England and the Midlands, and over a part of the North and of Scotland as well, the traveller would have seen the signs of intensely rapid urban development. Between 1920 and 1939 there were built in Great Britain over 4,000,000 new houses, whereas the total number of houses recorded in the census of 1921 was not much over 9,000,000. Moreover, nearly half these new houses had been built since the depression, so that the traveller could not have helped being impressed almost everywhere by the vast amount of quite new building. In pre-war England and Wales the peak year for new house-building was 1906, when 130,000 houses were built—or say 150,000 at the outside for Great Britain as a whole. Thereafter came the great housing slump; and in 1911 there were at the time of the Census only about 40,000 houses under construction. But during the middle 'thirties house-building was at the rate of over 360,000 houses a year. It began to fall off from 1937; but industrial building and the erection of garages, cinemas and public buildings were proceeding apace. If building is a sign of prosperity, Great Britain would appear to have been during these years an exceedingly prosperous country.

In fact, of course, this mass of new building was the consequence not of prosperity, but rather of low rates of interest which, brought in by the depression, had been maintained by an expansionist banking policy. It was a consequence, also, of the rapid migration of industry and population out of the old industrial areas to new centres, and above all to Greater

London and the Southern Counties. We have seen to what an extent the geographical distribution of the population was changing in the inter-war years. House-building was one of the objective manifestations of the shift of industry away from the old centres of the Industrial Revolution.

But it was not that alone. It was also a result of the clearance of slums, of the increased demand on land in urban centres for non-residential purposes, and of the growth of the salary-earning classes. The number of families that could just afford —or thought they could just afford—a house rather above the working-class standard of accommodation and amenity had increased very considerably as a result of the change in the proportion of blackcoated to manual workers. Smaller families, again, meant a need for more houses in proportion to population, and the possibility of spending a larger fraction of total income upon rent—because there were fewer children to feed and clothe. As a consequence of the falling birth-rate there was a larger proportion than there had been previously of earners in the total population.

Educational standards had risen with the spread of State secondary education under the Fisher Act of 1918. There were 174,000 pupils in state-aided secondary schools in England and Wales in 1913; in 1939 there were about 470,000. University education and technical education also expanded fast. The number of men and women educated and trained for jobs which carried a standard of payment above the working-class level was very much greater in 1939 than in 1913. It took fewer workers to produce commodities, and many more to organize their production and write letters and make book-entries about them. The one really noticeable change in the class structure of society was the relative increase in what is called the "lower middle class" of salary-earning technicians, clerks, typists and minor professional people.

Many of these blackcoats were not, in fact, earning a great deal more than the better-paid manual workers; but they spent their earnings differently, and to the casual observer the results of their spending *showed* a great deal more. Though even in 1939 the salary-earning class numbered only about 3,000,000, whereas the wage-earners in industry were about

10,000,000, the "commercial proletariat" of shop assistants and warehouse workers another 3,000,000, and the workers in personal service and miscellaneous wage-earning occupations yet another 3,000,000—in all 16,000,000 (or with the agricultural workers, 17,000,000) of wage-earners as against 3,000,000 of salary-earners—the 3,000,000 were very much the more visible to the traveller. They lived along the by-pass roads, they crowded more into the shopping centres, they thronged theatres and shows in the middle of the great towns much more than the wage-earners. They were above all visible in London; and their very obtrusiveness led easily to an over-impression of prevailing prosperity. Again, all over the country the richer a man was the more room he took, and the more he *showed*. The undiminished wealth of the British upper classes was very plain everywhere. It could be seen with the naked eye, whereas the precariousness of its foundations could not.

THE SECOND WORLD WAR

CHAPTER LI

EPILOGUE

IT is too soon, when this chapter is written, to give a balanced story of the common people of Britain in the second World War. We shall attempt, at this stage, no more than the briefest and most pedestrian outline of the main events and tendencies, as a sort of postscript, or as a reminder to the reader of what may be already in his mind but unco-ordinated or out of order.

The second World War shook the foundations of British society much more than the first. The strain on man-power and the call for industrial adaptation were much greater: evacuation and the development of war industry required much more migration and disturbance of family life: bombing from the air was on a quite different scale, in both its physical and its psychological effects. A higher proportion of the national income was absorbed by the war effort; and the realization of overseas investments in order to pay for war supplies cut more deeply into Great Britain's position as a creditor country. All classes, rich and poor alike, of both sexes and of all ages, were drawn much more completely into the struggle. Finally, there was very much less opposition, or even hesitancy and reluctant support, than at any time from 1914 to 1918. The first World War never was, but the second soon became, after a shaky start, a "total war."

At the outbreak in 1939, the Trades Union Congress, meeting at Bridlington, passed a resolution which expressed the almost unanimous view of its constituents. "The Nazi Government, having chosen the way of war, must be resisted to the utmost," it said. "Congress, with a united and resolute nation, enters the struggle with a clear conscience and steadfast purpose." But, however certain was that purpose, a dilemma at once followed. Almost equally unanimous was the decision that it was impossible to join a Ministry led by Mr. Chamberlain: distrust of the general line of his policy was reinforced by a growing conviction of the enormous incompetence of his administration, soon to be proved by an unexampled series of disasters. All that either the unions or the Labour Party could do was to offer collaboration with the Ministry from outside. Much of the record of the earlier months of the war consists of complaints, by deputations or in the Press, that this proffered co-operation was not used to a greater extent. The Unions operated a Joint Council with the employers for preventing stoppages, and worked with the Ministry of Labour and other government departments in fixing rates of wages and conditions of work, though up to the summer of 1940 there was still plenty of bidding against one another by employers seeking labour, and little attempt to prevent the waste of resources on unnecessary things, or to systematize the granting of war contracts. The Labour organizations gave active support to the voluntary schemes of civil defence, and demanded more effective "controls" in many other fields; but the Government still clung to its idea of reducing to a minimum the interference with normal ways of living. Dissatisfaction mounted during the "phoney war"; but it was a dissatisfaction with the ineptitude of the Government, not, as in France, a doubt whether the war was worth fighting at all.

On two occasions there was a major clash with the Government on matters of policy. In December, after the Soviet Union had attacked Finland, the Government was still so much living in fairyland that it concerted with M. Daladier's Ministry plans for intervening in the war on the Finnish side. Against this the Labour movement strongly protested, not so much out of sympathy with the Soviet, as from a clearer understanding of the military lunacy of such an action. It was, however, much more the obstinacy of Sweden than the protests of the Opposition which prevented the crowning folly of a war on Russia. In April 1940, when the unpreparedness and ineptness of the Government were clearly leading to the inevitable end in Norway, the Party in the House of Commons took part in a debate in which it severely and in detail attacked the conduct of the war both at home and abroad. The revelations and criticisms then made shook the credit of the Government in the country, but not in the House, where the Conservative majority which had approved of its policy since 1935 repeated its massive approbation.

There were two exceptions, numerically slight, to the general attitude of the British common people. The Independent Labour Party, by then a mere ghost of its former self, opposed the war on traditional "anti-capitalist" lines, maintaining that it should be regarded as an "imperialist" war and that no war should be supported except one waged for Socialist ends by a Socialist Government. The Communist Party, which had already outstripped it considerably in numbers and much more in influence, began by supporting the war with its usual vehemence, but within a few days reversed its policy, and went into opposition, presumably under orders from the Communist International in Moscow, and in harmony with the policy followed by the Soviet Union in pursuance of the Nazi–Soviet Pact. R. Palme Dutt replaced Harry Pollitt as general secretary, and soon the Party was calling upon the workers to recognize "Churchill and Daladier, Attlee and Blum" as their greatest enemies. This change of front was not easy to explain to the workers, and for a time Communist influence suffered a considerable setback. When Harry Pollitt presented his party's programme to a working-class electorate at the Silvertown bye-election in February 1940, he was rejected by a vote of 12 to 1. Mr. D. N. Pritt, the only Labour M.P. who followed the Communist lead on the war, was expelled in March 1940.

The end of the period of delusion came on 10 May, 1940. On that date, which was also the night on which the Germans broke into the Low Countries, the Labour Party pressed to a division its vote of censure. Mr. Chamberlain secured 281 votes, but the figure of 200 for the motion, including some 37 of his nominal supporters, was sufficient to make his retention of office impossible. Nine years of "National" Government, more disastrous than any nine years since Restoration days, had come at last to an end.

The new Government, headed by Mr. Churchill, was in essence a coalition of Conservatives and Labour, supported by the two small Liberal Parties in the House of Commons. Labour entered the War Cabinet with two members (Mr. C. R. Attlee and Mr. Arthur Greenwood) out of five, and four other Ministers at the head of important departments, including the Co-operator, Mr. A. V. Alexander, at the Admiralty and Mr. Ernest Bevin as Minister of Labour. Labour, despite its small representation in Parliament—a legacy of the deception of 1935—had played the vital part in enforcing the change of Government; and the Labour men came in, Mr. Attlee declared, bringing their programme with them and not leaving it outside. The Party Conference endorsed its leaders' actions by 2,413,000 votes to 170,000. Acts were raced through which empowered the Government, if it so wished, to put all property, including the land, under State control. Banks were taken under control. The books of private firms were to be subject to compulsory inspection. Recalcitrant employers could be forced to observe collective agreements with the workers. As against this, Labour accepted drastic obligations. The Minister of Labour could direct any person to any place and to do any work. There was widespread satisfaction that notorious Fascists, from Sir Oswald Mosley downwards, were at last rounded up and put away.

Little time was given to the new Government, to whom Churchill had promised, truthfully, nothing but "blood and sweat and tears." The Nazis were already in Holland and Belgium: in twenty days the Dutch had been crushed, the Belgian King had surrendered, and the British Army, without its arms, was being picked out from Dunkirk. Nine days later Italy, reading the signs, declared war: in a fortnight France had surrendered. On August 11, the Battle of Britain had started: the long night had begun.

In the period that began with May 10, the history of the British common people cannot be separated from that of all the nation. The unity so frequently promised or appealed to in politicians' speeches was for some time a reality: it is for once not untrue to say that few in any class failed to do their utmost for the community. The immediate programme promised by the bills announced in May was carried out: the rate of excess profits tax was increased to 100 per cent: for a while public interest did, within the limitations of human nature, override private interest. Momentarily, there was no time for dissension or recrimination. The workers in all essential industries worked, after Dunkirk, all hours that physical powers would permit—often many more than were wise. Gradually, some order was introduced into the organization of the industrial war effort. The A.R.P. services were enthusiastically performed, often by men and women who went back to work after nights spent in rescue. When the War Secretary asked for 150,000 volunteers to act as "parashots" to watch for parachute troops, 750,000 men joined what afterwards became the Home Guard, which within a month and a half passed the million mark and never fell below it. These, too, carried on with their work while being trained as an army. The task of re-equipping Britain was carried on underneath a nearly incessant bombardment from the air. There was very little defence for many months, and the A.R.P. protection provided was, until Herbert Morrison was transferred from Supply to the Home Office, almost intolerably inadequate. During all this period, there was almost no faltering, although the odds against the British were even to a lay observer terrific.

Yet, however united a people may be, there must always be some who are early exhausted by an ordeal of this kind, and some too, in a democracy, who will start an opposition. There was never in the second World War anything comparable to the wide anti-war movements of 1917 and 1918. But at the height of the "blitz," the Communist Party succeeded in uniting several heterogeneous elements in an attack on the war policy. On 10 January 1941, it assembled a considerable number of delegates (whose actual support in the country is a matter for debate) in a "People's Convention for a People's Peace," to be secured by overthrowing the Government. This action, and the resultant plans for a permanent organization, provoked the one major interference with Press liberty, the suppression of the Party's official newspaper, the *Daily Worker*, ten days later. However, when the Nazis attacked the Soviet Union in June of the same year, the Communist Party policy

changed instantly: it reproached the Government for not opening a second front in 1942, and the People's Convention disappeared almost in a night.

Before long a more deep-rooted opposition, of a different
kind, began to appear. British capitalism, it gradually became
clear, was enlisting only "for the duration." What was needed
for victory was indeed given. Profits were severely restricted,
factories forcibly concentrated, enormous taxation paid,
Government direction of policy and production implicitly
obeyed. Strict and fairly competent rationing of clothing and
food, with sumptuary regulations in restaurants, was observed
with (at the beginning at any rate) a minimum of evasion.
Even billeting of evacuees, a direct invasion of privacy, was in
most cases loyally accepted. But any action which threatened
any change of class relations in society or in the control of
industry after the war was, at first largely behind the scenes
and then more and more openly, resisted. It had been impossible for employers to stand out against the spread of
Trade Unionism, even in factories from which it had been
banned up to that time; but for a long period many firms, even
in the war industries, fought a rearguard action against the
acceptance of Joint Production Committees, which were
responsible for securing co-operation between managements
and workers in increasing war output, and against the parallel
growth of the Shop Stewards' Movement, which did not, as
between 1914 and 1918, take a political or anti-war shape, but
limited itself to safeguarding workshop conditions and recruiting members from the ranks of the new war-time workers in the
munitions trades. The Joint Production Committees, when
they were frankly accepted, did excellent work; but it was easy
for an employer or manager who disliked them to hamper
them at every turn, and then declare his disappointment at
what they had achieved. In general, despite these exceptions,
industrial relations remained much better than they had been
during the later stages of the first World War, because there
was a real unity of purpose throughout the nation. But this
did not apply to the coal industry, in which both relations and
output declined steadily, despite repeated announcements of
new schemes of control more effective than what had gone

before. There was so much distrust of the owners among the miners, who regarded public ownership as the only solution, and so determined an intention among the owners of resisting public ownership at any cost, that it was impossible for the two sides to pull together; and as the Tories in the Government would have nothing to say to nationalization during the war, matters were merely allowed to drift, though the shortage of coal was a severe handicap to war production as well as a source of hardship to the public, especially in the war-damaged areas.

Outside the coal industry, the chief complaints about war industry centred round the "Controllers" who, attached to the Ministry of Supply or to other war departments, were put in charge of particular materials or products of key importance to the war effort. These "Controllers" were mostly men who had been previously high up in the service of the profit-making industries they were now set to supervise in the national interest; and many of them continued to be paid by their firms and not by the Government. Complaints were soon heard, both from the general public and from smaller firms in the trades affected, that some of the "Controllers" were abusing their power by giving favours to their own firms on war contracts or in priority of supplies, or were stealing the trade secrets of their rivals with a view to post-war competition. There were other allegations that firms were giving to preparations for post-war trade attention which ought to have been given to war production. These latter charges were especially prevalent during the "export drive" of 1941, when goods were sent out of the country in considerable quantities in order to get foreign exchange for buying imports, and in consequence factories which could have been used for producing war supplies were left to get on with their normal, peace-time kinds of production. They died down as Lease-Lend from the United States eased the demand for dollars, and the "export drive" gave place to an increasing diversion of factories and labour of all sorts to direct war service.

Complaints about the "Controllers" continued longer, and in fact never wholly ceased. But they too died down as the tide of war turned, and as it became evident that the war-time structure of industry had become too firmly established to be altered without an upheaval that no one was willing to risk. There was undoubtedly, as the end of the war began to loom ahead, an increasing amount of jockeying for post-war position; but it attracted less public notice than a smaller amount had done at an earlier stage.

The political accompaniment to the suspension of industrial hostilities was the "electoral truce." The parties to the coalition reached agreement not to put up rival candidates for Parliament during the war, the candidate chosen by the party which had previously held any seat that fell vacant being allowed a walk-over, unless some "splinter" candidate insisted on challenging a contest. A General Election was prevented by prolonging the life of Parliament, which consequently grew older and more lifeless—the more so because some of the younger members were absent on war service, and many of the new war-time M.P.s were also veterans. In local government, even more drastic steps were taken, all contests being suspended and their place taken by co-options to fill vacancies by the existing councillors, who were given an indefinite term of service. At one time, it seemed more than possible that an invasion might so disturb the life of the country as to make not only local elections, but the working of local government on anything like the normal lines impossible. This underlay both the appointment of Regional Controllers, who were to take control in that event in their respective areas, and the handing over in many places of most of the functions of the local Councils to small Emergency Committees. Gradually, as the invasion danger receded, the full Councils began meeting again, and their various Committees resumed work. But local elections were not reinstated until the autumn of 1945: nor was the organization of the Regional Controllers wholly disbanded, though their functions gradually withered away, and the Government, in face of the strong hostility of the local authorities to the British "gauleiters," had again and again to reaffirm its intention of abolishing them finally at the end of the war.

In national politics, the "electoral truce" denied the electorate any right of choice when seats fell vacant and any means of influencing policy in the normal ways. Resentment at this "disfranchisement" led to the appearance of a number of "independents" of varying programmes, and to some kicking over of the traces by groups which rejected the discipline of the party machines; but only one new party emerged. This was Common Wealth, founded and led by a former Liberal, Sir Richard Acland, with a programme fully as Socialist as the Labour Party's and more insistently expressed, but with a following drawn mainly from the middle classes and the "blackcoated proletariat," though not a few Labour people in the constituencies gave it open or tacit support. Some official candidates at by-elections had narrow escapes, and a handful of Common Wealth and "left" independents found their way to the House of Commons. But for the most part the officially sponsored nominees of the older parties were returned.

For a time, discontent was intensified by the course of the war. The new allies secured in 1941 did not at first bring the hoped-for successes: the Germans thrust deep into Russia, driving the Soviet armies before them, and the Japanese threw the Americans out of the Philippines. But these disasters were followed by worse; the loss of Malaya, Singapore, the Dutch East Indies and Burma was not even an honourable defeat. It appeared as if the immense sums spent on naval and military defence there had been wasted, that neither the administrative nor the commercial and industrial castes were competent or able to defend themselves, and that British imperialism had made itself detested by the inhabitants, who in places openly helped the Japanese. Those who had for years attacked British imperialism felt that their prophecies were coming true and that a second harvest of Tory sowing was being reaped.

The delegate conferences of the Labour Party or the Trades Union Congress were almost the only remaining means by which popular opinion could still express itself democratically. It was thus significant that the Labour Party Conference of 1942 only rejected a motion to denounce the party truce by 1,275,000 votes to 1,209,000, a vote which marked the nadir of government popularity until then.

Thereafter, for several reasons, discontent abated. For one

thing, the war news became better. For another, a few plans for post-war reconstruction, of which the most famous was the Beveridge Report, were permitted to appear; though for the most part they remained plans. For a third, Sir Stafford Cripps was sent to India with a new offer from the British Government. When this was rejected by the leading Indian parties, even those who felt that the Indians had a case did not see what to do next; and an uneasy silence settled down upon the Indian problem.

Meantime, at home, the needs of the armed forces and of war industry had been making heavier and heavier demands on the limited man-power. It soon became indispensable not only to control the distribution of male workers between more and less essential industries, and to "direct" men to work for particular firms, even at long distances from home, but also to register and presently to control the movement of women's labour and to call up for industrial service married women and others who had previously not been engaged in paid work. The claims of the armed forces for additional recruits had to be balanced against the needs of industry, and in particular much effort went into ensuring that skilled men taken into the forces should not be wasted on work for which they had no special aptitude. Training schemes had to be improvised on a very large scale, both in the services—especially the Royal Air Force—and for industry; and workers—especially skilled workers—had to be extracted from every sort of factory and workplace and transferred to the great new war factories erected either by the Government itself or by private firms acting as its agents. These Royal Ordnance Factories and "Agency" factories were set up largely in remote areas out of the way of air attack; and immense difficulties arose in transporting workers to and from work and in providing accommodation near the sites in face of the large rival claims on the building industry for the construction of military camps, aerodromes, and other war works. Bombing caused dispersal of many other factories to less vulnerable areas; and very many thousands of workers found themselves labouring under extremely uncomfortable living conditions in factories which the black-out prevented from being properly lighted or there had been some surface changes in the class structure of Great Britain. During the 'thirties, the working classes, with the vast exception of those in the depressed areas, had made a real advance in their standards of living. There had been some shifting from the class of "proletarian" wage-earners to blackcoated salary-earners. During the war, though there had been great sacrifices, these sacrifices had been to some extent shared by the upper class. Moreover, the depressed areas had been, momentarily at least, reclaimed: dead towns in South Wales and the North-East had revived, and men who had never expected to work again had found jobs.

These were important changes. Nevertheless, two nations still confronted each other in 1946, though much less starkly than in the days of the Chartists when Disraeli wrote *Sybil* to point the contrast, less starkly even than in the years of depression between the world wars. Full employment, high direct taxation of large incomes, subsidizing of basic foods and improved social services were narrowing very greatly the immense gulf between the actual standards of living of the rich and the poor; and under the new Labour Government were to continue to do so, until about 1949 or 1951 at least. But there had been no equivalent change in the distribution of property. Industrial capital was still held mainly by a fairly limited class; rent, interest and profits still accounted for about one-third of the gross national product, as against two-thirds for wages, salaries and forces' pay; more than one-third of the total number of incomes over £135 were still under £250 a year. The great majority of those who died still had almost nothing to leave to their successors.

aileged. On the whole, this machinery worked reasonably well; and grossly inflated prices were not often charged except for certain kinds of luxury goods which were left outside the scope of control.

It was, however, necessary, in order to prevent the restrictions on production from leading to "black markets" on a large scale, to apply direct measures to limit consumption. Although rates of wages were not allowed to rise sharply, the achievement of full and continuous employment and the bringing of large numbers of additional workers into the labour market necessarily increased the total volume of money in the consumers' hands. One method of restricting consumption was the imposition of the purchase tax on a wide range of goods, other than food, at varying rates corresponding roughly to the more or less dispensable character of the articles. A second was the drastic raising of the taxes on beer, spirits and tobacco; and a third was the extension of income tax to the main body of wage-earners, presently coupled with a post-war rebate plan under which a small part of the tax paid was credited to the taxpayer in the form of a promise to repay in cash after the end of the war. At the same time the Government, fearful of a demand for wage-increases if it allowed the cost of living to rise sharply, soon began to keep down the prices of a number of necessary foodstuffs by means of subsidies, and these, at first small in amount, increased sharply as the war went on. In 1943 the Government collected £1,073,000,000 in indirect taxes levied specifically on consumption, but paid out £190,000,000 in subsidies on necessary consumers' supplies. In the same year, the total sums raised by national taxation rose to £2,807,000,000, out of a central government expenditure of £5,782,000,000, the balance being covered mainly by loans.

These loans were raised partly from the reserved profits of industry, which could not expend such reserves on new buildings and plant, and, in face of the control maintained over the capital market, had in effect no other outlet for them; partly from the banks—a form of borrowing which was kept within such limits as to avoid serious inflation; and partly—indeed to a remarkable extent—from the savings of the people. The

National Savings Movement organized vast savings campaigns; savings funds were instituted in the factories: war savings weeks were held in every area, often called by fancy names, designed to give people the idea that they were contributing to the supply of Spitfires, or tanks, or other war weapons— though, in fact, the output of these things was determined by the capacity of industry to produce them and not by monetary considerations.

By the end of 1944 the National Debt, which had stood at £8,300,000,000 in 1939 (as compared with £650,000,000 in August 1914) had risen to £22,000,000,000. But this total was much less formidable than it would have been if effective steps had not been taken to keep the rate of interest under firm control. In the first World War, interest rates were allowed to rise with each successive great loan, and in order to avert the charge of unfairness subscribers to previous loans were given a chance of converting to the higher rates, with the result that vast sums had to be found to meet the annual claims of the bondholders. By 1939 the folly of such a procedure had been understood; and the Government, keeping all competitors out of the capital market, fixed the rate of interest where it saw fit, and prevented it from rising as the war went on. Whatever criticisms can be advanced against the Government's conduct of the war on the home front, it is undeniable that on the financial side its management showed an immense improvement over the previous occasion.

As against this efficiency in finance, the mishandling of the coal situation stands in the strongest contrast. It should have been easy to foresee that, as the new war factories came into operation and the transport services were strained by the growing military requirements, the demand for coal would expand rapidly. Nevertheless, when with the collapse of France and the Nazi occupation of most of Europe the demand for coal exports dropped off, the Government, instead of using the opportunity to pile up big reserves, allowed large numbers of miners to join the forces and many more to drift away into other occupations. Nor was anything done to organize the industry effectively for its task. Control, of a sort, was imposed; but it was a control which not only left the ownership of the pits in the owners' hands, but also the management, under merely general supervision by the ill-staffed and unregarded Ministry of Mines, which was still a subordinate section of the Board of Trade. · Later on, when the coal shortage had become really acute, the control scheme was more than once tightened up, at any rate on paper. Managers were placed directly under the orders of what had by then become the separate Ministry of Fuel and Power; but they continued to be paid by the owners, to whom they had accordingly to look for their prospects of employment and promotion. The coal industry, owing to the long period of decline through which it had passed between the wars, was staffed by an ageing labour force ill-suited to stand up to the prolonged strain of war, and its evil reputation led to great difficulty in recruiting young workers. This was the reason for the introduction, from December 1943, of the "Bevin boys"—a body of young men chosen by ballot from those due to be called up for the armed forces, and sent to the mines instead. This form of conscription was acutely unpopular, and the dislike was aggravated by the bad conditions under which many of the "boys" found that they had to live in decaying and overcrowded mining villages. Nevertheless, the "Bevin boys" achieved a little in the way of checking the dangerous fall in output, though not nearly enough to prevent such stocks as there were from being used up at an alarming rate in the winter of 1944–5.

It was, indeed, evident that the organization of the coal industry was inefficient and obsolete, and that the Coal Mines Act of 1930, which had constituted what was in effect a statutory owners' cartel empowered to regulate prices and output, so far from bringing about an improvement, had enabled the owners more successfully to resist reorganization. The public ownership of the coal itself, brought about by the Coal Act of 1938, was a step forward; but the Coal Commission, set up under the Act to administer the coal as national property and to take over the largely abortive powers of the earlier Coal Mines Reorganization Commission to promote amalgamations, had not had time to produce any results when its operations were suspended at the outbreak of war. Nationalization of the mines, which was the obvious way of bringing about integrated development and improving technical efficiency, was excluded on political grounds; and there was no way short of nationalization whereby the industry could be brought into better condition. In 1945 the colliery owners produced a scheme, drafted by Mr. Robert Foot, who had been brought in from outside as Chairman of the Mining Association; but the scheme in effect involved conferring still more extensive powers on a Council to be appointed by the owners, with no means of assuring that these powers would not be used against the public interest. Meanwhile, the miners rejected it and the Government kept silence about its own views on the future of the industry. In truth, of course, its members disagreed.

There was a very similar impasse in the case of land. It was widely recognized that the old arrangement, under which the landowner supplied fixed capital as well as land to the tenant farmer, had broken down, and that to improve farming standards there was need for a larger investment of capital in agriculture than the landowners were willing or able to supply. Land nationalization was widely advocated as a remedy, but was strenuously opposed. Landlords, who were profiting by the increasing agricultural subsidies granted between the wars as well as by the higher agricultural prices brought about by the Agricultural Marketing Act of 1933, were by no means willing to lose their control of the land, which they hoped would enable them to receive yet larger subsidies in the future. In the case of urban land, the Ribbon Development Act of 1935, designed to check the undesirable spread of housing along main roads at the fringe of urban areas, was almost wholly neutralized by the onerous conditions of compensation imposed on local authorities which attempted to impose town planning regulations. This question of compensation and "betterment" was referred in 1941 to an expert committee presided over by Mr. Justice Uthwatt, which was instructed to consider it in relation to the entire problem of the use of land in connection with post-war planning. The Uthwatt Committee reported in 1942 in favour of easier procedures for public acquisition of land in areas already built-up, with the purpose of facilitating schemes of urban re-planning, especially in bombed cities, and in neighbourhoods likely to need extensive development in connection with the resettlement of congested populations. It also proposed a special tax on increments on land values in built-up areas, as an alternative to the usual form of "betterment" charge. In the case of land outside built-up areas it recommended public acquisition of all "development rights" and also actual public purchase of all land scheduled for development except for agricultural purposes. The Committee explicitly stated that it had ruled out the alternative of land nationalization as "politically impracticable"; but even the milder measures which it proposed were hotly opposed by landowners and anti-socialists, and after long delays were finally rejected by the Government without any alternative plans covering most of the ground being put forward in their place. As the war advanced it became increasingly plain that any measures of post-war reconstruction which in any way limited private property rights or proposed an extension of public ownership would be strenuously resisted by vested interests both in and outside Parliament and by the main body of Conservative and capitalist opinion.

During the war, however, it was indispensable to exercise a large minimum of control over the use of agricultural land. For the most part this control was exercised by paying farmers enough to induce them to produce what was wanted; but County War Agricultural Executive Committees, appointed by the Ministry of Agriculture and working under its orders, were given wide powers to dispossess inefficient farmers and either cultivate land themselves or hand it over to more efficient farmers. Agricultural wages were also raised substantially through the Agricultural Wages Board, with the declared object of bringing rural and urban standards of living closer together. It was left obscure to what extent the State would remain ready, when war conditions had ceased to exist, to continue subsidies in order to keep total agricultural production high; but it was evident that high production would have to be maintained, in face of world-wide scarcities, for some years beyond the actual cessation of hostilities in Europe.

The fate of the Uthwatt Report is only one instance of the

difficulties which arose as soon as the war-time Coalition Government had to begin facing the problem of preparing for the future, and could no longer concentrate exclusively on war issues. The task of making preliminary explorations of recon-struction problems was at first assigned, in 1940, to Mr. Arthur Greenwood, Minister without Portfolio in Mr. Chur-chill's War Cabinet; and a little later Lord Reith, who was Minister of Works and Buildings, was given a by no means clearly distinguished mandate to deal with problems of "physical reconstruction." At that time the regular public departments were all so preoccupied with war issues as to have little or no time to consider post-war problems; and neither Mr. Greenwood nor Lord Reith was given more than a purely nominal staff. Presently, Lord Reith, who had shown signs of energy, was superseded by Lord Portal; and soon after the section at the Ministry of Works which had been dealing with reconstruction problems was joined with the town planning department of the Ministry of Health to form the new Ministry of Town and Country Planning, which was, however, left with wholly inadequate powers. Mr. Greenwood was also removed from office in favour of Sir William Jowitt; but he too was left practically without staff or powers, to face the growing jealousy of the older departments, which were by this time setting up their own sections to deal with recon-struction and were determined that no functions previously entrusted to them should be allowed to slip out of their hands. It was impossible under these conditions to secure any co-ordinated planning of post-war policy—a state of affairs entirely satisfactory to the numerous interests which were set on preventing any such development.

The most important outcome of Mr. Greenwood's period of office in general charge of reconstruction was the appointment of the Beveridge Committee to report on the future of Social Insurance and allied services. This Committee, under the chairmanship of Sir William Beveridge, formerly a leading civil servant but later successively Director of the London School of Economics and Master of University College, Oxford, was virtually a one-man affair, as all the members except the Chairman were actual civil servants who were not allowed to express in public opinions on controversial matters. Accordingly, Sir William Beveridge alone prepared and issued the comprehensive Report which immediately became known by his name. In it he not only recommended a thorough recasting of the social insurance services so as to provide a comprehensive provision against want due to unemployment, sickness, disablement or old age, but also postulated the adoption of a system of children's allowances to begin with the second child, an all-in health service, including specialist and hospital treatment, for the entire population, and a constructive policy of "full employment," by which the Government would assume the responsibility for maintaining total employment at a high enough level to absorb all the available workers. This last item of his recommendations Sir William Beveridge subsequently expanded into a further elaborate report on "Full Employment in a Free Society," published in 1944. For this second report he had no official mandate, having indeed been publicly boycotted in government circles ever since the issue of his report on Social Security.

The first Beveridge Report was issued in November 1942, and at once aroused enormous public interest and resulted in heavy pressure on the Government to declare its attitude. In the parliamentary discussion which followed the Government accepted a number of particular proposals, but deferred committal judgment until the departments had been given time to examine its implications fully. This proved to be a most protracted business, and not till September 1944 did the Government issue a White Paper outlining its own proposals. These followed in the main the structure of the Beveridge Plan, but with certain very important differences. Sir William had proposed certain scales of benefit, which he related explicitly to a cost of living 25 per cent in excess of that of 1939. The Government accepted the actual figures, but made no provision for increasing them, though by that time prices had advanced to a considerably higher level, and seemed likely to remain up, if not to rise considerably further, for some time after the war. Secondly, Sir William had proposed that both sickness benefit and unemployment benefit should be made of unlimited duration, whereas the Government set a

time-limit to both and thus insisted on the retention of the
Means Test, which Sir William had wished to abolish. The
Government also rejected Sir William's proposal for Retirement Pensions on a rising scale, to be brought into force over
a period of twenty years, in favour of a flat rate of pension
intermediate between Sir William's initial and ultimate scales.
It further altered Sir William's plan for a system of accident
benefits in lieu of workmen's compensation by substituting flat
rates for scales of benefit based on previous earnings. It
reduced Sir William's proposed child's allowance of 8s. *plus*
allowances in kind to 5s., with a somewhat vague promise
that the allowances in kind would be increased. Finally,
while endorsing Sir William's view that funeral insurance
should be brought within the state social security scheme, it
rejected a further proposal that the business of industrial
insurance as a whole should be taken over from the insurance
companies and collecting societies and placed in the hands of
a public commission organized under the auspices of the State.
It did, however, accept Sir William's judgment that the
system of health insurance administration through separate
"approved societies," run by insurance companies, friendly
societies, trade unions and other bodies should be superseded
by direct state administration, in order to secure both economy
in cost and the provision of uniform benefits in return for
uniform contributions.

It is not possible here to give more than this meagre summary
of the Beveridge scheme or of the controversy which arose in
connection with it. Nor is it possible to enter into the even
further-reaching controversy which arose over the question of
"full employment." Up to 1944 Governments, as we saw,
refused to accept the view, advocated by the Socialists from
the 1880's under the slogan of the "right to work," that it was
the responsibility of the State to maintain total employment
at an adequate level, and both to offset adverse cyclical factors
by measures designed to expand employment and to deal
with more persistent forms of long-term unemployment. The
new doctrines associated with the name of Lord Keynes found
thoroughgoing expression in Sir William Beveridge's *Full
Employment in a Free Society*; but this was held up by war-

caused printing delays, and before it was published the Government had put forward its own much more cautious proposals in a White Paper on *Employment Policy*, issued in May 1944. This document accepted public responsibility for maintaining, not "full" employment, but "a high and stable level" of employment; but the positive proposals were vague and at some points self-contradictory, and it was left very doubtful how far the Government was really prepared to go in giving effect even to this diluted version of the "full employment" notions of the "new" economics.

In many other fields, throughout 1944, reconstruction policies were being left in a most unsatisfactory condition of suspense, mainly, no doubt, because there was no agreement about them among the members of the Government. We have seen that the Ministry of Town and Country Planning, set up at the beginning of 1943, was given totally inadequate powers; and the situation in respect of "physical" reconstruction was involved in further obscurities because of the Government's failure to give any adequate assurances to the areas badly damaged by bombing of financial help in facing their problems of rebuilding and re-planning. The problem was further complicated by acute controversies over Local Government and over public control of the location of industry. All over the country, the system of local rates was breaking down, partly on account of the effects of war damage and evacuation, but also because new burdens were continually being thrust on the local authorities without the means of financing them. It was generally agreed that local rates constituted an unfair form of taxation, especially since the partial derating of industrial properties by the Chamberlain Act of 1929, which had left householders to bear a disproportionate burden. But there was no agreement either upon any substitute for local rating or upon the proportion of the cost of locally administered national services that ought to be transferred to the central exchequer. Equally there was a failure to agree about the structure of Local Government. It was obvious that towns had in many cases—in London above all—outgrown municipal boundaries defined long ago; but the administrative County Councils strenuously resisted proposed extensions of county borough areas which threatened to rob them of some of the richer districts under their control. Each type of authority fought for its own hand; and all united to denounce proposals for any sort of regional administration designed to secure unification of essential services over wider areas. The Regional Commissioners appointed on the outbreak of war, primarily with the purpose of providing for the maintenance of services in the event of invasion, were denounced by the local authorities as an attempt to impose a permanent system of centralized government control; and the Government, in its eagerness to disarm the opposition of the local authorities, was induced to promise that no major changes in the post-war structure of Local Government would be introduced without their consent. As it was impossible to imagine any scheme of reform on which the various types of authority would agree, this was as good as saying that the main structure of Local Government was to be left unchanged; and when, early in 1945, the Government did at length announce its intentions, they amounted to no more than the establishment of a Commission with very limited powers to readjust local boundaries—and even so Greater London, in which the need for reform was greater than anywhere else, was to be excluded from the scope of the Commission's activities and left for separate treatment later.

There was similar confusion over the location of industry. The Barlow Commission, appointed before the outbreak of war, reported in 1940 in favour of a considerable measure of state control over the placing of new factories and extensions, above all in Greater London. But nothing was done about its report until 1945, when the Government at last introduced a Bill. This proved, however, to be little more than a strengthening of the pre-war legislation dealing with the "Special Areas," and to contain but few and weak provisions affecting the control of location elsewhere. There was in it no conception of using the powers of the State to bring about a balanced distribution of industry and population over the country, such as town planners and advocates of economic planning desired. Its provisions relating to "Development Areas"—the new name for "Special Areas"—were widely and on the whole generously conceived; but at the same time it was made clear that the Government had no intention of introducing any effective planning of industrial location, even to the limited extent contemplated in the Barlow Report.

Nowhere was the confusion over reconstruction policy worse than in the sphere of housing. The Government did indeed announce in February 1943, after strong pressure from a widely representative committee set up by the Ministry of Works, a plan for the gradual raising of the building labour force to a million and a quarter (as compared with rather more than a million in 1939). It was plain that the building industry would emerge from the war with a labour force reduced to at most a third of the numbers available in 1939, and would be immediately faced with urgent demands not only for repairing damaged dwellings and building new ones to accommodate displaced or new households, but also with the necessity of erecting new schools, factories, and structures of every sort in connection with every aspect of reconstruction. But, in face of these needs, government policy showed no clear direction. The building industry with its host of small employers, numbering about 100,000, and its lack of any effective common organization, seemed to be quite incapable of planning on the scale required of it; and here again the uncertainties concerning the financial help which the Government was prepared to offer, as well as the disputes between advocates of municipal and "private enterprise" housing, stood in the way of effective preparation for after-war tasks.

As the end of the German war drew nearer, the grave position of British export trade became clearer. In view of the heavy loss of overseas investments, it was clearly necessary either to face a heavy reduction in imports after the war or to bring about a large expansion of exports. Curtailment of imports presented great difficulties. Great Britain in the 'thirties was importing only small quantities of fully manufactured goods, the bulk of imports consisting of foodstuffs and of raw or semi-manufacturd materials essential for British industry. A policy of full employment would evidently increase the demand for imported materials; and accordingly the only possible field for substantial reductions was that of

CP: Z

foodstuffs. A policy of improved nutrition would, however, clearly increase total food consumption: so that, even if more food continued to be produced at home, there might be no fall in the demand for food imports. Moreover, a refusal to buy foodstuffs, especially from the Dominions, would be certain to react most unfavourably on exports, of which a large proportion were bought by the food-exporting countries. An export drive therefore seemed to be clearly required. The Government itself estimated that it would be necessary to expand the pre-war volume of British exports by at least 50 per cent (put later at nearer 75 per cent), in order to balance the international accounts; but the possibility of this evidently depended on the extent to which countries showed themselves ready to incorporate liberal commercial policies into the peace settlement and also on the amount of help given to devastated countries in restoring or developing their productive capacity. Great Britain had a strong interest in doing all that could be done to prevent a return to the pre-war policies of economic nationalism; but the main power in this field obviously rested with the United States, which would emerge from the war as the sole great creditor country. The plain danger was that the United States, with its high degree of self-sufficiency in manufactured goods, would not be willing to receive such goods in exchange for what it sent out—much less to enable its debtors to meet their obligations by selling more than they bought. To the extent to which this happened, the only way left of balancing accounts would be the making by Americans of huge foreign investments, which would ease the problem in the short run only at the cost of aggravating it later, when the Americans wanted to be repaid, or even to receive interest on their loans.

These were the issues which underlay the discussion of post-war monetary and international investment policy at Bretton Woods in 1944 and of post-war commercial policy in a number of different aspects. Monetary and commercial policies were closely connected. The Americans wanted other countries to promise a return to international monetary stabilization (that is, in effect, to some form of modified gold or dollar standard) before embarking on the discussion of commercial policy.

The British on the other hand could not well afford to promise to stabilize the pound sterling in relation to the dollar, or to give up control of foreign exchange transactions until they knew what the conditions of post-war commercial policy were to be. That was why throughout 1944 the commercial negotiations hung fire, and no step was taken towards British ratification of the draft monetary agreements drawn up by the experts at Bretton Woods. Only when the war was over, and the precipitate ending of Lend-Lease by the United States faced Great Britain with a peremptory need for dollars to purchase indispensable imports of food and raw materials, was a reluctant British Government compelled to accept both the Bretton Woods Agreement and the most drastic limitations on British financial and commercial policy as the price of a dollar loan.

We do not propose to enter further into the questions of international reconstruction that were under discussion in 1944 and 1945. This is the story of the British common people and not of Great Britain in all its aspects; and we have entered into the matter even so far only because the future standard of living of the British people obviously depended on the ability to build up an export trade large enough to meet the cost of necessary imports. By "necessary" we here mean such imports as must be brought in to avert a fall in the standards of living. If imports had to be reduced below this point, it would no doubt be possible to produce more food at home, but only at higher cost—that is, by using up more of the limited resources of British man-power in producing food under less advantageous conditions and thus leaving less man-power available for producing other things. Improvements in agricultural efficiency might make it possible to produce more food at home without raising the cost to the consumers; but there is a limit to this, and nothing had occurred by 1946 to indicate that the costs of home food-production were likely to fall. On the contrary, the accepted opinion that standards of living in the countryside ought to be brought nearer to the urban levels would raise costs.

There is another aspect of post-war standards of living to which we must refer briefly. State regulation of wages in 1939 was confined to trades subject to the Trade Boards Act (mainly, though not exclusively, trades employing a high proportion of women), to agriculture, and to a very few special cases (e.g. cotton weaving, road haulage) in which *ad hoc* legislation was in force. The war, of course, involved an enormous extension of the area of wage regulation. Wages continued ir most trades to be negotiated as before between employers' associations and Trade Unions, but with a reference to a publicly appointed body, the National Arbitration Tribunal, in case of disagreement—or in certain cases a direct reference to the Government or the department concerned. When "direction" of labour was introduced, it became necessary to safeguard the observance of fair wages and conditions by employers in the industries affected; and under the Essential Work Orders and other war-time regulations all employers in such industries were compelled by law to observe the wages and conditions laid down by collective agreement or arbitration. In addition, in certain industries, notably building, the enforcement of reasonable wage-conditions made it necessary to introduce the "guaranteed week," under which pay for a minimum number of hours was safeguarded even if work was interrupted by adverse weather, shortage of materials, or for any other reason beyond the workman's control. These regulations were all formally limited to the war period; but when concessions such as the "guaranteed week," which had been fought for long before the war, were gained in war-time, there was naturally a keen desire on the workers' side to make them permanent.

We have seen that Sir William Beveridge proclaimed as the main purpose of his Report the prevention of Want, which he desired the State to accept as a definite responsibility on behalf of all its citizens. Want, however, cannot be prevented only by providing incomes for the children, the sick, the disabled, the aged, and the unemployed. It involves in addition an assurance of a living wage for the worker who is actually in employment. The "guaranteed week" is one aspect of this problem; but another involves the minimum wage, for those classes of workers who are still outside the scope of either minimum wage law as it now exists, or effective trade union bargaining. In 1943 Mr. Ernest Bevin, the Minister of Labour, attempted to deal with one aspect of this question by introducing a Catering Wages Bill, designed to authorize the fixing of minimum rates and conditions for a large body of workers who were mostly unorganized. The Bill became law only after a tremendous struggle with a large section of the Conservative Party, which maintained that in introducing such a Bill, not limited to the war period, Mr. Bevin was breaking the spirit of the political truce. When, however, at the end of 1944, Mr. Bevin produced a much more drastic Wages Councils Bill, authorizing the establishment of wage-fixing machinery for any occupation not covered by effective arrangements for collective bargaining in which unfair wages were alleged to exist, there was no challenge from any quarter, and the Bill went through Parliament almost without debate, except on details. Nor was any powerful opposition offered to the empowering of the Wages Council to grant paid annual holidays of more than a week's duration, or to the common assumption that holidays with pay, which were being gradually introduced into one after another of the major industries before the war, were to be a normal part of the terms of the wage-contract for the post-war period. There occurred in fact, thanks partly to full employment and partly to Labour policy, a substantial levelling-up of wages for the worse-paid workers, accompanied by a decrease in real 'differentials' between the skilled and the less skilled. These changes had to a great extent taken place during the war; and they were continued after 1945 as long as Labour stayed in office.

So far, we have been dealing with such aspects of reconstruction policy as took shape in Bills, reports of committees, government White Papers, or other official pronouncements. Over the same period, of course, the political parties and a host of propagandist societies in many fields were also busy preparing and issuing plans for the post-war period. At the Labour Party Conference of 1942, a general statement of reconstruction policy, entitled *The Old World and the New Society*, was adopted, and special party committees there-after proceeded to work up the details into a series of reports on particular aspects of the policy therein approved.

But while Labour Ministers remained in the Government it was effectively impossible for the party to undertake independent action. Political initiative in consequence fell more than once to the Trades Union Congress—indeed political action was almost all that it was able to undertake. Efforts to get the Trade Unions and Trade Disputes Act of 1927 repealed, or even slightly modified so as to allow the Unions in the civil service to resume their affiliation to the Trades Union Congress, were defeated by the Conservative Party's inveterate refusal; and though a report recommending considerable changes in trade union structure was adopted at the Congress of 1944, the Unions were too busy with day-to-day war-time activities to have much time to spare for problems of internal reorganization. The only incident of importance in strictly trade union affairs was when thirty-five years of agitation reached its term in the merging at the end of 1944 of the Miners' Federation of Great Britain in one centralized National Mineworkers' Union.

Internationally, a mission was sent by Congress to Greece early in 1945, to do its best to help towards a reconciliation between the rival sections of the Greek Trade Unions; and shortly after a World Trade Union Conference, originally planned for the previous year, was held in London and agreed to form a new World Trade Union Federation to replace both the pre-war International Federation of Trade Unions and its Communist rival, the Red International of Labour Unions. The old I.F.T.U. had included neither the Trade Unions of the Soviet Union nor the United States Congress of Industrial Organizations. It had few affiliations outside Europe, except the strongly anti-Socialist American Federation of Labor, which refused to attend the 1945 Conference because the C.I.O. and the Russians were invited. The W.F.T.U. was launched in the hope that it would prove possible for Communist and non-Communist Unions to work together; but this hope was soon to be disappointed. Four years later the British, American and Dutch Trade Unions, objecting to the use made of the W.F.T.U. for Communist propaganda, seceded and took steps to establish an International Confederation of Free Trade Unions, to which most of the non-Communist movements soon adhered. Thereafter, there was sharp rivalry between the two bodies, especially for the allegiance of the growing Trade Union movements in the less developed countries. The Christian Trade Unions, mainly in Western Europe and in Latin America, maintained a separate International of their own; and all three were given consultative status by the United Nations and its specialized agencies.

When Germany was defeated in April 1945, it was clear to all that the burdensome alliance with the Conservatives could not long be maintained. Trusting that Winston Churchill's personal prestige would enable him to repeat Lloyd George's electoral *coup* of 1918, the Conservative leaders faced their Labour colleagues with an ultimatum requiring them to choose between an election forthwith or coalition till the end of the Japanese war, believed to be many months away. No more aware than they of the strength of the pent-up discontent, the Labour leaders made vain efforts to have the date postponed till October; they were almost as astonished as their foes at the result of the election. The holocaust of Conservative ministers was almost, though not quite, as complete as that of the Labour ministers in 1931; their party lost two hundred seats and the Labour Party gained as many. A Labour Government, headed by C. R. Attlee, took office, for the first time with a working majority; the verdict of the electors was repeated at the local elections in November.

Great difficulties faced the new Government, but it is not possible here to estimate either them or the steps it took to meet them. All that can be done here is to take a brief backward look, as from the beginning of 1946, at the road that has been travelled.

How had the common man changed in two hundred years? There was no doubt he was much freer than he had been in 1746, when all classes accepted "the grand scheme of subordination." He was freer too than he had been in 1846 when, though the grand scheme had been broken up beyond repair, he was wholly without political power and economically as badly off as ever in working-class history, though on the very eve of better times. Before the end of the second World War he had, as we have seen, begun to lose some of his freedom; but the encroachments were not as yet serious, and the freedom surrendered during the war had been deliberately handed over, as a loan to be returned intact.

True of a man, the above is even truer of a woman; the advance in freedom was so great that it is no exaggeration to say the whole pattern of her life had changed.

Vital statistics are insufficient, but it is fairly safe to say that he, or she, was probably taller than his forefathers, and heavier. He was better educated, certainly; probably better clothed, though it is a matter of opinion what is better clothing. He had, at the least, more choice of clothing; and he was unquestionably better housed than in 1846. He was healthier, and unless 1946 was to be the prelude to more war, he had a longer expectation of life.

His mind had changed more than his body. The common man of 1746, but for a small upper working class of skilled craftsmen, who were very largely Dissenters, had, it is not entirely unfair to say, no mind of his own. The time when the British common people first, *en masse*, show a political mind of their own separate from their rulers, is probably not earlier than the days of Cobbett. Cobbett's readers, as they appear to us from his columns, were neither foolish nor servile—much the reverse. But they were mainly countrymen, or had been so till very recently. They talked and thought as countrymen. They had to be spoken to in terms of grassland ploughed up by fools, of Squire Jolterheads who were in the hands of stock jobbers, and of the sly expressions of the pocket borough electors through whose streets they drove their masters' cattle. Vivid personal descriptions of individual villains they could understand—"squeaking Wilberforce," "nasty, canting, dirty, lousy Methodists"—but the organization of their oppression was something they never grasped; it was only "The Thing," an incomprehensible, tentacular power, which, it was fairly easy to see, could strangle them unless it was somehow kept in check.

Very few years later, the island seems almost populated by a different race. There is nothing left of solidity, except in the increasingly prosperous middle classes: no dignity, no earthy independence. The Chartists are more than anything else a *pitiable* people. The sufferings of the Early Victorian workers were abominable, and rent the hearts of even the hardened observers of the day. But the sufferers were without strength or tenacity; their threats were wild, because they were empty; their attacks on society collapsed at the first check.

A very different type begins to appear in later Victorian days. The Radical working man made the mould, which was not changed until the war of 1914. There is no essential difference in character between the supporters of Charles Bradlaugh and those of George Lansbury, though their political and religious belief had altered. There are characteristics common to Bradlaugh, William Morris, Tom Mann, John Burns, Keir Hardie, George Lansbury, and many others, which were immediately perceptible to those who met them. These are perhaps best described as a strong integrity of character, a determination (as though it was a personal duty) to put down whatever seemed to them to be inequality, superstition, injustice, or oppression, and an enormous strength of will with which to do so. Men of such strong personality could be, and often were, narrow; and in general their political or economic principles were cast in over-simple forms, were unchangeable by argument, and took little regard of countries or conditions outside their personal knowledge. But they seem, in retrospect, often to have been men of greater stature than their immediate successors.

It is difficult, for those who live among them, to estimate the men of 1946. Wiser, certainly, in a sense they were: the books which they demanded, the magazines they read, and even the daily journals they bought had been compelled to give more information, and about more subjects than ever before. That the technique of deluding the masses had had to be so much improved was in itself a compliment; it is difficult to deny that in the pre-war tangle the common man saw the truth more clearly than the richer classes: if an interest in world problems was a qualification, he was better able to face the more difficult problems of 1946. Courageous also: the course of 1940 to 1945 had silenced much chatter about "British decadence." But more than that it would be unprofitable to try to say.

One thing, however, was clear in 1946. In twenty years

there had been some surface changes in the class structure of Great Britain. During the 'thirties, the working classes, with the vast exception of those in the depressed areas, had made a real advance in their standards of living. There had been some shifting from the class of "proletarian" wage-earners to blackcoated salary-earners. During the war, though there had been great sacrifices, these sacrifices had been to some extent shared by the upper class. Moreover, the depressed areas had been, momentarily at least, reclaimed: dead towns in South Wales and the North-East had revived, and men who had never expected to work again had found jobs.

These were important changes. Nevertheless, two nations still confronted each other in 1946, though much less starkly than in the days of the Chartists when Disraeli wrote *Sybil* to point the contrast, less starkly even than in the years of depression between the world wars. Full employment, high direct taxation of large incomes, subsidizing of basic foods and improved social services were narrowing very greatly the immense gulf between the actual standards of living of the rich and the poor; and under the new Labour Government were to continue to do so, until about 1949 or 1951 at least. But there had been no equivalent change in the distribution of property. Industrial capital was still held mainly by a fairly limited class; rent, interest and profits still accounted for about one-third of the gross national product, as against two-thirds for wages, salaries and forces' pay; more than one-third of the total number of incomes over £135 were still under £250 a year. The great majority of those who died still had almost nothing to leave to their successors.

RECOMMENDED BOOKS

IN revising this bibliography I have tried to bear in mind the needs of students who are just beginning their work in modern English social history. When such people are confronted with long lists of books they are apt to feel much as Falstaff did about Mistress Quickly whom he compared to an otter. "Why, she's neither fish nor flesh; a man knows not where to have her." Accordingly, I preface my lists of books with this "talking bibliography" which I hope may help the reader to find the most useful and enjoyable books with the least effort on his part. My aim is to draw attention to the works which have the greatest general usefulness: to point to some of the most exciting and rewarding volumes, particularly ones which have been published since the first appearance of *The Common People*: and to explain how this bibliography has been compiled and how it works.

General histories of Labour

After seventy years, Sidney and Beatrice Webb: *History of Trade Unionism* (revised edition, 1920) retains its place as the best general history of this subject. Raymond Postgate in his own pioneering *The Builders' History* (1923) compared its importance for labour studies to that of the *Origin of Species* in biology. Certainly we still derive our chronology of trade unionism from the Webbs and their portrait of craft unionism has never been surpassed. The Webbs' *History* ought to be read in conjunction with their *Industrial Democracy*, 2 vols. (1897): a great analytical work which has justly been described as "the best single book ever written on the British trade unions."

Recently the Webbs' chronology has been called into question, although not very convincingly. Inevitably revisions have been made. One of the most important is G. D. H. Cole: *British Trade Unionism in the Third Quarter of the Nineteenth Century* in E. M. Carus Wilson (editor) *Essays in Economic History*, Vol. iii (1962). The work of correcting the Webbs and bringing them up to date has been begun by H. A. Clegg, A. Fox and A. F. Thompson: *History of Trade Unions since 1889*, Oxford 1964. So far only the first volume dealing with the years 1889–1910 has appeared. Those who feel they must have a short account of union history from its beginnings up to the present day can consult H. Pelling: *A History of British Trade Unionism* (Pelican), 1963.

The historiography of individual unions, or groups of unions, as distinct from general histories of the trade union movement, has made great strides since 1945. A list which is by no means exhaustive, will be found in Part I of this bibliography. H. A. Turner: *Trade Union Growth, Structure and Policy: A Comparative Study of the Cotton Unions* (1962), although not easy to read, is highly original and important. In so far as it stands in any tradition, it is in the one established by Postgate in his *Builders' History*. It treats, not one union, but a group of unions organizing in the same industry. S. Pollard: *History of Labour in Sheffield* (Liverpool) 1959, uses the region, rather than the industry, in order to develop a rich comparative study of trade union development. K. D. Buckley: *Trade Unionism in Aberdeen, 1878–1900* (Edinburgh 1955), although much narrower than Pollard, shows what can be done with the history of a Trades Council. Here labour and urban history come together and urban history has also been flourishing during the last fifteen years. A Briggs: *Victorian Cities* (1963), is an excellent example. There is still room for many more local histories of labour, not just organized labour, and this is a field in which the adult student who can track down the primary sources may be able to make an independent contribution to historical knowledge.

Returning to general histories, M. Beer: *History of British Socialism* (2 vols., 1919) and G. D. H. Cole: *A Short History of the British Working Class Movement, 1789–1937* (1937), are still attractive and essentially reliable guides. A few attempts have been made to compete with them on their own terms, but none has been very successful. E. P. Thompson: *The Making of the English Working Class* (1963), is the one really big book to have been published since the war which provides a continuous history of working class development over a substantial tract of time. (It stops about 1840.) It is in the tradition of J. L. and Barbara Hammond whose *Village Labourer* (1911), *Town Labourer* (1917), and *Skilled Labourer* (1919) remain, for all their deficiencies, classic works on the period 1760–1832. Thompson is splendidly indifferent as to where one sort of history starts and another begins. *The Making of the English Working Class* is an immense book, but gloriously evocative and exceptionally rewarding. While he teaches us much about the early history of the Labour Movement, Thompson greatly deepens our understanding of the material and cultural life of the labourer who had no direct experience of working-class organization. The same is true of E. J. Hobsbawm: *Labouring Men* (1964); another landmark is the post-war development of British labour historiography. Here Hobsbawm brings together a number of his outstanding essays and articles on such topics as *The Tramping Artisan, Custom, Wages and Work-load, The Labour Aristocracy*, and *The General Labour Unions 1889–1914*. His highly important and controversial essay on the *British Standard of Living 1790 to 1850* is also included. The essays on political topics are rather less impressive.

Labouring Men is a vitally important book which deals with topics over the whole range of general labour history, without pretending to supply such a history itself. There are four other volumes, bringing together contributions from several authors, of which the same might be said. J. Saville (editor): *Democracy and the Labour Movement* (1954) has many good things including an excellent essay on the Master and Servant Acts. A. Briggs and J. Saville (editors): *Essays in Labour History* (1960) is a well-planned work in which each chapter leads into the next in a way which is unusual in collections of this sort. L. S. Pressnell (editor): *Studies in the Industrial Revolution* (1960) and E. M. Carus-Wilson: *Essays in Economic History*, Vol. III (1962) are both exceptionally useful.

To the rule that there have been no great, general narrative histories since 1945, G. D. H. Cole himself provided the one outstanding exception. His *A History of Socialist Thought* (1953–1960) is encyclopaedic. It is nothing less than a history of the entire international labour movement. It is unrivalled and it is not likely to be challenged, at any rate not by a single scholar working alone and unaided. Despite its great length, it is a readable book and each volume can be taken as a work in its own right. The five volumes are organized as follows: I *The Forerunners, 1789–1850*: II *Marxism and Anarchism, 1850–1890* (1954): III *The Second International, 1889–1914* in two parts, (1956): IV *Communism and Social Democracy, 1914–1931* (in two parts) (1958): V *Socialism and Fascism, 1931–1939*. For those who must have a relatively brief sketch of the international Labour Movement there is H. W. Laidler: *Social Economic Movements* (1944).

Before leaving general histories of labour, mention should be made of three volumes which collect extracts from historical documents. The most comprehensive in relation to the years which it covers is G. D. H. Cole and A. W. Filson, *British Working Class Movements: Documents 1789–1875* (1951). H. Pelling: *The Challenge of Socialism* (1954) is a useful introduction without being very challenging. R. W. Postgate: *Revolution from 1789 to 1906* (1920) is mostly about France and Russia, but it includes other material and has a good collection from *The Revolutionary British Working Class, 1832–1854*. Other collections of documents such as A. Aspinall: The *Early English Trade Unions: Documents from the Home Office Papers in the Public Record Office* (1949) will be found in Part III where books are listed according to the period to which they relate.

General Socio-Economic Background

W. H. B. Court, *A Concise Economic History of Britain from 1750 to recent times* (Cambridge, 1954) is the best economic history text-book covering the two hundred years with which we are concerned. Those who are in search of rather more detailed text-book treatment of specific periods will find it in T. S. Ashton: *The Industrial Revolution, 1760–1830*. (This is a justly celebrated book, although H. L. Beales: *The Industrial Revolution, 1750–1850* (second revised edition, 1958) is shorter and easier to read). J. D. Chambers: *The Workshop of the World, 1820–1880* (1961) and S. Pollard: *The Development of the British Economy, 1914–1950* (1962) are both clear and helpful.

J. H. Clapham: *Economic History of Modern Britain*, 3 vols. 1930–38 is a classic work. M. Dobb: *Studies in the Development of Capitalism* (1946) is a valuable interpretation by a learned and latitudinarian Marxist, but will prove tough going for the beginner.

B. R. Mitchell and P. Deane: *Abstract of British Historical Statistics* (Cambridge, 1962), is one of those invaluable books which make it hard to imagine how we managed without it for so long. It brings together all the major historical statistics relating to economic development up to 1938. It contains sixteen sets of Tables relating to Population and Vital Statistics: the Labour Force: Agriculture: Coal: Transport: Overseas Trade: Wages and the Standard of Living: Prices, etc. There is a careful introduction to each topic explaining how the figures have been compiled and cautioning against their misuse. Each chapter closes with references to the principal books, articles and Government publications. Thanks to the appearance of this volume I have felt free to omit many of the statistical works which occupied much space in earlier editions of the *Common People*. Their principal conclusions have been incorporated in the *Abstract of British Historical Statistics* and all of them are referred to there. P. Deane and W. A. Cole: *British Economic Growth, 1688–1955* (Cambridge, 1962) is a companion volume.

General Socio-Political Background

There is no single volume which provides an adequate guide to the socio-political background. There are, however, three books which, between them, do the job. A Briggs: *The Age of Improvement* (1959) covers the period between the seventeen eighties and eighteen sixties. R. C. K. Ensor: *England 1870–1914* (Oxford, 1936) is dated but still worth while. C. L. Mowat: *Britain Between the Wars, 1918–1940* (1955) can be warmly recommended. A. J. P. Taylor: *English History, 1914–1945* (Oxford 1965) is good on the Wars themselves, but Mowat is the best guide to the inter-war period. E. Halevy: *History of the English People in the Nineteenth Century* (6 vols., 1924–1934) is a masterpiece. The first volume *England in 1815*, the fifth volume *Imperialism and the Rise of Labour 1895–1905* as well as the famous epilogue, *The Rule of Democracy* are of outstanding excellence.

Raymond Williams: *Culture and Society, 1780–1950* (Pelican, 1961) offers interesting interpretations of the relationship between intellectual developments and social change. He discusses several of the books which I have listed in Part III of this bibliography under the heading of "Contemporaneous and near contemporaneous writings." However, he is not concerned with culture in a bookish or arty way, but rather with it as a changing conception of "right knowing and right doing."

Plan of this Bibliography
The books which I have brought together in Part I of this bibliography (Special Subjects) either cover the two centuries 1746–1946 or else they relate to such a large part of it that they would have to be listed over and over again in Part III where works are grouped according to Periods. Thus, Henry Pelling's excellent *The Origins of the Labour Party* (1954) appears in the appropriate section of Part III (Imperialism and Socialism) because it relates only to that period: while Ralph Miliband's stimulating, but controversial, *Parliamentary Socialism* (1961) is placed in Part I because it begins in 1906 and extends beyond 1945.

In Part II (Biographies and Autobiographies) I have thought it useful to follow the practice adopted by Cole and Postgate in earlier editions and list the subjects in chronological rather than in alphabetical order. The student who enjoys biography may thus easily find one or more related to a period in which he is interested. Since biography is so popular I have listed "Lives," where they are available, of almost everybody who rates a mention in the text. (Those who don't get mentioned are excluded.) This has meant including books which are very uneven in importance, charm and merit. I have cast out some of the truly appalling contributions to this branch of literature such as G. J. Holyoake's: *Life of J. R. Stephens*, one of the worst biographies ever written, but it must be admitted that labour memoirs tend to be rather dull and pompous. Of course, there has been some great autobiographical writing. Most of it belongs to the last century. Cobbett, Bamford and Lovett are not to be missed by anyone who cares for the history of the English people. Nor for that matter should such delightful books as the autobiographies of Robert Dale Owen and John Stuart Mill be neglected. But in the present century only the Beatrice Webb diaries can be compared with them in point of fascination and value.

Matters are a great deal better when we turn from autobiographies to biographies. Since 1945 there have been several excellent ones. In particular, C. Driver: *Tory Radical: The Life of Richard Oastler* (Oxford, 1946) is a wholly satisfactory study of a great man and an indispensable work for any study of the Factory Movement. A. R. Schoyen: *The Chartist Challenge: A Portrait of George Julian Harney* (1958) is very exciting despite the fact that the author had the misfortune to discover some of Harney's letters only after the book had been published. A. Bullock: *The Life and Times of Ernest Bevin: Vol. I Trade Union Leader 1881–1940* (1960) is most important and very readable. Less important, but equally readable (in a quite different way) is M. Foot: *Aneurin Bevan, vol. I 1897–1945* (1962)

I have also followed Cole and Postgate in limiting this bibliography to books published in English which are either in print or are accessible in good libraries. This has meant omitting Blue Books and other Reports as well as articles. However, I have, in Part IV, listed guides and general works of reference. The student who acquaints himself with these indispensable tools of the trade will know how to find his way to the parliamentary papers referred to in the text: how to discover the whereabouts of periodicals and to learn about their contents: how to check up on statistical series and on biographical and other facts. The short-list of journals will help him to keep abreast of current research.

The place of publication of every book listed is London and the date is that of the first edition, unless otherwise stated. No book is included if it was published after October 1966. At the request of the publishers I have tried to keep this bibliography down to its original length. This has meant that the pleasure of including some new and exciting volumes has had to be matched by retiring others which are still worthy of attention and respect.

I am indebted to colleagues in Sheffield University and to fellow members of the Society for the Study of Labour History for many helpful suggestions. Raphael Samuel, Tutor in History at Ruskin College, Oxford and John Saville, Reader in Economic History in the University of Hull, made valuable criticisms.

Royden Harrison
Sheffield

October 1966

PART I SPECIAL SUBJECTS

(*a*) *Working-class Politics and Socialism.*
    COLE, G. D. H.—*British Working-class Politics: 1832–1914* (1946).
    COLE, G. D. H.—*A History of the Labour Party from 1914* (1948).
    MILIBAND, R.—*Parliamentary Socialism* (1961).
    BARRY, E. E.—*Nationalisation in British Politics* (1965).
    COLE, M. I.—*The Story of Fabian Socialism* (1961).

(*b*) *Collective Self-Help*
    HEDGES, R. Y. and WINTERBOTTOM, A.—*Legal History of Trade Unionism* (1930).
    ALLEN, V. L.—*Trade Unions and the Government* (1960).
    ROBERTS, B. C.—*The Trade Union Congress 1868–1921* (1958).
    TURNER, H. A.—*Trade Union Growth, Structure & Policy* (*The Cotton Unions*) (1962).
    JEFFREYS, J. B.—*The Story of the Engineers* (1945).
    BAGWELL, P. B.—*The Railwaymen* (1963).
    POSTGATE, R. W.—*The Builders' History* (1923).
    ARNOT, R. P.—*The Miners* (3 vols.) (1949–1961).
    WILLIAMS, J. E.—*The Derbyshire Miners* (1962).
    EVANS, E. W.—*The Miners of South Wales* (Cardiff: 1961).
    MUSSON, A. E.—*The Typographical Association* (1954).
    HOWE, E. and WAITE, H. E.—*London Society of Compositors* (1948).

GROVES, M.—*Sharpen the Sickle* (1949).

FYRTH, H. J. and COLLINS, H.—*The Foundry Workers* (1958).

CLEGG, H. A.—*General Union (G.M.W.U.)* (Oxford: 1954).

ALLEN, V. L.—*Trade Union Leadership (Important for T.G.W.U.)* (1957).

FOX, A.—*History of the National Union of Boot & Shoe Operatives* (1958).

CUTHBERT, N. H.—*The Lace-Makers Society 1760–1960* (Nottingham: 1960).

POTTER, B. (MRS. WEBB)—*The Cooperative Movement* (1899).

BONNER, A.—*British Co-operation* (Manchester: 1961).

COLE, G. D. H.—*A Century of Co-operation* (Manchester: 1945).

GOSDEN, P. H. J. H.—*The Friendly Societies in England 1815–1875* (Manchester: 1961).

HORNE, H. A.—*A History of Savings Banks* (Oxford: 1947).

(c) *National, Regional and Urban Studies.*

STRAUSS, E.—*Irish Nationalism & British Democracy* (1951).

CONNELL, K. H.—*The Great Famine: Studies in Irish History* (1957).

MARWICK, W. H.—*Scotland in Modern Times* (1964).

CAMPBELL, R. H.—*Scotland since 1707* (Oxford: 1965).

JOHNSTON, T.—*A History of the Working Classes in Scotland* (1929).

WILLIAMS, D.—*A History of Modern Wales* (1950).

JOHN, A. H.—*Industrial Development of South Wales 1750–1850* (Cardiff: 1950).

ROWE, J.—*Cornwall in the Age of the Industrial Revolution* (Liverpool: 1953).

POLLARD, S.—*History of Labour in Sheffield* (Liverpool: 1959).

BUCKLEY, K. D.—*Trade Unionism in Aberdeen* (Edinburgh: 1955).

BRIGGS, A.—*Victorian Cities* (1963).

BRIGGS, A.—*History of Birmingham Vol II 1865–1938* (1952).

DYOS, H. J.—*Victorian Suburb (Camberwell)* (Leicester: 1961).

CHURCH, R. A.—*Victorian Nottingham 1815–1900* (1966).

CHALONER, W. H.—*Social & Economic Development of Crewe 1780–1923* (Manchester: 1950).

BARKER, T. C. and HARRIS, J. R.—*St. Helens 1751–1900* (1959).

MARSHALL, J. D.—*Furness 1711–1900* (Barrow-in-Furness: 1958).

(*d*) *Industries and Economic Institutions.*

ERNLE, LORD—*English Farming, Past & Present* (6th revised ed.) (1961).

NEF, J. A.—*The Rise of the British Coal Industry*, 2 vols. (1932).

HEATON, H.—*The Yorkshire Woollen & Worsted Industries* (Oxford: 1920).

ROBSON, R.—*The Cotton Industry in Britain* (1955).

ARMYTAGE, W. H. G.—*Social History of Engineering* (1961).

MATHIAS, P.—*The Brewing Industry in England 1700–1830* (Cambridge: 1959).

VAIZEY, J.—*The Brewing Industry 1886–1951* (1960).

JACKMAN, W. T.—*Development of Transportation in Modern England* (2nd revised ed.) (1962).

BURN, D. L.—*Economic History of Steelmaking 1867–1939* (Cambridge: 1940).

HABER, L. F.—*The Chemical Industry during the Nineteenth Century* (1958).

JEFFREYS, J. B.—*Retail Trading in Britain* (Cambridge: 1954).

(*e*) *Social Conditions and Social Legislation.*

COLE, G. D. H.—*Studies in Class Structure* (1955).

DRUMMOND, SIR J. C. and WILBRAHAM, A.—*The English-man's Food* (2nd revised ed.) (1957).

SALAMAN, R. N.—*The History & Social Influence of the Potato* (1949).

COLLIER, F.—*The Family Economy of the Working Classes in the Cotton Industry 1784–1833* (Manchester: 1965).

PINCHBECK, I.—*Women Workers in the Industrial Revolution 1750–1850* (1930).

HEWITT, M.—*Wives & Mothers in Victorian Industry* (1958).

FRAZER, W. M.—*History of English Public Health, 1834–1939* (1950).

LAMBERT, R.—*Sir John Simon* (1963).

JONES, K.—*Lunacy, Law & Conscience 1744–1845* (1955).

OWEN, D. E.—*English Philanthropy 1660–1960* (Cambridge, Mass. U.S.A. 1965).

BRUCE, M.—*The Coming of the Welfare State* (1961).

(*f*) *Cultural, Educational and Religious Developments.*

ALTICK, R. D.—*The English Common Reader: a social history of the mass reading public 1800–1900* (Chicago: 1957).

HOGGART, R.—*The Uses of Literacy* (1957).

KLINGENDER, F. D.—*Art & the Industrial Revolution* (1947).

SIMON, B.—*Studies in the History of Education 1780–1870* (1960).

SIMON, B.—*Education & the Labour Movement 1870–1920* (1965).

HARRISON, J. F. C.—*Learning and Living 1790–1960* (1961).

INGLIS, K. S.—*Churches & the Working Classes in Victorian England* (1963).

WICKHAM, E. R.—*Church & People in an Industrial City* (1957).

WEARMOUTH, R. F.—*Methodism and the Working-Class Movements of England 1800–1850* (1937).

ARMYTAGE, W. H. G.—*Heavens Below* (1961).

MORTON, A. L.—*The English Utopia* (1952).

PART II

BIOGRAPHIES AND AUTOBIOGRAPHIES

L.—Life.   *Aut.*—Autobiography.   *C.P.*—Included in G. D. H. Cole, *Chartist Portraits* (1941). *VP.*—Sketched in relation to some theme or problem of mid-Victorian society in A. Briggs, *Victorian People* (Pelican) 1965.

Wesley, John (1703–91).—*Journals*, edited by M. Curnuck, 8 vols. (1909–1916).

L. by R. Southey, 1820 or by J. S. Simon, 1937.

Brindley, James (1716–72).—*L.* by S. Smiles, 1864.

Price, Richard (1723–91).—*L.* by R. Thomas, 1924.

Howard, J. (1726–90).—*L.* by J. B. Brown, 1818 or J. G. Rowe, 1927.

Wilkes, John (1727–97).—*L.* by R. Postgate (*That Devil Wilkes, 1930*) or by C. Trench, 1962.

Boulton, Matthew (1728—1809).—*L.* by S. Smiles, 1865.

Wedgwood, Josiah (1730–95).—*L.* by E. Meteyard, 1865.

Priestley, Joseph (1733–1804).—*Aut.* 1904 ed. and *L.* by A. D. Holt, 1931.

Tooke, John Horne (1736–1812).—*Aut.* Graham, J. A. ed., 1828 and *L.* by M. C. Yarborough, 1926.

Watt, James (1736–1819).—*L.* by S. Smiles, 1865.

Paine, T. (1737–1809).—*L.* by M. D. Conway, New York, 1892.

Cartwright, John (1740–1824).—*L.* by F. D. Cartwright, 1826.

Young, Arthur (1741–1820).—*Aut.* ed by M. B. Edwards, 1898.

More, Hannah (1745–1833).—*L.* by M. Gwladys Jones, 1952.

Bentham, Jeremy (1746–1832).—*L.* by Leslie Stephen (*The English Utilitarians*, vol. 1, 1900 or E. Halevy, *Growth of Philosophic Radicalism*) 1928.

Fox, Charles James (1749–1806).—*L.* by J. L. Hammond, 1903.

Holcroft, Thomas (1749–1809).—*Aut.* continued by Wm. Hazlitt, introduced by E. Colby, 2 vols., 1925.

Spence, Thomas (1750–1814).—*L.* by O. Rudkin, 1927.

Walker, Thomas (1751–1817).—*L.* by F. Knight, 1957.

Hardy, Thomas (1752–1832).—*Aut.* 1932.

Godwin, William (1756–1836).—*L.* by G. Woodcock, 1946.

McAdam, John Loudon (1756–1836).—*L.* by R. Devereux, 1936.

Wollstonecroft, Mary (1759–97).—*L.* by W. Godwin, 1798.—*L.* by E. R. Pennell 1885.

Birkbeck, George (1776–1841).—*L.* by T. Kelly, 1957.

Thompson, William (1775–1833).—*L.* by R. K. P. Pankhurst, 1954.

Pitt, William (1759–1806).—*L.* by J. Holland Rose, 1925.

Wilberforce, William (1759–1833).—*L.* by R. Coupland, 1945 (2nd ed.).

Cobbett, William (1763–1835).—*Aut.* (*The Life and Adventures of Peter Porcupine*), edited by G. D. H. Cole, 1927. *L.* by G. D. H. Cole (3rd revised ed. 1947).

Grey, Lord (1764–1845).—*L.* by G. M. Trevelyan, 1920.

Burdett, Francis (1770–1844).—*L.* by M. W. Patteson, 1931.

Place, Francis (1771–1854).—*L.* by Graham Wallas, 1898.

Owen, Robert (1771–1856).—*Aut.* 1857 (reprinted 1920). *L.* by G. D. H. Cole (revised ed. 1930) or M. I. Cole, 1953.

Hunt, Henry (1773–1835).—*L.* by R. Huish, 1836.

Brougham, Henry Peter (1778–1868).—*L.* by A. Aspinall (Manchester, 1927).

Stephenson, George (1781–1848).—*L.* by S. Smiles, 1857.

Attwood, Thomas (1783–1856). *C.P.*

Fielden, John (1784–1849). *C.P.*

Hunt, Leigh (1784–1859).—*Aut.* 3 vols., 1850.

Frost, John (1784–1877).—*L.* by D. Williams (Cardiff, 1939) and *C.P.*

Hodgskin, T. (1787–1869).—*L.* by E. Halevy (1956).

Bamford, Samuel (1788–1872).—*Aut.* (*Passages in the Life of a Radical*, 2 vols., 1844, and *Early Days*), 1849.

Oastler, Richard (1789–1861).—*L.* by C. Driver (Oxford, 1946) and *C.P.*

Carlile, Richard (1790–1843).—*L.* by M. C. Campbell (3rd ed. 1941).

Knight, Charles (1791–1873).—*Aut.* 3 vols. (*Passages of a Working Life*), 1864–5.

Durham, Lord (1792–1840).—*L.* by L. Cooper (*Radical Jack*), 1959.

Sturge, Joseph (1793–1859).—*L.* by S. Hobhouse, 1919.

O'Connor, Feargus (1794–1855).—*L.* by D. Read and E. Glasgow (1961) and *C.P.*

Wakley, Thomas (1795–1862).—*L.* by S. Sprigge, 1897.

Macaulay, Thomas Babington (1800–59).—*L.* by G. O. Trevelyan, 1876.

Hudson, George (1800–71).—*L.* by R. S. Lambert (*The Railway King*), 1934.

Lovett, William (1800–77).—*Aut.* 1876 (revised ed. by R. H. Tawney, 1920).

Chadwick, Edwin (1800–90).—*L.* by S. E. Finer, 1952.

Smith, James Elishamah (1801–57).—*L.* by W. A. Smith, 1892.

Owen, Robert Dale (1801–57).—*Aut.* (*Threading my Way*) 1874.

Roebuck, John Arthur (1801–79).—*L.* by R. E. Leader, 1897 and *V.P.*

Shaftesbury, Lord (1801–85).—*L.* by J. L. and B. Hammond, 1923 or by M. St. J. Fancourt, 1962.

Cobden, Richard (1804–65).—*L.* by J. Morley, 1881 or by J. A. Hobson, 1918.

Disraeli, Benjamin (1804–81).—*L.* by R. Blake, 1966 or by W. F. Monypenny and G. E. Buckle, 6 vols, 1910–20 and *V.P.*

O'Brien, James Bronterre (1805–64).—*C.P.*

Maurice, Frederick Denison (1805–72).—*L.* by J. F. Maurice, 1883–4

Cooper, Thomas (1805–92).—*Aut.* 1872 and *C.P.*

Mill, John Stuart (1806–73).—*Aut.* 1873. *L.* by M. St. John Packe, 1954.

Gladstone, William Ewart (1809–98).—*L.* by J. Morley, 3 vols. 1903 or P. Magnus, 1954.

Bright, John (1811–89).—*L.* by G. M. Trevelyan, 1913 and *V.P.*

Lowe, Robert (1811–92).—*V.P.*

Dickens, Charles (1812–70).—*L.* by J. Forster, 1928 and House, A. H. *The Dickens World,* 1941.

Harney, George Julian (1817–97).—*L.* by A. R. Schoyen (*The Chartist Challenge*) (1958) and *C.P.*

Holyoake, George Jacob (1817–1906).—*Aut. Sixty Years of an Agitator's Life,* 2 vols. 1892 and *Bygones Worth Remembering,* 2 vols. 1905.—*L.* by J. McCabe, 2 vols. 1908.

Marx, Karl Heinrich (1818–83).—*L.* by F. Mehring, 1936 or by I. Berlin, 1939.

Jones, Ernest (1819–69).—*L.* by J. Saville, 1952 and *C.P.*

Kingsley, Charles (1819–75).—*L.* by R. B. Martin (*The Dust of Combat*), 1959.

Ruskin, John (1819–1900)—*Aut.* Diaries. 3 vols. Oxford, 1856–9.—*L.* by J. A. Hobson, 1898.

Victoria, Queen (1819–1901).—*L.* by L. Strachey, 1921 or E. Longford, 1964.

Engels, Friedrich (1820–95).—*L.* by G. Mayer, 1937.

Ludlow, John Malcolm (1821–1911).—*L.* by N. C. Masterman (Cambridge), 1963.

Bagehot, Walter (1826–77).—*L.* by N. St. John-Stevas (1959) and *V.P.*

Arch, Joseph (1826–1919).—*Aut.* (edited by Countess of Warwick), 1898.

Butler, Josephine (1828–1906).—*L.* by E. M. Bell, 1962.

Cowen, Joseph (1831–1900).—*L.* by E. R. Jones, 1886.

Bradlaugh, Charles (1833–91).—*L.* by H. Bradlaugh Bonner, 1894 and W. L. Arnstein, The Bradlaugh Case (Oxford), 1965.

Morris, William (1834–96).—*L.* by E. P. Thompson, 1950 and by J. W. Mackail, 1899.

Applegarth, Robert (1834–1924).—*V.P.*

Chamberlain, Joseph (1836–1914).—*L.* by J. L. Garvin and J. Amery, 3 vols., 1932–1950.

Hill, Octavia (1838–1912).—*L.* by C. E. Maurice, 1913 or E. H. C. Moberly Bell, 1942.

Broadhurst, Henry (1840–1911).—*Aut.* 1901.

Hyndman, Henry Mayers (1842–1921).—*Aut. The Record of an Adventurous Life,* 1911 and *Further Reminiscences,* 1912.—*L.* by C. Tsuzuki, Oxford 1961.

Abraham, William (Mabon) (1842–1922).—*L.* by E. W. Evans (Cardiff), 1959.

Dilke, Charles Wentworth (1843–1911).—*L.* by R. Jenkins, 1958 and by G. M. Tuckwell and S. Gwynn, 2 vols., 1917–1925.

Soutter, Frederick William (1844–1932).—*Aut. Recollections of a Labour Pioneer,* 1923 and *Fights for Freedom,* 1925.

Parnell, Charles Stewart (1846–91).—*L.* by St. J. Ervine, 1925 or Barry O'Brien, 1898.

Rosebery, Lord (1847–1929).—*L.* by R. Rhodes James, 1963.

Besant, Annie (1847–1933).—*Aut.,* 1893. *L.* by A. H. Nethercot, 1961.

Graham, Robert (Bontine Cunninghame (1852–1936)).—*L.* by A. F. Tschiffely (*Don Roberto*), 1937.

Balfour Arthur James (1848–1930).—*L.* by K. Young, 1963.

Blatchford, Robert (1851–1943).—*L.* by L. Thompson, 1951.

Asquith, Herbert Henry (1852–1928).—*Aut.* 1928. *L.* by R. Jenkins, 1964.

Carson, Edward Henry (1854–1935).—*L.* by Montgomery Hyde, 1953.

Hodge, John (1855–1937).—*Aut.* (*Workman's Cottage to Windsor Castle*), 1931.

Hardie, James Keir (1856–1915).—*L.* by W. Stewart 1925 or E. Hughes, 1956.

Mann, Tom (1856–1941).—*Aut.* 1923. *L.* by D. Torr (vol. 1, 1856–90), 1956.

Shaw, George Bernard (1856–1950).—*Aut.* (*Sixteen Self-Sketches*), 1949. *L.* by A. Henderson, (New York, 1956) or St. John Ervine, 1956.

Sexton, James (1856–1938).—*Aut.*, 1936.

Burns, John (1858–1943).—*L.* by W. Kent (*Labour's Lost Leader*), 1950.

Law, Andrew Bonar (1858–1923).—*L.* by R. Blake, 1955.

Webb, Beatrice (1858–1943).—*Aut. My Apprenticeship.* 1926, *Our Partnership*, 1948, *Diaries*, 1912–24 (ed. by M. I. Cole, 1952) and *Diaries*, 1924–32 (ed. by M. I. Cole, 1956). *L.* by M. I. Cole, 1945.

Wilson, Joseph Havelock (1859–1929).—*Aut.* (*My Stormy Voyage Through Life*), 1925.

Webb, Sidney (1859–1947).—*L.* by M. I. Cole (ed.) *The Webbs and their Work*, 1949, or M. A. Hamilton, *Sidney and Beatrice Webb*, 1933.

Lansbury, George (1859–1940).—*Aut.* 1934. *L.* by R. Postgate, 1951.

Tillett, Ben (1860–1943).—*Aut.* 1931.

Bottomley, Horatio (1860–1933).—*L.* by J. Symons, 1955.

Gosling, Harry (1861–1930).—*Aut.* (*Up and Down Stream*), 1927.

Lloyd-George, David (1863–1945).—*L.* by F. Owen (*Tempestuous Journey*) 1954.

Henderson, Arthur (1863–1935).—*L.* by M. A. Hamilton, 1938.

Snowden, Philip (1864–1937).—*Aut.* 2 vols. 1934.

Jowett, Frederick W. (1864–1944).—*L.* by F. Brockway (*Socialism over Sixty Years*), 1946.

George V (1865–1936).—*L.* by H. Nicolson, 1952.

Macdonald, James Ramsay (1866–1937).—*L.* by Lord Elton, 1939 or L. M. Weir, 1938 or H. H. Tiltman, 1929

Wells, Herbert George (1866–1946).—*Aut.* 1934.

Baldwin, Stanley (1867–1947).—*L.* by G. M. Young, 1952.

Connolly, James (1868–1916).—*L.* by C. Desmond Greaves, 1961.

Chamberlain, Neville (1869–1940).—*L.* by K. G. Feiling, 1946.

Clynes, John Robert (1869–1949).—*Aut.* 2 vols, 1937.

Rowntree, B. Seebohm (1871–1954).—*L.* by A. Briggs, 1951.

Bondfield, Margaret (1873–1953).—*Aut.* 1949.

Chesterton, Gilbert Keith (1874–1936).—*Aut.* 1936 and *L.* by Maisie Ward, 1944.

Thomas, James Henry (1874–1949).—*Aut.* 1937.

Churchill, Winston Spencer (1874–1965).—*Aut. My Early Life*, 1930 and *Thoughts and Adventures*, 1932.

Larkin, James (1876–1947).—*L.* by E. Larkin, 1965.

Gallacher, William (1876–1965).—*Aut. (Revolt on the Clyde)*, 1936.

McLean, John (1879–1923).—*L.* by T. Bell (Glasgow), 1944.

Macarthur, Mary (1880–1921).—*L.* by M. A. Hamilton, 1925.

Cripps, Stafford (1880–1952).—*L.* by C. Cooke, 1957.

Bevin, Ernest (1881–1951).—*L.* by A. Bullock, vol. 1, 1881–1940, 1960.

Pankhurst, E. Sylvia (1882–1960).—*Aut. (The Home Front)*, 1933.

Keynes, John Maynard (1883–1946).—*L.* by R. F. Harrod, 1951.

Attlee, Clement Richard (1883–   ).—*Aut. As it Happened*, 1954 *A Prime Minister Remembers*, 1961).

Citrine, Walter M. (1887–   ).—*Aut. (Men and Work)*, 1964.

Dalton, Hugh (1887–1962).—*Aut. (Call Back Yesterday)*, 1953 and the *Fateful Years*, 1957.

Morrison, Herbert (1888–1965).—*Aut.* 1960.

Brockway, Fenner (1888—   ).—*Aut. (Inside the Left)*, 1942.

Cole, Margaret (1893—   ).—*Aut. Growing Up Into Revolution*, 1949.

Bevan, Aneurin (1897–1960).—*L.* by M. Foot, vol. 1, 1897–1945, 1962.

Cockburn, Claude (1904–   ).—*Aut. In Time of Trouble*, 1956 *(Communism)*.

PART III PERIODS

SECTION I. EIGHTEENTH CENTURY ENGLAND.

(a) Modern Books.

PLUMB, J. H.—*England in the Eighteenth Century* (1950).

COLE, G. D. H.—*Persons and Periods* (1938).

SYDNEY, W. C.—*England & the English in the Eighteenth Century* (Edinburgh: n.d.).

GEORGE, M. D.—*England in Transition* (1931).

GEORGE, M. D.—*London Life in the Eighteenth Century* (1925).

ASHTON, T. S.—*An Economic History of England—the eighteenth century* (1955).

MANTOUX, P.—*The Industrial Revolution in the Eighteenth Century* (2nd ed. 1928).

MATHIESON, W. L.—*The Awakening of Scotland 1747–1797* (Glasgow 1910).

MARSHALL, D. L.—*The English Poor in the Eighteenth Century* (1926).

HECHT, J. J.—*The Domestic Servant Class in Eighteenth Century England* (1960).

STEPHEN, LESLIE.—*English Thought in the Eighteenth Century* (1876).

BARKER, T. C.—"The Beginnings of the Canal Age in the British Isles" in Pressnell, L. S.: *Studies* (1960).

MANN, J. DE L.—"Clothiers & Weavers in Wiltshire during the Eighteenth Century" in Pressnell, L.S.: *Studies* (1960).

(b) Contemporary Descriptions.

DEFOE, DANIEL.—*A Tour Through the Whole Island of Great Britain* (1724–27).

MACKY JOHN.—*A Journey Through Great Britain* (1723–24).

POCOCKE, RICHARD.—*Travels Through England in 1750 and 1751* (Camden Society) (1888–9).

KALM, PETER.—*A Visit to England in 1748* (Translated: 1892).

YOUNG, ARTHUR.—*Six Months Tour Through the North of England* (1770).

YOUNG, ARTHUR.—*Farmer's Tour Through the East of England* (1771).

YOUNG, ARTHUR.—*Six Weeks Tour Through the Southern Counties* (1772).

YOUNG, ARTHUR.—*Annals of Agriculture* (for other tours).

CAMPBELL, JOHN.—*A Political Survey of Britain 1774* (2 vols.) (1774).

MORITZ, C. P.—*Travels in England in 1782* (Published in German in 1783). See Mavor: *British Tourists*, vol. 4 (1798–   ).

WESLEY, JOHN.—*The Journal* (Enlarged and edited by M. Curnock), 8 vols (1909–16).

DAVIES, DAVID.—*The Case of the Labourers in Husbandry* (Bath: 1795).

EDEN, F. M.—*The State of the Poor* (1797).

CHALMERS, G.—*An Estimate of the Comparative Strength of Great Britain* (1785 and later editions).

Section II.—SOCIO-POLITICAL MOVEMENTS IN THE EIGHTEENTH CENTURY.

THOMPSON, E. P.—*The Making of the English Working Class* (1963).

VEITCH, G. S.—*The Genesis of Parliamentary Reform* (1913).

RUDE, G.—*Wilkes & Liberty: a Social Study of 1763 to 1774* (Oxford: 1962).

CHRISTIE, I. R.—*Wilkes, Wyvill and Reform* (1962).

BOULTON, J. T.—*The Language of Politics in the Age of Wilkes & Burke* (1963).

BLACK, E. G.—*The Association: British Extra-Parliamentary Political Organisation 1769–93* (Harvard: 1963).

MACCOBY, S.—*English Radicalism*
The origins 1762–85 (1955).
From Price to Cobbett 1786–1832 (1955).

LINCOLN, A.—*Some Social & Political Ideas of English Dissent 1763–1800* (1938).

Section III.—THE INDUSTRIAL REVOLUTION AND THE FRENCH WAR.

(*a*) *The Agrarian and Industrial Revolutions.*
  CHAMBERS, J. D. & MINGAY, G. E.—*The Agricultural Revolution 1750–1880* (1966).
  THIRSK, J.—*English Peasant Farming* (1957).
  HAMMOND, J. L. & B.—*The Village Labourer* (1911).
  ASHTON, T. S.—*Iron & Steel in the Industrial Revolution* (Manchester: 1924).
  WADSWORTH, A. P. & MANN, J. DE L.—*The Cotton Trade & Industrial Lancashire 1600–1780* (Manchester: 1931).
  GRIFFITH, G. T.—*Population Problems of the Age of Malthus* (1926).
  SMELSER, N.—*Social Change in the Industrial Revolution* (1960).
  HAMMOND, J. L. & B.—*The Town Labourer* (1917).
  HAMMOND, J. L. & B.—*The Skilled Labourer* (1919).

(*b*) *The Response to the French Revolution: the Combination Acts and the Luddites.*
  COBBAN, A.—(ed.) *The Debate on the French Revolution* (1950).
  BROWN, P. A.—*The French Revolution in English History* (1918).
  MATHIESON, W. L.—*England in Transition* (1920).
  MEIKLE, G. L.—*Scotland & the French Revolution* (Glasgow: 1912).
  GILL, CONRAD.—*The Naval Mutinies of 1797* (Manchester: 1913).
  DOBREE, B. & MANWARING, A.—*The Floating Republic* (1935).
  ASPINALL, A.—*The Early English Trade Unions* (1949).
  PEEL, F.—*The Risings of the Luddites, Chartists & Plugdrawers* (3rd revised ed. 1895).
  FELKIN, W.—*A History of the Machine-Wrought Hosiery & Lace Manufactures* (1867).
  HOBSBAWM, E. J.—"The Machine Breakers" in his *Labouring Men* (1964).
  DARVALL, F. O.—*Popular Disturbances & Public Order in Regency England* (1934).
  ERDMAN, D. V.—*Blake, Prophet against Empire* (Princeton: 1954).

KIERNAN, V. G.—*Wordsworth & the People* in *Saville: Democracy and the Labour Movement* (1954).

BRAILSFORD, H. N.—*Shelley, Godwin and their Circle* (1927).

HASBACH, W.—*History of the English Agricultural Labourer* (1908).

HOSKINS, W. G.—*The Midland Peasant* (1957).

PRESSNELL, L. S.—*Country Banking in the Industrial Revolution* (Oxford: 1956).

HAMMOND, J. L. & B.—*The Rise of Modern Industry* (1925).

(*c*)   *Contemporaneous and near-contemporaneous writings.*

CHALMERS, C.—*The Comparative Strength of Great Britain* (1804).

COLQUHOUN, P.—*The Wealth, Power & Resources of the British Empire* (1812).

PAINE, T.—*The Rights of Man* (1792).

BURKE, E.—*Reflections on the Revolution in France* (1790).

GODWIN, W.—*Political Justice* (1793).

WORDSWORTH, W.—*The Prelude* (1798).

HAZLITT, W.—*Lectures on the English Poets: The Spirit of the Age* (1818) (Everyman 1910).

SHELLEY, P. B.—*Prometheus Unbound* (1820).

MARTINEAU, H.—*History of England 1800–1815* (1878).

SMILES, SAMUEL.—*Lives of the Engineers*, 3 vols, 1861–2.

Section IV.—THE PEACE WITHOUT A PARALLEL.

(*a*)   *Social Conditions after Waterloo.*

PIKE, E. ROYSTON.—*Human Documents of the Industrial Revolution* (1966).

MORRIS, M.—*From Cobbett to the Chartists (Select Documents)* (1948).

COLE, G. D. H.—*Life of William Cobbett* (1924).

WALLAS, G.—*Life of Francis Place* (1898).

EDWARDS, NESS.—*The Industrial Revolution in South Wales* (1924).

PEACOCK, A. J.—*Bread or Blood: A Study of the Agrarian Riots in East Anglia in 1816* (1965).

WHITE, R. J.—*Waterloo to Peterloo* (1957).

BEALES, H. L.—*The Early English Socialists* (1933).

(*b*)   *The Struggle for Reform.*

DAVIS, H. W. C.—*The Age of Grey and Peel* (Oxford: 1929).

BUTLER, J. R. M.—*The Passing of the Great Reform Bill* (2nd revised ed. 1965).

BRUTON, F. A.—(ed.) *Three Accounts of Peterloo* (Manchester 1921).

REED, D.—*Peterloo* (Manchester: 1958).

HAMBURGER, J.—*James Mill & the Art of Revolution* (Yale: 1963).

(*c*) *Contemporaneous and near-Contemporaneous writings.*

COLE, G. D. H. and MARGARET.—*The Opinions of William Cobbett* (1944).

COBBETT, W.—*Rural Rides* (Ed. by Martin, E. W.) (1958).

OWEN, R.—*A New View of Society* (Everyman edition) (1927)

WADE, JOHN.—*History of the Middle & Working Classes* (1833).

PRENTICE, A.—*Manchester 1792–1832* (1850).

COLLET, C. D.—*History of the Taxes on Knowledge* (1899).

Section V.—ENGLAND UNDER THE REFORM ACT.

(*a*) *Owen and the Trade Unions.*

POSTGATE, RAYMOND.—*The Builders' History* (1923).

POSTGATE, RAYMOND.—*Out of the Past* (1922).

COLE, G. D. H.—*Life of Robert Owen* (2nd ed. 1930).

COLE, G. D. H.—*Attempts at General Union* (1953).

TRADES UNION CONGRESS.—*The Martyrs of Tolpuddle* (1934).

SMITH, W. A.—*Shepherd Smith the Universalist* (1892).

(*b*) *The Economy, Poor Laws and Corn Laws.*

CLAPHAM, J. H.—*The Bank of England*, vol. 2. (1944).

PARRIS, H.—*Government & the Railways in the Nineteenth Century* (1965).

LEWIN, H. G.—*Early British Railways* (1925).

LAMBERT, R. S.—*The Railway King* (1934).

COLEMAN, T.—*The Railway Navvies* (1965).

HOBSBAWM, E. J.—"The British Standard of Living" in his *Labouring Men* (1964).

TAYLOR, A. J.—"Progress & Poverty in Britain 1780–1850": A re-appraisal in *Carus-Wilson: Essays III* (1962).

BEALES, H. L.—"The New Poor Law" in *Carus-Wilson: Essays III* (1962).

WEBB, S. & B.—*English Poor Law Policies since 1834.*

FINER, S. E.—*Chadwick* (1952).

BARNES, D. G.—*History of the English Corn Laws* (1930).

McCORD, N.—*The Anti-Corn Law League 1838–1846* (1958).

(c)   *Chartism and the Factory Movement.*

HOVELL, M.—*The Chartist Movement* (Manchester: 1925).

COLE, G. D. H.—*Chartist Portraits* (1941).

BRIGGS, A.—(ed.) *Chartist Studies* (1959).

SCHOYEN, A. R.—*The Chartist Challenge* (1958).

SLOSSON, P. A.—*The Decline of Chartism* (New York: 1916).

MATHER, F. C.—*Public Order in the Age of the Chartists* (Manchester: 1960).

SAUNDERS, L. J.—*Scottish Democracy, 1815–40* (1950).

WARD, J. T.—*The Factory Movement, 1830–55* (1962).

DRIVER, C.—*Tory Radical: the Life of Richard Oastler* (Oxford: 1946).

BREADY, J. WESLEY.—*Lord Shaftesbury and Social & Industrial Progress* (1926).

THOMAS, M. W.—*The Early Factory Legislation* (Leigh-on-Sea: 1948).

(d)   *Contemporaneous and near-Contemporaneous writings.*

ENGELS, F.—*Condition of the Working Classes in 1844* (1892). Translated.

CARLYLE, T.—*Chartism* (1839).

BAXTER, G. W.—*The Book of the Bastilles* (1841).

BRAY, J. F.—*A Voyage from Utopia* (ed. by N. F. Lloyd-Prichard) (1957).

GAMAGE, R. G.—*History of the Chartist Movement* (2nd ed. Newcastle-on-Tyne: 1894).

(ALFRED) KYDD, S.—*History of the Factory Movement* (1857).

LOVETT, W.—*Life and Struggles* (Introduction by Tawney, R. H.) 2 vols (1920).

SOMERVILLE, A.—*Autobiography of a Working-Man* (1848).

DISRAELI, B.—*Sybil, or the Two Nations* (1845).

GASKELL, E.—*Mary Barton* (1848).

KINGSLEY, C.—*Alton Locke* (1850).

DICKENS, C.—*Hard Times* (1854).

Section VI.—THE GREAT VICTORIAN AGE.

(a) *General, Economic Development, Social Changes and Legislation.*
    YOUNG, G. M.—*Early Victorian England: Portrait of an Age*
        2 vols. 1830–1865 (1934).
    READER, W. J.—*Life in Victorian England* (1964).
    HOUGHTON, F. W.—*The Victorian Frame of Mind, 1830–1870*
        (Newhaven: 1957).
    ROSTOW, W. W.—*The British Economy in the Nineteenth
        Century* (1948).
    SCHLÖTE, W.—*British Overseas Trade from 1700 to the 1930s.*
        (Oxford: 1952).
    FORMOY, R. R.—*Historical Foundations of Modern Company
        Law* (1923).
    BURN, D. L.—*The Economic History of Steel-making, 1867–1939*
        (1940).
    HOBSBAWM, E. J.—"The Labour Aristocracy in Nineteenth
        Century Britain", and, "Custom, Wages & Workload"
        both in his *Labouring Men* (1964).
    ASHBY, M. K.—*Joseph Ashby of Tysoe, 1859–1919: A study of
        English Village Life* (1961).
    SMITH, FRANK.—*A History of English Elementary Education*
        (1931).
    ARCHER, R. L.—*Secondary Education in the Nineteenth Century*
        (1921).
    HUTCHINS, B. L. and HARRISON, A.—*A History of Factory
        Legislation* (1903).

(b) *Trade Unionism, Cooperation and Working-class Politics.*
    JEFFREYS, J. B.—*Labour's Formative Years, 1848–1879, Select
        documents* (1948).
    (TATE, G.)—*The London Trades Council 1850–1950* (1950).
    COLE, G. D. H.—"British Trade Unionism in the Third
        Quarter of the Nineteenth Century" in *Carus-Wilson:
        Essays III* (1962).
    MUSSON, A. E.—*The Congress of 1868* (1955).
    SIMON, D.—"Master and Servant" in J. Saville: *Democracy &
        the Labour Movement* (1954).

REDFERN, P.—*The Story of the Cooperative Wholesale Society* (Manchester: 1913).

RAVEN, C. E.—*Christian Socialism, 1848–54* (1920).

SAVILLE, J.—"The Christian Socialists of 1848" in his *Democracy and the Labour Movement* (1953).

ROTHSTEIN, T.—*From Chartism to Labourism* (1929).

GILLESPIE, F. E.—*Labour & Politics in England, 1850–67* (Durham: 1927).

HARRISON, ROYDEN.—*Before the Socialists: Studies in Labour & Politics, 1861–1881* (1965).

COLLINS, H. & ABRAMSKY, C.—*Karl Marx & the British Labour Movement: Years of the First International* (1965).

ARMYTAGE, W. H. G.—*A. J. Mundella: the Liberal Background to the Labour Movement* (1951).

COLTHAM, S.—"The Bee-Hive Newspaper: Its origins and early struggles" in Briggs and Saville: *Essays in Labour History* (1960).

(*c*) *Contemporaneous and near-Contemporaneous writings.*

MAYHEW, HENRY.—*London Labour and the London Poor* 4 vols (1861–2).

LUDLOW, J. M. and JONES, LLOYD.—*The Progress of the Working Classes 1832–67* (1867).

PLIMSOLL, S.—*Our Seamen* (1873).

ARNOLD, MATTHEW.—*Culture and Anarchy* (1869).

BAGEHOT, W.—*The English Constitution* (Preface to the Second Edition, 1872).

RUSKIN, J.—*Fors Clavigera* (Oxford: 1871–84).

ELIOT, GEORGE.—*Felix Holt* (1866).

Section VII.—IMPERIALISM AND SOCIALISM.

HOBSON, J. A.—*Imperialism* (1902).

HOBSON, C. K.—*The Export of Capital* (1914).

CAIRNCROSS, A. K.—*Home & Foreign Investment, 1870–1913* (Cambridge: 1953).

BODELSEN, C. A.—*Studies in Mid-Victorian Imperialism* (Copenhagen: 1924).

FABER, R.—*The Vision & the Need: late Victorian imperialist aims* (1966).

THORNTON, A. P.—*The Imperial Idea and its Enemies* (1959).

BARRATT-BROWN, M.—*After Imperialism* (1963).

STRACHEY, J.—*The End of Empire* (1959).

SEMMEL, B.—*Imperialism & Social Reform*, 1895–1914 (1960).

(b) Trade Unionism and Socialism.

HOBSBAWM, E. J.—*Labour's Turning Point* (1948) (Select Documents).

CLEGG, N. A., FOX, A, and THOMPSON, A. F.—*A History of Trade Unions since 1889* (Vol. 1 1889–1910) (Oxford: 1964:).

LLEWELYN SMITH, E. and NASH, D.—*The Story of the Dockers' Strike* (1890).

STAFFORD, A.—*A Match to Fire the Thames* (1961).

HOBSBAWM, E. J.—"The British Gas Workers, 1873–1914" and "General Labour Unions in Britain" both in his *Labouring Men* (1964).

PELLING, H. M.—*The Origins of the Labour Party* (1954).

McBRIAR, A. M.—*Fabian Socialism & English Politics, 1884–1918* (Cambridge: 1962).

THOMPSON, E. P.—*William Morris* (1950).

THOMPSON, E. P.—"Homage to Tom Maguire" in Briggs and Saville: *Essays in Labour History* (1960).

TSUZUKI, C.—*H. M. Hyndman & British Socialism* (Oxford: 1961).

JOLL, J. B.—*The Second International, 1889–1914* (1955).

(c) Contemporaneous and near-Contemporaneous writings.

SMITH, GOLDWIN.—*The Empire* (1863).

DILKE, CHARLES W.—*Greater Britain*, 2 vols (1868).

BLATCHFORD, ROBERT.—*Merrie England* (1895).

BLATCHFORD, ROBERT.—*Britain for the British* (1902).

KIDD, B.—*Social Evolution* (1894).

SHAW, BERNARD (ed.).—*Fabian Essays in Socialism* (1889).

PEASE, E. R.—*History of the Fabian Society* (1916).

BOOTH, CHARLES—*Life and Labour of the People of London* (Poverty, 4 vols. 1902–4, Industry, 5 vols. 1903, Religion, 7 vols. 1902–3, Conclusion, 1902).

MORRIS, WILLIAM.—*News from Nowhere* (1891).

WILDE, OSCAR.—*The Soul of Man under Socialism* (1895).
GISSING, G.—*Demos* (1886).

Section VIII.—BEFORE THE FIRST WORLD WAR.

(*a*) *Edwardian Britain.*

DANGERFIELD, G.—*The Strange Death of Liberal England* (1936).
ADAMS, W. S.—*Edwardian Heritage* (1949).
JENKINS, R.—*Mr. Balfour's Poodle (House of Lords)* (1954).
MOWAT, C. L.—*The Charity Organisation Society* (1869–1913) (1961).
BRAITHWAITE, W. J.—*Lloyd George's Ambulance Wagon* (1957).
BEVERIDGE, W. H.—*Power and Influence* (1953).
FULFORD, R.—*Votes for Women* (1957).
LYONS, F. S. L.—*The Irish Parliamentary Party* (1951).
RYAN, A. P.—*The Mutiny at the Curragh* (1956).
BLAKE, R.—*Bonar Law* (1955).

(*b*) *Labour Movements.*

BEALEY, F. and PELLING, H. M.—*Labour and Politics, 1900–1906* (1958).
POIRIER, P.—*The Advent of the British Labour Party* (1958).
SAVILLE, J.—"Trade Unions and Free Labour: the Background to the Taff Vale Decision" in Briggs & Saville: *Essays in Labour History* (1960).
PHELPS-BROWN, E. H.—*The Growth of British Industrial Relations 1906–1914* (1959).
PRIBICEVIC, B.—*The Shop Stewards Movement and Workers Control 1910–1922* (Oxford: 1959).

(*c*) *Contemporaneous and near-Contemporaneous writings.*

COLE, G. D. H.—*The World of Labour* (1913).
BELLOC, HILAIRE.—*The Servile State* (1912).
PANKHURST, SYLVIA.—*The Suffragette Movement* (1911).
BEVERIDGE, W.—*Unemployment: a Problem of Industry* (1910).
MASTERMAN, C. F. G.—*The Conditions of England* (1909).
ROWNTREE, B. S.—*Poverty: a study of Town Life* (1901).
MONEY, G. J.—*Riches and Poverty* (1910).
REEVES, MRS. PEMBER.—*Round About a Pound a Week* (1913).

TRESSELL, R. (NOONAN, R.).—*The Ragged Trousered Philan-thropists,* ed. by F. C. Ball (1955).

Section IX.—THE FIRST WORLD WAR.

(*a*) *General.*
MARWICK, A.—*The Deluge* (1965).
BEAVERBROOK, LORD.—*Men and Power* (1956).
HURWITZ, S.—*State Intervention in Great Britain 1914–1919* (New York: 1949).
GRAUBARD, S. R.—*British Labour and the Russian Revolution* (Oxford: 1956).
DOWSE, R.—*Left in the Centre* (1966).
CLINE, C. A.—*Recruits to Labour, 1914–1931* (Syracuse: 1963).
MADDOX, W. P.—*Foreign Relations in British Labour Politics* (Cambridge, Mass. 1934).

(*b*) *Contemporaneous and near-Contemporaneous writings.*
COLE, G. D. H.—*Labour in War-time* (1915).
COLE, G. D. H.—*Trade Unionism and Munitions* (1923).
WEBB, S.—*The Restoration of Trade Union Conditions* (1917).
PANKHURST, S.—*The Home Front* (1932).
WELLS, H. G.—*Mr. Britling Sees It Through* (1916).
OWEN, WILFRED.—*Collected Poems* (3rd edition ed. by C. Day Lewis) (1963).

Sections X and XI.—BETWEEN THE WARS.

MOWAT, C. L.—*Britain Between the Wars 1918–1940* (1955).

(*a*) *The Political Economy.*
LEWIS, W. A.—*Economic Survey, 1919–1939* (1949).
ALLEN, G. C.—*British Industries & their Organisation* (1933).
AMBROVITZ, M. and ELIASBERG, V.—*Growth of Public Employment in Great Britain* (Princeton, 1957).
PEACOCK, A. T. and WISEMAN, J.—*The Growth of Public Expenditure in the United Kingdom* (1961).
HICKS, U. K.—*The Finance of British Government, 1920–1936* (Oxford: 1938).

MORGAN, E. V.—*Studies in British Financial Policy, 1914–1925* (1952).

SAYERS, R. S.—"The Return to Gold" in Pressnell, L. S., *Studies* (1960).

ARNDT, H. W.—*Economic Lessons of the Nineteen Thirties* (1944).

(b) *Labour Movements and Social and Political Developments.*

MEADE, J. E.—*Efficiency, Equality & the Ownership of Property* (1964).

CAMPION, H.—*Distribution of National Capital* (1936).

CARR-SAUNDERS, A. M., JONES, D. CARADOG and MOSER, C. A.—*Survey of Social Conditions in England & Wales* (1952).

ABRAMS, M. A.—*Condition of the British People, 1911–1945* (1945).

BECK, G. M. A.—*A Survey of British Employment & Unemployment 1927–1945* (Oxford: 1951).

HANNINGTON, W.—*Unemployed Struggles, 1919–1936* (1936).

CURTIS, S. J.—*Education in Britain since 1900* (1952).

BOWLEY, M.—*Housing and the State, 1919–1944* (1945).

SYMONS, J.—*The Thirties: A Dream Revolved* (1960).

COLE, G. D. H.—*History of the Labour Party from 1914* (1948).

MIDDLEMAS, R. K.—*The Clydesiders* (1965).

LYMAN, R. W.—*The First Labour Government, 1924* (1959).

SYMONS, J.—*The General Strike* (1957).

BASSETT, R.—*1931—Political Crisis* (1958).

DALTON, H.—*The Fateful Years* (*Memoirs*) (1957).

MINNEY, V.—*Viscount Southwood* (1954) (*Daily Herald*).

THOMAS, H.—*The Spanish Civil War* (1961).

WATKINS, K. W.—*Britain Divided: The Effect of the Spanish Civil War on British Political Opinion* (1963).

GILBERT, N. and GOTT, R.—*The Appeasers* (1962).

PELLING, H.—*The British Communist Party* (1958).

MACFARLANE, L. J.—*The British Communist Party, 1920–1929* (1966).

CROSS, C.—*The Fascists in Britain* (1961).

(c) *Contemporaneous and near-Contemporaneous writings.*

RUSSEL, B.—*Roads to Freedom: Socialism, Anarchism and Syndicalism* (1918).

COLE, G. D. H.—*The next ten years in British Economic &
Social Policy* (1929).

KEYNES, J. M.—*Essays in Persuasion* (1931).

MORRISON, H.—*Socialisation and Transport* (1931).

TAWNEY, R. H.—*Equality* (1931).

GARRATT, G. T.—*The Mugwumps and the Labour Party* (1932).

STRACHEY, J.—*The Coming Struggle for Power* (1932).

DUTT, R. P.—*Fascism and Social Revolution* (1934).

LAWRENCE, D. H.—*Nottingham: Mining Country* (1930).

AUDEN, W. H.—*Spain* (*1937*) (Must be read in this first
edition).

SPENDER, S.—*Trial of a Judge* (1938).

ORWELL, G.—*The Road to Wigan Pier* (1937).

PRIESTLEY, J. B.—*English Journey* (1934).

GREENWOOD, W.—*Love on the Dole* (1933).

Section XII.—THE SECOND WORLD WAR.

TAYLOR, A. J. P.—*English History, 1914–1945* (Oxford:
1965).

HANCOCK, W. K. and GOWING, M. M.—*British War
Economy* (1949).

POSTAN, M. M.—*British War Production* (1952).

INMAN, P.—*Labour in the Munitions Industries* (1957).

TITMUSS, R. M.—*Problems of Social Policy* (1950).

ROBERTS, B. C.—*National Wages Policy in War and Peace*
(1958).

COURT, W. H. B.—*Coal* (1951).

HARRISON, T. and MADGE, C.—*War Begins at Home* (1940).

TURNER, E. S.—*The Phoney War on the Home Front* (1961).

McCULLUM, R. B. and READMAN, A.—*The British General
Election of 1945* (1946).

PART IV GUIDES AND GENERAL
WORKS OF REFERENCE

Parliamentary Papers.

FORD, P. and G.—*A Guide to Parliamentary Papers; What they are;
How to find them; How to use them* (Oxford) 1955.

FORD, P. and G.—*Hansard's Catalogue and Breviate of Parliamentary Papers, 1696–1834* (Oxford) 1953.

FORD, P. and G.—*Select List of British Parliamentary Papers, 1833–1899* (Oxford) 1953.

FORD, P. and G.—*A Breviate of Parliamentary Papers, 1917–1939* (Oxford) 1951.

Biographical Facts.

—*The Dictionary of National Biography* (Oxford) 1885, etc. (See also *The Concise Dictionary of National Biography—an epitome of the D.N.B. down to 1950.*)

SAVILLE, J. (editor).—*Dictionary of Labour Biography.* (The first volume is promised for the Spring of 1968.)

See also Section II above, Biographies and Autobiographies.

Economic and Political Facts.

MITCHELL B. R. and DEANE, P.—*Abstract of British Historical Statistics* (Cambridge) 1962.

BUTLER, D. and FREEMAN, J.—*British Political Facts 1900–1960* (1963).

Periodical Literature.

Union Catalogue of the Periodical Publications in the University Libraries of the British Isles.

Palmer's Index to the *Times* 1790–1905, followed by the Official Index to the *Times* from 1906.

The Library Association: *British Humanities Index.* (This guide to work appearing in "learned" and other journals first appeared in 1915 under the title of *Subject Index to Periodicals.* It is now published quarterly.)

See also the Wellesley Index to Victorian Periodicals, 1965— and *Poole's Index 1883.*

The following periodicals regularly or frequently publish articles or bibliographies which will help the Student to keep abreast of current research:

Bulletin of the Society for the Study of Labour History (Sheffield).

Economic History Review (Utrecht).

International Review of Social History (Amsterdam).

Past and Present (Oxford).

Victorian Studies (Indiana).

LIST OF IMPORTANT DATES

[Dates are those of foundation in the case of organizations, publication in the case of books, discovery in the case of inventions, and accession in the case of monarchs.]

1746   Battle of Culloden—(final defeat of Jacobites).

1749   Huntsman's crucible steel process.

1758   Bridgewater canal.

1760   *George III.* Carron Iron Works.

1764   Hargreaves' Spinning Jenny (patented 1767). Wilkes expelled from the House of Commons.

1768   Wilkes re-elected, and repeatedly expelled.

1769   Watt's first steam-engine. Arkwright's water-frame.

1774   Wilkes Lord Mayor and M.P.

1776   Adam Smith's *Wealth of Nations.* American Declaration of Independence.

1779   Crompton's Mule.

1780   Gordon Riots. Cartwright's Constitutional Society.

1782   Burke's "Economical Reform" Act. Independence of U.S.A. acknowledged.

1784   Cort's puddling process. Watt's improved steam-engine.

1785   Cartwright's first Power Loom.

1789   French Revolution. Declaration of the Rights of Man.

1790   Burke's *Reflections on the French Revolution.*

1791   Paine's *Rights of Man.*

1792   France a Republic. London Corresponding Society.

1793   War with France. Scottish Treason Trials. Godwin's *Political Justice.*

1794   Acquittal of Hardy, Horne Tooke and others. Habeas Corpus suspended.

1795   Seditious Meetings and Treason Acts. Berkshire Justices adopt "Speenhamland" scale.

1797   Mutiny at the Nore. Cash payments suspended.

1798   Irish rebellion. Income Tax. Malthus's *Essay on Population.*

1799   Acts suppressing Corresponding Societies and freedom of the Press. First Combination Act.

1800   Second Combination Act. Act of Union with Ireland. Owen takes over New Lanark.

1801   First Census. General Enclosure Act.

1802   Health and Morals of (pauper) Apprentices Act. West India Dock opened. Cobbett's *Register.*

1803   Horrocks's Power Loom. *Charlotte Dundas* (steamboat).

1806   Death of Pitt: repression relaxed. Berlin Decrees.

1807   Orders in Council. Slave Trade abolished.

1808 Lancasterian Association (later became British and Foreign Schools Society).
1810 Durham Miners' Strike.
1811 *Prince of Wales Regent.* Luddite troubles begin.
1812 War with U.S.A. Luddite troubles.
1813 Bell's *Comet.* East India Company loses monopoly. Owen's *New View of Society.*
1813–14 Repeal of the Statute of Artificers. Stephenson's first engine.
1815 The Hundred Days. Waterloo. Corn Law. Davy's Safety Lamp.
1816 Acute Distress. Cobbett's *Twopenny Register.* Spa Fields Riot.
1817 Blanketeers' March. Derbyshire "Insurrection." Sidmouth's Gagging Acts.
1818 Trade improves. Lancashire Strikes.
1819 Peterloo Massacre. The Six Acts. First Factory Act. The *Savannah* crosses the Atlantic.
1820 *George IV.* Queen Caroline Case. Cato Street Conspiracy.
1821 Cash payments resumed. Grampound disfranchised. London Co-operative Society (Mudie). Owen's *Report to the County of Lanark.*
1823 Catholic Association formed. South American Republics recognized.
1824 Combination Acts repealed. Huskisson's tariff reforms. Gaol Acts (prison reform).
1825 Financial crisis. Combination Law made less liberal. Stockton and Darlington Railway opened. Northumberland and Durham Colliers' Union.
1826 Lancashire Power Loom Riots.
1828 Test and Corporation Acts repealed. O'Connell elected for Clare.
1829 Catholic Emancipation. Metropolitan Police established. Grand General Spinners' Union. Growth of Owenite Co-operative Societies begins.
1830 *William IV.* Whig ministry. French and Belgian Revolutions. Birmingham Political Union. National Association for the Protection of Labour. Liverpool and Manchester Railway. Agricultural Labourers' Revolt.
1831 Bristol and Nottingham Riots. First Cholera Epidemic. National Union of the Working Classes.
1832 First Reform Act. Operative Builders' Union. Owen's Labour Exchanges flourishing.
1833 First effective Factory Act. First State Grant for Education. Emancipation of slaves in British Empire. Grand National Consolidated Trades Union.
1834 New Poor Law. Dorchester Labourers convicted. The "Trades Union" defeated.
1835 Municipal Corporations Act.

1836   Newspaper Stamp Duty reduced to 1d. London Working Men's Association.

1837   *Victoria.*   Registration of Births, Marriages and Deaths. *Northern Star.*

1838   "People's Charter" issued. Manchester Anti-Corn Law Association.

1839   Penny postage. First Chartist Convention and Petition. Newport Rising. National Anti-Corn Law League. Queenwood (last Owenite colony).

1841   National Charter Association. Miners' Association of Great Britain.

1842   Second Chartist Petition. "Strikes for the Charter." Peel reduces corn and other duties. Income tax re-imposed.

1844   Rochdale Pioneers open Toad Lane Store. Bank Charter Act. Factory Act. Cheap Trains Act.

1845   Peel again lowers tariff. National Association of United Trades. Queenwood breaks up. Chartists adopt land scheme.

1846   Corn Laws repealed.

1847   Ten Hours' Act (textile mills). Commercial crisis.

1848   "Year of Revolutions" in Europe. *Communist Manifesto.* Third Chartist Petition. Second Cholera Epidemic. General Board of Health. Californian Gold Discovered.

1849   Navigation laws repealed. Society for Promoting Workingmen's Associations (Christian Socialists).

1850   Factory Act.

1851   Great Exhibition. Amalgamated Society of Engineers Australian gold discoveries.

1852   Third cholera epidemic. Industrial and Provident Societies Act (Co-operatives). Engineering lock-out.

1853   Blackburn Weavers' List. Preston Spinners' strike.

1854   Cardwell's Railway Act.

1855   Companies Act (Limited Liability). Newspaper duties repealed. Metropolis Management Act.

1856   Bessemer converter introduced.

1857   Transportation abolished. Aniline dyes.

1858   Public Health Act. Macdonald's National Miners' Association.

1859   Darwin's *Origin of Species.* London Building Strike.

1860   Gladstone's Free Trade Budget. Coal Mines (Checkweighing) Act. London Trades Council. *The Beehive.* Bradlaugh's *National Reformer.*

1861   American Civil War. Cotton famine begins. Paper duty abolished. Post Office Savings Bank. Amalgamated Society of Carpenters and Joiners.

1862   Kane's Ironworkers' Association. Working Men's Club and Institute Union. Companies Act.

1863   Co-operative Wholesale Society. Leeds Miners' Conference.

1864 International Working-men's Association ("First International"). First Trade Union Conference.

1865 Irish Fenian Movement. National Reform League.

1866 Atlantic cable laid. Overend and Gurney crisis. Sheffield
outrages. United Kingdom Alliance of Organized Trades.
Siemens open hearth process.

1867 Marx's *Capital*. Second Reform Act. Royal Commission on
Trade Unions. Master and Servant Act. Factory and
Workshops Acts. Housing Act. Conference of Amal-
gamated Trades ("Junta").

1868 First regular Trades Union Congress. Scottish Co-operative
Wholesale Society.

1869 Co-operative Union. Labour Representation League. Imprisonment for debt abolished. Suez Canal opened.

1870 Elementary Education Act. Civil Service made open to
competitive examinations.

1871 Paris Commune. Trade Union Act. Criminal Law Amendment Act. Local Government Board. Engineers' strike in
North-East.

1872 Ballot Act. Arch's National Agricultural Labourers' Union.
Trade boom. Public Health Act. Prosecution of London
gas stokers. Coal Mines Act.

1874 Women's Trade Union League. First Trade Union M.P.s.

1875 Conspiracy and Protection of Property Act. Employers and
Workmen Act. Cross's Housing Act. Public Health Act.
Merchant Shipping Act (Plimsoll Line).

1876 Trade Union Amendment Act. Elementary education made
compulsory.

1878 Factory Act.

1879 Irish Land League. Henry George's *Progress and Poverty*.

1880 Employers' Liability Act. Salvation Army. Bradlaugh
excluded from Parliament.

1881 (Social) Democratic Federation.

1882 Municipal Corporations Act.

1883 Fabian Society. Co-operative Women's Guild.

1884 Third Reform Act. William Morris's Socialist League.
Transvaal gold discoveries.

1885 Redistribution Act.

1886 First Home Rule Bill. Bradlaugh takes his seat. Unemployed
riots (Trafalgar Square). Broadhurst enters Government.
Daimler's engine.

1887 Jubilee. Coal Mines Act.

1888 County Councils Act. Bloody Sunday (Trafalgar Square).
Miners' Federation of Great Britain. Scottish Labour Party.

1889 London Dock Strike. Dockers' and Gasworkers' Unions.
Fabian Essays. Booth's *Survey of London Life and Labour*.

1890 Housing Act. Baring Crisis.

1891   Free elementary education. Factory Act (Workshops). *The Clarion.*

1892   Three Independent Labour M.P.s elected.

1893   Independent Labour Party. Shop Hours Act. Second Home Rule Bill. Royal Commission on Labour. National Mining Strike. Brooklands Agreement (Cotton Spinning).

1894   Parish Councils Act.

1896   Conciliation Act. Engineering lock-out.

1897   Workmen's Compensation Act.

1898   Imperial Penny Postage.

1899   General Federation of Trade Unions. London Government Act. Ruskin College.

1900   Labour Representation Committee. International Socialist Bureau.

1901   *Edward VII.* International Federation of Trade Unions. Factory Act. Taff Vale Judgment.

1902   Education Act. End of Boer War.

1903   Tariff Reform campaign begins. First effective aeroplane (Wright brothers). Workers' Educational Association.

1904   Women's Social and Political Union.

1905   Unemployed Workmen Act. Liberal Government.

1906   L.R.C. becomes Labour Party. Twenty-nine Labour M.P.s. Trade Disputes Act. Workmen's Compensation Act. School Meals Act.

1907   Education (Medical Inspection) Act. Small Holdings Act. First All-Grades Railway Movement.

1908   Old Age Pensions. Coal Mines Eight Hours Act.

1909   Osborne Judgment. Housing and Town Planning Act. Coal Mines Act. Labour Exchanges Act. Lloyd George's Budget. Miners join the Labour Party. Poor Law Commission Report. Blériot flies the Channel. Central Labour College.

1910   *George V.* Two General Elections. Transport Workers' Federation.

1911   Payment of M.P.s. Parliament Act. National Insurance Act. Second All-Grades Railway Movement. Big transport strikes.

1912   Miners' Strike and Coal Mines Minimum Wage Act. London Transport Strike. *Daily Herald.* Shops Act.

1913   Trade Union Act (political funds). National Union of Railwaymen. Dublin dispute.

1914   Triple Alliance. Outbreak of First World War.

1915   Strikes on Clyde and in South Wales. Shop Stewards Movement begins. Treasury Agreement and Munitions Act. Labour Party enters Coalition Government. National Guilds League. Rent Restriction Act.

1916   Conscription introduced. Clyde Deportations. Easter Week Revolt in Ireland.

1917 Russian Revolutions. Proposed Stockholm Conference. Corn Production Act (agricultural minimum wage). Whitley Report. Iron and Steel Trades Confederation.

1918 Representation of the People Act. Education Act. Trade Boards Act. New Labour Party constitution. Labour defeat in elections.

1919 Clyde and Belfast strikes. Sankey Coal Commission. National Industrial Conference. Cotton, Police and Railway strikes. Industrial Courts Act. Unemployment Insurance Act. Various "Reconstruction" Acts and schemes. Versailles Treaty. Washington Labour Conference. Third International.

1920 Great capitalist boom. Building Guilds. Amalgamated Engineering Union. Irish Civil War. Dockers' Inquiry. Communist Party. Council of Action stops intervention in Russo–Polish War. Trades Union Congress reorganized. Coal Dispute. Emergency Powers Act. Unemployment. Insurance Act. Deflation begins.

1921 Coal Mines Dispute. Black Friday. Irish Settlement. Unemployed Workers' Movement begins. Dispute over Poplarism. Corn Production Act repealed.

1922 Engineering lock-out. Hunger marches. Fascist *coup* in Italy.

1923 Occupation of Ruhr. Labour Election victory.

1924 First Labour Government. Agricultural Wages Act. Unemployment Insurance reorganized. Dawes Report. "Red Letter" Election.

1925 Return to Gold Standard. Red Friday. Locarno Pact.

1926 Coal Mines Dispute and General Strike. Electricity Supply Act ("The Grid").

1927 Trade Unions and Trade Disputes Act.

1928 Local Government Act (Guardians abolished).

1929 Second Labour Government. Wall Street crash.

1930 Young Plan (Reparations).

1931 Break-up of Labour Government. MacDonald forms "National" Government. Labour Election defeat. Gold Standard suspended. Means Test for unemployed.

1932 End of Free Trade. Japan seizes Manchuria.

1933 Nazi Revolution in Germany.

1934 Incitement to Disaffection Act. Shops Act.

1935 Abyssinian Crisis. Labour defeated at elections.

1936 *Edward VIII. George VI.* Public Order Act (uniforms and processions). Education Act. Spanish Fascist Rebellion. Labour Unity Campaign.

1937 Japan invades China. Labour Party Constitution revised Factories Act.

1938 Nazis seize Austria. Munich Agreement.

1939 Nazis seize Czechoslovakia. War.

1945 War ends. General Election. Third Labour Government.

INDEX